MANAGEMENT
The Key to Organizational Effectiveness

MANAGEMENT
The Key to Organizational Effectiveness

Clayton Reeser
University of Hawaii

Marvin Loper
University of Hawaii

Scott, Foresman and Company   Glenview, Illinois

Dallas, Tex. Oakland, N.J. Palo Alto, Cal.
Tucker, Ga. London, England

To: Freda and Pam
and
Jennifer and Matt

038312

Photo Credits
Cover: Howard N. Kaplan
Part opener photos: **1** Savage & Savage Studio **2** Peter Southwick/Stock, Boston
3 Ellis Herwig/Stock, Boston **4** Martin M. Rotker/Taurus **5** Patricia Hollander Gross/
Stock, Boston **6** Joel Gordon **7** George W. Gardner

Library of Congress Cataloging in Publication Data
Reeser, Clayton.
    Management: the key to organizational effectiveness.
    Published in 1973 under title: Management: functions
and modern concepts.
    Includes index and bibliographies.
    1. Management. I. Loper, Marvin, joint author.
II. Title.
HD31.R438   1978   658   77-22310
ISBN 0-673-15077-1

1 2 3 4 5 6 7 8 -KPK- 82 81 80 79 78 77

Acknowledgments

p. 63 Peter Lorange and Richard F. Vancil, "How to Design a Strategic Planning System," HARVARD BUSINESS REVIEW, September–October 1976, Copyright © 1976 by the President and Fellows of Harvard College; all rights reserved.

pp. 75–76 From "Sales Forecasting Methods and Accuracy" by Douglas J. Dalrymple from BUSINESS HORIZONS, Dec. 1975. Copyright 1975 by the Foundation for the School of Business at Indiana University. Reprinted by permission.

pp. 137–38 "If 'satellization' fails, try centralization" Reprinted from the August 2, 1976 issue of BUSINESS WEEK by special permission. © 1976 by McGraw-Hill, Inc.

pp. 161–62 From "Project Center: GM management system's new aid" by Charles Brady from CHICAGO TRIBUNE, February 27, 1977. Reprinted by permission.

p. 179 "Power and Politics in Organizational Life" by Abraham Zaleznik From DEVELOPING EXECUTIVE LEADERS, E. C. Bursk and T. B. Blodgett, editors, Cambridge, Mass.: Harvard University Press, Copyright © 1970, 1971 by the President and Fellows of Harvard College.

pp. 212–13 "The MOST way to time a job" Reprinted from the August 2, 1976 issue of BUSINESS WEEK by special permission. © 1976 by McGraw-Hill, Inc.

pp. 227–28 "A work force wins a travel bonus" Reprinted from the January 10, 1977 issue of BUSINESS WEEK by special permission. © 1977 by McGraw-Hill, Inc.

p. 252 Harry Levinson, "Appraisal of *What* Performance?" HARVARD BUSINESS REVIEW, July–August 1976, Copyright © 1976 by the President and Fellows of Harvard College; all rights reserved.

p. 303 David C. McClelland and David H. Burnham, "Power Is the Great Motivator," HARVARD BUSINESS REVIEW, March–April 1976, Copyright © 1976 by the President and Fellows of Harvard College; all rights reserved.

p. 324 Dick Bruner. WHY WHITE-COLLAR WORKERS CAN'T BE ORGANIZED. New York: Harper's Magazine, 1957.

p. 359 "Management by Objectives: Does It Really Work?" by Heinz Weihrich, Vol. 28, No. 4. Reprinted by permission from the July, 1976 issue of the *University of Michigan Business Review,* published by the Graduate School of Business Administration, The University of Michigan.

p. 415 Paul H. Thompson and Gene W. Dalton, "Are R&D Organizations Obsolete?" HARVARD BUSINESS REVIEW, November–December 1976, Copyright © 1976 by the President and Fellows of Harvard College; all rights reserved.

p. 431 and p. 440 Cortlandt Cammann and David A. Nadler, "Fit Control Systems to Your Managerial Style," HARVARD BUSINESS REVIEW, January–February 1976, Copyright © 1975 by the President and Fellows of Harvard College; all rights reserved.

pp. 471–72 "The pressure to compromise personal ethics" Reprinted from the January 31, 1977 issue of BUSINESS WEEK by special permission. © 1977 by McGraw-Hill, Inc.

pp. 500–03 From STARTING AND MANAGING A SMALL BUSINESS OF YOUR OWN by Wendell O. Metcalf. Small Business Administration, Washington, D.C. 1973.

Preface

The purpose of this book, as with the previous edition, *Management: Functions and Modern Concepts,* is to describe management with the student's frame of reference in mind. Professors want to know the methodologies and findings of empirical research, and to keep up-to-date on research advances in the field of management. However, it is our opinion that while students want to experience the full body of management knowledge, they have little interest in citings of research findings, and that such information is of minimal value to them.

Business students, and students from other disciplines who contemplate a managerial career, need an integration of the significant factors involved in managing an enterprise. The comments of one adopter of the earlier book sum up our position quite well: "The Reeser book is the first text that we have had that I have rather liked, including those I helped choose. My major approval deals with the fact that it is relatively short, easy to follow and understand, and is written for undergraduates and not to get the approval of other professors. In addition, it is the first book that my classes have approved (over 90 percent gave it a satisfactory to good evaluation, whereas previous texts had been evaluated as poor by about 90 percent)."

The book is structured in the format of most successful management textbooks; a treatment of early contributions to management is followed by analyses of the management functions of planning, organizing, staffing, leading, and controlling. Three innovative concluding chapters focus on the impact of the computer on management, corporate social responsiveness, and entrepreneurship, an important topic not found in most management textbooks. The entrepreneurship chapter outlines what students should know about starting and managing a small business. There are thirty-three short cases in the book, all drawn from real-life incidents, to give substance to the narrative text that precedes them. Up-to-date bibliographies are provided so that in-depth investigations of topics can be conducted at the student's or instructor's option. A revised instructor's manual is provided, with suggested answers to discussion questions. Short quizzes that have been validated with several thousand students are also included.

Second- or third-year college students are the primary audience for the book. It has also been used successfully to provide graduate students from undergraduate disciplines other than business an easy orientation to the area of management. In addition, the book is suitable for use in industrial and governmental training programs. Agencies sponsoring small business development programs would find the book especially useful in training aspiring entrepreneurs.

Consistent with many contemporary management textbooks, the book presents both the quantitative and behavioral approaches to management. The quantitative approach is treated nonrigorously, yet in a comprehensive manner. The chapters dealing with organizational behavior highlight modern views on leadership, motivation, and communication. The book is holistic; that is, it expresses the position that management has many parts, but that the integrated whole is greater than the sum of its parts.

The authors are indebted to many people who have encouraged the writing of this book. In particular, Dean David Heenan of the College of Business Administration at the University of Hawaii has been consistently helpful. Professor Harold Koontz at the Graduate School of Management at UCLA has been an inspiration in the writing of this book and its predecessor. Several users of the first edition provided helpful suggestions for the revision including Al Long, California State University; Charles Beavin, Miami-Dade Community College; J. David Harris, West Valley College; James E. Estes, C. Schulze, Jim Emens, and Mike Showalter, University of South Carolina; and Donald Hucker, Cypress College. Reviewers of the manuscript who have made important comments include Peter Hechler, California State University, and Stephen Miller, University of Maryland. The editorial work of Ms. Linda Brown of Scott, Foresman and Company has been unusually helpful. Finally, typing by Ms. Ruth Takahata and Ms. Jean Nakata has been outstanding.

Honolulu, Hawaii   Clayton Reeser
                                                       Marvin Loper

Contents

Part 2 PLANNING

Part 3 ORGANIZING

Case Studies

MANAGEMENT
The Key to Organizational Effectiveness

PART 1

Introduction to Management

This book is about management. Therefore, it starts with some introductory chapters intended to set the stage for the main body of management knowledge to be presented in subsequent Parts. Chapter 1 explains what management is, discusses various meanings for the term "management," and explores some different approaches to the study of management. It concludes with an investigation of the term "organization." Chapter 2 deals with the functions that managers perform, with the levels of management typically found in organizations, and with the complexities, advantages, and disadvantages of being a manager. Chapter 3 brings to the reader's attention some of the early contributions to management theory that serve as a foundation for modern concepts. As contemporary management is heavily influenced by the findings of psychologists, sociologists, and anthropologists, commonly called behavioral scientists, Chapter 4 examines the impact of these disciplines. Chapter 5, the last of the chapters in Part One, reviews the latest additions to management theory, which include mathematical concepts, the systems approach, and contingency views.

1 What Is Management?

Management is the process of integrating and coordinating resources in order to accomplish deliberate and purposive objectives. Imagine a situation where the physical and human resources necessary to get something done are available in adequate supply. Suppose there is a supply of money with which to pay bills (capital), a place in which work can be performed (plant), tools of all kinds (equipment), raw materials (steel, copper, plastics, etc.), and people with various skills (engineers, accountants, machinists, assemblers, salespersons, etc.). Yet, if there were no managers, any assembling of resources would be chaotic. However, introduce managers into the scene, and things will begin to happen. Managers will begin to

- set objectives for using the available resources.
- formulate plans for achieving these objectives.
- identify the various activities that will have to be performed.
- organize the activities into groups (departments).
- define the tasks to be done.
- group the tasks into jobs.
- establish compensation levels for the jobs.
- staff the jobs with people.
- initiate work performance.
- supply incentives to stimulate productivity.
- set up controls to measure the achievement of objectives.
- take remedial action if the objectives are not being met.

Thus managers, who are the people who practice management, direct and coordinate the use of resources to some planned end. However, the general relationship of managers to physical resources is indirect. It is through the people who are led by managers, the subordinates, that managers utilize capital, plant, equipment, and materials. Therefore, the management process is the utilization of physical and human resources through coordinative efforts, and it is accomplished by managers performing the functions of planning, organizing, staffing, leading, and controlling.

OTHER USES FOR THE TERM "MANAGEMENT"

Most students beginning their study of management are troubled by the various meanings that are used for certain key words. In this first part of the book, an effort will be made to clarify several confusing terms. A good place to start is with the term "management." It has already been defined as the process of coordinating resources. However, the following uses for the term are also accurate.

As Organizational Levels

All organizations are comprised of two basic levels. One level, and usually by far the largest, is made up of jobs which are nonmanagerial. People who perform these jobs work on individual tasks that pertain to the nature of the organization. They may sell, or operate machines, or maintain records. However, whatever they do, they do through their own efforts. They don't accomplish things through other people. The other level in an organization is management. People who occupy this level spend at least part of their time acting as managers, although they may also perform some nonmanagerial duties. Hence, management denotes the people who either partly or predominantly utilize resources by leading other people.

As a Career

Most business students are either consciously planning careers in management, or are at least indicating this choice by virtue of studying business. While it is true that the entry jobs for business students will likely be nonmanagerial, usually their first promotion will be to a job where they will have people reporting to them, and this will embark them on a management career. Although the work of the people whom they lead may vary (it might be construction, retail selling, accounting, or purchasing), the fact remains that probably for the rest of their lives they will be accomplishing objectives through other people. This fact establishes that their life work is fundamentally management.

As an Area of Study

Management is now recognized as a distinct academic discipline, with a strong body of literature to support it. All schools of business offer courses in management. Most schools have grouped courses and instructors into departments of management; and some universities, such as UCLA, have done away with the title College of Business Administration, and have substituted instead Graduate School of Management. This latter move suggests a possible trend for management to encompass the subdisciplines of marketing, production, accounting, finance, statistics, and even economics. There is at least surface justification for such a movement, because the modern manager must have a command of all of the subdisciplines in order to perform effectively. An understanding of management theory and a familiarity with the literature of management is becoming essential for the practitioner of management. However, study of management alone will not make a manager. In the final analysis, an individual becomes a manager by managing, and improves as a manager through a series of increasingly broadening and maturing experiences as a manager. No amount of study will replace practical management experience.

APPROACHES TO THE STUDY OF MANAGEMENT

Although there is general agreement by both practicing managers and management theorists that management is a process and that it is a distinct field of study, management theorists, or writers and teachers of management, have been sharply divided on the proper approach to the understanding of it. Virulent paper battles have raged for years in the management literature arena between disciples of different schools of thought. As with any evolving discipline, the foundation of management theory has been enhanced by innovative thinking and revealing research findings. Some of the figurative "plaster" on the original base has been thick and lasting. In other cases, it has been thin, and only vestiges remain of theories that once seemed monumental contributions. In this book we take the position that the traditional practice of studying management by examining what managers *do* provides a logical and useful framework. We've added, in the fashion of unifying cement, the behavioral and quantitative approaches to management to the framework. Support for this approach is afforded by the fact that curricula in most schools of business surround basic management courses with courses in the behavioral and quantitative areas. The study of the traditional model provides core work for studying management.

The Traditional Management Model

Despite numerous and highly vocal detractors, the model for studying management that focuses on what managers do has demonstrated remarkable staying powers in what has been called "the management theory jungle." Managers perform certain functions that enable them to coordinate and effectively utilize the various resources of the organization. As has been said, these functions are planning, organizing, staffing, leading, and controlling. These functions supply a structure of management that is descriptive of the total process. This structure is flexible; new thoughts can be added and specific functions can be changed or omitted to meet the varied characteristics of management in different types of organizations.

Critics of this model seem to concentrate their attacks on the principles that were formerly connected with it, and the notion that these principles implied that management had achieved the requisites of a science. Examples of principles include those cited by Fayol, a French writer on management, which are listed in Chapter 3. Like most contemporary books on management, this book does not offer principles for student memorization and later regurgitation on quizzes or examinations. However, something needs to be said in defense of principles. Possibly their worst defect was their name. "Guides" would have been a much better term for them. Their intended use for managers was to have been as a reference to help in making decisions relative to the planning, organizing, staffing, leading, and controlling functions. It was never intended that they be considered to be inviolate, like Ohm's Law in electricity. Moreover, the proponents of principles accurately denied that management was a science, or ever would be. Their stand on this issue, and the stand that is taken in this book, is that management is primarily an art. There are far too many variations in the way successful managers practice management to believe that there are discrete maxims that can be followed blindly. However, scientific methods for decision making have been developed that will lead managers toward solutions. From that point, managers will rely on their judgment, which is the art part of management, to conclude the decision process.

The Behavioral Approach

The evolution of the old human relations school of thought on management has culminated in the behavioral approach to management which places primary emphasis on the behaviors, attitudes, and motivations of the members of organizations, rather than on what managers do. This approach has had unquestionable impact on the study of management today. Management literature is bulging with the theories and research findings of psychologists, sociologists, and anthropologists, who have discovered organizational behavior to be a fertile field for the practice of their disciplines.

On the surface, there might appear to be an irreconcilable conflict between the organization goals implicit in the traditional management model and the individual interests and goals that are emphasized by the behavioralists. The traditional model stresses efficiency and optimal product or service quality and productivity, thus appearing to be impersonal and insensitive to the needs of the members of the organization. Conversely, the behavioral approach conveys the initial impression that economic outputs of organizations should be subordinate to social outputs. Such an objective would be considered unrealistic to the practicing manager, and really is a distortion of what the behavioralists are trying to do.

The time is long past when the human asset of organizations could be ignored. It is now firmly recognized that concern for the individual in organizations will produce as much, or more, creativity, productivity, and effectiveness as will efficient operating procedures. If this awareness were not enough to motivate managers to create organizational climates conducive to fostering human satisfactions, the threat of the regulatory powers of unions and government policing agencies would provide the necessary additional incentives. The original intent of unions was to improve the lot of the so-called "working man." Any relaxation by managers of their efforts to remove factors in the organizational way of life judged to be oppressive to the members would meet with union resistance. Moreover, the government has sweeping powers to eliminate impairments of human rights and privileges within organizations.

Therefore, in this book we contend that the traditional model of management and the behavioral approach are compatible, rather than mutually exclusive. In fact, the managerial function of leading is now totally based on the behavioral approach, and behavioral precepts figure largely in the performance of the planning, organizing, staffing, and controlling functions.

The Quantitative Approach

At the opposite pole is the school of thought that contends mathematical models and computer programs can be expressive of the whole of the management process. This quantitative approach is the ultimate in impersonal, optimal efficiency management models. While the behavioral approach seems to be on the ascent in management curricula and literature today, the quantitative school seems to have perhaps peaked in the 1960s, and to be in a stage of relative decline in the late 1970s. However, the omnipresent computer will effectively preclude any real diminishing of the importance of quantitative management methods.

Besides the computer and its many applications, practicing managers and management students are feeling the thrusts of statistical methods and operations research techniques. Business, government, institutional, and military organizations all employ staffs of quantitative specialists who develop mathematically derived solutions to operational problems. All business schools require students to pass courses in at least the rudiments of the quantitative methodologies. The quantitative approach to management has a strong position, and many persuasive proponents.

However, as with the contention that the behavioral approach is not in conflict with the traditional management model, so it is also claimed in this book that the quantitative approach complements the model of viewing management as a structure of functions that managers perform. The managerial functions of planning and controlling draw heavily on quantitative techniques for their performance. The digital computer is becoming an indispensable tool of most organizations today. There is no quarrel in this book with the advocates of the importance of the quantitative approach; in fact it is viewed that managers would unnecessarily handicap themselves if they failed to utilize these methods where appropriate.

MANAGEMENT AND ORGANIZATION

Hopefully, the meanings of the term *management* have been explained. However, another term, *organization,* has been prominent in our explanation of the term management. The term *organizing* has been defined as one of the functions that managers perform. Certainly some clarification is needed as to what is meant by organization and organizing in the vocabulary of management.

In the broad sense, an *organization* is a collection of people who are joined together by some common bond. Examined more narrowly, an organization is formal if the people are consciously joined together for the purpose of achieving some defined nonpersonal objectives. An organization is *informal* if the people come together spontaneously, and where the common bond is the satisfaction of individual personal objectives. The workings and power of informal organizations, which are present in all formal organizations, will be discussed later in the book. In this book, unless informal is specified, *organization* will mean formal organization. The management process is performed in all types of organizations. Although the thrust of this book is primarily directed to business organizations, other types of organizations that accomplish their objectives as a result of management include governments, churches, institutions (such as universities, hospitals, and prisons), the military, and social agencies (such as the Red Cross and the Salvation Army).

One way of classifying business organizations is to delineate companies primarily engaged in manufacturing and selling a line of products; companies primarily engaged in distributing products, which are called "wholesalers"; companies engaged in selling products to consumers, which are called "retailers"; and companies engaged in selling services, such as banking or insurance. In the United States, prominent manufacturing organizations include General Motors, U.S. Steel, and Boeing Aircraft. Because wholesalers do not deal with consumers, their names may not sound familiar. The grocery chain Smart and Final and the electrical distributor Graybar Electric are two large wholesale organizations. Well-known retail organizations include Sears Roebuck, Montgomery Ward, and J. C. Penney. Among service organizations, Bank of America and Metropolitan Life Insurance are familiar examples. These examples indicate that "organization," in the business context, may be used interchangeably with "the business company."

In addition to being a synonym for the business company, the term organization is often used to describe a collection of people consciously grouped to achieve planned objectives at various levels up and down the company structure. Thus, the accounting department, sales department, and the production department are all organizations.

Organizing is the function that managers perform when they create organizations. They must first plan the objectives they wish to accomplish. The determination of objectives will point to the activities that must be performed. If the objective is to sell furniture through a retail outlet, then there will be the activities of buying furniture, displaying it, advising customers as to style and color, consummating sales, making deliveries, and maintaining records. Organizing is the grouping of such activities into departments, establishing authority and responsibility relationships, and providing for coordination between the departments.

DISCUSSION QUESTIONS

1. Explain why management is essentially accomplishing things through people.
2. What makes management an academic discipline?
3. Speculate on why there has been such serious conflict over the proper approach to the study of management.
4. Explain how the traditional management model is complemented by the behavioral and quantitative approaches.
5. Explain the difference between a formal organization and an informal organization.

BIBLIOGRAPHY

Albers, Henry H. *Principles of Management,* 4th ed. New York: Wiley, 1974.

George, Claude S., Jr. *The History of Management Thought,* 2nd ed. Englewood Cliffs: Prentice-Hall, 1972.

Hertz, David B. "The Unity of Science and Management." *Management Science,* Vol. 11 No. 6 (April 1965), pp. B89–B97.

Koontz, Harold, ed. *Toward a United Theory of Management.* New York: McGraw-Hill, 1964.

Southoff, Herbert. "What Is the Manager?" *Harvard Business Review,* Vol. 42 No. 6 (November–December 1964), pp. 24–36ff.

Wortman, Max S., Jr., and Fred Luthans, eds. *Emerging Concepts in Management,* 2nd ed. New York: Macmillan, 1975.

2 The Manager's Job

The job of managing entails performing the functions of *planning, organizing, staffing, leading,* and *controlling.* These functions are performed to coordinate the resources of an organization so that the objectives of the organization can be realized. Actually, managers have direct contact with the human resource of the organization, so the effective utilization of the physical resources of the organization is achieved through managers working through people. This concept was explained in the preceding chapter. In this chapter we will take a more detailed look at the manager's job.

THE MANAGERIAL FUNCTIONS

The managerial functions model for studying management provides a logical structure that so far has not been equaled. It may be successfully argued that managers perform functions other than those that provide the framework for this book. Some activities managers perform, that are treated here as derivative of the main functions, may be considered by other writers to be main functions in themselves. For example, *representing* and *innovating,* treated here as derivative of the leading function, are activities occasionally categorized as functions. It is certainly accurate to say that all managers do not perform the functions in the same way. Specific performance will vary depending on the manager's level in an organization; the skill activity the manager is directing (such as finance, production, and marketing); whether the organization is business, military, government, or some other kind; and, if the organization is a business, whether it is manufacturing, wholesaling, retailing, or service. All of these variables will affect the exact way that the managerial functions are performed. However, the fact remains that, in some way, all managers plan, organize, staff, lead, and control.

Planning

While it is certainly not suggested that any function has primacy over any other (because any one of the functions may be the most significant in a given situation), it is generally true that if the management process is viewed as a continuum with a beginning and an end, planning comes first. Plans start with the determination of organizational objectives, for in any endeavor it is necessary to establish what is desired to be accomplished, if anything is going to be accomplished. Next, plans are needed to implement the objectives, to provide the step-by-step actions that will bring the objectives to fruition. Planning is concerned with the future; in effect it might be said to be an attempt to shape the future. Plans may be classified as those focusing on periods of three to five years hence, or they may bear more intensely on periods of just a few days up to twelve months. Another way of classifying plans is by the activities with which they are concerned, like finance, production, or sales. The determination of policies, procedures, budgets, and schedules is still another way of classifying plans. Finally, as planning is fundamentally choosing from among alternatives, planning is deciding on future courses of action.

Organizing

The managerial function of organizing was described in the preceding chapter, but additional elements of the function need to be clarified. As with all of the functions, organizing is a never ending process. All organizations are in a continual state of being reorganized. Activities change as a result of redirection in the organizational objectives. Departmental structures become outmoded as a result of growth in organizational size, or changes in the products or services offered. The coordinative process may lose synchronization, and systems adjustments will have to be introduced to reestablish stability and responsiveness in the network of team relationships. An organization might be likened to a machine. Planning involves deciding what a machine is to do. Organizing is the design of the machine; it involves getting all of its parts into cooperative working order, and keeping them that way.

Staffing

Staffing is the personnel function of managers. While it is true that most organizations above a certain size maintain a personnel department, such departments are intended to provide specialized personnel services for other departments. They do much of the basic recruiting of potential employees and they assist in the preliminary screening of job candidates. They design training programs as directed by the managers of other departments, and they administer wage and salary programs to assure equitable compensation. They also advise managers on systematic methods of performance appraisal. However, it should be clearly understood that the managers of an organization are ultimately responsible for their staffing performance. The fact that a personnel department will help them in performing this function does not relieve managers of this responsibility. It is a major part of their job to assure that their organization is staffed with qualified people.

Leading

Where planning is like determining what a machine is to do, and organizing is building the machine, the leading function involves getting the machine to run. A marginal operator will get some output of productivity from a machine, but the skilled technician can double or triple the marginal capacity. So it is with management. Managers who can lead subordinates to contribute maximum effort in job performance will leave the managers who rely exclusively on their formal authority figurative miles behind in the race for managerial success. Essentially, leading involves motivating subordinates to give their all. Leading seems to come naturally for some people, but it should not be assumed that it cannot be acquired. An understanding of the underlying nature of people's attitudes, behaviors, and needs is one requisite. Another essential part of leading is knowing how to communicate.

Controlling

Controlling completes the management process by comparing actual results with plans, seeking causes for deviations, and implementing actions to correct the deviations. It has been likened to the process of navigation. Navigators start with a plan as to where their ships or planes are headed, and make constant checks to determine if the vehicles are still on course. If they are not, the navigators make corrections to point them in the right direction. Up until about 1960, controlling primarily involved making measurements against quantitative standards, and calling people who were responsible to account for the detected differences.

Although there is an impersonal type of efficiency to such an approach to control, many people think it has threatening and debilitating aspects. Today controlling is also viewed as an attempt to identify and remove obstacles in the organizational climate that alienate people, or that cause anxieties and frustrations that inhibit people from performing with maximum competence.

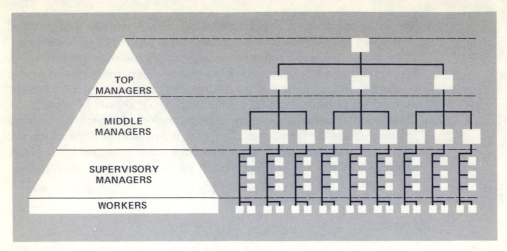

Figure 2-1. Organizational Levels.

ORGANIZATIONAL LEVELS

One feature that is common to all organizational structures is a shape like a pyramid. As depicted in Figure 2-1, at the bottom levels of organizations are the nonmanagers, or workers. (Workers is a convenient term, and should not be construed to mean that managers don't work.) At the supervisory level of managers, sometimes called the first level or the bottom level, are the managers who are on a face-to-face contact relationship with the workers. Above the supervisory level, and in large organizations frequently comprising many levels, is middle management. Middle managers direct specialized activities, specific product lines, or geographical areas. They implement the policies originated at the top management level through coordination of the managers at the supervisory level. The top-level managers are the policy makers and primary decision makers of the organization.

As can be seen from Figure 2-1, the pyramid shape of organizations derives from the narrowing of the number of jobs at each level, until ultimately at the top of all organizations there is only one job. In business organizations, the top job is titled either chief executive officer, chairman of the board of directors, or president. Although it has been said that managers at all levels perform the same functions, the following descriptions illustrate the differing degrees of importance attached to the performance of the same functions.

Top Management

Planning involves determining the kind of a company the firm is going to be, and deciding on profit, growth, and product line objectives. *Orga-*

nizing includes formulating the basic structure of the organization at the top level by function, product, or territory. *Staffing* involves selecting people for top management potential, providing opportunities for them to acquire general management experience, and establishing extra compensation and fringe benefits programs. *Leading* is providing the incentives and moral support to undertake highly significant and responsible endeavors. *Controlling* is assessing profit performance versus profit goals.

Middle Management

Planning is the formulating of second level plans for implementing the top level plans and developing broad budgets and schedules. Planning also involves developing and disseminating operating procedures. *Organizing* includes authority delegation, formulation of management spans, and development of lateral relationships. *Staffing* involves selecting people with middle management potential and assuring that they are exposed to policy implementation and other middle management development programs; assuring that there are equitable job evaluation and compensation systems; and conducting periodic performance appraisals. The middle management *leading* function is to induce subordinates to perceive that their personal need satisfactions are related to achieving the division or department objectives. *Controlling* involves measuring budget and schedule results in relation to plans.

Supervisory Management

Planning in supervisory management involves developing detailed budgets and schedules. Principally, organizing for this management level is complying with vertical relationships and maintaining lateral relationships, together with some grouping of operational activities. *Staffing* is selecting and training new employees, administering compensation policies, and carrying out periodic performance appraisals. *Leading* is overcoming worker resistance to the organization, recognizing above average achievement by workers, and occasionally acting in the role of the personnel counselor. Controlling is assuring that the necessary work gets done within cost and schedule estimates.

WHAT A MANAGER NEEDS TO KNOW

Organizations are becoming increasingly complex. This means that the contemporary manager and the manager of the future will have to possess a considerably broader range of knowledge than ever before. Just as the managerial functions vary from supervisory, to middle, to top management, so also does the manager's required breadth of knowledge expand as progress is made from the bottom of the pyramid to the apex. A compounding problem is that so much of what is involved in management cannot be taught in schools of business. As noted earlier, management is an art that can only be learned from experience. However, there is some information that all managers need to know.

Every organization provides a specific good or service. One organization might sell fruit, vegetables, canned goods, and meats in large volume. Another might make shoes. Another might sell life insurance. Still another might make appliances. But whatever the nature of the business, there is a unique technology associated with it. Practicing managers must be well acquainted with the technology associated with their organizations. Before they can ever be managers within an organization, they must develop an intimate knowledge of the activities the organization performs. Moreover, because the technology of most businesses is changing, after they become managers they must be constantly alert to these changes, and be prepared to implement them at the appropriate time. For example, it is predicted that the checkless economy is just around the corner in the United States and probably in other countries as well. This means that salaries won't be paid in checks to be deposited in banks, and that consumers won't pay their bills in checks that will be withdrawn from their bank balances. Instead, all transactions will be done electronically. Just think of the implications that this technological change will have for bank managers. The same kinds of changes are in the offing in dozens of other kinds of organizations.

The structure of authority relationships that define the *formal* organization becomes complex in companies as small as 500 employees. As business firms, or any other kind of organization, grow beyond this size, the groupings of product lines, services offered, and activities performed become intricate networks. An intimate understanding of how the organization is designed, and what provisions for coordination have been built into it are essential for a manager. Through this understanding, the manager can comprehend and interrupt the planned internal workings of the organization for his or her benefit, and for the benefit of subordinates and outsiders to the organization.

Later in this book the phenomenon of *informal* organizations is discussed. They are present in all formal organizations, and constitute powerful forces that an astute manager can use to his or her advantage. If they are not handled properly, informal organizations can effectively thwart a manager's efforts to successfully manage that part of the formal organization for which he or she is responsible. The formal organization structure of companies medium-sized and larger is difficult enough to understand, but the web of informal relationships are literally beyond comprehension. All a manager can do is understand the nature of informal organizations, and be constantly aware that a myriad of them are covertly in existence.

A working knowledge of psychology and sociology is essential for managers in the modern organization. Broadly defined, psychology is the study of individual behavior and sociology is the study of group behavior. Together, they constitute a large part of the discipline known as behavioral science, which, as was explained in the preceding chapter, is having an important impact on the management process in contemporary times. It should not be inferred that a manager must be a psychologist and a sociologist, but he or she must be acquainted with the central contributions to management thought that have come from these two disciplines.

The modern organization is not only being bombarded with technological changes, as has been mentioned, but also with social changes that are highly significant to managers. These changes generally fall into two categories: 1) responsibilities to women workers and workers from minority ethnic groups, and 2) responsibilities to the general public. Federal legislation intended to eliminate employment discrimination of all kinds stems from the Civil Rights Act of 1964. It is now unlawful to discriminate against workers, or applicants for employment, because of sex, race, religion, age, or political beliefs. Antidiscrimination means that women and members of minority groups must be assured of equal compensation with white males if they perform the same kind of work and must be afforded equal opportunities for advancement. So far, there is little in the way of specific legislation establishing business responsibility to the public at large, but pressures from activists like Ralph Nader and representatives of consumer and environmental protection groups make it imperative that managers keep up to date on these current social issues.

ADVANTAGES OF BEING A MANAGER

Considering how vigorously people in organizations compete to be promoted to a managerial job, and how the competition continues in the efforts to reach higher and higher managerial levels, it is apparent that lots of people already employed in organizations perceive advantages associated with being a manager. Moreover, the thousands of students enrolled in schools of business across the country further indicates that being a manager has desirable features. Some of the more obvious of these advantages are various forms of compensation that accompany a managerial position.

With few exceptions, managers make considerably more money than nonmanagers in the same organizations. One exception might be the occasional highly paid salesperson who works on a straight commission. Naturally, the higher the managerial level—the higher the salary. A rough estimate of managerial salaries in the United States in the late 1970s is around $20,000 annually for supervisory management, $25,000 to $60,000 per year for middle management, and $75,000 to

$500,000 yearly salaries for top management. (The annual *Business Week* survey of executive salaries shows few below $100,000, with the average running around $200,000; but these are for the top managers of the very large business firms in the United States.)

As individuals move up the managerial ranks, benefits that they receive in addition to generous salaries can be quite significant. Such benefits come in forms of indirect compensation and include attractive offices, company cars, expense accounts, club memberships, and comfortable pensions.

Finally, managers occupy positions in an organization that indicate achievement. Both within the organization and in their external relationships, managers are looked upon as being people who have succeeded. Frequently their implied abilities as a result of being managers will lead to other status positions in their churches, clubs, civic organizations, and on the board of directors of other business firms.

DISADVANTAGES OF BEING A MANAGER

A managerial job is not for everybody, even though most people would like to partake of the benefits associated with being a manager. Many people who become managers don't deliberately plan on management as a career; they simply happen to be on the scene when a managerial opportunity occurs, and they move naturally from nonmanagerial work into a managerial field. A large proportion of people who get into management this way are happy with their jobs, and have successful careers. However, there are some features of being a manager that are unattractive to some people. It is especially important that students who are contemplating a management career be aware of some of the disadvantages attached to managerial jobs.

Nonmanagers usually have a set number of hours that they work each week, and the rest of the time is theirs to do with what they wish. Not so with managers. Managerial jobs, and particularly top management jobs, are literally never ending. Average work weeks of 60 hours and over are the rule, rather than the exception. Personal life must be subordinated to the job, and the manager's family and hobbies naturally suffer as a consequence. This condition is really not as distasteful to top managers as it might sound because to most of them their jobs are the most fun thing that they do. Of course, not everyone can reach such a degree of dedication.

Some people thrive on responsibility, and the oftentimes oppressive responsibilities associated with being a manager do not bother them a bit. Other people are extremely threatened by responsibilities, and may actually develop physical and/or emotional responses to the demands of managerial work that may seriously damage their health.

Managers must play many roles, and the one that is most burdensome to some is that of counselor, confessor, or chaplain to other people. The members of a manager's organization look to him or her for help with their personal problems. They look to the manager for rewards and privileges. They vent their frustrations with their jobs and with the organization on the manager. They demand a great deal from the person who is their boss, but too often are unwilling to give anything in return. Dealing with other people's problems can be a very unattractive condition of the managerial job.

DISCUSSION QUESTIONS

1. Explain what is meant by the management functions model providing a logical structure for studying management.
2. Discuss the notion that planning is pervasively present in the other managerial functions.
3. Explain how the leading function might be basically similar at all levels of management.
4. How can an individual learn the technology associated with his or her specific organization?
5. What should a person do who wants a successful career in business and also a fulfilling life apart from the job?

BIBLIOGRAPHY

Dale, Ernest. *The Great Organizers.* New York: McGraw-Hill, 1960.

Katz, D. and R. L. Kahn. *The Social Psychology of Organizations.* New York: John Wiley and Sons, 1966.

Koontz, Harold. "The Management Theory Jungle." *Journal of the Academy of Management,* Vol. 4 No. 3 (December 1961), pp. 174–88.

Koontz, Harold and Cyril O'Donnell. *Principles of Management: An Analysis of Managerial Functions,* 5th ed. New York: McGraw-Hill, 1972.

March, J. G. and H. A. Simon. *Organizations.* New York: John Wiley and Sons, 1958.

3 Early Contributions to Management Theory

What is now formally known about management has accumulated from the findings of a host of contributors. However, formal knowledge of management lags behind working knowledge because theorists are not extensively aware of techniques developed by working managers. On the other hand, theorists have developed models which might be useful if they were known and applied by practicing managers. Although many past ideas about management have been misinterpreted, have become partially discredited, or now seem incomplete in the light of newer discoveries, much that is still valid can be gained from an understanding of what past thinkers have contributed to the development of management theory. The sections that follow summarize some of the important and influential contributions that have been made to management theory since the turn of the century.

MAX WEBER AND BUREAUCRACY

In the 1890s, a German sociologist named Max Weber prescribed a system for organization which he called "bureaucracy." In his description of this system, Weber in effect ushered in the era of the professional manager and bade farewell to the age of "patrimony," which, liberally interpreted, means owner-dominated management. The bureaucratic model is an impersonal, rational system that enables professional managers to efficiently assemble and control the human resources of an organization.

Although the concept of bureaucracy is now commonly associated with Weber, it is certain that it did not originate with him. Long before Weber's time military organizations, churches, and local governments were structured along the lines he proposed. Moreover, business organizations in the United States were taking on bureaucratic characteristics while Weber's writings were still waiting for translation into English. It may be that bureaucracy naturally evolves when efficiency in organization is the end objective. However, Weber is credited with the model, and his explanation of its typical operation is commonly accepted.

Essentials of Bureaucracy

Weber stated that a bureaucratic organization is characterized by the conduct of business in accordance with stipulated rules, a hierarchy of authority levels, the accountability of managers at each authority level for the uses of resources committed to them, and the conduct of business on the basis of written documents. To anyone with experience in modern organizations—either business, government, education, or military—these precepts must have a familiar ring.

Stipulated rules. The primary purpose of rules is to reduce the frequency of decision making. In a bureaucracy, rules, which may be broadened to include policies and procedures, are formulated to cover every possible situation. When an issue requiring action arises, one need only consult the rule applying to that type of situation to discover that the apppropriate action is spelled out. (This is popularly known as "going by the book.") Weber expanded the stipulated-rules concept to include the duties of each managerial position, denoting how much authority is assigned to each position and placing specific restrictions on the personal discretion permitted a manager. Thus, the objective in a bureaucracy is to assure predictable conformity of action throughout the organization.

Hierarchy of authority. Weber viewed the authority structure of a bureaucratic organization as an inverted pyramid. (See Chapter 2 for initial discussion of the pyramid shape of organizations.) Positions at the top of the structure have extensive authority, even though the content of the assignments would be specific and limited. In Weber's terms, the top people are responsible for supervision. Positions lower in the structure have less authority. The lowest levels have only the right of appeal. As we said in Chapter 2, in terms of the number of positions at the various organizational levels, the shape of the structure is a conventional pyramid. Thus, the effect of bureaucracy is a concentration of authority in a relatively few positions.

Accountability. Managers in a bureaucracy do not own the resources they employ. However, they are held accountable for the prudent use of them. Weber emphasized the necessity for professional managers to completely separate official business from their private affairs, and official income from their private income. In modern terms one would say that managers should act as trustees for the property rights of the owners, and scrupulously avoid conflicts between the organization's interests and their personal interests.

Written documents. Weber stressed that in a bureaucracy all business should be conducted on the basis of written documents, and that each transaction should be recorded for future reference. This principle is a control device to assure that the stipulated rules are followed and to restrain individuals from acting beyond their specified authority.

Professional managers. Weber characterized professional managers as appointed to their position, rather than acquiring it through property rights. Managers carry out their duties by adhering to impersonal rules. Their appointments to the jobs and their tenure depend on their technical qualifications. Their jobs are their full-time occupations. They have no right to the revenues of the organization, but are compensated for their work by a salary and the prospects of advancement. For the most part, this is an accurate portrayal of most business managers in the United States today.

Significance of the Bureaucratic Model

The extent to which bureaucratic concepts permeate all organizations makes the model perhaps the most significant of management theories. This does not mean that it is an ideal prescription. Its keynote is the depersonalization of work tasks at every organizational level. Weber used the term "specialized cogs" to describe individuals in a bureaucratic system. The model does not consider or accommodate human differences.

Bureaucracy is a rational response to the quest for systematic efficiency. Today, because of the increasing importance of the computer and the compatibility of the computer with impersonal systems, there may even be a trend toward an expansion of bureaucracy.

FREDERICK TAYLOR AND SCIENTIFIC MANAGEMENT

The term *scientific management* has come to be associated more with the mechanics its practitioners employed (time and motion study, for example) than with the concept itself. Actually, it was a philosophy dedicated to improving efficiency through the elimination of wasted effort. Its ideal was a constant growth in wealth achieved through productivity, a wealth which was to be shared by workers and management, and reflected by continual rises in the nation's prosperity.

Many important names are connected with the scientific management movement including those of Henry Gantt and Frank and Lillian Gilbreth. However, Frederick W. Taylor is the name that epitomizes scientific management. It is even common to speak of "Taylorism" rather than of "scientific management."

Taylor was a steel company engineer who had also worked as a trade craftsman and later became a widely known industrial consultant. He was convinced that workers perceived available work to be of a fixed amount (the "ball of work" concept) and that they believed it to be in their best interests to perform their work slowly in order to make the work last. His thinking led him to conceive an ideal condition where workers and management would cooperate to increase productivity, with both sides sharing the resulting growth in wealth. Thus, the inhibiting notion of the "ball of work" would be dispelled, and workers would be so satisfied with the larger absolute value of their share of profit that the traditional labor-management conflicts would disappear.

Taylor's Principles

Taylor's prescription for bringing about increased productivity was expressed in four principles which are fundamental to scientific management. These principles relate to job design, worker selection and training, worker motivation, and the separation of planning from performing.

Job design. Until Taylor's time (around 1910), managers did not give much thought to job design or to how work should be done. Work practices were passed down through generations of workers in the respective trades, and managers simply assumed that machinists, foundrymen, and shoemakers, for example, possessed the traditional skills that would enable them to produce an acceptable day's work. To Taylor, this approach was wrong. He believed that there was "one best way" to do any job, and that the primary responsibility of managers was to find it. The mass of knowledge related to every kind of work should be accumulated, studied, and recorded; superfluous elements should be discarded; then each job should be carefully redesigned via stopwatch time-and-motion study, among other techniques, to the point that no further improvements were possible. The "one best" method would be established as the standard way for performing the job.

Worker selection and training. Taylor's second principle focused on worker selection and training. Physical and mental attributes required to satisfactorily perform each job should be identified. Workers should then be selected for jobs on the basis of their possession of these qualities. (Before this principle was spelled out, no deliberate attention had been given to matching workers with jobs.) After it is assured that the workers selected for jobs have the potential for performing them, they should be carefully trained to do the work by the standardized method. The methods for doing each job should be specific enough so that each sequential movement can be learned and consistently followed.

Worker motivation. Taylor's third principle dealt with worker motivation. He said that once a standard method was established for doing each job and workers trained in following it, management was responsible for assuring that the workers conform to the standards. He asserted bluntly that workers who would not follow the instructions should be removed from the job. Today this is called "motivation by negative incentive": Workers either do things the way they are told or they are fired. On the opposite side, Taylor urged the offering of "plums" to workers who would follow the standard methods. One plum he suggested was a financial incentive. Minimum production rates should be established for doing every job according to the standard, and a base wage set for these rates. When workers followed the standard method and produced above the minimum rates, their wages should be increased to yield shares of greater productivity. Taylor is now identified solely with the idea of promising more money to workers as a way of motivating them to higher productivity. However, money was only one of the motivating "plums" that he suggested. Other motivators included better, more kindly treatment, more consideration for worker's wishes, and an opportunity for them to express their desires freely.

Separation of planning from performance. Taylor introduced the notion that planning should be separated from actual performance—that is, extensive preparation should precede actual work—and that management was responsible for such planning. Thus, organizing work, getting it started, and assessing its accomplishment should be taken away from the workers and set up as a separate activity. Presumably this division would lead to a spirit of team effort among workers and management. Taylor divided the planning phase into specialized segments, such as scheduling, employee selection, time-keeping, and training. Although not developing exactly as he had intended, this division did lead to the functional specialization that is characteristic of all organizations today.

Immediate Effects

Scientific management was enthusiastically accepted by industry, first in the United States, and eventually in all industrialized countries. It was a new and exciting way of viewing management and it invariably led to dramatic improvements in efficiency when properly applied. Bright young people gravitated to Taylor to learn his methods and many became well-known authorities in their own right as they developed and expanded Taylor's basic ideas.

On the negative side, workers rejected scientific management from the beginning. This was unfortunate because Taylor was apparently sincere in his belief that it was the best possible thing that could happen to labor. Instead of the labor-management cooperation Taylor sought, scientific management widened the schism between labor and management. Workers resented the depersonalization of jobs, with all of the individuality and craftsmanship taken out of them. They despised the speedup practices that evolved from wage-incentive systems. Intrinsic satisfaction in work was removed when the thinking part of jobs was taken over by management.

Lasting Effects

Some twenty years after Taylor's time, there began to be a wave of interest in human relations. It seemed that scientific management might disappear as a conceptual approach, although in practice it had spread through industry, with every organization following Taylor's principles in varying degrees. Eventually the human relations vogue reached its zenith and declined, and the two theories, together with others, are now viewed as mutually exclusive models to be examined in the abstract.

Today scientific management and bureaucracy are commonly viewed together as one impersonal, efficient model, with financial incentive as the primary basis for motivating workers. Scientific management is a convenient interpretation of what Taylor and his followers stood for, as it provides a basis for comparative analysis. However, it is incomplete because Taylor himself—and Gantt and Lillian Gilbreth to an even greater extent—were definitely concerned with the roles of the individual and the group in organizations. Scientific management was not nearly so devoid of consideration for people as it is usually made out to be, and any assessment of its defects ought to take note of the fact that at the time of its greatest popularity, psychology was just being accepted as a professional discipline.

HENRI FAYOL AND MANAGEMENT PRINCIPLES

The writings of the French industrialist Henri Fayol were first published in French, around 1916. These writings have a very important place in management literature. In fact, it is from Fayol that the framework of management functions has evolved as a basis for understanding management. He also originated the concept of the universality of management in his proposition that managers at all levels of business organization, whether they be senior executives, department heads, or foremen, perform the same functions. In addition, he suggested that there are certain guiding principles of management, a suggestion that greatly influenced management writers in this country in the 1950s.

Fayol's Definition of Management

Fayol perceived that certain activities are essential to any business organization. For instance, all firms must buy raw materials, produce and sell goods or services, raise capital and use it efficiently, protect resources, and accurately record transactions. However, he felt that another activity, that of management, was often overlooked. Management to him meant planning, organizing, commanding, coordinating, and controlling.

To Fayol, *planning* involved assessing the future and making provisions for it; it was the most difficult and important of the manager's tasks. He emphasized the need for primary plans and derivative plans. Fayol was using one-year and ten-year forecasts in his own organization fifty years before they became common among United States firms.

Fayol visualized *organizing* in a very broad sense. First, it involved providing a business with all of the necessary physical resources. Second, it concerned *human organization.* In describing it, Fayol focused on the way the management levels increase in proportion to increases in the number of employees. He defined the general duties at each organizational level; he stressed the need for organization charts; and finally, he included prescriptions for selecting and training employees and for developing managers, which are now customarily considered part of the staffing function.

Commanding, Fayol said, was the function of "getting the organization going," the function now called *leading.* It was the face-to-face interaction between managers and subordinates in accomplishing the goals of the organization. Fayol saw the need for managers to be personally involved with their subordinates as individuals, and the need for managers to lead by their own exemplary conduct.

What Fayol called *coordinating* is now usually identified as the purpose of all managerial functions, rather than a separate function. Fayol perceived it as harmonizing all the activities of a firm and achieving a balance between input and output factors. He urged conferences and liaison activities as methods of achieving coordination.

Controlling was seen by Fayol in very much the same way that it is now understood. To him controlling consisted of verifying whether everything occurs in conformity with the plan adopted, the instructions issued, and the principles established. He emphasized that controlling depended on plans. He also stressed that controlling can be effective only if it is done within a reasonable time after events, and that undesirable variations between plans and events must be corrected.

Fayol's Management Principles

In looking back over his long and successful career as a business manager, Fayol saw certain principles that he frequently applied. However, he stated that there is no limit to the number of principles, for any rule or procedure qualifies as a principle if the results it generates confirm its usefulness. He made the point that the difficult part of principles is knowing how to use them. The principles that he emphasized were

1. Division of work—large tasks should be divided into small ones, with people specializing in performing them.
2. Authority and responsibility—managers must have the right to give orders and the power to exact obedience. Responsibility of managers for their actions is the corollary of authority, arising whenever authority is exercised.
3. Discipline—managers must respect agreements made with employees, and employees must honor their commitments to the company.
4. Unity of command—subordinates should not receive orders from more than one supervisor.
5. Unity of direction—only one plan should exist for the achievement of any objective, and all members of the organization should follow the plan.
6. Subordination of interest—the interest of the organization should come before individual interests.
7. Remuneration—wages should rise or fall as a result of effort. Bonuses should be used to motivate extended effort.
8. Centralization—optimal centralization of decision making varies with the individual firm, but should be determined according to the best use of all of the abilities of the personnel.
9. Chain of command—authority is linked by a scalar (ladder-like) chain of supervisors and subordinates extending down from the highest management position to the lowest organizational level. Communication ideally flows up and down this chain, but in practice individuals in different chains must be able to communicate horizontally also.
10. Order—the qualifications of individuals and the requirements of jobs should be matched.
11. Equity—personnel should be dealt with on the basis of kindliness and justice.
12. Job stability—conditions should be provided to motivate employees to stay with their jobs.
13. Initiative—employees should be given the opportunity to think out and execute plans.
14. Team spirit—rapport among the individuals should be striven for and the setting up of divisive factors avoided. More reliance should be put on oral than on written communications.

The Importance of Fayol's Contributions

One especially significant feature of Fayol's writings is his approach to the "total job of managing." No one else really attempted such an approach until the management theorists of the 1950s. Taylor and his followers were preoccupied with improving the efficiency of workers at the operating level. Between 1900 and about 1950, valuable additions to management knowledge were made, but they were fragmentary, dealing either with organizing, planning and controlling, or staffing. Fayol, on the other hand, left a framework upon which the whole of management could be studied and analyzed.

THE HAWTHORNE STUDIES AND HUMAN RELATIONS

The most extensive and significant research ever conducted with social science methods was performed at the Hawthorne Works of the Western Electric Company over the interval of a few years before and after 1930. The research was sponsored by the National Research Council and made possible by the cooperation of Western Electric. Names that will always be remembered because of their association with the research are F. J. Roethlisberger, Elton Mayo, and T. N. Whitehead.

Originally, the research was designed to determine if there was a relationship between worker productivity and the lighting of the work area. Most of the workers involved in the experiments were women who performed routine assembly operations. The testing amounted to changing the intensity of light over work stations and measuring any corresponding changes in productivity. However, in this experiment the researchers invited the participation of the workers whose productivity was to be measured—carefully explaining to them the objectives of the experiment and asking for comments and suggestions while the investigation was taking place.

The experiment was conducted as planned. Lighting was increased, and productivity went up. Lighting was increased again, and again productivity went up. This pattern was repeated several more times. All during this period, the researchers demonstrated sincere interest in the workers, rather than treating them as impersonal research subjects.

At one point, the change in illumination was reversed. Although not telling the workers of the change, the researchers maintained their friendly, cooperative relationship with them. While the illumination was gradually being decreased, productivity continued to rise until it finally reached a plateau. Researchers concluded that any importance that lighting might have as a variable was obscured by other factors present in the experiment. These factors were plainly psychological, and suggested that the motivational effects of treating people as responsive individuals in their work environment offered exciting possibilities.

The research went on for a number of years, but with a different purpose. The new objective was to learn more about how the treatment of workers could affect productivity. The typical approach was to select a group of women workers to participate in an experiment in which changes in productivity could be accurately compared with changes in working conditions and with different attitudes toward the workers themselves.

Variations in working conditions included more precise control of work output, as well as changes in height and weight of stools and benches, hours of work, rest periods, methods of payment, and so on. The purpose of the experiment was explained to the workers and they were asked for their consent to take part. Traditional management attitudes toward workers also were altered; as in the lighting experiment, worker participation was conscientiously encouraged. There was no direct supervisor over the women. No attempt was made to limit conversation on the job, and the permissiveness extended to allowing birthday parties in the work area. Moreover, the women were invited in interviews to talk about their problems and what they wanted from their jobs.

The results of this research indicated that nothing that was done to change working conditions had any direct relationship with productivity. For example, productivity rose when rest periods were introduced, but it continued to rise when the rest periods were taken away. The work output by the experimental group increased until it reached an unpredicted high level, at which point it was sustained independent of any modification of work conditions.

The improved work performance by the experimental group could only be attributed to the worker's response to being personally involved in their jobs. The treatment they received made them like their work. They felt that what they were doing was important, and recognizing that the purpose of the research was to find out the effect of certain factors on productivity, they reacted by performing at a far higher level than they had ever performed before.

In addition to disclosing factors of individual behavior which were empirically supported for the first time, the research led to a greatly improved understanding of group behavior. In studying the various experimental groups, the researchers discovered that informal leaders always emerged. Although the groups were told by the researchers to work without strain, it was apparent that they set their own norms of effort, enforced by informal leaders. In these experiments, the group norms were set higher than the formal standards, apparently because the groups perceived a cause-and-effect relationship between productivity and the job satisfaction that came from being well treated. Other factors that became clear included the way a group worked harder to support workers having an off-day, and the close identification that the members felt with their group.

We should not conclude our discussion of the Hawthorne studies before noting that they are not above criticism. Shortcomings in the methods used have been uncovered. Nevertheless the work stands out as a high point of human relations research and has had a lasting effect on management study.

Development of Human Relations Concepts

The Hawthorne studies led to what has become known as "the human relations school" of management theory. The Great Depression, with its potential for causing social revolt, and the acute shortage of labor during World War II a decade later, made it necessary for business managers to view their employees from a new perspective. Application of the Hawthorne findings appeared to be the answer.

The human relations approach was misapplied, however, just as scientific management was distorted and misused by people who did not really understand it. For example, one approach used by managers to practice human relations was through "benevolent paternalism." Some managers actually tried to act as "father figures" in dealing with subordinates and became so engrossed with this role that they lost sight of their work objectives. This misguided paternalism also was observed in the practice of randomly granting fringe benefits—a practice that gained momentum with the imposition of wage controls during World War II. An analysis of the Hawthorne studies would have revealed that, as motivators, fringe benefits miss the point completely.

A second way in which managers misused human relations concepts was in trying to dupe workers into thinking that their participation was invited when they were really being manipulated. By the 1950s many managers had become so disillusioned by so-called human relations methods of management that the concept fell into some disrepute.

CHESTER BARNARD, TRANSITIONALIST

Although Chester I. Barnard, as president of New Jersey Bell Telephone Company, was a practical businessman, his contributions to management thought are academic and profound. His best known writing is the book *The Functions of the Executive* (1938), and while it is difficult reading, it is universally recognized as a valuable source of fundamental managerial concepts. Most lists of important contributors to management theory include Barnard's name, even though his managerial ideas are not a school of thought, as are those of Weber on bureaucracy, or of Taylor on scientific management, or of Mayo on human relations. Barnard acted as a bridge between the classicists in management theory who preceded him, and the modern behavioral writers who followed him. In effect, Barnard provides a transition between two eras—between the human relationists and the behavioral scientists.

Organization as a Cooperative System

Before Barnard, organization was viewed only in the rigid structural sense, with a focus on levels of managerial authority. Earlier writers called "authority" the "cement" of an organization. Barnard introduced a different theory, a theory that viewed organizations as "cooperative" systems. He pointed out that only a small number of people in an organization identify their personal objectives with the objectives of the organization; thus, most people must somehow be induced to contribute their individual cooperation. This common purpose is achieved by "communication," which is the "cement" that connects members of the organization and serves to transfer information and establish common purpose.

Barnard's emphasis on organizational purpose has been followed up by most modern writers on management, who see the need for clearly established objectives (purposes) as prerequisites to organizational planning.

Inducement-Contribution Balance

According to Barnard, each member of an organization theoretically gets some inducements from the organization in return for what he or she contributes. As long as the individual perceives that the inducements are as great as, or greater (measured in terms of the individual's values and the other options open to him or her) than the contributions asked to be made, he or she will continue to cooperate. Communication provides each individual with enough information to evaluate whether the inducements and contributions are in balance. Writers in the late 1970s are increasingly urging that managers extend the same or greater care in preserving the "human assets" of their organization as they do with their financial assets. Such a request is clearly a derivation of Barnard's work.

The Informal Organization

The informal organization is discussed later, in Chapter 24, so not too much needs to be said about it at this point. However, Barnard can clearly be seen as a transitionalist in the way he linked the findings on informal organization of the Hawthorne studies to the power of the informal organization now perceived by the modern behavioralists. Barnard apparently originated the idea that every formal organization necessarily overlies an informal one. When people realize that they cannot accomplish what they want to do individually, they get together to agree on a common purpose and intuitively set up a system of communication.

Strategic Factors

A significant feature of the modern concept of decision making is the search for the strategic factor in any decision situation. A *strategic factor* is one that most clearly obstructs the attainment of a desired objective. The manager must identify the strategic factors early in the decision process, and search for alternative solutions which will take care of them. Although Barnard admitted that he did not originate the concept, his insistent emphasis on it has done much to perpetuate it as one of the basic planning principles.

Acceptance Theory of Authority

Barnard's systematic approach to the study of organizations and the functions of executives was comprehensive. However, he is probably best remembered for his "acceptance theory" of authority. Briefly, Barnard awakened management thinkers to the possibility that authority may not come down from the top of an organization but may in fact rise upward from the bottom of the organization.

He said that managers only have as much authority as is granted to them by the people working under them. This authority falls within what Barnard called the worker's "zone of indifference." In other words, some orders given by a supervisor may be clearly unacceptable to the worker, and he or she will try to subvert or get around these orders in one way or another; some orders may be more or less neutrally accepted; and others are clearly acceptable. This last type of order lies within the worker's "zone of indifference" or acceptance.

According to Barnard, this zone of acceptance will be wider or narrower depending on how much the inducements offered by the organization exceed the contributions a worker is expected to make. That is, the more an employee thinks he or she is getting from the organization compared to what he or she is giving, the more the individual will be inclined to accept the authority of the organization.

DISCUSSION QUESTIONS

1. What evidences of bureaucracy have you observed in organizations with which you have been associated? Do you perceive any diminishing of bureaucratic tendencies?
2. What restrictive practices by trade unions provide evidence that the "ball of work" notion still persists?
3. What are the significant differences between Fayol's approach to management theory and the prescriptions offered by Weber?
4. What are some necessary objectives of managers that could be overlooked in a preoccupation with human relations?
5. Explain the "acceptance theory of authority" in terms of the student-instructor relationship.

BIBLIOGRAPHY

Barnard, Chester I. *The Functions of the Executive.* Cambridge: Harvard University Press, 1938.

Bennis, Warren. *Changing Organizations.* New York: McGraw-Hill, 1966.

Fayol, Henri. *General and Industrial Management.* New York: Pitman Publishing Company, 1949.

Gilbreth, Lillian. *The Psychology of Management.* New York: Macmillan, 1914.

Likert, Rensis. *New Patterns in Management.* New York: McGraw-Hill, 1961.

Rathe, A. W., ed. *Gantt on Management.* New York: American Management Association, 1961.

Roethlisberger, F. J. and W. J. Dickson. *Management and the Worker: An Account of a Research Program Conducted by the Western Electric Company Hawthorne Works, Chicago.* Cambridge: Harvard University Press, 1939.

Taylor, Frederick W. *The Principles of Scientific Management.* New York: Harper and Row, 1911.

Weber, Max. *The Theory of Social and Economic Organization.* trans. Talcott Parsons. New York: Oxford University Press, 1947.

4 Behavioral Science and Management Theory

Just when the management community had become disenchanted with the "human relations" approach, the applicability to management of a growing body of knowledge, based on research findings about human behavior, was increasingly recognized. On the other side of that coin, behavioral scientists recognized that substantial portions of human behavior occur in the organization context. Both parties shared an interest in a further understanding of organizational behavior. It is this loose collection of interdisciplinary approaches to human behavior which has come to be known as the *behavioral science* approach in management. This approach has an overall goal of understanding, explaining, and predicting human behavior, particularly as it occurs in organizations.

The boundary which defines what is and what is not part of the behavioral sciences is not universally agreed upon by practitioners and managers. One way of characterizing this approach is to consider the academic disciplines involved, the implications of the scientific procedures used, and the values underlying the research and applications of findings in organizations.

BEHAVIORAL SCIENCE AND SOCIAL SCIENCE

Berelson and Steiner[1] have made a useful distinction between the academic disciplines which are usually included in the behavioral sciences and the social sciences. The social sciences typically include anthropology, economics, history, political science, psychology, and sociology. The behavioral sciences draw heavily from psychology, sociology, and, to a lesser extent, from cultural anthropology. Within those broad areas, physiological psychology, archaeology, and physical anthropology are excluded. Social geography, psychiatry, economics, political science, and the law also deal with aspects of human behavior and are generally included in the behavioral sciences. "In short," Berelson and Steiner conclude, "we are concerned here with scientific research that deals directly with human behavior."[2]

The "Science" of Behavioral Science

Rather than base generalizations and conclusions about human behavior on personal preferences or beliefs about the way people are, the behavioral sciences rely on research findings for their explanations and understanding. Berelson and Steiner characterize the scientific approach with the following objectives:

- Well described research procedures which permit readers to follow them accurately.
- Precise definitions including a description of how procedures and variables were measured and explained.
- Data collection that is objective in that any biases are recognized and accounted for and inherent limitations imposed by data collection processes are identified.
- Research findings that can be replicated by another researcher who repeats the experiment.
- A body of knowledge that is increased by a cumulative, systematic approach.
- An endeavor to explain, understand, and predict human behavior.

Not all research will fully achieve all these objectives. To behavioral scientists these objectives represent ideals. Behavioral scientists strive to attain these ideals as they generate findings that may contribute to a more accurate understanding of human behavior.

VALUES UNDERLYING THE BEHAVIORAL SCIENCES

Like all people, behavioral scientists have values which influence their work and thinking. Additionally, as is also the case among all people, there is a wide range of values among different behavioral scientists. The following paragraphs describe values which are held by many behavioral scientists.

As behavioral scientists go about the practice of their profession, they are interested in obtaining an accurate view of the phenomena under consideration. On occasion, pursuing this objective can run counter to beliefs and preferences of management. In fact, in some situations dearly held management beliefs about the proper conduct of business are contributing to the problem.

For example, a manager who deeply believes that women should not supervise men would not welcome a behavioral scientist's research demonstrating that this belief is contributing to the low level of morale in the firm. The behavioral scientist, valuing accuracy, objectivity, reliability, and validity, will find it necessary to choose in favor of those values instead of management preferences. In the long run, managers will be better off if they have accurate information about the human behavior issues occurring in their organizations. However, managers, like most of us, sometimes find bad news or disconfirming data difficult to accept.

In their organizational work, behavioral scientists tend to avoid broad generalizations about human behavior. They are usually more tentative and speak in terms of propositions and hypotheses rather than principles or firm cause-effect relationships. Human behavior has been found to reflect many, many forces, some of which are subtle yet have a very complex effect on behavior occurring in organizational settings. This leads the behavioral scientist to be less certain about how people will behave than managers typically prefer. Managers need to know with as much certainty as possible the various if-then relationships which govern behavior in their organizations. Behavioral scientists are better at helping managers understand behavior that is occurring in the organization setting than they are at predicting the behavior.

The issues involved in the relationship between worker satisfaction and productivity are a good example of resistance on the part of behavioral scientists to make broad generalizations. Research has shown that it cannot be accurately argued that happy, satisfied workers will necessarily be more productive workers. There are too many variables with varying impact on both productivity and satisfaction to be able to establish a general cause and effect relationship. At the same time, worker satisfaction has turned out to be positively related to such things as absenteeism and employee turnover. Some managers will value increased worker satisfaction as an end in itself. However, other managers will be frustrated by the reluctance of the behavioral scientist to tell them "something that they can use." This usually translates to mean "I want to know that if I take actions A, B, or C, I can expect people in the organization to do X, Y, or Z."

A third value which most behavioral scientists share is an interest in the continued expansion of the frontier of knowledge about human behavior. This value is expressed in the research orientation of most of their interventions in organizations. Behavioral scientists will tend to gather information in the organization and use it to further understanding of both the organization's operations and behavioral dynamics. When that understanding is established, then action alternatives can be examined. This preference for understanding first is demonstrated in the situation where a manager has called upon a behavioral scientist for help in solving some organizational problem. The client will usually have identified a series of problems, which are presented to the behavioral science consultant for solution. A complication may arise because the manager's idea of what is wrong is not the real, basic problem in the operation. If it were, the manager probably could have solved it alone.

The first job of the behavioral science consultant is to help clarify what is occurring in organizational behavior terms. After that understanding has been achieved, the manager can lay plans for altering circumstances to align with what should be. The consultant may be able to assist in constructing the change plan with inputs and applications from the accumulated knowledge of the behavioral sciences.

The final set of values shared by a large number of behavioral scientists concerns their belief that the human being is the most critical and important part of the organization. Many behavioral scientists take a humanist posture similar to that found in the human relations viewpoint. This humanistic value leads to research and action applications which incorporate the goals of increasing the quality of life and reducing the dehumanizing aspects of work. Behavioral scientists holding these values will usually attempt to create work situations which help people fulfill their human potential for growth and development in such a way that organizational goal achievement is improved. It should be noted that there is a good deal of disagreement among practitioners of behavioral science as to what does and what does not contribute to growth and development in human beings.

Among behavioral scientists a controversy rages over the subject of organizational interventions based on the concepts of behaviorism in psychology. Simplifying the behaviorism approach almost too much, we could say the tenet on which behaviorism is based is that specific behavior can be brought out in people through the planned offering and withholding of rewards and punishments. This conceptual approach is viewed by some behavioral scientists as dehumanizing or as an approach that fails to acknowledge the higher virtues which human beings are potentially capable of expressing. Other behavioral scientists assert that organizational efforts to increase worker fulfillment could be improved with the application of knowledge from behaviorist psychology. Managers, like behavioral scientists, must remember that they view organizational behavior phenomena through the biasing filters of their own value systems. With this awareness, managers can better understand the behavior that occurs in their organizations. An awareness of value biases will permit managers to identify and evaluate action programs which may or may not be consistent with organizational objectives and the managers' values.

TOPICS IN BEHAVIORAL SCIENCES

There are a number of issues and topics in management to which the behavioral sciences typically contribute. The list presented here is not an exhaustive one; the intention is to describe behavioral science areas which are commonly included in management. Many of these topics are discussed in greater detail in later chapters of this book. The topics include

- The Individual—motivation, perception, personality, and behavior (Chapter 21).
- Small Groups—dynamics, leadership, interpersonal relations (Chapter 20).
- Large Social Organizations—cultural influences, organizational structure (Chapter 11).
- Concepts and theories that cut across all levels of behavioral analysis—
  Communications (Chapter 23).
  Conflict management (Chapter 13).
  Power relationships (Chapters 13, 24).
  Organizational design and change (Chapters 11, 24).
  Socio-technical systems (Chapters 5, 28).
  Contingency theories (Chapters 5, 20).
  Behaviorism and organizational change (Chapter 24).
  Industrial democracy and participation (Chapter 31).

The Individual

Questions and problems surrounding individual motivation are a constant concern of managers. It is in this realm that psychology has made a large contribution. Maslow's hierarchy of needs is an example. His theory, which is described in more detail in Chapter 21, holds that human motivation is a process of sequentially seeking satisfaction of certain basic needs. He suggested a possible ordering of these needs, beginning with basic physiological needs and proceeding through higher level needs for safety and security, for love and belonging, for esteem, and for self-actualization and fulfillment. These needs are activated in ascending order so that suitable levels of satisfaction of lower level needs must precede the emergence of higher level needs. Maslow's theory has exercised a powerful influence on the behavioral science assumption that the majority of members of organizations can be frustrated in satisfying their higher needs by the demands and structure of formal organizations. Behavioral scientists argue this is particularly true of self-actualization needs. In 1957, Chris Argyris proposed that the lack of congruence between the needs of healthy individuals and the demands of formal organizations results in human frustration, failure, short-time perspective, and interpersonal and intergroup conflict.

Closely related to problems of understanding human motivation is the problem of understanding the conceptual link between motivation and actual behavior. Managers have an idea of the way they would like their subordinates to behave in their jobs. Determining methods supervisors can use to elicit the desired behaviors is an area in which behavioral science knowledge can help. An understanding of the concepts and dynamics of individual personality has had a significant impact on managerial thought and practice.

The Theory X and Theory Y formulations of Douglas McGregor are widely known to managers. Theories X and Y refer to two distinct sets of basic assumptions that managers can make about basic human nature. Theory X assumptions assert that workers must be motivated and controlled by pressures applied by management. Managers embracing Theory X assumptions take the view that the typical worker is essentially lazy, lacking ambition, dislikes responsibilities, prefers to be led, and is passive or resistant to organizational goals when uncontrolled. Theory X assumptions suggest managerial practices which keep relatively tight controls on people and elicit the desired behaviors through financial incentives.

As an alternative, McGregor offered Theory Y, which assumes that, if given the opportunity, people will become self-motivated to achieve organizational goals as a natural consequence of their striving for personal growth and development. The similarities between the upper levels of Maslow's need hierarchy and the assumptions in Theory Y are apparent. Theory Y holds that the natural traits of people are the opposite of those represented by Theory X. Supporters of Theory Y contend that people acting in ways that are consistent with Theory X do so *not* because of their nature, but because stultifying experiences in organizations have repeatedly frustrated their attempts to express their positive potential. These experiences have resulted in Theory X behaviors. The essential task of management, therefore, is to arrange conditions so that people can satisfy their needs for self-actualization while accomplishing organizational objectives.

Small Groups

Committees, task forces, and other small groups are commonplace in organizations. Understanding how they operate and what dynamics are taking place as small groups operate is a necessary skill of today's managers. Similarly, knowledge of leadership in theory and in practice will enhance the effectiveness of managers. When dealing with other people in organizations, including subordinates, peers, and supervisors, the manager must continually use interpersonal relations skills. A knowledge of behavioral science research may help the manager in all of these phases of managing.

Large Social Organizations

In addition to concerns which focus on intra-unit issues, managers must concern themselves with events and relationships occurring between groups. A manager of a production department is intimately concerned with the relationship of that department to other units in the firm.

Managers in multinational firms have a particularly acute need to understand the effect of cultural influences and practices on the operation of foreign-based units.

Other Behavioral Science Concepts and Theories

The existence of "good" communications is often proposed as a must for successful organizational performance. It belabors the obvious to point out that most of the manager's activities are conducted through communications media. Behavioral science research has provided information to managers which can help them become more effective communicators. This information can help managers decide whether to write or telephone a message. With such information the manager can discern likely consequences of different communication networks, and take advantage of nonverbal communication possibilities.

In addition, this body of knowledge helps managers to achieve all their communications objectives more skillfully. The phenomenal increase in the speed of communication has brought significant changes in the manager's task and the organizational setting. Managers need to be able to use a broad range of communications media. In addition, they must understand subtle differences in media forms in order to select the most effective communications media, format, and presentation for their intended messages.

The understanding and management of organizational conflict has become an important aspect of the manager's task. Closely related to organizational conflict problems are issues involved in the power relationships which exist or which may develop in organizations. Managers have long recognized that formal organizational titles and positions do not always accurately reflect the real concentrations of power in organizations. Neither does the formal structure always indicate where the significant conflicts take place. With increased knowledge of organizational conflict and power, managers will be better able to chart a path for themselves and their units in their attempts to achieve their goals.

Decisions about how to structure the relationships among subunits in an organization are one of management's most powerful tools. At the same time, the complex issues involved in changing existing organizational structures and relationships represent one of the most critical management problems. Skill in effecting organizational change often differentiates the effective and mediocre managers. Techniques and strategies for organizational design and change that build on and use behavioral science knowledge are described in a later section of this chapter.

The manager's task has been described as one that involves coordinating the materials, people, and financial resources of the organization. One group of behavioral scientists[3] has combined these social and technological aspects in their analysis of organizations by using systems concepts. According to this conceptual approach, which will also be discussed in Chapter 28, organizations are understood to be collections of interrelated parts. *Inputs* to the system (in the form of raw materials, etc.) are operated on and transformed into *system outputs*.

The socio-technical systems view of an organization recognizes the importance of two essential subsystems, the human component and the technological component. This view focuses the manager's attention on the interaction of the social and technological subsystems of an organization. A person using a socio-technical systems approach to manage a service station would not attend entirely to either the mechanical details of servicing vehicles or to the customer relations that the attendants create. To successfully understand and manage this operation requires that both aspects be considered, as well as the interaction between the two. Thus, the success of the station, as measured by returning customers, would reflect the customer relations aspects, the quality of technical aspects of automotive service, and the recognition that each aspect influences the other.

As we saw earlier, a branch of psychology, generally termed "behaviorism," has had an increasing though controversial influence on management. The approach will be described in detail in Chapter 21. Briefly, the idea of behaviorism is based on the proposition that behavior which people find satisfying or rewarding in some way is likely to be repeated. Obviously, if managers can identify elements in the organizational context that are satisfying or rewarding, they can try to provide these elements and "link" them with organizationally desirable behavior. In a similar fashion, changes in organizational behavior can be influenced, using behaviorism theory, by rewarding and reinforcing new, desired behavior and by withdrawing or withholding rewards for undesirable behavior.

The final area which is commonly found in behavioral science approaches to management involves a commitment to increased participation by more organizational members in significant aspects of decision making. This commitment often takes the form of efforts to push the level of decision making down in organizations. Some strikingly successful experiments in industrial democracy in the U.S. and Europe have strengthened the enthusiasm for participative approaches to management in our post-industrial society. Behavioral scientists tend to value changes which will reduce the dehumanizing aspects of the workplace and which tend to help people reach their full potential.

BEHAVIORAL SCIENCE-BASED ACTIONS AND PROGRAMS

A number of behavioral science-based programs have generated a considerable following in the theory and practice of management.

Among these are Organizational Development (OD) programs, Job Enrichment, and Team Development.

Organizational Development (OD) efforts have the basic purpose of increasing organizational goal achievement through the application of scientific knowledge from the behavioral sciences. The process is described in Chapter 24.

The primary objectives in OD are usually increased productivity and decreased costs. Less directly, and often seen as intermediate objectives, are goals such as increased trust between people in the organization, better communication, decreased negative consequences of conflict, and increased participation. These intermediate goals are based on the idea that the chances for better organizational performance are improved if the quality of working relationships in organizations is improved.

Job Enrichment refers to the process of expanding the nature of task assignments in organizations. It has its genesis in the negative reaction of workers to task specialization, particularly the feelings of boredom that characterize many of today's jobs.

Job enrichment can be distinguished from *job rotation* and *job enlargement*. The latter techniques are also directed toward increased worker satisfaction and productivity. Job rotation deals most directly with the monotonous nature of many jobs by simply moving the worker into new jobs before boredom sets in. Job enlargement is designed to address similar problems. In this case, boredom and monotony are countered by providing variations which expand the scope of activities in jobs. In contrast, job enrichment involves a qualitative change in job definition. Rather than simply adding variety to jobs, this approach involves added responsibility and control over the job. An enriched job will require the worker to participate in the planning, organizing, and directing of the job. These activities call on the worker's initiative and achievement, and require that the worker accept responsibilities in the work and generally get more involved in the job.

Job enrichment is sometimes described as a vertical expansion of a job as contrasted to the horizontal expansion in task requirements that occurs in job enlargement. If a person has a job washing pots and pans, the expansion of the job to include washing silverware, plates, and floors will not do much to improve the essential nature of the job. Neither would any significant change in satisfaction be anticipated. In fact, it is difficult to imagine how such a job might be enriched very much. If, however, the job could include some control over hours worked, the sequence of work tasks and time off, and some opportunities to learn new skills, performing the job would be a little bit richer experience.

Team Development is a technique which is directed toward improving the effectiveness of small work groups. Team development activities draw heavily from the behavioral sciences, particularly psychology and sociology. The technique usually begins with a process of diagnosing existing team relationships and dynamics. With this data, the work group is encouraged to explore the strengths and weaknesses in their intra-team relationships and behavior. When this information is commonly held and generally agreed to by team members, the group is ready to proceed to work out ambiguities and differences that remain. As team development activities proceed, the group increases its ability to achieve its task assignments by improving the quality of its working relationships. Knowledge about individual behavior and group dynamics from the behavioral sciences has significantly guided activities designed to develop and improve the capacity of organizational teams to achieve their goals and perform assigned tasks.

SUMMARY

The behavioral sciences occupy a significant place in management theory and practice. Behavioral sciences address the problem of understanding and predicting human behavior—which is critical in the achievement of an organization's goals. Furthermore, the quality of people's efforts is directly related to the quality of organizational performance.

Behavioral sciences in management draw mostly from the academic disciplines of psychology, sociology, and cultural anthropology. The values and research procedures of these disciplines are incorporated in the study of human behavior in organizations. The focus of these investigations can include individual behavior and processes, small groups, large social organizations, communications, and conflict.

Finally, behavioral sciences address issues involved in planning and effecting constructive changes in organizational relationships and performance. The success of a planned organizational change is highly dependent on the actions of people who make up the organization. The behavioral sciences propose to assist managers in understanding, planning, and effecting desired organizational change.

NOTES

1. Bernard Berelson and Gary A. Steiner, *Human Behavior: An Inventory of Research Findings.* (New York: Harcourt, Brace, Jovanovich, 1964), p. 11.
2. Ibid.
3. Eric Trist, "On Socio-Technical Systems," in *The Planning of Change,* eds. W. Bennis, K. Benne and R. Chin. (New York: Holt, Rinehart and Winston, 1969), pp. 269–82.

DISCUSSION QUESTIONS

1. Describe a situation you have known in which an organization would benefit from the work of a behavioral scientist. What improvements in the operations might be expected?

2. "Increased accuracy and objectivity in our organization would be a terrible thing. We have too many skeletons in our corporate closet." Discuss.
3. List two or three values that you hold and describe how they might influence your perceptions and decisions as a behavioral scientist.
4. "Good management is really no more than the use of good common sense." Comment and discuss the place of the behavioral sciences in this management philosophy.
5. Discuss the pros and cons of managerial decisions which attempt to humanize jobs in an organization. Under what circumstances might such decisions be counterproductive?

BIBLIOGRAPHY

Argyris, Chris. *Personality and Organization*. New York: Harper and Row, 1957.

Argyris, Chris. "Some Limits of Rational Man Organizational Theory." *Public Administration Review,* Vol. 33 No. 3 (May 1973), pp. 253–67.

Bennis, W. G., et al. *The Planning of Change,* 2nd ed. New York: Holt, Rinehart and Winston, 1969.

Bennis, W. G. *Organizational Development*. New York: Addison-Wesley, 1970.

Berelson, Bernard and Gary A. Steiner. *Human Behavior: An Inventory of Scientific Findings*. New York: Harcourt Brace Jovanovich, 1964.

Davis, S. and R. Tannenbaum. "Values, Man, and Organizations." *Industrial Management Review,* Vol. 10 (Winter 1969), pp. 67–86.

Gibson, Charles H. "Volvo Increases Productivity Through Job Enrichment." *California Management Review,* Vol. XV No. 4 (1973), pp. 64–66.

Herbert, Theodore T. *Dimensions of Organizational Behavior*. New York: Macmillan, 1976.

Homans, George C. *The Human Group*. New York: Harcourt Brace Jovanovich, 1950.

Huse, Edgar F. *Organization Development and Change*. St. Paul: West, 1975.

Kast, F. E. and J. E. Rosenzweig. *Organization and Management: A Systems Approach,* 2nd ed. New York: McGraw-Hill, 1974.

Leavitt, H. *Managerial Psychology,* 2nd ed. Chicago: University of Chicago Press, 1964.

Likert, Rensis. *New Patterns in Management*. New York: McGraw-Hill, 1961.

Maslow, Abraham H. *Motivation and Personality*. New York: Harper and Row, 1954.

McGregor, D. *The Human Side of Enterprise*. New York: McGraw-Hill, 1960.

Skinner, B. F. *Beyond Freedom and Dignity*. New York: Knopf, 1971.

Zalesnik, A. "Power and Politics in Organizational Life." *Harvard Business Review,* Vol. 48 No. 3 (May–June 1970), pp. 47–60.

5 Modern Contributions to Management Theory

Three approaches to management are described in this chapter. They are similar in that they all draw on more recent developments in theory and applications in their prescriptions for managing organizations.

The mathematical school of management (begun about 1950) stresses decision making as the fundamental management process. Mathematical methods have been developed which, in theory, will point to the optimal decision from an array of all possible solutions. In practice, managers probably settle for satisfactory solutions rather than optimal ones in their decision making. Decision making in this school of thought calls for the use of conceptual models which describe and predict real-life conditions.

Systems management (begun during the 1960s) has evolved as a "modern" management theory. Essential features of this theory include identifying subsystems within larger systems, locating system boundaries, understanding the input-process-output sequence, and analyzing the feedback of systems as it influences the inputs and process of the system.

Contingency theories of management take the position that there is really no "one best way" to manage all organizations. There is too much variability within organizations and between the different situations managers face to be able to consistently prescribe one way of managing. The best management practice depends on the interrelationships among the tasks, technology, interpersonal relations, and on the nature of the environment in which the organization operates.

MANAGEMENT AND MATHEMATICS

What is now understood to be the mathematical approach to the study of management seems to have had its beginnings, during World War II, in efforts to improve military logistics. It attracted considerable attention during the 1950s, became implanted in the business curriculum at the college level in the 1960s, and appears to be gradually and inevitably becoming an important tool for the business manager.

Some of the methods of the mathematical school are described in Chapter 10, and a more detailed treatment of them in example form is provided in the appendixes of this book. If the mathematical school's prominent characteristics can be singled out, they are its focus on optimal decision making and its requirement for descriptive and predictive models.

Optimization

To the disciples of the mathematical school, management fundamentally consists of the process of decision making. Managers are constantly faced with problems for which solutions must be found. It is held that there exist many alternative solutions for every problem. The manager's challenge is to assemble every possible solution to a given problem, and from this array to select the one that will be most effective in terms of accomplishment and most efficient in terms of the costs required relative to the results achieved. An *optimal decision* is the choice of the best way to solve the given problem.

Optimal decisions are classified as either *maximizing* or *minimizing* functions. A maximizing function is one that generates the greatest possible profit, the highest output, and the maximum return on investment relative to the resources committed to the effort. When the function is minimizing, the optimal decision produces the desired result at the lowest possible cost.

There are also decisions that managers must make over and over again; that is, the decision conditions recur. For these kinds of decisions, the optimal solution can be formulated into a decision rule, which prescribes how the decision is to be made under the stipulated set of conditions. For nonrecurring decisions, or those where the conditions are not consistent, original optimal solutions must be sought.

Satisficing

Herbert Simon, a prominent management theorist, suggests that optimization cannot ever be more than a theoretical concept because making optimal decisions would require infinite time and perfect knowledge. He contends that managers cannot identify and examine every alternative to solving a problem. He notes that they can only consider the most obvious alternatives and select the course of action that will lead to a satisfactory solution.

This practice is known as *satisficing*. This does not mean, however, that managers do not attempt to assign measurable weights to variables involved in the possible courses of action and, through model building, try to develop an answer expressed in numerical terms.

Simulation

Consider a manager who must make a decision and who has identified three or four possible solutions. How can the one which will lead to the most satisfactory results be determined?

The manager has three options. The first is to implement each of the possible solutions and evaluate their effects. If conditions remained exactly the same throughout the experiment, presumably the manager would know the best alternative. However, in terms of time and money, this approach is rarely feasible.

A second option would be to apply personal experience, plus the experience of others, in trying to determine the best course of action. Unfortunately, experience does not often match up perfectly with the current situation. Thus, experience is an incomplete and unreliable guide to future action.

The manager's third option is to construct a model to simulate the solutions. A model may take many forms, but for decision making it is always an abstraction from real life. In addition, a model is predictive; that is, real-life conditions that a model describes can be assumed to recur constantly if conditions are unaltered.

One of the forms that a model may take is a physical replica, such as a scaled-down model of a turbine engine. A second form is graphic, such as a chart of the behavior of stock-market prices. A third form is schematic, such as an electrical wiring diagram.

The mathematical model uses symbols to represent the factors in a real-life situation. The symbols can be manipulated to study the interactions between the factors, or "variables," as they are usually called. The construction and use of a mathematical model consists of five steps: First, precisely define the system or problem. Second, determine some way of measuring effects. Third, construct the model by assembling the pertinent variables in their proper relationships. Fourth, examine various alternatives to the problem solution by plugging each one into the model. Finally, evaluate the results and choose the most promising course of action.

Suppose a hospital administrator wanted to maximize patient care on the pediatric ward within a specified annual budget. Let this serve as a definition of the administrator's problem. We can label patient care PC. Services that contribute to PC include skills of the physicians (M_D), nurses (N), and other ancillary personnel (P). Also contributing to PC are the physical surroundings (P_S) and special equipment (S_E). Relative quantities and qualities of these contributors to PC can be compared using dollar costs per unit of resource (C). The hospital administrator's model becomes:

$$PC = CM_D + CN + CP + CP_S + CS_E$$

Using the model, our administrator can evaluate different combinations of resources which contribute to patient care on the ward. Different levels of patient care can be compared and the relative mix of variables influencing care can be selected which satisfies the problem definition: maximum care within a fixed budget.

SYSTEMS MANAGEMENT

The idea of systems management, developed in the 1960s, has attracted a good deal of attention from management theorists and practitioners.

Systems management is difficult to explain, in part because of the specialized vocabulary that has developed for talking about it. Systems theory is discussed in some detail in Chapter 28, "Systems Approach to Control." For our purposes at this stage, a broad description of the central concepts and relationships of systems management will be presented.

Systems theory is simply a different way of looking at organizations. The goal is to gain an understanding of the organization, its subunits, their relationships, and the dynamics of their activities. This goal is not much different from the goals of more traditional views.

The traditional way of thinking, however, was to view the business firm as a complete entity within itself. In systems theory, the firm is seen as one system that is embedded in an environment that includes many other systems. These other systems can include other firms, customers, suppliers, governments, and competing firms. The important idea of systems theories is that all these parts within the system are interacting and are interdependent. Thus when a change occurs anywhere in the system, its effects are noticeable all through the system. If we call a corner service station our target system, then the petroleum wholesaler, the other stations on the other corners, and the customers will all be affected if the owners of our target station change their price, their operating hours, or the level of service provided.

Boundaries

The boundary concept is one of the unique notions in systems thinking. Recall that the goal in systems thinking is to gain understanding of organizational subunits, their relationships and processes. A system's boundary is conceptual; it is arbitrary and can be drawn to the convenience of the person using systems concepts. Returning to our service station example, the relevant boundary for understanding the operations of one station would conceptually separate that station from the other stations. However, if the issue to be understood were the characteristics of motorists who buy gasoline at a given intersection, then the appropriate conceptual boundary would include all the stations at the intersection.

Inputs-Process-Output

The *inputs-process-output* sequence is the usual description of the general operation of a system. The system boundary defines the place where inputs are brought into the system. Within the system these inputs are transformed and acted upon. The product of this transformation process is then exported from the system, across its boundary, into its environment in the form of system outputs. The sequence is diagrammed below:

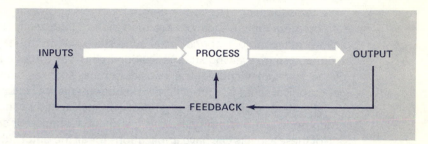

Figure 5-1. The Characteristics of a System.

System inputs are resources and can take the form of energy, people, materials, and information. Outputs can also be in these forms; the outputs of business firms are often classified as the goods and services produced.

Within a given system, as defined by its boundary, there can be a number of *subsystems*. These subsystems will all perform specialized operations and their outputs may be inputs for other subsystems. For example, the output of a production subsystem becomes the input for the shipping subsystem, which in turn can become an input for the sales subsystem.

Feedback

Another essential feature of systems thinking involves a *feedback loop*. This feedback loop implies that the system is regulated by information produced by the system. In Figure 5–1, the feedback loop illustrates that the system output has an impact on its own processing as well as on the inputs of the system. A simple example of feedback impact is illustrated by a working thermostat. When the temperature in a room drops below a predetermined level, the thermostat senses and communicates this information to the heating unit, which increases its heat output causing room temperature to rise. In similar fashion, the process is reversed when the room temperature becomes too high.

The feedback loop is an important aspect of systems theory. It has particular relevance to the control function in management. In systems terms, the outputs are evaluated and compared to established standards. When differences become apparent between outputs and standards, the measuring mechanism communicates this fact to the device that regulates inputs. The inputs are then adjusted to change outputs and bring them more in line with desired standards.

Socio-technical Theory

Systems management thinking has been expanded to include *sociotechnical systems theory*. This approach to management is firmly based in systems thinking. The major emphasis in this approach is on the fact that organizational endeavors are the result of interrelations and interactions of technological *and* social subsystems within the larger organizational system. Viewing an organization in this way forces a recognition of the fact that technological considerations, such as physical tasks, geographical settings, or mechanical requirements, will interact with the social system aspects of an organization, such as motivations, needs, group norms, and communications channels. A change or constraint in any of these aspects will have implications for all the other subsystems. A manager using social-technical systems to evaluate a proposed relocation of desks in an office to take advantage of given lighting facilities, for example, must recognize that the move will affect the work flow, communication relationships, traffic flow, and individual motivation.

On review, the systems management approach is a way of understanding organizational phenomena. Using the approach involves identifying the inputs, the processes, and the outputs of the system; defining the system and subsystem boundaries; and identifying feedback loops and influence mechanisms. Systems management thinking forces attention on the whole of the organization under consideration, as well as the interdependence of all its subsystems.

CONTINGENCY VIEW OF MANAGEMENT

Many of the classical approaches to management that have been discussed so far incorporate the idea that managerial performance could be improved if certain broad generalizations or principles were used to guide administrative decisions and practices. The contingency view of management stands in sharp contrast to this. The contingency, or situational, approach builds from a premise that, in the final analysis, there is no one best way to manage. In this approach, the best, most effective way to manage depends on the particular set of situational factors which surround and impinge on the organization at a given time. The contingency view continues with the premise that, for a given situation, more than a single way to solve administrative problems usually exists. In general, the contingency view holds that effective management results when managers accurately sense critical elements in the situation and match their decisions to them.

Woodward's Research

The concepts in the contingency approach have generated a great deal of interest within the management community. This interest has been in the form of enthusiastic support and criticism.

The contingency approach argues that organizationally effective management practices are situationally dependent. Paradoxically, it also argues that there is often a sufficient degree of similarity in different situations and that some managerial practices are generally more appropriate in a given situation than others. One of the early studies that revealed a contingent relationship was a study conducted by Woodward in 1965.[1]

She was interested in the applicability of classical theories of management to real-life situations. In order to study that question, she surveyed a number of firms to find which classical theories were being practiced. She also devised a measure of the firm's effectiveness so that the different theories being used could be compared.

Her results showed that there were no forms of organizational theories which were consistently effective in practice. However, when the firms were categorized by the type of production technology utilized, some consistent differences in effectiveness of different organizational structures became apparent. The three types of technology she identified were: (1) a job-shop, small-batch process, such as manufacturing a specialized piece of electronic equipment or a jumbo jetliner; (2) a large-batch process, such as an assembly line using mass production; and (3) a continuous-production process, such as an oil refinery or the generation of electricity. Woodward found that the effectiveness of different organizational structures depended on the nature of the basic process. For example, the number of levels in the management hierarchy were relatively low in successful job-shop type technologies and relatively high for successful continuous-process type technologies. Similarly, spans of control (see Chapter 12) tended to increase from narrow to wide as the basic technology of effective organizations varied from job shop through mass production to continuous process. The relative size of management groups also varied in the same way for successful firms in the study. These studies suggest that the effectiveness of different management practices depends, in part, on the type of production technology used in the organization.

Burns and Stalker's Research

The terms *mechanistic* and *organic* come from a study by Burns and Stalker.[2] In their research, they focused their attention on the conditions surrounding the organization. They identified and characterized the environments of organizations as being either relatively stable or relatively dynamic and changing. A stable environment would be one in which changes in the product or service, the marketplace and competitors, the level of innovations, turnover in employees, and social and political influences are slow and gradual. The opposite is true of a dynamic environment.

Burns and Stalker also identified two polar forms of management systems. A *mechanistic* system is one which involves

- a rigidly prescribed organizational structure including a great deal of specialization in problems and tasks.
- technical methods, duties, and powers which are precisely specified.
- a tendency for interaction in the organization to be vertical in nature between supervisor and subordinate.
- supervisors governing job performance.
- agreement that top management is the appropriate place for information to reside.
- a tendency for information to flow upward in the hierarchy and decisions to flow downward.

On the other hand, an *organic* organization will typically involve

- problems which do not conveniently break into parts for specialized attention.
- an unclear or ill-defined organizational hierarchy.
- individuals who tend to see their tasks as part of the whole organization's goals (as contrasted to a departmental or individual frame of reference that occurs in mechanistic systems).
- interaction that tends to run in all directions in the organization, horizontally as well as vertically.
- job methods, duties, and relative power that are continually being redefined by the participants as they interact on different problems.
- top management that is not seen as omniscient.
- a flow of information to points in the organization where that information is needed for decision making.

The essential finding of the Burns and Stalker study was that there is a consistent relationship between the nature of the environment and the type of management system practiced in successful firms. This finding suggests the following contingent relationships: In a stable environment, a mechanistic management practice is necessary. When the environment is rapidly changing, the organization will fare better with an organic practice.

Lawrence and Lorsch's Research

In any given organization, the various subunits within it may be in contact with different parts of the environment. The different parts of the environment can range from being relatively stable to dynamic. For example, a research and development department will typically be dealing in a more dynamic environment than an accounting department of the same firm. According to the Burns and Stalker findings, these differences in the nature of relevant parts of the environment should be accompanied by quite different management practices. The R&D group should be more organic and the accounting department more mechanistic as each strives for effectiveness.

From their research, Lawrence and Lorsch[3] have proposed that successful organizational units differentiate themselves along three dimensions in relation to requirements that are defined by the unit's environment. A fourth dimension of differentiation related to the goal orientation of the subunit. This dimension, however, was not found to be related to the environmental condition. The four dimensions include the following:

- the nature of the organizational units' structure, which involves such aspects as the number of rules, the breadth of span of control, and the levels in the hierarchy.
- a tendency to use a long or short time perspective.
- preferences among the people for task-related or for relationship-oriented interpersonal interactions.
- the nature of the goals being pursued by the unit, such as increased production, increased sales, or increased knowledge.

The paradox which results is that with increased differentiation between subunits in an organization, there is also an increased need for coordination between the subunits. Organizational endeavor, by definition, requires coordination; coordination is essential if organizations are to be effective. Lawrence and Lorsch found that successful firms whose environments required a great deal of differentiation among subunits also had specific and effective devices for integrating the subunits' efforts. Integrating devices included the formal management hierarchy, procedures and routines, committees, task forces in teams, and subunits whose specific mission was to contribute to the coordination of various subunits.

Where organizational subunits are quite different from each other, conditions are ripe for a good deal of organizational conflict. Successful firms were found to be distinguishable on the basis of the kind of conflict resolution procedures used. Lawrence and Lorsch identified four modes of conflict resolution:

- resort to power to force a solution using either formal position power or expertise/knowledge power.
- smooth the conflict over; suppress it; pour oil on troubled waters.
- compromise, which can result in solutions in which all subunits lose something and the total organization's needs are suboptimally filled.

- problem solving in which differences are openly confronted and solutions are sought.

The more successful firms tended to use the last approach.

Contingency Ideas in Leadership

The notion that different styles of leadership are equally effective depending on the nature of the situation developed from Fred Fiedler's work at Ohio State. His approach is discussed in more detail in Chapter 20. His research suggests that the degree of favorableness in the situation for the leader determines whether authoritarian or participative leadership is apt to be more successful. Favorableness of the situation is defined by the power of the leader's position, the relative degree of structure in the task at hand, and the qualitative nature of the leader-member relationship. The most favorable situation is one in which the leader has considerable power over the members, where the task is well defined and structured and where the leader enjoys good interpersonal relations with the members. An unfavorable situation would have the opposite characteristics along these three dimensions.

When a situation is either highly favorable or highly unfavorable, a more directive, authoritarian approach is suggested. When the situation is in the middle, between favorable and unfavorable, then a more participative leadership style is recommended.

Tannenbaum and Schmidt expand the contingencies for effective leadership to include forces in the manager and the subordinate, as well as forces in the surrounding situation. They suggest that leadership style can range along a continuum from manager-centered to subordinate-centered. The appropriate place along this continuum for the leader will depend on these sets of forces. For example, if the situation calls for an immediate action or decision, then it does not matter too much what leadership style is preferred by the manager and the subordinates. A need for quick decision or action calls for manager-centered styles; there is not sufficient time to discuss alternatives. On the other hand, if the necessary information rests with the subordinates, if there is sufficient time, and if the members are prepared to assume decision-making responsibilities, the leader can share the decision making effectively.

NOTES

1. Joan Woodward, *Industrial Organization: Theory and Practice* (Oxford University Press, 1965).
2. Tom Burns and G. M. Stalker, *The Management of Innovation* (Tavistock Publications, 1961).
3. Paul R. Lawrence and Jay W. Lorsch, *Organization and Environment: Managing Differentiation and Integration* (Division of Research, Harvard University Graduate School of Business Administration, 1967).

DISCUSSION QUESTIONS

1. Assume you want to maximize your learning and minimize wasted time in school. What factors might you want to consider to optimize these objectives? Do you find you "satisfice" in relation to these objectives in the management of your own education? Discuss.
2. Try to construct a mathematical model that simulates the process of earning a B average in college.
3. Select a relatively simple organization or situation (such as a small supermarket, a college athletic team, a retail clothing store, etc.) and describe it using systems terminology and concepts.
4. Describe an example of a socio-technical system. What advantages and limits does the socio-technical systems approach seem to have for your example?
5. Identify the production process in an organization you know using Woodward's categories. Does the organizational structure match that process as Woodward's research suggests it should? Discuss.
6. Do you believe there is a general belief in our culture that organic organizational forms are inherently better than mechanistic? Discuss the managerial implications of your answer.
7. "Organizational conflict only occurs when managers are not properly performing their jobs." Comment.

BIBLIOGRAPHY

Degreene, Kenyon B. *Sociotechnical Systems: Factors in Analysis, Design, and Management.* New York: Prentice-Hall, 1973.

Katz, Daniel and Robert L. Kahn. *The Social Psychology of Organizations.* New York: Wiley, 1966.

March, James and Herbert Simon. *Organizations.* New York: Wiley, 1958.

Perrow, Charles. *Organizational Analysis: A Sociological View.* Belmont: Wadsworth, 1970.

Rice, A. K. *Productivity and Social Organizations: The Ahmedabad Experiment.* London: Tavistock Publications, 1958.

Trist, E. L., et al. *Organizational Choice.* London: Tavistock Publications, 1963.

Summary

Management is the process of integrating and coordinating resources. The term "management" can also be used to identify the organization level that managers occupy, to identify a specific career, and to specify an area of study. Main approaches to the study of management include the traditional functional model, the behavioral model, and the quantitative model. The term "organization" can mean a collection of people joined together by some common bond, but also can be a synonym for a business company and to identify different groupings of specialized activities.

Managers perform the functions of planning, organizing, staffing, leading, and controlling in order to achieve coordination. Top, middle, and supervisory management levels can be found within organizations. Generally, managers need to know the technology of their particular organization, the formal organization structure and the workings of the informal organization, something about psychology and sociology, and the nature of current social issues. Managers receive higher financial and indirect compensation than nonmanagers, and also enjoy higher status and prestige. On the other hand, managers must work long hours, face demanding responsibilities, and have to deal with the problems of other people.

One early contributor to management theory was Max Weber, who prescribed the bureaucratic system. The main tenets of bureaucracy are stipulated rules, hierarchy of authority, accountability of managers, and written documentation. Frederick Taylor introduced the era of scientific management, with its emphasis on "the one best way" to do any job, scientific selection and training of workers, providing incentives to workers to improve productivity, and management's responsibility to plan how work should be performed. The French industrialist Henri

Fayol made lasting contributions to management theory with his identification of functions that summarize what managers do. He is also credited with initiating the idea that there are principles of management. The Hawthorne studies focused attention on the importance of worker participation in decision making which affects them, and on recognizing workers as human beings with individual feelings and attitudes. Chester Barnard is now perceived as the transitionalist who bridged the human relations school that emerged from the Hawthorne studies with the concepts of the modern behavioral scientists.

The various academic disciplines and methodologies that make up the behavioral sciences include psychology, sociology, and, to a lesser extent, cultural anthropology. Parts of geography, psychiatry, economics, and political science are also included. Behavioral scientists specialize in various managerially related topics. These topics include the individual and related issues of motivation and perception, the small group, larger social organizations, the communications and conflict that arise in those settings, and the concepts of social systems and behaviorism. Managerial programs and actions that are based in behavioral science concepts include organization development, job enrichment, and team development.

The management concepts and theories that stem from a base in mathematics are the heart of the mathematics school of management. These concepts are directed toward the goal of improving the quality of decisions that managers make. The concepts centered around the systems approach to understanding organizations were developed around 1960. Such concepts include system boundaries, feedback, and socio-technical systems. In the contingency view of management the best or most appropriate management action is determined, in part, by the nature of the surrounding circumstances. Effective management, therefore, is contingent upon many conditions over which the manager has little or no control.

PART 2

Planning

Part Two focuses on the managerial function of planning. Planning includes a range of activities that must be performed to reach decisions. It is always forward-looking; if future efforts are to be effective, plans must be made today.

It is difficult to imagine any organization existing for long without planning, for depending on random happenings to produce results is an unreliable prescription. In a very real sense, planning provides the manager with some power over the future; even incomplete power is far better than no power at all.

Chapter 6 explains the importance of establishing objectives as a first step in planning and discusses the characteristics of objectives. Chapter 7 is devoted to sales forecasting, which is the determination of the future demand for the product of the organization. Chapter 8 reviews various types of plans which must be formulated to assure achievement of the organization's objectives. Chapter 9 develops the steps in decision making, a process which is recognized as possibly the key process of management. The chapter explores the conditions present in decision making and examines various kinds of decisions. Chapter 10 presents some analytical techniques which managers may use to improve their performance of the planning function.

The chapters that comprise Part Two do not exhaust discussions of planning contained in this book. The pervasiveness of planning and the existence and use of various types of plans are evidenced throughout later chapters dealing with the functions of organizing, staffing, leading, and controlling.

6 Setting Objectives

Plans are predetermined ways for accomplishing certain results. Obviously, before a manager can plan, the desired results have to be known. These results, which are the reasons for any organization to exist, are called its goals or objectives. Objectives are essential for all organizations, regardless of their nature. Business firms, governments, churches, schools, and military forces have all been created for specific purposes. Clear identification of these "reasons for being" is necessary if planning is to proceed systematically and effectively.

Planning is the primary managerial function. The other functions—organizing, staffing, leading, and controlling—derive from the formulation of comprehensive plans. These functions must be coordinated to accomplish harmonious results and to avoid conflict. A *plan*, simply stated, is a predetermined concept of how a result will be accomplished.

This chapter will address itself to the general nature of organizational objectives; subsequent chapters will deal with sales forecasts, various types of plans, decision-making processes, and specific techniques that have been developed to help managers plan and make decisions.

SIGNIFICANCE OF OBJECTIVES

Unless the managers of organizations have clearly decided what they want to accomplish, it is unlikely that they will accomplish anything. Therefore, objectives are extremely significant. Let's examine four specific results that can be traced to a carefully designed and well-communicated set of objectives.

Objectives help integrate plans. Well-constructed objectives become the basis for all future planning action. When they are understood and accepted by all levels of management, they will lead to harmony in the management process and will counter conflicting values and disunity that can so easily infest an organization when main purposes are unclear.

Objectives become standards of performance. Objectives inform members of an organization what is expected of them and, hopefully, motivate people to live up to these expectations. Objectives build teamwork, because the various organizational units can see that if they mesh together to achieve the standards, the overall result will be better than if they were individually striving for uncoordinated standards.

Well-formulated plans act to facilitate control. In any endeavor where standards are known, actual results can be compared to standards and the extent of accomplishment can be determined. When the objectives of an organization are clear and sharp, the product of the organization's efforts can be easily compared with what was planned.

Objectives reflect the company's desired image. They describe how the company wants to be perceived by external observers. Sometimes it is difficult to achieve this desired image in a short period of time and without dedicated commitments from all members of the organization. Although the vision may never be fully attained, if at least the desired image is established as an objective it can become, in an idealistic sense, a driving force that will motivate a large proportion of the total organization.

PRIMARY OBJECTIVES

The primary objective of any business organization is, of course, to make more money than it spends, or, in other words, to produce a profit. However, a definition of what profit really is and how it is accurately measured have bothered economists for years. For example, when we speak of profit as the surplus that is left after paying the expenses of a business enterprise, do we just consider out-of-pocket expenses, or do we include depreciation, a noncash allowance used to replace assets when they wear out? Also, over what period of time is profit to be figured? By avoiding advertising and research and development, a firm might show a handsome profit for a few years, then plunge into a high loss situation when its loose standards of operation catch up with it. Thus, a statement such as "the objective of this firm is to make a profit" is too general to serve as a basis for planning. Objectives must be spelled out in considerable detail before realistic planning can be done.

The planning function should start with decisions on the primary objectives of the firm. This may seem obvious, but a surprising number of companies, both large and small, avoid facing up to these decisions. One way of determining primary objectives is to have senior managers of the firm develop thoughtful answers to such questions as

- Do we want to concentrate on a single product or service, or should we diversify and spread our efforts over a variety of products or services?
- Should we focus on high quality and high prices but low volume, or should we concentrate on high volume at low prices and sacrifice quality?
- What should our market be? Should it be the general public or some specialized segment? Should our market cover a wide geographical area, or should it be local?
- What are our size ambitions? Do we want to grow rapidly or do we want slow but steady growth? Are we satisfied with our present size, or do we wish to expand the scale of our operations?

Expressing Objectives

To the extent possible, answers to the preceding questions should be developed in verifiable terms. A firm's objectives—in prices, volume, markets, growth, and so on—should be described by standards that are measurable. For example, a furniture store might have as its objective to "strive to have the lowest prices for comparable quality of any furniture store in town." This statement can be verified by the firm's own personnel. Comparative shopping will readily establish whether this objective is being met. It also can be verified by customers. Another firm might express a major objective in terms of sales volume, such as "a 10 percent growth in sales each year." This objective is also not open to question; it is either achieved or it is not.

A firm that has traditionally been in the defense industry may revise its objective, and state that "over the next five years we will diversify our product line to the extent that our markets are equally divided between defense and consumer goods." The advantage of setting measurable objectives should be apparent. It is easier to plan when clear, measurable objectives have been set. The reverse is also true. It is difficult to develop plans for objectives expressed in general terms, because there is no way of knowing whether they have been achieved.

The tendency to express ideals in platitudes and call them objectives is a failing of many companies, although such ideals are often highly desirable from a social standpoint. The senior managers who declare "we want our firm to be a good place to work," or, "to us, the customer is king" are making statements with which few would quarrel from a societal viewpoint. However, for planning purposes objectives should be quantifiable. The managers who decide "we will strive to keep voluntary terminations by our employees to less than 3 percent of the total personnel per year," or, "we want continuing repeat business from every customer to whom we make a sale" can actually verify the success or failure of their objectives.

How to Design a Strategic Planning System

Goal-setting process

From the division manager's viewpoint, should he or corporate management set the division's goals? This issue is sometimes cast as a choice between "top-down" and "bottom-up" goal setting. Actually, of course, management at both levels must agree on divisional goals. An important issue, however, remains: Which level in the hierarchy should initiate the process? In a homogeneous company, the same issue arises concerning the general manager and functional managers. The design of the planning system can strongly influence how this issue is resolved.

The goals that emerge from the programming process in *a small company* are tied to an approved set of action programs. Until the president has decided on the programs, no functional manager can set goals for his sphere of activity. Selection of a set of action programs, therefore, more or less automatically determines the performance goals for each functional unit. In many small companies a "package" of action programs spells out the functional goals for every department, because of the interdependence of all the departments.

In a sense then, functional goal setting is a top-down process. The functional managers propose action programs, but the president with his business-wide perspective determines the programs and goals for his functional subordinates.

In *a large company* with a relatively diversified group of businesses, "capacity limitations" at the corporate level dictate a more or less bottom-up approach. The divisions initiate much of the goal setting, since it requires intimate knowledge of the industry-specific set of business conditions.

Establishing an effective corporate-divisional goal-setting climate in a large company is not easy. For the first year or two of a formal planning effort, the best approach in most situations is to allow the initiative for recommending divisional goals to rest with the division manager. This approach gives him support in running his business and encourages strategic thinking at the divisional level.

Later, after the corporate and divisional managers have gained experience in hammering out a mutually agreeable set of divisional goals, the division manager's annual proposal for divisional goals will become more constrained than in the early years. In a divisionalized, consumer goods manufacturer we know of, the first years of carrying on the planning process were viewed frankly as a learning experience for division managers in making plans operational as well as for top management in learning to appreciate the strategic problems of each business of the company.

The cumulative experience of negotiating the goal setting over the years improves the effectiveness of the process. Corporate management can help nurture this development by creating a system that maintains a proper top-down/bottom-up balance. One way to achieve this balance is by withholding an explicit statement of corporate goals for the first year or two, while requiring the division manager to recommend goals for his division.

PROFIT: THE ULTIMATE OBJECTIVE

By determining its product; the price, volume, and market of its product; and its growth objectives, each firm defines how it will go about achieving the ultimate objective of profit. For profit to be an adequately planned objective, it must be expressed in precise terms. Expressing profit as a certain number of dollars is not enough; it must be expressed as a proportion of the resources required to generate it. *Profit ratios expressed as a percentage of net worth, of assets, or of sales are commonly found.* For example, one very large chemical company in the United States requires a 20 percent return on assets on every product in its line. Big chain supermarkets set their profit objectives to be at least 1 percent of sales.

Moreover, profit-ratio objectives should be established for different products. For example, a new product or service just being introduced might have one set of profit ratios; an established product with wide demand might have another set; and a product nearing the end of its life cycle might have still another set. In addition, profit ratios for specific markets and for planned growth are objectives that can be planned discriminatingly. For instance, a manufacturing firm subcontracting in the competitive auto parts market might plan a profit objective of 3 percent on sales in this field; in another market, where the firm has patent protection on a proprietary item, it might aim for a 15 percent return on sales. Also, a firm with a product line just beginning to peak in its demand cycle might project a profit objective of 20 percent on net worth for the next five years, then realistically scale this down for a subsequent period, when a sales decline for the original product can be predicted and if new products are not expected to be ready to pick up the slack.

A HIERARCHY OF OBJECTIVES

Primary objectives, as has been indicated, are formulated at the top level of management. These objectives determine the major courses the organization intends to follow and, as mentioned earlier, include the kind of a company the firm is going to be, profit goals, product line, market growth, and social objectives of a highly crucial nature. However, for these objectives to be met, each successively lower level of management must set its own objectives. Middle management objectives, for example, derive from and are intended to implement major objectives. Therefore, they are more specialized in nature. They will concern quality, capacity levels, sales quotas, and budgets. At the supervisory level, objectives are relatively short term and are made in response to immediate demands. Fundamentally, they will be minor schedule revisions, handling of customer complaints, and relationships with subordinates. In short, they will center on day-to-day operating requirements.

Communicating Objectives

Unknown objectives can not be achieved. Since a firm's major objectives become the starting points for setting the goals of the organizational units lower in the hierarchy, it is imperative that they be effectively communicated downward. Managers of such operations as finance, production, engineering, marketing, and personnel should all know the overall results desired in order to be able to work together and avoid conflict. If this communication is accomplished as it should be, the entire organization from top to bottom will be synchronized to plan in a common direction.

A managerial technique called "management by objectives" came into popular usage in the early 1960s, and is discussed in rather full detail in Part Five of this book, which is devoted to the Leading function. We mention it here because of its unusual capacity for communicating objectives. Throughout the organizational hierarchy, subordinate managers formulate their short-term objectives and gain approval of them by their superiors. In this way, a network for communicating objectives is developed and formalized from bottom to top, thus complementing the traditional top to bottom communication.

DISCUSSION QUESTIONS

1. Explain why all organizations must have objectives.
2. Discuss why having objectives is essential if an organization is going to be under control.
3. Explain how short-term profit objectives will differ from long-term profit objectives.
4. Why should a firm try to express its objectives in verifiable terms?
5. Why is profit more meaningful if it is expressed in ratio terms rather than in absolute terms?
6. Discuss how top-level objectives differ from middle-level objectives.

BIBLIOGRAPHY

Ackoff, Russell A. *A Concept of Corporate Planning.* New York: Wiley, 1970.

Chambers, John C., Satinder K. Mullick, and David Goodman. "Catalytic Agent for Effective Planning." *Harvard Business Review* Vol. 49 No. 1 (January–February 1971), pp. 110–19.

Granger, Charles. "How to Set Company Objectives." *Management Review* Vol. 59 No. 7 (July 1970), pp. 2–7.

Jones, Reginald L. "Executives Panel: Practical Business Planning." *Managerial Planning* Vol. 21 No. 2 (September–October 1972), pp. 32–40.

Schleh, Edward. *Management by Results.* New York: McGraw-Hill, 1961.

The Case of the Many-Headed Monster

On March 31, 1976, the end of Tredco's fiscal year, Harold Greely, president, held a meeting of his senior managers. "The trouble with this company," he said, "is that there are no definite objectives. We always eventually seem to do all right, but we have never set standards by which we can judge our performance. Starting this coming year, our objective is to increase profits annually by 10 percent." He went on to say, "You are all experts in your fields. I expect each of you to develop plans for implementing this objective in your own divisions."

Tredco (Transmission Engineering and Development Company) designs and manufactures a line of power transmission equipment such as gears, gear reducers, sprockets, and drive chains. It had been founded by two brothers, Otto and Ben Hilga, in 1937, and by 1976 served a national market. Upon the deaths of both of the founders in 1967, their families, who together owned 55 percent control of the company, brought in Greely to head the firm's operations. Greely had been Tredco's attorney for about ten years. Although he admitted to not knowing much about the company's product, he prided himself on his good relationships with the local banking institutions. He was extremely interested in civic affairs, which took a great deal of his time.

The response of Tredco's division managers to Greely's announcement was that he "meant business" about a consistent annual increase in profits. Roy Johnson, manufacturing vice-president, called his staff together to break the news. "Personally, I am glad Greely has taken this stand," he stated. "One thing we are going to do here in manufacturing is stop catering to the customer's preferences. We are going to reduce the different options that we have been offering on all of our various products, and standardize on those items where we can get long production runs. Efficiency is going to be the password in our shops. When we get our schedules adjusted to mass production, I am going to expand our industrial engineering staff, and invest in automated equipment."

Ned Bannister, cost analyst, spoke up, "One of our heaviest costs is from parts that are rejected because of minor deviations from the quality standards set by engineering. Is there anything that we can do about that?"

"You bet there is," replied Johnson. "From now on if there is a good chance of a part working we are going to let it go through, even if it doesn't quite come up to specifications."

Don Hayes, marketing vice-president, left on an extended trip where he visited each of his nine regional sales managers. "Increasing sales is the name of the game as far as I am concerned," he told them. "Profits are a direct function of sales. In our line, in order to sell more we have to offer the customer more. That means if he wants 51 teeth in a gear instead of our standard 50 we give it to him. If he wants immediate delivery on a special order, we tell manufacturing to break into their schedule. If he wants extended credit terms, we authorize them. Doing these things might cost us a little more, but the added profit that we get from the increased sales will more than offset the expenses."

Elmer Richardson, engineering vice-

Tredco
Confidential Memorandum
To: Division Vice-Presidents   Date: 4/4/76
From: G. Stearns, Controller
Subject: Implementation of the 10% annual profit improvement objective

1. A 10% reduction in all division personnel is to be accomplished within 90 days.
2. There will be a moratorium on all salary increases for the next fiscal year.
3. No capital equipment expenditures will be authorized in the next fiscal year.
4. Salesmen's traveling expenses are to be reduced 25%. Customer entertainment expenses are to be reduced 50%.
5. The maximum age for accounts receivable is 40 days before aggressive collection action is undertaken.
6. Expenditures for office supplies last year totaled $4719.63. Division vice-presidents are requested to give their personal attention to cutting this figure 50% next year.

Countersigned: Harold Greely, President

Figure 6-1. Memorandum of Tredco's Controller.

president, thought about what Greely had said for a long time before he called his department managers together. "It is finally clear to me that the answer to higher profits ultimately lies in a better quality product than is offered by our competitors," he said. "We are considering a design as being finished too soon. In the future we are going to test and change, then test and change again until no more improvements are possible before we release production drawings.

If I have my way, our product will be the Rolls Royce in the power transmission industry."

Tredco's controller, George Stearns, had been largely responsible for planting the profit objective idea in Greely's mind. In fact, he had a memorandum (Figure 6-1) already prepared which he distributed on April 4, 1976.

On April 20, 1977, Carter Drusig of the firm Drusig, Hall, and Pierce, Certified Public Accountants, presented

	Period			
	4/1/75–6/30/75	7/1/75–9/30/75	10/1/75–12/31/75	1/1/76–3/31/76
Net Sales	$2,167,956	$2,554,221	$1,983,348	$2,236,609
Net Profits	85,173	127,050	79,316	111,500

	Period			
	4/1/76–6/30/76	7/1/76–9/30/76	10/1/76–12/31/76	1/1/77–3/31/77
Net Sales	$2,341,992	$2,156,712	$1,564,447	$1,317,371
Net Profits	70,040	64,500	25,618	(2,038)

Figure 6-2. Comparative Summary, Tredco's Sales and Profits.

Greely with a comparative summary of Tredco's past year of operations (Figure 6-2). It tells a dismal story.

DISCUSSION QUESTIONS

1. Did Harold Greely take the appropriate first steps in planning?
2. Were there any defects in the implementing plans of each of Tredco's division managers in response to Greely's overall objective?
3. How would you integrate the plans in order to establish the kind of company Tredco should aspire to be?
4. Having decided on the kind of company, what might be some derivative objectives for Tredco?
5. What was the single most important reason for Tredco's decline in both sales and profits?

7 Forecasting Sales

Forecasting sales is second only to setting objectives in importance for planning. For our purposes, sales forecasting can be broadly defined as estimates of the future demand for an organization's goods and services. All organizations operate with a number of different goals and objectives. Business firms need to sell their product to remain viable. Nonprofit organizations have a comparable need in that if their product, such as health care, or governmental services, is not needed or demanded, the reason for its existence will eventually disappear. It is in this sense that all organizations need to know, as best as they are able, the future demand for their products.

Because the future cannot be known with certainty (save death and taxes, it is said), firms are vitally interested in estimating the likely demand for their goods and services. Without such an estimate, it is virtually impossible to plan and arrange for the orderly conduct of organizational affairs.

In some cases, an assumption is made that the future will be essentially the same as the past. In that case, there is little for managers to do in preparing for the future, except to be sure that the organization is ready to continue along in the same old way. The trouble with this easy and simple assumption is that economic conditions, political status, and consumers' tastes are all changing at an ever increasing rate. Where it might have taken five years to see much change in a given technology in the past, today's rates of change make similar assumptions naive. Organizations that base their well-being on an unexamined assumption that the future will be like the past run inordinate risks.

FORECASTING TECHNIQUES

It has been suggested that there are four broad groups of sales forecasting techniques. While all have the same objective, each has its own approach, statistical sophistication, assumptions, and costs. The four groups consist of

- polling people for their estimates of the future.
- looking for trends from the past.
- analyzing data with statistics.
- testing to see what people will buy.

Polling

The essence of polling techniques for arriving at sales forecasts lies in asking people what they believe will happen. Obviously, *who* is asked is important. When there is a relatively steady set of customers for an organization's product or service, they can be polled to get an idea of their planned use in future time periods. Sales forecasts generated this way must be evaluated conservatively, since the customers have only indicated what they believe they intend to do regarding purchases. What they *actually* do will not necessarily match what they said they planned to do. Similarly, the sales force, which is in the field and usually has a good feel for the pulse of the market, can give estimates of future sales. Sales-force-generated sales estimates should be viewed with the salesperson's compensation in mind. If evaluation of sales force performance is based on forecasts established by the sales force itself, then there is reason to expect that some bias has been introduced to the forecast. The sales force may build in a bit of a cushion for themselves by underestimating the potential sales. On the other hand, an unrealistically optimistic sales force may overestimate sales potential.

For some products, it is possible to empanel a group of experts and charge them with the task of developing a sales forecast. This technique is particularly useful in areas where there is a specialized product or select clientele. It can happen that the technology surrounding a good or service is sufficiently complex and rapidly changing that only experts in the field have both the background and current knowledge of the product. Where this "state of the art" is a critical factor in the demand for a good or service in future time periods, the use of experts knowledgeable in the area can be a useful forecasting technique.

Finally, it is important to gather the opinions of an organization's executives about potential sales. These executives will generally have critical knowledge of and experience with the firm's operations, market, environment, and potential. Judgments of the executive group can provide a sound measure of confidence to forecasts when there is agreement. Forecasts that do not agree with executive judgments signal a time for caution and a reexamination of both the forecast and executives' assumptions.

Look for Trends

The purpose of a forecast is to predict the future environment. Factors in this environment include conditions external to the firm making the forecast. Among such factors are prosperity or depression, war or peace, government spending, unemployment, population growth or decline, and the political party in power. These conditions are critical in determining the demand for the firm's product or service.

Over the short run, changes in external conditions that affect demand are minor. That is, tomorrow will be almost exactly like today, next month will not be much different from this month, and even next year will probably be more like this year than different. Therefore, firms wanting to develop a short-term forecast of their sales can do it with some reliability by determining present sales trends, adjusting the trends for known influences, and then projecting the trends for a period as far as a year ahead.

The easiest way to project a trend is to simply plot the sales figures for each of the past several time periods. The general direction of these plots can be extended to the next few time periods to become the sales forecast.

Sometimes predictions of future sales based on the past are difficult to make because any general trends may be hidden by quirky jumps and depressions in the data. These jumps and depressions in the data can be suppressed by quantitative techniques such as the use of a moving average. When using the moving average, instead of plotting sales for each specific time period, the average sales for a given period of time are plotted. Each successive data point drops the oldest and adds the newest figure in the computation of average sales.

A common cause for cyclical variation in sales is the seasonal nature of the good or service. Winter and warm weather sports equipment will have different seasonal sales patterns. General trends in their sales may be clouded by the seasonal variations and effects of unpredictable weather. By using techniques such as the moving average, the otherwise jumpy and irregular plots of past sales may disclose a general trend for the future.

Statistical Analysis

This third group of forecasting techniques, statistical analysis, is closely related to the trend-identifying techniques outlined above. This technique tries to go one step beyond trend analysis. When estimating from trends, there is usually no attempt made to sort out factors contributing to the trends. Statistical analysis techniques attempt to isolate specific factors which tend to vary consistently with sales. The major statistical tool used in this kind of forecasting is regression analysis.

Basically, *regression analysis* is an attempt to identify factors that are relatively easy to research and which are related in some way to a firm's sales. It is important to recognize that regression analyses do not identify cause-and-effect relationships. They do show how closely the variations in one set of data, sales of the firm's product or service, can be predicted from another set of data.

Firms large enough to hire economists will often compare industry sales (or the firm's sales if the firm is big enough) to what are known as leading indicators. Leading indicators are economic statistics which are easily accessible and are fairly current. Examples of leading indicators include gross national product (GNP), the various sectors of GNP, the Federal Reserve Board Industrial Production Index, the supply of money, and interest rates. Other factors, such as population trends, construction awards, and freightcar indicators, can be predicted with usable accuracy for periods extending several years into the future. The task in selecting leading indicators centers on finding those that are relevant to the sales forecast. Once an indicator has been found to vary in a consistent way with sales variations, it can be used to arrive at an estimate of sales. For example, the supply of money in the United States is regulated by the Federal Reserve Bank. The money supply is expanded in times of business depression to stimulate buying and is contracted during inflationary periods to curtail spending. The cost of borrowing money (that is, the interest rates charged for loans) tends to be a function of the money supply; it strongly influences sales trends in some industries, such as housing. If the money supply can be predicted, sales forecasts can be developed for firms in the housing industry and other industries whose sales are sensitive to interest rates.

Test the Market

The final group of techniques for estimating future sales involves a test of the market. This activity is most commonly associated with the introduction of a new product. The strategy involves selecting a relatively small and representative part of the total market for the product. The product is offered in this limited market and a careful record is kept of sales. The outcome of this test is used to construct the larger forecast for the firm's sales of the product.

The testing technique is essentially a research technique and shares all the advantages and limits of that approach. The problems associated with defining an appropriate segment of the market to test are critical. If the relationship between a selected community or geographical area and the firm's larger target market area is not accurately determined, any generalizations from the test would be invalid. Results from market tests can be upset by unforeseen natural events as well as by actions of competitors. A competitor's special promotion or price changes made during the test will throw off the results and make predictions based on them less useful.

Combination of Methods

Often a firm will use some combination of the various forecasting methods in developing their sales forecasts. The combination used is usually a *narrowing down* process or one of *building up*. In the narrowing down case, changes in the leading indicators for the natural economy are estimated: Is GNP expected to increase? Will the interest rate be lower? Will disposable personal income be larger in the coming time period? Once a forecast is made for the general economic conditions, the sales potential for the industry is estimated. This estimate is used, in turn, to develop an estimate of the firm's market share within the industry. With market share estimated, sales forecasts can be developed and supporting budgets and operational plan developed.

The building up method typically begins with an estimate of a firm's sales potential for a geographical area or on a product-by-product basis. These estimates can be generated by any of the methods outlined above. A common practice is to obtain estimates by the sales force in the field about their potential in the coming period. These areas or product forecasts are then summed and adjusted to reflect the influence of estimated changes in the firm's economic environment. This leads to a sales forecast for the firm which can then be used in planning strategy and operations.

CRITERIA FOR SELECTING A FORECASTING METHOD

The National Industrial Conference Board has developed a list of criteria which can be applied in making a decision about forecasting methods.[1] The five criteria are

- comprehensibility.
- accuracy.
- timeliness.
- information availability.
- cost-benefits of forecast.

Comprehensibility

Forecasting sales is essentially a part of the larger planning process. If the forecasting method is so complex or so technically limited that the planners either cannot use it or run the risk of erroneously using the forecast, then the method is probably inappropriate. The resolution of such a problem would involve either the adoption of a simpler, more easily understood forecasting technique, or embarking on an educational venture to train the users so they could take advantage of the technique.

Accuracy

Obviously, for a sales forecast to be of value, it must be sufficiently accurate for its intended purposes. Specific situations will vary, so the level of accuracy needed in a forecast for different firms will vary. For example, suppose the owners of a well-established restaurant have used their available space and have no intention or opportunity to expand their operations. A sales forecast for the restaurant might simply be based on the observation that there are no apparent economic changes on the horizon which would upset the continued level of business. If sales vary some from week to week it will not upset the operations or financial well-being of the restaurant. On the other hand, for a newly established restaurant, with a growing clientele and the cash-flow and financing problems so common to new, small businesses, an estimate of sales should be considerably more accurate and specific in order to avoid troubles.

Timeliness

Unless the forecast can be made in time for the user to incorporate it in the planning process, it becomes useless. The time factor affects the kind of data gathering techniques that are appropriate. If it takes six months to poll and coordinate a sales force estimate of sales, the resulting forecast will probably be less useful for planning and operational decisions.

Information Availability

When selecting a forecasting method, it is important to recognize limits in the firm's ability to gather necessary information. Information about a competitor's plans might be very useful in constructing a sales forecast. This information is often not available. A reliable sales forecast depends on information in which the firm can place confidence.

Cost-Benefits of Sales Forecast

Costs and benefits have application to each of the preceding criterion. Essentially, the forecasting method selected must generate benefits to the firm which outweigh the costs of producing the forecast. It could be that the costs of explaining a forecast to decision makers are greater than the benefits that would accrue from using the forecast. Increases in forecast accuracy are usually possible, with commensurate increases in costs. It is common for increments in accuracy to be increasingly costly; the cost

Sales Forecasting Methods and Accuracy

Predictions of future revenues are important to business planning, and sales forecasts are often used to set production schedules, budget capital, and allocate resources to marketing programs. Recently, forecasting accuracy has, on the one hand, been hurt by unstable business conditions, while on the other hand, has been improved by the greater availability and use of computers. This past summer a survey was conducted to find out what methods businessmen use to predict sales, and how accurate their forecasts have been using these techniques. This article summarizes the findings of the study, and suggests ways in which businessmen can improve their own sales forecasts. From an initial mailing of 500 questionnaires (plus a follow-up letter to nonrespondents) a sample of 175 Midwestern businessmen was obtained, a 35 percent response rate.

Preparing Forecasts

The development of sales forecasts tended to be a group effort by the firms responding to this survey. Also, sales forecasts are most often prepared annually, with 27–30 percent of the firms forecasting sales on a monthly or quarterly schedule. Revisions to sales forecasts are made frequently, usually every one to three months. About half of the firms in this study said that seasonal factors are important enough to necessitate adjustments in their sales forecasts.

Respondents were also asked to evaluate the importance of a selected list of factors commonly used in preparing sales forecasts. Forty percent of the companies indicated that past sales are very important. Among variables for which projections are frequently available, industry sales and customers' attitudes were the most popular. Surprisingly, the three factors that are used to make up the popular buying power index (retail sales, income and population) were not given high ratings in this survey. There was some interest in inventory changes, interest rates and housing starts as indicators, but businessmen have only a very limited faith in the stock market as a forecasting tool.

Two resources supposedly often used by businessmen preparing sales forecasts are consultants and computers. The study indicated that consultants are used infrequently in forecasting, and computers are employed on a regular basis by less than half of the firms in the study. The computer programs used in sales forecasting are usually developed by company personnel. The computers themselves are owned or leased by 57 percent of the firms, with some companies using a time sharing arrangement or obtaining access through consultants.

Forecasting Errors

Some of the most useful data collected in this study were estimates of the forecasting errors experienced by respondents. Eighty-one percent of the firms maintain records on forecasting success and could report their past errors. The current survey showed the average error on a one-year forecast is 6.9 percent, considerably greater than the 5 percent average forecasting error reported by the 1967 survey. Reasons for increased errors mentioned in the current study were unstable business conditions, inflation, shortages of materials and unstable customer demand. Some firms indicated their errors have declined due to better data, probably from computers and improved forecasting techniques.

In contrast to previous research, forecasting errors reported in this study did not vary inversely with the size of the firm. In the 1967 study, the largest firms had the lowest errors and the smallest firms had the highest errors. In the current study, the lowest errors were reported by medium-sized firms and the highest errors by some of the largest firms.

Since some firms reported that consultants and computers helped reduce forecasting errors, a special tabulation was made to see if this was true for firms in the study. Although only fifteen firms said they always or frequently use consultants, these companies reported lower errors than firms who never use consultants. About one-third of the firms in the study do not use computers for forecasting, and have average errors of 7.6 percent. This contrasts sharply with an average error of 6.5 percent for companies that use computers for forecasting. Firms that always use computers had average errors (6.9 percent), but they are still below the forecasting errors reported by companies that never use computers.

---

to move from 60 to 70 percent accuracy will usually be less than the costs to move from 70 to 80 percent. Similar limits apply to the information availability and timeliness criteria. In each case, the costs of creating timely forecasts and gathering relevant data must be offset by benefits that accrue to the firm from the forecast.

ENSURING RELIABILITY OF LONG-RANGE FORECASTS

When a sales forecast arrived at by one method is confirmed by a forecast using another method, there is a higher level of apparent reliability. The decision maker can be more confident when more than one method points to the same conclusion.

The farther into the future a forecast extends, the more necessary it is to use sophisticated and expensive methods. However, the longer the period of the forecast, the less reliable it will be, in spite of using varied and sophisticated methods. The passage of time brings additional unpredictable elements into the situation, reducing a forecast's accuracy. For this reason, it is important to use short-term forecasts to critically adjust the longer-range forecasts.

NOTES

1. *Forecasting Sales: Studies in Business Policy,* National Industrial Conference Board, No. 106 (New York: 1963), pp. 100–103.

DISCUSSION QUESTIONS

1. What forecasting method(s) would give a good estimate of demand for
   (a) popcorn sales in a movie theater?

(b) wristwatch sales in a jewelry store?

(c) ticket sales to a college football game?

2. Why might it be important to smooth out seasonal variations when using past records to forecast sales?

3. Suppose you managed an urban department store. It has come to your attention that your rival and only competitive department store is test marketing a new line of women's clothes that you heard was highly successful in other cities. Women's clothes represent 18 percent of gross sales in your store. What, if anything, would you do? Why?

4. "Sales forecasts are nothing more than a prediction of the future disguised by scientific sounding jargon. It is just a fancy crystal ball." Comment.

BIBLIOGRAPHY

Chambers, John C., Satinder K. Mullick, and Donald D. Smith. "How to Choose the Right Forecasting Technique." *Harvard Business Review,* Vol. 49 No. 4 (July–August 1971), pp. 45–74.

Enis, Ben. *Marketing Principles: The Management Process.* Pacific Palisades: Goodyear, 1974.

Forecasting Sales: Studies in Business Policy No. 106. National Industrial Conference Board, New York: 1963, pp. 100–103.

Wheelwright, Steven C. and Darral G. Clarke. "Corporate Forecasting: Promise and Reality." *Harvard Business Review,* Vol. 54 No. 6 (November–December 1976), p. 40.

The Case of the Unpredicted Variable

"Actually, our forecast wouldn't have been too bad except for one thing," said Harry Moore to his brother, Dinty, as they looked over the past year's sales figures of the Central Texas Welding Supply Company. "We knew business was going to fall off in the last half of 1976 and the first half of 1977, but what we missed was what Weld Gas was going to do. And nobody could have predicted that."

Harry and Dinty had started Central Texas Welding Supply just after World War II. Both of them had been sales representatives for a national manufacturer of welding equipment before the war, and they had the experience, personal drive, and capital to make their business successful. They had experienced only two periods of anxiety about their company, one in 1954 and the other in 1958. In retrospect, they realized that on both occasions they had failed to detect signs of a general decline in business, and as a result had been caught with inventories and overhead expenses so large that if there had not been a quick business recovery in each of the following years, their firm might have been in serious trouble. After the 1958 incident, they felt that they had learned a lesson, and from then on they had diligently prepared an annual sales forecast, in which they tried to predict the behavior of as many variables that would affect their sales as they possibly could.

Characteristically, a welding supply company is franchised by one of the large manufacturers of welding equipment and supplies to sell that manufacturer's products in a specified marketing area. The bread-and-butter items in the welding supply business are oxygen and acetylene, and electrodes and gas rods. Although these are low-profit items, if a welding supply firm can generate enough sales volume for them, they will come close to covering fixed costs. There is no quality differentiation between competing lines of oxygen and acetylene, and, except for the personal preferences of welders, very little between the various brands of welding rods. Despite the quality and performance similarity of these basic products, customers tend to remain loyal to one manufacturer's make, primarily because of convenience. Oxygen and acetylene are delivered in cylinders which are returned to the supplier, and customers find it inconvenient to be responsible for the property of more than one supplier.

In addition to the security of the gas and rod business from a loyal customer, a welding supply company gains in another way. When a customer is considering the high-profit items in the welding line, such as welding machines, generators, and torches, the natural inclination is to favor the supplier of the staple items. Therefore, the thing that a welding supply company hates most is to lose a gas and rod customer. Next to keeping those customers happy, the second priority goes to capturing the customers of its competitors. The specter that haunts the industry is that some supply firm will use price cutting to accomplish the latter objective.

In March 1976, Harry and Dinty had begun spending several nights each week preparing a sales forecast for the fiscal year starting July 1. Harry, being the firm's outside man, had focused on gathering data from existing customers and from prospective customers who were then being courted. Dinty, who watched over the inside operations of the office, shop, and warehouse, had concentrated on the trends of regional and national statistics. To assist him in his work, he had engaged Dr. Paul Hastings, an economics professor.

Central Texas Welding Supply employed twelve salesmen, who worked under two sales supervisors. Harry directed the sales supervisors, as well as personally handling the high-level contacts with the firm's ten largest accounts. These accounts were vital to Central Texas, as they accounted for close to 40 percent of the total sales volume. Harry had cultivated friendships with policy-making executives in each of these companies, which he nurtured with golf games, lunches, and evening entertainment. Two salesmen handled five of these accounts each, and their duties were to assure perfect service, as well as to entertain the respective buyers, engineers, and shop superintendents. The other salesmen and the sales supervisors serviced the bulk of the company's remaining accounts, over three hundred, which were arranged by geographical territories.

Harry had called a meeting of the supervisors and salesmen to explain how to gather information for the sales forecast. "First of all, we are going to assume that we are not going to lose any accounts," he began. "I have a card here for each customer with whom we have done business this year, showing by item and date what each one has purchased

from us. What I want you to do is to talk with your contacts in the accounts that you handle, and learn what they think their own business will be like next year in comparison to this year. If they think it will be better, or worse, try to find out how much as a percentage. Enter this information on the cards. In addition, each one of you is working on some new accounts. Make a strong effort to find out what their annual gas and rod volume is and then estimate the probability that you will capture the account. Make out a card for each one of them. We can approximate their hardware purchases from their gas and rod business. I will do the same thing for the accounts I call on."

The approach Dr. Hastings had used in working with Dinty was to identify and project the key variables affecting the sale of welding equipment in the local area. One variable was construction awards, which showed a definite downward trend. Defense spending was another variable, and this one seemed headed downward even more sharply than construction. Agricultural production, in which welding supplies are involved because of repairs to farm machinery, appeared to be stable for the next year. No important change was noticed for expenditures by state and local governments. Capital spending by transportation firms was estimated to fall off, but this suggested more repair work on old equipment, which meant a possible increase in welding supply purchases. The integration of all of the projections had pointed to a potential decrease in the demand for welding supplies of as much as 12 percent.

A careful recapping of the figures collected from the company's customers had showed a similar decline, which were projected to drop off even more sharply in the last half of the year. "Well, at least we know that we are headed for lean times," Harry had said to his brother. "If you agree, let's expect that our sales will fall off by as much as $200,000 next year. This means that we are shooting for a $1,000,000 year, and with our overhead costs what they are, we had sure better get it."

In the meantime, something important had been taking place at Weld Gas, one of Central Texas' smaller and less bothersome competitors. Marguerite Burke, who had been running the company since the death of her husband, had sold Weld Gas to a syndicate of wealthy investors headed by a former vice-president of the leading welding equipment manufacturer in the country. He had said that, as he had always wanted to manage his own business, he was going to build Weld Gas into the strongest welding equipment supply house in Texas. With his powerful financial resources, and some disregard for industry ethics, he had begun picking off the big accounts one by one by installing free bulk-storage gas tanks in their plants, eliminating charges on overdue cylinders, and consigning inventories of rod that would not have to be paid for until used. In addition, his entertainment capacities for wooing important customers appeared unlimited.

Small wonder that at the end of the year Harry and Dinty were crestfallen.

"Just look at those figures," Harry said to his brother. "Sales just over $800,000 for last year, with most of the loss coming from my own pet accounts."

DISCUSSION QUESTIONS

1. If the future is so difficult to predict, why should a business firm invest time and money trying to develop a sales forecast?
2. Did the Moore brothers do all that they could to develop a reliable sales forecast?
3. Was there any way that the entrance of a strong competitor in the local market could have been predicted?
4. Speculate on some external factors that would be particularly important in sales forecasting in the following industries:
   a) public utilities
   b) color television sets
   c) toys
   d) aerospace
   e) ethical drugs
5. Who should be made aware of the assumptions about the future upon which a sales forecast is based?

8 Types of Plans

The achievement of a business firm's objectives depends on the inter-locking effectiveness of so many plans that failure of any one of them would probably be a major setback. However, three plans stand out as being crucial: the sales plan, the production plan (for providing the service, or buying or manufacturing the goods that are to be sold), and the financial plan. In addition to these *major* plans, a number of *supporting* plans—involving organization, labor needs, capital investment, and so on—must be developed. Finally, both major and supporting plans can be classified as either *long-* or *short-term,* or as *standing* or *single-purpose* plans. Each type of plan is discussed in this chapter. As you go through the chapter it is important to keep in mind that all planning, regardless of the type of plan being used, occurs concurrently and must be tied into overall organizational objectives.

THE SALES PLAN

As was discussed in the preceding chapter, the sales forecast is an assumption about the probable future demand for a firm's products or services. It can be prepared in such a way that it is both a forecast and a plan; but if it is, two steps have been taken, not just one. The basic plan for all business firms derives from the sales forecast; and, although it can be called a number of names, let us call it the sales plan.

The *sales plan* details the actions that must be taken to make the sales forecast a reality. Probable sales do not become real sales until action by the firm makes them so. The type of sales effort that a firm exerts varies with the nature of its business. Efforts to produce sales for a restaurant, a retail store, a trucking firm, and a manufacturing company are different;

however, the purpose of each is to effect an exchange of the firm's products or services for the customer's dollars. Therefore, every firm must either formally or informally define and schedule the actions that will be taken to produce sales.

Regardless of the kinds of sales actions that individual companies undertake, one thing that is common to all actions is that they cost money. Therefore, an essential feature of the sales plan is a time schedule of the costs of actions that will be taken to produce sales. This part of a sales plan is usually called a *budget.*

In some businesses, sales are made at a constant rate, but in many other businesses, the rate of sales varies. In either case, a time-phased schedule of expected sales should be developed. Some companies receive payment at the time a sale is made. Other companies, particularly manufacturing and industrial supply firms, must wait to be paid for sales made earlier. For firms of this kind, an additional *collection schedule* showing income from sales by time period should be prepared.

Working from a sales forecast, a sales plan becomes a firm's basic planning document. This plan should detail four basic elements: sales actions, costs, resulting sales, and income—all scheduled by time.

THE PRODUCTION PLAN

A business firm sells either a product or a service, or both. In the case of a service, the source of what is sold lies in the skills of the firm's employees. This involves manpower planning, and will be discussed later in this chapter.

The sales plan is essential in developing the production plan. Whether a firm obtains a product by making it, as with manufacturing firms, or by purchasing it and then reselling it, as with retail stores, it is imperative to develop a production plan. This ensures that the product will be available for sale at the time specified by the sales plan.

Purchase Plan

Resellers of goods made by other firms, such as retailers, require a purchase plan in order to have goods available when customers want to buy them. Manufacturing firms require a purchase plan for the raw materials which they will convert to a finished product. Developing a purchase plan involves determining, from the sales plan, the quantity and quality of the items expected to be sold, and when they are expected to be sold. Lead times, or the length of time between placing orders and receiving them, must be calculated; and inventory levels, or the amount of unsold goods that the firm is willing to have on hand in any particular period, must be set. One way of determining lead times is to examine past records showing how long it took to receive goods after placing orders. In certain instances, such as the purchase of steel from the mills, the common practice is to get an approximation of lead times when orders are negotiated. Finally, suppliers must be selected, and the times scheduled for placing orders, receiving goods, and making payments.

Manufacturing Plan

For manufacturers, a production plan can be a highly involved process, especially if the product is made of many parts. The sales plan specifies when, what, and how many kinds of products are to be sold, thus defining when finished products must be available for delivery. Figuring backward from that target date, the time needed for assembling the finished product must be estimated, and assembly operations set early enough to have the finished product ready on schedule.

Preliminary steps that must be planned in an overall manufacturing process include determining dates for starting and completing product assembly, gathering the parts so that they are available when assembly is scheduled to start, ordering and receiving raw materials in time to start making the parts, and having required manpower and equipment available. Although the sales plan usually shows that sales will vary, it is undesirable to have abrupt fluctuations in the production rate. Therefore, the manufacturing plan must provide for some goods to be held in inventory when sales are slack.

Services

The planning for providing services, whether it be a bank, a law firm, a CPA firm, or whatever, must start with a plan for the volume of services that will be provided over some time period, usually one year. As a bank's services are primarily lending money, a plan for having lendable funds available is crucial. However, the common factor in the planning of all service firms is to have sufficient people with appropriate skills available to provide the services that are anticipated. Thus, planning for service companies becomes essentially manpower planning, which is discussed later in this chapter.

THE FINANCIAL PLAN

Although the sales plan is regarded as the basic planning document because all other plans derive from it, the most critical plan to a firm's survival is its financial plan. Costs must be scheduled for all aspects of the sales and production plans, for no matter how successful a company's sales record may be, if it does not have money to pay its bills, it will eventually become bankrupt.

There is a time lag between the costs incurred in making or buying a product and the receipt of payment for sales. This fact was mentioned earlier in the chapter. Also, there are investments that must be made in manpower, plant, and equipment. Thus, all companies must carefully schedule the outgo of cash for all purposes by time periods. Balanced against this schedule is a schedule of income from sales and other known sources. That way, if at any time accumulated cash outgo exceeds accumulated income, managers will know that additional cash must be obtained from sources outside the firm. If this is not possible, it will be apparent that the firm's scale of operations must be cut back.

SUPPORTING PLANS

It is difficult to imagine any business firm that should not plan its operations—at least to the extent of having a sales plan, a production plan, and a financial plan. This is possibly enough planning for a small company. However, as the scale of a firm's operations increases, it is necessary to develop other plans—such as organization, manpower, management development, capital investment, and research and development plans—to support its major plans. These plans are described below.

Organization Plan

As a firm grows beyond the size where all activities can be directed by the owner, it becomes necessary to divide the work into departments. Therefore, an organization plan is an important supporting plan for companies larger than the owner-operator type. There are alternative ways of departmenting, such as grouping activities by the kind of work done (finance, manufacturing, sales), the geographical area where the work is done (northwest region, central region, southwest region), and the requirements of different products or services. (The issues that must be considered in organizing will be discussed in Chapters 11–14, the "Organizing" chapters.)

Manpower Plan

Another important supporting plan for the larger company is a manpower plan. Even if the firm intends to remain the same size, it will lose employees over time through resignation, firing, retirement, ill health, and death. But the managers of most companies realize that growth is essential for survival, so their sales plan will reflect the objective of some projected increase in size. Thus, a plan is necessary not only to replace employees who are lost to the firm for some reason, but to add to the complement of salespeople, production workers, clerical personnel, buyers, accountants, and others required to meet the increased demands imposed by a constantly growing scale of operations. (Details of a manpower plan, including recruiting, selection, training, and compensation, are described in Chapters 15–19, the "Staffing" chapters.)

Management Development Plan

The availability of competent managers is such an important factor in a firm's ability even to survive, let alone successfully grow, that a special plan is necessary to assure an adequate supply of managers. The number and qualifications of managers needed in the future at each organizational level can be determined from the company's organization plan. An inventory of current and potential managers now employed should be maintained. Such an inventory should include details covering their backgrounds and their potential for promotion. A comparison of managers currently employed with the number needed in the future, as identified in the organization plan, will indicate the number of potential managers that must be brought into the firm each year. In addition, the further education and experience needed by each managerial candidate must be determined, and the entire findings put together in a management development plan. (Management development is discussed in Chapter 18.)

Capital Investment Plan

A firm's use of its capital funds, the money available to finance its operations, is crucial to its success. A good manager has the ability to continuously produce good *candidate investments* for capital funds. (In this case, candidate investments go toward improved production equipment and facilities.) A well-managed company will always have more candidate investments than it has capital funds. Therefore, a capital investment plan involves a careful analysis of the cost of each candidate investment relative to the savings produced by the investment over its economic life.

Several methods for establishing a numerical index of each investment's savings relative to its cost have been invented. One, called the *discounted rate of return,* is discussed in a later chapter. A firm's capital investment plan can be developed by rationing available capital funds among the candidate investments, starting with the investment with the highest rate of return, then proceeding to the next, and so on, until either the supply of capital funds is exhausted or the next candidate investment promises an unsatisfactory rate of return.

Research and Development Plan

This discussion, which in no way covers all of the supporting plans that business firms may make, will conclude with some comments on a kind

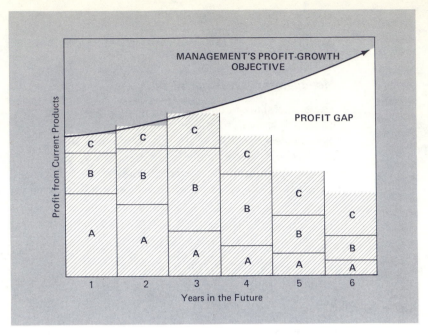

Figure 8-1. The Profit Gap.

of plan that is becoming increasingly important in these times of dynamic change—the research and development plan. This plan, by its nature, is most relevant to manufacturing organizations.

Change in products of all kinds is taking place at such a rapid rate that the average market acceptance of even a fantastically successful product is less than twelve years. Competition between products is so keen that some 80 percent of the new products brought on the market are failures. Therefore, for a firm to stay alive, it must constantly develop new product ideas to replace those on the market that will eventually become obsolete. Figure 8–1 illustrates the gap that develops between projected profit growth and the profit contributions of current products.

A firm uses the basic objectives and premises of its forecasts as foundations for its research and development plan. For example, a printing company which produces checks for bank customers might have as a premise that electronic systems are going to do away with the use of checks, and have an objective of getting into textbook printing. Its R&D plan would be shaped by these considerations.

One restraint on the magnitude of an R&D plan is the money that can be allocated. The details of such plans vary with individual firms, but the goal of all such plans is to come up with enough new ideas annually to keep the company alive and growing. (See Chapter 27 for a treatment of R&D from the perspective of the controlling function.)

LONG- AND SHORT-TERM PLANS

Plans, both major and supporting, can be further classified according to the period of time over which they are projected. The common time classifications for plans are *long term* and *short term,* although some companies also have what they call *intermediate* plans. A firm's long-term plan is really a set of alternative courses of action, any one of which, depending on external conditions, could lead the firm to achieve its basic objectives over an extended time period. A short-term plan is for an immediate time period and is designed to meet objectives for that period. Therefore, short-term plans derive from long-term plans, and can be set only after long-term plans are made.

Long-Term Plans

Long-term plans tend to be strategies designed to achieve the firm's objectives and to thwart competitor's objectives. They are also designed to enable firms to accommodate predicted trends in their industry. For example, firms in the aerospace industry, such as Boeing, North American Rockwell, and Aerojet-General, foresaw a steady lessening of defense orders in the early 1970s and began to formulate strategies to diversify their product lines. Such plans are subject to change, and, therefore, should be flexible and need not be spelled out in detail. They are usually stated in gross, yearly terms. The type of thinking that goes into long-term plans has been called "nonprogrammed" decision making. That is, the strategies devised are novel, opportunistic, and uninfluenced by past actions.

Developing long-term plans is almost always the responsibility of the top managers of the firm, although they may enlist a planning staff or lower-level managers in the plan's preparation. Since a firm's major plans are concerned with sales production and finance, its long-term plans will focus on these areas in broad perspective. Long-term supporting plans also stress objectives and policies more than they do details.

Apparently the current practice among business firms is to give increasing attention to the development and maintenance of long-term plans. Except for extremely large companies, this is a fairly new practice. The theory of long-term planning for business has been around for some time, and there has not been significant change in the concepts that Henri Fayol advanced (see Chapter 3). However, it has been only during the past twenty-five years that most companies have practiced long-term planning of any consequence. Probable reasons for the developing popularity of long-term plans include accelerating rates of change in products and markets, improved forecasting methods, computerization of data, and the increasing sophistication of business managers.

Surveys show that the majority of companies doing long-range planning arbitrarily pick a period of five years as the time span for such plans. Some companies select shorter periods, others longer. The period should not be selected arbitrarily, and there are objective criteria that a firm can use to determine the length of a long-term plan. One such criterion is how far into the future the firm's fixed commitments extend. Such commitments would include contracts and long-term indebtedness. For example, if the firm is obligated to make debt payments covering principal and interest over ten years, it would seem wise to plan for a ten year period. Another criterion is the life cycle of its existing product line, as well as the life cycles of products in development.

As we noted earlier, long-term plans spell out alternate actions. Assume that a firm's basic objectives have been set, and that they focus on a certain rate of growth and a certain return on investment. There are different ways these objectives can be achieved: (1) capture a larger share of the market; (2) broaden the product line and enter new markets; (3) acquire other companies. The long-term plan might include thoughtful analysis of all three alternatives. The final choice is made later on the basis of data obtained concerning factors in the environment in which the firm operates, such as changes in market demand, changes in competitors' strategies, or changes in government policy.

Short-Term Plans

Short-term plans can be made with the long-term plan serving as a guide. Short-term plans tend to be implementations of the long-term plans over the period immediately ahead. Because it is the function of the short-term plans to contribute to the realization of the long-term plan, they should be consistent with it. Opportunistic ventures, tempting though they may appear in the short run, must be avoided if they are in conflict with what has been planned for the long run.

Unlike long-term plans, short-term plans are prepared in detail and are supposed to be carried out exactly as stated. Managers working under short-term plans are usually permitted only limited freedom to

CROCK

CROCK by Bill Rechin and Brant Parker. Reproduced through the courtesy of Field Newspaper Syndicate.

make changes. The plans are developed in at least monthly terms, and it is not uncommon, especially with the advantages now offered by the computer, to develop them in weekly terms. The best way to explain short-term plans is to say that they are budgets and offer a means of control, permitting actual results to be compared with projected performance.

Long-term plans are strategic, and short-term plans are tactical. The decisions involved in short-term planning might be called "programmed"; that is, they are routine, repetitive, and highly influenced by the action of those preparing the long-term plan. Short-term planning decisions are made at the operational level by middle managers or supervisors.

STANDING PLANS AND SINGLE-PURPOSE PLANS

Besides classifying plans as major or supporting, and long-term or short-term, another way to classify plans is to separate those that are used over and over again—called *standing plans*—from *single-purpose plans*. While the latter are applied to a single and probably nonrecurring series of future decisions, *standing plans* are composed of policies, procedures, and rules that are intended to apply to decisions made regularly, so that planning need not be repeated each time a decision situation recurs.

Policies

A firm's policies tend to reflect its attitude on various issues, some highly important and others relatively minor. Actually, a firm's most important policies are its objectives, which set the course for all managerial actions. Lower-level policies perform the same function; that is, they serve as guides to action.

Some of a firm's policies are the result of deliberate management decision. Examples of such policies include requiring at least a 20 percent estimated return on all capital investments, restricting inventories on hand to one fifth of expected annual sales, and stipulating that all contracts, negotiations, and agreements with suppliers be made only by the purchasing department. Policies of this kind are usually written, and deviations from them usually must be cleared in advance.

Some policies simply evolve from precedent. Without conscious managerial planning, various policies accumulate as a result of past behavior and actions, such as aggressive retaliation to a competitor's price cut, favoring graduates of a particular college when hiring new employees, and continued use of machinery until it is completely worn out. Evolved policies can have a great deal of influence in shaping a company's image, and they can be dangerous if they are in conflict with its stated objectives. Since evolved policies are usually not written, managers are often not fully aware of the extent to which they influence actions.

A third kind of policy, largely beyond a firm's control, is imposed on it by outside forces, such as governments and labor unions. Such policies include regulated wage and hour requirements, restrictions on the hiring of nonunion employees, and prohibition of misleading advertising. A firm's actions are strongly influenced by such policies, which are almost always expressed in written form, such as in published government regulations and in union contracts.

Procedures

Procedures are detailed, step-by-step methods for performing specific actions. The logic of routinizing actions that are consistently being repeated can be traced back to Weber's bureaucratic model and to Taylor's scientific management theory (see Chapter 3). The one best way for performing any action is determined, and becomes the procedure to be used every time the action is performed thereafter.

Procedures are set up to reduce the need for planning. Once the decision to standardize a procedure is made, the action governed by that procedure becomes routine. No further time need be spent on planning that particular action until the procedure becomes obsolete. The key to efficient use of procedures is that they must be continually reviewed, and revised when necessary.

Generally speaking, the larger the company, the more extensive is its use of procedures. They are designed to govern every kind of repetitive action, including payroll checkwriting; requisitioning materials, supplies, and equipment; hiring new employees; processing a quality control report; and requesting a budget increase.

Rules

Procedures specify how repetitive work activities are to be performed, while *rules* tend to stipulate what personal conduct is required of employees. Thus, firms have rules covering such matters as the care of company property, times for starting and stopping work, safety precautions, and drinking and fighting on company premises. Most rules are accompanied by penalties for violation, which vary in degree according to the seriousness of the rule and the number of violations. Some rules and penalties are written and formally communicated; others are only informally understood.

Single-Purpose Plans

Single-purpose plans are often called *programs* or *projects*. Such plans have an identifiable beginning and end. They often extend beyond a year from start to finish. For example, building a new factory, development of an advanced and unique weapon system (like the B-1 bomber plane), or a drive for increased long-term capital would all require single-purpose planning.

Program planning involves a detailed determination of each step required to accomplish the end objective. The sequence with which each step must be performed; the time and resources required to accomplish each step; the measurements to determine that a step is accomplished; and the dates for completion of each step must all be determined. Program plans tend to be as detailed as short-term plans, but extend over long-term periods. Individual managerial responsibility for a total program, and parts of a program, are usually specified. Programs frequently cut across functional lines, that is, they represent a complex of plans for engineering, production, procurement, and other departments.

DISCUSSION QUESTIONS

1. Explain why a firm's sales plan is its basic planning document.
2. Discuss the importance to a firm of its financial plan.
3. Do all business firms need some kind of a research and development plan?
4. Explain why the formulation of long-term plans must necessarily precede the development of short-term plans.
5. How far in the future should long-term plans extend?
6. Differentiate between policies and procedures.

BIBLIOGRAPHY

Ackoff, Russell A. *A Concept of Corporate Planning.* New York: Wiley, 1970.

Cleland, David I. and William R. King. "Organizing for Long Range Planning." *Business Horizons,* Vol. 17 No. 4 (August 1974), pp. 25–32.

Meier, Arthur P. "The Planning Process." *Managerial Planning,* Vol. 23 No. 1 (July–August 1974), pp. 1–5, 9.

Robertson, John F. "Try Strategic Planning for Measurable Results." *Industry Week,* Vol. 174 (August 21, 1972), pp. 20–21.

Schoeffler, Sidney, Robert D. Buzzell, and Donald E. Heaney. "Impact of Strategic Planning on Profit and Performance." *Harvard Business Review,* Vol. 52 No. 2 (March–April 1974), pp. 137–48.

Warren, Kirby. *Long Range Planning.* Englewood Cliffs: Prentice-Hall, 1966.

The Case of the Markets That Will Fade Away

"I don't mean to suggest that the two primary uses for petroleum products, namely, internal combustion engines and gas and oil furnaces, are going to disappear in the near future. In fact, the markets that they create for petroleum may not change much in our lifetimes. But, inevitably, gasoline will not be the fuel source for future modes of transportation, and nuclear or solar energy will heat our homes and factories. Plans must be made to enable Petro Corporation to cope with these changes." Thus, Paul Rosetti, chairman of the board of Petro Corporation, addressed the other four members of the newly formed planning subcommittee of the firm's board of directors.

"As I see this committee's role," Rosetti continued, "it is, for one thing, to establish the planning premises. The eventual disappearance of our markets is one planning premise, but we should time-phase the events leading up to this demise, which become premises themselves. We should also identify alternate strategies for use when each of the premised events occurs. This committee should then pass along the premises and the strategies to lower-level planning committees made up of operating managers."

"My thoughts are that there will not be dramatic impacts on either of the petroleum industry's two main markets for at least ten years," said Philip Coates, a director of Petro, and president of American Bank. "Over the very short run—say for the next year—I premise that gasoline marketing will be characterized by promotion of pollution-reducing additives. The board should autho-

rize our president, Mr. Love, to adopt appropriate tactics to assure that Petro does not lose market position in the additives race."

"I subscribe to Mr. Coates' views," said Dr. Peter Benz, a director and vice-president for research and development. "A promotion plan for our special brand of lead-free gasoline is ready for implementation. The next thing that we must be ready for is reduction of other contaminants in gasoline. This will be forced on the petroleum industry, first by taxation, and later probably by legislation. The effect on Petro, and all other oil companies, will be obsolescence of our high-octane refineries, and a requirement for major capital expenditures for low-octane refineries."

"The need for a probable large amount of outside capital is a premise for your financial planning," said Rosetti to Justin Kast, another Petro director, and the firm's vice-president for finance.

"Our present financial plan extends to 1988," said Kast, "but will have to be revised, and stretched out in gross terms to the year 2000, in light of what this committee is developing."

"The reason that I agree with Mr. Coates' premise of a minimum ten-year period of little change," volunteered Dr. Neil Rogers, one of the outside directors, and president of the state university, "is that the equipment to replace gasoline engines and oil furnaces has really not been designed yet. I suggest that plans be developed separately for what must be done about the elimination of the internal combustion engine, and what actions must be taken to compensate for the loss of the natural gas and heating oil markets. I put the serious effects of the latter contingency well into the next century, and suggest this as a premise. Moreover, I recommend two plans for the sustained sale of lead-free gasoline, one for a ten-year term, and another for a twenty-year term."

"If there is agreement, let us adopt the premise that nuclear or solar energy will not be a threat to natural gas or heating oils on a major scale for forty years," said Rosetti. "This gives us some time, but your people, Dr. Benz, should start planning on how Petro can fit into a new heat-source industry. Now, let's start talking about what Petro can do about the eventual decline in the market for gasoline."

"As the company's greatest resource is its oil reserves, we must develop other uses for petroleum," answered Benz. "We have expanded heavily in the petrochemical industry, but so have our competitors, both domestic and foreign."

"One area in which Petro has gone too far is fertilizers," said Coates. "Fertilizer plants all over the world are operating under capacity. I think that we might be better off getting out of this business."

"At least one of our competitors has sold its fertilizer subsidiary," Kast supported, "and our own operations have lost money."

"Well, it looks like we have another product with an unfavorable market," said Rosetti. "I will ask Mr. Love to have a detailed study made of fertilizer prospects. There is one obvious step that Petro can take, and that is gradually to change from strictly a petroleum com-

pany into a conglomerate. It will not be the complete solution, but one strategy that I suggest is that we begin acquiring firms in other industries. Perhaps the goal that in ten years Petro's sales should be 50 percent from products other than petroleum would be a desirable one to propose to the board."

"There is no question that Petro will have to go this route," said Neil Rogers, "but we must consider many additional strategies. Some of them may seem pretty wild at the present time. For example, this firm is in an extractive industry. The ocean floor is abundant with some minerals that are nearing exhaustion on the earth's surface. I suggest that serious thought be given to Petro becoming an ocean-mining company."

"Detailed planning for something like this would take years, and cost millions of dollars," said Rosetti thoughtfully. "But, I think it is something that should be done. I will ask Mr. Love to have a preliminary estimate and prospectus made for presentation to the full board of directors."

"One factor that should be kept in mind," Kast said, "is Petro's association with transportation. I think we should try to connect the firm with whatever modes of transportation will supplant the gasoline-powered automobile."

"I certainly agree that Petro shouldn't abandon transportation," remarked Benz. "What I suggest that this committee do is speculate on all possible replacements for gasoline-powered automobiles, and then determine how Petro can use its resources to associate with the new devices."

"It sounds like an excellent approach," said Rosetti. "Who would like to get the discussion started?"

DISCUSSION QUESTIONS

1. Would a five-year plan be adequate for meeting the problems faced by Petro Corporation? If not, why not?
2. How might Petro's planning subcommittee of the board of directors utilize a planning staff?
3. What short-term plans will derive from the long-term planning that Petro Corporation has begun to formulate?
4. Why would some of the plans being developed by Petro's top-level planning committee be called "nonprogrammed" decisions?
5. In view of the directions taken by Petro's planning committee, what major long-term plan stands out as an imperative?

The Case of the Impending Disaster

Jim Brewster sat uncomfortably in what he now knew to be the overly plush outer office of Transcon, Inc. It occurred to him that it was just like Eric Waino and Jefferson Hill, president and executive vice-president, respectively, of Transcon, to keep him waiting, because from the beginning they had been unenthusiastic about engaging his services as a management consultant. It had only been his proposition that he would do a five-day study for one third the normal consulting fee that induced them to hire him at all, and then it had been with the remark that the only reason they were doing it was to satisfy their curiosity as to what function a consultant thought he performed. Jim had been trying to build his own consulting practice for three months, after having worked two years for a national consulting firm, and was beginning to wonder if he would ever get to like the selling part of the profession. He certainly knew that he didn't like having to cut his fee in order to get an assignment.

"Well, I guess that you have found out what a promising company we have here," was Waino's opening comment when Jim was finally admitted to the inner office. Waino and Hill had started Transcon about nine months previously with $50,000 of their own savings, $250,000 raised from a group of small business investors, and some outstanding ideas for the design and manufacture of transistors, diodes, and semiconductors. Both men had brilliant backgrounds as research and development engineers.

"In the time you allowed me, I decided to concentrate on your cash position over the next twelve months," said Jim.

"Because you said that you were not interested in reading a long, wordy report, I have condensed my findings on a single page. I have backup for all my figures, however."

"You seem to avoid Mr. Waino's comment, which was really in the form of a question," said Jefferson Hill.

Jim paused for a moment before replying. "I carefully checked the basis for your sales forecast, and if anything, it is conservative. There is an excellent potential market for your products. I used your own sales projections to do my cash forecast."

"You don't expect a fee for telling us something we already know, do you?" asked Waino.

"No, I have earned a fee for finding out that your company will probably go broke in May or June of next year," was Jim's calm response.

"Utterly absurd!" Waino exploded. "Don't you know that we have over $140,000 in cash right now, that our investment group is going to put in $200,000 more month after next, and that I am dickering for a $200,000 additional loan from the bank to be credited in January? And you have admitted that our sales will total over 3.5 million dollars over the next twelve months."

"I have taken all of those things into consideration," Jim said, "even including the highly improbable bank loan. If you will let me go over the figures with you, you will see what is going to happen. First of all, the average collection period on accounts receivable in this industry is forty-five days. In other words, you can expect to receive cash from one month's sales in the middle of

	OCT.	NOV.	DEC.	JAN.	FEB.	MAR.	APRIL	MAY	JUNE	JULY	AUG.	SEPT.
CASH INFLOW:												
Cash Balance	143											
Sales	75	100	125	150	200	250	310	375	450	525	540	550
Receipts from Sales	25	40	75	100	125	150	200	250	310	375	450	525
Receipts from Loan				200								
Receipts from Stock			200									
TOTAL RECEIPTS	168	40	275	300	125	150	200	250	310	375	450	525
CASH OUTFLOW:												
Payroll	50	60	75	100	125	155	185	225	265	270	225	225
Purchases	35	40	50	60	80	100	125	150	180	210	220	225
Plant & Equipment	2	1	3	100	5	1	2	4	1	1	1	1
Loan Payment	8	8	8	8	25	25	25	25	25	25	25	25
Interest	1	1	1	1	2	2	2	2	2	2	2	2
TOTAL DISBURSEMENTS	96	110	137	269	237	283	339	406	473	508	473	478
Cash Surplus (INC.)	72	(70)	138	31	(112)	(133)	(139)	(156)	(163)	(133)	(23)	47
Cash Surplus (CUM.)	72	2	140	171	59	(74)	(213)	(369)	(532)	(665)	(688)	(641)

Figure 8-2. Transcon, Inc., Cash Forecast, 12-Month Period, October 1975–September 1976 ($000).

the second following month. As you will notice, I have realistically lagged the cash receipts from sales in the forecast." (See Figure 8–2.)

"Maybe we can press our customers for faster payment," said Hill.

"Your customers are giant corporations, and can't be pressed," Jim replied. "What you had better start doing right now is try to talk them into some sort of an advance payment arrangement.

"Your main problem is that you will incur the expenses for generating sales before the sales are made," Jim continued, "and the buildup of payroll and purchase payments will be as impressive as the potential sales themselves. Wages and salaries must be paid when due, and payroll taxes must be paid at the end of each quarter. Trade creditors can only be stalled for so long before they will begin to take action. This firm is simply undercapitalized for the sales volume that you are trying to reach. As for the doubtful bank loan, you will observe that half of it will go out for new machinery in the month that you hope to get it, and that then you will have to start paying it back, which will be a further drain on cash. I see no feasible way for you to last until September, but if you could, and if you don't overexpand further, you would begin to reduce the negative cash balance at that time."

In view of the cavalier way that Waino and Hill had treated him, Jim couldn't help gloating a little as he watched their deflated faces. Finally Waino spoke up. "What do you recommend that we do about the situation?"

"As I have mentioned, you can try to get advance payments," Jim said. "This would certainly help, but you would still need to add substantially more permanent capital. You can try to get your investors to put in more, but there is the risk that you and Mr. Hill will end up as only very minor stockholders in your own company. I suspect that several of your customers might be glad to acquire your firm, but there again, you would be back to working for someone else. At the present time, long-term debt is out of the question. My best suggestion is that you drastically cut back on your sales growth. Be the size of company that you can afford to be, and expand gradually as your resources permit."

"Would you consider coming to work for us, and helping us get this company soundly established?" Hill asked.

"Right now I am interested in getting my own practice established," said Jim, secretly glad that he had a hedge on the venture. "But I will be glad to help you as a consultant. It will be at full fee, of course."

DISCUSSION QUESTIONS

Reference Case A: The Case of the Unpredicted Variable (Chapter 7)

1. Explain how, in Reference Case A, the Moore brothers had developed a sales forecast but had apparently not implemented it with a sales plan.

2. In Reference Case A, what would be the effect of the expected reduction in sales volume on Central Texas Welding Supply Company's purchase plan? What would be the effect of the unexpected sales decrease?

3. In the Case of the Impending Disaster, how could the partners Waino and Hill have built a successful company, yet

be so blind to the seriousness of their cash position?

4. Why would Jim Brewster tell Waino and Hill that it was improbable that Transcon would get a bank loan?

5. Speculate on some disadvantages of Transcon's getting advance payments from its large customers.

9 Decision Making

Decision making is the conscious process of selecting a course of action in response to some presently recognizable problem. It is a choosing process, because there is always more than one way of coping with most problems. Although in the simplest terms the choice can be either to try and handle the problem or ignore it, in the real sense, *decision making* means doing more than hoping the problem will go away; it means choosing some positive series of steps which will lead to a desirable result. A decision, then, implies a pledge or promise to resolve some defined problem and attain an end that is consistent with the goals of the organization.

Decision making is essential to the survival of any organization, but, unfortunately fear of making decisions leads to a tendency to postpone decisive actions, and it tends to make decision making exasperatingly slow. However, there are techniques managers can use to make decision making easier and better. In this chapter we will explore the general process of decision making, including a "scientific method" for making decisions, types of decisions, and factors that may hinder effective decision making.

THE SCIENTIFIC METHOD OF DECISION MAKING

In Chapter 1 we explored the argument as to whether management is an art or a science. When managers base their decisions on their own intuition or hunches, management becomes wholly an art—without a vestige of science. Decision making on this strictly subjective basis, though rarely exclusively relied upon in modern management, does exist to some degree. A stage beyond relying on intuition and hunches is

basing decisions on judgment, which involves a reasoning that seems to be inborn in some individuals. These individuals achieve best results when they supplement this natural gift with the maturity and wisdom that comes with experience. As with intuition and hunches, reliance on judgmental experience as a basis for decision making also places decision making in the category of an art. However, management has borrowed from the physical and life sciences the technique of identifying a problem, searching for alternative ways to solve it, examining the alternatives, and choosing the apparent optimal (best) solution. When heavy reliance is placed on this technique for decision making, management approaches being a science. The following discussion centers on each of the steps involved in this scientific approach to decision making.

Diagnose the Problem

Managers become aware that problems exist or are lurking in the future when they notice indications that hoped-for results may not occur. For example, a business firm might have as an objective a growth rate of 10 percent per year in sales. Suppose tallies of sales for the first six months show that sales are 10 percent less than for a comparable period last year, and a forecast for the next six months reveals that the downward trend will continue or even worsen. Thus, a problem has raised its ominous head. It might go away of its own accord, but problems are rarely so cooperative.

The first step in solving such a problem should probably be to search for its causes. Once discovered, the causes may not be subject to management control. For instance, they may center on a recession like the one of 1974–75, which resulted in sales declines for thousands of businesses. To some extent, heroic measures by management may counter problems resulting from external pressures, but there are some conditions where a manager is helpless. Business depressions, loss of government contracts, and natural disasters are some of the situations where management action is largely ineffective. Under such conditions, objectives may have to be reset and new measures of accomplishment established.

Some problems are caused by factors that *can* be controlled by management. Problems may be the result of the internal working of the firm or of external relationships that can be directly influenced by managerial action. Managers faced with internal causes for declining sales might reassess their organization's product or service, looking for product obsolescence, inferior quality, or excessive production costs. Managers who suspect external causes might investigate possible overpricing, unpopular advertising, or poor distribution channels.

In summary, when managers detect a problem they should try to define causes and predicted results clearly. If there are factors that limit the number of possible solutions to the problem they should be sharply delineated. For example, a solution to the problem of declining sales might be a reduction in selling price, but this might cause the firm to suffer such losses that bankruptcy would be inevitable. Limits on possible solutions should be kept in mind as the next step is undertaken.

Search for Alternatives

Finding alternative solutions once a problem has been identified is often handled routinely, but has the potential for being an exciting, creative endeavor. A popular method for producing alternatives is *brainstorming*. Brainstorming is a group process in which members call out solutions to a problem as thoughts occur to them. There is no evaluation of proposals, regardless of how absurd they may seem, until the creativity of the group is exhausted. Then each solution that has been generated is examined, and those that are clearly unworkable are discarded. Those that are left are candidates for really serious examination. Whether brainstorming in its pure form is used is incidental; the idea itself should be the starting point for bringing out all possible options for closing the gap between what was expected and what now appears to be the undesirable reality—in short, the problem.

Compare Alternatives

Alternatives are separate and distinct approaches to solving a given problem. Presumably, any one of them will lead to a solution of the problem. However, some of the alternatives will reach a solution faster, more comprehensively, and with less cost and disturbance to the company—that is, more efficiently and effectively than other alternatives. Theoretically, of all the alternatives, one of them will be optimal, or better than all others. Therefore, a comparison must be made in order to screen out all but the most attractive ones from which the final choice will be made.

Advantages and disadvantages should be compared. In some cases alternatives that possess the most advantages may also have disadvantages serious enough to rule them out. The significant consequences of each alternative should be identified and considered in light of all phases of the organization's operation. The crucial differences in alternatives should be brought to light and examined for their specialized impacts. Whenever possible, the differences should be expressed in quantifiable terms, such as dollars.

Make the Choice

Before choosing from among the alternatives, the manager should reexamine the problem and think through the solution objectives. The manager should then focus on the projected results of the alternatives that survive the comparison step. With careful examination the manager should be able to find the best fit between the objectives and an alternative. In this final narrowing-down process, other possible consequences that might be generated by alternatives still in the running should be uncovered. Sometimes there are highly desirable side effects that might not have been considered. The word that is often found in management literature to describe the occurrence of unforeseen positive events is *serendipity*. Conversely, a highly acceptable alternative might produce very undesirable side effects.

Let's go back to our example of the decline in sales and assume that the cause was diagnosed as a noncompetitive selling price, forced up by rising costs. A search for alternatives uncovered these cost-cutting possibilities: (1) cut back on quality, (2) invest in additional automated machinery, (3) build additional plants in order to get closer to the markets and thus save on transportation, and (4) reduce overhead by laying off half of the engineers engaged in the research and development (R&D) effort. Let us say that a comparison of the alternatives narrowed the choice down to an increase in automation or a reduction in engineering personnel. Affecting the final choice is the finding that an investment in automated machinery will not only reduce costs but will also improve product quality. A final analysis of the effects of laying off engineers leads to the strong suspicion that such a cutback would adversely affect the company image, and an analysis of the local labor market discloses that the workers displaced by the automation can be readily absorbed. Therefore, in view of all the facts, more automation appears to be the best solution to the problem.

Delimiting Factors in the Scientific Method

The scientific method provides an ideal model for describing how decision making should be done. However, in real life decision making must work around factors that make it impossible to stick to the scientific method. Some of these factors are: (1) the frequent absence of a clear definition of the decision problem, (2) incomplete goals relevant to the decision, (3) the impossibility of collecting an accurate definition of all feasible alternatives, and (4) an absence of freedom to choose some form of the apparent optimum alternative. Another highly significant factor—the question of relative certainty, risk, and the uncertainty of the future domain within which the decision will be implemented—also limits the use of the scientific method in decision making. We shall discuss this factor, uncertainty, in terms of *bounded rationality* and *states of nature*.

Bounded rationality. The limitations of scientific decision making have caused decision makers to substitute realism for idealism in decision making and have led to the concept of *bounded rationality*. This reasoning accepts the appeal of decision making in its optimal form, which is implied by the scientific method. At the same time, however, this reasoning is pragmatic enough to recognize that there are almost always factors present that make it impossible to use the scientific method. Therefore, rationality is "bounded," or, more frankly, it is compromised. Something less than the optimal decision is probably always reached, if only because decision makers can never be completely aware of all the facts that combine to lead to the perfect solution. Bounded rationality is by no means an abandonment of the scientific method, but seeks a practical balance between how decisions are reached ideally, and how, as a result of conditions, they may be reached with some bypassing of pure theory. It is an attempt to find a workable solution to a problem, even though that solution is recognized as probably not being the best.

In real life, a problem assumes an identity without being completely diagnosed. Significant aspects make it stand out, but there is rarely a complete investigation of all of its facets. A search for alternatives is conducted until one or perhaps a few that promise satisfactory solutions are found. The pressures generally bearing on solving the problem usually leave an insufficient amount of time to conduct an unlimited search. The evaluation of alternatives is usually more superficial than is suggested by the scientific method because of the difficulties of anticipating all consequences precisely, and because of the impossibility of quantifying all of the variables. Finally the best choice available is made. Hopefully, it will be a choice that will lead to desirable consequences, but not necessarily to optimal consequences.

For example, let us assume that the problem is identified as the need to find a new senior executive. This is an inexhaustive diagnosis, because more diligent investigation might reveal that a reorganization would point to no need for the position, or to the need for several new key managers. A search for available candidates will be carried on until there is a list of perhaps twenty or thirty available applicants. This would be far from uncovering all possible individuals who have the necessary qualifications. A screening process that usually includes biases, predetermination, and personal preferences narrows the list to perhaps three or four individuals. Often the first or second choices reject the ultimate employment offer, but finally an offer and a candidate are matched, and a satisfactory solution to the initial problem is reached. This is the typical mechanism of bounded rationality.

States of nature. Decisions are made in anticipation of some field or sphere of activity that will exist in the future. Conditions that determine the future domain of decision making have come to be called *states of nature*.

One state of nature is *relative certainty* about future conditions. For example, a relatively certain state of nature exists when plant capacity and output are predictable, when the number of man-hours needed to complete a work task can be accurately estimated, when the amount of capital available for asset investment is actually on hand, and when the price of crucial raw materials has been established by a firm contract. Relative certainty relaxes some of the limits implied in bounded rationality and allows the manager to work within rational constraints when making decisions. Therefore, the scientific method can be followed more closely under relative certainty than any other state of nature. However, when the future state of nature is relatively certain, the number of alternatives becomes fairly apparent and the choice generally becomes routine.

A second state of nature exists when a number of widely different conditions could exist in the future, with none of them relatively certain, but where the probability of each one of them occurring can be objectively determined. When the probability of an event happening is less than 100 percent, there is a risk. However, if the probability is known, then the extent of risk is known, and the decision maker can make a rational approach to solving the problem.

The knowledgeable gambler who takes a chance on drawing a red card out of a deck of fifty-two provides us with a simple example of risk. Since half of the deck is black clubs and spades, and the other half red hearts and diamonds, the gambler knows that there is a 50 percent probability of drawing a red card out of a well-sorted deck. This is a lesser risk than that of drawing a heart, which has only a 25 percent probability.

More practical examples of decision making under risk conditions include stocking an inventory when past records indicate the probability of demand for specific items; in deciding on production quantities for baby foods when demographic data on infant population are available; and when planning for tourist expenditures when disposable income has risen dramatically. However, the fact that there is risk will dilute the strict adherence to the scientific method.

The state of nature of *relative uncertainty* occurs more often than either relative certainty or risk. When future conditions are relatively uncertain one cannot predict conditions with any high degree of reliability. The ability to identify the consequences of any action is limited, but it should not be assumed that when relatively uncertain states of nature exist the decision maker is totally ignorant about possible events and their consequences in a future that may be fuzzy. The decision maker is never without some indicators of probable future conditions.

It is always possible to develop some subjective feeling about practically any event that will take place in the future. The probability of future events is not as certain as the annual one-shift output of a machine tool, for example; nor do the decision makers know the risk they are taking when they assume that consumer buying will be at least at as high a level this coming Christmas season as it was last year. But they can usually glean enough data from internal and external sources to come up with a subjective but usable assumption about the future. When the future is relatively uncertain decision makers will be less sure of the problem, more likely to consider the alternatives that are most readily apparent, do a less exhausting comparison of the options open to them, and choose more impulsively the first satisfactory solution that presents itself. This will occur more often when decision makers are looking toward uncertain states of nature than when relative certainty or risk are the predictive states of nature. Decision making under relative uncertainty is always less routine, and demands far more creativity, than under more certain conditions.

KINDS OF DECISIONS

Managers at all levels spend a major part of their working hours making decisions. In fact, it is often observed that managing is essentially decision making. It is important to understand that decision making encompasses a wide range of intellectual processes. For example, when a manager chooses to deal with one crisis rather than another, he or she is making a decision. When a manager settles a labor dispute by referring to provisions in the union contract, a decision has been made. Thus, decisions vary widely in significance and complexity. A convenient way of categorizing them is to separate them into two groups: (1) the host of automatic responses, or reflexes, to familiar situations requiring conditioned choosing, and (2) authentic decision making requiring the establishment of new foundations and guiding principles to discriminate between previously unexplored alternatives.

Routine Decisions

In terms of actual frequency, by far the greatest number of decisions concern issues similar to those that have been encountered in the past. In this sense, they are recurring decisions, because the need for them to be made occurred before, and probably will come up again. Conditions

© King Features Syndicate Inc. 1976 and 1977.

and assumptions surrounding them will become well-known, in fact the predictability of some situations arising again and again is so certain that procedures for handling them are put in written form in operating manuals.

In computer language, which is becoming ingrained in modern vocabulary, such decisions are "programmable." That is, the optimal procedures for treating them are determined, and these become the patterns of response that are triggered whenever a situation of a similar nature requires resolution.

The following situation is an example of a recurring decision. A new middle-level manager requests a monetary allowance for moving expenses. This request necessitates a decision, but because it is of a nature that will predictably reoccur, a standard practice for dealing with it probably has been developed. The incoming executive will be advised of the compensation he or she can expect for moving and of the paperwork necessary to acquire the allotted funds.

Genuine Decisions

Lower-level managers are constantly faced with decisions, but they are generally of the routine variety. In fact, it is probable that managers below the upper-middle range rarely make original decisions. The answers to the issues they resolve have usually already been figured out. Their fundamental challenge is to be sure they fit the right decision to the appropriate problem.

At higher organizational levels, decision making is typified by conscious, deliberate, pioneering thought processes on the frontiers of unexplored problems and alternatives. These are really authentic decisions that have "make or break" implications for the decision maker, and often for the organization itself. Genuine decisions are never of the "routine" variety; instead they tend to set the pattern for the subsequent development of routine decision-making procedures. While routine decisions are made in a static framework, genuine decisions are formulated under dynamic conditions where there are few, if any, precedents for guidance and the variables impinging on the situation are diverse and little understood at the beginning of the decision-making process.

Genuine decisions can be grouped into three classifications. There are *strategic decisions,* which involve the relationship of an organization with its external environment. These decisions are made at the top level of the management hierarchy and, because of their significance, once made tend to exist for some time. Examples of strategic decisions include those faced by the United States steel industry when trying to cope with the increasing pressures of foreign imports, or the automobile industry which has two government-imposed problems to solve: improve the safety of vehicles and reduce the pollution generated by the internal combustion engine.

A second classification of genuine decisions is *operating decisions.* This classification includes internal decisions which bear primarily on improving the efficiency of the system. In business organizations, operating decisions resolve pricing, marketing, and production problems which focus on reducing costs and improving profitability.

Finally, there are *administrative decisions* which deal with information flows, work flows, structure, plant, and facilities in all types of organizations. For example, universities have the problem of a high incidence of tenured faculty in conflict with the very real probability of a decline of student enrollment in many disciplines. Both operating and administrative decisions, while important, are generally made within the domains of middle and upper-middle management.

BARRIERS TO EFFECTIVE DECISION MAKING

So far in this chapter we have examined a method for decision making and the types of decisions managers are called upon to make at various levels in an organization. We have also noted that decision making is an essential part of all of the managerial functions. Because managers must make decisions daily they should be aware of factors that may prevent effective decision making. Let's examine some of them now.

Decision making is subject to a variety of pressures that can develop in an environment where the personal interests of decision makers conflict and where objectivity is often subordinated to impulse. The following are some of the extraneous influences that dilute the effectiveness of decision making.

Biases

All people have preconceptions or biases that prejudice them in spite of efforts to be strictly rational. For example, the choice of a new location for company headquarters is often finally resolved by the personal preference of the chief executive officer. Few individuals are completely unbiased when considering solutions whose economic consequences will benefit them personally. Also, the pride of authorship of a solution may arouse defensive maneuvers that could obstruct consideration of other solutions that have been proposed.

Inaccurate Comparisons

Present and predicted future events may bear superficial resemblances to events of the past, but total reliance on the assumption that the past will repeat itself can lead decision makers to solutions that are reached while wearing figurative "blinders." It is too tempting to analogize and compare; experience is worthwhile, but it is imperative that the conclusions reached on this basis be kept under tight control.

Generalizations

Decisions must be made with respect to their specialized characteristics. Generalizations are convenient and easy approaches, but too often appear to be solutions to problems that actually require far more attention. Frequently biases and generalizations become companion weaknesses. For example, a bias in favor of people with an MBA degree can lead to the generalization that all things being equal, an MBA degree holder will prove to be a better performer on a prospective job.

Inappropriate Issues

Decision making can be bogged down by the introduction of issues into the analysis that really don't belong. For example, managers engaged in deciding how to conform to legal requirements for employing women can be completely sidetracked by the entry of thoughts on how women are more emotional in handling work problems than men.

Misapplied Statistics

It is unfortunately true that statistics can be convincingly assembled to prove any argument. One example is employment data. A 7 percent unemployment rate can be made to sound threatening, while the fact that 93 percent of the work force is gainfully employed can be presented with optimistic connotations. Decision makers must be extremely wary about statistics that are used in misleading ways.

Managers should be aware of these barriers to effective decision making when using the scientific method and the analytical techniques for planning—techniques that are the topic of the following chapter.

DISCUSSION QUESTIONS

1. Explain why decision making is a choosing process.
2. Discuss how the scientific method of decision making is supplemental to making decisions by managerial judgment.
3. Give some examples of problems that are caused by factors controllable by management.
4. What is meant by serendipity?
5. What factors in real life make sticking strictly to the scientific method impossible?
6. What is meant by bounded rationality?
7. Discuss the three states of nature.
8. Differentiate between routine and authentic decision making.
9. How do inaccurate comparisons obstruct effective decision making?

BIBLIOGRAPHY

"A Better Basis for Better Decisions." *Business Week,* No. 2245 (September 9, 1972) pp. 137–39.

Alexis, Marcus and Charles Z. Wilson. *Organization Decision Making.* Englewood Cliffs: Prentice-Hall, 1967.

Ferber, Robert C. "The Dark Side of Decision Making." *Management Review,* Vol. 60 No. 3 (March 1971), pp. 4–13.

Greiner, Larry, D. Paul Leitch, and Louis B. Barnes. "Putting Judgment Back Into Decisions." *Harvard Business Review,* Vol. 48 No. 2 (March–April 1970), pp. 59–67.

Simon, Herbert A. *Administrative Behavior.* 2nd ed. New York: Macmillan, 1957.

Steiner, George A. *Top Management Planning.* New York: Macmillan, 1969.

Swalm, R. O. "Utility Theory—Insights Into Risk Taking." *Harvard Business Review,* Vol. 44 No. 6 (November–December 1966), pp. 123–36.

The Case of the Clogged Filter

By the summer of 1970, Sidney Green, president of Green Wholesale Grocers, Inc., knew that some drastic steps had to be taken to reduce operating costs or the firm was going to be in serious trouble. He first thought of imposing some enconomizing measures on his department managers, but then decided to let them develop a cost-reduction plan on their own. He called them together, and with complete frankness explained that the decline in business made a plan for running the company at considerably lower overhead costs absolutely essential.

"I appreciate the old man's confidence in us," said Jack Trask, warehouse manager. "Whatever we decide to do, we should try to communicate to the troops with the same candor that he has used. My personal contribution will be to stop putting in for the overtime that I work, which Mr. Green didn't have to pay, but always did. This might set an example for the guys in the warehouse to donate their overtime hours. Another thing that can be cut out is the cafeteria, which has always been much too small an operation to come close to breaking even."

"I am going to do the same thing with overtime," supported Al Mann, office manager. "If my people see me not charging my overtime, they should be able to sense the seriousness of our situation. Of course we should cut out all frills like the children's Christmas party and the Labor Day picnic. I think that if we just run the air conditioner in the late afternoon we could save some money. Also, I am going to ask my people to be especially careful with office supplies.

What thoughts do you have for the sales department, Ike?" he asked Ike Comstock, sales manager.

"Well, we can't do the things that you fellows are planning," Ike responded, "and anyhow we must keep up appearances so that our customers won't suspect that Green is in trouble. I am going to tell the salesmen to try to work a little harder, however."

"I'll tell you what you can have your people do to reduce costs, and also eliminate what the other employees think is a gross inequity," Jack replied. "That is, do something about the salesmen using company cars and company gas for personal business. I don't know how I am going to get my people to work overtime without pay when they see your salesmen lining up their cars at the company gas tank every Friday afternoon. Who do they think they are kidding? They sure aren't calling on customers on Saturdays and Sundays."

"That's right, Ike," said Al. "Unless you put the clamps on the salesmen abusing their car privileges, this whole cost-reduction plan will go down the drain. How about having the company cars parked in the lot at night and over the weekends, and let the salesmen get to work and get back home the same ways that the rest of us do?"

Comstock suddenly became very unhappy. He figured the use of the company car was worth about $250 per month to him, especially when his weekend trips to his mountain cabin at Big Bear Lake were considered. "Absolutely absurd," he shouted. "The salesmen wouldn't stand for that for a day. They count the personal use of company cars as part of their compensation, and would look at your scheme as a wage cut. Besides, quite a few of them live in their territories, and they would have to get in here and then drive back each morning before they could start to work."

"They would take it a lot better if you explained why the company has to reduce costs, and what the rest of the employees are doing," Jack said. "I concede that some of the salesmen live in their territories, and perhaps their cars should only be parked in the company lot over the weekends. Many of them come in here in the morning before going out to their territories, and their cars could be parked overnight. I think the key to getting this accepted would be for you to set the example with your company car."

Ike Comstock was trapped, and he knew it. He realized that if he presented any more arguments, Jack and Al would bring out what was really on their minds, namely that as he spent most of his time in the office, why did he need a company car at all?

"I'll see what the salesmen say," Ike snapped. "But I can tell you right now that they won't go for it."

That afternoon at the sales meeting, Ike made his announcement, "Green doesn't think he is making enough money," he said, "and he is trying to squeeze more out of the sales department. He begrudges us the use of company cars, and we are all going to have to park them here at night. I suppose the next thing that will happen is that you guys will have to walk to call on your accounts."

The response of the salesmen was predictable. They voted unanimously to refuse to call on their customers unless the overnight and weekend parking requirement for company cars was rescinded.

On the following day Ike reported back to Stan and Al. "I tried my best to convince the salesmen that it was for the good of the company," he said. "But they voted to strike if they are denied their personal use of the company cars."

"That's too bad," Stan said, and Al nodded in agreement. "Both my people and Al's agreed to cooperate 100 percent with our plan, provided that the salesmen would do their share. However, unless the salesmen will knock off using the cars and the gas as their personal property, the warehouse and the office workers will have no part of the plan. I guess we will have to tell Mr. Green that we can't do much for him."

"I really am disappointed," was Sidney Green's response when Stan, reluctantly acting as spokesman, outlined a greatly modified plan that promised only minor savings. "I was really counting on you men coming up with an emergency plan that would keep the company profitable. Now I am afraid that I am going to have to accept a purchase offer for the firm that has been made to me. My hope was that you three could show me that you could successfully manage the company, and I had a plan whereby you could eventually buy me out."

DISCUSSION QUESTIONS

Reference Case A: The Case of the Many-Headed Monster (Chapter 6)
1. What is the likely effect of compromise

on the quality of decisions? How eager are people to support the decisions of the majority, when their own plans have been defeated?

2. In Reference Case A, why were there so many interpretations of Harold Greely's statement of Tredco's objective?

3. In the Case of the Clogged Filter, did Sidney Green go as far as he should have in communicating to his key subordinates the need for a cost-reduction plan?

4. How could Ike Comstock have been prevented from deliberately distorting the sense of the plan when he communicated it to the salesmen?

10 Analytical Techniques for Planning

Over the past ten to twenty years, there have been influences from two distinct directions on the way management is practiced. The first influence has come from an improved, although still incomplete, understanding of human behavior. Some of the implications of behavioral science for management have already been described, and are discussed in greater detail in the sections on organizing and leading. The second influence on management has come from the development of quantitative techniques for assisting in decision making.

Decision making, as noted earlier, is fundamentally the act of choosing from among alternatives. It would be rare for any goal not to have alternative means of achieving it. In real life there are usually so many alternatives that relatively few can be known or examined; consequently, decision making becomes a matter of evaluating those alternatives that stand out and choosing the one that appears to be best.

This chapter briefly describes tangible and intangible factors of such alternatives, and some useful quantitative techniques for making decisions and plans.

DECISION FACTORS

There are a number of quantitative techniques that managers can use to reach a workable solution to a new problem. When using these techniques, managers must identify the tangible and intangible factors that shape the situation.

Tangible factors are those that can be expressed numerically, such as hours of labor, units of production, and dollars of profit. Quantitative techniques arrange tangible factors into logical relationships and derive numerical solutions.

Intangible factors bear heavily on many decisions, but they cannot be expressed numerically. Reputation, community relations, and employee morale are examples of such factors.

Critical-path scheduling, linear programming, simulation, and probability decision theory are all quantitative techniques for decision making. Detailed examples of each of these techniques are presented as appendixes of this book, but will be generally described in this chapter. One less quantitative method for making decisions is cost-benefit analysis. Let's start with it.

COST-BENEFIT ANALYSIS

One method of choosing among alternatives, cost-benefit analysis, does not necessarily involve or require highly sophisticated quantitative techniques. The method can be compared to an old-fashioned balance scale. On one side of the scale are placed the costs involved in the decision in question. On the other side of the balance are placed the benefits which could be expected to accrue were the decision effected. The direction that the scales tip then suggests which way the decision should be made.

For a scalelike comparison of cost-benefits to be useful, the units of measure must be the same on both sides of the scale. Suppose a firm was considering relocation. The costs of relocating any office cannot really be directly compared to the motivational benefits of a new physical work situation. Therefore, units of measurement need to be converted to a common denominator. For most purposes, dollars are the common evaluative measure. In many cases, it is possible to convert otherwise different units of measure to dollars. Problems in measurement occur when subjective goals or benefits such as creativity, commitment, or industry are involved. In these cases, managers must simply make their best estimates and proceed.

On the other side, it is also difficult at times to account for all the costs implied in a decision. For costs which have dollar value equivalents, there is not much problem. However, when the managers must consider costs of a less tangible nature, such as inefficiencies that come with instituting new procedures, social or environmental costs, or other unanticipated events, then the problem is greater.

On balance, the exercise of enumerating costs and benefits, in terms of a common denominator where possible, is a useful one for the decision maker. Once the issues in the decisions which share a common base are compared, consideration of the more subjective, judgmental aspects can be made. The final decision should reflect the comparison of all those elements in identifying the relative merits of an array of alternatives. The

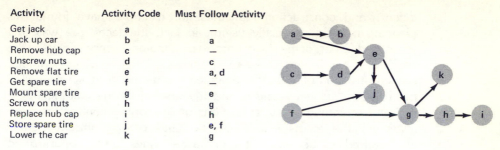

Activity	Activity Code	Must Follow Activity
Get jack	a	—
Jack up car	b	a
Remove hub cap	c	—
Unscrew nuts	d	c
Remove flat tire	e	a, d
Get spare tire	f	—
Mount spare tire	g	e
Screw on nuts	h	g
Replace hub cap	i	h
Store spare tire	j	e, f
Lower the car	k	g

Figure 10-1. A Precedence Diagram for Changing a Tire.

judgment of the manager is critical at this point. The significance and relevance of the quantitative data must be evaluated along with the more subjective issues. When benefits seem to outweigh the costs, the contemplated course of action is an appropriate one to pursue. Obviously, managerial judgment is a critical element in this process.

CRITICAL-PATH SCHEDULING

Critical-path scheduling, a program type of plan, employs the concept of network analysis to plan and control the performance of events in a time-phase relation to one another. The first step defines the program objectives. Then each event to be accomplished is identified, the time for accomplishing each event estimated, and finally, the events are arrayed in a diagram (see Figure 10-1).

The network diagram uses circles to depict events. Those that must be accomplished first (preceding events) are placed on the left side, and those that cannot be started until preceding events are finished (succeeding events) are placed at their right. Sequential events are connected by arrows.

For a program of any complexity, the resulting network will contain a number of paths from the start of the program to the finish.

The path through the network that takes the longest time from start to finish is called the *critical path.* The total time for the critical path is the time needed by the program.

The benefit of critical-path scheduling for planning should now be clear. Once planners know the time of the critical path, they can shorten it by shifting resources from events not in the critical path to events that are in the critical path, or by other devices, such as using overtime work to speed up critical-path events.

The detailed plan that is drawn up for the program; time estimate; identification of critical program events; and the isolation of potential bottlenecks are among the benefits of critical-path scheduling.

The use of critical-path scheduling has spread to all kinds of firms that must plan for the performance of activities in sequence. Firms in the defense and construction industries, for example, have found this planning method especially useful. In fact, the technique was first developed as part of the Polaris program, a major defense project of the late 1950s. Major parts of this program were the design, development, and construction of a nuclear-powered submarine, a rocket-propelled missile with a nuclear warhead, and advanced electronic guiding, tracking, and operating subsystems. Four or five prime contractors were involved in the Polaris project, plus thousands of subcontractors. Literally hundreds of thousands of sequential activities had to be performed to allow schedules for all of the parts to mesh. It has been said that critical-path scheduling was one of the key factors in making the Polaris program successful.

LINEAR PROGRAMMING

The resources a manager has available (labor, material, capital) are limited. Moreover, these resources can be allocated to a number of uses and in different amounts. Labor and material, for example, can be allocated to any or several product lines within the firm's product mix; capital can be rationed to a number of different investment opportunities. How can the best use of limited resources be determined? The problem can be truly staggering in its complexity; fortunately, there is a mathematical technique, *linear programming,* which can help.

A detailed example of linear programming is provided in Appendix B; what follows is a general, though far from simple, explanation of this technique.

The purpose of linear programming is to maximize (or minimize) some objective of the firm, like profits (or costs) by prescribing the relative amounts of various resources that should be applied to that objective. The process is called linear programming because the relationships of the different, varying amounts of resources to their respective outcomes are stated in directly proportional terms. A linear relationship between two variables will plot as a straight line on regular graph paper. Once the relationships between different amounts of resources and the associated outcomes are identified, a computation is made. All of the linear relationships, stated in terms of equations, are taken into consideration and a solution is generated which conforms to the limits of the linear relationships and also maximizes (or minimizes) the objective or goal. Suppose a firm had two products. Each has a certain set requirement for capital, labor, and material for its manufacture. Furthermore, each product has a different profit margin. A linear programming solution to this problem would involve expressing the relationship between resources and output of each of two products, the limits on resources available to the firm, and the relative mix of the two products which will maximize the firm's profits. Despite its complexity, linear programming is being used by an increasing number of companies for some parts of their planning effort. One example is a company like Sears, which has thousands of retail stores scattered over the country, and perhaps dozens of central warehouses from which goods can be shipped to retail outlets. From which warehouse is it most economical to ship to each of the stores? This question can be formulated into a linear programming problem, and the most efficient allocation of goods from warehouses to stores determined.

SIMULATION

Simulation is a term that covers many different techniques, all of which are designed to imitate a set of real conditions in order to predict the outcome of real conditions. Simulation techniques are much less expensive than actually trying out different alternatives, and the results are known much sooner.

One simulation technique is called "Monte Carlo." It is based on the assumption that events will occur with the same frequency in the future as they have in the past. To use Monte Carlo simulation, it is necessary to have records that show the frequency with which certain events have occurred in some time period; this is known as a *frequency distribution*. It is possible to project from such a distribution the average number of times each event will occur in the future. However, averages alone are not useful with many kinds of plans, where it is desirable to know how events will occur at random, the way they really do occur. This can be handled by relating numbers drawn at random (via a random number generator or a table of random numbers, in a manner like that described in Appendix C) to the cumulative frequency distribution. From this operation, projections can be made of the probable occurrence of events in some future time period, and comparisons of alternative decisions can be made on the basis of these projections.

Monte Carlo simulation is not nearly so complicated as it sounds. One example is offered in Appendix C. Another practical business example of the use of Monte Carlo might have to do with preventive maintenance. Assume that the gear box of an important piece of equipment contains three main bearings. One of the bearings fails, and the gear box must be opened for the bearing to be replaced. Now the question occurs: Should one or both of the other two bearings be replaced along with the defective one? Through relating numbers drawn at random to the frequency distribution gained from past performance records, the likelihood of needed replacement of the other two can be simulated, cost comparisons of the alternative actions made, and an optimal decision reached.

PROBABILITY DECISION THEORY

The technique for decision making that is generally called *probability decision theory* utilizes the concepts of certainty, risk, or uncertainty described in the previous chapter. Recall that if certainty is the state of nature, only one set of future conditions is possible. Knowing exactly what will happen, a manager need only select the planning strategy that will produce the biggest payoff in terms of the use of the firm's resources. This kind of planning is relatively easy. Unfortunately, however, it is rare to have such certainty about future conditions. Very few absolutely certain conditions exist in the world, but there are many things that are relatively certain—for example, that actual time for doing work will conform to well-engineered work standards.

When risk is the state of nature, possible future conditions can be identified, and it is frequently possible to assign occurrence probabilities to each of them from data obtained from past records. The next step is to determine the firm's alternative strategies, and then to calculate the maximum payoffs that will occur for each combination of strategy and conditions. The optimal strategy will be the one for which the greatest payoff is produced by the summation of each condition's probability times the payoff for that strategy/condition combination. Because risk occurs more frequently in business planning than certainty, this technique can substantially improve the planning effort.

Most planning, however, is not done under certainty or risk, but when the state of nature is uncertainty. Under uncertainty, thoughtful analysis will uncover the conditions that possibly can occur, but records or other sources will be lacking to establish objectively the occurrence probabilities of each. However, decision makers can identify the firm's alternative strategies. If, for the moment, each possible set of conditions is considered to be certain, the payoff for each strategy/set of conditions combination can be calculated. From this point on, there are numerous suggested methods for selecting the apparently superior strategy. The method that seems to be most popular is calling upon managers to use their best judgment to assign subjective occurrence probabilities to the possible conditions. When this is done, the final decision is made as though under risk conditions.

This technique is used frequently. In fact, people constantly assign subjective probabilities in their daily lives without realizing they are doing it. For example, when most people undertake an important financial commitment, such as buying a new car or house, they will have intuitively determined the probability of continued income from which to make payments.

DISCUSSION QUESTIONS

1. Suppose you have a quiz in this class scheduled for tomorrow and an exceptional film is being screened for the last time this evening. Discuss the costs and benefits of your decision to study or see the film.
2. Explain why a process like linear programming, which helps in allocation-of-resource decisions, would appeal to the business planner.
3. What is the outstanding advantage of simulation techniques?
4. What are some decisions you routinely make in your daily life in which you intuitively assign subjective occurrence probabilities?

BIBLIOGRAPHY

Buffa, Elwood S. *Basic Production Management.* 2nd ed. New York: Wiley, 1975.

Kabus, Irwin. "You Can Bank on Uncertainty." *Harvard Business Review,* Vol. 54 No. 3 (May–June 1976), pp. 95–105.

Koontz, Harold and Cyril O'Donnell. *Principles of Management.* 5th ed. New York: McGraw-Hill, 1972.

Levin, R. I. and C. A. Kirkpatrick. *Quantitative Approaches to Management.* New York: McGraw-Hill, 1975.

Summary

The basic step in the planning function is setting objectives. First primary objectives are spelled out, which involve, in addition to making a profit, what kind of company the firm aspires to be. To the extent possible, objectives should be expressed in measurable terms. Objectives established at the top management level tend to set the pattern for lower management level objectives.

Sales forecasting involves various techniques, including polling, trend analysis, testing, and combinations of these methods. Managers can select appropriate forecasting models using the series of criteria outlined.

A business firm has three major plans—the sales plan, the production or service plan, and the financial plan. Supporting plans include the organization plan, the manpower plan, the management development plan, the capital investment plan, and the research and development plan. An organization must start with the development of long-term plans, and from these formulate short-term plans. Standing plans, single-purpose plans, policies, procedures, and rules are additional ways of classifying plans.

Fundamentally, decision making is choosing from alternative solutions to a problem. Ideally, the scientific method is the approach managers should use in making decisions, but there are restraints that limit the scientific method as a working tool. Decision making may be done under conditions of certainty or risk about the future, but more likely it is done where the future is uncertain. Decisions are most often of a routine nature but at higher management levels the decision-making process tends to be original and pioneering. The decision-making process is weakened by the pressures of various environmental factors.

Tangible and intangible factors must be considered when making decisions; then specific planning techniques such as cost-benefit analysis, critical-path scheduling, linear programming, simulation, and probability decision theory may be used.

Organizing

Managers group work activities into departments, assign authority over these departments, and coordinate the activities of the separate departments so that objectives can be met and conflicts minimized. When managers do these things, they are organizing. However, not all of an organization's activities can be wholly controlled by managers. Some of the variables that are considered part of any organizing effort are only partially controlled by managers. And some organizational variables are completely out of managers' hands. Thus the chapters in Part 3 not only cover the managerial activities involved in the organizing function, Chapters 11–14 also examine characteristics and behaviors commonly found in organizations that help shape the organization.

Chapter 11 presents ways to determine work activities, explains alternative ways to group activities within departments, and analyzes the pros and cons of both centralization and decentralization. Chapter 12 focuses on the concepts of vertical authority and span of control. The lateral relationships that are deliberately formulated, such as those between central, supporting, or service departments, as well as less controllable lateral relationships are discussed. We conclude the chapter with a discussion of the informal organization. Chapter 13 begins with a discussion of conflict in organizations and explores power politics and human alienation—two causes of conflict in organizations. The last section of Chapter 13 focuses on coordination. Chapter 14 examines the nature of committees and their advantages and disadvantages.

11 Departmentation

Typically, the organizing function is executed within an existing framework. The exception, of course, is the company that is just getting started. However, organizing is not a one-time function that, once accomplished, need never be tackled again. It is a continual process, performed by managers to keep their operations attuned to changing conditions.

The first step in any organizing process is the identification of the various work activities or work elements performed by members of an organization when carrying out their jobs. Determining exact work activities is one of the most important functions of the manager. It is also one of the most neglected; such neglect sometimes allows unnecessary activities to creep into the operation of an organization. These unnecessary activities could be performed better and at less expense by outside companies.

PEANUTS ®   **By Charles M. Schulz**

After all necessary activities have been determined, departments are formed by grouping activities, which is the process of *departmentation,* or identifying the levels in an organization at which activities are grouped. Various terms may be associated with higher or lower levels. Thus, a hierarchy of descending levels might be *plant, division, department,* and *section.* The various labels for organization levels suggest the relative importance of activity groupings, but there is no set pattern used in business firms. Therefore, in this book the general term *department* is used to refer to any organizational unit, regardless of level.

We will begin the chapter by examining ways to determine activities. Then we will take a look at ways activities can be grouped into departments; ways in which these departments can be arranged in organizations; and lastly, we will consider the topic of decentralization and how it affects departmentation.

DETERMINING ACTIVITIES

One way to determine necessary work activities is to critically examine the work elements currently being performed. Two approaches are possible. To be really effective, both should be employed, for the results obtained will differ to some extent.

One approach might be called "the top-down method"; it starts with the highest manager in the organization and identifies the activities of that position. Next, managers who report to the top manager are identified, and their activities determined. This is continued until the lowest level of employee in the organization has been identified and activities for that level determined. The opposite approach is obviously, "the bottom-up method." Here the starting point is the people who do the basic work in the organization, such as machine operators, salespeople and clerks. The activities each of these people perform are determined. This proceeds through the first level of supervision, such as foremen, crew chiefs, and head clerks, identifying what they do and determining their work activities. This procedure is continued as high in the organization as desired. This process does not have to be done with an entire organization; any segment of an organization can be examined.

There is a problem in asking people what they do. Generally, people cannot be objective about their own jobs. Being human, they are motivated to protect their personal interests. Therefore, when they are asked what they do, their natural tendency is to exaggerate. The manager, or an organization analyst appointed by the manager, has few standards for discriminating necessary activities from those which could be readily discarded. Since requirements for activities will vary greatly between different-sized companies, and between companies in different industries, there is nothing resembling uniform guides or policies to assist the manager or analyst. The problem of evaluating supporting activities—

activities that are *not* central to the organization's main purpose—is especially difficult.

Central and Supporting Activities

The structure of every business organization contains *central* and *supporting activities*. In a manufacturing firm, central activities include those concerned with engineering, producing, and selling a product; supporting activities include work elements associated with personnel procedures and records, accounting, and quality control. In an insurance company, central activities are those involved in generating premiums and investing funds; supporting activities would be those involved in office management and public relations. A similar breakdown could be developed for every kind of business organization.

Determining the necessary central activities is a relatively straightforward process. Deciding which are the necessary supporting activities, and the extent to which they should be performed—by asking the people whose jobs and careers depend on performing these activities—is an entirely different matter. Generally speaking, to them, everything they do is necessary and important. In fact, managers of support departments, given the chance, are usually prepared and eager to institute new supporting activities.

An alternative approach is to ask the people concerned with central activities which supporting activities are necessary and how much of each are needed. This practice has its limitations, however. The managers of central departments are also biased in favor of their own interests, and are often unfavorably disposed toward *any* supporting activities. This is a major source of conflict in organizations. These managers tend to look upon supporting activities both as a cost which their operations must bear, and as a source of potential rivalry. Actually, some supporting activities are essential to an organization's survival, and are becoming even more so in these days of advancing specialization.

Actually, the approach should be one that defines activities that must be performed to accomplish the organization's objectives under future conditions, rather than an attempt to find out what activities have been performed under past conditions. For example, firms in the aerospace industry, who found their past market for business drying up, are trying to develop new products for different industries. They should project required, future activities rather than perpetuate aerospace-type work. This approach challenges a manager's organizing ability, and must start with a sound long-term plan. It requires an intimate understanding of the firm's central activities and the impact on these activities of changing conditions and technological improvements. After this has been done, a thoughtful projection of the necessary support activities should be made. The whole process is one of determining what should be done, divorced as much as possible from the influence of what is currently being done.

CONVENTIONAL DEPARTMENTATION

Once central and support activities have been determined, managers may use a conventional method to form departments. "Conventional" is used here to differentiate the methods for grouping activities predominantly used in the past, from a relatively new concept in organization, namely project organization, which is discussed later in the chapter. Conventional groupings occur at both primary and secondary levels of management. The primary level of management is that level of managers who report directly to the top executive; secondary level management are those levels between top management and nonmanagers. Traditionally, there have been three alternative activity groupings at these levels: functional organization, product organization, and geographic organization.

Functional Organization

Functional organization groups activities by the kind of work done. Thus, all sales activities are grouped into a sales department, all production activities are grouped into a production department, and so on. Figure 11-1 illustrates a simple functional organization.

Functional organization is the method for grouping activities most widely used by small firms. It is the method that is intuitively chosen when a small company begins to grow beyond the size where the owner/manager can handle everything alone. Departments can be created by grouping central activities into departments and appointing subordinate managers to run them.

The advantage of functional organization is that it facilitates specialization in work tasks. Because it provides increased specialization, it is the organization best calculated to optimize the performance of individual functions. When it is employed at the primary level, it ensures that the main functions to be performed get top management attention.

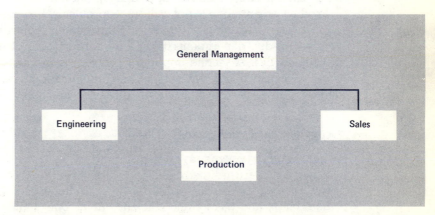

Figure 11-1. Functional Organization at the Primary Level.

However, as firms become larger and more complex, this *advantage* of functional organization at the primary level becomes a disadvantage. The top manager of a small company with a single product can personally coordinate the activities of functional managers so the goals of the firm are met. But at some stage of size and complexity, coordination of relatively independent functional departments becomes virtually impossible. At this stage, there must be provision for directing top management's attention to broader dimensions, such as geographical areas, rather than to specialized departments, such as engineering, production, and sales. At this point, an alternative method for grouping activities at the primary level must be chosen. However, regardless of the method used for grouping activities at the primary level, activities will be grouped functionally at some level in the organization—and always at the operating level.

Product Organization

A second organization form, *product organization*, groups activities at the primary level by specific products, or product lines. This form of organization permits companies to grow very large, as evidenced by such corporation giants as General Motors, General Electric, and Du Pont. In product organization, the central activities pertaining to a specific product, and often the supporting activities, are grouped together under a product manager. Product departments tend to be semiautonomous, and often grow to the size of large companies themselves.

Specialization is the outstanding advantage of product organization, but it is a different kind of specialization than that found in functional organization. In product organization, human skills and production equipment can be specialized to meet the requirements of individual, and often highly complex products. In addition, because of the location of the product departments at the primary level, as illustrated by Figure 11-2, each product receives top management attention.

Product organization is not without its problems, however. The main problem is maintaining effective top-management control over independent product departments (techniques for such control are discussed in Chapter 27). A second important problem is product-organization costs. Because it duplicates skills and equipment for each product department, costs run higher than those for functional organization.

Geographical Organization

Widely scattered operations often justify a third form of organization, in which activities are grouped at the primary level by the territorial location at which they are performed. This form is known as *geographical organization*, and has logistic efficiency as its outstanding advantage. *Logistic efficiency* means that a company may locate operations close to

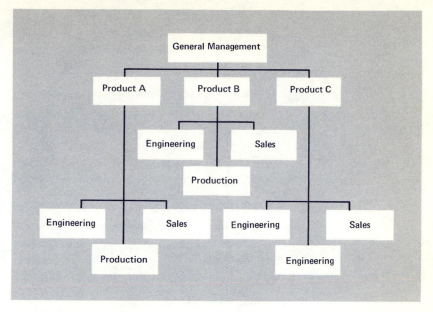

Figure 11-2. Product Organization at the Primary Level; Functional Organization at the Secondary Level.

the source of raw materials, or close to the markets being served, or both, and thereby significantly reduce transportation costs. A second advantage is the opportunity to provide specialized local services. Examples would be the southern division of a national steel company that employs salesmen with southern backgrounds, or national supermarket chains that cater to the food-buying habits of people in the areas they serve. The main problem with geographical organization, as with product organization, is controlling the dispersed operations. Figure 11-3 illustrates a simple geographical organization.

Organization of Supporting Activities

Finance is one supporting activity that is always organized functionally at the primary level. This is done because top-management attention to the control of funds is crucial to every firm's survival. Other strong candidates for primary-level location on a functional basis are personnel and purchasing activities in respective departments.

However, there is no set pattern for the assignment of supporting activities. If central activities are grouped functionally at the primary level, supporting activities may also be grouped functionally at the primary level, or under central activities at the secondary level. A product or geographical department manager may have supporting activities at the same level as central activities, or at a lower level, under

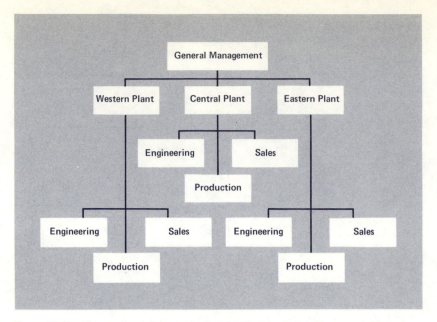

Figure 11-3. Geographical Organization at the Primary Level; Functional Organization at the Secondary Level.

central activities. The implications of such locations of central and supporting activities are discussed in Chapter 12, which is concerned with vertical and lateral relationships.

PROJECT ORGANIZATION

Sometime around 1955, industries working under government contracts became interested in project organization, which they thought was a new organization form. However, project organization had been around awhile. The theatrical and construction industries, for example, have used the form, since they first became organized activities. Today, it is being used extensively by marketing and distribution companies; banks and insurance firms are experimenting with it; and some retail stores, laboratories, and hospitals have adopted it, at least in part.

Project organization is the team or task-force approach to getting a particular job done. It works this way: There is a specific goal, with complex requirements, (involving diverse skills) that must be accomplished in a limited time period. Examples of such goals include a product that must be developed and produced, a consumer product or service that requires a special marketing effort, or an unusual task with large and significant dimensions, such as a corporate merger or the creation of a new degree program in a university. The effort mounted to accomplish the requirements of the goal is called a *project*. The project is given a name—usually one associated with the goal—and a project manager is chosen.

The project manager must have access to various skills to achieve the goal. These skills are assembled by recruiting people as full-time staff members for the life of the project. These people tend to be specialists, and are usually drawn from permanent departments. They are under the direct authority of the project manager. The remainder of the work to be done, which is often the bulk of the project task, is executed by people temporarily assigned to the project who are also permanent members of other organizational units. Although directed in their work on the project by the project manager or appointed deputies, they remain under the line authority of the manager of their parent department. The whole idea is to bring top efficiency to a convergence of specialized and varied skills—temporarily applied as needed—to produce a specific end item by cutting across organizational boundary lines and disregarding traditional organization theories.

Project organization has a marked resemblance to product organization, in that activities are grouped according to the requirements of a specific product or service, rather than by the kind of work or where it is done. As in both product and geographical forms of organization, activities are grouped on a functional basis at some level in the project organization. Within a project organization, there may be a level of activities grouped on a subordinate product basis; or a grouping may be made on a geographical basis, above a functional grouping of the kinds of work done.

A significant difference between the project organization concept and other organization forms is the life of the organization. Permanence is the normal intent in setting up a functional, product, or geographical organization. Project organizations are purposefully temporary. They are created to accomplish specific goals, and when those goals are achieved the project organization is disbanded.

Project organization differs from conventional organization in another way. It is not usually employed for grouping of activities at the primary level. In the aerospace and electronics industries, for example, activities are usually grouped at the primary level according to product classification. Project organizations are created beneath the product level in a matrix relationship to secondary functional levels. Figure 11-4 illustrates this matrix relationship, and points to the major distinguishing feature of project organization, which is plural command relationships.

Subordinates in a direct, formal relationship to one supervisor, who are permanent members of one organization (in Figure 11-4, an engineering department) may be temporarily assigned to a project department, and be in an authority relationship to at least one additional

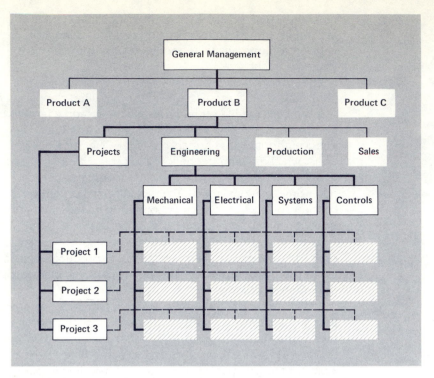

Figure 11-4. Product Organization at the Primary Level; Functional Organization at the Secondary Level; Project Organization in a Matrix Relationship to Functional Organizations.

supervisor. In Figure 11-4, engineers would be reporting both to the manager of the functional engineering department and (temporarily) to the manager of the project department.

Advantages of Project Organization

Optimal solutions to difficult problems can be attained through project organization, which pools talent from various functional units. The people recruited for a project are freed from the constraints and prejudices of departments preoccupied with a single function, and become highly involved in contributing their share to a goal which depends on the successful performance of multiple functions. Project organization focuses group attention on a total process, rather than focusing individual attention on subprocesses.

Stages of project development can be completed faster and with greater integration of skills because the shortened lines of communication facilitate information feedback. Cumbersome formal organization channels are bypassed, and many reviews and approvals necessary when crossing traditional organization boundary lines are simply eliminated.

People assigned to a project identify strongly with the total process, an identification which tends to act as a motivator. They see themselves as part of an effort that has definable and measurable results, and know that a successful effort reflects credit on those who helped make it possible. They tend to get personally involved with a project, and perceive that, to some extent, their own needs are satisfied in meeting the objectives of the project.

In addition, permanent and costly organizational "empires" are avoided. In essence, the project system draws on skills as they are needed—only for as long as they are needed—and releases the skills for some other productive use as soon as the goals are achieved. The system is deliberately set up to gain maximum efficiency from human resources. The need to complete the project successfully pressures the project manager to efficiently deploy the skills of the people assigned to it.

Problems of Project Organization

It would be unrealistic to assume that project organization does not have some unique problems. One is that setting up a project is potentially disturbing to the total organization. Managers must accept giving up some of their key personnel to the project, often for an indefinite time. Functional managers find they are no longer in a key position but have been relegated to serving a project, or projects. When there are many projects, the project managers tend to compete vigorously with each other for the services of functional departments.

Another problem unique to project organization centers on authority. The authority delegated to the project manager is often ambiguous. In theory, the manager is supposed to act with all of the authority of the president or senior officer of the enterprise in getting the project job done. However, in practice this authority is often more apparent than real, and the manager's accomplishments tend to be a result of personal persuasiveness and personality. On the other hand, the responsibilities are clearcut: The project manager normally is blamed for anything that goes wrong on the project. To make project organization successful, a new state of mind must be achieved by all of the managers involved. The old system of command authority must be forgotten, and a new system substituted; a system based on coordinated lateral relationships. (These alternative relationships are discussed in the next chapter.)

One of the major problems of project organization is that it can cause frustrations and anxieties for the people connected with it. Ideally, a forecast is made as to when a project organization must be broken up, and plans are developed for placing project workers in some other organization at comparable status. But often, in practice, after a project organization is disbanded, its people are either laid off or placed in lower-status jobs.

This can cause a number of serious problems. The known temporary life of a project organization can generate unusual worries about loss of employment or career setbacks. When individuals experience a successive series of bosses, they can become concerned that there is no one person looking out for their personal development. Also, people who are continually being transferred from one department to another may not develop a sense of loyalty to the larger organization.

Intuitively, it would appear that people would be frustrated by dual-command relationships. However, there has not been enough good research on the subject to reveal much about the effect on people of having to report to more than one direct supervisor.

GUIDELINES FOR THE MANAGER

While project organization offers advantages other methods of grouping activities are also viable. Keep in mind that project organization may not be applicable to all business firms and social institutions. The problems of project organization are indeed formidable. However, proponents of the system urge that the problems are more than offset by the possible efficiencies. The challenge to managers considering project organization is to balance potential gains against potential losses in each case. Managers should let the greatest weight determine the decision. Project organization has had an impressive record of success, but only when it was thoughtfully and properly applied; managers must recognize where it is appropriate and where it is not. The following criteria may assist in deciding for or against project organization.

- Scale of operation. Project organization is generally appropriate for a unique endeavor, one that is
    a. definable in terms of a specific goal.
    b. large enough to warrant special management attention.
    c. measurable in terms of having a definite beginning and end.
- Unusual need. Conventional organization forms are appropriate for meeting familiar needs. The choice of project organization is indicated when there is uncertainty, or even ignorance, about how to meet performance, cost, and schedule parameters. It is also warranted when unusual management controls are necessary.
- Integration. Project organization is best for tying together dependent, diverse, and complex skills. It is especially appropriate when these skills must be applied simultaneously, rather than one after the other.
- Significance. The project should be so important that a failure would represent a serious setback. In such a case, management might well decide that adopting project organization to cope with the problem is warranted.

We have seen that there are various ways to determine work activities. We have also examined ways to group these activities into departments. The following section is concerned with decentralization, and with its opposite, the location of decision making at the top of the organization, both of which also affect the departmentation process.

DECENTRALIZATION VS. CENTRALIZATION

A *decentralized* organization permits more decisions by lower-level managers, while a *centralized* organization is one in which the bulk of the decisions are made by top-level managers. The terms are relative; an organization cannot be completely decentralized, because all decisions would be made at the lowest level of the organization, and would therefore be uncontrolled and without an integrated direction. Nor can an organization, other than a very small and simple one, be completely centralized, because all decisions would be reserved for the top manager, and would significantly restrict the scale of operations in the organization. The terms refer to tendencies to either disperse or concentrate the location of decision making within the vertical relationship structure. They have no connection with the geographical location of decision making.

Factors Involved in Decentralization

The primary requisite for a decentralized operation is maturity on the part of the organization, and the people in it. An undeveloped organization, still trying to find its place in the larger social system, has a strong need for the central determination of goals, along with plans for achieving them. In such a case, decisions should be restricted to the most experienced managers, who, presumably, would be at the top level. An organization should take the risk of decentralizing in order to capitalize on increased growth and success opportunities. However, the risk should not be taken until the organization could survive the mistakes likely to be made by less experienced managers. Not only does decentralization require maturity on the part of the subordinates to whom the decision-making responsibility is entrusted; it also requires maturity on the part of the higher managers, who, though still responsible for the outcome of their subordinates' decisions, must refrain from interfering with their decision processes. The higher managers need, above all else, to have faith in the axiom that management is accomplishing things through others, not doing the things themselves. Managers must never decentralize, however, until they have means for objectively evaluating and controlling the performance of their subordinates. The subordinates must possess demonstrated judgment, confidence in themselves, and a drive to be on their own.

Actually, decentralization is the dispersal of certain amounts of the planning function. This can be accomplished in various ways and degrees. One way is to have the firm's long-term plans developed from the integrated contributions of the lower-level managers. Another is to disseminate the centrally developed long-term plan to the subordinate managers, and hold them responsible for implementing it with short-term plans. Still another way is to specify the areas in which subordinates can make decisions, such as whether to produce or buy parts and larger components, which channels to use in marketing distribution, and even what style and characteristics should identify the product line. There is also a growing tendency to decentralize by forcing profit-making responsibility down into the organization. In this approach, human and physical resources are made available to lower-level managers, who are challenged to utilize these resources to yield some expected profit.

How Far to Decentralize

Textbooks on management are replete with guides on how much a company should decentralize. Generally, these guides approve the delegation of decision making to a level at which

1. the facts needed for making a decision can be readily and accurately obtained.
2. individuals have a proven capacity to make sound decisions of the order required.
3. costs would occur if the decision in question were delayed.
4. the probability of costly mistakes is low.

Advantages of Decentralization

One outstanding effect of decentralization is democracy in industry. People become involved in decisions which affect them, and therefore, in a sense, are masters of their own destinies rather than pawns to be manipulated. Another advantage, both to individuals and the firm, is that decentralization provides excellent opportunities for the development of managers who may rise higher in the organization. And to the firm itself, decentralization permits almost unlimited size and scope of operations, and it might lead to improved profitability.

The Present Trend

Some companies are re-centralizing decision making. One reason is the difficulty of controlling highly decentralized operations. Over the past ten to fifteen years, a number of large corporations in the United States have encountered serious problems because decentralized divisions got out of control. Another reason for re-centralizing decision making is the difficulty of coping with the pressures of big government and big labor

If 'satellization' fails, try centralization

Since merging erstwhile auto maker Studebaker Corp. with equipment manufacturer Worthington Corp. in 1967, Chairman Derald H. Ruttenberg has been casting about for the right formula to manage Studebaker-Worthington Inc. In the early 1970s Ruttenberg tried what he called "satellization," a program in which minority interests in the billion-dollar conglomerate's subsidiaries were spun off to the public and managers were given virtual autonomy in running their operations.

Now, however, rebuffed by slumping stock prices and encouraged by expanding markets, Ruttenberg has done an about-face. Last week he mailed out proxies to stockholders in a move to begin buying back the seven minority interests, merge the subsidiaries, and impose centralized control. Ruttenberg has proposed three mergers involving the expenditure of $30 million in cash to the shareholders, who vote on them at the annual meeting next month.

The mergers, though, are just the latest in a series of moves by the 60-year-old chairman. Already, sw has been reorganized into two operating groups: a raw-materials processing group composed of five subsidiaries—Worthington Pump, Masoneilan International, Turbodyne, Worthington Service, and Worthington Compressors—that account for 55% of the company's sales; and a consumer and industrial group consisting of Onan, Clarke-Gravely, STP, Wagner Electric, and Campbell Chain. Ruttenberg has decided to get out of all businesses not fitting into these two groups and several subsidiaries have been sold.

Pasco Inc., an oil company 55%-owned by sw, is in the midst of liquidation. sw acquired Pasco, formerly Pan American Sulphur Co., four years ago for about $31 million. From the liquidation, however, the company expects to receive about $125 million ultimately, for a $90 million pretax gain and about $63 million after taxes.

Debt reduction

The major portion of the proceeds from Pasco and the divestitures has gone to reduce sw's debt. Last year the company paid off $6 million, lowering its total debt to $246 million. According to Ruttenberg, the total debt should be less than $100 million by the end of 1976, compared with a net worth of $400 million.

The three mergers of Wagner, Clarke-Gravely, and Turbodyne should help Ruttenberg centralize the company. For one thing, sw will then be able to interchange facilities among the subsidiaries without worrying about minority shareholders and possible conflicts of interest. For another, cash management can be centralized.

The centralization is necessary, Ruttenberg says, because several subsidiaries in a group often sell to the same customers. Most important, Ruttenberg foresees an "unprecedented upsurge in the worldwide demand for raw-materials processing equipment," for irrigation and drainage projects, new oil refineries, pipelines, and petrochemical and fertilizer plants. Already, sw has established a central service and maintenance organization in Europe for raw-materials processing.

The company's earnings, up 141% in the first half of 1976 to $22.7 million or $4.50 a share, should get an additional boost from the reduction in minority interests—which penalized earnings by $7.6 million last year. Ruttenberg, for his part, could take a pay cut when Pasco is liquidated: $119,000 of his $459,000 salary last year was paid for his service as Pasco's chairman.

Big benefits
But the balance is more than likely to be made up by the dividends Ruttenberg receives on his 160,000 shares of sw stock, now selling at about $56. At the annual meeting next month, the shareholders will also be asked to ratify a three-for-two stock split that would not only increase the number of shares by 50% but would also increase the dividend, since the pay-out per share will be held at $1.32 annually.

The benefits of centralizing sw, Ruttenberg feels, outweigh those of the satellization of several years ago. Then, the theory went, public minority interest would give sw more visibility and show investors its operation in greater detail. The public companies, moreover, would be able to attract top management talent that would prefer to run a separate entity rather than just another division of a conglomerate.

But the stock market did not endorse the concept, and sw is paying just about what it received for those minority shares. "Selling those minority interests never did make good business sense," says an investment banker familiar with the company. "The minority shareholders complicate management, create potential conflicts of interest, and nobody wants to buy stock in a company 80%-controlled by someone else."

---

unions. These two forces are making business firms operate under uniform policies, strictly administered by top-level managers. A third reason for centralization is associated with the increasing use of the computer. The computer is said to be eliminating some middle-management positions and causing others to be reduced in importance, and it is at this management level that decisions are made under decentralization. Primarily, however, the computer influences a firm to centralize bacause it can furnish information regarding all phases of the company's operations to top managers with incredible speed. No longer is it necessary to have "the man on the spot" make the decisions; through the computer the firm's most experienced managers can keep abreast of every decision-making situation.

DISCUSSION QUESTIONS

1. Why should an analyst be careful in asking people what they do on their jobs?
2. Give examples of what you consider to be central and supporting activities in any organization with which you are familiar, and explain your reasoning.
3. Differentiate between functional and product organization.

4. Discuss the characteristics of project organization.
5. When should an organization tend toward decentralization and when is a tendency toward centralization more appropriate?

BIBLIOGRAPHY

Davis, Keith. "Trends in Organization Design." *Arizona Business*, (November 1963), pp. 3–7.

Drucker, Peter. "New Templates for Today's Organizations." *Harvard Business Review*, Vol. 52 No. 1 (January–February 1974), pp. 45–53.

Fulmer, R. M. "Product Management: Panacea or Pandora's Box." *California Management Review*, Vol. 7 No. 4 (Summer 1965), pp. 63–74.

Galbraith, Jay R. "Matrix Organization Designs: How to Combine Functional and Project Forms." *Business Horizons*, Vol. 14 (February 1971), pp. 29–40.

Morris, William T. *Decentralization in Management Systems: An Introduction to Design.* Columbus: Ohio State University Press, 1968.

Reeser, Clayton. "Some Potential Human Problems of the Project Form of Organization." *Academy of Management Journal*, Vol. 12 No. 4 (December 1969), pp. 459–67.

The Case of the Function That Wouldn't Fit

Bob McNulty was twenty-five years old, and just out of the Navy, when his father died and left the McNulty Steel Construction Company for Bob to retrieve from its creditors. The older McNulty had been a good engineer, and had built his company, which specialized in custom storage tanks, into an industry leader in the Phoenix area. Because of the virtual impossibility during World War II of getting steel for nondefense purposes, McNulty had successfully bid on a subcontract for making a bomber landing-gear component. He would have been all right on the contract if he had not tried to improve the design of the component at his own expense, and the pressure of trying to pay back the money that he had borrowed was probably the cause of his death.

Young McNulty began his industrial career by calling a meeting of the firm's creditors. The argument he gave them was that if they foreclosed on the company's assets they would be lucky to get back fifty cents on the dollar, but if they would give him time to reorganize the company to take advantage of the promising markets that were plainly visible, they would get back all of their money, and in addition have a good future customer.

The creditors seemed agreeable to the proposition; however, one of them raised the question: "It sounds fine, Bob, but are you going to try to do everything yourself like your father did?"

"No, I'm not," Bob replied. "I'm going to organize the company around the main functions of finance, engineering, manufacturing, and sales. I'm going to put good men in charge of these func-tions, and my job will be to keep everything coordinated."

With the blessings of his creditors, Bob started to build the company. Thanks to his father, there were both specialized equipment and a skilled work force for constructing steel tanks, and the firm branched out into pressure vessels of all kinds. A contemporary product using similar resources was steel buildings, such as gasoline stations and warehouses, and Bob moved aggressively into this field. The firm's engineers and salesmen, who were also engineering-oriented, fitted nicely into the expanded pattern that the company was following.

During the Korean War, Bob saw an opportunity to get into a new business that not only had a good profit potential of its own, but would also help the existing product line. The new venture was steel jobbing, which is buying steel in carload quantities from the mills, carrying it in inventory, cutting it to customer specifications, and selling it in small lots at prices substantially over the mill cost. The advantage to the tank and building business was the low cost of steel bought in large quantities.

A problem with the new business was that steel jobbing required a different kind of selling effort than tanks and buildings, and involved different customers—some of whom were actually competitors of McNulty Steel Construction. The apparent answer was to set up a steel supply division, in which the activities associated with steel jobbing would be independently grouped. Thus began the change from a functional to a product type of organization, although the question of where steel procurement and inventory control activities would be located did not have a really acceptable answer. As an expedient, these activities remained under manufacturing.

Bob McNulty had retained the engineer primarily involved in working on the landing-gear component design, and had subsidized a modest research and development effort until a payoff finally came in 1967. A design that was a marked innovation for both military and commercial aircraft was achieved, and excellent patent protection was granted. The firm had generated sufficient capital by this time to handle the complete manufacturing and marketing of the product, but its process characteristics did not integrate at all with the manufacturing capabilities for tanks and steel buildings, and the marketing effort for the aircraft component was entirely different from that of either of the firm's other product lines. Therefore, it was decided to create an aircraft products division, with its own engineering, manufacturing, and marketing functions.

The one thing that the new division had in common with the construction and supply operations was the requirement of large quantities of steel purchased at the lowest possible price. At the time of forming the aircraft division, it seemed appropriate to group the engineering, manufacturing, and marketing activities for the tank and building line under a product division designated as "construction." Strong pressure was then exerted by the manager of the steel supply division to have procurement and inventory management activities placed under his control. He persuasively reasoned with Bob McNulty that his operation would act as a steel supplier to the construction and aircraft divisions just as with any of the firm's large outside customers. The procurement manager countered with the argument that steel buying and storing, together with the purchasing and inventory of all of the other of the company's required supplies and equipment, was important enough to be set up as an independent functional division directly under McNulty. The view of the construction division manager and the new aircraft division manager was that they should each have their own procurement and inventory departments. For the time being, McNulty elected to go along with the supply division manager, so this organizational change was effected.

In the 1970s the company's name was changed to McNulty Steel Products, Inc., and its product-line expansion went in two directions. One was the fabrication of steel pipe for the transmission of petroleum and natural gas, and the other was a proprietary line of standard liquid petroleum gas (LPG) storage tanks for home use. Both the pipe and the LPG tank lines were complementary to the engineering and manufacturing capabilities of the construction division, and were dependent upon extremely efficient buying and storing of steel. However, they both required distinctly separate marketing organizations. McNulty set up two new product divisions, oilfield and LPG, with the respective managers reporting to him. Although this organizational arrangement solved some problems, it also created others, because the inevitable conflicts between the oilfield and LPG division managers, who had

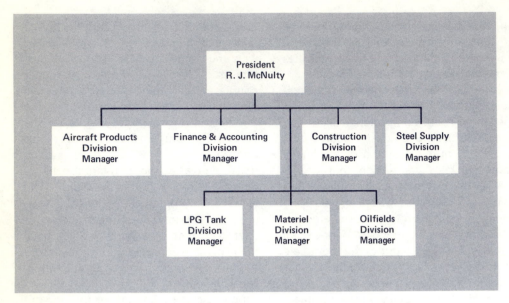

Figure 11-5. Organization Chart at the Primary Level, McNulty Steel Products, Inc.

the responsibility for selling their respective products, and the construction division manager, who had the responsibility for making them, could only be resolved by McNulty himself. In addition, the construction division manager was increasingly critical of steel procurement and inventory being under the supply division manager. Finally, in 1974, McNulty centralized all procurement and inventory activities in a functional division called "materiel," and the company's organization chart at the primary level became as shown in Figure 11-5.

In the summer of 1977 Bob McNulty called in a management consulting firm for assistance with an organizational problem. "What I am thinking of," he said, "is setting up two decentralized materiel operations—one in the construction division and the other in the supply division. Making a centralized materiel division work in a company like this seems to be impossible. Please make a study and give me your recommendations."

DISCUSSION QUESTIONS

1. In the Case of the Function That Wouldn't Fit, was Bob McNulty right in organizing on a functional basis when he first began to run the company?

2. After the introduction of the steel supply division, no good answer was available for where to put procurement and inventory, so as an expedient these activities were just left where they were. Do you think it likely that many organizational decisions are made this way?

3. In the argument concerning the proper

location for procurement and inventory management prior to 1970, take the side of each of the contending managers at McNulty Steel, including the procurement manager, and argue for their views.

4. If you represented the management consulting firm called in by Bob McNulty in 1977, what recommendations would you have made in response to his request?

5. In addition to the problem of where to locate steel procurement and inventory management activities, what other organizational problems might be caused by supporting activities? Name the supporting activities that you think may be sources of problems.

The Case of the Chicken With Its Head Cut Off

As Charles Leghorn often remarked, "With my last name, and the nickname of 'Chick,' there was really no way that I could stay out of the chicken business."

Chick Leghorn got started in business for himself with a catering service in a large midwestern city. He would undertake to provide every detail connected with banquets, weddings, conferences, etc., including the room itself, food, beverage, waiters, bartenders, decoration, and transportation to and from the location, if required. He developed an outstanding reputation for the quality of his service, and he became particularly recognized for the fact that the final bill that he presented never exceeded his original estimate. As was to be a characteristic of his later business life, he developed a system for handling every size and kind of a catering assignment, and he would meticulously check the performance of his employees, whom he informally called his "arrangers," and who supervised the actual work at the catering occasions. By 1973, he had seven arrangers working for him in the city in which he started, and three in each of two smaller cities within a radius of seventy-five miles.

The success of the catering business convinced Chick that many people in the United States were affluent enough to be willing to pay for the convenience of having things done for them. Take-out food service shops, which were then just beginning their phenomenal growth, especially attracted his attention. Through his contacts with local restaurants, he met a chef who was unusually proud of his ability to prepare fried chicken. Chick commissioned the chef, Tony, to experiment with his recipe until he developed an original process for the mass frying of chickens that really had superior qualities. Chick paid Tony $5,000 for exclusive rights to the process.

After an intensive study to determine the most promising location sites for take-out food shops, interior and exterior architectural styles, pricing, advertising, kitchen equipment, and even attendants' uniforms, Chick opened his first shop under the copyrighted name of Chick's Heavenly Chicken. He had a long-term lease on the site, but owned the building and all of the equipment. As he said: "I'm going to spend a year with this one operation until I feel that I really understand the business." He hired and trained employees to prepare the food and wait on customers, and methodically tried different approaches to increasing sales and reducing costs. In the meantime, he remained extremely active in his catering business.

In the middle of 1974, Chick felt that he was ready to expand the Heavenly Chicken operation, and he decided to do it on a franchise basis. He ran display advertisements in the financial sections of local newspapers, and in the newspapers of neighboring cities. The minimum requirements were $35,000 in cash, an impeccable character background, and some business experience. Chick interviewed each applicant intensively, and found that he was accepting only about 20 percent of those who met the minimum standards. Those who were accepted were obligated to a contract wherein Chick would select and negotiate for the site, specify the architecture, prescribe all operating methods, and retain the option to terminate the franchise if, on the basis of periodic reports and his regular visits, he found that the franchisee was departing from established procedures. In spite of the rigid requirements, franchises were in great demand because Chick's Heavenly Chicken shops were making the franchisees prosperous.

The growth of the take-out food industry made desirable sites increasingly difficult to find, and Chick was required to widen his geographical sphere of operations. By 1977 there were 89 franchised Chick's Heavenly Chicken shops in 11 states, with 13 as far away as California, and 7 in Florida. The strain on Chick's personal time was tremendous, and he tried to meet it partially through agents whom he would engage as needed in the various geographical areas. For example, there was an attorney whom he would call on to help with new franchise deals in Los Angeles, a retired ex-banker often did similar things for him in Miami, and around his headquarters city he had trained one of his catering arrangers to relieve him of some of the load.

The huge annual payments by franchise holders to poultry wholesalers made Chick realize that he was missing a bet by not raising, processing, and distributing his own chickens. With his typical thoroughness, he first studied poultry raising, and then started an experimental farm near his headquarters city. Initial results were highly satisfactory, and he expanded the original farm to mass-production scale, and started two others, one in southern Oregon and another one in Florida.

A small wholesale restaurant-supply firm in Los Angeles got into financial trouble in 1978, and Chick's attorney friend mentioned to him that it could be picked up at a bargain. Chick had been thinking for some time that the thousands of take-out food shops all over the country offered a virtually untapped market for an aggressive supply operation, and he figured he could learn how to capture this sales potential with an already going business in a closely related field. Therefore, he made an offer which was accepted, and after spending about three months personally running the company, he found the prospects were really better than he had estimated. He decided that when sales doubled, which he calculated would be by 1980, he would start a branch in the midwest.

One day as Chick and his architect were flying to Seattle to get construction started on three new Chick's Heavenly Chicken shops, the architect remarked: "I admit that I don't know much about management, but it seems to me that what you need more than anything else is an organization. You are personally stretched to the breaking point."

Chick's reply was: "My physician tells me the same thing, but I can't get things done the way I want them with an organization chart and fancy titles."

In the early afternoon of Tuesday, April 27, 1978, Chick walked into his office and said to his secretary, "Miss Forrest, please remind me to get to the banquet hall for the political party meeting by five o'clock. I want to be sure to check out the catering details."

Ten minutes later a call came in from San Francisco, where it seemed that a lease on a new shopping center site had bogged down. He buzzed Miss Forrest, "Get me on the late afternoon flight to San Francisco."

Just before 2:30 P.M. he received a call from the poultry farm in Florida. A trucking strike had stopped the delivery of chickens, and nobody there knew what to do about it. "Miss Forrest," he said, "get me to Florida as soon as possible, and arrange for a car to meet me."

A few minutes later Miss Forrest came in and said: "Mr. Leghorn, I simply have to ask you a question."

"Yes, what is it?" replied Chick as he impatiently looked up from his study of the fast-growing "fish and chips" shops.

"Just which part of you is going to the banquet, which part to San Francisco, and which part to Florida?" answered Miss Forrest in a resigned voice.

DISCUSSION QUESTIONS

1. *Decentralization* and *centralization* refer to the location of decision-making authority within the organization structure—irrespective of geographical location. What effect on the locus of decision making, however, would geographical dispersal of a firm's operations have?
2. Why should a young and struggling company avoid much decentralization?
3. Argue from the position that the computer may foster decentralization, rather than centralization.
4. In the Case of the Chicken With Its Head Cut Off, what criteria justify decentralizing Chick Leghorn's enterprise?
5. Should Chick undertake the organization of his enterprises himself?

The Case of the Misguided Organization Study

"And I promise that if I am elected mayor, I will do everything in my power to reorganize the city government and reduce its costs of operation." This was the message that Frank Fawcett dinned into the ears of prospective voters in the city of Glenbank during the weeks preceding the 1974 election, and which ultimately was a major factor in his election victory.

Like some incorporated cities in central California, Glenbank had, up until 1968, enjoyed a period of prosperity dating back to the early 1940's. The reason, of course, was the presence in the immediate area of a large number of companies working on defense contracts. The employment opportunities generated by these firms had caused the population in Glenbank to more than triple. However, by 1968 the severe cutbacks in the defense industry had been felt in the form of significant reductions in the city's tax revenues, and the incumbent mayor did nothing to adjust Glenbank's governmental operations to a scale consistent with lower revenues and a shrinking population. This explains why economy in the city's management became a key issue in the mayoral election of June 1974. Some three months after the election, Mayor Fawcett began to be forcibly reminded by the City Council and Glenbank's newspaper and radio station of his campaign promise to reorganize the city government. This was a bothersome thing to the mayor because actually he was a retired dentist, and although he had enjoyed participating in civic affairs during the thirty years of his practice, he did not have the vaguest notion of how to go about reorganizing some quite substantial city departments. However, he knew he had to do something, so he decided to give the assignment to Anita Dale, a young attorney who had been his campaign manager, and who was now employed in Glenbank's Legal Department.

"I suppose one way to do it would be to just order a 10-percent reduction in personnel for all departments," mused the mayor as he acquainted Dale with the assignment, "but I did promise the voters that I would handle the reorganization on a systematic basis, and I think that is what the Council, and some others, are looking for. What ideas do you have?"

"I read somewhere that when you attempt to reorganize an organization already in existence, you should first find out what activities are absolutely essential, combine them, and then drop the ones that can be dispensed with. The newspaper editor and some other business people have been complaining for some time about what they claim is a ridiculously large maintenance department. I just happened to find out that salaries in that department amount to over $800,000 a year. Suppose I start there by asking people what activities might be done away with."

Anita Dale obtained a copy of the Maintenance Department's organization chart (Figure 11-6) before meeting with Jim Jonish, maintenance superintendent. She was somewhat surprised to find that there were eighty-one employees in the department, and noticed that in all cases the activities performed were offered as part of the services of private business firms in Glenbank. As she had

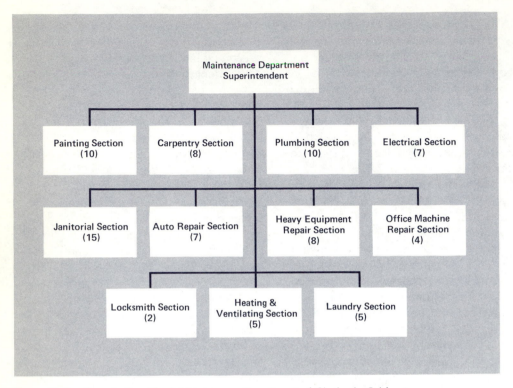

Figure 11-6. Organization Chart, Maintenance Department of Glenbank, California. (Numbers = amount of filled positions.)

found Jonish to be very cooperative in several previous contacts, she expected an open mind when she suggested that Jonish identify activities in his department that could be dropped.

"Eliminate some activities! You must be out of your mind," exclaimed Jonish when Dale made her proposal. "Why, what we should do is add some. I have been trying to get a machine shop in this department for years, and we still have to send our machining out. We are having the computer maintained by the leasing company, and we should be doing that work in-house. I could go on

and on telling you of activities that should be brought into this department. If you don't believe me, go out and ask some of the section foremen. They will tell you how much money the city is losing by not having an adequate size maintenance department."

With her enthusiasm considerably dampened, Dale began to make the rounds of the foremen. Dave Grier, electrical section foreman, almost exploded when Dale pointed out that four of the six electricians were obviously not doing any work at the time that they were talking. "Of course they're not,"

Grier said. "We have to keep them on standby. Do you think that if there is an electrical emergency in city hall that they don't want it taken care of right away? And, you talk of activities that can be cut out. I'll tell you some, like motor rewinding, that we should be doing and are not."

Every foreman said fundamentally the same things about his own section, but the plumbing foreman did not see too much need for the city to maintain a laundry, and the heavy equipment repair foreman thought that auto repairs could be better done by the service departments of the local auto dealers. He obviously had a grudge against the auto repair foreman, however.

Dale then went to the Public Works Department and the Parks and Recreation Department and talked to people there about activities needed to be performed by the Maintenance Department. She detected a wariness on the part of everyone she discussed the matter with—almost as though they were defensive about something.

"I thought that Fawcett was promising things that he couldn't do," said Luigi Ferraldi, head groundskeeper. "Just try to name one activity done by Maintenance, or any other department, that the city could get along without."

The city engineer, Melvin Rogers, was even more emphatic. "What Fawcett is going to do with your help is mess up the entire city organization. These departments have been carefully built up over the years, and nothing is being done in any of them that isn't essential."

As Dale began to write her report to the mayor on the findings of her organization study, her spirits began to rise. After all, she rationalized, organization was not her field, but she had carried out the study on a logical basis. It was not her fault that the mayor had made a campaign promise that could not be kept, or that some people in town were biased against what appeared to be an efficient city government. She had carefully looked for activities in a sample department, Maintenance, that could be done away with, and could not find any. She felt she was justified in reporting to the mayor that any reorganization would be detrimental to Glenbank.

DISCUSSION QUESTIONS

1. Explain how prosperity can lead to the buildup of unnecessary activities within organizations.
2. Was Mayor Fawcett's idea of a blanket 10 percent reduction in personnel for all departments any worse than the approach that Dale used?
3. Speculate how you would feel if you were Jonish or any of the foremen, and someone suggested to you that some of your organization's activities might be expendable.
4. Explain why people in Public Works and Parks and Recreation might seem defensive to Dale.
5. If you were given Dale's assignment, how would you go about it?

12 Organizational Relationships

The act of departmentation sets in motion a wide variety of relationships within an organization. Most obvious, perhaps, are vertical relationships—those between manager and subordinates. Crucial issues here, to be discussed in this chapter, are span of control (how many subordinates can a manager deal with effectively?) and authority. There are a number of relationships beyond this strict hierarchical one. Therefore, we will also examine lateral relationships and, finally, informal relationships.

VERTICAL RELATIONSHIPS

Vertical relationships in an organization are those between individual managers and the subordinates reporting directly to them. The act of departmentation creates these vertical relationships; when activities are grouped into departments, managers are appointed to head them, and are granted authority over the subordinates reporting to them. Earlier notions on management theory perceived vertical relationships as practically the whole of organization, and authority as the cement holding an organization together. The predominant organizational interest in those days was with the hierarchy of supervisor-subordinate relationships. Modern thinking is that there is a great deal more to organization than this, but vertical relationships and authority are still recognized as highly important factors.

To understand the workings of vertical relationships it is necessary to have a working knowledge of two key concepts: *span of control* and *authority*. Let us start by establishing definitions for these concepts.

Span of Control

The number of subordinates that report directly to a manager determines the manager's *span of control*. In the early days of management theory—almost up to 1950—a great deal of attention was directed to this issue. It was thought that an effective span of control involved some fixed number of subordinates, usually six. Often one of the first things an organization analyst or consultant did was to count the number of subordinates reporting to each manager. In each instance where the number exceeded six, the analyst would recommend narrowing the span.

It is now clearly recognized that no general prescription can be made of an arbitrary number of subordinates. The fact remains, however, that each manager can effectively control only a limited number of direct subordinates. When this number is reached a new management level must be created. Thus, the typical organizational structure is developed, with the top manager having authority over a certain number of subordinate managers, who thereby form a level. These managers, in turn, have a certain number of subordinate managers reporting to them, thus forming another level, and so on down to the lowest level of managers, who have only nonmanagers reporting to them. The number of management levels is determined by the spans of control. If spans of control are narrow, there will of necessity be many levels. As spans of control are widened, the number of levels will be reduced, and the organization structure will have a flatter look. Figure 12-1 illustrates the difference between a "deep" organization and a "flat" organization.

Factors Affecting a Manager's Capacity

Ideally, each manager's capacity for handling subordinates should be determined exactly, and a new organizational level created when this optimal number of subordinates is reached. However, this perfect arrangement can not be achieved in the real world. There are simply too many variables that bear on finding each manager's optimal span of control. Some of the more important of these variables merit brief discussion here.

1. The experience, personality, and attitude of the manager. A manager who is inexperienced and is learning the assignment cannot supervise as many subordinates as the manager who has been through all of the problems many times before. Some people have personalities that enable them to give direction to subordinates quickly and concisely, thereby enabling them to handle more subordinates than the deliberate and painstaking type. Some managers are inclined to delegate authority, which permits subordinates to make more decisions. Such delegation not only reduces the decisions the manager must make, but also increases the number of

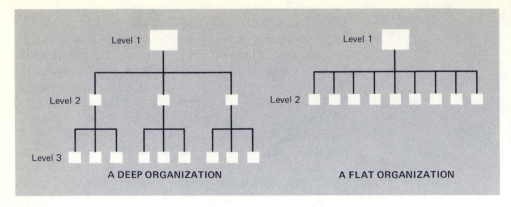

Figure 12-1.   A Deep Organization vs. a Flat Organization.

subordinates the manager can supervise effectively. Managers who are inclined not to delegate authority must spend more time making decisions, which restricts their span of control.

2.   The experience and training of the subordinates. The extent to which subordinates are capable of performing their duties with a minimum of supervision and coordination influences how many subordinates a manager can control. The more time that a manager must spend in directing individual subordinates, the fewer the number of subordinates who can be effectively directed.

3.   The incidence of change within the work environment. Frequent and dramatic changes in the nature and scope of work assignments will restrict the number of subordinates. If changes are few and job routines can be established, the span of control can be substantially increased.

4.   External pressures on the manager's time and attention. Contact with direct subordinates is only one of a manager's continuous relationships. The manager will also have highly demanding contacts with an immediate superior and, through lateral relationships, with other managers in the organization. If these contacts (which are external to the manager's relationships with subordinates) are too time consuming, they will act to restrict the number of subordinates that can be handled effectively.

Arguments for a wide span of control.   Current thinking appears to favor wide spans of control, as contrasted to the general belief, thirty to forty years ago, that narrow spans were the most efficient. The question of how wide the span should be is really best answered by considering the tangible and intangible costs of wide spans of control in comparison with the alternative, which is an increase in the levels of management.

Tangible costs resulting from stretching the span of control are difficult to pinpoint. We might consider the costs of mistakes that subordinates might make by not getting adequate supervision as tangible costs. Intangible costs might result from subordinates' feelings of insecurity and frustration from not receiving as much of their boss's time as they would like. But, the advantage of a manager having a large number of direct subordinates is that the subordinates have to be left relatively on their own. They get a chance to learn and develop by making decisions, and may get more job satisfaction as a result.

There are some definite tangible costs associated with excessive management levels. An increase in the number of managers is accompanied by an increase in managerial salaries. In addition, managers require secretaries and extra office space, both of which add to overhead costs. A significant intangible cost results from communication distortion—distortion that occurs when communication passes through multiple filters, which is what each management level tends to resemble. At each succeeding level downward, members are apt to feel less important in the organization and more like anonymous contributors. This feeling damages their motivation to produce effectively. Their job satisfaction may be further diluted because their managers, having few subordinates, will tend to exercise close supervision. As a result, all decisions affecting the subordinates are made for them, and their opportunity to grow by learning is blocked. On balance, there appears to be substantial justification supporting wide spans of control.

A manager's span of control determines the number of subordinates over whom he or she exercises direct authority. Let us examine some concepts of authority.

Authority

Authority can be defined in many ways. One is that authority is the right to command. Another is that authority is the power to limit choice. One that seems particularly meaningful to our discussion is that authority is a right granted to a manager to make decisions (within certain limitations), to assign duties to subordinates, and to require subordinates' conformance to expected behavior. There is a theoretical dispute over the source of authority. The conventional view that it flows downward is at odds with the *acceptance theory*.

Conventionally, authority in business organizations has been viewed as having its origins in private property rights. Consider the following: The ownership of a corporation is vested in its common stockholders, whose individual authority is proportionate to the number of common shares they own. The stockholders centralize their authority by electing a board of directors. The directors, having possession of all the authority granted to them by the stockholders, delegate a large part of that authority to the corporation's chief executive. This officer, in turn, delegates portions of that authority to subordinate managers on the primary level, and they delegate pieces of their authority to their subordinates. And so on through the organization.

Sharply conflicting with the "downward" view of the source of authority is one which holds that authority is a right granted to a manager *by subordinates.* The extent of the authority thus granted is determined by the subordinates' judgments concerning whether they stand to lose more by conforming to the manager's commands than by not conforming. This acceptance theory was discussed in Chapter 3, in our discussion of Chester Barnard's contributions to management theory.

Actually, the downward-upward dispute over the source of authority tends to oversimplify a highly complex relationship. A strong argument could be made for the case that authority derives from both poles, with effective authority being that which is generally supported by both a manager's supervisors and his or her subordinates. And it is highly probable that the recognition that at least some authority may rise from below has had a modifying influence on the behavior of managers who otherwise might have acted despotically toward their subordinates.

Authority and responsibility. If we accept the premise that authority is a right granted to an individual, then *responsibility* is the individual's obligation to execute the right properly. In the traditional theory of management, authority and responsibility were viewed as fixed qualities. It was assumed that authority and responsibility could be spelled out exactly in job descriptions, and it was emphasized that the two must be equal. It is now recognized that rarely does a manager have any unilateral authority, either in decision making or in relations with subordinates. The modern manager may expect to be held responsible for departmental actions, even though the actions may be effected through a pooling of authority with that of other managers. The project manager, discussed in Chapter 11, is a case in point.

The Manager's Roles in the Vertical Structure

Two management functions, leading and controlling, derive from the formation of vertical relationships within the organization. (These functions are discussed in detail in later chapters of this book.) In addition to the obvious vertical relationships, in which the manager gives direction to subordinates' activities and monitors their performance, a web of less apparent relationships is created. These relationships cast managers in various roles, each with different requirements.

Subordinates seek assurances about their security and career development. They need reinforcement of their perceptions of their role status; they want help in resolving personal conflicts; they often need technical assistance in performing their jobs; and they want to be represented effectively on such issues as raises and promotions. These requirements put varying pressures on the manager. Sometimes the manager is cast in the role of a parent, other times as a psychologist, and occasionally as a judge, a teacher, or a promoter. Each of these roles calls for a different supervisor-subordinate relationship; and it appears clear that authority for leadership and controlling work performance has no primary significance in any of these other roles. Yet, the way the manager performs them will influence the way the subordinates respond in their formal duties. Merely having a supervisor tends to generate conflicting feelings on the part of subordinates—respect, admiration, and affection are often at odds with fear, frustration, and contempt.

Managers perform still another role in the formal vertical relationship structure—they transmit messages upward and downward in the organization. The manager connects the two organization levels, serving both as an amplifier and a filter for the communication.

LATERAL RELATIONSHIPS

Perhaps an analogy using the human body will illustrate the significance of lateral relationships. The heart, and its blood-pumping function, might be likened to an organizational subsystem of vertical relationships. There is no question that this process is important, but consider the countless additional subsystems of organs, nerves, and muscles that relate to make the total system of the human body. Lateral relationships within organizations are the counterparts of these human subsystem relationships. All of the lateral relationships that exist in an organization cannot possibly be described, but members of the organization are either consciously or subconsciously affected by them. The work completed within an organization, and its success or failure, is as much—or possibly far more—the result of lateral relationships as of vertical relationships.

Advisory Relationships

Advisory relationships represent one interaction between members of an organization that is distinguished from the supervisor-subordinate relationships described in preceding sections. Typically, an advisory relationship is established when a member or members of one department (usually a supporting department) counsels a member or members of another department (often a central department) on some specific subject area. The counseling function may carry with it some authority, but the authority is confined to the subject area.

Reasons for advisory relationships. There are two principal reasons for instituting advisory relationships: They make specialized knowledge available to every department and they assure uniform interpretation of policies. The necessity for advice based on specialized knowledge derives from the ever growing complexity of the activities performed within a business organization. It is no longer possible for a single individual to be relatively well informed about more than a few of an organization's activities. Thus, specialists in such areas as public relations, office procedures, and employee compensation have been developed. Their specific competence is made available to other people within the organization. The complexity of organizations also makes it necessary to follow policies intended to guide decision making consistently. Policies governing such affairs as labor relations, contacts with vendors, and overhead cost allocation need to be explained, and questions regarding the policies satisfactorily answered.

The line-staff concept. *Line-staff* is a traditional management concept that implies a sharp distinction between two key areas. Historically, *line* has been used in reference to two things: (1) vertical authority relationships and (2) departments in which central activities have been grouped. *Staff* has been used in reference to (1) the locus of a type of authority ambiguously called "the authority of advice," and (2) departments in which supporting activities are grouped. Literally dozens of management writers have struggled with the contradiction that their so-called staff departments are involved in many more relationships besides advisory ones.

In this book, as we saw in Chapter 11, we take the position that in any organization there are two kinds of departments, central and supporting. Vertical relationships always exist within both kinds of departments. In addition, there are relationships that take place between departments, including advisory relationships, wherein advice is tendered by a supporting department—either central or supporting. For example, the personnel department, a supporting department, may advise the production department, which is a central department, and also the purchasing department, another supporting department.

Change in role—advisory to prescriptive. Since one purpose for setting up specialized supporting departments is to make expert advice available to other departments, the conduct of newly established supporting departments will be confined to providing information and counseling others on how to use it. However, this level of effort tends to be unsatisfying after a while, because highly trained specialists get greater satisfaction out of telling people what to do than from merely advising them. Thus, they often begin to move toward having prescriptive control over the way their specific activities are practiced. Frequently they gain this authority through the formal edict, issued by a manager high in the organization. Such edicts note that other departments shall abide by the specialist's prescriptions for doing things in their areas of specialization. The superior manager in such a case is motivated to grant this limited authority to the specialists either because of a conviction that things will be done better, or because of the influence of their personalities and persuasive arguments. Specialists will often be highly aggressive in changing their roles from merely advisory ones to ones of limited formal authority.

Specialists can also gain the right to prescribe specific conduct in departments other than their own when another manager grants it voluntarily. This often occurs when the manager is so impressed by the specialists' technical competence that they envision improvements in their operations if the specialists are permitted to implement their advice. Managers may also grant specialists authority over some activity within their departments because they simply do not want to be bothered with it themselves. Their sensitivity to the power of a supporting department manager, and their doubts concerning who would win in case of a direct confrontation, is another reason some managers grant authority to specialists.

Reactions to advisory relationships. Obviously, the authority of the central department manager will be reduced when specialists have prescriptive control over the performance of certain activities in the department. However, as indicated earlier, the manager's responsibility will probably remain the same. In addition, there will be a disruption of the department's vertical relationships. Subordinates, for example, will receive direction not only from their own supervisor, but also from each of the specialists in their respective areas of authority. Thus, a subordinate in the production department may receive instructions from the production manager and also from a personnel department specialist, an accounting department specialist, and an industrial engineering department specialist. The reality of this situation violates the traditional concept that no subordinate should have more than one boss.

The pure advisory relationship can be highly successful if managers have the right to request the advice, and if specialists make sure that managers get credit for any benefits achieved from following their advice. Similarly, when managers grant specialists certain authority within their departments, the relationship can be quite productive. There is no question that many managers resent having advice forced on them, and having specialists make a big show of how valuable their advice is. The practice by top management of authorizing specialists to prescribe certain policies and procedures in other managers' departments has become so common that it is tolerated, but it carries the potential for explosive conflict. (Conflict, as a general subject, will be discussed in Chapter 13.)

Service Relationships

Like advisory relationships, service relationships set up within an organization induce a type of interaction that does not involve the supervisor-subordinate authority question. Service relationships derive from the service activities that must be performed in the organization.

Any supporting department will probably engage in both advisory and service relationships with other departments. You will recall from the previous section that when involved in advisory relationships, supporting departments guide other departments as they perform an activity. However, in service relationships a supporting department is responsible for the performance of a group of specialized activities. Although the activities will be in the same functional area whether the relationship is an advisory or service one, the nature of the relationships will be distinctly different. For example, the personnel department, in an advisory relationship, may inform the production department concerning the prevailing wage rates in the industry for schedulers, or may go further and specify that schedulers be restricted to some maximum wage rate. In a service relationship, the personnel department may recruit and screen applicant schedulers to fulfill a request by the production department.

Reasons for service departments.   In a small organization, the necessary service activities, such as personnel, purchasing, and maintenance, will probably be performed on a part-time basis by members of the central departments. Accounting activities will almost always be an exception, for, when forming even simple organizations, accounting is usually set up as a supporting department.

For the service activities that are performed in the central departments, problems will begin to appear as the organization becomes more complex. First of all, when an activity is only performed as a sideline by individuals, it will not be executed as well as it would be by people who are specifically trained in its routines, and who give it full-time attention. Second, when an activity (such as one pertaining to personnel or purchasing) is performed in two separate departments (such as production and sales), many aspects of the activity will be similar, but a different policy may be applied with respect to its accomplishment. And third, costly equipment and facilities will be duplicated when various central departments independently perform services that are commonly required throughout the organization.

In order to reduce these problems, at some point in the development of any organization specific service activities will be broken out of the central departments and grouped into semiautonomous supporting departments. It is important to note that the creation of different supporting departments will not usually happen simultaneously; the establishment of each should occur at a time when the advantages of having the department appear to justify the outlay of effort and expense.

Characteristics of service departments.   Although in many respects service relationships resemble conventional buyer-seller relationships—with the object of the service being to meet the standards of those to whom it is rendered—they differ from the buyer-seller relationship in an important way: The services are arbitrarily imposed. Usually there is no option in the matter of utilizing this service or some other one; the specialized services of a supporting department are utilized to the exclusion of all alternatives. Thus, the supporting departments, in effect, have captive customers. For example, central departments within the organization in need of industrial engineering, or market research, or traffic activities, may not choose whether to do the work internally, hire an outside company for the service, or use the service of the respective supporting department. Not only must the supporting departments be patronized, usually the costs of operating the supporting departments are arbitrarily allocated to the production and sales department budgets as well.

As implied above, managers of central departments would often prefer to have direct control over their own service activities. The production and sales managers, for example, will reason that their authority has been diluted when they are not permitted to perform important activities in such areas as personnel and purchasing. Therefore, these managers are quick to point out flaws in the quality, quantity, and timing of the various services that they are forced to use.

Currently, service activities are distinguished by the fact that they must be performed by specially trained people. Many of these people believe that their skill is at the professional level, and perhaps several degrees above the status level of the people in the departments they serve. This preoccupation with status often breeds an attitude of superiority, which places an additional strain on service relationships.

The combined pressure from outside the supporting departments for faster and better service, and from the specialists themselves for wider scope and increased professional recognition, often causes the size of supporting departments and the number of services offered to expand far beyond original expectations. This seems to be particularly true with business firms in the United States, where the entire subject of service relationships appears to have a far greater significance than it does with firms in foreign countries.

Resolution of problems. When expansion of a service activity is being considered, the problem of how large a service department to provide arises. The problem can be handled by comparing the costs of any expansion proposal to the expected benefits. In addition, the costs of alternative ways of providing any proposed expanded service, such as by purchasing the service from outside firms, should be compared.

The supporting department managers must prevent "prima donnas" in their ranks from destroying necessary service relationships. Managers can prevent this by impressing upon the people responsible for performing specialized activities the fact that their organizational purpose is indeed to serve, and that their success is measured in the way their services are received by other departments. Other departments' frequent resentment of being captive customers can be handled, in part, by the supporting department. These managers should provide the best service possible. If the problem becomes aggravated, and especially if the organization grows large enough to adopt the product form of departmentation (see Chapter 11), the next move may be to relocate the service activities under the central managers.

Other Lateral Relationships

From the foregoing descriptions of relationships within an organization, one might conclude that the typical organization is composed of relationships so complex and numerous that any attempt to describe them graphically with a very fine pen on a very large chart would produce a solid background of undifferentiated lines. Indeed, this is the case for all organizations—nonbusiness as well as business. Until very recently, writers on management were preoccupied with the supervisor-subordinate relationships in organizations, and gave varying attention to the so-called line-staff concept. In this book, part of the old line-staff relationships are identified separately as advisory and service relationships. These are *lateral relationships,* in that no resemblance to supervisor-subordinate relationships is present. However, they do not represent all possible lateral relationships. Just a few of the other important ones include functional-sequence, evaluative, plural, and nonvertical, unequal-status relationships.

Functional-sequence relationships. Highly important nonvertical interactions between members of organizations occur as a result of functional-sequence relationships. These relationships exist because the tasks necessary to produce an end product or service must usually be performed in series. Again resorting to a manufacturing firm for purposes of illustration, assume that the engineering design of a product is the initial task in a series. Immediately following is the task of developing a prototype model. Thus, there will be interactions between individuals involved in the two tasks with regard to schedules, drawings, and so on. The development people depend on the design people doing their job on time, and doing it in such a way that the prototype can be made, but they have no real authority over design people to assure desired performance. In turn, the task of producing an approved product will follow the development of the prototype. If the development work in either the design or prototype stage is delayed, the manufacturing schedule will be affected, so production people will engage in interactions with individuals in both development areas. Finally, the people involved in selling the product will depend on the whole series of preceding tasks to provide a salable item in the quantities and at the times desired, so, they too will

Project Center: GM management system's new aid

For many years GM has operated under the philosophy formulated by Alfred P. Sloan in 1920, the concept of "decentralized operations with coordinated control."

Following Sloan's precepts, the GM organization developed separate units, which competed with each other as well as with outside companies. A central management coordinated the general activities of the many separate units.

Now, the Project Center has been developed as a management tool to help GM satisfy the sometimes conflicting demands of growing customer requirements and the governmental energy, safety, and environmental laws. It also is aimed at achieving reasonable levels of profit in the face of spiraling costs in every phase of its business.

The center still employs the traditional General Motors philosophy of decentralization with coordinated control—with some changes. GM is centralized where it is most effective, and still decentralized where that is most effective.

The objectives of the Project Center are:

- To use the best technology to design and develop products that meet stringent requirements;
- To ensure that areas such as buildability and serviceability requirements are properly addressed;
- To lower costs by using common parts while retaining saleability and divisional identity features.

The Project Center is at the General Motors Technical Center, where GM divisions and staffs pool their technical expertise. And design and development facilities are set up to work on a new car design program, such as the new line of B and C body full-size GM cars for 1977. Responsibility for the Project Center system has been assigned to the engineering staff.

The car division chief engineers are the technical directors. They choose the program manager, who is directly in charge of the new car program.

The program manager must set up an organization using division and staff personnel. The center will have a number of system managers reporting to the program manager; they are each responsible for an area such as body, electrical, chassis, structure, etc.

One of the center's most important functions is to establish a set of engineering specifications for the new lines being designed.

This is when various ideas of the major divisions are combined into a single set of specifications that engineering will use to design and develop the vehicle; items such as passenger and luggage compartment dimensions, weight goals, engine sizes and types, fuel economy goals, and building methods.

When the product definition and engineering specifications are completed, they are presented to the various levels of management for approval.

Next, styling, engineering and development begin. Master layout work, along with that on seating, trunk, and engine bucks, is done at the center. The styling is done by the design staff, which is at the Technical Center near the Project Center.

The Project Center is built around the lead division responsibility concept, which gives engineering coordination and development responsibility for specific vehicle components and systems to one of the car divisions.

For example, Oldsmobile has the steering system, Buick has brakes, Pontiac has air conditioning, Chevrolet has front suspensions, Cadillac has electronic fuel injection. The component divisions of General Motors support the car divisions by providing design expertise for the products their divisions manufacture.

The lead division concept has four major objectives:

- To minimize redundancy of specialized engineering facilities and technical personnel.
- To develop greater expertise at each division in its own area of responsibility.
- To lower GM's costs by optimum use of common parts.
- To maintain close liaison between engineering and manufacturing personnel.

The Project Center conducts a monthly review of the program's progress and status for engineers, and executives.

---

engage in a complex network of relationships. People late in a series will influence their peers who are early in the series by every possible tactic, including friendly inquiry, referral to a higher manager, bullying, pleading, and reciprocation.

Evaluative relationships. Members of organizations, particularly those at some managerial level, are continually involved in evaluative relationships with peers in other departments. These are not formal evaluations having to do with raises and promotions (which will be discussed in Chapter 18). Nevertheless, these informal evaluations have an important bearing on career progression, and on the evaluee's ability to get support for his or her department's objectives. Evaluative relationships are two-directional, in that while person A is evaluating person B, the evaluation of person A by person B is also taking place. The evaluations are sometimes based on objective, measurable parameters, but often they are founded on superficial judgments. Typically they are not kept private but are communicated throughout the organization by the "grapevine," an organizational phenomena which will be discussed in the section on informal organizations.

An example of evaluative relationships can be drawn from the context of the project type of organization. The project manager will evaluate the manager of the functional engineering department according to the way engineers assigned to the project from that department have performed. Simultaneously, the engineering manager will be evaluating the project manager according to the project's engineering accomplishments.

Professional ability is one criterion for performance evaluation. Another is the opinion of peers; do they mark an individual as someone who is going to move ahead in the organization, or as someone whose proper level has been reached or passed? This latter judgment is based largely on how a person behaves in the various organizational relationships—a factor that is vague, at best.

Plural relationships. Group meetings tend to be a way of life in the modern organization. Here the individual is exposed to plural relationships, which require interaction with two or more members of the same or other departments. In the departmental meeting, people may propose or defend issues that have a bearing on their personal roles. In the interdepartmental meeting, an individual represents the department and must try to serve its needs. While the apparent purpose of the meeting will be to coordinate various activities for the good of the organization, personal and departmental pressures will motivate the individual to gain something for the department, or at least prevent it from suffering some loss.

Group relationships are often characterized by friction—friction resulting from the divergent motivations of the participants, and from alliances which pit participants holding sympathetic views against those with strongly opposing views. Unless controlled, such friction can impair the coordination which is supposed to result from the group meetings. Fundamentally, four outcomes can result from friction. The first is that one faction will win and the other faction, or factions, will lose. Second, there can be an impasse, and all factions will withdraw. A third possibility, and a very common one, is compromise. Finally and ideally, the factions may discard their parochial interests and try to work together toward mutually agreed-upon goals.

Nonvertical unequal-status relationships. We have already considered vertical, unequal-status relationships which exist between direct supervisors and their subordinates. Within an organization, there are also many occasions for nonvertical, unequal-status relationships to occur. These take place when individuals in one department must interact with individuals in another department who are at a level as high, or higher, than the first individual's supervisor. Both individuals are aware that authoritative directions need not be followed, but both are also conscious of a status differentiation. The lower-level individual will characteristically be somewhat subdued, although there will be instances when hostility is expressed. Some condescension might be evident in the attitude of the higher-level individual. An example of this kind of relationship would be the production manager who proposes a drawing change to a nonmanagerial design engineer. The two individuals can resolve the problem together, but stress can result if there are sharp differences of opinion. If stress does occur, the issue will probably be referred to the manager in design engineering at the production manager's level, and fresh negotiations will begin.

THE INFORMAL ORGANIZATION

Until now, the discussion of organizing as a managerial function has focused on the processes, concepts, and relationships of the formal organization. Formal organization, as has been indicated, is the deliberate and conscious grouping of activities and melding of relationships for the purpose of achieving some predetermined objective. We will now direct attention to informal organizations, which are a part of every formal organization.

Roots of Informal Groups

Maslow's theory of needs, and the implications of needs for motivation, will be discussed in some detail in Chapter 21. However, parts of his theory are pertinent to the present discussion. Informal groupings represent an unconscious attempt by individuals to satisfy a special kind of need. This is the need that virtually all people feel for close relationships with other people. It is the need for sociability, for emotional support from other people, for a sense of a personal identification, for protection against feeling alone. The larger the formal organization, the more impersonal it becomes; members feel some isolation even in belonging. Therefore, they form informal groups instinctively, without analyzing what makes them do it.

The work environment within the formal organization naturally fosters informal groupings. For example, workers on an assembly line, clerks in a specific area of an office, engineers in a "bull pen," and managers on the same corridor of the executive suite will tend to be found associating off the job. Cultural ties also bind people together. Thus, groups will form made up of people with similar ethnic, racial, or religious backgrounds. Outside interests represent another basis for informal groups; golfers, stamp collectors, and garden enthusiasts, to name a few, will naturally gravitate to their respective interest groups. Dissenters, or persons with unresolved grievances, will be inclined to merge their dissatisfactions and find some solace in collective unhappiness.

There are countless other bases for informal organizations. Some are formed just for sociability, some for exchanging information, and some for gaining allies for future action; and some combine these functions. It should be plain, also, that a given individual may belong to many such groups.

Distinguishing Features

Informal organizations originate spontaneously rather than deliberately. Members of informal organizations may or may not be conscious of the fact that they are members. But often they are not. Relationships among members are never spelled out, but somehow status and position distinctions do exist and are perceived as highly important. If informal organizations have goals, they are undefined, and reflect the personal goals of members. In short, informal organizations differ in every way possible from formal organizations. However, in every formal organization, whether it be a business firm, a military unit, or a church, to name a few, the members will instinctively join together in informal groups disassociated from the formal structure. The force that causes such groups to form is a need that cannot be satisfied through the formal organization.

Inner workings of informal groups. An interesting characteristic of each informal group is the way in which status hierarchies develop. An individual's position within a group is, of course, in no way formally designated. But through some subtle process of perception and understanding, members have a rank and status accorded to them by the group.

Each group will have an informal leader, or, possibly, leaders. These leaders are neither appointed nor elected. They are leaders simply because the other members of the group—somehow perceiving that the leader can either help them advance toward their personal goals or hold the group together, or perform both functions simultaneously—simply become followers.

Another characteristic of informal groups is their tendency to separate themselves from other groups and withhold coveted membership. The word which describes this element in grouping is *clique*. Cliques will compete with each other, and an individual's status in some large informal organization will be largely determined on the basis of membership in a particular clique. Cliques will be perceived by outsiders as snobbish, but their members might not even recognize that they are in a clique. A clique system and a caste system have marked similarities.

The cohesiveness that a group develops has significant implications for group conduct. That is, the group will set norms of conduct and behavior to which all members will be expected to adhere. These norms are extremely important to the formal organization because they are applied to quantity and quality of work produced; responses to authoritative commands by the formal supervisor; dress, punctuality, and absenteeism; competition with other groups; and so on. Thus, an informal group has power to facilitate or thwart the attainment of the formal organization's objectives.

Grapevine. The grapevine is the unofficial, unauthorized channel of communication in the informal organization. It flourishes on information which is not openly available and which appears to have indications of privilege and confidentiality. The grapevine comes alive when two or more people gather informally and exchange rumors, gossip, or vaguely supported items of opinion. Information channeled via the grapevine proceeds with amazing speed and incredible penetration. Like the informal organization in which it has its origin, the grapevine is inevitably and unavoidably present in *every* formal organization.

DISCUSSION QUESTIONS

1. What circumstances help create vertical relationships?
2. Discuss the variables that affect a manager's span of control.
3. Compare the advantages and disadvantages of wide and narrow spans of control.
4. Evaluate the various views on the source of authority.
5. Explain lateral relationships. Discuss some significant lateral relationships.
6. Discuss the features and operations of informal organizations.

BIBLIOGRAPHY

Barnard, Chester I. *The Functions of the Executive.* Cambridge: Harvard University Press, 1938.

Blau, Peter M. "The Hierarchy of Authority in Organizations." *The American Journal of Sociology,* Vol. 73 No. 4 (January 1968), pp. 453–67.

Jacques, Elliott. "Too Many Management Levels." *California Management Review,* Vol. 8 No. 1 (Fall 1965), pp. 13–20.

Koontz, Harold and Cyril O'Donnell. *Management: A Systems and Contingency Analysis of Managerial Functions.* New York: McGraw–Hill, 1976.

Sayles, Leonard R. *Managerial Behavior.* New York: McGraw–Hill, 1964.

The Case of Piggyback Management

The organization structure of the contracts administration division of Philips-Aerodyne Corporation evolved as the firm acquired more and more space weapons contracts. In the company's early days, Jim Mario personally handled all of the activities associated with contract negotiation and administration. As the company grew, it became necessary for him to hire contract administrators to do the actual work, and his role became that of a manager. Despite continued expansion of the firm's defense contracts, Mario resisted for a long time adding a second level of management to his organization. He personally supervised his administrators until he finally had nine reporting directly to him. Most of them were new to contract administration work, so there was much training that he had to perform. In addition, changes were taking place on all of the contracts constantly, which necessitated Mario's close involvement with each of his administrators. Finally, when one administrator neglected to request a progress payment from the Navy far enough in advance and the company had to borrow money for working capital for ninety days, it became apparent that a reorganization was essential.

Jim Mario separated the current contracts into three groups according to the nature of the work required, namely, development, production, and field support. He appointed a supervisor over each group to report to him, which meant that he had reduced his span of control to three subordinates, and each of them supervised three contract administrators. At the time, this was a needed innovation, and there was a considerable improvement in the performance of contracts administration, which had now gained the organizational status of a department.

The contracts on which Philips-Aerodyne was the successful bidder continued to increase, and each of Mario's supervisors had to hire additional contract administrators. When the number of subordinates reporting to the development contracts group supervisor reached eight, he came to Mario with the request that he be allowed to reorganize. He wanted to add a level of three supervisors to report to him, with each of them being responsible for approximately one third of the development contracts. They would supervise two or three contract administrators.

There was some logic to this appeal, but Mario perceived that if he granted the request of this particular supervisor, he would have a problem with his production and field-support group supervisors, who would feel that a former peer had moved a level above them. A solution was to add an additional management level to each group. Mario was secretly motivated in this direction anyway, because the company's controller had recently been made a division manager, primarily on the basis of adding personnel to his organization. So, Mario effected this new reorganization.

After about a year, some subtle differences began to occur in the work characteristics of Philips-Aerodyne's contract administration. One difference was that the contract administrators had become highly skilled in their duties. Another was that the contracts themselves began to stabilize, and significant changes were the exception rather than the rule. A third difference was that the total number of contracts began decreasing, so that each administrator had fewer contracts for which he was responsible. Jim Mario either didn't know, or didn't want to know, about these things that were happening.

One day Mario was told by his boss, the plant general manager, that a doctoral candidate named John Moore had requested permission to collect data from various divisions within Philips-Aerodyne. Mario was asked to cooperate in this endeavor.

"The purpose of my research is to investigate human problems within organizations," Moore told Mario, "that is, problems that cause people to become frustrated and upset."

"Young man," said Mario condescendingly, "we have no human problems in the contracts administration division. However, if you wish, you have my permission to talk with the administrators."

Moore had developed a research instrument comprised of ten problem statements. He would read a statement to a research subject, and then ask two questions: First, is this a problem in your organization, and second, if it is a problem, what is the perceived severity of it on a scale of from 1 to 5? He invited the research subjects to make any comments that would explain their responses.

There was nothing particularly significant about the responses of the twenty-one participants to any of the statements except the last one. This one read: "The number of management levels in the organization causes a stifling of individual initiative." Only two of the administrators said that this was not a problem, and they were both new to the organization. The mean perceived severity was 4.

As Moore analyzed the comments to the management-level statement, he found marked evidence of considerable frustration. Quite a number were in this vein: "The supervisors don't have enough real managing to do, so they stick their necks into our work." Another common one was: "Everything that comes down to us is filtered through those guys, and then they screen and distort everything that goes back up." One comment was: "Can you believe formal morning section meetings when there are only two people in the section?" Three responses were in almost identical words: "My supervisor religiously comes to my cubicle twice every morning and twice every afternoon to check on my work." A comment with important implications went: "The company is now screaming about reducing costs, yet it tolerates this piggyback management. If it wants to cut costs, why doesn't it eliminate one whole level of supervisors?"

DISCUSSION QUESTIONS

1. If it could be determined what is the optimal number of subordinates that a given department manager can effectively handle, would it mean that the manager should continue with that same span of control in the event of a promotion? Or should the new job carry with it the same number of subordinates who reported to the previous manager?

2. In the Case of Piggyback Management, did Jim Mario have an alternative to establishing a second management level when his personal span of control stretched to nine subordinates?

3. Can you explain why the top management of Philips-Aerodyne could have accepted the adding of management levels when the principal reason for the reorganization appeared to be the improvement of the status of individuals?

4. How could Jim Mario not know that the real work in his division was shrinking? Why might he not want to know?

5. How could the attitudes learned by researcher John Moore be related to Philips-Aerodyne's declining business?

The Case of the Subtle Takeover

Curtis Tool Company, a leading manufacturer of oil field equipment, employed about 1500 workers. A new president, Loren Whipple, had been appointed in early 1974. Whipple was a former senior partner in a large management consulting firm, and had extensive ideas about introducing up-to-date methods in all of the company's operating divisions. In June of 1974, he issued a memorandum to all division managers announcing the establishment of a new department, Management Controls, to be headed by a former junior associate of his, Bill D'Agostino. In the memo Whipple told the division managers that the new department's function would be to help them in the areas of systems, organization, and planning. He urged them to cooperate with D'Agostino and his staff.

"Actually, I don't think it's going to be too bad," said Bob Mill, manufacturing division manager, to his assistant, Ken Beeson. "Remember how apprehensive we were under the old regime when a labor relations department was appointed. Now we wouldn't think of doing anything that would have an effect on our various union contracts without getting the advice of the labor relations people. Let's hope that we have the same good relationship with this new advisory department."

Bill D'Agostino arranged a meeting with Bob Mill for the purpose of explaining what his department's role would be. He brought along three of his assistants: Gail Drinkwater, a systems specialist, Ralph Thompson, whose forte was organization, and a planning specialist, Ed Litvak. "What you should do," D'Agostino told Mill, "is think of us as being your own private consultants. We are here to take some of the load off your back. Our only purpose is to give you help when you need it. A way of getting started would be for you to let my people roam about your organization in order to learn what is going on."

After about a month, each of D'Agostino's specialists requested separate conferences with Mill in order to present their findings. Mill asked Ken Beeson to sit in. The first meeting was with Gail Drinkwater.

"I have spent most of my time studying your inventory and production control systems," Drinkwater said, "and I have some ideas that should help you. For one thing, your inventory policy is a two month's coverage for all items. I suggest that the carrying costs for many of the high-value items could be reduced by shortening the coverage period, and the ordering costs for the low-value items could be reduced by increasing the quantities carried in stock. Another thought is that instead of having expediters reporting the progress of work in process in the shop, you could require the foremen to phone notice of completion of operations to the production control office."

Ralph Thompson was next to describe what he had done. "I have prepared charts of authority relationships for your organizational units, starting with the sections, then leading into the departments, and finally culminating with the division itself. Each chart shows the number of people in various experience and educational brackets, and the subordinate/supervisor ratios."

Mill next heard from Litvak. "My work

has been to get your supervisors to start thinking about planning in two dimensions," said Litvak. "First, I have been helping them plan the extent and timing of their section's effort in terms of labor hours for each of the current and potential work orders. Second, I have been advising them on how to project their section's total operating expenses by month in terms of the aggregate of the work orders for which they have some responsibility."

"See how well it's working out," Bob Mill said to Ken Beeson when the two of them had finished studying the three written reports that had been submitted. "These reports contain some really good ideas."

"It's working out well for D'Agostino too," said Beeson reservedly. "You will notice that a copy of each of these reports went to Whipple, and they might make him wonder why we haven't thought of these ideas."

Over the next year, changes began to take place gradually in the relationships between Management Controls and all of the operating divisions of Curtis Tool Company. The following are some examples of things that happened in the manufacturing division:

Drinkwater first began selling Bob Mill on the notion of a computerized inventory and production-control system. Before long his presentations got beyond Mill's technical competence, but they sounded plausible. Without fully realizing the consequences of the action, Mill authorized Drinkwater to implement a computerized system. Ken Beeson finally brought to Mill's attention the fact that the inventory and production con-

trol personnel were taking their operating orders directly from Drinkwater.

Ralph Thompson partially convinced Mill that the educational level of the supervisors in the manufacturing division was too low. With some reluctance, Mill approved a policy statement prepared by Thompson to the effect that two years of college was the minimum educational requirement for a supervisory job.

D'Agostino and Litvak together presented Mill with a new planning system. It was keyed around a five-page input form which was to be filled out by each supervisor, approved by the department heads and finally by Mill, and submitted to Management Controls quarterly. Mill's objections that the system involved too much red tape were quelled by D'Agostino's remark that it had been developed by Loren Whipple, the president, when he was in the management consulting business.

In July 1977, a memorandum was sent to all division managers by D'Agostino. It was countersigned by Loren Whipple. The thesis of the memorandum was expressed by the following statements:

1. Sole authority to design and implement an integrated information-flow system, cutting across all divisional lines, is vested in Management Controls.
2. Organizational changes in all divisions, including expansions, promotions, transfers, subordinate/supervisory ratios, etc., must first be approved by Management Controls.
3. All variations between a division's plans and subsequent events must

be explained by the responsible division manager in quarterly reviews conducted by Management Controls.

"Well, Ken, it looks as if the division managers' jobs have been pretty much taken over," Bob Mill commented as he handed Ken Beeson the memorandum.

"That's a polite way to say it," was Beeson's tight-lipped reply.

DISCUSSION QUESTIONS

1. Is the term *staff department* necessarily obsolete?

2. Why would members of a supporting department strive to expand their role from advising to prescribing?

3. In the Case of the Subtle Takeover, could Loren Whipple have had a personal motive in establishing and expanding the authority of the new department, Management Controls?

4. Was there anything apparently wrong with the way Drinkwater, Thompson, and Litvak executed their advisory relationships in the beginning?

5. Would the authority vested in Management Controls (as expressed in D'Agostino's memorandum of July 1977) be detrimental to the future operation of Curtis Tool Company?

13 Conflict and Coordination

Much has been written on the subject of organizational conflict. Management literature abounds with treatments of conflict between the organization and external systems, such as trade unions; between individuals in organizations over cultural, ideological, and racial values; and between subsystems (or departments) within an organization. In this chapter we continue our examination of the organizing function focusing on conflict between subsystems. It is this form of conflict that managers face as they work to develop the efficient departments and effective relationships described in preceding chapters. *Conflict* can be defined as feelings of rivalry and hostility between subgroups whose goals are incompatible and who, therefore, work against each other.

A discussion of conflict and its possible consequences begins the chapter. The section on conflict is concluded with an examination of two sources of conflict, namely power politics and human alienation in organizations. We will then turn to the process that enables managers to avoid and/or resolve conflict, the process of coordination.

CONFLICT

The Development of Conflict

Any of a number of factors may cause conflict between work groups to develop. One major contributor to conflict in organizations is their hierarchical structure. Departments are established like independent little islands, with highly effective boundaries separating the duties and prerogatives of each group of activities. In complex organizations, activities at the top management level may be grouped by function, by product line, or by geographic location. However, at some place in all organizations, departments are formulated according to the function performed. Thus, as has been noted earlier, there are central functional departments, such as engineering, production, and sales, and supporting functional departments, such as accounting, personnel, and purchasing.

Each functional department has goals—both assigned and internally developed—associated with the performance of its specific function. One internally developed goal is to perform its function efficiently, thereby gaining status within the organization. Thus, each department as a whole is more concerned about its function than about the functions of other departments. In addition, each functional department is staffed by specialists who are inclined to be prejudiced in favor of their own department's function. That is, an accountant would be more concerned with an organization's debits and credits than with the organization's public image (that would be the concern of the community relations department). The members of each functional department will also have personal goals—goals that are likely to be different from the department's goals. However, department members will perceive that some of their personal goals can be achieved through the achievement of departmental goals. This too causes department members to favor their own department's function.

When members of different functional departments survey the availability of organizational resources and status symbols, they will note that the supply is limited. For example, there can only be so many departments at the primary (top) level of an organization. Competition between departments naturally arises; and when there is competition there is the chance of losing. Therefore, each department will feel threatened by other departments—feelings that can cause conflict.

Likely Locations for Conflict

Management literature stresses the incidence of conflict between line and staff departments, which, in the terms of this book, are central and supporting departments (see Chapter 11). Some writers contend that advisory departments try to prove their worth too aggressively; that they are condescending to personnel in the central departments; and that they resent being measured by values set by the central departments. And for their part, the central departments are described as fearful lest the advisory departments usurp some of that authority, and jealous of the rising importance of the advisory departments.

However, observations by many experienced managers suggest that the degree of conflict between departments tends to reflect personality differences between department managers rather than differences in the functions performed. Departments whose managers are driving, domineering, and highly motivated toward goal achievement will reflect these characteristics and will be continuously involved in a high degree of interdepartmental conflict. Conflict will be at a much less stressful level between these departments and departments whose managers are placid and easygoing; and it will be practically nonexistent between departments whose respective managers are both of the latter type.

Possible Consequences of Conflict

A certain amount of competition, and hence conflict, is essential within organizations. Constructive competition is a motivating force and ensures efficient achievement of objectives. It is when competition becomes an end in itself that the conflict becomes destructive. Destructive conflict drains energies away from productive effort, and directs them almost exclusively toward strategies of defense and attack. Such conflict can cause continuous and violent win-lose struggles, in which neither party will capitulate, so each issue must be referred to a third party for resolution.

Often, after a win-lose struggle has been resolved, the losing party will begin plotting retaliation. A real-life example of such conflict, related to one of your authors by a company vice-president, took place between an engineering department and a production department. The managers of both departments assigned first order of importance to their respective functions and continuously fought for supremacy over such issues as final authority over part configuration, make-or-buy decisions, quality deviations, and work-order responsibility. Each conflict precipitated an impasse, which had to be resolved by a higher-level manager. The loser in each case then would begin developing strategies to assure success on the next occasion.

If the losers of destructive conflict do not react by plotting retaliation, they may take a position of isolation. Often this attitude develops in a department which is a constant loser in win-lose struggles. Its manager takes the position, which is adopted by the other members, that the department will perform only those duties precisely spelled out in the operations manual and sever all nonspecified contacts with other departments. One real-world example of such withdrawal concerned a reliability department that was withdrawn by its manager from all but formal interdepartmental contacts because it was not accorded primary-level status.

Compromise is a less disruptive consequence of conflict, but one which still can thwart organizational objectives. Like win-lose struggles, a compromise usually involves a third party. To avoid the bitterness inevitable in win-lose situations, the third party will try to find a solution both parties will accept. Often this conclusion is not really satisfactory to either party, and is only partially satisfactory in terms of the goals of the organization.

Reduction of destructive conflict. As noted earlier, the structure of organizations makes conflict inevitable. Conflict-free, productive cooperation should *not* be expected from an organizational network in which each department's boundaries are rigidly defined; in which the members of each department identify more with their functional goals than with the goals of the organization; and where efficient lateral relationships betweeen departments are left to chance. Since these conditions are so common in organizations where departmentation is functional, an entirely new approach to organization is needed. The first step might be to relax functional boundary lines, and create loosely knit organizational subsystems that are oriented toward an end item or product, rather than toward functional specialization. Such subsystems would be multifunctional, rather than single-functional. A second step might be to study the necessary lateral relationships between the subsystems and define how they should be conducted. And finally, a third step should be taken—a step that seems completely obvious—that is, to build into the organization's formal appraisal structure a system of rewards for managers who accomplish their objectives without destructive conflict, and sanctions for managers who do not.

We have seen that the hierarchical structure of organizations contributes to conflict within them. Now let us examine two additional sources of conflict, namely power politics and human alienation.

Power Politics in Organizations

All organizations are arenas for power struggles, and politics is the means for gaining mastery in these struggles. Any person experienced in the affairs of organizations will testify to the dominant influence of power politics, and will also identify power politics as a source of conflict.

Most people have an intuitive knowledge of the existence and workings of power politics; however, there is little textbook information on the subject. One of our best sources is Machiavelli, who developed a classical prescription for the use of power politics in *The Prince,* written over five hundred years ago. Although Machiavelli's purpose in writing *The Prince* was to advise his benefactor, the dictator of an Italian city-state, on the use of political strategies, his precepts may be seen operating in any modern quest for power.

Striving for power may be instinctive in human beings or it may be a cultivated drive resulting from a cultural emphasis. For example, many people are impressed from childhood with the idea that competition is the mode for goal achievement. Whatever its source, the will for power appears to be at least latent, in most people. If managerial success is to be attained, the will for power must be accompanied by the ability to obtain and manipulate power.

Power may be defined as the capacity of an individual to restrict the alternatives available to other people to those of his or her choosing. It follows then that *politics* is the complex of intuitive and deliberate strategies and tactics through which power is acquired and manipulated. We can also look at politics in another way—as a means of gaining promotions and status other than by, or in addition to, demonstrated job competence or nepotism.

Both *power* and *politics* have somewhat unpleasant connotations. However, the fact is that people who govern the affairs of organizations seek power and know how to use it. This does not necessarily imply that they are immoral or unethical; the simple truth is that, from a practical standpoint, they can gain the power to rule most readily through politics.

Stages in the Development of Organizational Politicians

At least three stages, through which an aspiring organizational politician must pass, can be identified: the preparation, planning, and tactical stages.*

Preparation stage. The power-seeking individual must first go through the preliminary stages of preparation. This may be done intuitively; however, the truly professional politician makes it a deliberate and thoughtful process. It is essential that the manager create a unique personal image from the beginning. Components of this image, which is the way that the manager wants to be perceived by others, will include physical characteristics, interactional behavior, past accomplishments, and a projection of potential accomplishments. The manager will want to convey a sense of ease and quiet confidence and to be consistent in behavior, so that every attitude and action reinforces the desired image.

The next preparatory stage involves the development of external power resources. These resources will include individuals and cliques who can be relied on for support. The individual's existing power will be increased and strengthened by pooling the power of these supporters, who will be characterized by loyalty and positive response to requests.

Following the enlistment of a personal team, the power seeker will need to develop an efficient intelligence system. Privileged information, although not readily available, is the key to power. In addition, the power seeker will want feedback regarding the effect of self-initiated moves and of retaliatory moves by opponents. To a large extent, the personal team will represent an information-gathering system.

The most important information that the aspirant to power will need concerns individual rivals—their strengths and weaknesses, their approaches to situations, and their defense mechanisms. Their social connections, their enemies, and their sponsors and protégés will also be matters of utmost importance, for above all the power seeker will want to

---

*The steps outlined are based chiefly on an unpublished analysis by Norman Martin of New York University.

know where obstacles will occur and how difficult it will be to remove them. With the development of this intelligence system, all the steps in the organizational power seeker's preparation stage have been completed.

Planning stage. Next, political strategies must be developed. A clear statement of the individual's ultimate objective in the organization should be the starting point. Then, by working backward to the present, the sequence and timing of the subgoals that must be accomplished in order to reach that final goal must be established. Involved in this process is a projection of the general lines of conduct to be pursued, including a forecast of possible obstacles and a description of means to overcome them. Thus, the political plan will not be confined to a single course of action, but will include contingency paths to be followed in the event of power shifts within the organization.

Tactical stage. Finally, the power seeker will reach the tactical stage. It is at this point, when the political plan goes into motion, that the individual will proceed patiently and carefully to negotiate the required actions in their predetermined sequence—typically following certain practices that date back to Machiavelli. Some of these Machiavellian maneuvers are listed below:

1. Maintain mobility. Be able to switch to alternative plans readily, without apparent compromise or loss of face.
2. Maintain tempo. Always be one move ahead of opponents in the power arena.
3. Avoid entanglements. Seek counsel only when you want it, not when others wish to give it.
4. Beware of being overwhelmed by success. Never relax; always move forward; do not drop guard.
5. Beware of friends. Use people; do not be used by them.

You can personally decide whether people actually behave in this manner. Think of a membership you've held in some organization. Did the behavioral patterns of individuals who rose in the organization resemble the Machiavellian prescriptions listed here?

Human Alienation in Organizations

The following discussion summarizes the nature of human alienation in formal organizations, another possible source of organizational conflict. Possible resolutions of the problem, together with a discussion of what is known about human needs, are presented in sections of this book dealing with the managerial function of leading.

Formal organizations are formed, in part, by the deliberate actions of managers. However, as has been pointed out, the development of such

Power and Politics in Organizational Life

Whatever else organizations may be (problem-solving instruments, sociotechnical systems, reward systems, and so on), they are political structures. This means that organizations operate by distributing authority and setting a stage for the exercise of power. It is no wonder, therefore, that individuals who are highly motivated to secure and use power find a familiar and hospitable environment in business.

Political pyramid

Organizations provide a power base for individuals. From a purely economic standpoint, organizations exist to create a surplus of income over costs by meeting needs in the marketplace. But organizations also are political structures which provide opportunities for people to develop careers and therefore provide platforms for the expression of individual interests and motives. The development of careers, particularly at high managerial and professional levels, depends on accumulation of power as the vehicle for transforming individual interests into activities which influence other people.

A factor which heightens the competition for power that is characteristic of all political structures is the incessant need to use whatever power one possesses. Corporations have an implicit "banking" system in power transactions. The initial "capitalization" which makes up an individual's power base consists of three elements:

1. The quantity of formal authority vested in his position relative to other positions.
2. The authority vested in his expertise and reputation for competence (a factor weighted by how important the expertise is for the growth areas of the corporation as against the historically stable areas of its business).
3. The attractiveness of his personality to others (a combination of respect for him as well as liking, although these two sources of attraction are often in conflict).

This capitalization of power reflects the total esteem with which others regard the individual. By a process which is still not too clear, the individual internalizes all of the sources of power capital in a manner parallel to the way he develops a sense of self-esteem. The individual knows he has power, assesses it realistically, and is willing to risk his personal esteem to influence others.

A critical element here is the risk in the uses of power. The individual must perform *and* get results. If he fails to do either, an attrition occurs in his power base in direct proportion to the doubts other people entertained in their earlier appraisals of him.

elements in formal organizations as informal groups, the maze of lateral relationships, politics, and conflict are largely beyond the control of the manager engaged in the function of organizing. But, to the extent that organizing is controllable, it is geared toward achieving maximum efficiency. Departmentation, job design, vertical authority relationships, policies, procedures, and rules are calculated with this objective in mind. However, the entire process is at odds with the individual's needs for security, self-esteem, and opportunities to grow to the limit of his or her capability.

Indifference to efficiency. It is probably not so much that people are opposed to efficiency as they are indifferent to it. While high-level managers feel a sense of personal involvement with the organization, people at lower levels in the organization do not. They are frustrated by the means employed to achieve efficiency. And although most people in organizations know that they are frustrated, few can point to the reasons. All organizations of which they have ever been a part, starting with kindergarten, have been fundamentally structured the same way. Most people have little trouble adapting to new organizations because the regimen is the same; it is merely the paperwork that is different. So people infer that the organizational way of life is normal, including the business organization through which they earn a living. The realization that the mechanics of organizational efficiency are unnatural to us, and induce frustrations, has come to us from the studies of psychologists and sociologists.

Frustrations. Consider the following conditions in a formal organization. They suggest a number of reasons for human frustration.

1. Monotony. Division of work is one principle of efficiency. It is based on the theory that if work is fractionalized into parts and people are trained in performing the various parts, the end result will be better than if people were to learn all the variables in the total job. This is undoubtedly true—in some cases and for some people. However, to individuals possessing more than basic intellectual qualifications, such jobs become repetitive and boring. Moreover, after a few years of such work they become known as specialists in it, and will have great difficulty breaking out of the rut.

2. No room for individual differences. Work assignments are designed for some conceptualized "average person." People whose aptitudes and education seem to fit the requirements for particular jobs are trained in performing the carefully engineered work tasks. Recognition is rarely given to the probability that a job would be a great deal more satisfying if an individual's qualifications were considered first, and a job designed to fit them. As a result, most individuals rarely have a chance to use more than a few of their abilities. There is no place in organizational efficiency for individual differences.

3. Lowering of self-esteem. The conventional vertical authority relationships are assumed to be the logical way to organize, with little thought ever given to the fact that such a relationship cannot fail to have a psychological effect on the subordinates. Self-esteem is a major human need—a need that cannot be fulfilled by feelings of submissiveness built into the supervisor-subordinate relationship.
4. Regimentation. Although it is undoubtedly highly efficient to routinize repetitive decisions by adopting policies, procedures, and rules, such regimentation is stultifying to individual growth. Little, if any, personal satisfaction can be derived from looking in a manual to find the prescribed action for a particular situation. The need that individuals feel to have some control over their work environment, and to be able to create something on their own, cannot be fulfilled when everything must be "run by the book."
5. Pressures for conformity. A tenet of organizational efficiency stresses the need for conformity, because conformists are predictable and therefore controllable. Individuals soon learn that rewards are given for conformity and that nonconformists are passed over for raises and promotions. Therefore, they conform.
6. Status discrepancies. Defects in a firm's system of promoting employees will be readily perceived by individuals in the ranks, and their resentments will fester when they see people rise higher for reasons other than merit. Status discrepancies will be particularly galling when individuals, to keep their jobs, must appear contented to take orders from a supervisor whom they do not respect.

Effect of goal divergence. If conditions in an organization are as described (and they frequently are), the result, paradoxically, will be low efficiency in an efficiently designed system. If organizational efficiency requires individuals to have no goals other than those associated with their organizational roles, then their response typically will be to learn whatever the organization expects of them, do it at the specific level of performance required and do nothing more. Their own needs will be unsatisfied; or if they are satisfied, it will be in some system other than the formal organization. Sometimes the external system that provides satisfaction conflicts with the formal organization (a labor union is such a system). Improved coordination of organizational and individual goals is the objective of the managerial function of leading. This improved coordination can also be achieved by breaking away from strictly mechanistic organizational models.

COORDINATION

It should now be clear that organizations are made up of subsystems, or groups of activities, conveniently called *departments*. Within each department there are smaller subsystems, with the smallest being the job roles of individual members. Each subsystem has a defined contribution to make, in a certain form and at a certain time, to the total system that is the organization. Coordination could be viewed as the process of assuring that the contributions from the subsystems are made as required, and are linked into a harmonious whole.

Coordination could also be viewed as the management of change. Through the managerial functions of planning and organizing, objectives are established and the means are created for implementing them. Among these means are defined divisions of work, vertical authority relationships, managerial spans of control, decentralization of decision making, and the definitions of some lateral relationships. Plans are disseminated downward through the organization, and channels are provided for feedback of the results of plans upward. Policies to guide nonroutine decision making, and procedures specifying how to make routine decisions, are established. Theoretically, at one static moment in time, the system is synchronized; every gear is apparently in mesh, and there is a high probability that all events will conform to plan. But an organization operates in a dynamic environment, not a static one. Changes of all kinds that cause the system to get out of synchronization take place continuously. Thus coordination is the effort to manage changes in such a way that the system is brought back into a state of synchronization.

Actually, coordination is the essence of management. The functions of planning, organizing, staffing, leading, and controlling are performed to achieve coordination. Therefore, coordination is the composite of the functions performed by all managers at all levels. However, the importance of coordination seems to stand out more in the organizing function than in some of the others. Fundamentally, there are three approaches to achieving coordination. These include planned coordination, corrective adjustments resulting from the analysis of feedback, and motivated coordination. These approaches are not mutually exclusive; all three must be employed continuously within an organization in the never ending battle to eliminate the obstacles to coordination.

Planned coordination is the deliberate action taken by managers to hold the organization together as a single working unit. Coordination must be planned because it will not automatically result from even the most perfectly defined structure of departments, policies, and relationships. Misinterpretation of organizational goals, and divergent subgoals, can cause various subsystems to move in opposing directions unless they are tied together. Therefore, formal groups composed of representatives from different subsystems are either permanently established, or provisions for them are created as required. These groups, commonly called *committees,* will be discussed in Chapter 14.

Committees permit the airing of various views on goals and on the means for accomplishing them—views which often conflict. The act of meeting together reveals to the members that there are objectives bigger than their own narrow ones; and the exchange of information and viewpoints often discloses more similarity than dissimilarity in personal interests. Because committee decisions are normally reached by consensus, even dissenting members will be deterred from actively working against the expressed views of the majority.

A manager's day-to-day work activities consist primarily of exposing existing or potential friction points in the subsystem. Managers are sometimes notified of them by subordinates or higher management, or by fellow managers in a lateral relationship. Friction points are signs that the system is getting out of synchronization and corrective action is needed. The manager may decide on the appropriate action alone, or may confer on remedial means with vertical and lateral contacts. Coordination takes place when the prescribed action is communicated to all persons who must respond to the action and when positive response is obtained. The communication may be channeled via face-to-face instruction, speeches to assembled groups, written memoranda or directives, or written changes in policies or procedures.

Managers try to coordinate motivation. They try to persuade individuals to identify with the goals of the total organization rather than some subsystem of it. Obviously, for this to happen, organizational objectives and plans for implementing them must be communicated to the individuals and be understood and accepted by them. Then, benefits to be derived from working with members of other subsystems toward common goals must be made to appear of greater personal value than those to be gained from specialized goals. One way of achieving this end is to break down the boundaries between subsystems; this would facilitate problem solving by teams made up of various specialists. This is the project management concept, as discussed in Chapter 11. Another approach is to rotate individuals among subsystems on a periodic basis. In this way, they will come to see the necessary interactions of all parts of the organization, and avoid becoming biased toward any one segment.

Certainly no problem involving the coordination of the parts of a physical system, such as the parts of a machine, is comparable in complexity to that of coordinating human organizations. Some progress has been made as a result of findings by the behavioral scientists. The more important of their contributions toward an understanding of people and how they can be motivated are summarized in the parts of this book devoted to the staffing and leading functions. The subject is of such depth, however, that only the surface has been scratched; much more investigation needs to be done.

DISCUSSION QUESTIONS

1. Explain how conflict between various departments within an organization might develop.

2. Can conflict within an organization ever be productive?
3. Discuss ways to reduce destructive conflict.
4. Discuss the nature of power politics. Have you seen power politics at work in any organization with which you are familiar?
5. Explain how people in formal organizations may become frustrated.
6. Discuss coordination and explain why it might be called the essence of management.

BIBLIOGRAPHY

Argyris, Chris. *Personality and Organization: The Conflict Between the System and the Individual.* New York: Harper and Row, 1957.

Holder, Jack J., Jr. "Decision Making by Consensus." *Business Horizons,* Vol. 15 (April 1972), pp. 47–54.

Kast, Fremont E. "Organizational and Individual Objectives." in *Contemporary Management,* ed. Joseph W. McGuire. Englewood Cliffs: Prentice-Hall, 1974.

Likert, Rensis. *The Human Organization.* New York: McGraw-Hill, 1967.

Pondy, Louis R. "Organizational Conflict: Concepts and Models." *Administrative Science Quarterly,* Vol. 12 (September 1967), pp. 296–320.

Seiler, John A. "Diagnosing Interdepartmental Conflict." *Harvard Business Review,* Vol. 41 No. 5 (September–October 1963), pp. 121–32.

The Case of the Mexican Crazy Quilt

"The mission of the project which you will head is to get our new Mexican subsidiary company ready for take-over by Mexican managers. My hope is that you will be able to do this in about two years," explained Robert Linderman, president of Linderman Industries, Inc., to Carl Conway, newly appointed project manager for "Operation Mexicano." Conway had been hired specifically for this assignment because of his experience in managing large defense projects in the aerospace industry.

"The first thing that I will have to do is put a project team together," said Conway. "I imagine that you have in mind my drawing people from the functional divisions."

"Yes, and I have already sent memoranda to the division managers informing them that you will be asking for some of their key people to work under you for about two years," said Linderman. "In addition, I have advised them to be prepared to process work orders from Operation Mexicano with the personnel and equipment of their organizations. Later on in the project's life, you will begin to get Mexican personnel, both managers and technicians, into your organization. These people will have Mexican supervisors, but until the mission is accomplished they also will report to you. I will have to admit that you are going to have some complex authority relationships, especially as you personally will be responsible to the president of the subsidiary, Felix Delgado, as well as to me."

Conway began to make his plans for the project team. The plant building was available and empty in Mexico City, and it was important to get equipment pur-chased and installed as soon as possible. A plant layout would have to be prepared, but before that could be done there would have to be a manufacturing plan. Therefore, he needed to recruit an industrial engineer, a production planner, and an equipment buyer. They, in turn, would have to build their own staffs.

He made an appointment with Sam Sargis, corporate manager of industrial engineering. "I have had a preliminary talk with Bob Cates about his joining Operation Mexicano, and he is quite interested," Carl said. "Will you release him to me?"

"Why, I'm grooming Cates to take over my job when I retire," replied Sargis. "He is my best man. Let me pick someone else for you, or better still, you just tell me what industrial engineering work you want done, and I will have it done for you."

"Sorry, I want Cates," said Carl firmly. "And besides, you are not due to retire for five years. This will be good experience for him."

For production planning, Carl had in mind Bert Mill, an older man with extensive experience in managing production operations, but Mill rejected his offer. "I talked it over with my new wife," he said, "and we feel that at my age I shouldn't take a chance on not having a job to come back to when Operation Mexicano is finished."

Carl next talked to Blanca Banowetz, who was assistant to Jim Burke, the vice-president for manufacturing, and Banowetz decided that she would like to join the project team. However, Burke told Conway that if Banowetz were forcibly taken away from him, he would give Mr. Linderman his resignation, so Carl decided to back down. He finally accepted a man that Burke recommended.

Filling the equipment buyer's slot was easy. The director of procurement phoned Carl and said that a senior buyer, Humberto Guzman, had requested permission to ask for the assignment, and that he strongly recommended him. Guzman had been purchasing agent for a large mining company in Mexico for about ten years.

Carl had about the same experiences in getting the people he wanted for the functions of engineering, quality control, cost, marketing, and advertising as he did for the first three positions; in other words, he won some confrontations with the division managers, and lost some. For personnel, he got Dr. Juan Perez, who was slated to be personnel director of the subsidiary company, to affiliate temporarily with the project team.

The first brush that Project Mexicano had in getting a functional division to do work for it came when Carl's engineering man, Frank Fong, reported to him that the engineering vice-president, who was formally Fong's boss, refused to authorize top priority to the changing of dimensions in the production drawings to the metric system. Carl had to take this issue to Linderman, who ruled in his favor. The defeated vice-president, of course, did not take kindly to the decision.

The next incident revolved about Carl's desire to have a pilot run of products made with metric measurements for shipment to Mexico. The purpose was to test the market acceptance of the Linderman articles. Jim Burke stated flatly that there was no way that his production workers could be trained to work with metric drawings. Carl quickly saw that this was an issue that he was not going to win, so he had his buyer, Guzman, work with the newly appointed manufacturing manager for the subsidiary in getting a run of the products subcontracted in Mexico City.

Bob Cates made a special trip from Mexico City to present Carl with an interesting problem. The Mexican industrial engineer, whom Bob was supposed to be training, had his own ideas about plant layout. When they differed from Bob's, as they usually did, he would take his complaint directly to Felix Delgado, the president of the Mexican subsidiary. Because Delgado's competence was primarily in finance, he would not know how to decide the argument, and would simply table it. Carl took samples of some of the disagreements to Bob's formal boss, Sam Sargis, who quite unexpectedly ruled against Bob's proposed methods. Carl saw that there was bad feeling by Sargis against Bob for leaving his department, which boded ill for Bob's return. To solve the immediate problem, however, Carl asked Dr. Perez to try to reconcile the situation in Mexico City.

Despite these problems, and many more of a similar nature, Project Mexicano was successful, and the transition to Mexican management was made in just a little over two years. By a curious twist, through Dr. Perez' intercession Felix Delgado became very impressed by Bob Cates and convinced him to accept the job of director of industrial engineering for the Mexican company. Humberto

Guzman also stayed on to head the procurement operation.

Other members of the project team were not so fortunate. Linderman Industries was laying off personnel when the project ended in 1970, and only the project production man was able to get a job in the company at as high a level as the one he had when he joined the team. The cost expert elected to leave Linderman because he said the glamor of Project Mexicano has spoiled him for any routine job.

Carl Conway had a difficult decision of his own to make. Robert Linderman said that he was extremely pleased with his performance and that something good would open up in the company for him soon. In the meantime, there was a staff assignment available for him. Carl had seen enough project managers in the aerospace industry who had figuratively rotted on staff assignments when their projects were completed to be somewhat wary.

DISCUSSION QUESTIONS

1. Was Linderman Industries' adoption of project organization an appropriate one for getting the Mexican subsidiary started?

2. In consideration of Robert Linderman's letting the division managers know that the project manager would be asking for some of their key people, why would Conway have any difficulty in getting the ones he wanted?

3. Would you expect that many people would turn down a chance to join a project organization, as Bert Mill did?

4. Why would Conway take his problem with the engineering vice-president to Linderman and have it resolved in his favor, yet back down in two disputes with the manufacturing vice-president?

5. What could Linderman Industries have done to assure good jobs for the people coming off Project Mexicano, including Carl Conway, the project manager?

14 Committees

The frequent ineptness of committees is burlesqued by the saying that "a camel is a horse designed by a committee." Fearing such an outcome, managers in many organizations view membership on a committee as a chore to be avoided rather than an honor to be sought. Yet despite the dim view that many managers have of them, numerous forms of managerial action require the group decision making that is the distinctive function of committees. So committees, those groups of people that assemble for some management purpose, are becoming increasingly prevalent in most organizations, including those of business, health, government, and education. Aided by the popularity of the "participative management" concept, and by the size and complexity of modern organizations, the use of committees has continually increased. An understanding of committees is essential for students of management. In this chapter we will examine the types of committees found in organizations, conditions justifying their use, limitations of committees, and, finally we will take a look at a type of committee mandated by law, namely, the board of directors.

KINDS OF COMMITTEES

Within most organizations, there are numerous varieties of committees ranging from ones that are formal, permanent, and powerful to others that are relatively informal, temporary, and powerless. In addition, specific organizations have their own specialized committees which are not found in other organizations. For example, there is no apparent parallel to the curriculum committee of an educational organization in either a business or a governmental organization. Because there is such a wide range of committees, we will present only brief descriptions of the three general classifications of committees: formal standing committees, ad hoc committees, and informal temporary committees. Most organizations have a certain number of permanent committees with formally structured charters, and in many cases, with a considerable amount of power. In business organizations, the board of directors is an example of such a committee, and will be discussed in some detail later in this chapter. Other business committees in this category often include the pricing committee, the long-range planning committee, and the compensation committee.

Formal-standing government committees include those formed to consider budgetary, taxation, and welfare proposals. Universities have faculty senates and promotion and tenure committees. Though the character of formal committees in different organizations will vary, they have the common characteristics of regular meeting times, defined goals, and membership created on some systematic basis. The issues they deal with are of a recurring nature, are customarily specialized as to topic, and are usually significant to the organization.

A growing number of modern organizations are using ad hoc committees. These are committees formed to deal with significant but nonrecurring issues requiring high-level problem solving. "Task force" is often a synonym for "ad hoc" committee. Committees identified by either of these terms are created to accomplish specific goals. When the goals have been reached such committees are dissolved.

Ad hoc committees could be formed to search for a chief executive officer; to devise a means for coping with a temporary financial crisis or other impending disaster; or to consider the implications and strategies needed to handle some emergency arising from a source external to the organization like a strike, or a new government regulation. To understand the type of problems handled by such committees, remember that they are usually important matters that have terminal solutions.

Routine organization processes generate numerous issues that require action by a group of interested persons rather than by an individual. Sometimes such groups form spontaneously; in other instances they are appointed by an individual manager or by a higher level committee. The primary difference between an ad hoc committee and the informal temporary committee lies in the significance of the mission for which they are formed.

Informal temporary committees deal with mundane matters, in fact often with matters for which no particular resolution is required. They might be assembled to review general purchasing procedures, to consider optional starting and quitting times, or to plan for the annual Christmas office party. The reasons for forming temporary committees within organizations are virtually limitless, and the continual formation of temporary committees often constitutes a problem that may have to be handled by a committee created to prune a surplus of committees.

CONDITIONS JUSTIFYING COMMITTEES

Despite often heard complaints about the ineffectiveness of committees, and the frustrations that may be experienced from serving on them, there are definite conditions justifying the use of such bodies. The use of committees when they should be used, and the assignment of action to individual managers when committees would be obstructive or impotent in reaching the goals desired is a sign of organizational maturity. Management literature dealing with committees usually identifies some or all of the following criteria which support the use of group action.

When Integrated Group Judgment Is Needed

In the continuous network of organizational processes, the pooled judgment of a group of individuals often produces results that are superior to any sum of judgments reached by individuals acting separately. When this condition can accurately be determined to be present, a committee should justifiably be formed. In trying to assess the need for integrated group judgment, the following questions should be considered:

1. Does the situation require more experiences and skills than any one individual could be expected to muster?
2. Have significant aspects of the situation been overlooked or only superficially treated when the situation has been previously handled by individuals?
3. Is it a situation where no individual manager feels competent or comfortable in taking it on alone?

There are many cases where individuals selected to serve on committees personally feel that group action is unnecessary; however, if there is a strong consensus for the need for integration, the formation and possible continuance of a committee can be carried out with optimism. Integrated group judgment can be effective when considering a product line expansion, a plant relocation, or, in a government context, a change in tax assessments.

To Ensure Coordination

Subsystems of an organization inevitably develop specialized goals and approaches for achieving them. As a consequence, managers can lose sight of the goals of the total system. Committees can fill an essential role by coordinating diverse goals and random modes of operation, thus enabling all parts of a total system to work in harmony. Teamwork achieved through committees might be accomplished by the orchestration of a skilled manager. However, such teamwork often comes about more naturally through group interaction. Coordination achieved by committee action is exemplified where individuals from different functional areas, such as engineering, production, purchasing, and marketing meet regularly to decide which components of the product line should be made in-plant, and which should be purchased from subcontractors.

To Invite Participation

Resistance to change is a natural human response, but it is substantially reduced when people affected by changes participate in considering alternative courses of action and in choosing a final solution. Group action facilitates bringing all facets of a situation out in the open. It also helps in getting inputs and feedback from people who might resist any decision in which they had not had an opportunity to make their opinions heard.

A decision reached by group participation might not be superior to a decision reached unilaterally by an individual manager, but resistance to its implications can be considerably lessened. For example, the dean of a college might expeditiously and competently select a new assistant professor, but resistance to the individual picked for the position will be greatly reduced if all members of the faculty are given the opportunity to present their views of the candidate.

To Facilitate Communication

One purpose of the hierarchical structure of organizations (where one level of managers reports to a higher level, and a lower level reports to it, in turn) is to foster the form of communication that comes about through vertical authority relationships. In other words, a boss transmits information to his or her subordinates, and receives information from them. A defect of this medium of communication is the exclusion of the people who are not in the specific scalar chain of messages being communicated. In addition, the hierarchical line of authority is far from perfect in permitting clear communication between boss and subordinates. Therefore, a valid use for committees is to provide a meeting ground where information can be shared by people in the organization who need it. For instance, after marketing people glean information from their market contacts, a temporary committee, or sometimes one of a permanent nature, may be formed to transmit this information to members of other functional or product departments within the organization. The marketing organization may also create its own committee to disseminate information derived from different customers, geographical areas, and indirect competitor contacts.

For Representation of External Interest Groups

Modern organizations, except for the most simple ones, exist in an open system characterized by hosts of contacts with external interest groups. Those groups include creditors, customers, suppliers, stockholders, and the general public. Even medium-sized organizations are no longer entities unto themselves. This transformation is not confined to business organizations alone. Governments are becoming more sensitive to the interests of its constituents, and universities are conscious of the need for dialogue with students, the state legislature (if it is a state school), federal government agencies of all sorts, the business community, and private potential donors. Therefore, special committees are set up to facilitate contact between the organization and external groups. The usual annual stockholders' meeting is an example of a business committee of this form in action.

For Executive Development

A certain amount of gamesmanship is essential in organizational politics. The give-and-take of committee action provides an arena in which the skills needed by top executives in face-to-face confrontation over controversial issues can be developed. In addition, membership on committees can broaden the perspectives and technical knowledge of blossoming managers, and give them a cross-sectional insight into the workings and frames of reference of associate members from diverse subsystems of the organization. For example, a promising young executive representing his or her department on a middle-level capital budgeting committee can observe and engage in the infighting for scarce capital funds as well as learn about the needs, problems, and motivations of people from other departments.

CONDITIONS WORKING AGAINST COMMITTEES

Committees are usually criticized when their costs exceed benefits derived from them, or when they are set up for purposes in which their ineffectiveness is inevitable, and the action intended would be handled better by individual managers. As has been described, conditions can be present where group action can produce results that are substantially better and more efficient in long-term costs than reliance upon the performance of managers acting individually. Therefore, as in all aspects of management, a balance must be made of the advantages and disadvantages of alternatives. Such a balance will sometimes show that individual problem solving is superior to committee deliberation. Some of the disadvantages of committees are discussed below.

Committees Cost Money

Because managers serving on committees must take time away from other organization activities, the direct and indirect compensation of the managers is assignable to the committees. Therefore, while it might be more accurate to focus on the time consumption of committees, money cost becomes the tangible unit of measurement. Let us consider just the direct cost of committees. Assume a committee meets in the company control room for four hours every Monday morning to review the performance of various projects or cost centers. Assume that the committee is comprised of ten members, and their individual average salary is $750 per week. This amounts to a total of $750 per week, or $37,500 per fifty-week year.

An alternative to this expenditure would be to have the weekly performance reviews conducted by the manager to whom the project or cost center managers report. The evidence is far from clear that a committee is more effective at detecting deviations from plans and implementing corrective action than a really competent manager would be. The more money saved by abolishing this committee could be repeated many times in organizations just by an objective assessment of whether various committees are really worth the money they cost in direct terms. When the costs of having the members away from their regular jobs, staff time to prepare for committee meetings, and often travel, meals, and lodging costs are included, the actual costs of all but vital committees can amount to shocking money drains.

Compromise—or No Decision

Occasionally, committees are set up with the provision that all decisions must be unanimous. The membership committee of private clubs are often governed by this requirement. However, the conventional procedure for committees is to require a majority vote in favor of a decision in order to pass it. Either requirement—unanimity or majority—may lead to watered down, compromised decisions, or to such an impasse that no meaningful decision is possible.

The politics of committees is best exemplified by the cumbersomeness of the U.S. Congress which, scaled down, is the pattern of virtually all committees. Congressional committee members have both their personal interests and the interests of the subsystems that they represent as prime motivators. To gain their ends they negotiate deals with each other in which something is gained for themselves and their constituents. Too often in such negotiations either a lesser gain is achieved for the total system, or any gain for the whole organization is obstructed. Observe, for example, two division managers who are each vying for a $1 million capital expenditure approval. Only $1 million can be made available for all capital additions to the organization. If both managers are members of the capital budget committee, two interesting possibilities may occur. One is that each manager may agree to support the other manager's proposal for a $500,000 expenditure, but either investment at $500,000 may be ineffective for the total organization. The second possibility is that both managers may lobby against each other so successfully that neither proposal will be approved by the committee, and the organization suffers by not getting the advantage of the proposal that an unprejudiced evaluation might have proved highly beneficial.

Minority Domination

The advantages of group interaction are defeated if one powerful individual, or two or three dominating persons acting in concert, totally subordinate the free participation of the other committee members. An autocratically inclined manager often attempts to disguise unilateral decision making by giving the pretense that a permissive and open climate has been established for committee action. What often happens is that the manager continues to run the show, even though the committee processes are adhered to superficially. Similarly, a small coalition of persons with specialized interests can be so aggressive and overpowering that the majority of the committee are unwittingly or unavoidably swayed to accept this minority point of view. Whenever a committee is ruled by a minority, committee advantages—except possibly some form of communication—are eliminated, and the committee might just as well be dissolved.

Diffused Responsibility

When an action item is assigned to an individual manager, his or her performance can be clearly measured; if the manager drops the ball it is the manager's reputation and possibly continued employment that is in jeopardy. This clarity of responsibility is not possible with a committee. When the decisions reached by a committee lead to mistakes, which can be horrendous, no one person can be held accountable, and it is usually difficult to fire or otherwise censure all of the members of a committee.

When a mistake is made by a committee, members become very protective of each other. It is, in effect, as though they were all holding hands. Their instinctive response is to collectively rationalize or minimize the mistake, so that punitive action is circumvented—and the opportunity for future mistakes perpetuated. Some interesting research using the laboratory approach suggest that because of this absence of responsibility groups are more prone to make risky decisions than individuals. The hypothesis seems at least intuitively possible. The relative freedom to walk away from responsibility is a serious defect of committees.

THE AMBIVALENCE OF COMMITTEES

Thus far, it has been established that there are conditions favoring committee formation, and other conditions that militate against their use. These are white and black positions, either completely for or completely opposed to committees. Unfortunately, there are also gray positions, that is, conditions that can be argued as having both favorable and unfavorable aspects.

Social Pressures

Groups exert both conscious and subconscious pressures on members. The behavior of even the most obstinate of the legendary "one man gang" type of autocrat will be somewhat modified by group pressures for conformity. Subtle coercion to adopt group norms can have the effect of reducing minority pressures and opening the door to the beneficial features of group action. On the other hand, bright, aggressive, innovative people can experience a suppression of their drive and enthusiasm by finding themselves sentenced to a committee informally dedicated to oppose any hint of progressive action.

The Attractiveness of the First Acceptable Alternative

Groups often become restive in attempting to cope with problems that seem insoluble. Sometimes the search for alternatives is abandoned too soon—before more fruitful options have been uncovered. So many solutions can be nominated and discussed with the eventual conclusion that the deficiencies outweigh the benefits, that when an alternative is proposed that seems to offer a solution without glaring weaknesses, it is accepted.

Conversely, there is a saying in engineering design that at some point further efforts at improvement must stop, and what has been done must be adopted. When an acceptable alternative has been discovered, the cost and time advantages of not investigating further can counterbalance the benefits of a slightly improved option that may never be brought to view.

Disagreements

Committee meetings can be battlegrounds where bitter disagreements turn into lasting feuds that render the group incapable of productive action. On the other hand, healthy differences of opinion can often lead to a melding of ideas that represent an improvement of parts that started out widely separated. Disagreements may actually be more apparent than real, and healthy innovation may develop as sincere group action is permitted to wear off the initial points of friction.

Slowness

A rumor circulated during the early days of World War II had to do with a meeting between President Roosevelt and Prime Minister Churchill. At a time when the United States' entry into the European war seemed imminent, Mr. Roosevelt is supposed to have asked Mr. Churchill for his best single piece of advice for guiding the United States through the impending fearful conflict. Mr. Churchill's Delphic reply was "never reveal the impotence of a democracy." It is certainly true that the democratic process is frustratingly slow, and that individuals acting unilaterally can move with comparative lightning-like speed in choosing from among alternatives. However, in committee work this very fault for which group action is so often condemned can be one of its greatest strengths. More comprehensive, better analyzed, long-term decisions can eventually emerge from the laborious process of giving every representative the opportunity to make his or her views heard, and then work toward a consensus opinion.

THE INGREDIENTS OF SUCCESSFUL COMMITTEE ACTION

Productive and useful committees don't just happen, skillful planning and organizing must go into their assignments and composition. Too often committees are formed randomly, with little real thought given to whether group action is truly appropriate, what the end product of the committee's action should be, and what should be the qualifications and interests of the members. The checklist that follows is a composite from management literature and compiled real-life experiences of what should be done to assure that committees have a chance to be effective.

- *Assignment of duties best handled by groups.* As has been mentioned, some managerial processes and types of decision making are facilitated by group action. It is our opinion that a far greater number of situations are better handled by individual managers. Therefore, form committees only where they have the potential of being more productive than if the duties were assigned to individuals. In other words, avoid forming committees unless they are absolutely necessary.
- *Prior determination of committee goals and standards of measurement.* At the very outset think carefully about what the committee is expected to accomplish. The next step is to formulate criteria by which the accomplishment will be assessed. Commit these objectives and terms of measurement to writing and make sure every member of the committee understands and accepts them.
- *Appropriate membership.* Old-time buddies might generate a comfortable comradeship, and bitter enemies might spark some exciting conflicts. However, neither compositions would necessarily lead to an

effective committee. Appropriate members should have an interest and a skill related to the stated objectives; they should represent all vital groups; they should be experienced in group interaction; and they should have the time, dedication, and objectivity to work together as a team.

- *Appropriate size.* Groups of six to eight members seem to work best. Small groups suffer from a paucity of ideas or single member domination, and larger groups become cumbersome. A productive technique that large groups can employ is to allow subgroups to work on a subject, and report findings and recommendations to the main body.
- *Efficient procedures.* Probably the first item of business for all committees after the determination of a chairperson and recording secretary is to decide the procedures for conducting committee meetings. Formal rules of order are necessary for some kinds of committees, and relaxed procedures along these lines are probably essential in moving and controlling any committee.
- *An effective experienced chairperson.* No committee can be better than the skill and competence demonstrated by the chairperson. His or her role is like that of a conductor of a symphony orchestra. Although his or her behavior is probably best if it is low key, the chairperson must be the catalyst that keeps the committee progressing in synchronization toward its goals. He or she must learn the strengths and weaknesses of all the members intimately and should capitalize on the strengths and avoid the weaknesses so that each member contributes with maximum effectiveness. The chairperson must keep the meetings on course, handle conflicts so that they become productive, and be the power that creates unity out of potential chaos.
- *Agenda and follow-up.* One way to assure useless committee meetings is to keep the members uninformed as to the topics to be discussed until they arrive at the meeting time and place. Before the meeting, prepare and distribute an agenda of the meeting topics and suggestions for data sources needed to prepare intelligently for the agenda. After the meeting, a summary of conclusions reached on each agenda topic, and action items assigned, should be distributed to all committee members.

THE BOARD OF DIRECTORS

The board of directors is a committee mandated by the corporate laws of most states. Therefore, as most business organizations above the very smallest in size are corporations, the board of directors assumes importance in any discussion of committees. However, other than their legal necessity very few generalizations can be made about boards. Their functions and power range from being nothing more than figureheads to comply with corporate charter requirements, to being the main policy and strategy determining body of the company. Nonbusiness analogies to boards of directors include boards of regents for universities, and boards of trustees for donor-sponsored institutions such as museums. Probably the duties, authority, and composition are as variable with these super nonbusiness committees as they are with corporate boards. However, the significance of the corporate board of directors when it is empowered to act, and does act, as it is increasingly being thought that it should, should be brought to the attention of business students. The following discussion centers on the proper function of the board of directors. It is probably more idealistic than totally realistic, because the transition from figurehead to optimally effective board is far from easy.

The Proper Functions of Corporate Boards of Directors

- *Select, and determine the compensation of, the chief executive and the chief operating officer of the company.* There is an immediate ambiguity here, because the growing trend among United States corporations is for the chief executive officer to be the Chairperson of the board of directors. Obviously, to avoid a conflict of interest, the Chairperson of the board should be absent from any discussion of his or her compensation. Once that point is clarified, the board of directors should select the Chairperson and the President, who is increasingly becoming the chief operating officer. There is also a trend for boards to appoint a subcommittee from within the board to be the Executive Compensation Committee, whose recommendations for compensation for all top-level managers of the corporation are presented to the total board for approval.
- *Formulate the fundamental policies and strategies of the firm.* In a sense, this means philosophically determining the kind of company the firm is going to be. It involves deciding the basic strategies the company will employ to become that kind of company, and communicating these objectives and strategies to the operating officers of the company to be carried out. The board legally represents the owners of the corporation, and the future of the company should be in the direction that the owners, through their elected representatives, want it to go. In today's organizations, the operating managers, who are essentially high-level employees because of the small number of shares of stock that they typically own, are responsible for implementing the objectives and strategies originated by the board.
- *Advise and guide all major policies and strategies.* Ideally, the board of directors should be the senior counselors of the organization. (Senior is used in the context of ability and experience, which do not necessarily correspond to chronological age.) In a broad sense, the board should be the firm's internal consulting body. Its members should make themselves available for personal consultation with the operating officers. From an ethical and practical standpoint these

consultations should probably be confidential. Company officers should feel confident that their problems and frustrations have a private audience when they go to a director for help.

- *Evaluate and ask discerning questions.* The Socratic method of asking a general question, then from the cue of the answer, asking a more probing one, subsequently followed by a question probing in even greater depth is an outstanding technique for directors to use to ferret out weaknesses that lie waiting for an external stimuli to bring them to light. Knowledge that such intensive interrogation is in prospect will do more than anything else to force the operating officers to do their homework. Discerning questions should be asked on a continuous basis; supplemental to this technique should be comprehensive periodic reviews in which the manager and his or her staff inform the board of directors of progress and problems relative to their responsibility for operating results and achievement of the organization's long-term plans.

Board Size and Compensation

The size of boards of directors varies from the usual legal minimum of three to as many as twenty or thirty. As mentioned before with committees, large boards become unwieldy, but can be effective if broken up into investigative or problem-solving subcommittees.

Compensation of directors is ridiculously small relative to what it should be if their proper duties and authority are granted to them and commensurate responsibility exacted from them. Fees run from $100 per meeting—and it is understandable that not much effort will be obtained for that price—to retainers running into thousands of dollars annually. In view of current managerial salaries, it would seem appropriate for a working director to receive at least $1000 to $1500 per day. On the average, meetings occur once a month. Often, in addition to being top-level officers of their own companies, directors are on the boards of as many as ten to thirteen other business firms. This fact is a sad commentary on how little work many directors do as directors.

Contemporary Attitudes About Boards of Directors

A Security and Exchange Commission regulation prohibits interlocking boards of directors, that is, boards of competing companies comprised of the same members. This constraint has gone a long way toward alleviating the monopolistic practices that were detrimental to the public interest prior to the 1930s. However, various militant groups, including the consumer protection group headed by Ralph Nader, contend that boards of directors need further cleaning up before they merit the confidence of the public at large.

A characteristic of many boards that meets with criticism from stockholders as well as dissident public factions is the number of corporation officers who also serve as directors. There is an obvious potential for conflict of interest when individuals acting in the role of directors attempt to evaluate their roles as officers responsible to the board of directors. Many corporations are indicating their awareness of this irregularity, and are increasing the proportion of "outsiders" on the board relative to the number of "insiders," or operating officers.

The choice of outsiders is also under attack. Critics of U.S. corporations, and there are hosts of them, argue that there is insufficient representation of the various publics whose interests are affected by corporate policies on boards of directors. Corporations are taking these challenges seriously—a seriousness that is illustrated by the number of new board members of leading corporations being chosen from among women, blacks, ministers, and other public segments unthinkable for board recruits twenty-five years ago. There are encouraging signs that transitions in corporate boards of directors may be in the vanguard of changes in business conduct that may alleviate some of the distaste toward business that has surfaced so virulently over the past twenty years.

DISCUSSION QUESTIONS

1. Compare an ad hoc committee and the project form of organization.
2. Should a decision on where to locate the company's purchasing department within the organizational structure be assigned to an individual manager or to a committee?
3. What benefits would a promising young manager gain by serving on several different committees?
4. What are the problems of compromise? Are there any instances where compromise might be justified?
5. What problems would you expect a new outside director to encounter in trying to effectively represent the public interests?

BIBLIOGRAPHY

Beloviez, W. W., F. E. Finch, and Halsey Jones. "Do Groups Make Riskier Decisions Than Individuals?" *Academy of Management Proceedings,* (December 1968), pp. 73–85.

Filley, A. C. "Committee Management: Guidelines from Social Science Research." *California Management Review,* Vol. 13 (Fall 1970), pp. 13–20.

Golde, Roger A. "Are Your Meetings Like This One?" *Harvard Business Review,* Vol. 50 No. 1 (January–February 1972), pp. 68–77.

Koontz, Harold. "The Corporate Board and Special Interests." *Business Horizons,* Vol. 14 No. 5 (October 1971), pp. 75–82.

Rush, Francis M. and Victor E. Phillips, Jr. "Getting the Most Out of Meetings." *Business Horizons,* Vol. 17 (October 1974), pp. 55–61.

Van de Ven, Andrew and Andre L. Delbecq. "Nominal Versus Interacting Group Processes for Committee Decision-Making Effectiveness." *The Academy of Management Journal,* Vol. 14 (June 1971), p. 205.

Zald, Mayer N. "The Power and Functions of the Board of Directors: A Theoretical Synthesis." *American Journal of Sociology*, Vol. 75 No. 1 (July 1969), pp. 97–111.

The Case of the Out-Moded Vice-President

The other officers of Weber Corporation found various ways of distracting their attention from Bob Reith's disjointed harangue at the weekly meeting of the executive committee. Some doodled, one or two looked out the window, several engaged in whispered conversations, and a few simply stared down at the conference table before them. "Before any of you start interrupting me," Reith rambled on, "let me remind you that I was here when the old man was running the show, and I know what he would have said about acquiring a company that is losing money. All this talk about its tax loss carryover and its leverage position doesn't make any sense to me."

As he had done many times in the past, Verne Weber, son of the founder of Weber Construction Company, and president of Weber Corporation, the successor company, patiently let Reith have his say before directing the committee's discussion into productive channels.

Bob Reith had started to work for the senior Mr. Weber when he was eighteen years old. His drive soon became apparent to Weber, and by the time he was in his early twenties he was successfully managing construction projects. The military building boom caused by World War II resulted in a tremendous growth of Weber Construction Company, and Reith's ability to force a project to completion gained him a vice-presidency and the designation of Weber's "right hand man" when he was just thirty. When the war ended and young Verne Weber joined his father's company, he was as-

signed to work for two years under Reith's tutelage.

Upon his father's death in 1954, Verne Weber succeeded to the presidency of the company. After several years of making certain that the company was firmly established in a growth position in the construction industry, Weber began to consummate his plans for diversifying the company's operations. He had hoped that Reith, who was the only remaining top manager from the old company, would be able to run the construction division of the new company that he envisioned, but came to the reluctant realization that Reith's ability level was to boss an individual construction project, and that managing an international construction organization was completely over his head. Weber's expansion plans were delayed for two years until he finally attracted Tom Hoslett, a highly experienced manager in the largest construction company in the country, to accept the challenge of building Weber's construction division.

In 1960 the company's name was changed to Weber Corporation, and the firm branched out into equipment distributorships, auto leasing, resort hotels, and insurance. Weber was very careful not to enter a new field until he was able to entice the most competent managers that he could find to align their interests with the corporation in heading the diversified operations. As a result, Weber Corporation grew on a foundation of highly qualified top managers. The only exception was Bob Reith, who still held the title of vice-president, and whose role was formally defined as advisor to

Mr. Weber. In a practical sense, the scope of the company's operations had gone beyond his ability to contribute anything of value, but he lacked the perception to recognize his inadequacies. His constant meddling in the firm's affairs was a source of increasing resentment to the other senior managers.

Many times during the prosperous 1960s, Verne Weber's thoughts dwelt on the problem of what to do with Reith. He regularly suggested early retirement, but Reith's predictive reply was always, "I'm too healthy to think of retirement yet. And besides, I promised your father that I would always be around to give you a hand when you needed it." Once in 1967 he talked Reith into taking over the managing of the construction of a huge shopping center, thinking that would get him back into the area where he had shown ability as a young man. However, construction technology had passed Reith by, and when Hoslett finally demanded that he be replaced as head of the project, Reith's bungling had caused such delays that the shopping center resulted in the largest loss that the corporation had ever suffered.

Weber's success in putting together an industrial empire earned him the respect of all of the managers he had reporting to him. The only time there was serious disagreement was when they periodically, either individually or collectively, asked him to get rid of Reith. On an objective basis, Weber knew they were right. He realized that he should have discharged Reith years before. Had he done so, the man might have been able to build a new career at a job level compatible with his abilities. Thus, as Weber reasoned, his own weakness had caused the situation to get beyond the point where a discharge was an equitable solution.

One day in 1972, shortly after Reith's emotional stand against the acquisition that all of the other company officers strongly favored, Weber asked the advice of Lane Smith, a management consultant who was doing some work for the company. "Actually, Mr. Weber," said Smith, "many companies have drones in their management ranks. You might even be surprised to learn that some of them are much worse than Mr. Reith. For example, he apparently is neither an alcoholic, a compulsive gambler, or a woman chaser—and that is more than can be said for the problem of personnel of other firms. What trouble is he really causing?"

"Actually, it is just his talking at the meetings," Weber answered. "I can keep him away from the other managers except for those occasions. He has no decisions to make that could cause problems for the company. The dollar cost of his salary and office expense to this company is meaningless. I can put up with his well-meant counsel to me without any personal difficulty. It is just that the other managers can't stand him, and my conscience won't let me fire him."

"How about removing him from the executive committee, and all other committees that he might be on," Smith suggested. "You could think of plausible reasons to explain the action to him, and it would at least be a lot less damaging to him personally than a discharge."

DISCUSSION QUESTIONS

1. What do you think of the consultant's advice to simply remove Reith from any contact with the other senior managers?
2. If you think the best decision would have been to discharge Reith, when was the most appropriate time to have done it?
3. What effect do you think Verne Weber's reluctance to discharge Reith would have on the attitudes of the senior managers toward Weber himself?

Summary

Organizing starts with the identification of the activities that need to be performed in an organization. Activities are then grouped to form departments. Departments may be organized functionally, by product, geographically, or sometimes by the relatively new form—project organization. Organizations may be typed as *decentralized,* where the tendency is to force decision making down into the lower management levels, or *centralized,* where decision making tends to be restricted to top management.

A vertical authority relationship exists between managers and the subordinates reporting to them. The number of subordinates that a manager can effectively handle is known as his or her span of control. Authority may be viewed as a right to command that flows downward; as a consent to be managed that flows upward; or, more realistically, as a combination of both. Lateral relationships exist between members of an organization who must interact, but who are not in a superior/subordinate relationship. The relationships between central and advisory departments provide examples. Informal organizations are present in all formal organizations. They form spontaneously, and have the potential for being extremely powerful.

Conflict between departments is a characteristic of all organizations. One cause is the loyalty that people tend to feel toward their departments. Conflict can have dysfunctional effects on the organization's goals. Another behavior found in organization is power politics. Power seekers use organization politics to reach their personal goals. Organizational structure can alienate people, and contribute to conflict. Coordination links the contributions of the subsystems of an organization into a harmonious whole, and involves the management of change. Actually, coordination is the essence of what managers do.

Committees are created when group deliberation is needed. They can take a variety of forms. Committees should be used to get integrated judgment, to assist in coordination, to invite participation, to facilitate communication, and to develop managers. They are costly, are slow to reach decisions, and can be irresponsible. The board of directors is an important committee in business organizations.

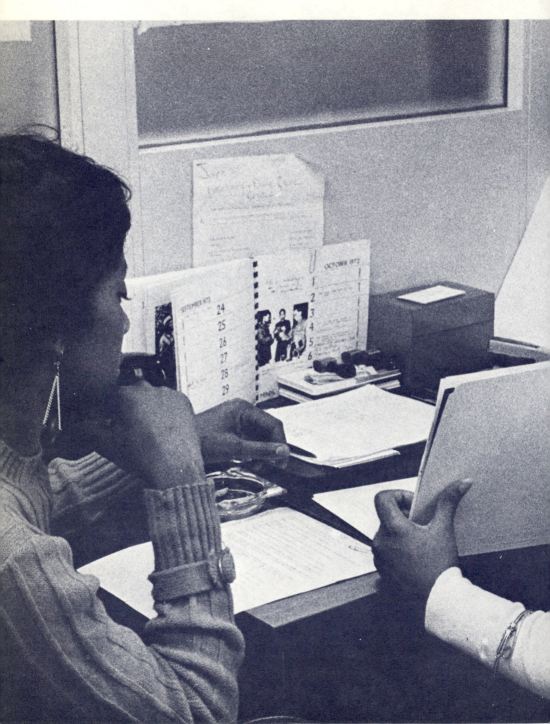

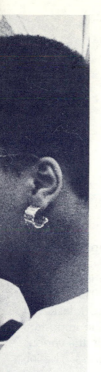

PART 4

Staffing

An organization's success depends on how well its managers develop and maintain all its various resources. The managerial function of staffing is concerned with development and maintenance of an organization's human resources. For a business organization, as in all organizations, the most important resource is people. Other resources, such as capital, raw materials, plant, and equipment, are essential—but they require the human element to bring them to bear on organizational goals.

The chapters in Part Four address the important activities which concern managers as they develop and maintain the human resources of the organization. Managers will be involved in the following activities as they perform the staffing function:

- Determine what work has to be done and segregate this work into identifiable jobs. This task will be discussed in Chapter 15, Job Design.
- Analyze and determine the relative worth of jobs so that equitable compensation levels can be established. Compensation is the topic of Chapter 16.
- Forecast future job openings that must be filled.
- Recruit and select people for these openings. Manpower topics are treated in Chapter 17.
- Appraise job performance.
- Provide training opportunities for employees to increase their value to the organization and to enhance their self-image.
- Provide management development opportunities within the organization to insure availability of this critical resource. Performance appraisal, training, and development are discussed in Chapter 18.

Human reactions to organizational practices are explored in Chapter 19, the last of the chapters on staffing.

Managers can become impatient with the time demands of staffing activities and be tempted to relegate them to the personnel department. While the details of many of these activities can be appropriately delegated and valuable assistance of modern personnel experts can be obtained, managers compromise an important dimension of their managerial role and responsibilities when they neglect the staffing function.

15 Job Design

It is convenient to visualize the *job* as the smallest subsystem or group of activities within an organization. A job is made up of a combination of work tasks which are performed by individuals. Each job is distinctive from other jobs in terms of its component work tasks. The primary reason for creating jobs is to make sure that necessary work tasks get done. This chapter addresses the issues that surround the important process of determining what activities should be included in the various jobs that must be performed to ensure organizational success. The job requirements provide the basis for selecting, training, evaluating, and compensating members of an organization. These activities are discussed in Chapters 16, 17, and 18.

There is a distinction between a *job* and a *position*. Basically, the terms are convenient for differentiating between a classification of work tasks, which is a job, and the number of slots authorized for that particular classification, with each of these slots being a position. Thus, it might be said that in a firm there are ten positions authorized for the job of machinist; of these ten positions, seven are presently filled and three are open. Each person performing a job occupies a position. Sometimes organizations use the terms to differentiate between high and low status work. A manager, for example, would be said to have a position, while a machinist would be said to have a job.

Generally, a job can be defined by its specific content, a particular method for carrying out specific work tasks, and relatively predictable social relationships within the organization. Job content refers to an explicit collection of tasks and outputs for a given job. In addition, with most jobs, tasks are to be completed in a certain way. Defining the appropriate way for the job to be done is partly under the control of the manager, partly the job holder, and partly by the relevant technology and state of the art. Jobs will typically have social relationships which are relatively constant, regardless of who holds the job. Typically, the job of plant manager will require the job holder to engage in social interaction with other specific positions in the organization. The manager will need to relate to both higher management, immediate subordinates, and significant portions of the organization's environment.

As job design has progressed over the years, jobs have tended to become more specific and narrower in scope. The general trend has been toward simpler, more specialized jobs. The term "work simplification" refers to a process in which the scope of jobs is reduced to achieve maximum efficiency. This has resulted in many jobs which are highly repetitive and for some people very boring.

THE COMPOSITION OF A JOB

In performing staffing functions, managers must first ask which tasks should be included in a specific job. Job analysis, which includes job description and specifications, has been the traditional manner to reach an answer. Recent developments in industrial democracy and participation have raised the additional question of *who* should provide answers to these questions of job content. These issues are addressed in the latter part of this section.

Job Descriptions and Specifications

The techniques used to record job components (job descriptions) and those used to set forth the necessary qualifications for the jobs as so described (job specifications) are complementary. Both techniques fall in the general category of job analysis. Job analyses in organizations should be on-going so that the organizational goals can be achieved, replacements for workers can be recruited, and appropriate compensation can be made for work performed.

Job descriptions. Although there are various forms for devising *job descriptions*, they generally provide the following:

- Job title and classification grade, the latter being an identification of the relative worth or significance of the job.
- A concise summary of the nature of the job, often specifying the person to whom incumbents on the job report.
- A description, in intentionally broad terms, of the duties of the job—the objective being to describe the average duties of many individuals occupying job positions.

Job descriptions are used to inform and remind individuals what is expected of them; they serve as a basis for training people to perform

The MOST Way to Time a Job

Production managers need to have accurate measurements of the time workers need to do their jobs. But jobs change, new jobs arise, and the analysis and documentation that work measurement requires takes time itself—making the effort costly.

Now H. B. Maynard & Co., a Pittsburgh consulting firm, is aggressively marketing a new, simplified system first developed and applied at SaabScania in Sweden in 1967. Called MOST (for Maynard Operation Sequence Technique), the system already boasts an impressive list of U.S. users and some glowing testimonials. Like other work measurement systems, MOST is based on so-called predetermined time standards—the fragments of time that studies have shown are normally needed for such basic human motions as grasping with the fingers, reaching with the arm, lifting, and turning. Many such systems are on the market, but MOST differs from its predecessors enough so that one textile executive privately calls it "the most exciting work measurement tool developed in the past 10 years."

Maynard claims two big pluses for MOST:

Speed
The company says the method is 5 to 15 times faster than MTM-2 (MTM stands for Methods-Time-Measurement), the most widely used "simplified" work measurement system, and 30 to 50 times faster than MTM-1, the basic, detailed method. Speed makes it worthwhile to measure some jobs that otherwise would be uneconomical to measure and also makes it easier to keep time standards up to date.

Comprehensibility
Users agree that the method of analysis and the fact that even a complex job can be documented on one page make the system easy to learn. And the method is easy to explain to higher management, to workers, and to their unions.

So far, MOST has been used mainly to measure production jobs. Kjell B. Zandin, who invented MOST and is now Maynard's director of work measurement systems, claims it is highly accurate for work cycles exceeding two minutes. He is now adapting it to measure such functions as maintenance and shipping. Joe LaBadie, industrial engineering manager at Blue Bird Body Co., the bus builder in Fort Valley, Ga., says that MOST is "an extremely helpful time saver, and we'll be able to go into almost all jobs."

Sequences
Zandin found, in a computerized statistical analysis, that a large number of industrial jobs can be described in terms of a few simple sequences. And he found that as work cycles increased in length, it was possible to let an "average" time fragment represent ever-wider, real-time intervals without any significant loss in over-all accuracy. So, while an analyst needs to know 400 time values for MTM-1 and 39 for MTM-2, MOST is built around only nine time fragments and three basic sequence models: general move, controlled move, and tool use. Installing a carburetor float in its housing, for example, is a couple of simple "general moves" in MOST, but in MTM-2 is a string of such minute steps as inserting a screw, grasping a screwdriver, putting it on the screw, tightening, and so forth.

Eaton Corp. has probably done more with MOST than any other U. S. company. In one test, Melvin Schaffer, the Industrial Truck Div.'s manager of industrial engineering, compared MOST against more detailed studies of a task that consisted of setting up the three jaws in the chuck of a lathe used to make a part for lift-trucks. The task itself takes about six minutes. With basic MTM, an analyst needed about 20 hours and 13 pages to develop and document a time standard for the task. With MOST, the job was done in 1.4 hours and on a single page. And the task time, as measured by MOST, was only 3.6% longer than the time measured by MTM-1.

Dissent

Still, consulting firms that rely on MTM or other, proprietary work measurement systems bristle at Maynard's claims for MOST. James P. O'Brien, executive director of the MTM Assn. for Standards & Research, of which Maynard is a member, says flatly: "We disagree with their claims on accuracy and speed."

Zandin, meanwhile, can point to several dozen customers, among them Baldwin Piano, Johnson & Johnson, Parke Davis, and Steelcase. Says William R. Harrison, manager of industrial engineering at Cornell-Dubilier Electronics, a division of Federal Pacific Electric Co.: "It's amazing to me that someone didn't think of it before." He adds, half-jokingly, "The biggest problem is explaining to an operator how a rate can be valid after the analyst has spent so little time on the floor."

---

jobs; and they provide criteria for measuring performance. In addition, they provide a basis for preparing job specifications; and they are used in still another way, namely to assist in *manpower planning* as outlined in Chapter 17.

Simple jobs can be described quite adequately because the duties are routine and interactions with other jobs are minimal. Problems occur in describing complex jobs, where there are hosts of unpredictable and indescribable lateral relationships, and where each position of the job is performed differently by the incumbent. Thus, descriptions of complex jobs are rarely precise, and, as a result, are not as useful as they should be for their intended purposes.

Job specifications. *Job specifications* derive from job descriptions. For a given job, the specification enumerates the personal qualifications needed to perform the job. These qualifications are described briefly under such headings as education, experience, ability to work with other people, capacity for responsibility, initiative, and the like. Next, the physical demands of the job are identified. These might include such items as descriptions of physical exertion required, noise and contaminant levels, and heat or ventilation needed. If appropriate for the particular job, the specification will attempt to describe the mental effort required.

Job specifications are used in the recruitment and selection processes to differentiate between people who have the potential for performing particular jobs and those who do not. In addition, they are used in *job evaluation*, the process of determining the relative worth of jobs.

Most job specifications are unnecessarily restrictive regarding applicants' qualifications. The required qualifications are either inferred from the job descriptions or are determined through induction, by checking the qualifications of people who are performing or have performed the jobs. Both approaches tend to inflate the qualifications unnecessarily. For example, college graduates are becoming so prevalent that an impressive title on a job description usually leads to an assumption that only a degree holder can do the job.

The increasing emphasis on fair employment practices is affecting job specifications. The traditional assumption that jobs require either men or women to perform them has increasingly been brought into question and successfully challenged. Managers who make staffing decisions must insure that inappropriate or inaccurate assumptions about necessary qualifications are not being made. Not only might it be illegal but the organization may be unnecessarily overlooking potentially valuable human resources by limiting access to jobs. Managers must realize that the very best job descriptions and specifications will never completely and accurately describe what and how jobs are performed. Decisions about the nature and content of organizational jobs rest with the managers in charge and will require constant updating.

Job Expansion

The traditional, and allegedly efficient, approach to designing jobs has been to combine a limited number of similar work activities. Jobs designed in this way require minimum skills. Simple techniques can be used to train people to perform the jobs. The repetitive nature of the job presumably leads to improved quantity and quality of work produced. While it is easy to see how this technique can be used in grouping routine, manual tasks, it must be recognized that similar design processes have been used in all types of organizations for designing jobs in such categories as engineering, personnel, accounting, and other white collar classifications.

Growing recognition of the fact that many people become frustrated by highly specialized jobs, and thereby alienated toward the organization, has led to managerial attempts to move away from narrow job definitions. These attempts have developed into different ways of responding to the negative impact of boring jobs. The approaches have included job rotation, job enlargement, and job enrichment.

Job rotation simply refers to the practice of encouraging holders of repetitive jobs to change to new, repetitive jobs. If the decision to rotate can be well timed, this practice will alleviate some of the worst aspects of highly simplified work. When the authority to decide when to rotate can be placed with the job holder, the timing for the individual will be most appropriate.

Job enlargement refers to a process of adding dimensions to a job which do not materially reduce the efficient design and which help relieve the boredom.

Job enrichment is a process similar to job enlargement; however, it goes further and adds dimensions of decision-making authority and increased responsibilities in the job. An enriching component was suggested in the job rotation discussion above, where it was suggested that the job holder decide when to rotate jobs. Job enrichment can be seen as a vertical expansion of a job compared to the lateral expansion of job enlargement. Job enlargement typically puts more variation and activity in the job; it may expand the job to cover larger segments of the task. Job enrichment permits the job holder to exercise more control over the job environment and make the job richer in terms of variety, interest, and significance.

Related to these job-expanding approaches to job design is another approach called "human engineering." It aims to design jobs, and the equipment and work environment associated with them, that fit human physiological, psychological, and sociocultural characteristics. This idea is incorporated in the sociotechnical systems concepts of structuring organizations. (See Chapters 5 and 28.)

Increased Employee Participation

In simple organizations, job design has traditionally been performed by the worker's immediate supervisor. In more complex organizations, professional job designers, such as industrial engineers or management consultants, have performed the task. Some recent changes in job design involve enlisting the participation of the people who are going to do the work in deciding the content of jobs. Reports from firms that have tried this approach suggest that it has exciting possibilities for improving worker satisfaction and performance.

A trend which often implicitly accompanies expanded job designs is increased participation in organizational affairs, participation even beyond the boundaries of the particular job. Increased industrial democracy will often run counter to the preferences of managers who feel strongly about the preservation of "traditional" managerial rights and perquisites. In countries where socialism has been more common, the experiments with increased industrial democracy have met with less managerial resistance. However, many companies in the U.S. are also experimenting with various forms of expanded jobs and preliminary findings suggest impressive improvements in worker performance as well as in their attitudes toward their jobs and the organization.

There is an underlying conceptual polarity in the various approaches managers use in arriving at the composition of a job. At one extreme, the composition of a job will be designed so that it fits ideally with organizational needs, tasks, and relationships. At the other extreme, the jobs in an organization can be tailored to the strengths, skills, and preferences of present and potential organization members. Actual practice will fall somewhere between these extremes. Demands on the organization, the availability of workers' skills, and managerial preferences will all influence decisions on job composition.

DISCUSSION QUESTIONS

1. Take a job you have held or know of and write a job description and a set of job specifications for it. What problems would you anticipate if you were really going to use these for the job you selected?
2. Some organizations seem to operate adequately and in some cases quite well, without a recorded set of job descriptions. Speculate on this situation: How does it come about? At what costs and benefits?
3. Briefly, describe a job with which you are familiar. How could job rotation, job enlargement, and job enrichment be applied to that job?

BIBLIOGRAPHY

Foy, Nancy and Herman Gadon. "Worker Participation: Contrasts in Three Countries." *Harvard Business Review*, Vol. 54 No. 3 (May–June 1976), pp. 71–83.

Hackman, J. Richard. "Is Job Enrichment Just a Fad?" *Harvard Business Review*, Vol. 53 No. 5 (September–October 1975), pp. 129–38.

Miner, John B. and Mary Green Miner. *Personnel and Industrial Relations: A Managerial Approach*, 2nd ed. New York: The Macmillan Co., 1973.

Reif, William E. and Fred Luthans. "Does Job Enrichment Really Pay Off?" *California Management Review*, Vol. 15 (Fall 1972), pp. 30–37.

The Case of Picking the Right Words

In the summer of 1975, Skil Mor, Inc., a manufacturer of power lawn mowers, hedge trimmers, and chain saws, employed about 200 people in all job classifications. The highly satisfactory market acceptance of the firm's products had warranted an approved plan to expand the work force to 500 employees by 1977. Before any substantial recruiting or hiring was to be started, however, the company's managers agreed that objective descriptions and specifications should be prepared for all new jobs. The personnel manager, Dick Awenius, offered to lend his help in designing new jobs, and many of the managers volunteered to help each other. Among the new jobs that would have to be designed was that of buyer in the purchasing department. Up until then, all of the purchasing work had been handled by Ralph Smith, the purchasing agent, and his secretary, but the firm's expansion necessitated filling three positions in the job classification of buyer.

"I have asked Mrs. Scheuler to join us while we talk about the buyer job, Dick," said Ralph Smith. "She knows the purchasing part of this company as well as I do. In fact, she would be a prime candidate for buyer if it weren't for the fact that she has decided to move to the West Coast."

"Fine. To get started, Ralph, what do you generally see a buyer doing?"

"Well, first of all, I have in mind three different kinds of buyers—one for raw materials, one for supplies of all types, and another for subcontract parts. Should there be separate descriptions and specifications for each one?"

"A case could probably be made for separating the job of buying subcontract parts from the others, but let's try to write a blanket description and specification covering all three," said Awenius. "I suggest that the description start out: 'Under the general supervision of the purchasing agent, the buyer . . . ,' and then go on to specify the duties."

"I am afraid of the word 'general.' As I am ultimately responsible for all purchasing, I feel that I should exercise close supervision," said Smith.

"Mr. Smith," said Mrs. Scheuler, "the main reason for having buyers is to relieve you for more important matters, such as policy. If you exercise close supervision you will get so bogged down that you can't get past the routine details. And another thing, if you put the buyers pretty much on their own, within a policy framework, they will be motivated to better effort."

"I must agree," replied Awenius, "and besides, if you specify 'close' supervision the job will be evaluated lower than if you say 'general' supervision."

"All right. At least on paper I will go along with it. Well, a buyer will maintain a list of qualified vendors. He will receive and evaluate purchase requisitions. He will . . ."

"Excuse me for interrupting, Ralph," said Awenius, "but about the word 'evaluate.' Does this mean that a buyer can question a requisition, or that he can change what someone in a requisitioning department has asked for?"

"The issue revolves primarily around requisitions that specify brand or vendor. We must allow the buyer to make the decision as to what make is best for a particular purpose, and from whom to buy it," replied Smith.

"Perhaps we can take the threat of a change out of the wording by saying 'receive and process,'" said Mrs. Scheuler. "Then we can leave any possible interpretation conflicts to the individual buyers."

"We are going to have to find people for the buyer positions who are particularly good at handling potentially explosive situations if we are going to even imply that the production manager, for example, can't have his steel bought from a certain source, if that is the way that he wants it," said Awenius. "Somehow, we will have to get this qualification written into the job specification. However, let's be straightforward and say 'evaluate,' if that is what a buyer really does."

"To go on," said Smith, "a buyer will send requests for quotation to approved vendors, and analyze the returned quotations. He will select the vendor, with the approval of the purchasing agent, and issue a purchase order."

"Now we are back to the matter of the closeness of your supervision," said Awenius. "Are you saying that you are going to make the final selection of every vendor?"

"No, of course not. In many cases the buyer will simply award the purchase to the vendor with the lowest price. However, with some of the things that we buy I want to spread the business among several vendors, provided that the prices are the same. There will also be occasions when we will select the vendor with

the lowest price to start negotiations for a better deal. These are the kinds of situations where I want to be consulted before a purchase order is sent out."

"Those are contingencies that are rather hard to spell out in a job description," said Awenius. "I guess we will have to say it your way, and then you will have to work out understandings with each of your buyers."

"I think that will be best," replied Smith. "Finally, a buyer will follow up on all purchase transactions to assure that the terms are met, and authorize the payment of the vendor's invoice."

"I guess those duties are clear enough in general terms," said Awenius. "Now about the job specification. I suggest that for minimum education we specify four years of college. This is so that we can fit the job into the proper salary grade."

"I don't have four years of college myself," conceded Ralph Smith, "and I don't think that it is necessary for a buyer. A bright, aggressive individual with some good work experience, like inventory or production control, is what I would like for the job, regardless of his formal education."

"How about saying 'four years of college or equivalent'?" said Awenius.

"What exactly is the equivalent of four years of college?" asked Mrs. Scheuler. "It seems to me that this will always be a matter of personal judgment."

"You are probably right, but we have to specify some educational level. Now about experience. We should specify some number of years, such as five, in similar or related work," said Awenius.

"Suppose we get an applicant with

three years of intensive experience. Do we screen him out because he lacks two years?" asked Smith.

"That will be another matter of judgment," admitted Awenius.

"How are we going to say that the buyer must have high ethical standards, and make it meaningful for hiring? You can only tell whether an individual is susceptible to commercial bribery after you have worked with him awhile," was Smith's next comment.

"And, getting back to the kind of personality that a buyer should have," said Mrs. Scheuler, "just saying 'must have the ability to get along with people' is pretty vague. I don't suppose Skil Mor would hire a person for any job who did not have the apparent ability to work with others. How do we say in the specification that a buyer must be reasonable, but be firm when he thinks he is right, and must be able to make people—perhaps higher in the organization—defer to his opinions? Moreover, how do we screen people for this quality?"

DISCUSSION QUESTIONS

1. In the Case of Picking the Right Words, will Dick Awenius' insistence on the words *general supervision* in the job description change Ralph Smith's views on how he will supervise the job? What are the implications of Smith's comments?

2. How useful will the buyer's job description be if understandings must be worked out privately with each buyer concerning vendor selection?

3. What potential problems are being created by setting the specification for education as "four years of college or equivalent"?

16 Job Evaluation and Compensation

When people are organized to work toward a common set of goals, the tasks the people do become differentiated. The different jobs which need to be done in an organization have differing degrees of value to the organization. This chapter first addresses the issues and problems involved in evaluating the jobs that are performed in an organization. Second, the chapter takes up problems and issues that surround the process of determining the proper type and amount of compensation to be given the job holders.

JOB EVALUATION

In every organization, all members have the implicit understanding that the various jobs are not equal in worth or significance. This worth or significance does not refer to the performance by individuals on different jobs, but to the jobs themselves. With some jobs, of course, value differentiations are obvious; no one would deny that the job of general manager is more important to a firm than that of stock clerk. With many other jobs, however, distinctions are not nearly as clear. Since the relative worth of a job is reflected in the compensation paid for doing it, job evaluation is extremely important; and since in all organizations there are compensation differentials between jobs, somehow job evaluation always occurs. However, the methods used to evaluate jobs vary. They may be highly subjective judgments, formal application of objective standards, or something in between these two.

When there is no formal job evaluation program, salaries of the managers at the first level will have a ceiling that is a specific percentage of the chief executive's salary. Salaries below this ceiling will be determined by the compensation level of similar titles in the industry, the effect on company image, and the managers' ability to negotiate in their own interest. Salaries for managers at lower levels will be determined in the same pattern. Where managerial jobs are formally evaluated, the criteria and terms are different, but the systems themselves are quite similar to systems used to evaluate nonmanagerial jobs. Therefore, in the following discussion of evaluation systems, no job level distinctions will be made.

Job Evaluation Systems

When a firm adopts a formal system of evaluating jobs, it does so with the intention of providing an equitable basis for compensating people according to the worth of the job they perform to the organization.

Ranking. The simplest job evaluation system, and one that is only a slight step beyond not having any system at all, is ranking. This system classifies jobs in the order of perceived importance. A simple way to rank would be to use cards on which job titles have been entered, or to use the job descriptions, and try to decide which job is most important, which is next, and so on. This approach does not involve any detailed analysis of the components of the job, and a request for an explanation of a ranking can often be difficult to fill.

Grade. The system just above simple ranking is a *grade*, or classification, method. Concise descriptions of a number of different grades are developed, and requisite degrees of such factors as skill, experience, and responsibility are assigned to each grade. Using job descriptions as a guide, the method fits jobs into the grades which appear to be most appropriate. This system can have enough substance built into it to be quite workable for an uncomplicated organization, such as a university, where there are only four academic grades—instructor, assistant professor, associate professor, and full professor.

The point method. At the opposite pole of evaluation systems, so far as complexity is concerned, is the *point method* of evaluation. This method involves the use of a manual, or guide, which should be custom-made for a specific company. There are also many standard manuals available which a company might use with varying degrees of success. The main features of the manual are the thoughtful development of the elements that are common, to some extent, to all of the jobs that will be evaluated, and clear descriptions of a number of gradations of each element.

Examples of elements include education, experience, physical effort, mental effort, responsibility for equipment, and responsibility for the safety of others. Gradations, using experience as a typical element, might look like these: (1) Job can be learned in less than three months. (2) A minimum of one year's experience is required in order to perform the job satisfactorily. (3) Progressive experience totaling two years leading up to the job, plus three years of experience on the job, is necessary for expected job performance. (4) A complex of related job experiences totaling five years, plus five years of experience on the job, is the minimum required to assure acceptable competence.

After elements and grades within elements are established, some number of points must be assigned to each gradation of each element. It should be noted that each element does not require the same number of gradations, and that the total points assigned to the various elements will probably be different. This happens because the elements will not usually be of the same importance.

The final step is to group the various jobs into grades, or classifications, according to total points. Thus, Grade I might include jobs with less than 100 points, Grade II, jobs with point totals of 100 to 125, and so on. After that, wage or salary ranges must be developed for each grade (a discussion of wage or salary ranges is included in later sections of this chapter).

Evaluation of Top-Level Jobs

While there appears to be a trend toward introducing objective evaluation methods for high-level managerial jobs, many companies still use completely subjective methods for setting executive salaries. These salaries are used as an index of a job's worth. The salary of a chief executive of a business organization is often based on the salaries of other chief executives in the same industry. Another basis for setting the chief executive's salary is the effect it will have on the company's desired image. In other words, it might be set low to indicate that the firm is sober and prudent, or it might be high to suggest that the firm is prosperous enough to afford only first-class managerial talent. The chief executive's salary might also reflect an ability to negotiate to personal advantage.

Problems in Job Evaluation

The point method does have defects, for although there is the appearance of being objective, the method is based on what may be described as "systematized subjectivity." Every step in the point method, for instance, actually requires a value judgment. Answers to such questions as what elements should be included, how many points should be given for each gradation, and which gradation best fits a particular job, are all influenced by human biases. The detail of the analysis, and the use of group judgments, compensate for this subjectivity to some extent. It has been suggested by some experts that participation on the part of job incumbents will offset the negative aspects of the inherent subjectivity. It is very important that people sense a basic equity in the compensation system. This sense of equity can begin with a thorough evaluation of jobs with emphasis and attention directed on the job itself, *not* on the performance of the incumbent.

Another significant obstacle that must be overcome is resistance by the people in the organization to formal job evaluation. Whoever is sponsoring the program must gain the confidence of the people who will be affected by the evaluations. Ideally, those affected should perceive that the program is fair, will not be prejudicial to them, and that, despite its weaknesses, it is better than no system at all.

Another problem arises when there are sharply different groupings of jobs within the organization, such as factory, clerical, and technical. Should different evaluation systems be used for each job type, or should the same system cover all types? Problems will arise no matter what action is taken.

FINANCIAL COMPENSATION

After job design and job evaluation have been completed, wage or salary ranges for each grade of jobs must be determined. It seems to be general practice to use the term *wages* when compensation is on an hourly basis, and *salary* when compensation is based on a longer period, such as a week, month, or year.

A *range* is the spread between the minimum and maximum compensation for a job grade. Ranges permit merit compensation increases. The maximum is usually some fixed percentage increase over the minimum for the grade; thus, each higher grade will have a larger range value in dollars. Ranges usually are established for nonunion jobs only, because, typically, unions are not in favor of merit increases and prefer raises to be on an across-the-board basis.

As we mentioned earlier, the purpose of identifying the relative worth of each job is to develop an equitable basis for compensation. However, other factors external to the organization may also help determine compensation. That is, the relative worth of jobs within the organization will be the starting point, but after that adjustments will commonly have to be made because of demands by unions, the going market value of jobs, and government legislation.

Using Scatter Diagrams

The first step in equating compensation with job worth is to construct what is called a *scatter diagram*—job evaluation points are measured on the horizontal axis and existing compensation on the vertical axis. Figure 16–1 illustrates this type of diagram. Coordinates derived from the intersection of the number of points evaluated for a job and the compensation currently paid for the job are marked on the diagram. The

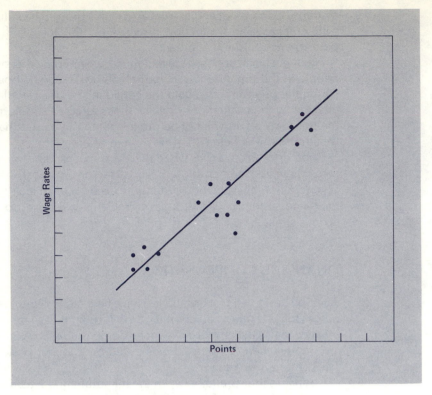

Figure 16-1. Wage/Points Scatter Diagram.

marks will tend to cluster around a diagonal line that rises as the number of job evaluation points increase. In other words, there will be a strong tendency for job evaluation points to be proportional to compensation, even at the start of systematizing the compensation structure. However, there will be some marks that are significantly below the diagonal line, which indicates that the associated job is being underpaid. Other marks may be considerably above the line, and this condition suggests that the associated jobs are being overpaid.

Adjusting marks above or below the line. When an organization finds it is paying less or more than its jobs are worth, the first step should be to carefully check evaluations for possible errors. The next step for most companies is to increase the compensation of jobs that are underpaid to bring them up to the average. Jobs that are overpaid present more of a problem. If compensation is reduced to where it should be, workers will be dissatisfied and productivity will probably suffer. If compensation is left where it is, workers whose jobs are worth more than the overpaid workers, but whose pay is the same, will feel inequitably treated. Most firms elect not to change the compensation until all existing workers on

the overpaid jobs have left the company or have been transferred to other jobs.

Reviewing and adjusting the compensation paid for jobs, relative to the worth of the jobs as indicated by the evaluation points, will bring the jobs into proper internal balance. From this point on, raises can be applied proportionally for individual jobs without disturbing the balance.

Factors That Necessitate Adjustments

As indicated earlier, external factors such as union demands, labor supply, and government legislation will create imbalances in a firm's compensation system.

Union pressure. Management's strategy in wage negotiations with unions will be to try to keep the wages paid for jobs in proper balance with their worth. Often union pressure will force wages for union jobs higher than their relative worth. If this occurs management can either provide relatively inequitable compensation for nonunion jobs, or management can restore the balance by raising compensation for nonunion jobs. Choosing the first alternative will cause the nonunion people to be dissatisfied with their pay, and election of the second alternative will significantly boost the company's total cost for compensation. Management will be faced with the dilemma of choosing between two unattractive alternatives.

Labor supply. If a review of a job's evaluation shows that its compensation is internally equitable but the firm still cannot attract new people—or hold existing employees—then the demand for qualified applicants must be greater than the supply. The company's alternatives include hiring people with less than required qualifications, but at the compensation established for the job, or increasing the compensation in order to get qualified people. The first alternative will probably cause performance to suffer, and the second will cause an imbalance in the compensation structure.

Government legislation. Overtime pay under specified conditions for stipulated kinds of jobs is one well-known form of government legislation that necessitates compensation adjustments. However, the main impact of government legislation comes from the minimum wage requirement, which was established under the Fair Labor Standards Act of 1938, as amended. Jobs, which formerly were not evaluated as worth the legal amount of compensation, must be paid legal minimums. Thus, the minimum wage requirement has forced the compensation of higher-grade jobs up proportionally, and has, in effect, increased the total compensation cost.

Other Forms of Financial Compensation

Financial incentives to produce more or better work were briefly discussed in Chapter 3 as part of the management concepts promoted by Frederick W. Taylor. These incentives can be built into either a piece-work system, in which individuals or groups receive increased compensation for production beyond a certain standard, or into the commission system, in which salespeople, for example, are paid in direct proportion to what they produce.

Various profit-sharing systems seem to be increasing in popularity among firms in the United States. The objective in such systems is to increase the total net profits of the company by motivating the employees to greater productivity. The share of profits going to employees is usually distributed on an individual basis by a formula. Usually, the direct compensation paid to the job is the key variable in these formulas. Other variables are the employee's length of service and, of course, the profits available for distribution.

INDIRECT COMPENSATION

Indirect compensation refers to the fringe benefits that individuals receive from employers as supplements to wages or salaries. The amount tends to reflect an individual's relative worth to an organization; pension contributions, for example, are based on direct compensation. However the amounts of some other forms of indirect compensation do *not* vary with job grade, and are equally available to all. An example of this form would be a company's recreation program.

Two aspects make indirect compensation a highly significant factor to managers.

- As a percentage of total compensation costs, fringe benefits rose from an average 14.6 percent in 1941, to 32.7 percent in 1973 in a representative sample of companies in the United States. This striking increase suggests that management control over indirect compensa-

A Work Force Wins a Travel Bonus

Perhaps the most unusual incentive-bonus for faithful work yet devised by a grateful boss will be paid out this March by Data Terminal Systems Inc. of Maynard, Mass. DTS will close down its bustling factory for a week and send all 400 employees who want to go—from president to lowliest assembler—on company-paid trips to London or to Walt Disney World in Orlando, Fla. The estimated cost of this largess is $100,000, but DTS figures that the return to shareholders is worth the price.

The trips are a reward for workers' help in doubling profits this year from the $1 million of 1975. "We ask a lot of our employees, and when we set a goal of doubling profits, I wanted a memorable reward to generate a real team effort," says Robert F. Collings, 38, the founder-president of DTS. Now six years old, the nonunion manufacturer of electronic cash-register systems expects a sales volume of $20 million for 1976.

The company already pays employees a generous cash bonus, based on production goals set jointly by supervisors and workers. The quarterly bonus can add up to six weeks of pay per year for top performers. The long-distance trips were added as "a means of getting an extra burst of adrenalin from everybody here," Collings says.

The company points to gains other than rising profits that have resulted from these incentives. Collings says sales per employee—his gauge of productivity—amounted to $63,000 at DTS last summer, far greater than the much larger NCR Corp., he says. Such a comparison may overlook the fact that NCR produces many products, while DTS is a one-product company—but NCR is its chief rival in that product. DTS's absenteeism has also been cut in the past year, and Collings maintains that some of his workers have rejected higher-paid jobs at other companies because of the incentive programs at Data Terminal.

DTS does seem to have a happy shop at Maynard. Supervisor Ruth Coutu was undismayed by having to work two straight overtime shifts during Christmas week because of late parts deliveries. "I'm off to London and I can't wait," she said. Glancing at Collings, she added: "I love that man."

"Everybody is talking about it," says an enthusiastic Jennie Walsh, who tests subassemblies at DTS. She decided immediately to go on the junket to London because "I can visit relatives and take a side trip to Scotland." Like most other employees, she was undeterred by the fact that she will have to pay federal income taxes on the $400 cost of the trip.

While many of the production workers chose the trip to London, which was originally planned for all employees, a number of engineers, technical writers, and other middle managers wanted alternatives. An employees-activities committee rejected ideas such as trips to Rome and Paris or cash in lieu of travel, but finally approved the trek to Disney World for those who wanted it.

Almost 100% of the young singles and older married workers are opting for London, while employees with young families are choosing the trip to Walt Disney World. More than half of the 400 workers have signed up for one of the trips so far, and those who want to stay home will simply get a week off without pay. Workers with less than one year of service must pay a portion of the trip cost.

"I've never heard of any company sending its entire work force on a trip like this—never, never," says Keith Rogal, co-owner of Rogal Associates, a large Boston group-incentive agency. "But you know these technical types, they're all sort of crazy," he adds. "I think that it is the niftiest thing that I've seen."

Collings concedes that doubling profits will get tougher as time goes on, but he is convinced that a goal-reward mechanism forces managers to deal with workers' problems and thus keeps productivity high. "We're constantly thinking about motivation," Collings says, "and if this trip is a success, then we'll consider another trip in return for meeting some other objective."

---

tion is seriously needed. Other studies on the magnitude of fringe benefit payments do not show them to be as high as 30 percent of total compensation costs. The other estimates fall in the 20 percent range, which indicates that indirect compensation represents one out of every five dollars of total compensation costs.

- Generous fringe benefit programs have come to be expected by workers, and firms whose programs are relatively austere will experience much difficulty in competing for skilled personnel in the labor market.

Classifications of Fringe Benefits

There is one category of indirect compensation which a firm must provide. A firm must provide the legally required payments to federal and state social welfare programs, which include Old Age, Survivors, and Disability Insurance, Unemployment Compensation, and Workmen's Compensation. The estimated proportion of this category of indirect compensation to total compensation cost is about 7.5 percent.

The next two categories of indirect compensation are not legally imposed, but may either be volunteered by the company or negotiated between the company and the employees' bargaining representatives. The first of these includes the service costs of deferred or contingent monetary payments by the company to its employees, including pension plan costs, life, accident, health, and hospitalization insurance costs, and termination pay allowances. The average cost of these benefits is about 10.5 percent of a company's total cost for all compensation.

The second category of benefits that may either be volunteered by the company or result from negotiation includes the cost of payment for time not worked by employees, including rest periods, get-ready time, wash-up time, vacations, holidays, and sick leave. Employees have come to expect benefits of this nature, which, on the average, represent about 12.7 percent of all compensation costs.

A final category of fringe benefits includes such elements as recreational and educational programs, suggestion awards, and parties and picnics. Generally, these benefits are not negotiated, but tend to be granted at the company's discretion. In the total compensation picture, they average about 2 percent.

Returns to the Company

Business firms appear to get little in the form of improved performances in return for the costs of indirect compensation, except by way of attracting and retaining qualified employees. At the same time, benefits do tend to bind the marginal workers to the company. There is virtually no evidence linking higher productivity to fringe benefits, but lower productivity may result if a fringe benefit program is reduced.

Indirect compensation has evolved to its present magnitude without any deliberate management aid. The increases began during the World War II wage freeze, when employers competing for workers offered them so-called fringes. Those fringes have now grown into what many managers perceive as a Frankenstein. Paradoxically, fringes are also resented by some workers who complain that the employer is exercising discretionary choice over part of their merited compensation. Thus, the argument runs, the company should add a pro-rata share of the costs of indirect compensation to each paycheck and allow individuals to decide whether to spend the additional amount for insurance, a retirement income plan, or anything else that they might have in mind.

The opposing argument, in favor of fringes, is that they are tax free to the employee. As the income tax bite on direct compensation increases, the attractiveness of indirect compensation is magnified.

Control of Fringe Benefits

Fringe benefits are uncontrolled in many companies because the objectives of such benefits have never been established, nor plans made for administering them. Certainly, the first thing a company should do is carefully determine the cost of each item in a fringe benefit program. The next step should be an attempt to assign a priority to benefits. That is, the cost of each item might be related to the value that the company might receive from it, and the items arrayed in the order of their estimated return. Another vitally important step is to project the amount of money the company will have available for all items in a fringe benefit program over some future period of time.

After these steps are completed, the program is formed by rationing available future funds to the items in the order of their priority. The first rationing would be to the legally required items, the next to items already agreed to by contract or other commitment. If there is not enough money to cover these second priority items, then the company should renegotiate. When all of the money that the company can afford for indirect forms of compensation has been rationed, then the items to which funds have been assigned will comprise the fringe benefit program.

Future Considerations

A number of studies have been conducted in which experts in the field of employee benefits were asked to predict future trends in the field. Their predictions suggest the following benefits will become more prevalent:

- Increased health insurance including allied health care such as dental coverage, drug costs, eye care and glasses, and preventative health care such as physical exams.
- Group auto insurance.
- Longer vacations.
- Flexible work schedules.
- Higher pensions, cost of living escalators in pensions, early vesting and transferability in pensions.

It is obvious that providing any of these newer fringe benefits will increase the labor costs of an organization substantially. Managers will be required to effect increased efficiencies in their organizations to support the added costs. Adding benefits which influence the number of hours at work and the times that people perform work will require managers to call on their best skills to achieve organizational goals. Managers will need to be innovative and adaptable as these new types of influences on the work situation become increasingly prevalent.

DISCUSSION QUESTIONS

1. Suppose you were in your early sixties and the chief executive as well as a large stockholder of a company whose stock was on the stock exchange. What would your inclinations be about setting your own salary? How would the amount you decide upon affect your subordinate managers?
2. In show business, there is an expression that holds, "There are no small parts, only small actors." Comment from the point of view of job evaluation.
3. What impact can the legislated minimum wage have on job seekers?
4. What impact do you believe fringe benefits have on productivity? Discuss your answer.
5. What justification is there for not reducing the compensation of jobs found to be overpaid? Identify pro and con arguments.

BIBLIOGRAPHY

Belcher, D. W. *Wage and Salary Administration,* 2nd ed. Englewood Cliffs: Prentice-Hall, 1962.

Brennan, Charles W. *Wage Administration,* rev. ed. Homewood: Richard D. Irwin, Inc., 1963.

Chamber of Commerce of the United States. *Employee Benefits, 1973.* Washington, D.C., 1974.

Gordon, T. and R. LeBleu. "Employee Benefits: 1970–1985." *Harvard Business Review*, Vol. 48 No. 1 (January–February 1970), pp. 93–107.

Kraus, David. "The 'Devaluation' of the American Executive." *Harvard Business Review*, Vol. 54 No. 3 (May–June 1976), pp. 82–94.

Lawler, Edward E., III. *Pay and Organizational Effectiveness: A Psychological Review* New York: McGraw-Hill, 1971.

Patton, A., "What is an Executive Worth?" *Harvard Business Review*, Vol. 39 No. 2 (March–April 1961), pp. 65–73.

Paul, Robert. *Employee Benefits Factbook*. New York: Martin Segal Co., 1970.

Salter, Malcolm S. "What Is 'Fair Pay' for the Executive?" *Harvard Business Review*, Vol. 50 No. 3 (May–June, 1972), pp. 6–14, 144–46.

The Case of the Heated Furnace Repairmen

Workers in a number of job classifications at the Littleton Steel Company had been disgruntled for some time over what they held were wage inequities between their jobs and other jobs in the company. By far the most vocal were the 23 holders of the job classification "furnace repairman," who argued that the conditions under which they had to work warranted top wages in the mill. Furnace repairmen are required to don asbestos clothing, crawl into a furnace in which the temperature had been allowed to cool to around 180° F., dig out bricks that had deteriorated under up to 3000° F. operating temperatures, and cement in new bricks. The workers were in a furnace for fifteen minutes, then were out for thirty minutes to recuperate from the heat exposure. There was no disagreement by anybody that it was a miserable job.

Ray Miller, personnel director of Littleton Steel, and Sharon Frank, job analyst, had recognized for some time that the grade system of job evaluation that the company used was inadequate for the number and varieties of jobs in a steel mill. The many complaints by workers that their jobs were unfairly rated induced Miller to request sufficient funds to design and install a more comprehensive system. Upon approval of his request, he held a meeting with the union stewards to let them know that the company was going to try to do something about the alleged inequities. He went a step further and invited the stewards to select three of their number to make up an ad hoc job evaluation committee with him, Frank, and another management representative. The purpose of the committee was to select a new system, and then to reevaluate every job in the mill. Concurrent with the study of various possible systems was a review and updating of all job descriptions.

The committee finally selected a point system tailored after the one approved by the National Metal Trades Association, but with the wording of the gradations, or degrees, for each element written in the context of steel mill work. The committee then spent almost one year in careful reevaluation of each job. Particular attention was given to such jobs as furnace repairman, where gross misjudging of worth under the old system was claimed.

When the final scores for each job were tabulated, it was found that the new system established the relative worth of furnace repairman one classification lower than it had been under the old system. The immediate response of the furnace repairmen was to file a formal grievance, after which a meeting was arranged between the union grievance committee and the ad hoc job evaluation committee, not including the union members.

Joe Graber represented the furnace repairmen and was supported by the two shop stewards and the local union business agent. The meeting had not even been called to order when Graber burst out, "Miller, you and the rest of these fancy pants guys had better learn to crawl in a furnace because I and the rest of the gang are going to walk out."

The business agent, Bob Chewning,

Factors	Point Values for Job Factors				
	1st Degree	2nd Degree	3rd Degree	4th Degree	5th Degree
Skill					
1. Education	14	28	42	56	70
2. Experience	22	44	66	88	110
3. Initiative	14	28	42	56	70
Effort					
4. Physical Demand	10	20	30	40	50
5. Mental Demand	5	10	15	20	25
Responsibility					
6. Equipment	5	10	15	20	25
7. Material	5	10	15	20	25
8. Safety of Others	5	10	15	20	25
9. Work of Others	5	10	15	20	25
Job Conditions					
10. Working Conditions	10	20	30	40	50
11. Hazards	5	10	15	20	25

Figure 16-2. Littleton Steel Company Job Evaluation System.

said calmly, "Now let's not talk about walking out. We're here to learn if your job was not properly evaluated."

Ray Miller first went over the table of point values for each of the factors considered important in steel mill jobs (Figure 16-2). He was about to go over the way the committee had evaluated the job of furnace repairman, starting with the factors where the job had received a high number of points, but Graber beat him to it.

"How about working conditions and hazards?" he demanded. "How did you rate the jobs on those?"

"Furnace repairman was rated at the 5th Degree for working conditions, which is 50 points, or maximum," said Miller. "It also received the maximum points for hazards, but the 5th Degree for this element is only 25 points. This is because our safety program has eliminated really serious hazards; Littleton's extremely low accident rate confirms this. Another element for which the job of furnace repairman received the maximum number of points was physical demand, which is also 50 points at the 5th Degree. So you can see that everything that you claim makes your job worth more has been agreed to by the evaluation committee."

"Now for the factors where furnace repairman did not receive a high evaluation," Miller continued. "It was rated at the 1st Degree for education."

"As I only have an 8th-grade education myself, I guess I can't complain about that," conceded Graber.

Miller went on, "There are four new

men on the job who are doing satisfactory work with experience that compares to the 2nd Degree, so we think that is a fair rating. About the only initiative that is required for the job is deciding whether a brick has started to crumble, so it is also rated at the 2nd Degree for that element. For the three skill factors, furnace repairman has 86 points out of a possible 250 points."

"Do you see anything unfair about this, Joe?" asked Chewning.

"No, but I know the job isn't being paid enough," said Graber.

"To continue," said Miller, "the job was rated at the 1st Degree for mental demand. It was rated fairly high, at the 3rd Degree, for both responsibility for equipment and for material, but at the 1st Degree for responsibility for safety of others and work of others. To summarize, the job received a total of 256 points out of a maximum of 500 points. 256 points places it in the fifth highest classification in the mill, which means that it is considered to be an important job to the company."

"Not important enough to be paid what it is worth," said Graber heatedly. "I might admit that the job rates are low on some of those things, but not enough points are given for others like working conditions."

"That is a matter of opinion," said Miller.

"Yeah, and my opinion is as good as yours. The boys and I are walking out," shouted Graber.

"Oh no, you're not," was Chewning's response to this outburst.

DISCUSSION QUESTIONS

1. Suppose you were in your early sixties and the chief executive and a large stockholder of a company whose stock was on the stock exchange. What would be your inclination for setting the amount of your own salary? How would the amount affect your subordinate managers?
2. What reason would there be for a company's having a different evaluation system for factory, clerical, and technical jobs?
3. In the Case of the Heated Furnace Repairmen, what were some evidences of good judgment shown by Ray Miller in implementing an improved job evaluation system?
4. What foreseeable problem came up in explaining the evaluation of the furnace repairman job to Joe Graber?
5. What have you noticed to be an obvious result of Ray Miller's careful planning for the implementation of the job evaluation system?

17 Manpower Planning, Recruitment, and Selection

People are the most important resource of any organization, yet business organizations frequently rely on chance to provide proper quantities and quality for future needs. While the trend is toward more effective planning, most managers feel that the effort can be improved still further. This chapter will first cover issues managers must face as they plan the organization's manpower needs. Once a manpower plan has been drafted recruiting additional people becomes important. So problems surrounding recruitment of and selecting among candidates for open positions are also addressed in this chapter.

MANPOWER PLANNING

Manpower planning is a complex process. It involves gathering information about the manpower needs of the organization and matching it to an estimate of the available manpower supply. Estimating the organization's manpower needs should start with information concerning all the different jobs that must be performed within the organization, the qualifications needed for each job, and the total compensation cost of each job. Developing this information was the topic of the preceding two chapters.

The next step requires an assessment of the current manpower inventory within the organization and the nature of the manpower supply outside the organization. A prerequisite to manpower planning, then, is a detailed appraisal of the organization's current human resources.

Using Manpower Replacement Charts

In appraising current human resources, managers will examine selected aspects of an organization's employees. These aspects reflect the organization's goals and tasks. However, most manpower inventories take into consideration an individual's present position, age, promotion potential, need for additional training or development, and health. These aspects and the potential movement of people within the organization can be displayed in a manpower replacement chart similar to the one in Figure 17-1.

Replacement charts indicate existing positions and potential replacement inadequacies should they be vacated. Keep in mind that use of the chart assumes that it accurately portrays the necessary jobs and relationships for organizational goal achievement.

Skills Inventory

A skills inventory is another device an organization can use to track its human resources. Skills inventories range in complexity from relatively simple to very complex. At the relatively simple end is the practice of listing people's names and major skills they possess. The manager maintains the list in his or her head. An intermediate system involves keeping a set of cards with varying amounts of information about individuals recorded on their card. The most complex forms, most often used by large organizations such as the U.S. Army, involve computer and electronic data processing systems that retain and provide access to skills needed by the organization. The complexity of the skills inventory will usually be directly related to the cost of setting up and maintaining the system. In determining the appropriate type of inventory, an organization should compare maintenance costs with the benefits it will accrue by knowing what and where its human resources are. The decision may be difficult to make for the benefits may be difficult to measure. Typically, benefits will come in the form of reduced recruiting and training costs. Improved employee performance may also result for managers would be taking advantage of existing skills rather than developing them from scratch.

A beginning step in manpower planning might be to hold the existing scale of operations constant. Obviously, voids will begin to appear immediately and become increasingly manifest as the projection extends farther into the future.

There are several reasons for this. First, there is the firm's normal attrition rate, which can be calculated from past records. A certain number of employees will quit each year and another predictable number will be fired. Absenteeism is another factor; each year a proportion of the labor force will be absent from their jobs for lengthy periods because of accidents or sickness. Promotions will account for

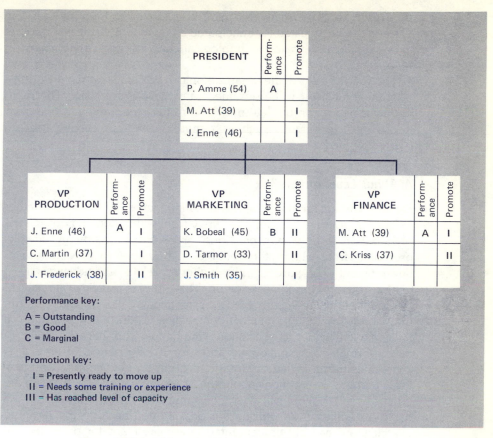

PRESIDENT	Performance	Promote
P. Amme (54)	A	
M. Att (39)		I
J. Enne (46)		I

VP PRODUCTION	Performance	Promote
J. Enne (46)	A	I
C. Martin (37)		I
J. Frederick (38)		II

VP MARKETING	Performance	Promote
K. Bobeal (45)	B	II
D. Tarmor (33)		II
J. Smith (35)		I

VP FINANCE	Performance	Promote
M. Att (39)	A	I
C. Kriss (37)		II

Performance key:

A = Outstanding
B = Good
C = Marginal

Promotion key:

I = Presently ready to move up
II = Needs some training or experience
III = Has reached level of capacity

Figure 17-1. A Manpower Replacement Chart.

some vacancies; employees will be promoted to higher jobs, for which they will need some training, leaving voids in their old jobs. Eventually, employees who stay long enough will either retire or die.

In systems terminology, entropy is occurring in the organization. Recall that entropy means that a system has the built-in tendency to run down unless it is rejuvenated. In the case of an organization, this rejuvenation can come in two forms. The organization can hire new employees at a rate comparable to the occurrence of voids and it can upgrade existing employees through training, to assume jobs of greater responsibility.

Forecasts of human resource needs, like skills inventories, can range in complexity and sophistication. Let us examine some of the different ways these forecasts can be made.

- Get an expert to estimate the needs. The expert could be the manager, the owner, or an agency external to the organization such as a trade publication or a consultant.

- An estimate of future needs can be based on trends from the past. The trend can be adjusted for anticipated changes in product lines, size of operations, anticipated technological changes, and capital expenditures.
- The specific tasks of the organization can be detailed, then the appropriate structure can be designed to achieve those tasks. The manpower needs can be determined from the structure.
- Statistical techniques such as regression analysis can be used to predict needs.

At What Level to Hire?

In their planning for manpower needs, managers should decide whether to follow a policy of promoting entirely from within, looking outside the organization to fill vacant positions, or a combined strategy. Ideally, promoting from within starts people at their level of capability, uses development to prepare them for higher-level jobs, and advances them up the structure through promotion. This policy is usually well received by organizational members. However, managers following that plan run the risk of generating a narrow perspective within the organization, if they only staff higher-level positions with people who share the quality of having remained in the organization for a long period of time. It is sometimes useful for an organization to import new people, with new ideas and few assumptions about the "proper" ways to do things. As a practical matter, there will always be some jobs at higher levels that will have to be filled from outside the organization because the required qualifications can not be generated internally. Plans for providing the people and skills the organization will need each year must be developed by comparing the manpower inventory, both present and forecasted, with the predicted job openings.

Plan for Change

If the manpower plan has begun with an assumption of constant scale of operations, it must be revised to account for changes that can be foreseen. Clearly, the manpower plan will need to be adjusted in accord with the firm's long-term objectives. Does the firm plan to expand the magnitude of present operations? Will there be new markets, new products, new acquisitions? Or, does the firm plan to contract its operations, concentrate in an area, drop some products, divisions, or subsidiaries?

The usual and traditional approach has been to assume that growth is the only alternative available to the firm. This assumption is being challenged by a growing number of economists who predict a steady-state economic environment in which every expanding firm cannot survive. Managers must make genuine decisions about the size and direction of a firm's activities rather than simply assume more is better. To make these decisions, managers will need to incorporate the limits and strengths identified in the manpower plans.

Integrate with other plans. After a determination has been made of the number and kinds of new employees that must be assimilated into the firm each year, and systems provided for continual upgrading of the company's human resources through training and development, the costs of the manpower plan must be assessed. Projections must be made of the future increases in both direct and indirect compensation for each job. These projections must then be extended by multiplying compensation by the number of future positions for each job to arrive at the firm's total wage and salary bill. This final amount then becomes an essential element in the cash flow forecast and income statements.

The process may reveal that the company's objectives are too ambitious—that it cannot afford the manpower to carry them out. If this happens the organization's long-term plans may have to be cut back. Or, other plans, such as those for equipment and research and development, may have to be reevaluated in light of an unexpectedly high rate of expenditure for personnel. Another crucial plan that may be affected is the firm's projection of permanent capital needs. The organization may have to increase its capital base to carry out its long-term plans.

Decisions about the company's whole complex of plans will result in a manpower plan that must be approved by top management. Such approval will authorize managers to perform subsequent processes of the staffing function.

RECRUITMENT OF NEW PERSONNEL

Managers are authorized to acquire new employees for unfilled positions in their organization within the limits set by the firm's manpower plan. The plan's limits will usually establish the number of positions of each job that may be filled during a specified time period. Some positions will be filled by people from within the firm. In this section of the chapter we will deal with recruiting applicants from outside the company.

Recruiting, in most medium and large companies, tends to be a centralized service performed by the personnel department, with actual hiring decisions subject to the requisitioning manager's approval. Many managers would prefer to recruit applicants personally; for example, sales managers might feel that they know best how to look for potential salespeople. By and large, however, they must cooperate in the recruiting function. Most managers can suggest likely sources or names of likely applicants, but ordinarily, they must leave the mechanics of recruiting to the specialists. However, the recruitment of new managers is often removed from the personnel department and assigned to a top-level manager or a committee of top-level managers.

Sources of Applicants

Sources of applicants will vary according to the types of jobs to be filled. Jobs can be divided into the three classifications: (1) wage and commission jobs, such as clerks, machine operators, and salespeople; (2) jobs for management trainees and professionals; and (3) jobs for experienced managers.

Class 1. Wage and commission jobs. Applicant sources for jobs in this class include

- *Public employment agencies.* There is no known way of arraying sources in the order of their effectiveness. However, the fact that all persons applying for unemployment insurance benefits must register with their state employment agency as being available for work, makes listings of job openings with agencies in different locations a productive source.
- *Newspaper classified advertising.* As this source involves an expense for the recruiting company, its use tends to increase as the supply of qualified applicants decreases. When unemployment is low, prospective employers try to outdo each other in the size and number of their advertisements, and in descriptions of benefits to be derived from working for them. In times of short labor supply, this is also a very popular source of professional applicants (who are grouped in Class 2).
- *Commercial employment agencies.* Although the applicants from this source usually must pay a fee if hired (unless the recruiting firm assumes all or part of the obligation), the charge made for the placement services often makes applicants more serious about performing well on a job. Commercial agencies also do some screening of applicants for qualifications before referring them to a prospective employer.
- *Union hiring halls.* In many industries, such as the construction, transportation, steel, and automotive trades, the union hiring hall constitutes virtually the only source of applicants for certain jobs. One problem the employer might face when using this source is that these applicants are usually referred on a basis of "first on the list, first referred;" the top of the list might be occupied by the least desirable workers because unions tend to resist differentiating between workers on the basis of ability.
- *Educational institutions.* Trade schools, high schools, and junior colleges are usually cooperative in referring qualified applicants to recruiting employers. An advantage of this source is that the applicant's grades, if released by the student, provide one indication of their ability.
- *Referrals by present employees.* When present employees refer their friends or acquaintances for employment, it is some indication that

they are satisfied with working conditions. A potential problem that must be considered, however, is the build-up of informal groups in the organization whose interests and actions are directed more to the social needs of the group than toward achievement of organizational goals.

- *Unsolicited applications.* The number of people who just "drop in" looking for jobs varies with the supply of labor, and in times of high national or regional unemployment provides a good source of qualified applicants. However, the task of maintaining an active file of such applicants can be costly and relatively unrewarding, because in many cases the applicants become unavailable soon after making their application.

Class 2. Jobs for management trainees and professional employees.
Sources of applicants in this class include

- *Universities.* By far, the leading technique for generating a supply of young applicants for managerial jobs, and applicants educated in some engineering or scientific discipline, is a formal recruiting campaign on college and university campuses. Depending on the level of demand, these campaigns can be highly competitive, as trained recruiters strive to interest the most qualified senior and graduate students in joining their respective companies.
- *Professional societies.* Technically trained individuals frequently register with societies representing their particular discipline, indicating that they are seeking employment. Recruiters often find these organizations to be productive sources of specialized kinds of applicants. In addition, many of these societies publish journals in which advertisements of job opportunities can be presented.
- *Newspaper classified and display advertising.* The competition for management trainees and professional employees with high potential is acute enough at times to prompt recruiters to go beyond classified advertising into more expensive display advertisements to attract applicants with outstanding qualifications.
- *Professional placement agencies.* In most large cities, there are some agencies that specialize in finding engineers and scientists for client companies. During a shortage of this type of worker during the 1960s, the fees were paid by the employing firms. Because of the oversupply of technical workers in the early 1970s, however, many of these agencies began charging the fees to the applicants whom they placed in jobs.

Class 3. Jobs for experienced managers.   Sources of applicants in this class include

- *Industry contacts.* Often, the names of individuals throughout the country who are qualified for certain management jobs can be learned, either through published information on their accomplishments, or through underwriting houses, banks, law firms, management consulting firms, or comparable sources. Inquiries may be made of these individuals as to interest, and more direct approaches undertaken if they offer some encouragement.

- *Executive recruiting firms.* Since the early 1960s, many hundreds of firms specializing in executive placement have developed lists of managers with the required qualifications who might be interested in relocating. The cost to the companies using such firms is high—running as high as a full year's salary for an applicant who is placed as a consequence of the service.
- *Display advertising.* Publications specializing in financial news—*The Wall Street Journal* in particular—are serving as clearing houses for executive talent via display advertisements. These advertisements are inserted either by the firms seeking managers or by managers looking for a change in jobs.
- *Second career people and "40 plus" associations.* Many people, particularly government employees, find themselves retired from their first jobs with many productive years remaining. Other competent managers, for a wide variety of personal reasons, find themselves embarking on second careers. Both of these categories represent excellent sources of mature, seasoned executives.

MANPOWER SELECTION

The recruitment process is intended to produce enough applicants for job openings to permit differentiation between those who appear to have the necessary qualifications and those who do not. The word "appear" is used because, despite the diligence with which the selection process is conducted, the job performance of applicants chosen for employment cannot be known before they begin work.

Validity of the Selection Process

Only after the applicant's actual performance in the job has occurred can the validity of the selection process be known. In many cases, it can be several years before that actual performance has reached the proper level. Selection techniques can be considered valid if employees who were hired on the basis of predictions that they would do well on the job in fact do well. The selection process can also be considered valid if applicants it predicted would not do well on the job in fact did not do well. This assumes that the signs predicting poor performance were ignored and the applicants were hired anyway.

Preliminary Screening

Typically, the preliminary screening of applicants is done by the personnel department. The final choice among qualified applicants is usually made by the immediate supervisor of the vacant job.

The screening procedure will vary according to the level of jobs for which applicants are being considered. Usually, the first step is to let the applicants know something about the particular job for which they are applying. At this point, some applicants will automatically remove themselves from further consideration because they are not interested in the job or are obviously not qualified.

Next, most companies will request that applicants complete application forms. These forms vary in the extensiveness of the information requested, but usually the information asked for includes name, address, phone number, physical characteristics, work experience, and education. Generally, different application forms will be used for higher-level jobs than for those at the lower grades. A practice being used by many firms is to have a short form filled out at the preliminary stage, followed by a more comprehensive form later, if mutual interest toward employment develops between the company and the applicant.

Care must be exercised to insure that information requested in the application form is critical to job performance and that the requested information does not violate current antidiscrimination laws and regulations.

Courtesy toward job applicants is an accepted standard by most companies, so the completion of the application form is almost always followed by an interview. These interviews are customarily conducted by the personnel department in the preliminary screening, and some applicants will be weeded out at this stage because of readily apparent deficiencies in qualifications. Again, courtesy requires that applicants be told, tactfully, the reason for their rejection. Implicit in continuing the selection process, or stopping it at the initial interview, is the understanding that the information contained on the application form and supplemented in the interview is in some degree predictive of success on

The Wizard Of Id by permission of Johnny Hart and Field Enterprises, Inc.

the job. Applicants who are not rejected at this stage are almost invariably referred to the departments with the job opening for which they are applying.

Subsequent Screening: "The" Interview

For lower-level jobs, a second interview conducted by the person under whom the applicants would work if employed often terminates the selection process; that is, an employment agreement is either reached or it is not. However, even for lower-grade jobs, psychological testing, physical testing, and reference checking are sometimes used to reinforce what is decided in the interview. In addition to these testing and checking techniques, the number and comprehensiveness of interviews tends to increase as the job grade for which the applicant is being considered rises in importance. Thus, an applicant might be (1) given a series of interviews by superiors on successively higher levels; (2) interviewed by a group of potential superiors together; or (3) asked to talk with potential peers, either individually or in groups. It should be clear by now that the interview is a vital part of the selection process.

Interviewing methods. Probably the most important requirement for effective interviewing is a plan. In other words, random conversation will not produce much in the way of benefits for either the interviewer or interviewee. The plan must start with objectives, which are usually twofold. The plan should be designed to

- Find out more about the applicant's qualifications than has been revealed thus far.
- Convince a promising applicant that the employment opportunity under discussion is better than others that may be available.

Accomplishing both objectives in the same interview requires considerable skill, regardless of the interview technique used.

Among the interviewing techniques that have been devised, the "patterned" interview has become widely accepted. Patterned interviews are conducted by asking the applicant questions contained on forms and summarizing the applicant's answers after the questions. Forms vary for different jobs, but all applicants for the same job are asked identical questions. Consistency is the outstanding advantage of this method because all applicants are evaluated on the basis of the same criteria. Although patterned interviews are not guaranteed predictors of job performance, they are particularly useful where consistency in information and comparison among many different applicants is required.

The nondirective interview involves asking broad questions which permit applicants to carry the response in the directions they prefer. Nondirective interviews allow the interviewer to discover some of the "real" thoughts of applicants rather than their "proper" responses to predetermined questions. The nondirective interview may be useful in predicting job performance where the prospective employee would have considerable autonomy or where there will be a great deal of verbal exchange with clients or the public.

The "stress" interview is designed to test the applicant's tolerance for unpleasantness, nonroutine situations, and threats to personal defenses. Some jobs involve a high order of these variables, and the stress interview is intended to predict how well the applicant is able to cope with them. For example, applicants for selling jobs may be deliberately insulted and otherwise treated rudely in an attempt to learn their tolerance for this kind of behavior. Stress interviews have a low validity in predicting job performance, and, generally, have fallen into disuse in industry.

Interviewing mistakes and pitfalls. A common misconception is that interviewing skill comes naturally to people, but the fact is that it requires intensive training. Personnel department specialists usually have developed their skills so that they can predict an applicant's success or failure on a job with a fair degree of accuracy. The problem is that managers who are not trained in interviewing must usually make the final decision concerning selection or rejection of applicants. "Don'ts" of interviewing include the following practices:

- *Unplanned interviews.* Often the inexperienced interviewer will do most of the talking, and when realizing at the interview's conclusion that very little information has been learned about the applicant, will make a snap judgment from some superficial bit of evidence.
- *Basing judgments on stereotypes.* The tendency in some people to base judgments on stereotypes leads to many selection errors. Stereotypes are fixed assumptions which people develop about the characteristics of individuals of certain appearance or background. To make selection decisions according to these assumptions is morally unjust and rationally insupportable. In fact, such decisions can prove to be a waste of the firm's resources.
- *Placing undue emphasis on one characteristic.* Untrained interviewers tend to be influenced by the "halo effect;" that is, if one of the applicant's characteristics is liked or disliked, all other characteristics will be judged on the basis of that feature. For example, some managers find it difficult to evaluate fairly those applicants who happened to graduate from the school they attended.

Other Screening Techniques

A physical examination is often required of applicants, both to assure that they are physically capable of doing the work, and to preclude persons with chronic ailments from being potential financial burdens to the company. Reference checking is another highly important selection technique.

Checking references. Certainly past employers constitute a prime source of information about applicants who have a previous work history. An easy way to utilize this source is to mail a standard form, requesting that criteria such as industriousness, loyalty, and initiative be graded. These forms are of relatively doubtful value, however, because past employers usually will not give a bad written referral to any but the most derelict of employees. Somewhat more useful is a request from past employers for letters describing the applicant's attributes and weaknesses. This technique develops more specific information than a checked-off form. However, it still requires that negative judgments about the applicant be put in writing. A third alternative, which can be productive, is to call past employers by telephone to learn their opinions of an applicant. Finally, face-to-face discussions with past employers tend to yield the most candid appraisals of the applicant's performance, and may be among the best predictors of the way an applicant will perform on the job if hired.

In addition to past employers, former teachers and work peers or subordinates can provide illuminating information about job applicants. Here, also, face-to-face communication produces the best results but is not often feasible.

Personal references listed by the applicant are of questionable value except to affirm the applicant's good points, because a person would be foolish to name as a reference someone who would stress, or even point out, negative characteristics.

DISCUSSION QUESTIONS

1. Should manpower planning be performed in small businesses?
2. Locate an employment advertisement in your local paper. What sort of applicant is being solicited? How effective do you believe the ad to be?
3. Suppose you were assigned the task of designing a patterned interview for applicants for the position of manager of a medium-sized ice cream parlor. What questions would you ask and why?
4. Referring to question 3, would you recommend using a patterned interview? Why?

BIBLIOGRAPHY

Churchill, Neil C. and John K. Shank. "Affirmative Action and Guilt-Edged Goals." *Harvard Business Review*, Vol. 54 No. 2 (March–April, 1976), pp. 111–16.

French, Wendell. *The Personnel Management Process.* Boston: Houghton Mifflin Co., 1970.

Patten, Thomas H., Jr. *Manpower Planning and the Development of Human Resources.* New York: John Wiley and Sons, 1972.

The Case of the Defensive Defense Contractor and the Pitiful Pawn

It was in the early 1960s that Dr. Charles Lane, planning director for Spacetech, made his plea for a relaxation in the manpower ceilings before the top managers of the company and their staffs. The main thrust of his address was as follows:

"In summary, my warning is that unless Spacetech drastically increases its ability to apply direct labor hours, particularly engineering, according to our proposal schedules, we are going to lose out in the race for the weapons contracts coming up. On some of our present contracts we have charged only 50 percent of the engineering manhours that we said we would have committed by this date. We have promised the customer for so long that the big surge in our engineering effort is just ahead of us, that the government negotiators are beginning to joke about it. I can see the space weapons business booming for at least the next ten years, but we are not going to get our share unless we double the number of engineers that we now have on board."

Ralph Stevens, engineering vice-president, led the applause that followed Lane's somewhat emotional presentation. "What I urge," Stevens said, "is that we start building an inventory of engineers, so that when we submit a proposal we can actually identify the technical people who would work on the project by name and badge number. There is no question that the Department of Defense is committed to a long-term program of building and improving the nation's space weapons arsenal, and we simply must get ready for it."

The vice-president and general man-ager of Spacetech, Dr. Lloyd Allison, looked quizzically around the room before quietly commenting: "It appears that my manpower ceilings are not as popular as they might be. However, I am not nearly as confident as the rest of you seem to be that the government will, or can, continue the present rate of defense spending much longer. Does anyone else have anything to say?"

Bob Blake, personnel director, got to his feet. "Forecasting defense spending is not a strength of mine, as it is Dr. Lane's, so I won't attempt to differ with him. I do know this, however, that if we expand our personnel base and the defense contract well does dry up, we are going to cause some human suffering. In our relatively isolated location, we will have to import any additional engineers that we hire from other parts of the country. Suppose that they go to all of the stress and expense of moving, then after a year or two we have to lay them off. They can't get any other job in this area, and will have to move again, with probably a house to sell. Let me ask Don Hyde, our professional recruitment manager, what he thinks."

Hyde had prepared some statistics in case he was asked to talk. "Like Mr. Blake," he began, "I don't know how long these weapons contracts are going to go on. I am familiar with the supply of engineers in this country right now, and it is unbelievably tight. Dr. Lane suggests that we double our present number of engineers, which is approximately 400. There is no way that I can conceive of getting 400 qualified people in the foreseeable future. I will stick my neck way out and say that we can have a net increase of 100 engineers in eighteen months, if we are willing to incur any expense in order to obtain them."

Dr. Allison studied the flip charts arrayed along the walls of the room showing manpower assignments to existing contracts and to proposal efforts, as well as Dr. Lane's projections of future requirements. Somewhat reluctantly he finally said, "I am willing to authorize requisitions for 100 additional engineers, as well as requisitions for 100 positions in other job classifications. Before any of you start complaining that this isn't enough, let me advise you that I would feel a lot more comfortable if I could predict job security for the bulk of the people already employed by Spacetech."

• • • • •

The following is taken from the exit interview with Jim Wilson, one of the eighty-seven engineers hired by Spacetech recruiters between the time of Dr. Allison's opening of the additional engineering requisitions and the time, fifteen months later, when he cancelled the remaining unfilled positions.

"Getting my layoff notice didn't come as a surprise, but what makes me sick is the five years of my life that I literally wasted at Spacetech," was Wilson's opening remark as he took a seat in Tom Trump's small interviewing cubicle.

Tom answered sympathetically, "We have talked together several times since you have been here, Jim, and I think I know how you feel. Dr. Allison knows generally what the conditions have been like at Spacetech over the last five years, but he would like to give each person who has to be laid off an opportunity to express his personal feelings. Please believe that anything that you tell me will be reported anonymously."

"Well, at least it will give me a chance to get some things off my chest," Jim began. "Would you believe that when I got here in 1963 there were already rumors about impending layoffs. This really startled me, particularly when I found out that I hadn't been hired for any specific job. I was assigned to a section in the engineering controls department, but the section supervisor told me that he was so busy personally doing engineering work on a contract that was having slipped schedule and overrun costs that he couldn't take the time to train me. He suggested that I read the contract work statement and the proposal and acquaint myself with what was going on. I read these documents so many times that I almost memorized them, and finally in desperation began to spend my days in the company library, reading anything that happened to interest me. This went on for about six months before I got any kind of a job assignment. By this time I knew I had made a mistake signing on."

Tom said, "If there were layoff rumors, and you didn't like not having definite work to do, why didn't you either complain or look for another job?"

Jim flushed slightly, "I guess I have to admit that it was the money—about $250 a month more than I had been making. But, to go on, my first work assignment was on a new proposal. I was given the job of estimating part of the engineering costs."

Tom commented, "I've often wondered how you, as an engineer, ever got into cost work."

"Of course this is one of the things that gripes me," Jim replied. "As long as I have been here I have never done any real engineering. The proposal got me typed as a cost man. When we negotiated the contract I went on the project to work on the budget. Then the company layoffs really started, but I had a secure job as long as the project lasted, and finally became cost supervisor. Now the contract is finished and I am laid off. I have a house to sell, and I have been out of engineering for so long I'm obsolete. And in nondefense companies, they want accountants for cost work, not engineers."

"Forgive me for saying this, Jim," Tom said, "but I can't help wondering how many of your present problems you could have avoided by looking to the obvious future, and doing some good, sound reasoning of your own."

DISCUSSION QUESTIONS

Reference Case A. The Case of the Markets That Will Fade Away (Chapter 8)

1. In Reference Case A, what is a formidable manpower planning problem?
2. In the Case of the Defensive Defense Contractor and the Pitiful Pawn, what example do the remarks of Lane and Stevens provide of an engineering approach to manpower planning?
3. Unemployment resulting from curtailed defense spending is a problem in the United States. Could not Spacetech, and actual aerospace companies, have foreseen the decrease in defense contracts?
4. Other than the miscalculation of the defense contract market, what was a major mistake in Spacetech's manpower planning?
5. Spacetech's manpower planning was obviously deficient. But what about the personal planning of the engineers who were hired, if Jim Wilson is a typical example?

18 Performance Appraisal, Training, and Development

A significant portion of a manager's staffing responsibilities involves efforts to improve the job performance of people within the organization. To achieve improved levels of performance, managers must make judgments about the desired quality of job performance. Where performance is not up to a desired level, action should be initiated which helps organization members improve their job performance.

The chapter first discusses performance appraisal. This process is designed to help managers identify areas where job performance of subordinates is less than ideal. The latter parts of the chapter deal with training and development. These two activities are designed to bring actual organizational performance in line with desired levels of performance.

PERFORMANCE APPRAISAL

Very likely, the performance by individuals of their assigned duties has been appraised by supervisors since the beginning of any form of organized activity. When performance can be measured in numerical terms, such as length of ditch dug in a day, it is easy to evaluate. Assessment of nonquantitative performance, on the other hand, has always posed a problem.

Historically, evaluation of nonquantitative performance was made on the basis of overall impressions, scaled into relative degrees of good or bad. Efforts have been under way—dating back to about World War I—to reduce the subjectivity of such performance appraisals through the development of techniques that apply numerical measurement to components of the performance. The resulting techniques—still largely unsatisfactory—differentiate individual performance by developing a method to "score" individuals on the performance of job components. These "scoring" techniques are examined below.

Appraisal Techniques

Determination of scores has varied with the appraisal technique used. Some of the most widely used appraisal techniques include the graphic rating scale, rank order, critical incident, and forced-choice methods.

Graphic rating scale. One of the oldest appraisal methods, and the most frequently used, employs the graphic rating scale. The essentials of this technique include a list of traits or characteristics that are deemed important to job performance. Categories commonly found on appraisal forms include quality of work, quantity of work, dependability, initiative, and cooperation. Descriptions of gradations of each characteristic are also provided on the form, ranging from various synonyms for outstanding to terse euphemisms for poor. A certain number of points is established for each gradation of each trait. In using the form, the appraiser considers the performance of the subordinate relative to each trait, and decides on the proper gradation. The sum of the points given for the various traits becomes the total score of the individual being appraised. For example, suppose employee A was being appraised and the scale of excellent to poor for each characteristic ranged from 10 to 1. Employee A's manager felt that A's quality of work was pretty good, so the manager gave A an 8 for that. However, A does not produce as much as the others, so a 4 goes in the "quantity of work" category. Similar ratings of each trait are made and employee A's overall rating is simply the sum of the numerical ratings in each trait.

Rank order. Like the graphic rating scale, the rank order method also involves rating employees according to characteristics of performance, but here all employees in a given job classification are rated against each other. The employee showing the best performance in any category is given a score equal to the number of employees being rated. The others receive successively lower scores according to their relative performance. From this analysis in each category, the appraiser is able to develop a total score for each person. For example, in the rating of five customer service employees on the basis of such characteristics as quality of work, quantity of work, dependability, and customer contacts, the appraiser would rank each person from 1 to 5 for each characteristic, and then add the individuals' scores in all categories to determine their standings.

Critical incident. The critical incident method departs from characteristics of performance, in that the manager keeps a record of extreme impressions formed of each subordinate over some past period. Both unusually good and unusually bad impressions are recorded. This

Appraisal of *what* Performance?

In order for performance appraisal to be effective for coaching, teaching, and changing those aspects of an employee's behavior that are amenable to change, an employee needs to know about each piece of behavior that is good, as well as that which for some reason is not acceptable or needs modification. Such incidents will occur randomly and be judged randomly by his manager.

So that there will be useful data, the manager needs to quickly write down what he has said to the subordinate, describing in a paragraph what the subordinate did or did not do, in what setting, under what circumstances, about what problem. This information forms a *behavioral* record, a critical incident report of which the subordinate already has been informed and which is now in his folder, open to his review.

This critical incident technique is not new. In the past it has been used largely for case illustrations and, in modified forms, has been suggested as a method for first-level supervisors to evaluate line employees. Supervisors already record negative incidents concerning line employees because warnings and disciplinary steps must be documented. However, efforts to develop scales from critical incidents for rating behavior have not worked well. Behavior is too complex to be scaled along a few dimensions and then rated.

But instead of scaling behavior, one might directly record the behavior of those being appraised, and evaluate it at a later date. There are other good reasons for adopting this technique as well. At last, here is a process that provides data to help managers perform the basic functions of performance appraisal systems—namely, provide feedback, coaching, and promotion data. Another plus is that recorded data live longer than the manager recording them.

Examples of critical incidents

On May 15, the director of manufacturing, together with the president of the union, met with a group of shop stewards and the international business agent who were irate about the temporary 10% cutback in working hours. The cutback had been prematurely announced by corporate personnel without local consultation. The director of manufacturing heard them out, did not get hot under the collar about their tirade, and then explained the need to use up inventories. By reassuring them of the company's true intention, the director of manufacturing reduced tension in the plants.

Executive Vice President

The director of manufacturing and I met today (August 13th) to review his development plans for his subordinates. While these are broadly defined on paper, the director does not hear enough from his subordinates about *their* objectives or ask enough about what *they* are up against. He is impatient with this aspect of his responsibility. I suggested that he allot regular meeting times for such discussions and take more time to listen. He agreed to do so.

Executive Vice President

---

method does not involve totalling a score, but presumably a preponderance of either favorable or unfavorable incidents leads to some overall impression.

Forced choice. Although the forced-choice method is not widely used, proponents urge that it has significant advantages. The appraisal form consists of four sets of statements. The appraiser does not know the value assigned to any of the statements, but is asked to check the statement in each set that best describes the individual being evaluated, plus the description that is least appropriate. Some of the statements have good connotations; others, bad; and a scored evaluation can be developed after the appraisal checks have been entered on the form. It should be noted that forced choice is rarely used due to the difficulty and expense of developing valid scales specific to a particular job and company.

Use of Performance Appraisals

Most companies that employ formal appraisal methods require periodic performance interviews. Ideally, in these interviews the supervisor carefully reviews each appraisal statement with the individual concerned. Again ideally, the scene involves the wise and patient supervisor not only counseling the attentive and earnest subordinate on correcting deficiencies, but also stressing competencies and offering encouragement concerning advancement. From most reports, however, the situation rarely is so constructive. For one thing, neither supervisor nor subordinate has much confidence in any of the appraisal methods that have been described. All of the methods we've described lack objective standards against which performance can be compared.

The typical performance interview is characterized by a supervisor who feels embarrassed and defensive because the appraisal cannot be backed up if challenged, and a subordinate who feels resentful of the vagueness and subjectiveness of the appraisal. The subordinate may also feel indignant at being appraised by a person perceived to be quite fallible.

Often the performance interview will culminate with the supervisor identifying the amount of the merit increase that the subordinate will receive for the next period. In many cases, this is all that makes the experience palatable to the subordinate, and the typical interview ends with both parties being glad that it is over.

The director of industrial relations for a large aerospace company reported that over a twenty-year period his company had gone full circle in the types of appraisal systems used. The firm started with the graphic rating scale, then abandoned it in favor of rank order, next tried critical incident, went next to forced choice, and finally readopted the rating scale. According to this senior manager, none of the methods tried were satisfactory, but the rating scale method was being readopted because company directors felt an appraisal system was needed, and the graphic rating scale technique was the easiest to administer.

Shortcomings of Appraisal Techniques

While the appraisal techniques that have been described share some deficiencies they each have some unique shortcomings as well.

The graphic rating technique sums scores over a series of traits to determine an overall individual rating. In this process, an individual's strengths tend to balance out weaker areas. As a consequence it does not reflect the different degree of importance a particular characteristic may have for good job performance. For example, punctuality may not be as critical as initiative in evaluating the performance of a person in sales. Or quality of work might be relatively more important than quantity for a medical technician or physician.

The rank order procedure compares subordinates on the same scale. The shortcoming inherent to this procedure is that even the best job performance among the group may not be as good as it should be. Even if no one in the group is performing at a satisfactory level of output, someone will get the top rating possible in that category using the rank order method.

The critical incident method requires the manager to keep a current written record of events. This task can have a very low priority in the rush of a day's activities and would be easy to defer. As a consequence, the number of critical incidents in a person's dossier will reflect, in part, how busy the manager was when potentially notable incidents occur. If incidents are not noted and recorded soon after they occur, the manager will be required to recall incidents from memory. All of the pitfalls and subtle changes that the passage of time imparts to our memory of events are introduced when this occurs.

All of the techniques share the potential problems of a halo effect, of personality and performance, and of variation among evaluations. The halo effect refers to the unconscious tendency to rate a person in all categories in a way similar to the person's strong rating in any single category. For example, suppose a manager prefers highly-cooperative subordinates. When the halo effect is operating, individuals who are judged high on that dimension will tend to be judged high on other dimensions, such as quality of work regardless of the real quality of performance. Similarly, an uncooperative employee's quality of work might be judged inappropriately low.

The tendency to appraise personality traits, rather than job performance is inherent in the various techniques. In many cases, it is difficult to separate the two. Some people are simply not geared to being on time, so punctuality on the job may not be high. Dependability is a characteristic which can describe both job performance and personality.

When using these techniques to judge subordinates' job performance, the unique preferences and personality of the manager will be involved. Where an individual might be rated high by one manager, a low rating might be awarded by another. This "rater" bias is a serious shortcoming shared by all the evaluation techniques.

Methods Under Development

There are new methods of performance appraisal that are still in the development stage. Let's examine some of them.

Peer rating. One method that has been used extensively in military organizations, and which is now being experimented with by some business firms, is peer rating, or sometimes called "buddy" rating. As the name implies, in this system all members of a group with equal status evaluate each other. So far, the value of peer rating seems to be restricted to identifying potential leaders; this is a benefit not to be lightly regarded. Leadership is an important characteristic of successful managers, and if individuals who have this capacity can be discovered early in their careers and provided with management experience, the future supply of qualified managers will probably be increased.

Appraisal by specialists. Apart from some inherent weaknesses in the conventional appraisal methods, an additional problem in making them effective is that most managers are not well trained in using them. A relatively new approach being taken by some companies is to have appraisal specialists from the personnel department or from outside the firm gather information on the performance of individuals in all departments. These specialists compile the information through patterned interviews with each employee's superior, peers, and sometimes subordinates. They then prepare an appraisal, usually of the graphic rating scale type, and have it approved by the superior of the respective subordinates.

Appraisal within management by objectives. A concept that is partially an appraisal system, but primarily a view on how to perform the managerial function of leading, is management by objectives (MBO), or results-centered management. MBO is described in more detail in Chapter 24, "Organizational Development." However, some MBO characteristics are relevant to the present discussion. MBO encourages subordinates to decide upon goals to be accomplished over some future time period, (subject to their superior's agreement that the goals are appropriate). At the end of the period, the superior and subordinate assess the degree to which the goals have been reached. Thus, MBO includes a built-in method for performance appraisal.

EMPLOYEE TRAINING

The skill level of new employees hired into a business organization will vary from virtually none at all, to a high degree of occupational competence. Individuals in the first category obviously must be taught some rudimentary skills, otherwise they would have no productive value to the firm. Individuals at the opposite extreme of initial capability, and at all gradations of skills between, should have opportunities to upgrade their capacities in order to satisfy their personal needs for growth, to keep abreast of new information and changing technology, and to provide a pool of steadily improving workers upon which the company can rely in moving toward its objectives. For these reasons, the role of formal training programs within industry is growing in importance.

Getting Started

If a firm has constructed a comprehensive manpower plan, this document would be the starting place for designing a training program. It would detail the kinds and quantities of skills needed at stated times in the future, plus an inventory of skills possessed by workers currently employed. An analysis of these categories of information would identify the required scope of the training program. However, most companies do not have manpower plans that have been developed in such depth.

An alternative method for determining training needs, and the programs to satisfy them, is through initiation by top management. After an analysis of performance records, perception of skill deficiencies in the labor force, and observation of training programs adopted by other companies, senior managers may recognize the need for formal training opportunities, and put the mechanism into action via policies, appointments, and budgets. Recognition of a need for training may also occur at the foreman or supervisor level. These managers may be frustrated by their inability to meet performance standards with the level of skill that their workers possess, and will communicate recommendations for formal training upward until they reach a management level at which positive action is taken. Others who may recognize the need for upgrading workers' skills may be specialists in the personnel department. Their inability to recruit applicants with required qualifications will be a strong factor pushing them to urge for a comprehensive program of skill training.

An essential first step, and one that is, surprisingly enough, not always taken, is to identify the specific goals of a training course. Designers should also provide a method to validate goal achievement. For example, assume that a course in welding is being considered. Before the course is started, it might be established that the criterion for measuring the effectiveness of the course is that all persons completing it be capable of performing three-position welding in accordance with specifications.

Training Methods

Probably all business firms, large or small, rely most heavily on on-the-job training. Sometimes an experienced worker is assigned the duty of teaching a newcomer; at other times, the foreman or supervisor takes responsibility for on-the-job training. Such training may advance the new worker to the stage of adequate performance, but because the training is usually unplanned, it may result in significant voids in the trainee's preparation.

An opposite approach is to use formal classroom teaching methods. With this approach, considerably more of the theory underlying the optimal performance of various jobs can be imparted to the trainee. To be effective, however, this method must provide for the theory to be supplemented by practical experience under simulated work conditions.

A relatively new technique for classroom instruction is *programmed instruction*, often used with a teaching machine. The technique involves organizing course subject matter into a sequence of dependent steps. Material in each step, which may be in the form of narrative, graph, or formula, is printed on a frame, and all the frames together make up the program. To describe the principle simply, the trainee digests the material frame by frame. To progress from one frame to another, the trainee must correctly answer a question concerning the preceding frame. In case of a wrong answer, advice may be given to go back and review material in earlier frames.

A balanced training approach would combine on-the-job training with formal classroom instruction. Many of the apprenticeship programs leading to journeyman status in a craft or trade now incorporate the two methods, and the practice seems to be followed in less formal training programs as well, such as short-term training in a specific skill.

The trainee's desire to learn is essential if any training is to be effective. And if trainees are going to want to learn, they must see that they will benefit from the training. In some cases, tangible benefits, such as promotions or raises immediately following completion of some specific training, provide the incentive. In other cases, the only immediate tangible reward might be a certificate of completion. However, if the trainees perceive that the certificates will lead to more money or higher status in the long run, they can be effective incentives. Success is another powerful motivator. If the trainees' confidence in their ability to complete a training course is periodically reinforced, they will be much more inclined to stick with it until completion than if they perceive themselves as failing. Therefore, training must be organized so that the trainees can perceive incremental progress.

MANAGEMENT DEVELOPMENT

Up until as late as the first years after World War II, few U.S. business organizations were involved in planned efforts to develop managers. This absence of management development programs suggests that either managerial ability was considered a talent that certain individuals were born with; or that the task of developing such programs appeared to be too awesome a challenge. However, the situation has definitely changed since the early 1950s. Today all but a few of the companies beyond those of simple scale have some kind of program for management development.

Despite this emphasis on management development, there are too few well-planned, systematic programs. Indeed, the current popularity of the notion of "management development" has led many companies to randomly adopt unintegrated courses, so-called packaged training programs, and out-and-out gimmicks, all in the mistaken belief that they will "train" managers. A better understanding of the complexities of developing managers is needed before programs are undertaken if real, tangible benefits are to be gained.

It is important to distinguish development and training. Skill training implies teaching, in accord with known principles, how to do some technical tasks that require determinate physical and/or mental effort. Training can be undertaken with good reason to believe it will be successful. Management ability, on the other hand, being in large part an art, cannot be taught with the same predictive success. Potential managers can be exposed to the existing body of knowledge about management, as summarized in this book, but this exposure will not insure they will be successful managers. However, with this knowledge and sufficient motivation and judgment, they may grow to be successful managers, particularly if they are provided successive management experiences. This is the way management development should be viewed; any notion that people can be trained to be managers is oversimplified and in many ways misleading.

Development Opportunities

It should be recognized that there are gradations of management jobs within an organization which, for the sake of simplicity, can be categorized by levels—supervisory, middle management, and top management. In order to survive, every organization must assure that there is continuous accession of qualified individuals to each level. However, the required qualifications at the successive levels will differ; therefore, the developmental experiences must also differ.

Supervisory positions. It may be presumed that individuals being groomed for positions at the supervisory level have had no previous management experience. They will tend to come from two sources—either technical jobs within the organization, or college campuses. The former will know something about the company, but together with the recent graduates, they will need to learn the details of company policies and procedures regarding personnel, budgeting, scheduling, and other matters. These policies and procedures can be taught via classroom instruction, reading assignments, and instruction provided by the candidates' supervisors.

The next step should be to gradually expose the candidates to management problems, and permit them to participate in their solution. This experience could be gained by assigning the candidates to the role of "assistants to" their immediate supervisors. At this stage some candidates will find that management is not to their liking and disqualify themselves. Others will be disqualified because of lack of potential not apparent to them. The remainder will succeed to their supervisor's job, or some other job at a comparable level, when an opening occurs and their performance indicates that they are ready for such responsibility. The experience that first-level supervisors gain is primarily in directing technical workers, making routine decisions within the framework of procedures, and facing the sobering results of mistakes in judgment.

Middle-management positions. Opportunities for experience in middle-management jobs are usually reserved for individuals who have demonstrated managerial competence at the supervisory level. By this time, they will be familiar with the routines of the company's operation, but will need closer acquaintance with its objectives and policies. In addition, they will need to acquire a broad view of management theory. The first requirement is usually fulfilled with instruction by the managers immediately above them—to whom, in their first exposure to middle-management responsibilities, they will likely be assistants. The broadening of these employees' theoretical knowledge of management is facilitated by university programs geared to the development of managers, by conference programs offering more condensed instruction, and by courses sponsored by the company itself. The experience that individuals gain in middle-management positions includes leading subordinate managers, pooling judgment and authority with peers in arriving at group decisions, and participating in setting goals, along with guides for implementing them. It is becoming increasingly popular to rotate middle managers from job to job in order to broaden their experience.

Top-management positions. The criterion for consideration of individuals for top-management posts is almost always singularly impressive performance in middle management. Some outstanding middle managers may have a general management background as a result of job rotation or of experience in product management. More often, however, their experience will tend to be specialized, and what they will need most at the top level is a general management background. Here again, the "assistant to" role can be used to provide this rounding and maturing exposure. In addition, top-level committee appointments and special study assignments can have a broadening effect. Assignments in which the individual is put in contact with systems external to the firm, such as government, labor unions, the public at large, or potential foreign markets, are also of substantial benefit. And finally, many university programs, some lasting as long as a year, are especially adapted to providing managers headed for the top echelons with a broad theoretical base in both management and cultural subjects, and are well suited to supplementing the planned management experience.

Cost-Benefit of Training and Development Programs

Like other decisions to commit organization resources, the decision to engage in employee training or management development should follow a cost-benefit comparison. Costs of such programs will vary as will the time commitment involved. If internal training and development resources are to be established, more time will need to be committed than if external trainers or development consultants are utilized. The costs of not having the employee on the job during training sessions will also need to be included.

On the benefit side, the full results are less easily put in dollar terms. Increases in productivity should follow successful efforts; reduced recruiting expenses should result from a well-trained pool of human resources in the firm. Employees' general attitude toward their jobs and the organization may improve and reduce turnover and absenteeism costs. It has been suggested that training costs be treated conceptually as investments and that decisions about alternative investments of an organization's financial resources reflect that view.

DISCUSSION QUESTIONS

1. Develop either a graphic rating or rank ordering scale that you believe would form an accurate appraisal of performance in this course. Discuss the benefits and shortcomings you see.
2. Discuss the ways that the performance appraisal process is importantly different in an MBO context as compared to the other techniques described in the text.
3. Describe the circumstances that might lead individuals to decide that a managerial career is an inappropriate one.
4. What problems may develop when an experienced manager is assigned to train a newcomer?
5. What obstacles, psychological and otherwise, might a company encounter in an attempt to retrain employees whose skills have become technologically obsolete?

BIBLIOGRAPHY

Beer, Michael and Robert A. Ruh. "Employee Growth Through Performance Management." *Harvard Business Review,* Vol. 54 No. 4 (July–August 1976), pp. 59–66.

Blum, M. and J. Naylor. *Industrial Psychology, Its Theoretical and Social Foundations.* New York: Holt, Rinehart, and Winston, 1962.

Cummings, L. L. and D. P. Schwab. *Performance in Organizations: Determinants and Appraisal.* Glenview: Scott, Foresman and Co., 1973.

Levinson, Harry. "Appraisal of *What* Performance." *Harvard Business Review,* Vol. 54 No. 4 (July–August 1976), p. 30.

Miner, John B. and Mary Green Miner. *Personnel and Industrial Relations: A Managerial Approach,* 2nd ed. New York: Macmillan, 1973.

Patten, Thomas H. Jr. *Manpower Planning and the Development of Human Resources.* New York: John Wiley and Sons, 1972.

The Case of Four Roads to the Top

It was the evening of the bimonthly dinner meeting of the presidents of the member stores of International Department Stores, Inc. As was their custom on these occasions, four of the executives who had become fast friends over the years met for cocktails in one of their hotel suites before joining the other officers at dinner.

"I have a problem at my store which is not a new one, and I am sure that it is shared by the rest of you," said John Hopkins, president of Hunt-Marshal. "That is, how to develop qualified managers. We have two stores now, and a third one under construction, and we badly need managers at all organizational levels. I have tried pirating good ones from our competitors, but they simply reciprocate by pirating from us. We have experimented with various kinds of management development programs, but with indifferent success. What does it take to develop good managers?"

"You're right, it is one of our most difficult problems," answered George Moranian, president of Huntley Brothers, Inc. "But I have an idea of something that we can talk about while we are enjoying our drinks. Suppose each of us tells the others the steps that he took on the road to the top job in his company. John, since you brought up the question, perhaps you would like to start."

"Well, I got out of college in 1940. Hunt-Marshal had what they called a management training program, and I was hired for it along with five other new college graduates. The philosophy of the company at that time was that management trainees should have the experi-

ence of working at the lowest jobs in the store before very gradually moving up. I suppose the vague objective was to expose the trainees intimately to every activity in the company. Anyhow, my first assignment was unpacking dishes. I suppose there is some value in knowing how to unpack dishes, but the knowledge can be learned in a day. I was kept on this task for over three months. After numerous complaints, I was transferred to men's suits. There my training consisted of assuring that suits in different sizes were carefully segregated. After two months of this, I was about to quit the company, as three of the other trainees had already done, but I got drafted into the Army. When the war was over, I told the people at Hunt-Marshal that there was only one job that I would take, and that was selling appliances. I not only sold on the floor during the days, but I followed up prospects by calling at their homes at night. My record was good, and in a year I was made department manager. Within four years I was assistant merchandise manager, and from there became merchandise manager, and so on up. Other than the first abortive training experience, the only company-sponsored development that I had was at some American Management Association Conferences."

"I joined the Navy right out of high school," said George Moranian, "and when my hitch was over I started to work under my father, who was head carpet buyer at Huntley's. I also began to study accounting at night school. My father retired about the time I got my degree, and I moved into his job. I heard about the summer management training program at Stanford, and I asked the then president of the company to send me. About two years after that experience I was asked if I wouldn't like a change from carpets, and was made assistant controller. Next came the controller's job, which carried a vice-presidency, and then finally I became president six years ago."

"I think there was a lot of planning to the trainee program that I got started on," said Richard Johnson, president of Scott-Anderson Company, and the youngest of the four men. "In the first two years after I joined the company out of college, I worked as an assistant to five different buyers. During this time I was really given some responsible assignments. Then I was made buyer for the notions department, which was one of the buyers' jobs reserved exclusively for trainees. The company usually kept a trainee on the buyer's job for about a year, while watching his performance very closely. My next assignment was at the corporate office, where I became involved in appraising European department stores that seemed ripe for acquisition. That was really an interesting job and I hated to leave it after three years, but the people at central headquarters felt that I should have more experience in store operations. I came back to Scott-Anderson as buyer of men's shoes, and in two years was made assistant to the president. Three years on this job led to merchandising manager, and four years later I was made president."

"I think you all know most of the story of my life," said Irving Levine, president of Goldblach-Levine, Inc. "I dropped out

of high school and began selling pots and pans door to door. When the Korean War ended, I opened a war surplus store. This operation did extremely well, and I got three others started. When I saw my sources of supply drying up I took a long trip to Japan and made hundreds of contacts for good, cheap merchandise. I gradually converted my surplus stores to discount houses just when the boom in this kind of merchandising was taking off. Goldblach's had been the principal department store in the area, and was expanding to the suburbs. However, every time they built a department store, I built a discount house close enough to capture the market for low-cost merchandise. Finally Goldblach's decided that I should be on their team, so we merged. I was executive vice-president for a couple of years, and then moved to the top job. I haven't had a day of formal management development in my life, but I feel that a good part of my personal development has been through my interest in the arts."

"Those are certainly four entirely different stories," said John Hopkins. "Dick obviously had the best company guidance, and he has given me the kind of ideas that I was hoping to get. Let me ask you this question, Dick. Would the kind of program that you were on make good managers out of anyone with the normal prerequisites?"

"I saw too many apparently good men who didn't make it to reply yes," Dick answered. "No matter what kind of program that a company sets up for developing managers, the only individuals who will ultimately be able to handle senior managerial responsibilities are those who are more motivated by the drive for success than by anything else."

DISCUSSION QUESTIONS

1. How can you explain the emphasis given by most medium-size and large companies to management development programs?
2. What kind of experiences do you suppose are most valuable in the development of managerial ability?
3. In the Case of Four Roads to the Top, John Hopkins got into management as a result of an outstanding record as a salesperson. What would you think of a company policy requiring that all managerial aspirants prove themselves through outstanding performance in some technical function, such as selling, accounting, or engineering?
4. Apparently, business firms cannot rely on getting good managers by looking for individuals with the "knack" for managing of an Irving Levine. Explain why not.
5. What do you think of Richard Johnson's statement that "drive for success" is the most important quality that managers must have?

19 Human Reactions to Organizational Practices

The final chapter in the staffing section examines two areas that are indirectly related to each other. The first area concerns the managerial issues that arise when people change jobs within the organization. The second area addresses the issues generated when organizational practice is deemed unjust, unethical, illegal, or inefficient by organization members. Both of these areas involve managers in organizational staffing decisions about the members and the reactions of the members to those organizational practices.

CHANGE IN ORGANIZATIONAL ASSIGNMENT

Moves upward, downward, or laterally within the organizational hierarchy are made as a result of a managerial decision to make a change in organizational assignments. Decisions about these kinds of moves will usually be based on job performances judged to be meritorious or deficient or the moves may be made on the basis of seniority in position. Seniority as a basis of deciding changes in assignment is a great deal easier to establish than is merit in job performance.

Promotions

The job changes that are probably the most crucial to the organization are promotions because they provide a significant source of qualified personnel flowing into jobs of ever greater responsibility. Promotions represent significant changes to most qualified people too, since they represent recognition for performance and progress. In addition, promotions usually are accompanied by more tangible rewards such as more pay.

An organization will always seek to staff open, needed positions with the most competent people available. In practice, this means that all promotions should ideally be decided on the basis of merit. It would also be ideal to determine the relative merit of individuals by an analysis of performance appraisal system records. The problem is that weaknesses in the existing appraisal systems make the determination of relative merit difficult. In practice, most managers must proceed to make promotion decisions with the imperfect means they have available.

Many promotion decisions are made more on the basis of seniority than decision makers would prefer. The assumption that length of service is directly related to ability to perform the next higher job is the organization's rationale for these decisions. Clearly this will be true for some jobs and situations. There are also many instances when the relationship does not hold. The most senior foreman may not be the candidate for department manager because different skills, preparation, and behavior may be necessary to succeed. There is only a little better chance that a person's excellent performance at one job in an organization will accurately predict successful performance in the next higher level task in the organization.

Promotions serve a dual function in organizations: They are (1) rewards for outstanding past performance of its members and (2) devices by which vacancies in the hierarchy are filled. These two functions may not be equally served by a single promotion decision. Attempts to utilize the reward function may be perceived as unjust or inappropriate. These issues are discussed in the second section of this chapter. When seniority is the sole criterion used, the promotion decision is easily understood by the employees and very little controversy will be generated. Seniority is obvious and objectively determined. It does not require unsuccessful candidates to accept the idea that someone else *merits* the promotion more than they do.

Whatever the criteria used to make promotion decisions, it is important that they be as explicit as possible. Since selecting one person for promotion will usually also require not selecting other candidates, the manager is faced with a situation in which one person is pleased and several are disappointed by the decision taken. If the decision is deemed a fair one and is understood to have direct impact on organizational well-being and success, the negative consequences of the disappointment will probably be minimized.

Demotions

As with promotions, questions of merit and seniority enter into demotion decisions. When individuals have been assigned to jobs for which they are obviously not qualified, they need to be relocated to a level in the organization where they can perform satisfactorily. It is rare that demotion actions are satisfactory to the person being demoted. If the action is taken unilaterally by the organization, the employee will probably be sufficiently resentful and disgruntled to make job performance at the lower level less than satisfactory. On the other hand, a skilled manager might, through careful counseling, be able to assist the employee in recognizing the futility in pursuing a job that is over the employee's head and the benefits, in terms of self-esteem, which might accrue from a work assignment at a more appropriate level. This counseling process will usually break down when the employee recognizes that compensation will be reduced as well as assignment level.

When a company is forced by economic conditions to cut back its scale of operations, reductions in the size of the work force can be accomplished by releasing the most junior employees and moving others down to lower level positions. Again, the basis for the decisions will be critical; where merit-based decisions are feasible, managers will make them. Where merit distinctions are ill-defined, those individuals with the least seniority will be the ones who are demoted or dismissed.

Terminations

The finality of a termination action may be one of degree, as indicated by the terms discharge and layoff. An employee who is discharged has either been considered to be incompetent in the performance of a job or has seriously violated company rules. The decision to discharge an employee should be faced carefully by the managers involved because of the potentially damaging effects on the individual. Loss of earning power and self-esteem can work severe hardships.

The decision to discharge an employee should be the final act in a series of actions designed to correct the situation. It is unwise to permit infractions to occur repeatedly and then finally and suddenly move to discharge the employee. A discharged employee who is a union member may ask the union to contest the action as unfair, or a discharged union employee may take the case to court. Either action could result in a reversal of a decision to discharge if the firm cannot objectively support it. The problem is aggravated if the discharged employee has had extended service with the firm. Management may be found wanting for failing to detect the basic problem early enough so that corrective action could be undertaken rather than a discharge.

Layoffs are usually made necessary by the contraction of a firm's business. They can be caused by a downturn in economic conditions or may simply be a decision to reduce the scale of operations. Layoffs are often considered temporary, with the laid-off employee expecting to be recalled. Union contract provisions regarding how layoffs are to be handled are usually explicit. Typically, the contracts specify that seniority shall be the single basis for determining who goes last and returns to work first. Given the option, management would prefer to base layoff and recall decisions on merit. Very often, however, management will resort to seniority, even with the merit option available, because of limits in making merit distinctions among several employees.

Lateral Changes

Occasionally people make job transfers in which a lateral move in the organization is made. The transfer may be from one kind of a job to another, with equal pay and status, or may be from one location to another in the same job.

A strong reason for transferring individuals from one job to another, particularly managers, is to broaden their base of experience. Employees who have first-hand experience with a number of different facets of an organization are better able to keep organization-wide benefits a critical element in their decision making. Transfers of these kinds tend to reduce the parochialism in managers' thinking. Such lateral transfers benefit both the employees and the organization.

Employees may not fully appreciate the advantages of lateral transfers. A transfer represents a substantial change in a major element of peoples' lives and an unsolicited transfer may be perceived as a threat, particularly if there are no direct, tangible rewards connected with it. People may have formulated their own ideas about career plans and paths of advancement. Sudden, unanticipated changes in career-path expectations will probably generate resistance. Managers are well advised to engage in constructive counseling with people who may have opportunities to make lateral transfers. Costs and benefits of the proposed move should be openly discussed and objectively evaluated.

Transfers from one geographical location to another in the same job classification are frequently made for the convenience of the company. When a firm's operations are dispersed, the demand for particular job skills will vary over time from place to place in the total organization. Individuals will be transferred to the points where the current demand exists. These transfers can be temporary or permanent in nature. When permanent, employees and their families may resist such moves because they mean uprooting and severing ties with friends, schools, and neighborhoods. Companies with operations requiring frequent location transfers often stress this as something to be expected and tolerated as they interview applicants for employment.

Transfers may also be made with the employees' needs as a primary factor. When people are assigned jobs for which they are not suited, it makes sense to try and effect a transfer to more appropriate kinds of tasks. People and jobs may not match because of over or under qualification, disinterest, or personal, emotional stresses unrelated to the job. If the people involved are judged to have potential value to the firm, efforts will often be made to transfer them to assignments that are more suitable. Sometimes transfers are necessary because of irreconcilable differences among people in a particular location.

The problems associated with the different roles managers must undertake in the staffing process call for the expression of the highest managerial skill. Managers must define the tasks and goals for their organizational units and members. They must also aid members in their efforts to achieve personal and organizational goals. At the same time, it falls to managers to evaluate the performance of their subordinates and provide feedback so that needed improvements can be instituted. Finally, managers must make the staffing decisions about promotion and pay increases based on the data generated in the earlier phases of the process. Shifting from the role of leader and coach to judge and dispenser of rewards is sometimes a difficult transition for managers to make. Some managers have been uncomfortable when faced with these dual responsibilities. They have found it useful to be explicit about which set of roles is operative in meetings with subordinates and not try to do both in the same meeting.

ORGANIZATIONAL JUSTICE

Where the first section of this chapter dealt with the issues managers face in their staffing decisions, this section deals with the organization members' judgments of organizational acts, including pay and promotion decisions. In broad terms, this section deals with the various alternatives that the employee and the organization have when the employee believes the organization has acted in an illegal, immoral, unjust, or simply inefficient way. The issue of social responsibility that organizations owe to external factors is treated in a later chapter. Attention in this section will be directed to the member-organization relationship.

The Constitution and the Bill of Rights define rights available to all citizens of the United States. However, members of U.S. organizations have not had a uniformly accepted set of rights spelled out. Neither have organizational members usually enjoyed the degree of freedom relative to their employing organization as they enjoy as citizens of the U.S. One reason people join trade unions is to gain assurance of fair treatment through collective means when it can not be attained individually. Nonunion employees of business firms have also joined forces to exert leverage for the same level of justice in their job environment as promised by the national social system.

Classification of Rights

The rights that individuals have in their organizational setting can be classified by the nature of the social device supporting and maintaining the right. At one extreme, individuals' rights are determined by the members of the organization itself, in a democratic fashion. These democratically determined rights are constrained only by the limits of the larger social system of which the organization is a part. A second group of rights are established by law and government. Formal constitutions and contracts spell out the boundaries for organizational members. Less formally, some organizations will have formal rules, such as employee handbooks, or informal rules about things employees may and may not do. Usually, rights are classified so that the organization can exercise its authority in determining members' rights and the sanctions to be imposed when the boundary of acceptable behavior is crossed by an employee.

Meanings of Justice

Justice is a concept which has been treated for centuries by philosophers. One idea of justice refers to the fair and impartial distribution of rewards and punishments according to how they are deserved or merited. More precisely, this form of justice is known as "distributive" justice. Distributive justice will often need to be supplemented with "corrective" justice which attempts to reverse errors made as rewards and punishments have been distributed. In most organizations the final authority for distributive decisions rests with the organization. Employee attempts to adjust these decisions give rise to the corrective aspects of justice.

In a business organization, distributive justice is associated with assuring that

- Pay raises, promotions, and other tangible benefits are awarded without discrimination except by supportable merit variations or seniority.
- Differentiated privileges are decided by equitable standards.
- Disciplinary actions are administered impersonally and without bias.

Many of the staffing processes that have been discussed in the preceding chapters are either directly or indirectly intended to assure distributive justice. For example

- Job evaluations are attempts to determine in a fair and just way, the relative worth of different jobs to the organization and to establish compensation scales proportional to their worth.
- Modern selection policies are designed so that relative ability to perform on a job is the only discriminatory factor in choosing among applicants, and so that race, religion, age, or sex are not used as employment factors.
- Training programs are generally open to all employees who are interested in improving their skills in areas related to their jobs, or to jobs that they might hope to be promoted to.

- Performance appraisals are attempts to place an objective value on the worth of individuals to the organization, and to differentiate the compensation and change of status on the basis of worth, except where seniority is an overriding factor.

Other means for assuring justice are the formal rules that specify acceptable conduct and penalties for violations; these are often distributed in booklet form so that all employees may be informed of them. If some of a company's employees are union members, the labor contract will spell out criteria applying to wages, hours, working conditions, change in organizational assignment, and disciplinary action in an attempt to guarantee fair allocations of rewards and penalties to all union members.

Problems in Administration of Justice

Trouble arises in a system of distributive justice primarily because of conflicting opinions on what is fair between the people who make the decisions and the people who are affected by them. The processes designed to assure distributive justice have the appearance of being objective. They are based, however, on human judgment which is fallible and inconsistent.

Human judgment is variable; that is, if only one individual in an organization were administering justice, decisions on a single issue would be inconsistent to some degree from case to case. This inconsistency is compounded when various individuals make independent decisions on the same issue. Inconsistencies are compounded further when there are a variety of issues on which decisions must be made. Thus, justice is usually administered in a variable, rather than constant, way in organizations.

In addition, the recipients of justice have varying perceptions of what is fair and what is unjust. Individuals will be inconsistent in their evaluations of fairness on an issue from case to case. The more people involved, the greater will be the variations in the perceptions about justice that is administered. The differences of opinion on what is fair cannot fail to generate friction. Consider the single issue of merit increases. Assume that Manager A is a "low grader" and regards what would be superior performance to another manager as only average. Moreover, this manager is strongly influenced in evaluating subordinates by their "loyalty," which means their willingness to work overtime, for which they are compensated. Now assume that Manager B tends to be a "high grader," and places top priority on the qualities of punctuality and regular attendance. In this manager's view, if people are never late or absent from work, overtime will not be necessary, and if it is, it is the fault of the workers and they should not be paid for it.

Some subordinates of Manager A will feel unjustly treated because their merit wage increases are low in comparison with their counterparts in the other department. Some of Manager A's other subordinates will not perceive inequity, because to them the overtime pay more than makes up for the merit increase discrepancy. Subordinates of Manager B will show similar variations in their opinions of how they are treated. To some, high performance ratings satisfy both their desire for a little more money and their need for recognition. To others, punctuality and attendance will be shallow criteria for appraisal, and the refusal to pay for overtime work will be perceived as unjust.

Corrective Justice

When the standard procedures and practices have resulted in action deemed unjust by the employee, corrective justice processes can be brought to bear. Our discussion of corrective justice will examine union and nonunion employees separately. Virtually all union contracts specify a formal procedure whereby union employees may file a grievance for alleviation of what they perceive to be unfair treatment. The typical procedure comprises a series of steps that the aggrieved employee and the union representatives may take in the effort to get satisfaction. The steps move the dispute up through the levels of management until it reaches top management (if decisions unsatisfactory to the employee are rendered at the lower levels). However, a decision unacceptable to the employee and the union even at this level does not necessarily end the matter, because the ultimate step is to submit the grievance to arbitration. At this step, an impartial person, or a tripartite board comprised of a union representative, a management representative, and an impartial person acceptable to both union and management, listens to the arguments of both sides, and renders a binding decision.

Surveys indicate that about 50 percent of the medium-sized and large companies in the United States have some kind of formal grievance procedure for unorganized employees. These procedures tend to follow the general lines of those specified in union contracts, although it appears that they offer less protection to the aggrieved employee. For one thing, the nonunion worker is not buttressed by a powerful representative. Second, nonunion grievance procedures restrict the issues that may be presented. Finally, procedures for taking the dispute outside the organizational hierarchy for settlement generally do not exist.

In lieu of formal grievance procedures, most business organizations, at least in theory, provide some means for redress of unfairness. There is the so-called open-door policy, whereby dissatisfied employees may bypass their immediate superior and go to a higher manager to present their case. Many companies provide that serious disciplinary actions must be reviewed by a panel of managers higher in the organization than the manager who meted out the punishment. In addition, there appears to be a trend for firms to offer their personnel departments as places to which an employee who perceives injustice may submit a grievance for impartial review and decision.

There has been an increasing tendency for employees who feel the organization has acted in an unjust manner to turn to agencies outside the organization for redress or correction. In some instances, it has simply been a public statement which describes the corporate act and the person's judgment about it. These appeals to external sources for justice or correction of errors made by the organization have included acts outside the staffing areas discussed above. Employees have been known to tell the press or governmental regulatory agencies about intra-organizational affairs that are deemed unjust. Employees of defense contractors have reported on gross inefficiencies in operations. Leaks of information about activities within government organizations are common. Publicizing organizational activities raises the question of loyalty. And, more specifically, what degree of loyalty can the organization expect and demand? There is a tradition that a good employee is a good team member and as such is expected to keep the organizational dirty linen in the closet. This expectation for loyalty increases with higher levels in the management hierarchy. A very real dilemma is posed for managers who find activities being undertaken by their organization which violate their own sense of justice and values.

Presently, there is generally more legal protection for government employees who decide to go public with their views than there is protection for employees of firms in the private sector. Some legal scholars are predicting increased protection in the latter case. A few landmark cases have held that employees may not be fired when the substance of their disclosure has resulted in a significant public service or reduced a significant public danger. Usually employees will turn to resources outside the organization when it seems that justice cannot be gained through internal systems. To prevent this, skilled managers will insure that

- Organizational expectations do not interfere with employee political freedoms.
- The internal systems for assuring justice are adequate; that they operate fairly and in a timely way.
- Where possible, employee rights are documented and limits to the organization's power over the individual are specified.

DISCUSSION QUESTIONS

1. Do you consider your movement from freshman to sophomore standing a promotion based on merit, seniority, or some other criteria? Discuss.
2. Chairpeople of committees in the U.S. Congress are selected on the basis of seniority. Discuss advantages and disadvantages you see.

3. What would lead a person who was demoted to work effectively and well in a new, lower ranked position?
4. Why are lateral transfers in an organization deemed desirable? Discuss.
5. Pick a business firm in your community and describe the organizational rights the firm's employees might enjoy.
6. "If you don't have anything nice to say, don't say anything at all." Discuss the organizational implications of this statement.

BIBLIOGRAPHY

Schein, Edgar N. and J. Steven Ott. "The Legitimacy of Organizational Influence." *American Journal of Sociology,* (May 1962), pp. 682–89.

Scott, William G. *The Management of Conflict: Appeal Systems in Organizations.* Homewood: Richard D. Irwin, Inc., 1965.

Walters, Kenneth D. "Your Employees' Right to Blow the Whistle."
Harvard Business Review, Vol. 53 No. 4 (July–August 1975), p. 26.

The Case of the Encroaching Rut

Sally Inouye felt her familiar impatience growing as she read the newly received insert page for the Standard Practices Manual entitled "Rules of Personal Conduct for Female Buyers." In fact, she had to muster her sense of humor in order not to be insulted at some of the instructions, for example, "2.2. Female buyers are requested not to accept evening entertainment from suppliers' representatives." She thought to herself that her husband had some prescriptions of his own on that issue. Another nagging thought crossed her mind, which was that five years ago when she started as assistant chinaware buyer for Rinehart Department Store, she would have been far less resigned to receiving instructions from her employer as to her personal behavior. Yes, she was becoming brainwashed, or maybe just more realistic about the present state of affairs.

Inouye was a thirty-year-old, highly intelligent college graduate who had started her business career with visions of becoming one of the first woman presidents of a large merchandising organization. Beginning as assistant to Mary Tilford, chinaware buyer, Sally thought that she would soon be promoted past the older woman, and move solely on the basis of ability through successively higher levels on the way to her goal. Her discovery that although Rinehart had a lot of women at the buyer level, there was an unwritten law in the company that said that no woman can ever rise higher, was a bitter pill for her to swallow. Being single at the time, she had been willing to leave Rinehart's and start over in a different store in another

city, but her investigations disclosed that she would probably encounter the same discrimination wherever she went.

Now, still working under Mary Tilford, Sally found herself tormented by a complex of frustrations. She had a grudging respect for Mary Tilford's efficiency in running her department, but rebelled at having to take orders as though she were an insignificant underling. In the earlier years at Rinehart's she had had several opportunities to transfer to other departments, but then she thought that she soon would succeed to Ms. Tilford's position. In any case, two incidents in which she was involved diminished the enthusiasm of other buyers to have her in their departments.

One incident occurred when Sally was acting in her role as salesperson. Her taste in all beautiful things, including fabrics, fine furniture, and paintings, attracted some of the store's most valued customers, and in serving them she became intolerant of departmental boundary lines, and would take them from department to department, landing large sales. The personnel in the other departments became extremely resentful of the way she would ignore them as she escorted customers through.

Sally's reputation as a nonconformist reached the attention of the store's top managers when she submitted a written proposal to the effect that certain customers be assigned to her for all of their shopping. The flat rejection of this idea met with her barely concealed contempt, because it had been inspired by the customers themselves.

Another unfortunate incident occurred at a semiannual buyers' market in New York. Mary Tilford was ill and could not attend, and Sally handled her selections and negotiations with marked ability. The trouble came when she observed Ted Egan, buyer for flatware, trying to negotiate a large purchase in an obviously drunken condition. She overheard a term being entered in the contract that she knew would be prejudicial to Rinehart's, and moving Egan aside, she negotiated with the supplier's representative until the term was finally resolved in Rinehart's favor. She might have picked up some credit with the senior buyers had it not been for her remark: "I don't know why Rinehart's always sends a bunch of lushes on these buying trips."

In Inouye's fourth year at Rinehart, the company opened a branch store in a suburban shopping center, and there were many managerial positions to be filled. She requested an appointment with the company president, Wilbur Rinehart III, and asked for his personal intercession in getting one of these posts. He was polite but reserved in his conversation with her, and when the staff for the new store was announced, her name was omitted.

One day soon afterwards, Mary Tilford asked Sally to meet her after the store closed. "I suppose you feel mistreated because you didn't get a promotion," Mary began. "Well, let me tell you something. I had in mind recommending you up the line. But, instead, you had to go over the heads of about five people to try to get Mr. Rinehart's help. This irritated the personnel vice-president, the merchandise manager, the assistant merchandise manager, the group buyer, and me. One thing you have never learned, young lady, and that is how to play the organizational game. You have refused to conform ever since you have been here, and that's the cause of all of your problems. You have one chance left, and that is for my job when I retire in five years. However, the only way you are going to get it is to drastically change the way you act."

The following year saw Sally outwardly begin to adjust to the system. In fact, she began to receive a few mildly favorable comments from persons more highly placed in the organization. Inwardly she felt contempt for herself. By her values, she had put a price on her self-esteem in resigning herself to wait five years to get a job that would be a complete dead end.

One day she snapped at a sales clerk: "Haven't you read the Standard Practice Manual on how to handle a charge sale when a customer doesn't have her charge plate? It might do you some good to find out how things are supposed to be handled around here."

Mary Tilford, overhearing the remark, smiled triumphantly. Sally Inouye wished that she could crawl into a hole.

DISCUSSION QUESTIONS

1. Describe some system, organized for maximum efficiency, that has been extremely frustrating to you as a student.
2. What inefficiency will probably occur when an organization strives for conformity by its members?
3. In the Case of the Encroaching Rut, Sally Inouye suffered one frustration in finding that women could advance only so far in the company. Can business firms justify such a policy?
4. What is the effect on people when, as with Ms. Inouye, their jobs permit them to use only part of their abilities?

Summary

Staffing an organization with its human resources is a critical management function. The process involves a number of related activities which occur simultaneously and repeatedly in organizational life. In Part Four, staffing is defined as a group of managerial activities that includes the design of jobs, their evaluation and compensation; planning for, finding, and choosing the right people; evaluating and improving job performance; and, finally, providing for human reactions to staffing decisions.

The design of jobs provides a good starting point for grouping jobs that must be performed in an organization. An early trend in job design was to make each job increasingly narrow and simple. A developing staffing practice is toward expanding the content and scope of jobs in order to decrease the boredom and dehumanizing aspects of work. Additionally, people who perform jobs are being asked to participate in the design of those jobs. This is in contrast to the traditional practice of having a job design come down from above in the organization. Job descriptions and job specifications are different, related components of the job. Job descriptions refer to the composition of the job while job specifications refer to the capacities people must have to be able to perform the jobs.

After jobs are designed, it becomes necessary to determine the worth of the job to the organization. All other things being equal, compensation paid the jobholder should be proportional to the worth of the job. A number of systems have been designed to evaluate jobs. These systems range from a simple ranking method to a complex point method.

In determining the financial compensation level for jobs, an attempt is made to relate compensation to their worth. However, many factors intervene which require exceptions to this ideal. Inappropriate compensation levels can occur when too high a level has been set by precedent; when union pressure has forced wages for particular jobs above their real worth; and when labor scarcity requires adjustments in compensation to attract people with needed skills. In some cases the minimum wage established by government has exceeded the value of the job to the firm.

Fringe benefits are indirect ways of compensating people for their efforts. Some fringe benefits are mandated by social legislation. Other fringes have come about in response to other forces in the job market. Indirect compensation must be viewed as a real cost to the organization and should be subjected to critical cost benefit analyses. It appears that demands for increased indirect compensation will continue, both in terms of larger amounts of currently received fringe benefits and in a broader range of services.

The development of a systematic manpower plan is a central facet of the managerial staffing function. Such plans are essential to insure the future availability of needed human resources. Elements of a manpower plan include an analysis of the jobs performed in the organization's operations, development of a current manpower inventory, and a projection of job vacancies over successive time periods. Manpower plans must be integrated with other major organizational plans in order to insure the plans' feasibility.

Usually, an organization cannot rely on qualified applicants to show up at the time job openings occur. Most organizations must seek out such applicants. Sources of applicants vary with the type of job being filled and include employment agencies, educational institutions, advertising media, unions, professional societies, and industry contacts.

Once recruited, applicants must be screened and the new employee selected. The screening processes in selection decisions tend to be increasingly discriminating and typically involve information provided by the candidate, a series of interviews, and often reference checks. Interviews tend to be the most used screening device. Good interviewing skill can be learned and with it, many selection errors can be avoided.

An employee's job performance in the organization must be evaluated. The organization needs to know that the necessary tasks are being performed and how well they are being performed. Employees need to know how they are doing. This information is generated through performance appraisals. The information becomes a basis for the very important pay and promotion decisions a manager must make. Several techniques for reaching objective evaluations of performance have been proposed. Each type has some strengths and shortcomings. Management by objectives (MBO) is a technique which emphasizes a performance evaluation process.

New employees rarely possess all the skills at the level of proficiency needed to give an outstanding performance on the job. Present employees should have their skills upgraded to improve their contribution to the organization and their self-regard. For these reasons, organizations need to institute and maintain skill training programs. For programs to be successful, it is crucial that there be a clear understanding of the results to be obtained from the training. Furthermore, the trainees themselves must see the value in the training and be motivated to undertake it.

Developing management potential is somewhat different than skill training, because managerial ability cannot be taught. Skillful management comes from management experience of increasing breadth and responsibility. Development of managerial ability can be supported and enhanced by formal studies in management theory. For maximum development of management ability, opportunities for experiences should be planned, should include rotation to different managerial assignments, should involve increasingly complex decisions, should involve participation in policy determination, and should involve exposure and interactions with agencies and people outside the organization.

Staffing decisions usually involve very sensitive and critical aspects of peoples' working lives. A promotion, demotion, transfer, or termination is usually a significant event with far-reaching consequences for people. Organizational members will not treat such decisions lightly; neither will the competent manager.

Many employees will be intolerant of treatment they receive which seems unjust. This intolerance seems to be spreading to increasing numbers and levels of employees in organizations. People want and expect the rewards to which they feel entitled, and they resist being punished or treated in a manner they feel is undeserved or inappropriate. When an employee feels a management decision is unfair, unjust, or simply in error, there should be an organizational procedure in place so that corrections can be made and fairness achieved in the distribution of rewards and penalties.

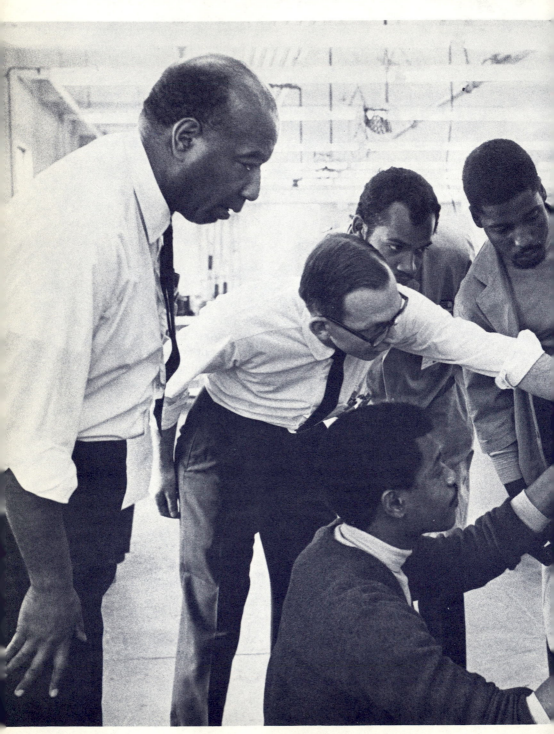

Leading

Part 5 of the text examines the leading function that managers perform. The managerial functions discussed up to this point can be seen as essential and preliminary to the leading function: planning must be accomplished so that goals and directions can be established; organizing must occur so that specialization of effort and coordination can be achieved; staffing must take place to ensure that the organization has the essential human resources needed to make it work. When these functions are even minimally performed, an organization can begin to work toward its goals. Keep in mind that it is the action and behavior of the people in the organization that will determine the degree of goal achievement attained. When managers perform leading functions they are addressing the problems of influencing the performance of organization's members.

Issues managers will be required to consider as they perform the leading function include

- Concepts and theories of leadership in organizational settings, the subject of Chapter 20.
- Concepts and theories about human needs and motivation, that are examined in Chapter 21.
- Problems and considerations that are unique to managing professional employees which are explored in Chapter 22.
- Concepts and practices in organizational communication, the subject of Chapter 23.
- Concepts and practices that support and encourage the growth and development of an organization to better achieve its goals and objectives are examined in Chapter 24.

As this list of issues and topics suggests, the leading function deals with the behavior of people in an organizational setting and the efforts of managers to influence that behavior into organizationally desirable channels.

20 Leadership

Managers are responsible for the quality and effectiveness of their organization's performance. To shoulder this responsibility managers rely on a wide range of skills and knowledge. Managers have long recognized that their organization's performance is directly related to the effectiveness of their own leadership behavior. However, there are a wide variety of descriptions and prescriptions for effective leadership and they do not provide consistent advice.

Three viewpoints can be identified in approaching the problem of leadership. We will examine each of them. They involve the identification and measurement of the

- traits of the leader, both innate and learned.
- various leadership styles, usually ranging from task/problem-centered styles to relationship/people-centered styles.
- situational variables which combine in different ways and call for different, specific leadership behavior.

TRAIT THEORY

Research attempts to identify particular personality traits necessary for good leadership have not produced a consistent list of such traits.

Part of the difficulty in establishing a consistent list of leadership traits stems from differences among conceptual approaches of researchers and differences in the situations that require effective leadership. Conceptual problems arise when trying to identify common meanings for the traits involved. For example, everyone has a general feel for the trait known as "industriousness." However, it is difficult to get everyone to agree on a consistent definition which can be used in research. Measuring the traits is a second methodological problem in leadership trait research.

The setting in which leadership occurs will affect its effectiveness, so even if we could identify and measure a leadership trait, its importance will be partly determined by the different situations in which it takes place. For example, the traits which separate effective and ineffective leaders on high-school basketball teams, in automobile repair shops, and in research laboratories are probably different in very important ways.

Some general factors which seem to recur in trait studies indicate successful leaders tend to be

- a little more intelligent than their followers.
- reasonably self-confident and socially mature.
- motivated to get things done.
- human-relations oriented.

One trait which, by definition, is effective in leading is charisma. Each of us has known someone who, by virtue of personal magnetism, is able to elicit an extra measure of performance from his or her followers. The charismatic manager is fortunate. Since this quality is not widespread among people, most managers must rely on other dynamics as they perform their leadership function.

An important consideration for the manager turns on the issue of whether or not necessary leadership traits can be learned. Some aspects of personality are innate and cannot be learned. One's intellectual capacity and predispositions seem to be either innate or established very early in one's life. There are, however, a wide range of attitudes and behavioral skills which can be influenced by a person's surroundings and which, by implication, can be learned.

A particular situation may call for a particular trait, such as patience, or aggressiveness, or decisiveness. When managers recognize a need for a particular trait in particular job situations, they will be able to select appropriate people to fill those positions. Managers will search for a person who possesses the desired leadership traits or who seems able to learn them. However, real-life situations are mischieviously unpredictable. Just about the time a manager identifies desirable leadership traits, the situation may change. This is the major problem managers face when applying the trait approach to leadership.

LEADERSHIP STYLE

A second approach for understanding leadership involves an analysis of the way leaders generally behave—their style. In one formulation, leadership style has been described as varying along a continuum ranging from authoritarian to democratic. The authoritarian leader makes the important decisions, tells subordinates what to do, and keeps close control over subordinates. Leaders adopting a democratic style will encourage wider participation in decision making, at both the policy and operational levels.[1]

Another common way of describing leadership style involves the identification of two different dimensions.[2] The leader's concern for the task, for production, and for procedures is one dimension; the leader's concern for people and relationships with them is the other. A major point to recognize in connection with these multi-dimensional style approaches is that while the two dimensions are different, they *are not* mutually exclusive. Thus the effective leader is usually described as adopting a style which is high in concern for task accomplishment *and* high in concern for the people involved.[3]

Another important point to recognize is that in the style approach to effective leadership, the emphasis is on what people do rather than on the formal, organizational positions they hold. Therefore, "task" leadership might shift within a group to different members at different times. Ideally, various members would have different styles—each style would be appropriate to the immediate group goals. For example, if a management team were considering a commitment of financial resources to a new product or production process, leadership in the group might shift between members possessing particular knowledge and skill in the areas of finance, production, and marketing, depending on the dimension of the problem under consideration at the time. The person chairing the meeting or the formal leader of the team might not provide technical leadership or special skill in any of these areas.

At the same time, the style approach to leadership recognizes the need for groups to maintain themselves while they work. For a group to continue to be productive and remain viable for a period of time sufficient to accomplish its task, some leadership effort should be directed toward maintaining the competence of the group. Leadership effort toward this end is the second major dimension mentioned in the style approaches to leadership.

When a group of people work together, differences of opinion, individual preferences and values, reactions to personalities, and unique behavioral characteristics will inevitably create barriers to continued, effective group work. A group's ability to deal with differences of opinion, conflicts among members, and individual preferences will directly influence the group's productivity. Therefore, group "maintenance" leadership is critical to effective group performance. It is important to recognize that leadership efforts directed toward group maintenance have a positive influence on group performance. It might appear, for example, that an unnecessary amount of committee time is being spent in idle chit-chat and conversations which are not directly related to the group's task. To prohibit all such seemingly idle talk might be dysfunctional to the group's performance in the long run. Quite unconsciously, people in the group may be using the idle conversation to gain time and perspective, to sound out each other, or to relieve unstated, tense interpersonal issues which, if unresolved, would reduce the quality of the group's output. Activities which are often included in the group maintenance styles of leadership are those that

- encourage group members to contribute.
- help the group work through conflicts and differences.
- assist in keeping communications flowing within the group.

SITUATIONAL-CONTINGENT CONSIDERATIONS

The common-sense notion that effectiveness in different situations calls for different leadership behaviors is at the heart of the third general way of looking at leadership. Elements in the situation, such as time limitations, requisite knowledge and skill, preferences, inclinations and expectations of leader and followers, the certainty of environmental circumstances, and the rapidity with which things are changing, will all influence the choice of an appropriate leadership style. Adding situational considerations to the leadership problem provides managers with greater flexibility and more options in achieving desired levels of effectiveness. Leadership styles can be matched with situational requirements.

The Fiedler Research

The work of Fred Fiedler[4] emphasizes the importance of the situation in leadership effectiveness. In his writings, Fiedler maintains that a leader's style can range from highly task-oriented to highly relationship-oriented. The leader's style is assumed to be relatively fixed. The leader's ability or capacity to vary his or her predominant style is deemphasized. Fiedler says, ". . . While the position that an individual's interpersonal behavior is largely outside his control is not very popular among laymen or most psychologists, the problem demands attention and is likely to remain highly controversial. Our data suggest that leader behavior is more strongly determined by the situation than by what the individual would like to do or thinks he ought to do."[5]

Instead, Fiedler maintains, effectiveness depends on the interaction of the leader's style and the relative favorableness of the situation for the leader. This favorableness will be determined by three major dimensions in the situation:

- The nature and quality of leader-member relationships.
- The amount of power in the leader's formal position.
- The amount of structure in the task itself.

Leader-member relations refers to the leader's evaluation of the degree of compatibility in the working relationships between the leader and the group members. If this relationship is deemed workable and promising, then there is an increase in the general favorableness of the situation for the leader. Similarly, when the leader has a relatively high degree of position power over the rewards and punishments and when the task has obvious and easily specified procedures for accomplishment, the situation is also described as favorable for the leader.

The essential point of Fiedler's theory is that when the situation is either highly favorable or highly unfavorable for the leader, the most effective leadership style will be a task-oriented one. A highly relationship-oriented leadership style is called for when the situation tends to be neither extremely favorable nor unfavorable. For example, the chairperson of a committee appointed to advise a mayor about actions that should be undertaken to reduce noise pollution in the city is in a highly unfavorable situation. The leader of this group may not have highly compatible relations with all the members; the formal power in the leader's position is weak; and the task is not an orderly one. On the other hand, a well-liked and admired general, conducting a field exercise, is an example of a leader in a highly favorable situation. In both these situations, Fiedler's theory suggests that task-oriented leadership would be more effective than a relationship-oriented style.

Implications for managers. Since Fiedler's approach to leadership emphasizes the interrelations between style and situation, it is possible in his view to increase effectiveness by altering either of the two variables. It has been argued that it is usually easier to alter the nature of the situation than to alter the personalities and styles of individuals. Managers, therefore, are encouraged to identify the dominant leadership style being exhibited by the leader and then to create a situation to fit. If leaders tend to be task-oriented, then they should be most effective when the situation is either highly favorable or highly unfavorable. The nature of leader-member relationships can be influenced by altering the composition of the group—people can be moved into and out of the group. The amount of power the leader has over rewards and punishments in the situation can be increased or decreased. The group can be assigned tasks that are more or less structured to vary the third dimension of the situation. Altering these variables in the organizational setting in order to match them to a predominant leadership style may be more efficient and effective than undertaking efforts to change the leader's style.

Tannenbaum-Schmidt Model

The central ideas of a situational approach to effective leadership are presented in a classic article by Tannenbaum and Schmidt.[6] In their view, the effective leader selects appropriate behavior from a continuum of styles which ranges from highly manager-centered to highly subordinate-centered. The continuum is illustrated in Figure 20-1.

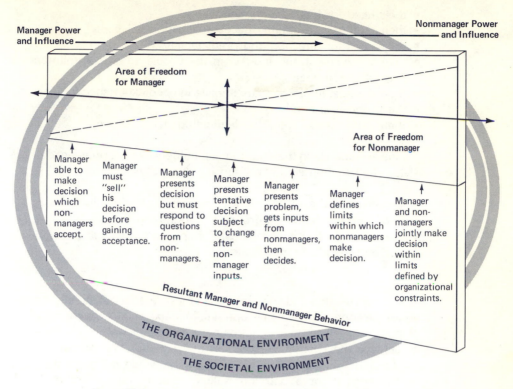

The figure shows:

Manager Power and Influence — **Nonmanager Power and Influence**

Area of Freedom for Manager

Area of Freedom for Nonmanager

| Manager able to make decision which non-managers accept. | Manager must "sell" his decision before gaining acceptance. | Manager presents decision but must respond to questions from non-managers. | Manager presents tentative decision subject to change after non-manager inputs. | Manager presents problem, gets inputs from nonmanagers, then decides. | Manager defines limits within which nonmanagers make decision. | Manager and non-managers jointly make decision within limits defined by organizational constraints. |

Resultant Manager and Nonmanager Behavior

THE ORGANIZATIONAL ENVIRONMENT

THE SOCIETAL ENVIRONMENT

Figure 20-1.   A Continuum of Manager-Nonmanager Behavior.

The first major point to recognize in this approach is that there is no implication that either end of the continuum is inherently more effective than the other. The appropriate balance between levels of manager and subordinate power and influence in decisions is determined by the forces in the manager, in the subordinate, and in the particular situation.

Forces in managers which contribute to a determination of appropriate balance between manager and subordinate power and influence include

- the manager's background, knowledge, and experiences.
- the values held by the manager, particularly about participation in decision making, efficiency, and company profits.
- the manager's confidence in the subordinates' competence.
- the manager's preferences for a directive or team approach to leading.
- the manager's need for predictability and stability in his or her environment.

Forces in the subordinate which can influence appropriate leadership style include

- their need for independent action.
- their readiness to assume necessary responsibility.
- their need for direction and predictability.
- their involvement and interest in the problem and commitment to organizational goals.
- their possession of necessary knowledge and experience to deal with the problem at hand.
- their expectations about the leadership style.

Finally, variance in the situation can influence appropriate leadership style. The situation could vary among these dimensions:

- Organizational expectations for appropriate leadership styles.
- The effectiveness of the group in working together.
- The problem itself that may call for special knowledge or require a person to work it through alone.
- The pressure of time.

The interrelation and combination of these factors will identify a place along the continuum which is optimal. Managers who gear their leadership style to reflect an optimal balance of influence will be most likely to achieve the desired outcome in that situation. A captain preparing to land a jetliner with a disabled engine would not invite the crew to the cockpit for a decision-making session. On the other hand, the same captain might find that, when chairing a PTA committee, wide participation by members is highly beneficial to the quality of decisions made.

A second point that is suggested in the Tannenbaum and Schmidt approach is that it is unlikely that any of us is so flexible or has such a wide-ranging repertoire of behavioral style that we can behave credibly across the whole range of possible leadership styles. What seems more common is that each of us has a relatively narrow band of preferred ways of leading and we tend to use these styles over and over. The implication for leader training is obvious. Learn to lead in a wider range of styles; be decisive when the strengths and limits in yourself, in your subordinates, and in the situation call for it. Similarly, move toward participation and collaboration when that style of behavior is appropriate.

A third point to note about the continuum concerns the nature of decisions being made. At the extreme left, the manager has the major portion of the influence over deciding both the problem and the action to be taken. At the far right, subordinates have the lion's share of deciding what the problem is as well as selecting courses of action. Delegating problem identification shifts to subordinates an activity that has traditionally fallen within the realm of management prerogative and responsibility. It is important, therefore, to recognize the limitations in all three aspects of the leadership situation. Even if the leader is prepared to share problem definition with the group, group members may be unprepared or unwilling to assume that responsibility.

Look again at Figure 20-1. Notice that neither the manager nor the subordinates has complete control. Some influence always remains with the other party. The subordinate always has the option of noncompliance with orders and directives. Costs associated with noncompliance can be extremely high, such as leaving the job or being fired. At the other extreme, managers can never relieve themselves of all responsibility for the actions and decisions of their organizations.

GUIDELINES FOR THE MANAGER

Generally, managers achieve better long-run results by leaning toward a democratic leadership style. This assumes that the skills and style of the leader, the abilities and preferences of the followers, and the elements in the situation form an appropriate environment for this style. An outstanding advantage of democracy and participation in organizations is that they offer people an opportunity to grow to their full potential.

Recent studies have shown that the meaning of work is a wider and deeper concern among people in our culture than has been generally recognized.[7] When work is viewed as being more than simply an economic necessity for survival, the benefits of a democratic approach to leadership become more obvious. Thoughtful managers recognize that the chances of meeting desired levels of performance are improved if all members of the organization are working toward similar objectives. Cooperation in those efforts can best be achieved if subordinates can see that they stand to gain personally when organizational goals are met.

NOTES

1. K. Lewis, R. Lippett, and R. K. White, "Patterns of Aggressive Behavior in Experimentally Created Social Climates," *Journal of Social Psychology* Vol. 10(1939) pp. 271–299.
2. R. M. Stogdill and A. E. Coons, "Leader Behavior: Its Description and Measurement," Research Monograph No. 88, Ohio State University, 1957.
3. R. Blake, and J. Mouton, *The Managerial Grid* (Houston: Gulf, 1964).
4. F. E. Fiedler, *A Theory of Leadership Effectiveness* (New York: McGraw-Hill, 1967).
5. F. E. Fiedler and Martin M. Chemers, *Leadership and Effective Management* (Glenview: Scott, Foresman and Company, 1974), p. 96.
6. R. Tannenbaum and W. H. Schmidt, "How to Choose a Leadership Pattern," *Harvard Business Review*, Vol. 51 No. 3 (May–June 1973), pp. 162–68.
7. *Work in America.* Report of a special task force to the Secretary of Health, Education, and Welfare (Cambridge: The MIT Press, 1973).

DISCUSSION QUESTIONS

1. What leadership traits do you possess? For each trait you identify, discuss its relative strength and consistency in your behavior.
2. What would you consider your typical leadership style to be? Could you (and people in general) learn other styles? Discuss.
3. Discuss the positive and negative implications you see for a leader in a highly favorable situation, in the sense used by Fiedler, who adopts a relationship-oriented style.
4. Assume you've accepted an invitation to lecture on "leadership training." Prepare a brief topic outline of your address. Discuss your major points.
5. "The nature and quality of leadership is of *no* consequence as far as the overall quality of working life in the situation is concerned." Discuss.
6. "Good leadership and organizational goal achievement generally go together. If the organization fails to meet its objective, good leadership cannot have taken place." Discuss.

BIBLIOGRAPHY

Berelson, Bernard, and Gary A. Steiner. *Human Behavior: An Inventory of Scientific Findings.* New York: Harcourt, Brace, and World, 1964.

Bowers, David G., and Stanley E. Seashore. "Predicting Organizational Effectiveness with a Four-Factor Theory of Leadership." *Administrative Science Quarterly,* Vol. 11 (September 1966), pp. 238–63.

Carlisle, T. *On Heroes, Hero-Worship, and the Heroic in History.* Boston: Houghton Mifflin, 1907.

Davis, K. *Human Behavior at Work,* 4th ed. New York: McGraw-Hill, 1972.

Fiedler, Fred E. "Engineer the Job to Fit the Manager." *Harvard Business Review,* Vol. 43 No. 5 (September–October 1965), pp. 115–22.

Fiedler, F. E., and Chemers, M. M. *Leadership and Effective Management.* Glenview: Scott, Foresman, 1974.

Likert, R. *The Human Organization.* New York: McGraw-Hill, 1967.

Stogdill, R. M. *Handbook of Leadership: A Survey of Theory and Research.* New York: Free Press, 1974.

Tannenbaum, R., and W. Schmidt. "How to Choose a Leadership Pattern." *Harvard Business Review,* Vol. 51 No. 3 (May–June 1973), pp. 162–75 and 178–80.

The Case of the Loyalty-Loving Ex-Colonel

The sixty-year-old Taggart Construction Company had reached the point in 1970 where it was doing about $25 million in construction business annually. The firm was headed by Alex Taggart, grandson of the founder. Except for approximately 5 percent of the common stock that was dispersed among employees, the company was owned by members of the Taggart family.

Alex Taggart decided in 1970 that he was trying to personally watch over too many of the company's activities. The bids on construction jobs which the firm regularly submitted were often as high as $7 million, and because of the magnitude of the stakes Taggart wanted to spend most of his time reviewing and approving estimates and checking the progress of the major projects. He felt that if he could group the purchasing, personnel, safety, and equipment maintenance functions in a department to be called Administration, he could direct more of his own attention to the activities that he considered central to the firm's operations. Purchasing was headed by Ted Reeves, fifteen years with the company, who supervised two buyers, a chief storeskeeper, and a secretary. A ten-year man, Sid Cohen, handled the personnel activities with the help of a secretary. The safety engineer, Frank Tanada, had been with Taggart eight years, and had an assistant and a secretary. John Petersen, also with eight years' seniority, supervised five foremen, and had a total equipment maintenance organization of about forty people.

Among the applicants for the newly created job of manager of administration was Lt. Col. Bob Laird, who was retiring from the Air Force. Laird served his last tour of duty at the local air base, and as Taggart knew many of the senior officers, he was able to get some first-hand information about this promising candidate. The officers under whom Laird had served spoke extremely well of his administrative experience and ability, and each singled out loyalty as one of his outstanding traits.

In due course Laird retired, and he immediately started to work for Taggart Construction Company. On the first day Laird said to Taggart: "The people who will be working under me seem to be loyal, and with that quality, plus their good experience, we're going to have a great team."

It was in early 1972 that Taggart called Bob Laird into his office to have a serious talk: "I have been putting off saying this to you for a long time," he began, "but it is obvious that something is wrong between you and the men reporting directly to you. I sense it when we have meetings. Before you came, Ted, Sid, Frank, and John always had worthwhile contributions to make to agenda items in their particular areas. Now they don't say anything, but merely look down at the table. This happens even when I specifically ask for their opinions of some of your proposals. When I try to talk to them in the hall, or in the coffee room, or out on the construction sites, it's the same thing. They either find an excuse to move away, or change the subject to some trivial topic. The climax came this morning when Frank Tanada asked to be allowed to go back to his old job of running a survey gang, which he was promoted out of five years ago. Can you tell me what the trouble is?"

"Mr. Taggart, I have made one mistake since I have been here," Laird heatedly replied, "and that was in assuming that these men would be loyal. They don't know the meaning of loyalty, and that is one thing that I cannot stand."

"Well, I owe it to them to hear their side of the story. With your consent, I am going to have a talk with them as a group," said Taggart.

Taggart opened the afternoon talk cautiously.

"Ted, and Sid, and Frank, and John, we've known each other for a long time. I used to think that we knew each other pretty well. Lately you have put up a barrier between us, and you seem very unhappy. I suspect that has something to do with Mr. Laird, and although I have never before asked people to talk about their superior, this time I am breaking my own rule. What is the matter?"

There was nothing but silence. Taggart finally broke it by saying: "Ted, you have been with this company for almost as long as I have. Can't you help me figure this thing out?"

Ted looked away, and then said: "Mr. Laird is one of the hardest working men I have ever known. In addition, he always tries to help the people working under him—like getting me authorized to have a company car."

"That's right," John spoke up, "he has been helping my son with algebra for the past six months."

Taggart thought for a moment before he commented: "One thing that I have observed about Mr. Laird is that he makes up his mind on things pretty quickly."

The others looked sharply at each other. Sid then made the opening remark: "I guess that's it in a nutshell, Mr. Taggart. He makes his decisions off the top of his head. Then, once he has made them, he is absolutely convinced they are right."

"I go along with that," Frank put in. "I'm scared every time an issue comes up that has to be decided. He doesn't even start to think something through before he has an answer. Then he gets mad at me if I suggest that we should consider some alternative."

"An example that comes to my mind," John supported, "is when I suggested that we start thinking about a winter repair program. He immediately decided that we should schedule a major overhaul for every piece of equipment with over 2000 hours on it. When I mentioned that this would include equipment we plan to sell in the spring, he said that this would help us get more money for it. He then refused to look at figures showing that we only recoup about half of an overhaul cost even when we trade in equipment on a new purchase."

"I have no confidence in his decisions," Ted reluctantly said. "He is smart enough, and he has plenty of experience. But when he decides something as capriciously as he did the other day, I lose respect for him. We were trying to objectively decide between three makes of tractors. He was sitting in the meeting, and became more and more impatient as we compared specifications, past equipment records, dealer spare parts inventories, and so forth. He finally broke up the analysis by saying he thought we should have an equal number of each make of tractor in our fleet, and therefore we should buy tractors of the make that we have fewest of."

The following morning Taggart entered Laird's office and sat down. "Bob," he said, "this is a question that I should have asked you two years ago. What is your definition of a loyal subordinate?"

"One who doesn't debate and question every single thing that his superior decides," Bob Laird replied.

DISCUSSION QUESTIONS

1. What is a drawback of the "natural leader" concept?
2. Why study leadership from the standpoint of the evaluations of subordinates?
3. In the Case of the Loyalty-Loving Ex-Colonel, was anything unacceptable to Laird's subordinates in the way he interpreted organizational objectives?
4. What qualities did Laird have that could have made him an effective leader? What factors were present in the situation that could have helped make him a leader?
5. What quality essential for effective leadership did Laird lack?

The Case of the Leopard That Couldn't Change Its Spots

Al Kirschman became interested in rocketry and rocket design while he was in high school, and when he began his engineering education it was with the intention of entering the then budding aerospace industry. After receiving his engineering degree, he spent two important years with a small developmental laboratory, and then five years in the aerospace division of a large aircraft company. By the time he joined Consolidated Technology he had established a reputation as a successful manager of rocket engineers, rather than as an engineer himself, and despite his youth had an impressive record of projects that he had managed.

Al drove himself relentlessly to get a goal accomplished, and expected the same kind of discipline from the people working under him. When a project was in trouble, an 80-hour work week was normal with him. In fact, he often made the comment: "If I weren't married, I would put a cot in my office and spend my entire time on the job." Just as he demanded perfection from himself, so also did he demand it from his subordinates, and as he suspected that most persons' performance standards did not measure up to his, he ran his organization with an iron hand.

He held many meetings, but they were of an interrogation type, rather than group discussion. He was indifferent to people's feelings, and, in a room filled with people, would sarcastically probe into a subordinate's defense until it was plain to everyone that a blunder or oversight had been committed. It couldn't be said that Al was very well liked person-

ally, but he was respected because he was almost always right in the final outcome. His superiors and the Air Force representatives thought he was great, because his project was one of the few aerospace missions that was successful by any criterion.

Al had been with Consolidated Technology for about two years, and the project he headed was about half completed, when the company employed Dr. Hugh Stetson to set up and administer a management development program. Dr. Stetson's approach to management development was through sensitivity training. He would form groups of peers within an organization, take the group to an isolated retreat away from the day-to-day operations, give them copies of the contemporary literature on human relations, and then through informal group processes enable each member to become aware of his own behavior as other people perceived it. He would then individually counsel the managers who had gone through the experience on changing their managerial shortcomings, as measured by human relations norms.

Al Kirschman was a member of the first group to experience Dr. Stetson's session, and he had a rude awakening. Most of the other members had at one time or another been temporarily assigned to Al's project, and in that sense had been subordinate to him. In the group discussions Al's way of managing was identified as the worst possible managerial behavior. He became the butt of jokes, many of which were not meant to be too funny, with the result that the exposure to what other people thought of him made quite an impact. He was most receptive to Dr. Stetson's offer of counsel.

"Al, your problem is that you are 'thing' oriented, rather than 'people' oriented," Dr. Stetson began. "To you, people are just tools that you use to get things done. Your attitude is that people won't produce unless they are driven, which is not true. You would be surprised to find out how much can be accomplished by getting your subordinates to work with you, rather than for you. Let them bring out their ideas, not just obediently follow yours. You plainly saw in the group discussions how those people resented the way you have made fools out of them. That's not the way to manage. Why don't you try complimenting them instead of tearing them down? You will find that your projects' performance will be greatly improved."

Al was a confused young man. For the past seven years he had received raises, promotions, and bonuses because of the accomplishments of the projects he had managed. Now it had been forcefully brought to his attention that everything he did as a manager was wrong. He was intelligent enough to know that he was not perfect, and to accept the possibility that a way of managing different from his might be better. He decided to find out.

"Fellows," Al began at the next meeting that he held, "I hate to say this, because I know how hard you have all been working, but the Air Force wants much better performance out of the pump. You are all the best in your respective fields, and I invite you to state what you think is wrong, and what you would do to correct it."

For a while the group sat in shocked silence. They were so used to being told what to do that they didn't know how to respond. Finally some thoughts began to be expressed, and as Al didn't rip them apart, the discussion picked up momentum. Al inwardly fumed, as he thought they were only scratching the surface of the problem, but he let the discussion run its course. When all of the ideas seemed to be exhausted he said: "I have confidence that you can work this out by yourselves, so see what you can do. And another thing, I am going to stop calling Saturday and Sunday meetings. I know that a lot of you would like to spend the weekends with your families, and if you think you can spend the time away from your jobs, that's up to you."

Al continued like this for about three months. His cigarette consumption went from two packs a day to four as the project's progress reports got progressively worse. There were no signs of a correction of the pump problem, and Al observed that each weekend there were fewer pump engineers working. Inevitably, Al was called to the office of his own boss, Ray Wilt.

"What is going on out there?" Wilt demanded. "All of a sudden I have another sick project on my hands, and it is the last one I would have expected."

Al explained how he was trying to change his managerial style to conform to what Dr. Stetson said was right. He said that he was so frustrated that he was thinking of leaving management and going back to research work.

"Al, what Stetson says might suit some people, but it won't work for you, and it wouldn't work for me," said Wilt. "I want job results, not well-balanced people. Now you get out there and run that project like you used to."

Al called a meeting that afternoon. "Heath," he said, "How do you solve an engineering problem?"

"Why, I do an analytical overhaul."

"Are you sure that you know what an analytical overhaul is?" asked Al.

"Of course I do," Jack Heath heatedly replied. "It is tearing a system down, part by part, examining for actual or potential malperformance, making the necessary corrections, then rebuilding the system."

"Have you done that with the pump?" said Al.

"Absolutely," said Heath.

"Is the hydraulic seal part of the pump?" Al probed.

"You know it is," Heath said, as he became more angry.

"What did you find with the seal?" Al continued.

"It was worn, and we replaced it," Heath spit out.

"Why was it worn?" Al asked.

"I don't know," Heath almost yelled. "Maybe because it isn't the right material."

"Maybe," Al sneered. "Don't you think that an expert like you should find out?"

The meeting went on like this until two o'clock the next morning, with each member receiving his share of Al's seething interrogation. When it finally broke up, one member remarked to Jack Heath: "Well, it looks like the vacation is over, doesn't it?"

"I know damn well it is for me," said Heath grimly.

DISCUSSION QUESTIONS

1. In what way does the limitation of a manager's span of control necessitate some delegation, or departure from pure authoritarian management? (See Chapter 12.)
2. What is missing in most reward systems that might motivate managers to try harder to cast off authoritarian tendencies?
3. Would you have liked to work under Al Kirschman?
4. What was wrong with Al's attempt at democratic leadership? Could he have made it work? What other style might he try?
5. If you were in the position of Ray Wilt, and saw the efficiency of Al's project drop off suddenly, would you have done as Wilt did? If not, what would you have done?

21 Human Needs and Motivation

Managers are vitally concerned with supporting and encouraging productive organizational behavior of subordinates. They are also interested in discouraging behavior that is counterproductive to organizational objectives.

Before managers can act on these concerns they need an understanding of what is, and what might be, in the work setting that would motivate subordinates to perform their jobs well.

We will begin our study of motivation by examining a simple model of motivation. The desire to understand human motivation has led to many research projects and theories which involve some or all of the elements in the model as well as the relationships among the elements. Abraham Maslow proposed an influential theory on the structure of human needs.[1] His "hierarchy of needs" will be described and we will study other theories that have been proposed to explain why people behave as they do. We will also study the motivational implications of behavioral modification theories. Finally, the problems managers face when making decisions are reexamined in light of human needs and motivation. We are taking another look at these decisions because they will reflect the theories and explanations of motivation the manager adopts while attempting to elicit the best job performance possible from subordinates.

A SIMPLE MODEL OF MOTIVATION

A simplified model can be used to illustrate conceptual components and their relationships in human motivation. A typical representation of the motivation process involves *needs* which stimulate *behavior* which results in an *outcome* which satisfies the original need.

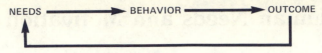

NEEDS ━━━━━▶ BEHAVIOR ━━━━━▶ OUTCOME

Figure 21-1.   A Needs/Behavior Model.

People behave with a purpose, even though they may not be fully conscious of the extent and ramifications of those purposes. Working backwards from that observation, it can be inferred that behavior is not random, formless, or accidental. Rather, behavior is goal oriented. Generalizing, we could say that people strive to achieve some desired end, or to avoid an undesirable outcome or condition.

The "law of effect" is a commonly accepted propoposition in psychology which holds that people tend to repeat those behaviors which have resulted in satisfactory outcomes in the past. From our experiences we learn which behaviors give us pleasure or satisfaction. All other things being equal, the law of effect says that we will usually try that behavior again when faced with a similar need or situation. For example, a baby soon learns which behaviors will result in food being provided to satisfy hunger needs. Similarly, people in organizations are quick to recognize what kinds of behaviors will result in expressions of the supervisor's approval.

Look again at the model. We can retrace the links from outcomes through behavioral acts to some initial set of needs. These needs are internal to the individual and are inferred from observable behavior. The model now looks like this: People have needs—these needs come into a position of prominence and mobilize energy in the person to act—this action/behavior is directed toward things that will satisfy the need. If the consequences of the behavior are appropriate, the original need is satisfied and reduced.

It is important to recognize the oversimplification of this model. For example, many different needs can be satisfied by the same outcome. Eating a prime cut of meat at a first-class restaurant will satisfy many needs besides simple nutrition. Similarly, if a person is hungry there are a number of actions that can be taken to satisfy the need. Hamburgers, prime rib, or even insects can satisfy hunger. Outstanding job performance may result in pay increases and promotions which can satisfy a host of needs ranging from food and shelter to status and self-esteem.

Managers should understand the major job-related components in the needs → behavior → outcome model of motivation.

We will end our discussion with a warning about the motivation process. Needs are not necessarily rational. Many times the needs that are operating to stimulate behavior are not obvious to the individual nor to another person observing the behavior. It has been said that a sadist is someone who is kind to a masochist. A manager must be careful to recognize that needs are unique to the individual. A subordinate's needs

may vary from a manager's own needs in many important ways. Furthermore the subordinate will not necessarily go about satisfying a need similar to the manager's, in the same way the manager might.

A HIERARCHY OF NEEDS

A widely accepted classification of human needs was developed by the psychologist, Abraham Maslow. The following discussion is based primarily on his theory. That theory makes a few basic assertions about the structure of human needs. It holds that

- human needs can be grouped into five categories; physiological, safety, love, esteem, and self-actualization.
- these categories are arranged in an ascending hierarchy.
- humans are generally motivated to satisfy these needs in an ascending order.
- a satisfied need is no longer a motivator of behavior.

Physiological Needs

The most primary needs are for the physiological elements which sustain life, such as air, water, and nourishment. When needs in this class are not being met, the individual is simply not concerned with higher level needs. Managers can influence elements in the job situation which would touch on physiological needs. Physical conditions, such as clean air and ventilation, fall in this category and can be influenced by the manager.

Safety Needs

When life supporting needs are relatively well satisfied, the next level of need emerges. Safety needs usually refer to our need to establish and maintain conditions that preserve and insure basic needs over time. Shelter, clothing, and protection from physical danger are examples of safety needs. Economic security is often included in this category also.

Clearly, for many segments of our society, the threat of danger from predators, the elements, and grinding poverty is not severe. It is not as clear that psychological safety needs are as well met. Change in an organization, especially unexpected change, is a definite threat to a need for security that people in organizations have. Even the most modern senior manager will feel twinges of insecurity and will probably be less productive at the prospect of some dramatic organizational change, such as a takeover of a firm by another company.

Managers must be aware that such change can lead to insecurity and that people who feel their security threatened will act in ways to reduce that threat. They will be inclined to focus their attention and energy on behavior that will fulfill security needs. Managers can anticipate that those threat-reducing behaviors may not be productive in terms of organizational goals and processes. By remaining alert to indications of threat-reducing behavior, managers can control the nature and pace of organizational changes to minimize the negative impact on organizational performance.

Need for Love and Affiliation

Following the need for securing the necessities of life are needs reflecting the social aspect of humans. Maslow's theory holds that humans have a basic need for giving and receiving affection and experiencing relationships with other people. The expression of these needs is evident in all organizations. Coffee breaks are typically occasions for social contact and conversation rather than quiet, solitary refreshment. Groups and needs for group membership are a powerful set of influences on people in organizations. These influences are discussed in more detail in a later section.

Need for Esteem

As people satisfy most of their needs for affection and affiliation, the need for esteem will become important. The need for esteem involves two, related dimensions. On one hand, people need self-esteem and self-respect. At the same time, much of this self-respect is based on the judgment of others. To fulfill a need for esteem, people work to be favorably regarded by both themselves and others.

Job performance is an important source of fulfillment of esteem needs. Most people take pride in doing their job well. The sense of accomplishment associated with good job performance is an important source of satisfaction for esteem needs.

Managers have control over many aspects of the job situation which can be important to the subordinate's esteem. Material aspects (e.g. pay and bonuses, a well-appointed office, access to an executive dining room), and nonmaterial aspects (e.g. praise and recognition) are all potential sources of esteem. Each of these aspects has a unique potential for satisfying esteem needs in different people. Managers are well-advised to remember this as they attempt to improve the organizational performance of subordinates by appealing to esteem needs. What works for one person may not be at all desirable to another.

Need for Self-Actualization

The ultimate set of needs in the hierarchy are the needs for self-actualization. These needs center on those activities and conditions which make it possible for individuals to fully express their potential—to become all they have the capacity to be. At this point in a person's development, needs cease to be deficiencies which call for satisfaction. Instead, people are said to be motivated by creative, "being" needs.

These self-actualization needs are probably not very active in much of the population. At the same time though, Maslow's theory holds that it is the activation and potential for satisfying these needs that is an ever present direction underlying human behavior. This assertion has significance for those aspiring to manage. The organization presents an excellent environment for the expression of an individual's finest potentials. It is also true that organizations need plans, structure, and sufficient stability to conduct its affairs in a coordinated fashion. These requirements can often impinge on an individual's fullest expression of his or her own potential. It is the manager's very difficult task to orchestrate the situation so that individual and organizational needs and goals are appropriately balanced and met.

MOTIVATION THROUGH NEED FOR ACHIEVEMENT

A somewhat different view of needs has been developed by David C. McClelland.[2] His theory is that there are some people who have a compelling need to achieve simply for the sake of achieving rather that for whatever benefits and symbols of success might follow high achievement. Two additional needs, the need for affiliation and the need for power, are the other main needs which McClelland proposes for understanding human behavior.

These latter needs relate to the social and interpersonal aspects of organizational life. Achievement needs focus on the task aspects in organizations.

People who have a high need for achievement can be distinguished from those whose needs for affiliation and power are stronger. McClelland estimates that only about 10 percent of the population possess a strong need for achievement. These people characteristically prefer to set their own goals or be influential in setting them. They do not want to be without goals. These high need-for-achievement (n Ach) people tend to set goals which are moderately challenging. Their goals are neither so easy as to represent no significant accomplishment nor so difficult as to be unattainable. Achieving a too-easy goal does not provide sufficient satisfaction and a too-difficult goal does not provide an opportunity to achieve. Finally, people who have a high n Ach also need to know often and in concrete terms how they are doing. Feedback about performance is critical to someone who needs to achieve. Because of this, people with a high n Ach often choose careers in sales, enter a profession, or undertake entrepreneurial activities.

As managers attempt to provide leadership they should try to recognize the predominant needs of their subordinates. If a subordinate has high n Ach it would be a mistake to place him or her in a position which does not lend itself to frequent and concrete feedback about performance, or one which does not permit a fair degree of control over setting of job goals. Similarly, if the subordinate's needs seem to be predominantly in other areas, such as needs for affiliation or power, the manager should not anticipate a greater than average expression of achievement motivation. The manager's challenge is to match the task requirements with the central needs of those who may be charged with the task in order to get optimal organizational performance.

Recently, McClelland has addressed the need for power in more detail.[3] He suggests that the *relative* need for power separates people with managerial potential from those who are not likely to be good managers. Individuals with high n Ach will find it difficult to get tasks done through and with other people. High needs for affiliation and friendship can make it difficult for an individual to make unpopular necessary decisions in organizations.

MOTIVATION AND JOB SATISFACTION

Both managers and behavioral scientists have been concerned with the question of the relationship between productivity and the level and kinds of satisfaction people find in their jobs. A common hypothesis about this relationship says that the greater the level of satisfaction in the job the more productive a worker will be. This relationship is assumed to hold because it seems to make sense that people who are satisfied in their jobs are going to be motivated to do a good job. Unfortunately, this statement oversimplifies the situation, and is generally inaccurate.

Part of the reason the "higher satisfaction leads to higher productivity" model has not been solidly confirmed by research lies in the many and varied definitions of job satisfaction that can be used. Recall the discussion of the multiplicity of needs and outcomes early in the chapter. Different aspects of the same job can satisfy different people. Furthermore, one aspect of a job could be satisfying different needs. For example, one person might find a carpeted office an important symbol of

Power Is the Great Motivator

The manager's job seems to call more for someone who can influence people than for someone who does things better on his own. In motivational terms, then, we might expect the successful manager to have a greater "need for power" than need to achieve. But there must be other qualities beside the need for power that go into the makeup of a good manager. Just what these qualities are and how they interrelate is the subject of this article.

To measure the motivations of managers, good and bad, we studied a number of individual managers from different large U.S. corporations who were participating in management workshops designed to improve their managerial effectiveness.

The general conclusion of these studies is that the top manager of a company must possess a high need for power, that is, a concern for influencing people. However, this need must be disciplined and controlled so that it is directed toward the benefit of the institution as a whole and not toward the manager's personal aggrandizement. Moreover, the top manager's need for power ought to be greater than his need for being liked by people.

Principally, we have discovered what motive combination makes an effective manager. We have also seen that change is possible if a person has the right combination of qualities.

Oddly enough, the good manager in a large company does not have a high need for achievement, as we define and measure that motive, although there must be plenty of that motive somewhere in his organization. The top managers in our study have a high need for power and an interest in influencing others, both greater than their interest in being liked by people. The manager's concern for power should be socialized—controlled so that the institution as a whole, not only the individual, benefits. Men and nations with this motive profile are empire builders; they tend to create high morale and to expand the organizations they head.

But there is also danger in this motive profile; empire building can lead to imperialism and authoritarianism in companies.

The same motive pattern which produces good power management can also lead a company or a country to try to dominate others, ostensibly in the interests of organizational expansion. Thus it is not surprising that big business has had to be regulated from time to time by federal agencies.

For an individual, the regulative function is performed by two characteristics that are part of the profile of the very best managers—a greater emotional maturity, where there is little egotism, and a democratic, coaching managerial style. If an institutional power motivation is checked by maturity, it does not lead to an aggressive, egotistic expansiveness.

For individuals, this checking means they can control their subordinates and influence others around them without resorting to coercion or to an authoritarian management style. Real disinterested statesmanship has a vital role to play at the top of both countries and companies.

success and, therefore, satisfying. Another person, though, may be relatively indifferent to the carpet and instead find great satisfaction in a large number of subordinates or in a large budget.

Even if we assume that we have a solid fix on aspects of the job situation an individual finds satisfying, there remains the problem of relating satisfaction to productivity. Referring to our earlier examples, it does not necessarily follow that productivity of any of the individuals would increase were better carpeting laid, more subordinates assigned, or the budget increased.

TWO-FACTOR THEORY

Frederick Herzberg and his associates have done a great deal of work in the area of motivation and work. His major conclusion is that there are two sets of factors into which motivational aspects of jobs can be placed, namely satisfiers and dissatisfiers.[4]

Dissatisfiers

One set of factors in the work place is composed of all those things which, if absent, would create dissatisfaction. Herzberg called these hygiene factors and they include

- acceptable company policies and rules.
- tolerable management methods by the immediate supervisor.
- equitable compensation.
- desirable interpersonal relations with co-workers.
- agreeable working conditions.

One thing to remember about hygiene factors is that if present in the job situation they will help prevent dissatisfaction. Another characteristic of hygiene factors is that they tend to become expected conditions. Once in place, hygiene factors must be continued. Assume for example that top employees have been awarded a new company car each year for a number of years. If the new car is not provided in some year, great dissatisfaction would likely follow even if the reason for the decision had nothing to do with the particular employee. In fact, many people would feel they had suffered a cut in pay were this to happen to them.

Real Motivators

The second set of factors in the job situation that Herzberg described corresponds to the kinds of needs found at the top of Maslow's hierarchy of needs. While the hygiene factors deal with people's interest in avoiding the painful and uncomfortable aspects of work, the true motivators appeal to the needs of people to grow and to develop to their full potential. These motivators include

- a sense of achievement, or the knowledge of having done something worthwhile.
- recognition, by persons whose opinion is valued, that one's work has merit.
- the satisfaction that comes from challenging work.
- a high degree of responsibility on the job.
- an opportunity for advancement, growth and development.

For example, the real motivation to provide outstanding customer service comes from a sense of achievement in a job well done, the recognition that comes from a pleased customer, and the knowledge that a difficult task was handled well. An important thing to remember about this set of motivating factors is that they are *intrinsic* to the job or task being performed. The quantity and intensity of these factors is changed mainly by changing the essential nature of the job.

Criticism of the Two-Factor Theory

It should be noted that the theories and research methodology of Herzberg and his supporters have not been without criticism. Most of the criticism centers on the research methodology used to test and support aspects of the two-factor theory. Herzberg based his research findings on the reports of people about what they felt motivated or dissatisfied them. This method overlooks the fact that human beings are not always aware of all their needs and motives; neither are people always willing to tell all these things to a researcher. Also, people may tend to take credit themselves and find aspects of the job very positive when things are going well. When things are not so rosy on the job, people may tend to lay the blame on the situations surrounding the job—the hygiene factors.

The prudent manager and student of management will recognize that the last word on motivation in the work place will not be in for a long time. In the meantime, work goes on and decisions must be made. If a manager perceives that enriching jobs along the lines of self-actualization will be well received by subordinates, and that the costs or risks of such changes are reasonable, then an organization may gain from the expression of that extra measure of potential which people so often hold in reserve.

EXPECTANCY THEORY OF MOTIVATION

The work of Kurt Lewin and later V. H. Vroom[5] is the basis of another theory which attempts to explain why people behave as they do. In this theory, emphasis is placed on the *expectancy* a person has about the outcome of his or her behavior and on the perceived desirability of the outcome. The expectancy theory holds that people act on the basis of their *subjective* estimates of the probability that certain behaviors will yield a particular outcome and that the outcome will provide some degree of satisfaction.

Thus, if a file clerk wanted to be considered for promotion to secretary, the clerk would be motivated to file quickly and accurately to the extent that it seemed (1) extra efforts would lead to quick and accurate filing and (2) quick and accurate filing would lead to promotion. Expanding this example to the entire organization, then, people will engage in productive behavior when they believe that their efforts will probably lead to some desired behavior *and* that the behavior is likely to be followed by a desirable outcome. An important aspect of this formulation for the manager to keep in mind is that it is the relationships between effort, behavior, and consequences which people *believe* exist that govern their choices and behavior. The objective reality of the situation may be very different from what is perceived to be the case. To understand their subordinates, managers must understand what the subordinates believe those relationships to be.

MOTIVATION THROUGH THE WORK GROUP

Informal organizations were discussed in Chapter 12 in connection with their impact on the organizing function of management. In this section, the influence that work groups have on the motivation of their individual members will be discussed.

Norms in Groups

The term *norms* is frequently used when discussing peoples' behavior in groups. The term refers to standards of behavior, both job-related and otherwise, which the members of the group generally share. Norms are the ways a "good" group member typically behaves. Conformance with group norms is affected by powerful social sanctions and pressures. These pressures are increased as individuals violate group norms more frequently. When a group member has deviated too far, too often from the established norms, his or her membership in the group will usually be terminated.

Group norms which influence subordinates actions in areas such as productivity standards, attendance, tardiness, and respect for rules are concerns for the manager. But managers must recognize that group norms develop as a consequence of the group's interaction. The formal position of the manager does not provide a basis for establishing group norms. Groups can establish norms for behavior which can be either favorable or unfavorable to goals that the manager feels are in the best interests of the organization. The manager can work to develop an organizational climate and setting in which desirable norms will develop.

Cohesiveness in Groups

Groups will vary in the degree to which their members want to remain in and committed to them. When these things are high, a group is said to be more cohesive. A consequence of a highly cohesive group is the perception among group members of similarity between their personal goals and the objectives of the group or, if these elements differ, a willingness to subordinate personal goals.

Conformity in Groups

It is sometimes assumed that highly cohesive groups will, by definition, be characterized by a high degree of conformity among its members. While this is possible, the manager should remember it is not always the case. A research and development project team, for example, can value and support very divergent and different behavior among its members, particularly when the achievement of group objectives is felt to be a likely outcome. On the other hand, a platoon of Marine Corp recruits, through their boot camp experience, becomes a very special, cohesive, and conforming group.

BEHAVIOR MODIFICATION

In the preceding sections it was suggested that managers might look to the internal needs of people in order to understand and influence organizational behavior. An alternative approach to the problem of influencing human behavior is presented by a collection of theory and practices generally known as "behavior modification." This approach is often associated with the work of psychologist B. F. Skinner. The behavior modification approach does not rely on inferences about internal states of individuals as do Maslow, Herzberg and others. Instead, it deals with the linkages that can be observed between behaviors and the consequences of these behaviors. This point of view draws heavily on the idea that the tendency to repeat behavior is dependent on the consequences of that behavior.

If a person does something on the job that leads to a pleasing consequence or if the behavior tends to stop a displeasing consequence then, chances are, the behavior will be repeated. Thus, if accurate typing is followed by praise or by a reduction in complaints from the boss, then accurate typing is apt to be repeated. These two outcomes of accurate typing are examples of *positive* and *negative reinforcement* of behavior respectively. In both cases, the effect on the behavior is to support its repetition.

Two other potential relationships between behavior and its consequence are identified in behavior modification. One is *punishment* and the other is usually called *extinction*. In situations where behavior elicits these consequences, the behavior will cease. In the case of punishment, a displeasing consequence follows the behavior. The manager who warns, "If you are late to work three times you will be terminated," hopes the threat of punishment will prompt the subordinate to cease the behavior. The essential difference between negative reinforcement and punishment is that negative reinforcement tends to increase the probability of a behavior being exhibited while punishment tends to diminish the behavior that results in punishment.

There are, in addition, substantial side effects to punishment which tend to make its selection as a managerial strategy somewhat less desirable than other reinforcement strategies. The effects of punishment are generally so variable, and interdependent with other conditions in the situation, that it is not easy to predict their ultimate impact and effect. The intensity of the punishment, the strength of the behavior being punished, and the timing all have to be considered. Punishment may elicit other, related behavior that is less desirable than that being punished. If a manager punishes tardiness by withholding pay, employees may resort to petty theft to restore what they would consider equity in the situation.

The final strategy for diminishing behavior is called *extinction*. In this case, there is no regular relationship between the behavior and its consequences. When nothing predictable is apt to happen after a specific behavior, no strengthening of the chance for repeating that behavior has occurred. Again using the office example, it is not uncommon to hear people complain, "Nobody appreciates what I do around here." This complaint contains the implicit statement that without recognition the "things done around here" may not continue to be done, the behaviors may become extinct.

To sum up, there are four general relationships between behavior and its consequences. In two instances, positive and negative reinforcement, the tendency is to encourage more of the behavior. In the other two, punishment and extinction, the tendency is to reduce the occurrence of the behavior.

Reinforcement Schedules

There are different ways in which the occurrence of consequences in relation to behavior can be delivered, or "scheduled." Generally, a reinforcer of behavior has its greatest effect if it comes immediately after the behavior is exhibited. In the simplest schedule, called continuous reinforcement, the consequence follows each time the behavior occurs.

Managers who consistently convey their genuine appreciation for comments and suggestions of subordinates are following a continuous reinforcement schedule. Continuous reinforcement is not particularly common in organizations.

A more common set of schedules are intermittent in nature. In one case the consequence can follow a consistently repeated interval, either in terms of time or number of behavioral occurrences; pay is an example. In the second case, the interval may vary so that the amount of time that passes or the number of times the behavior occurs before the consequence occurs, will vary. It is this latter schedule which operates at the slot machines in gambling casinos. The positive aspects of occasional payoffs and jackpots are sufficiently rewarding to the players that they continue to feed coins to the machines even though they know the odds are against them.

The Manager and Behavior Modification

Whether or not the behavior modification model of behavior appeals to the manager, the fact remains that people will behave in ways that they think will achieve pleasing outcomes. Managers can improve organizational performance by reinforcing, as much as they are able, those behaviors which contribute to organizational goal achievement. Similarly, they may find that there are counterproductive behaviors occurring which can be discouraged by (1) punishing them, (2) by removing the rewards that the behaviors are associated with, or (3) by providing alternative consequences which are contingent on productive behaviors.

Shaping. The preceding discussion assumed that behavior was occurring which the manager views as either productive or counterproductive in terms of organizational performance. It can also happen that the manager would like some behavior to occur which is not forthcoming. This becomes the occasion for applying the concept of *shaping behavior*. Shaping is applied to reinforce behavior that is headed in the direction of the desired behavior. We often do this naturally when we encourage someone with phrases like "You are improving" or "Now you're getting the idea." The basic idea for managers is that they can shape subordinates behavior by reinforcing successively closer approximations to the behavior they ultimately wish to elicit.

Premack Principle. Another technique the manager can use in efforts to encourage organizationally productive behavior comes from the *Premack Principle*. Essentially this principle holds that behavior-consequence relationships can be chained so that desired outcomes become contingent on the performance of less desirable behaviors. Parents have long used the principle when they tell children, "You may have your dessert when all of your vegetables are eaten." Managers can arrange work assignments so that the more desirable ones follow and are contingent upon the completion of the less desirable tasks.

MOTIVATIONAL MIX OF THE MANAGER

The manager can choose among a dazzling, and in some instances contradictory, array of theories of motivation with derivative prescriptions for action to guide important organizational decisions. The difficulty in choosing is amplified because it seems that no single approach to the issue has a clear, consistent edge over the others. Each approach has its adherents, some more vocal and assertive than others. The fact remains, however, that managers will select (either explicitly or implicitly), a set of strategies and theories about motivation which guide their organizational decisions. These decisions will be influenced by the manager's own career experiences and the motivational aspects of subordinates' jobs.

Implications for the Manager

Each manager has a preferred style of management. This style will be based, in large part, on the beliefs the manager holds about what motivates people and on values the manager thinks are important. Thus, the decisions and behaviors of effective managers will reflect their choices of and preferences for different theories of motivation.

Implications for Subordinates

It is virtually impossible for one person to know, except superficially, another person's needs and motives. We may be able to guess or infer a certain need or motive based on our observation of particular sequences of behaviors. In addition, we may rely on some global assumption about universally basic needs, such as needs for security, mastery, power, affiliation, and self-actualization. Nevertheless, to prove which need is operating to stimulate the particular behavior observed at a particular time relies on a set of cause-effect relationships whose validity is tenuous at best.

The manager must decide and act, even in the absence of consistent, proven theories of motivation. As a consequence, managers have to be eclectic in the adoption of motivation theory. As a guide to managerial decisions and actions, managers should rely on those theories and derived prescriptions for action which in their experiences seem to work. Each manager will bring a different set of needs, skills, and values to the work situation. The combination of these factors will call for a unique combination of actions which will appeal to the needs of the manager's subordinates.

Managers, then, have to decide on which occasions and under what circumstances they will invoke prescriptions of the different theories in their attempts to influence the motivation of subordinates. A manager's job is to generate a successful mix of motivational theory and practice. This mix should match the manager's own preferences, beliefs, and values, with varying situations and with the preferences of his or her subordinates. To do so, managers will sometimes have to exercise social power. This aspect of managers' activities cannot be ignored or avoided. At other times, however, they must be highly tolerant. They must know when to challenge subordinates and when to give them breathing room. They must know when to reward desirable behavior and when to ignore undesirable behavior.

NOTES

1. Abraham H. Maslow, *Motivation and Personality* (New York: Harper & Row, 1954).
2. D. C. McClelland, *The Achieving Society* (Princeton: Van Nostrand, 1961).
3. David C. McClelland and David H. Burnham, "Power is the Great Motivator" *Harvard Business Review* Vol. 54 No. 2 (March–April 1976) pp. 100–110.
4. F. Herzberg, "One More Time: How Do You Motivate Employees?" *Harvard Business Review* Vol. 46 No. 1 (January–February 1968) pp. 53–62.
5. Victor H. Vroom, *Work and Motivation* (New York: John Wiley and Sons, Inc., 1964).

DISCUSSION QUESTIONS

1. How can acts of heroism, in which great physical danger is voluntarily undertaken, be explained by Maslow's need hierarchy?
2. Discuss the factors that seem to motivate you to do your best school work. Would these same factors apply to your job performance?
3. Describe a norm that exists in a group to which you belong. How would you go about trying to change that norm?
4. Discuss your conclusions about the motivation of spectators at a sporting event such as a little league baseball game, a boxing match, a college or professional football game, a tennis match, or a golf tournament. Relate your comments to different theories of motivation.

BIBLIOGRAPHY

Armor, Thomas. "A Note on the Peak Experience and a Transpersonal Psychology." *Journal of Transpersonal Psychology,* Vol. 1 No. 1 (Spring 1969), pp. 47–50.
Cartwright, Dorwin and Alvin Zander, eds. *Group Dynamics,* 2nd ed. Evanston: Row, Peterson and Co., 1960.

Fry, Fred L. "Operant Conditioning in Organizational Settings: Of Mice or Men?" *Personnel,* Vol. 51 (July–August 1974), pp. 17–24.

Herzberg, F. "One More Time: How Do You Motivate Employees?" *Harvard Business Review,* Vol. 46 No. 1 (January–February 1968), pp. 53–62.

House, R. J. and L. A. Wigdor. "Herzberg's Dual-Factor Theory of Job Satisfaction and Motivation: A Review of the Evidence and a Criticism." *Personnel Psychology,* Vol. 20 No. 4 (Winter 1967), pp. 369–89.

Knowles, Henry P. and Borje O. Saxberg. "Human Relations and the Nature of Man." *Harvard Business Review,* Vol. 45 No. 2 (March–April 1967), p. 224.

Levinson, Harry. "Asinine Attitudes Toward Motivation." *Harvard Business Review,* Vol. 51 No. 1 (January–February 1973), pp. 70–76.

Luthans, Fred and Robert Kreitner. *Organizational Behavior Modification.* Glenview: Scott, Foresman and Co., 1975.

Maslow, Abraham H. *Motivation and Personality.* New York: Harper & Row, 1954.

McClelland, D. C. *The Achieving Society* Princeton: Van Nostrand, 1961.

McClelland, David C. and David H. Burnham. "Power is the Great Motivator." *Harvard Business Review,* Vol. 54 No. 2 (March–April 1976), pp. 100–110.

Olmstead, Michael S. *The Small Group.* New York: Random House 1959.

Vroom, Victor H. *Work and Motivation.* New York: John Wiley and Sons 1964.

Zaleznik, Abraham. "Power and Politics in Organizational Life." *Harvard Business Review,* Vol. 48 No. 3 (May–June 1970), pp. 47–60.

The Case of the Contrary Conscience

Amos Hull's family had farmed the same rocky forty acres in an isolated area of Vermont for nearly three hundred years. The original Amos Hull had left England with other members of a small religious sect in order that they might worship God and interpret the Bible in the manner of their choosing. The valley they selected for settlement had enough resources to provide a frugal living, and the sect was able to stay in existence and remain relatively independent of outside material influences through nine generations.

The congregation survived the minor disasters of nature that a farming community could expect over the time that it occupied the valley, but in 1968 two catastrophes occurred in series that destroyed its means of livelihood. First, a fire swept across the fields ready for harvesting, the orchards, and the grazing lands. Several lives were lost, much of the livestock was killed, and the homes and barns were leveled. Then came an early blizzard that killed most of the remaining livestock; and without shelter, the families were forced to flee to the nearest town. The congregation's way of living had not been calculated to generate much cash, and the communal wealth, of which Amos Hull was custodian, was slightly over $1100.

Through the efforts of some of the leading townspeople, the valley was declared a disaster area, and the inhabitants were entitled to a rehabilitation loan at low interest. When this information was communicated to the valley residents, Amos Hull, acting as spokesman, explained their refusal: "In our religion we consider debt to be a sin. The heads of the families are going to find work. We will pool our savings, and when we have enough we will rebuild our farms."

Although Amos Hull had no specific job skill, he could work with hand tools, and he moved his wife and three daughters to Waterbury, Connecticut, where he got a job as an assembler at the National Valve Company. Although Amos was not by inclination a friendly man, his co-workers sympathized with his plight, and helped him acquire the skills necessary to perform his duties. In fact, they might have taught him too well, because within a few months he was progressively exceeding the daily output of every other worker in the assembly crew.

One day Sam Bolton, who seemed to be the informal leader of the work group, came over to Amos' work bench. "Huh! Sixty valves assembled so far today, and there are still two hours to go," Sam said as he looked at Amos' tally sheet. "Didn't I let you know last week that the gang has set about fifty valves a day as the bogey? What are you trying to do—mess things up for everybody?"

"I'm sorry you feel that way," said Amos, "but I can't do less than a full day's work for a full day's pay. I feel an obligation to turn out as many valves as I can."

"Buddy, we don't go for guys like you," Sam replied. "You either cut back to fifty valves per day, or it's going to be pretty rough for you around here."

Amos' daily production continued to increase, and things began to happen. The freeze was put on—not one member of the assembly crew said a word to him.

His tools would mysteriously disappear. Sometimes when he opened his lunch pail he would find it filled with greasy rags. One evening as he walked home he was grabbed from behind, and punched in the stomach. His productivity finally leveled off, but at a rate almost double the standard set by the work group.

Bill Eztey, assembly lead man, met Amos one morning as he entered the shop. "Well if it isn't the tin hero," said Bill. "The guy who shows up everybody, including me, his boss. Now the foreman wants to know why I let the rest of the gang get away with doing only about half the work that you do. You had better get in line, or I'm going to find some reason to get rid of you." Amos proceeded to his work bench, and knelt to pray as he did each morning. He then turned to his work, and assembled more valves that day than he had ever managed to produce in a single day.

About two weeks later, the company's personnel manager passed down word that he would like to talk to Amos. "You know, you are the only employee who has not made a donation to the Community Chest," he said to Amos. "The company prides itself on getting 100 percent participation each year. Why don't you make a small donation, like $5.00, just so that everybody will be in."

"I don't believe in accepting charity, or in giving to charity except to my own congregation," Amos answered. "This is a deep conviction with me."

At about this time, after several attempts to get a union shop, the International Association of Machinists received a majority vote by the employees of National Valve Company. Amos cast his vote against the union, and made up his mind that he would never join, regardless of the outcome of the election. Because of the completely ostracized conditions under which he worked, he knew little of the implications of National Valve Company being certified as a union shop by the NLRB. He disregarded the form that he received in his pay envelope, which he was supposed to sign authorizing the deduction of union dues from his paycheck.

Once again Amos was called to the office of the personnel manager. "Secretly I applauded the way you stood up for your rights on the Community Chest matter," the personnel manager said to Amos, "but this issue is different. Unless you authorize the check-off of union dues, the company will have to let you go."

"Badly as I need the job, that's what you will have to do," Amos said. "My principles are against an individual having to belong to anything."

DISCUSSION QUESTIONS

1. How could the process of motivating be simplified if people's behavior were consistently rational?
2. Argue against Freud's thesis that the behavior of humans is largely determined in childhood by impressions on the unconscious mind.
3. In the Case of the Contrary Conscience, Amos Hull's precept against going into debt seems completely out of date. However, what constrains you, and most of the people you know,

from using credit to the limit in getting material things?

4. Do you believe Amos Hull was acting rationally, or irrationally, when he refused to conform to the pressures of his work group and his boss to reduce his production of valves?

5. Do you agree or disagree with Amos that an individual should have the right to accept or reject membership in any organization? What makes you think as you do?

The Case of the Invisible Hand

The invoice processing section of the New York Wholesale Hardware Company's accounting department had a normal complement of seventy-five women clerks who were divided into five groups. Each group was headed by a woman group leader, and they in turn reported to Walter Miller, section supervisor. The section occupied one wing of the top floor of the company's Brooklyn headquarters building. The invoice clerks' desks were arranged in rows facing the desks of the group leaders. Miller occupied a glassed-in cubicle in a corner of the wing. The work performed by the invoice clerks consisted of deriving the details of sales from the customers' purchase orders and the shipping reports, and typing invoices to be mailed to the customers.

One day in the summer of 1977, Miller was visited in his cubicle by Harvey Smith, payroll section supervisor. "Walt, I have a problem with one of my clerks," said Smith. "She has the potential of being a good worker. However, she seems to rebel at conforming to any standards or rules of conduct. The groups in my section are not very closely knit, perhaps because I have purposely kept moving individuals from group to group to prevent them from developing loyalties other than to the total section. Some of the others are beginning to copy this girl's behavior. Her name is Linda Jones, and although I don't want to, I will have to discharge her unless you will be willing to give her a trial. I am asking you because of the excellent morale that you have developed in your section."

"The morale in my section is more the result of what I call 'the invisible hand,' which is an inaccurate paraphrase from Adam Smith's 'The Wealth of Nations,' than from anything that I have done," replied Miller. "By 'invisible,' I mean that the employees are motivated by some force that exists within their groups. I'll be glad to give this girl a chance. What does Linda look like?"

"She is in her early twenties, and is small and pretty."

"She sounds like a perfect fit for the 'Mighty Mites,'" said Walter Miller.

"What do you mean, 'Mighty Mites?' That sounds like a name for a girls' softball team."

"Well, I used to designate my groups by the letters of the alphabet corresponding to the names of the customers that they handled," Miller replied. "For example, there was A–E Group, F–L Group, and so on. One day, quite by accident, in complimenting the F–L Group I called them 'the mighty mites,' because they are all rather short, petite types. The name stuck, and the girls seemed to take more pride in belonging to the group. And surprisingly, the group's productivity began to improve. Pretty soon the other groups began to invent names for themselves, so now instead of having cold alphabetical designations, we have the Valkyries, the Suffragettes, the Florence Nightingales, and the Gray Ladies, in addition to the Mighty Mites."

"Do these names pose any personnel problems for you?" asked Smith.

"They definitely do," answered Miller. "I have to be extremely careful when I assign a new employee to a group to put her where she fits. Each group has taken on distinctive characteristics. For example, the Gray Ladies are all older women, the Suffragettes are in their thirties and early forties, the Valkyries all have last names like Olsen, Kruger, or Hackenschmidt. The Florence Nightingales have the highest educational level and the largest proportion of black women. It's remarkable, but the women in all groups are obviously pleased when I make a perfect fit in placing a new employee. On the other hand, performance of the entire section drops immediately if I don't fit a new person to the proper group. For instance, productivity would fall 50 percent if I put Linda Jones in the Gray Ladies."

"Do you think the Mighty Mites can change her behavior?" asked Smith.

"She will either conform to the group's norms, or she will be made so miserable that she will quit," said Miller. "All of the groups have set productivity standards in terms of average number of invoices processed each month, average number of errors, etc. The groups compete with each other to have the best monthly records. In addition, the Mighty Mites have adopted a certain style of dress. They use low-key makeup. They don't smoke at their desks. If Linda flaunts these norms, the other girls won't talk to her. She will eat lunch by herself. She won't be invited to parties and the other things the girls do together. I think

she will change, not only to keep the job, but in order to belong to the group."

On the next day when Miller interviewed Linda Jones, he made the following mental observations: Her appearance was seemingly in defiance of conventional business standards. She wore no makeup, tight, tattered jeans, and a t-shirt. She chain-smoked. She was defensive, with slight undercurrent indications of fear. On the positive side, she had better than average grades from high school, her typing proficiency was high, and her responses to questions were quick and articulate.

About a month later, Miller came to the office early, and to his surprise found Linda at her desk working. "What are you doing here at this time of the morning?" he asked, noting a complete change in her dress and general appearance.

"I didn't make my quota yesterday, and I came in early to be sure to get it out," she answered.

"How do you like your job?" asked Miller.

"I hated it the first week," she replied. "Now I love it. Can you believe that the group got together a donation to send flowers to my mother who is in the hospital? And one of the girls got me a blind date with her brother, and now we are going steady." She looked up shyly: "I like being a Mighty Mite."

DISCUSSION QUESTIONS

1. What can a manager do on finding that the productivity norms set by the group are lower than the standards established for the group?
2. Are cohesive subordinate groups a help or a hindrance to effective management?
3. In the Case of the Invisible Hand, what factor is leading to high morale and productivity, in addition to the "invisible hand" that Walter Miller modestly identifies?
4. What practical problems hinder attempts to fit a new employee to the group for which he or she appeared to be most suited?

22 Managing Professional Employees

Our society has been experiencing a striking increase in the amount of specialization in its educational programs. Specialists in subareas of traditional professions are more the rule than the exception. Changes in technology and knowledge occur at ever increasing rates. This has contributed to organizations' need to include more and more specialists in the ranks of their employees.

Specialists in professions have begun to practice in groups. Physicians, attorneys, and accountants have a history of group practice. Less common, but increasingly found, are groups of dentists, consulting engineers, and management consultants. These groups provide an opportunity for a team of related specialists to provide a broad spectrum of services in a central location. The specialists benefit from their professional interaction and the breadth of skills they can apply to a client's problem. Both the professionals and their clients can realize financial benefits that flow from combined practices.

Managing a group of professionals, whether they are organizational employees or a voluntary association of professional people, calls for the application of principles common to all management situations. There are also some unique characteristics and issues in managing professional people. We will focus on these issues in this chapter.

UNIQUENESS OF PROFESSIONAL EMPLOYEES

Two kinds of factors set professional employees apart from other organization members. One has to do with what they represent to the organization. The other has to do with the characteristics which profes-

319

sional people seem to share which make them different from other organization members.

Meaning to the Organization

For an organization, its pool of professional employees represents an extremely valuable asset. Their value is derived from at least two sources. One source is the dependence of business organizations on the continuous generation of new ideas that can be incorporated into future products or services. These new ideas, and their development, often come from an organization's professional employees. Hiring and keeping professional employees represents a substantial investment by the organization in maintaining the flow of new ideas.

A second source of value to the organization comes in the form of skills and expert knowledge the professional brings to the job. There are usually intensive educational processes and evaluative hurdles which the person must pass to gain professional standing. The professional can exercise these skills and knowledge on the part of the organization.

Characteristics of Professionals

People who have entered professions often share a unique set of characteristics, assumptions, and expectations. While there will be obvious exceptions to such a listing, the following seem to set professional employees apart from other nonmanagerial employees:

- Professionals have invested heavily in terms of time, energy, and often salary foregone, in order to prepare themselves in their area.
- The number of potential employers is relatively large for the professionally trained individual. If employment in an organization does not suit the professional it is often possible to go into private practice or to simply change organizations.
- Professionals will usually have strong loyalties to and identify with their profession. These loyalties can be in conflict with loyalties to their employing organization.
- Professionals often have strong needs for recognition. They usually prefer to be deeply involved in their work and in many cases will have substantial needs for self-actualization (see Chapter 21).

ISSUES IN MANAGING PROFESSIONAL EMPLOYEES

An important consideration for maintaining job satisfaction with professional employees involves selecting the right manager. Managers in this role must possess an unusual combination of talents. In some quarters, it is felt that people who are *not* trained in a particular profession can rarely be successful managing a group of professionally trained people. The gap in vocabulary and, more importantly, the potential absence of regard for people working in, but not trained in, the profession are major obstacles to such a manager's success. There are, however, notable exceptions to this argument. For example, there are a number of graduate schools of management that have seasoned business executives as their deans. It would be rare, though, to find someone chairing a department who was not an academician. The use of a nonphysician manager for a group medical practice is not uncommon. Both physicians and nonphysicians hold positions as hospital directors. It seems clear that people who are not trained in the profession have to do more to insure their managerial success. Sophisticated, sensitive management skill will go a long way to overcome disadvantages associated with not being a member of a particular profession.

Another important consideration in managing these employees involves the increasing authority they exercise in high-level decision making. Because professional people have special knowledge and skills they enjoy a degree of influence in their organization which is broader and stronger than their formal, organizational positions might suggest. Senior managers cannot know all the facets of the many specialized areas so they must rely on the judgment of their professional employees. This informal influence can create interunit problems for the manager. A professional employee's direct access to management higher in the hierarchy can pose situations which are not easily resolved by traditional, bureaucratic methods, as well. For example, changing tax considerations could result in the accountant of a manufacturing firm having as much influence with top management as the vice-president of operations.

JOB PREFERENCES AND REWARDS

Professional people usually place a high priority on work assignments that are challenging and sufficiently stimulating to provide them with a sense of achievement. They want to receive recognition for outstanding performance from the organization and from their colleagues. They rate highly the opportunity to exercise considerable personal discretion in carrying out their work. While not universally true, professional people in organizations tend to expect working conditions generally equivalent with those enjoyed by others in private practices. This could involve perquisites such as office and equipment of a certain quality, relatively unstructured working hours, and some freedom from routine tasks.

To be effective, managers must have a good understanding of the preferences of the particular people in their sections. Work assignments should be geared to individual preferences, abilities, and interests and at the same time they should be consistent with the goals of the organization. Some people prefer to work alone; others prefer to work with colleagues. Organization structure should be arranged to follow these preferences rather than to run counter to them.

To foster creativity, managers should provide a work environment that is relatively open and permissive. There should be a climate in which criticism of ideas is delayed and judgment is deferred. New ideas are often fragile. They may need to be shielded in their early stages from the harsh criticism and detailed evaluation that characterize some organizational climates. Open communications is a must for the encouragement of new, creative ideas. Ideal conditions for creativity include a substantial degree of cooperation within units which are working on the same or similar projects.

Finally, managers of creative people will usually need to provide some degree of insulation for those people from the rest of the organization. Creative people often do not work well under structured conditions. Their behavior, dress, work habits, and attitudes may be substantially different from those in the balance of the organization. Other parts of the organization may pressure creative people in an attempt to bring their behavior and procedures in line with more traditional ones in the organization. Creative people and organizations will need some shelter from these pressures so that the creative output is not impaired.

Reward Structure Issues

Professional employees present unique problems for the manager with regard to the reward structure in the organization. Typical promotional paths in organizations involve the transition from technical proficiency and performance to assignments that are managerial and administrative. This sequence can be a real dilemma for professional people who are competent in their field, prefer to practice their profession, but do not aspire to management roles. Special promotional paths can be considered for employees in this situation. Typical examples of this process occur in the field of engineering and nursing. In some hospitals, for example, the promotion ladder for nurses has been divided into two tracks. This split usually occurs at the point where the nurse, in order to be promoted, would typically move up to a supervisory position. Rather than require a shift from professional activities to the assumption of managerial responsibilities, the alternative path makes it possible for the nurse to earn increases in pay and organizational stature as a clinical nurse. The clinical nurse's responsibilities do not include administration and supervision. Instead the position calls for high-level performance in the professional practice of nursing.

There have been some innovative adjustments in organizational structures which have accommodated the need to formally recognize, through promotions, outstanding performance without imposing managerial tasks. By creating parallel paths of advancement, one managerial and the other based on excellence in professional achievement, the dilemma can be resolved. Implementing this type of structure requires that the traditional rule that "no one should make more than the manager" will have to be discarded. It has been pointed out that this rule was not carved in stone. Furthermore, it is mainly within the ranks of business organizations that a great cloud of secrecy is maintained around salaries people earn. In public sector organizations, salary levels are public knowledge. The concern for managers being the most highly paid in their organization may stem from a subtle association assumed to exist between the amount of money received in compensation and the amount of authority in the position (or person occupying the position).

Salaries for professional employees in an organization are also influenced by the fact that people in private practice in the same profession are very highly paid. Professional employees are usually brought into the organization at salaries that are high relative to other organizational salaries. The premium must be offered to attract competent and skilled professionals. A consequence of this practice is that the typical band of salary increases is relatively narrow, so that as a percentage of a large base, increases may seem incrementally small. This perception tends to make fringes and benefits other than salary relatively more important in maintaining satisfaction with this aspect of the job. The organization can subsidize professional development, encourage such things as attendance at professional meetings, and provide recognition to individuals who present research papers.

Teamwork Among Professional Employees

Professional employees can be grouped into two kinds of teams. Each has different implications for the manager. Teams may be composed of members who are from the same professional area. The legal or medical staff of an organization is an example of this kind of group. When managing this sort of group, emphasis should be placed on permitting individual preferences and unique skills to guide decisions.

Teams may also be interdisciplinary in nature. The group may have members from several separate professions. In an organizational context, the teams may be grouped in matrix form, or in a product/project format (see Chapter 11). In this situation the organization has the opportunity for reaping huge benefits from the skills of its professional employees. Interdisciplinary teams can apply a wide range of skills and education to particular questions. There is also the potential for great misunderstanding and conflict in these groups due to the differences in training, outlook, and values. Managing interdisciplinary teams calls for well-developed skills in facilitating communication. Team members will need to be assisted in dovetailing their specialized work in the service of team goals. Managers of these teams will need to be skillful in resolving conflicts.

The Dilemma of the White-Collar Worker

No one likes strikes. However, a factory worker's life is not so closely tied to a regular weekly income as the white-collar worker's. When an Auto Workers representative was trying to explain the guaranteed annual wage to an audience of union members' wives, he asked the question, "How many of you women here can go into a store and buy something and tell the man that you'll be able to make a regular weekly payment for the next fifty-two weeks?" Not a single woman in the audience raised her hand. Certain periods of unemployment— whether through lay-off or strikes—are an accepted part of a blue-collar worker's life. However, to a white-collar worker—who mortgages his regular paycheck months in advance and has to meet installments due on his house and refrigerator—a period of unemployment is catastrophic.

Catastrophe, crisis, and militancy are scare words to white-collar workers. They want to be dignified, professional, and loved. They want to be promoted; they want to be secure; and they don't want to have to fight. Actually, they are probably not sophisticated enough to know when they are being exploited.

White-collar workers are the most exploited group in our economy. Tied to a fixed nonnegotiable salary, victims of every price rise (with no escalator clause to help them), without a political voice raised on their behalf, they are truly "on the short end." But, like Steinbeck's tenant in *The Grapes of Wrath*, whom do they shoot? Mr. Turner, the head of the accounting department, who is so grouchy when he comes to work in the morning? The Steelworkers who always get those big wage raises for their members and thus—according to steel executives—force prices up all along the line? The politicians who never keep their promises? The company for which they work?

No, instead of shooting the company executives or joining a union, they mouse along and live with their hopes.

In a general way, every manager's assignments include the task of coordinating the activities of the organization. This is also a part of the assignment for managers of professional employees. However, for these managers an equally important task includes managing the environment in which professional employees practice. Professional employees possess specialized skills which are relatively expensive. The manager should provide working conditions and support services which permit professionals to concentrate attention and time on their practice rather than on activities which do not require specialized background, education, and training.

DISCUSSION QUESTIONS

1. Suppose that an organization established separate personnel policies for its professional employees. How would employee relations in other departments be affected?

2. What criteria should be used when selecting a manager for professional employees?
3. What problems would you have if you were a manager of a department in which the salaries of many of the people were higher than yours?

BIBLIOGRAPHY

Anderson, H. H., ed. *Creativity and Its Cultivation.* New York: Harper & Row, 1959.

Charnot, Dennis. "Professional Employees Turn to Unions." *Harvard Business Review,* Vol. 54 No. 3 (May–June 1976), pp. 119–27.

House, R. J., A. C. Filley, and S. Kerr. "Relation of Leader Consideration and Initiating Structure to Research and Development Subordinate Satisfaction." *Administrative Science Quarterly,* Vol. 16 No. 1 (March 1971), pp. 19–30.

Levinson, Harry. *Executive Stress.* New York: Harper & Row, 1964.

Patton, Arch. "The Coming Flood of Young Executives." *Harvard Business Review,* Vol. 54 No. 5 (September–October 1976), pp. 20–38, 178–80.

Steiner, G. A. *Creative Organization.* Chicago: University of Chicago Press, 1965.

Thompson, Paul H. and Gene W. Dalton. "Are R and D Organizations Obsolete?" *Harvard Business Review,* Vol. 54 No. 6 (November–December 1976), pp. 105–16.

The Case of Why Some Engineers May Join Unions

"The reason I have asked you to come here," said Preston McNair, senior vice-president of engineering, Amalgamated Aircraft Corporation, to Sharon Cloud, industrial psychologist in the personnel department, "is to see if you can help me understand why any individual with an engineering degree would join a union. When I was a young man moving up the ladder, engineers looked at themselves as professionals, just like physicians or attorneys, and considered that unions were for the blue-collar workers. We got everything that we needed, such as security, status, and challenge, from our jobs. Yet, the bulk of the engineers in this company have voted for a union. Why?"

Cloud glanced about McNair's luxurious office. With its drapes, thick carpet, oil paintings, and expensive furniture, it looked like a room in a private club. "Tell me, Mr. McNair," she asked, "how long has it been since you have had any contact with the working engineers in this company?"

"Well, to tell you the truth, it has been a long time. My responsibilities center on engineering policy at the corporate level. There are engineering division managers for the product groups whom I see frequently, and sometimes I have contact with a few of the managers of engineering departments. However, I haven't talked with a first line engineer in years."

"I suggest that we take a walk through one of the engineering buildings," said Cloud. "You may get the answer to your question through your own observations."

As McNair and Cloud opened the door leading to the interior area of the Commercial Aircraft Division engineering buildings, their view was obstructed by a large bulletin board. Despite the warning, "Use of this board for nonbusiness messages is expressly forbidden," a page from that morning's newspaper had been thumb-tacked to the board. The headlines of an article, which had been circled in red, were: "TEXAS AIRCRAFT TO LAY OFF 2000 ENGINEERS."

"I suppose the implication is that if a layoff can happen at our competitor's plant, it can also happen here," remarked McNair. "Let me take a minute to read this company communication." The communication was headed: "RULES OF CONDUCT FOR ALL ENGINEERING JOB CLASSIFICATIONS," and listed fifteen statements, of which the following are examples:

1. Hours of work are from 7:30 A.M. to 4:00 P.M., with a lunch break from 11:30 A.M. to 12:00 noon. A ten-minute coffee break is permitted in the morning and in the afternoon.

2. Except for the designated breaks, all employees are expected to be at their work stations during the work day, unless authorized to leave by their supervisors, or for the relief of personal discomfort.

5. Nonbusiness conversations between employees at their work stations or in the corridors is not permitted.

8. Incoming personal telephone calls will not be transmitted by the control switchboard. With the approval of their supervisor, employees may place outgoing personal calls of not more than three minutes' duration at the pay telephone booth.

"Those are rather restrictive conditions for people that I called 'professional,'" McNair commented. "Let's see what the inside of this place looks like."

The scene that met his eyes would be staggering to a person not accustomed to it. The windowless interior covered acres of space. Half of the area was occupied by rows of drafting tables placed end to end. A draftsman was busily hunched over each table, with the exception of some groups of two or three people who appeared to be discussing the drawings on the tables. The other portion of the huge room was partitioned into cubicles. The portable walls of the cubicles were six feet high, and there were two sizes of cubicles in the main area, one sized to accommodate four desks and the other sized to hold eight desks. A labyrinth of corridors permitted access to the various cubicles. Each of the four walls of the building were lined with cubicles large enough to hold one desk, a table, and four chairs. These were the offices of the supervisors.

"I know what you are thinking, Cloud," said McNair, "but let me remind you that when I started out as an engineer I worked in an airplane hangar. Of course, I'll have to admit that I would rather work in a hangar than in this place. By the way, who is that guy walking around with the clipboard?"

"His job is to take notes at random of what the people in this room are doing at all hours of the day. He notes what proportion appears to be working, what proportion seems to be occupied with nonbusiness activities, what proportion is away from the assigned work stations, and so on. The results are tabulated into comparative scores for the various supervisors' sections. Each week the five highest and the five lowest sections are listed on the bulletin board. Supervisors of sections with low scores are reprimanded, and they in turn chew out their subordinates. It's supposed to be a motivating device."

"It sounds about as motivating as a rawhide whip," said McNair caustically. "What is the education level of the people working in these cubicles?"

"Seventy-eight percent have at least a bachelor's degree, 35 percent have a master's degree, and 17 percent have their doctorate," replied Cloud. "Perhaps you would like to talk to some of them," she said as she directed McNair into a cubicle occupied by four men.

After the introductions and some opening conversation, McNair asked the question: "What about the work itself? Are the assignments that you are given challenging to you?"

"Sir, I am willing to speak for all four of us," said Tom Jefferson, who had a master's degree. "The practice here is to force engineers into specialization on fragments of work. As a result, we simply do the same things over and over again. We become good at some micro portion of our engineering field, but we don't have the opportunity to expand our abilities. Actually, I haven't been stimulated by my work in over two years."

Just then the 11:30 bell rang, and the men reached for their metal lunch containers. McNair and Cloud walked out of the building. "Before going back to your office," said Cloud, "let's take a walk through the machine shop."

At the entrance to the machine shop,

there was a bulletin board with a rules of conduct list prominently displayed. The shop was a vast windowless area filled with rows of machine tools. Several analysts could be observed entering work-sampling notes on clipboards. Because the machine shop was on a different schedule, the bell rang at noon, and the workers reached for their metal lunch containers.

Back in his office, McNair sat thoughtfully for a few minutes. Finally he said: "You are right. I did get the answer to my question, Cloud. Except for higher pay and cleaner clothes, there is no difference in this company's treatment of engineers and machinists. The engineers are worried about being laid off, the working conditions couldn't possibly make them proud of their status, and their work is boring to them. Why shouldn't they think that a union might satisfy some of their needs?"

DISCUSSION QUESTIONS

1. Explain why individuals might leave a secure job where they have many friends and risk their savings to start their own businesses.
2. What are the implications, for a manager trying to motivate subordinates, of the tenet that a satisfied need is not a motivator?
3. In the Case of Why Some Engineers May Join Unions, what evidence is there that Amalgamated Aircraft's engineers may feel a threat to their security need?
4. Has Amalgamated Aircraft accorded professional esteem to its technically trained employees?
5. What needs of Amalgamated Aircraft's engineers could a union satisfy?

23 Communications in Organizations

Communications is the tool managers use to achieve coordination among organizational units. Managers use communications to perform planning, organizing, staffing, leading, and controlling functions. The chapter first reviews topics and concepts in communications of a general nature. Then the important area of interpersonal communications is discussed. These interpersonal, face-to-face exchanges are a critical aspect of a manager's job. Much of the success, or failure, a manager experiences is a consequence of interpersonal communication.

A COMMUNICATIONS MODEL

Communication, in its most simple state, is the exchange of information among units and/or people. Successful communication has occurred when an idea or piece of information has been accurately transferred from a sender to the intended receiver. Figure 23-1 represents a typical schematic representation of the communication process.

This schematic could be extended to include machines as senders or receivers of information and ideas. Since the majority of organizational communications involves a human being in some way at each end of the process, our discussion will refer to people.

Encoding and Decoding

The communicative process begins when there is some idea or information that a potential sender wishes a receiver to understand. This idea is "encoded" into a message format within the sender. Basically, the encoding of an idea involves the conversion of an experience into a

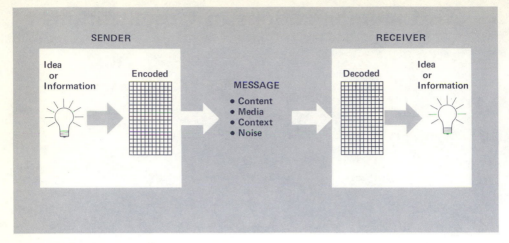

Figure 23-1.   A Communications Model.

series of words. Suppose, for example, you are trying to describe a beautiful sunset to a friend. In many ways, words fail to capture the whole meaning.

The encoding is isolated in the schematic because it is through this encoding that so much of the variation from intentions are introduced. Variations are introduced because people can perceive a limited amount of stimuli. If this were not the case we would be unable to discriminate between the different sensations which bombard us constantly. This perceptual filtering of sensory data is also at work when an idea is encoded for transmission to another person. The *message* is a symbolic representation of the idea, not the idea itself; as a consequence the translation of an idea into a message symbolizing that idea will involve a large component of bias unique to the sender.

The same sequence happens at the receiver end of the process. The message is filtered through the decoding process which has influences that are unique and unpredictably different in many ways from the sender's filter. Thus an idea in the sender is filtered twice before it emerges from the process as an idea with the receiver.

© 1962 United Features Syndicate Inc.

The encoding and decoding of ideas is affected by all the following:

- Sender/receiver attitudes and value systems.
- Sender/receiver perceptual processes which are influenced, in turn, by the person's needs.
- The sum of sender/receiver experiences and the assumptions made about the situation.
- Judgments about the receiver's or sender's credibility, trust, worthiness, integrity, and intentions.
- The culture, including vocabulary and language, surrounding the communications process.

A message may use a vocabulary entirely unfamiliar to the receiver. Terms such as LIFO, FIFO, and EBIT would make sense to an accountant while they would probably baffle an electrical engineer. Some concepts are unique to a language and do not translate well into other languages. Eskimos for example, have nine words for snow which convey subtle yet important differences in meaning.

The Message

A number of things can happen to a message on its way from sender to receiver. The content of the message may overload the receiver's ability to decode it. Or the content of a message may be so poorly organized that it is almost meaningless.

The selection of a medium for the message will also affect the message itself. Actually, it is impossible to convey the smell of a rose or the intent of a simple smile in words. The selection of media—written, sign, and nonverbal—will all influence the message itself.

Written messages have the advantage of permanence. The receiver of a written communication can go over the message at a convenient pace and as many times as necessary. Written communication tends to be one-way, so that questions raised or clarifications needed are often delayed or nonexistent.

Verbal messages contain additional information provided by vocal intonation. The verbal message "That's a good job" can differ in meaning depending on whether it is said in a sarcastic or genuine way.

Nonverbal messages can involve gestures that are intentionally made as well as movement and body language that are not particularly planned. Examples of the former include the wave of the hand or shaking the fist. Less intentional gestures are also potent influences on messages. For instance, drumming the fingers, a relaxed or tense posture, and nodding the head signal that you are listening. Nodding can also signal affirmation and agreement—or sleepiness.

The context within which the communication occurs will also influence the message. Noise in the communication process will reduce the quality of message received. For our purposes, *noise* is the extra energy in a communication channel which is not a part of the message but which is nevertheless carried along, usually interfering with the message. Static over a radio is an example of noise in that communication system. In an effort to curry favor with a newly elected official, a political appointee might introduce noise into the communication of information about the state of the agencies under his or her direction. In a business organization, noise can be introduced at the various levels that may be involved in the communications chain. For example, a department manager communicates a new production schedule along with some additional items of his or her own, such as a need for fewer grievances to the foremen. The foremen communicate the schedules along with the manager's noise to workers, maintenance staffs, and union officials while adding their own "extra" noise.

Timing is another contextual issue influencing messages. A message delivered so late as to make it impossible to appropriately respond will probably generate resentment and accomplish little else. Distributing a memo informing middle-level managers of a major change in policy and goals of a firm, after an announcement to that effect has appeared on the financial page of a local newspaper, will probably make some managers wonder how they are viewed by top management. This situation is an example of multiple messages being received simultaneously, an occurrence that is often not intended by the sender. Nonetheless, people are generally quick to infer a great deal from what is *not* in an organizational communication. To prevent misunderstandings, a climate of mutual trust and integrity is invaluable to both sender and receiver for an accurate transfer of ideas.

DIRECTIONAL FLOW OF COMMUNICATIONS

In this section we will address some of the unique qualities of the directional flow of communications in organizations. In general, the type of message that flows downward in the organization involves telling people what is going to happen and what to do. Upward-flowing communication tends to be informative in nature. Lateral messages also carry "news" rather than orders and directives. The information in lateral communications helps coordinate the activities between units in the organization.

Downward-Flowing Communications

Managers often use downward-flowing communication to tell subordinates about

- expectations and directions for performing work tasks.
- information about the company, including prospects, goals, product news, and operational developments.
- personnel policies and procedures.
- important changes in the goals or operations of the organization.

When communicating downward, managers must select wording which meets the level of the subordinate. They can use verbal, written, or a combination of both media. The verbal mode could range from an address to a group, a conference, or face-to-face meetings with individuals. In general the questions of need for accuracy, time available, and relative costs in the various media are criteria useful in deciding these issues. A written communication could range from widely disseminated ones such as newsletters or bulletin board announcements, to more intimate forms such as personal letters and memos.

The Upward Flow of Communication

Upward-flowing communication is critical to organizational goal achievement. Communications moving in this direction tend to be informative in nature. In addition to all the influences described so far that can garble a message, upward-flowing communications are particularly sensitive to distortions and influences due to the organizational hierarchy. For instance, it is often difficult for subordinates to convey bad news to their supervisors. The supervisor controls rewards and punishments in the job situation. Consequently, there is a natural tendency to avoid communicating those messages upward which might reflect badly on one's job performance. (Managers are faced with a dilemma in that they need to know the quality of job performance in their organization and they cannot continually ignore poor performance.) Sometimes, the person bearing bad news receives the immediate negative reaction of the recipient of the news. This occurs whether or not the bearer of bad tidings caused the condition. Managers should carefully separate the quality of job performance from the information-conveying requirements of subordinate positions.

Lateral Communications

Lateral communications are the third important directional-flow category. These messages occur between individuals and hierarchical levels that are comparable, or nearly so, in the organization. This form of communication often takes place outside the formal hierarchy. It is a means of coordinating a large part of the organization's work. For example, suppose a local branch manager of a bank needed information about planned changes in the bank's policies regarding loan eligibility requirements. The manager would typically pick up the phone and call someone at a comparable level in the central office to get the information. When matters can be handled at this level, their resolution is usually speedier than it would be if formal channels were used. In addition, the time and attention of people in higher positions in the organizational hierarchy are not required. Lateral communications are particularly useful in conveying information across an organization about its goals, plans, and activities. Messages between people in different departments may be obstructed by formal organizational relationships. These obstructions will reflect the emphasis communicators place on the relative role and status of the departments they represent. In some ways, organizational subsystems always rival each other. This rivalry can lead to bias and confusion in the construction and interpretation of messages between them.

ONE-WAY AND TWO-WAY COMMUNICATION

A major distinction between communication processes is one that differentiates one-way and two-way communications. One-way communication limits the flow of messages from a sender to a receiver— no response is expected or necessary. Examples of one-way communication include formal speeches, company newspapers, notices on bulletin boards, and most mass media. This mode is usually used when there are many intended receivers of the message, when there is a high probability that the intended message is not confusing, or when a speedy transmission is necessary. Written communications are usually one-way. When it is important for managers to have a record of their messages, written, one-way communication is preferable. At a simple level, the issue for managers is whether to telephone (two-way) or send a memo (one-way). The simple communication model illustrated in Figure 23-1 is a one-way model. By adding a second, returning message from the receiver to the sender in response to the first message, the communications becomes two-way.

When accuracy of understanding is paramount, two-way communication is essential. In two-way communication, the feedback of receivers is sought to confirm that the message was accurately understood. The receiver's commitment to act in accordance with the intention of the message is another advantage of two-way communication. In the case of one-way communication, the sender does not know whether the absense of action is a result of a receiver's decision to ignore the message or a result of an "unreceived" message. Radio commercials often ask consumers to indicate that they heard about the product on the radio when they make a purchase. This feedback is useful in judging the effectiveness of the message. When complex task instructions are being given, a two-way mode of communication will usually result in a higher level of receiver satisfaction than one-way. This occurs because the receiver has an opportunity to clarify the parts of the instructions he or she does not understand.

The sender is generally more vulnerable in the two-way mode than in one-way. Responses from the receivers may include questions which point out unanticipated weaknesses in the content or idea behind the message. Responses may range beyond the scope of the initial message, causing the sender to deal with issues he or she might prefer to leave unaddressed.

Finally, one-way communication is relatively more neat and orderly than two-way. The latter tends to be noisy and unpredictable. A manager's communication efforts will be more successful when his or her intent is clear—whether it be to achieve full understanding or to persuade the receiver. Two-way communication is more successful in the former, one-way in the latter.

Communications Nets

Senders and receivers can be placed in different relationships to each other. The structure of these relationships has been referred to as *communication nets*. Research has been conducted to determine some of the effects of these different configurations of senders and receivers.[1] Three different nets are illustrated in Figure 23-2.

The person at the hub of the "wheel" is able to communicate with each of the other members of the group. They, in turn, are only able to communicate with the central person. This makes the central person very powerful since that position really controls the direction and content of information flows within the net. For the circle and star networks social power is less clearly a product of network design. Social power evolves from the group's interaction and the personalities of group members.

When given simple and repetitive tasks, the wheel-type group tends to be more efficient. This type of net is usually the most accurate of the three and performs the tasks faster as well. The free-flowing communications in the star network seem to diminish their effectiveness on simple tasks. Groups placed in this configuration for research purposes tend to voluntarily restrict their communications, choose a central person, and solve problems in a manner similar to procedures used by wheel groups. The level of task satisfaction among members is significantly higher for the star networks. This parallels the high level of satisfaction the central, hub person reported in the wheel network.

The circular or chained network is the least desirable for simple tasks. It is slower and there are more errors made in this type than in the other networks. People in the circular network have difficulty organizing their relationships. The chained, circular network is not a common organizational design. However, it does have an analog in organizational communications such as the practice of sending a memo or letter through

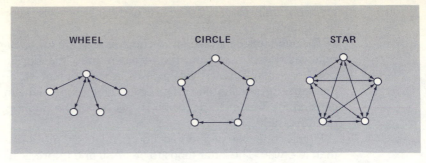

Figure 23-2.   Communications Nets.

several people before directing it to its intended recipient. Addressing memos via intermediate people is fairly common in organizations. For example, a memo from the manager of a production department to the vice-president of sales might be sent via the vice-president of production in an effort to keep the production vice-president informed.

Solving Complex Problems

When the networks are assigned complex problems involving value judgments, the quality of performance in the nets changes from that described above. The star communications networks are able to reach a decision much more quickly. These findings suggest that managers will benefit by organizing the communication structure in task groups depending on the nature of the tasks which face them. For simple, repetitive tasks, a group with a specified leader is most appropriate. When the task is more complex, like deciding on a department's budget, a more free-flowing, star-shaped communication network would be more appropriate.

INTERPERSONAL COMMUNICATIONS

Effective interpersonal communication is critical to productive leadership. Interpersonal communication is face-to-face, it involves verbal and nonverbal signals, and it is usually two-way. It is sometimes directed toward understanding, sometimes toward persuasion. In a sense, managers cannot avoid engaging in interpersonal communications. Whenever they speak, or for that matter, whenever they fail to speak with subordinates, interpersonal communications will be taking place. These communications will be characterized by the exchange of information and reactions to each new bit of information. In that sense they are not programmable in nature.

The content of interpersonal communications includes information about the topic, information about how the speaker feels about the topic, and sometimes information that suggests what expectations the sender has for how the receiver should deal with the message. An important component of interpersonal communications involves the nonverbal signals which are being sent. Gestures, such as a pointed finger or a clenched fist, emphasize information about the sender's feelings on a topic. People are curious, and appropriately so, about their supervisor's attitudes toward organizational issues. This is particularly so for issues that are felt to be critical to the success of people in the organization. Managers should realize that their nonverbal signals will be carefully "read" by subordinates in order to get an idea of the manager's full thinking.

Listening Skills

Effectiveness in interpersonal communication relies as heavily on good listening as it does on good message sending. The essence of interpersonal communication lies in the interaction between the people. Effectiveness in leading will often depend on the manager's listening skills. One factor in good listening includes an awareness of elements of the message being sent. When people talk with each other, there is a wealth of information being conveyed besides the words themselves. The feelings associated with the message are often subtle and the listeners may be aided in understanding by trying to hear from the sender's point of view. It is easy to turn off the listening as soon as it seems that we have the essence of a message. Since we think so much faster than we talk, the listener has extra time in conversations. That time is often used to construct and word responses and rebuttals to the message. The danger in that procedure is that some part of the whole message is lost. A good listener carefully attends to the other person and tries to understand the entire message. Attention should be paid to all the cues being sent, including the words, the intonation, the gestures, the meanings, and the feelings.

Barriers to Interpersonal Communication

The two biggest barriers to effective interpersonal communication are an evaluative stance on the part of the listener and responses which tend to generate defensiveness. When people sense that the message receiver is being critical or judgmental of what is being said, or of the sender, senders will be inclined to limit and edit their communications. This reaction will be more pronounced depending on the degree of power or control the receiver exercises over the message senders. Managers are clearly in this kind of relationship with their subordinates. To the extent that managers are felt to be evaluative, critical, or judgmental in their interpersonal communications, others will be less than open, candid, and sincere. Further exchanges will be resisted and increasingly strained.

Defensiveness is not consistent with effective interpersonal communication. Defensiveness is a natural reaction to a perceived threat. People can be threatened when they sense that others

- are trying to exert what is seen as inappropriate control over them.
- are trying to manipulate them; appear untrustworthy; seem to be dishonest or less than candid.
- hold an attitude of superiority.
- are dogmatic and rigid in their thinking.
- are indifferent to the idea they are trying to communicate.

Managers can improve the quality of their interpersonal communications by lowering the degree to which they may be threatening others. Managers may be threatening in ways that they are only slightly aware of and do not intend. Managers may exercise their authority in such a way that is highly intimidating to others. Nonverbal behavior may communicate very aggressive messages which can seem very threatening. Behavior which is in a direction opposite from those listed above will contribute to a positive cycle in the interpersonal communication process. The manager's efforts to establish a positive relationship will typically generate reciprocal positive behaviors in subordinates and the positive cycle is further encouraged.

Before interpersonal communication can be improved, a degree of trust must exist between parties. As trust between parties is violated or diminished, the quality of communications will begin to diminish. People will begin to feel threatened, they will act to defend themselves, and the candid, open quality of their communications will decrease. As the more powerful party in the relationship, managers have the opportunity to initiate behaviors which will begin the cycle moving in a positive direction. Subordinates will typically feel they have too much to lose to be able to take the risk necessary to initiate this process.

Empathy, unconditional positive regard, and sincerity in a relationship are qualities which, if expressed, can improve interpersonal relationships.[2] Empathy is the ability to accurately experience the world as another person does. It is not the same as sympathy or intellectual understanding. When you are speaking with someone who is truly empathetic, you *know* the other person really feels what you are experiencing. Now, if that person who is empathetic also conveys to you the idea that your experiences and your feelings are acceptable, and not to be judged, then you would probably feel safe enough that defensiveness is not necessary. Finally, if that other person shares some of his or her own feelings and experiences, you will probably feel that the person is trustworthy and that you are valued by that person. All of these qualities, then, enhance the chances for improved interpersonal relationships and communication.

Relationships as deep or personal as those described in the preceding discussion are rare and probably inappropriate in most organizational settings. The conditions, however, do point the direction for managers who wish to improve the quality of their interpersonal communications. Managers will need to recognize their own psychological preferences for closeness and openness in interpersonal relationships as well as their subordinates' preferences and expectations. In addition, the organization will have norms of expected behavior which must be taken into account. If managers wish to improve the quality and intensify the interpersonal dimension of their communications, attempts to demonstrate empathy, unconditional positive regard, and sincerity, will help.

Risks in Interpersonal Communications

Open interpersonal communications involves two forms of risk to the participants. When people are candid and reciprocal in their communications one party has information which could be used against the other. To trust another person in this case also means accepting the risk that the other may prove to be untrustworthy.

The second form of risk that good interpersonal communications involves has to do with changes in opinions, attitudes, and beliefs which can occur. To fully understand another person's meaning is to take the chance that you might end up agreeing with that person's views. In this sense, the manager who moves toward improving interpersonal communications must be sufficiently courageous and possess sufficient ego strength to assume these risks.

NOTES

1. Alex Bavelas and Dermott Barrett, "An Experimental Approach to Organizational Communication," *Personnel,* (March 1951), pp. 370–71.
   M. E. Shaw, "Communication Networks" in *Advances in Experimental Social Psychology,* Vol. 1, ed. M. E. Shaw (New York: Academic Press, 1961), p. 123.
2. Carl Rogers, *On Becoming A Person* (Boston: Houghton Mifflin, 1961).

DISCUSSION QUESTIONS

1. Using the communications model, describe and label the communication that occurs in a large lecture-type class. What do you consider to be effective and ineffective aspects? Why?
2. Suppose you wanted to protest a grade you received. Describe how you would communicate your message and why you selected that means.
3. Describe an experience you have had with one of the communication nets described in the chapter. Was your experience consistent with the text description of research findings about that form of net?

4. Do you consider yourself a good listener? Why? Describe an instance when better listening skills would have improved the situation.
5. Suppose you were applying for a part-time clerk position in a department store. How important would it be for you to be a good interpersonal communicator? Why?
6. Describe and discuss the quality of communications you observe in a local service station. Should the quality be improved? Why or why not?

BIBLIOGRAPHY

Applebaum, R. L., and K. W. E. Anatol. *Strategies for Persuasive Communication.* Columbus: Charles E. Merrill Publishing Co., 1974.

Fabun, Don. *Communications: The Transfer of Meanings.* Riverside: Glencoe Press, 1968.

Giffen, Kim, and Bobby R. Patton. *Fundamentals of Interpersonal Communication.* New York: Harper & Row, 1971.

Knapp, Mark L. *Nonverbal Communication in Human Interaction.* New York: Holt, Rinehart and Winston, Inc., 1972.

Newman, Ruth G. "Case of the Questionable Communiqués." *Harvard Business Review,* Vol. 53 No. 6 (November–December, 1975), p. 26.

Rogers, Carl, *On Becoming a Person.* Boston: Houghton Mifflin, 1961.

Rogers, Carl R., and F. J. Roethlisberger. "Barriers and Gateways to Communication." *Harvard Business Review,* Vol. 40 No. 4 (July–August 1952), p. 46.

The Case of the Un-Merry Widow

The widow of Patrick Moynihan was a diminutive Korean who had married Pat when his Army unit was stationed near Seoul. Soon after their son was born, Pat was transferred to Fort Lewis, and the Moynihans settled in an apartment in Tacoma. Then, tragically, Pat was killed in an automobile accident, and Ms. Moynihan was left with the decision of whether to try to make a life in the United States or to return to Korea. For the sake of her son, she decided to stay in the States.

Ms. Moynihan's father was a professor of English at the university in Seoul, and she had been a legal secretary for three years in a Seoul law office. Therefore, in seeking the employment that was absolutely necessary, she had two things going for her, a proficiency in English and a high competence in typing, shorthand, and office procedures. However, she knew nothing about the customs that have become ingrained in the process of getting a job in the United States.

Upon the advice of her landlord, Ms. Moynihan took a bus into Seattle and went directly to the Acme Employment Agency. She arrived there at 11 o'clock on a Monday morning, and the office was jammed with people. It was early afternoon before an interviewer finally got to her, and after a short discussion about her employment background, she was asked to return the following day to take a typing test.

To a former legal secretary, the typing test was ridiculously easy, and the interviewer was quite impressed with Ms. Moynihan's performance. "I think I will send you to Washington Equitable Insurance Company," the interviewer told

her. "They are looking for someone like you, and the offices are on the top four floors of this building. The starting salary is $450 per month, and you should be there at 9:00 A.M. Friday."

In her naivety, Ms. Moynihan thought she was being told that she had a job. She spent the balance of that day finding a day nursery for her son, and paid a deposit. She located an apartment near downtown Seattle and the nursery on the following day, and moved in on Thursday. On Friday morning she reported to the Washington Equitable Insurance Company to go to work.

"If you will make out this short application form, an interviewer will see you in about thirty minutes," was her greeting by the receptionist in the personnel department of the insurance company.

"But I came here to start to work," said Ms. Moynihan.

"I'm sorry, but there must be some mistake," said the secretary. "You have been merely referred to us by the employment agency."

The interviewer talked with Ms. Moynihan only briefly, but seemed to be interested. In any event, he was quite polite, and finally said: "This shouldn't be necessary, but this company has a requirement that all applicants for a secretarial job must take a typing test. Could you arrange to do this on Monday?"

"Please tell me when I start to work," answered Ms. Moynihan, and then told the interviewer about the apartment and the nursery.

"I can't tell you how sorry I am that we have unintentionally inconvenienced you, but due to the layoffs in Seattle there are a lot of people available, and we are intending to screen a number of applicants for this job opening," was his reply.

After resignedly telling the interviewer that she would take the test on Monday, Ms. Moynihan stopped in at the Acme Employment Agency. There she was told about three other job openings, but they were all in the suburbs, and she had paid the first month's rent on the downtown apartment. She knew that she couldn't afford to forfeit this money, and was further shocked when the agency interviewer said to her: "I'm sorry you didn't understand that you were just referred to the insurance company. Perhaps you also don't know that if you get a job through the agency you will owe us 35 percent of your first month's gross salary."

On Monday, Ms. Moynihan took the typing test and passed brilliantly. She was then asked to fill out a four-page application form, and bring it in the next day for an interview with the personnel manager.

"Tell me in your own words, Ms. Moynihan, why you want to work for us," this gentlemen purred in a friendly way.

Ms. Moynihan was momentarily speechless. Other than to tell him that she desperately needed a job, and that because of the apartment she had committed herself to work in the downtown Seattle area, she couldn't think of anything else to say.

The personnel manager frowned slightly as she somewhat embarrassedly stated these reasons. "The kind of people that we really like to employ here at Washington," he said gently, "are those who feel dedicated to the objectives of the company, rather than just wanting a job. However, you appear to have exceptional ability, and I would like to have you meet the man whose department has the job opening. Can you arrange to be here on Friday afternoon?"

Feeling increasingly discouraged, Ms. Moynihan spent the next two days calling on other employment agencies. She had one referral, but at that company she was asked to return the following day to take a typing test, which she elected not to do. On Friday she kept her appointment with Mr. King, who was her prospective employer.

"Do you think that you may be *too* well qualified?" asked Mr. King, after he reviewed Ms. Moynihan's background and described the duties of the job that was open. "The girls in this office have a pretty tight little group," he went on, "and are apt to resent someone who might show them up, especially if the new person happened to be a foreigner."

"What mistakes have I made now," thought Ms. Moynihan. She then proceeded to try to play down the qualifications that she had so carefully built up a few minutes earlier.

"I like your determination," said Mr. King finally, "and would like to see you get the job. However, there are a few more things that the personnel department has to do. Suppose you go back to their office."

Ms. Moynihan dutifully waited to see the personnel manager. "Well, it looks like you are getting close to being a member of our happy family," he said to her. "You will have to have a physical examination, which you can do next week."

"Will that be all? If I pass will I get the job?" asked Ms. Moynihan.

"Not quite yet," answered the personnel manager. "We will have to wait for a reply to the letter that we sent the law firm that you worked for in Seoul."

"I will be in Seoul on Monday, and will probably be back on my old job the next day," said Ms. Moynihan quietly. "Korea is really not such a bad place to raise a boy."

DISCUSSION QUESTIONS

1. Did Ms. Moynihan encode the first interviewer's message correctly?
2. The interview, a form of interpersonal communication, is a widely-used staffing tool. Why?
3. What forms of "noise" can creep into an interview?

24 Organization Development

Organization Development, called OD in the management community, includes a broad spectrum of activities and procedures which are designed to bring about an improvement in an organization. Many different criteria are used to gauge improvement. This practice reflects the multiplicity of goals which OD efforts are undertaken to achieve. Typically, the OD process begins when an organizational client decides to try to improve organizational performance in some way. The question, "Who is the client?" is an important issue in OD and is discussed later in the chapter. Various techniques which fall within the band of OD activities are described in the final part of this chapter. OD efforts usually involve a consultant to the organization. Generally, this consultant *does not* "solve" the organization's problem and present a report. Instead the consultant works within the organization, trying to help its members develop the capacity to solve its problems.[1]

Basically, OD activities change organizations. These change efforts differ from many other organizational change efforts in that the members of the organization have a substantial amount of influence over the direction and degree of change. Traditional methods for achieving organizational change tend to rely on institutional power vested in the higher levels of the hierarchy. The boss says change, so some change occurs. The change may be greater than, less, and different from those intended by the boss. However, the organization reacts to the boss' directive. In an OD effort, an attempt is made to develop the capacity *in the organization* to diagnose and make necessary changes to achieve improved effectiveness and efficiency.

Since OD is a relatively new phenomenon, the boundaries which define what is, and what is not OD, are fuzzy. There have been many definitions proposed in attempts to impart more order to the field.

Beckhard's definition is representative and gives a good idea of what activities are included in OD.[2]

He asserts, "Organizational development is an effort (1) *planned,* (2) *organizationwide,* and (3) *managed* from the top, to (4) increase *organization effectiveness* and *health* through (5) *planned interventions* in the organization's 'process,' using *behavioral science* knowledge."

Generalizing from this definition it can be seen that the goals of OD efforts are usually changes in the organization that are beneficial or desirable to the management of an organization and its membership. The values that underlie many OD efforts have led to goals which include

- improved interpersonal communication skill and competence of members.
- recognition of emotions as a legitimate part of organizational behavior.
- improved understanding of group operations and development of teamwork skills.
- improvement of the capacity to manage conflict in the organization.

At the center of most OD efforts is some procedure which involves the client group in the diagnosis and action-taking process. This quality of involvement on the part of the target group in problem identification distinguishes OD from most other efforts aimed at organization change. The OD process usually is designed so that the diagnosis and action sequences are recycled several times with successive outcomes; each of which is closer to the ideal state.

The desired outcomes of OD efforts involve improved organizational performance. The specific criteria used to measure general objectives will vary, depending on the philosophy of the management, and the OD consultant. Specific criteria which have been used include increases in profitability, efficiency, and effectiveness, and decreases in employee turnover rates, labor costs, and employee alienation from the job.

OD is a relatively new organizational phenomenon. Its beginnings can be traced back to the activities taking place at the National Training Laboratories (NTL) in the 1940s and to activities occurring about the same time at the Survey Research Center of the University of Michigan.[3] Each of these early predecessors to OD has left its mark on current OD practice.

The NTL influence is most obvious in the OD activities which use values and techniques developed in the T-group format. T-groups (T stands for training) are small informal groups formed to allow participants to learn from the observation and experience of the group's own behavior and process.

A T-group usually has no agenda imposed by the leader or the organization. What the group does and what is discussed is left to the group to work out. This uncommon absence of group structure is often sufficient to stimulate members to question and seek understanding of

(1) one's own behavior and interpersonal relationships, and (2) the dynamics and processes of groups. Typical questions that arise about issues of self are: Who am I? What influences are predominant in influencing my behavior? Questions about group-process issues are: How does the leadership of the group develop in the absence of structure? How do different communication styles impact group performance? How are group decisions made? What seems to help groups attain their goals? What hinders them? As T-groups discuss and explore these issues, members learn the importance of interpersonal openness, trust and trustworthiness, and acknowledging and expressing feelings in interpersonal relations.

The importance of T-groups to current OD efforts resides less in their direct use and more in their contribution of a set of values and laboratory learning techniques. These topics are discussed in later sections of this chapter.

The survey research influence in OD history contributed a technology for intervention in an organization's usual way of conducting its affairs. This technology involves gathering data about the target group, summarizing the data, and feeding the data back to the group itself. The idea behind the approach is that the group, with current, accurate information about its performance, attitudes, or beliefs, will be able to make changes in its own performance to bring it in line with the group's objectives. The group decides if there is sufficient reason for change, what those changes should be, and what action should be undertaken to effect the desired change.

BASIC OD VALUES

Laboratory learning is a device commonly used in OD efforts.[4] As a consequence, many of the assumptions and values that surround laboratory learning have been transferred to OD practices. Among the most commonly transferred are lab learning values placed on a spirit of inquiry, open communications, confrontation of organizational problems, and a tendency to prefer democratic, participative action strategies that encourage collaboration of effort. The spirit of inquiry shows up in OD efforts in the early, diagnostic phase of a project. Recall that OD efforts rely on the organization to provide the information needed to diagnose the organization's state of affairs. The group needs such information to generate and select from alternative action steps. As a result, the action steps and the judgments involved in figuring out what is amiss in the organization are not handed down by the chief executive officer or by an outside consultant. Rather, these activities are performed by organization members. If members are to engage in these activities, the organization must value a spirit of inquiry. Members must feel that they can and should seek out information relevant to the organization's performance. Furthermore, once preliminary action steps have been taken, their effect should be examined so that additional corrections can be made as needed. When the spirit of inquiry is fully operating, it would be rare to hear, "Oh, we cannot get into that issue; the XYZ department always takes care of that," or "We'd better not survey that department's morale; it's better to leave them alone."

The laboratory learning value that is placed on open communications is closely related to a spirit of inquiry. Much of the communication that takes place in OD efforts is interpersonal (see Chapter 23). All of the benefits and pitfalls of that mode of communicating are present in OD efforts. Essentially OD communications are based on a philosophical position which holds that facts and the truth about organization affairs are better in the long run than deceit and deception. This position recognizes that working with the actual situation, rather than organizational fictions, may present problems and may involve difficult choices. However, the value of a truthful approach is supported by the argument that these problems and choices remain whether or not they are openly addressed, and, unless addressed they will usually continue to be unproductive consumers of organizational energy.

Organization members, including managers, often make the assumption that certain problems and issues must be avoided in communications. Those who support the open-communications value maintain that if a department discovered morale problems—problems caused by a particular manager's style or behavior, it would be inappropriate to avoid informing the manager. Of course, there are appropriate and inappropriate ways to deliver feedback about the negative impact of a person's organizational behavior. The point here is that once the information has been discovered, it is inappropriate to withhold, deny, or distort it.

Open communications in organizations about positive events and behavior are also valued. If a person has done well or has been instrumental in achieving organizational objectives, this should also be communicated. In general then, when open communications are valued in an organization, the flow of information will not be impeded by organizational hierarchy, structure, or untested assumptions about the consequences of people having information.

When an organization is questioning its performance and the communications within the organization are flowing openly, it is difficult for the organization to avoid confronting its problems. OD efforts generally place a value on dealing directly with organizational problems in an open, problem-solving way rather than trying to smooth over problems or creating the illusion that they do not exist.

The final value of laboratory learning that is commonly found in OD efforts is a general tendency toward democratic, participatory strategies for making decisions that will effect organizational change. In general, those involved in such decisions need sufficient experience and knowledge, and a desire to be involved to provide for successful participation of group members. OD efforts generally value participation that is as wide as is feasible in the given situation.

Limits to participation are defined by the willingness of people to become involved, their possession of required skills, knowledge and information, and availability of time. Fortunately, a practical implication of increased participation in organizational decision making is that the same people who are called on to identify and prescribe the organizational change are the ones who effect the change. A second dimension of the value placed on wide participation reflects the opportunity that such participation offers for the personal and professional growth and development of organization members. Wider participation in organizational affairs can result in jobs that are more challenging and rewarding. It is an excellent professional opportunity for middle- and lower-level managers to become more involved in identifying problems in their organization and later developing and effecting positive changes. In general, increased involvement by all organization members will permit them to create a climate and working situation which fulfills their growth and development needs more effectively.

Implications for Managers

The values described above have implications which managers must take into account when considering an OD effort. In the first place, it is critical that top management be prepared to accept behavior in the organization that is consistent with the values described earlier. When people are learning new ways of behaving, particularly when those ways are different from the "usual" ways of behaving in organizations, their early attempts may be awkward and inappropriate. It takes time for an organization's members to learn and become proficient at new ways of working in organizational contexts.

When an OD effort is undertaken in an organization, it is important to estimate the degree to which members are prepared, and willing to behave in a manner necessary for the OD effort to succeed. It is difficult to be certain of the depth of commitment to the OD effort in its early stages. People may be initially attracted to OD by the idea of increased involvement in organizational change. However, as the realities of the work, risks, and personal changes involved become apparent, people may become hesitant to press on. It is at this point that subtle and powerful factors forcing compliance with the OD effort may develop. In order to be consistent with its values, and indeed for OD to have a chance to succeed in accomplishing its goals at all, the participation of the group must be genuinely voluntary. Compliance cannot be forced. Even if legitimate and serious reservations are maintained, group members must choose to become involved. In their enthusiasm to institute new programs and to achieve desired changes, managers sometimes create powerful incentives for members to appear involved and in agreement. However, if commitment is in form only and not substantive, the OD effort will probably fail.

Finally, the value issue that surrounds the idea of collaboration has implications for managers. The benefits of collaborative actions and styles in organizations are clear. Much of a manager's job involves the coordination of various subunits to achieve common goals. If a wide number of the members in an organization are committed to and value collaboration, it would seem that, probably, the manager's job would be made that much easier. However, there is another value position which holds that competition for scarce resources within an organization is good. In the long run, better use of those scarce resources will be insured if competition for them is keen. Subunits which ultimately win the resources will be the ones which are the most efficient and effective, thereby permitting the larger unit to approach its most effective and efficient operation. To do away with this healthy competition by encouraging collaboration among subunits, the argument goes, is to encourage the firm to operate at less than its best and in the long run endanger its survival. In organizations which place a high value on the benefits of competition, it may be difficult to institute an OD effort which requires and values a high level of collaboration on the part of individuals and subunits within the organization.

ISSUES RELATED TO OD EFFORTS

There are a number of issues which occur in most OD efforts regardless of organization or OD technology employed. Managers should consider these issues as they contemplate initiating an OD procedure in order to maximize the chances of its success.

OD practitioners have maintained that certain minimal conditions should exist before an OD effort is undertaken. There are some descriptive models which are helpful in designing and understanding the organizational change process. The nature of organizational change using an OD strategy has been criticized for paying insufficient attention to the realities of power and conflict in the organizational environment. Issues such as these which surround OD efforts are discussed in the following sections.

Need for Minimum Conditions for OD

Since the process of change is clearly a part of an OD effort, a necessary preliminary condition is that there be a certain degree of dissatisfaction with present conditions of performance. This dissatisfaction on the part of those who control organizational resources should be translated early into feelings that there is a need for change. It is not essential that the present situation be abominable or intolerable. If there is a sense that somehow conditions might be better, even though they may be adequate at present, the necessary energy is probably available to consider an OD effort. It is not crucial that the key people in the organization have a clear idea of what is wrong or what to do about it. Those questions can become part of the OD effort itself.

A basic tenet in OD is "to begin where the client is." To do so, existing organizational climate and practices must be understood and considered as the effort is designed. Planners may be tempted to ignore hard organizational realities while formulating an ideal OD effort. If an organization has a management philosophy that requires that communications be made through authorized channels only, an OD effort that calls for direct interunit interaction would probably fail. Similarly, an OD effort designed to improve productivity in a unit by increasing commitment to organizational goals would receive scant attention if the predominant concern in the organization was an announced budget cut and reduction of the work force.

Time considerations are an important dimension of OD efforts. Often managers who undertake changes in an organization are impatient if events do not occur quickly. OD efforts typically involve a complicated diagnosis and action cycle which takes time to work through. Managers who undertake OD programs should anticipate long-term benefits rather than immediate, next-week changes in organizational performance. Most OD efforts involve restructuring some very basic ideas and assumptions held in the organization. Change of this proportion requires some getting used to in terms of acceptance and in terms of implementation.

Models of Organizational Change

Making important changes in organizational relationships and operations is not easy. Many built-in factors contribute to a general resistance to change. Such factors should not be seen as wrong or necessarily inappropriate, for organizations need stability and predictability in order to accomplish tasks in a coordinated manner. At the same time, the need for change in an organization must overcome resistance to change.

Among the most common forms of resistance to change in organizations is simply habit and repetition. People get used to functioning in patterned, routine ways. In addition, all new behaviors have an unknown quality about them.

When individuals or organizations contemplate substantial changes in the way they function, they are often not sure the new behavior will be beneficial. Furthermore, as individuals or organizations behave in new and unaccustomed ways, other individuals or organizations must make adjustments in their own expectations and actions. Often the "others" will put subtle pressure on the original unit to return to its old ways— ways that were comfortable for the other organizations or individuals.

Both the ambiguity associated with a change and the environmental pressures result in a natural hesitance to adopt a change.

Dynamic equilibrium model. The dynamic equilibrium model of an organization is a useful way to develop an understanding of organizational stability and change.

Organizations have been described as being in a state of dynamic equilibrium. Generally, major relationships and activities in an organization are fairly stable and predictable even while the organization is moving to achieve its objectives. A gliding paper airplane can be said to be in such a state. If it is flying in stable air, the net of the forces acting on the plane will carry it in a fairly predictable path. If any of the forces are altered, so is the resultant glide path. If a wind current blows, if the tail section is bent, or if the balance is altered by additional folds, the flight characteristics will be changed. An organization can be likened to the plane. As long as no new forces are introduced, the organization will tend to continue on in its usual way. A change in any of the forces influencing the organization will be reflected in the organization's performance.

Unfreezing-change-refreezing. The dynamic equilibrium model has been used to describe a strategy for changing organizations.[5] This strategy introduces a change in the organization which upsets the equilibrium state. This is done purposely to loosen up established organization operations or relationships. With routine structures or procedures unfrozen, and in a less fixed state, the new, desired set of relationships or activities can be tested. These new forces are then maintained long enough for the system to rebalance itself in a new equilibrium state. The new equilibrium state will refreeze with the desired changes incorporated.

In OD efforts, it is often the generation and feedback of information about organizational behavior and issues which serves to unfreeze the system. If a management team is surprised to find that 65 percent of its employees are dissatisfied with the working conditions and would change jobs if they were able, there is a good chance that management assumptions about working conditions may be unfrozen. Once there is a recognition that there may be a problem, the equilibrium has been disturbed and changes designed to address the problem may be introduced.

Force field analysis. The technique known as Force Field Analysis[6] carries the dynamic equilibrium concept another step and uses it to help identify specific forces which can be altered to effect desired changes in the organization. The force field is characterized as described in Figure 24-1. The equilibrium is depicted by the solid vertical line and the desired state after the change is represented by the dotted line.

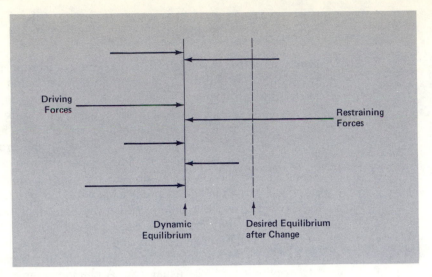

Figure 24-1. The Force Field Model.

The model implies that the equilibrium state of the organization can be altered by changing the number or magnitude of either the driving or restraining forces. *Driving forces* are those pushing toward the new position. *Restraining forces* are those that resist movement of the organization. For example, a college department might decide that it should increase the quality of instruction in its classes. A force field analysis of the department would try to identify factors in the department that encouraged good teaching, factors that hindered good teaching, and the relative strengths of the factors in both categories. Once this information were available, it would be possible to initiate changes in practiced instruction methods which would tend to increase the strength and number of driving forces and similarly decrease the number and strength of restraining forces. Examples of driving forces in this case might be the rewards in terms of pay and promotion that are associated with excellence in teaching, the psychic rewards from positive responses of students, light teaching loads, and few preparations. Restraining forces could include time commitments required for committee service, professional aspirations of professors to research and publish, inadequate resources for preparation of material, and organizational rules requiring suboptimum teaching assignments.

The force field model also implies that change associated with a decrease in restraining forces is accompanied by a decrease in the net pressure in the system. If change is effected by simply increasing the driving forces, the new equilibrium point is determined by the sum of stronger driving forces and the original restraining forces. If the same change is accomplished without additional force, the negative side effects of increased pressure in the organization can be avoided. For example, if a manager wants to reduce tardiness, he or she could increase the severity of penalties associated with unexcused late arrival at work. However, people may begin to react to the penalties by covering for each other, falsifying reasons for tardiness, or some other sub-optimum reaction to the increased pressure to be on time. An alternative strategy, suggested by a force field analysis of the situation, would be to identify forces which make it difficult for employees to arrive on time. For example, starting work 30 minutes earlier or later might permit employees to beat or miss rush-hour traffic, allowing them to spend less time getting to work.

Power and Conflict in Organizational Change

OD practice and theory have been criticized for being somewhat silent on the issues of power and conflict involved in organizational change. Stronger criticism has been that, generally, the practitioners of OD in the U.S. have naively assumed away these very powerful organizational realities.[7]

The idea that people have a need for power was introduced in Chapter 21 on human motivation. The organization, with its hierarchical structure and intense need for coordination, is an ideal setting for the expression of this need. Power and its implications for relationships among people in organizations is intimately tied to the leading function.

Response to the exercise of power is at the other end of the power relationship. There is no single explanation which accounts for why people respond to attempts by others to exert power. One argument holds that it is simply in the best interest of the less powerful to go along. In that way the negative sanctions or unpleasant consequences associated with losing a power struggle can be avoided. Another hypothesis suggests that we have an innate tendency to follow the directions of those we deem powerful. Supporting this position is disturbing research in which research subjects, who believed they were administering severe electric shocks to unidentified people, continued to do so at the request of the researcher even though the shocks were apparently causing severe physical pain to others.[8]

It is important to recognize that power is an organizational reality of substantial magnitude. People in organizations exert power over others, and subunits vie for budget allocations and influence in decision making. OD practice and theory are beginning to come to grips with this pressure in organizational life and to include power issues in its own processes of organizational change.

OD has often taken the position that effective organizational change is top-down. This is true predominantly for business organizations; voluntary organizations, such as churches and service organizations, are somewhat more responsive to the wishes of the membership. Decisions and commitment for change in business organizations usually originate at the highest levels and then filter down the hierarchy. OD theory, and most practice, has tended to ignore the substantial alternative organizational change processes that do not follow the top-down pattern. Examples include both nonviolent dissent and more violent political revolutions that have resulted in vast organizational changes.

There have been a few OD efforts mounted which involve the initiation of change from middle or lower levels in the organization. These efforts, however, are not common. It is more common to find a prescription that asserts top-management commitment is essential for success. This position overlooks the rapid social and cultural changes that have occurred in this country since the 1960s. These changes have forced organizational changes in response. Legal and moral expectations for organizational action regarding fair employment and environmental impact of operations are two examples of widespread changes in organizations that have been generated by forces other than top-down, internal decisions of the organization.

The history of the labor movement in the U.S. has been one of employees expressing power by way of strikes, and the threat of strikes. This influence has resulted in a host of organizational changes over the years including a constant redefinition of managerial prerogative, acceptable work practices, and changes in wage levels and structure. These changes have all come about without top-level initiation.

People do fight and compete in organizations. To ignore that reality in an attempt to foster cooperation and collaboration in organizational effort is foolish. Managers should try to strike a balance between a realistic recognition of power and conflict issues in an organization and a recognition of where and when the possibilities for increased cooperation and collaboration exist. When there is sufficient reason to believe the benefits of collaboration will outweigh the costs and risks of attempting them, a manager's decision is clear. If an OD effort is undertaken, the manager's decision-making methods will have a powerful influence on its outcome.

Role of the Consultant

A very common characteristic of OD efforts is the presence of a consultant. The consultant's role is to assist in the process of changing the client's organization. In OD efforts, the consultant is a resource to the client. The consultant can supply expert knowledge of the applied behavioral sciences and can serve as a facilitator in fostering open and honest communications. The consultant can assist the client in efforts to confront and constructively handle problems of conflict and power in the organization. In all of these activities, the consultant is a facilitator, making every effort to help the client achieve stated OD purposes and objectives. This assignment is somewhat different than the more common consulting assignment in which a problem is presented with the expectation that the consultant will solve it. Assisting organizations develop the capacity to solve their own problems and develop into entities with desired characteristics and capacities is the OD consultant's job. The OD consultant may offer suggestions to the client about how to identify problems and search for viable action alternatives. The task of solving the client's problems, however, always remains with the client. Some OD practitioners hold that they are most successful when they have helped a client to the point that the consultant is no longer needed.

Internal and external consultants. Some organizations, in both the public and private sectors of the economy, have developed an internal staff of OD consultants. Other organizations hire external consultants. Both external and internal consultants usually have the same objectives. There are important differences, however, between the two kinds of consultants. External consultants are not members and therefore not subject to the influences of long-term employment in the organization. Therefore, the external consultant may bring fresh viewpoints to an organization. This may make it easier to question existing organizational dynamics and processes which the client has assumed to be essential. On the other hand, internal OD consultants usually understand and appreciate the subtleties in various organizational relationships and practices. A major advantage consultants have, whether internal or external, is that they are not permanent members of the client organization. As temporary members they are able to take the extra risks needed to openly address sensitive organizational issues. When consultants' concerns for losing a very good client begin to overpower their commitment to developing the capacity of the client to be independent, the relationship will begin to deteriorate as will the consultants' contribution to the client organization.

Identifying the Client

A common dilemma for OD consultants is one of clarity about who the client is. This dilemma is usually anticipated by OD consultants who insist on clarity and agreement about allegiances and commitments early in the consulting relationship. Many times consultants will be brought in by one level of management and work with other, usually lower level, personnel in the organization. Or one subunit in an organization will employ a consultant who must resolve conflicts that arise between the subunit's goal achievement and the goals of the larger organization. These complications are occasioned by the OD consultant's role of "improver." Changes that improve one subunit of an organization may not be particularly beneficial to another. Or, changes that may be helpful to a particular manager in a given unit may be detrimental to the growth and development of other members of the unit.

OD TECHNIQUES

In this section several different OD techniques that are in use in organizations will be described. It is important to recognize that most OD efforts in organizations will be a combination of some or all of the techniques described in this section. This occurs because each OD effort should be tailored to fit the organization, its particular needs, and the unique situation. The four OD techniques discussed in this section are Action Research, Management Grid, Management by Objectives (MBO), and Organizational Behavior Modification (OB Mod).

Action Research

One of the earliest techniques developed for organizational change was the form known as action research.[9] The basic idea in *action research* is to investigate the organization, summarize the findings, and report those findings to the client organization. The client then uses the feedback as information for decisions that guide the organization's action steps. The process is recycled after the impact of the decisions can be assessed. New data is collected, fed back, and new action is decided upon and effected.

The research is usually of a social science nature, involving opinions, attitudes, or beliefs. Methodologies for collecting this data include interviews, questionnaires, and observation of ongoing organizational activities. The researchers can also collect data on organizational performance measures such as productivity, absenteeism, profitability, and cost increases or decreases.

Some form of data gathering and feedback will be found in practically any OD change effort. It would be futile to try to design and implement a plan to change the organization unless the important elements in the present organizational situation are relatively clear. Without a good idea of "what is" in an organization, it is not possible to design a strategy to reach "what should be."

Management Grid

A copyrighted technique for organizational development has been widely adopted. Management Grid[10] takes its name from the figure of a grid which describes basic types of management. Figure 24-2 is adapted from *The Management Grid* by R. Blake and J. Mouton. The OD process is

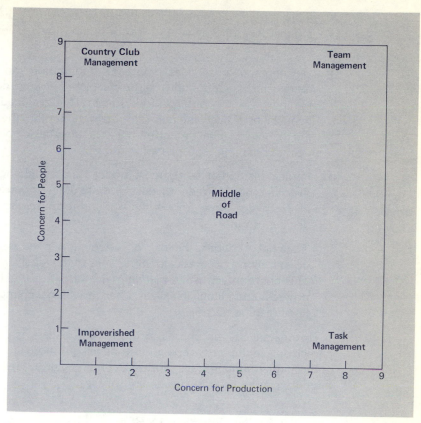

Figure 24-2. The Management Grid.

designed to move an organization to a 9,9 position on the managerial grid. At that region, management is both acting with concern for the people in the organization as well as attending to the production/performance of the organization. To achieve this change, the organization is sequenced through six phases of Grid training. These phases are

1. The Grid Seminar. Here top management learns about the Grid process and about how they can be more objective about their management styles, communications skills, and values. Increased understanding of organizational issues including problem solving and conflict management are stressed. After top management completes this training they return and teach comparable sessions to the next level of managers.

2. Teamwork development. During this phase of training, managers learn how to develop and work in effective teams.

3. Intergroup development. This phase takes the effectively functioning teams of phase two and teaches them how to work with each other effectively.

4. Development of an ideal strategic organization model. The top management team studies strategic planning then does strategic planning for the organization. Plans are developed concerning financial objectives, the nature of the organization, the character of the market, an ideal organizational structure, basic policies to guide decision making, and plans for growth.

5. Implementation of the strategic model. All of the changes implied in the difference between the current state of the organization and its ideal strategic state are worked out in this phase. Action steps are decided upon.

6. Systematic critique. Finally, a systematic review is made of the organization's progress along the lines of the ideal strategic model. This phase serves as the managerial control function by measuring progress and identifying areas where additional changes or corrections may be necessary.

Throughout the six phases, a great deal of data is collected from participants in the form of paper and pencil questionnaires. The results of these questionnaires are reported in training group meetings so that the data can be used in succeeding phases.

Management by Objectives (MBO)

Peter Drucker is generally credited with the authorship of MBO.[11] As the name implies, MBO is the accomplishment of objectives which distinguish good and poor organizational performance. Some MBO features are not always found in an organization's usual operating procedures. One feature of MBO is its interactive goal setting. In the MBO process, people sit down with their supervisors to negotiate and agree on a set of objectives for themselves to be achieved during a specific time period. The supervisor is guided by broad organizational directions and boundaries that have been set by people in higher levels of the organization. At the very top of the organization, broad policy and boundaries for objectives are set by top management. More narrow boundaries for objectives and subobjectives are successively defined by subsequent levels in the organization. The time period set aside for achievement of the agreed upon objectives typically is one year, though other spans of time have been used when appropriate. Ideally, neither the boss nor the subordinate has the complete say-so in the goal-setting process. It is truly one of negotiation.

A second MBO feature has to do with the way the goals are stated. When an agreement has been properly reached, the objectives will be

Management By Objectives: Does It Really Work?

1. *Achievement of objectives may not accurately indicate performance.* A manager may miss or overachieve his objectives as a result of bad or good luck. Changes in the economy may make it impossible to reach the agreed-upon target. Even within the same organization, individual managers may be affected differently by external circumstances. For example, a bank branch office located near aerospace installations may not reach the goal of attracting savings at a time of high unemployment in that industry.

2. *The MBO administrator can be very valuable in the difficult task of setting objectives and implementing the program.* It should be pointed out, however, that subordinates must remain accountable primarily to their immediate superior. The administrator should function in an advisory role in order not to undermine the authority of the line manager.

3. *Tying MBO directly to an incentive system may have negative side effects.* A manager may learn to play the game to maximize his reward. This may be done by ignoring important activities that are not directly related to his objectives or by setting objectives that can be achieved easily. Therefore, the wise administrator should carefully consider the pros and cons of relating performance directly to the achievement of objectives.

4. *There is also the possibility of inflexibility.* When properly applied, MBO should promote flexibility. MBO facilitates planning and gives direction. But planning should be a continuous process which requires reevaluation in light of changing circumstances. For example, a change in basic factors such as money rates may require a change not only in objectives but also in strategies and tactics.

    To pursue obsolete objectives for the sake of achieving agreed-upon results is absurd. But goals should not be changed lightly, either. If nonachievement is corrected by changing the standards, then goal-setting is meaningless. What is needed is a check from time to time to see whether the assumptions underlying the plans have changed. If so, goals should be adjusted to fit reality.

5. *Finally, MBO must be viewed as a managerial system.* It should not be a burdensome addition to the manager's job, but rather a way of managing. Then, and only then, can the advantages of MBO be fully realized and problems overcome. The purpose of MBO is to make managers more effective and promote the achievement of their professional potential.

described in terms which can be verified objectively. This means that the subordinates will not be evaluated in terms of subjective impressions held by their bosses. Instead, the degree of achievement of agreed upon objectives determines the quality of performance. As the time period reaches its conclusion, a review of achievement is made. It is likely that some objectives will remain unattained. A new set of objectives is negotiated for the next time period in light of the past experience. This process is recycled through time and downward through the organizational hierarchy.

MBO considerations. To effect an MBO procedure, the top management must be willing and able to set broad guidelines within which organizational objectives are to be met. This is often a difficult task and may require the assistance of an OD consultant familiar with the MBO process.

Organization traditions and style may make collaboration in goal setting and implicit delegations of authority difficult to achieve. In MBO activities, managers do not tell their subordinates what to do or what their objectives must be. Instead, the manager represents higher levels of management in an objective-setting process. As such, the manager is responsible for defining the limits within which goals are to be set and negotiating a reasonable level of satisfactory performance.

While it may not run counter to general style preferences of some managers for them to share the objective-setting process, it may be difficult for their subordinates to accept the added responsibility. There is a commitment and vulnerability in the public expression of performance quality that is involved when people engage in the MBO process. For some, this vulnerability may make it difficult or impossible to be realistic about objectives and the degree of difficulty involved in achieving them. It may take a complete cycle or two of the process before people become skilled at this kind of goal setting.

A common stumbling block for OD efforts that incorporate MBO is the multiplier effect on time involved in the process. Managers engage in the process with their supervisors as well as setting goals with each of their subordinates. By the time all these objectives have been hammered out and committed to paper, a great deal of time will have been consumed. Difficulties in time are also compounded by the difficulties involved in specifying objectives in precise measurable terms. To be effective, the objectives must be described so that achievement or failure is obvious to the subordinate and to the supervisor. It would be insufficient to set an objective to increase employee satisfaction, even though the objective may be worthwhile and the change needed. The difficulty is that when stated in that way, neither the manager nor the supervisor would know if or when it was achieved.

A final issue that may hinder MBO programs involves changes in the environment which may occur. In a rapidly changing and volatile environment, goals agreed to in July may be inappropriate by December.

Organization Behavior Modification (OB Mod)

OB Mod, a term coined by Fred Luthans,[12] denotes an OD process which is based on the theory and practices of behavior modification in psychology. Behavior modification was discussed in Chapter 21. We noted then that behavior modification practices rest conceptually on the law of *effect*. This psychological proposition says that people will tend to repeat behavior that they find satisfying and they will tend to discontinue behavior which has a neutral or negative consequence. Positive and negative reinforcement involves consequences to behavior which tend to cause the individual to repeat the behavior. Thus, praise for being on time or criticism for tardiness are positive and negative reinforcers, respectively, designed to increase the incidence of on-time behavior. The majority of OB Mod efforts focus on positive reinforcement of desired organizational behavior.

Behavior modification techniques used in one successful OD effort involved the following four steps:[13]

1. An audit of present performance was conducted. The audit revealed where change was needed and where that need was the greatest.

2. Second, a set of standards for each person was determined. Unlike MBO programs, this standard was not set by the people involved; however, like MBO goals, they were specific and measurable.

3. Third, the members of the organization were given the data they needed to track their own performance in light of their goals.

4. Finally, the supervisors praised the good performances of individuals. When a goal was reached or nearly reached, positive reinforcement was applied in the form of supervisory recognition.

Like MBO, a central difficulty with OB Mod lies in the goal/objective definition process. To be successful, goals must be identified which can be measured. This task is much easier when the work is routine and repetitive. However, defining measurable objectives for design engineers, for advertising copy writers, or for airline pilots would not be as easy. Where it has been tried, OB Mod has enjoyed moderate success. The final word is not in on this new OD process. It continues to be controversial and to attract substantial attention. Managers may be able to incorporate facets of the process in their leadership activities.

NOTES

1. Edgar F. Huse, *Organizational Development and Change* (St. Paul: West Publishing Co., 1975), p. 21.

2. R. Beckhard, *Organizational Development: Strategies and Models* (Reading: Addison-Wesley, 1969), p. 9.
3. Huse, op. cit., p. 24.
4. Huse, op. cit., pp. 247–60.
5. K. Lewin, *Field Theory in Social Science* (New York: Harper and Row, 1951).
6. Lewin, op. cit.
7. Huse, op. cit., pp. 68–69.
8. Stanley Milgram, *Obedience to Authority* (New York: Harper and Row, 1974).
9. R. Lippett, J. Watson, and B. Westley, *The Dynamics of Planned Change* (New York: Harcourt, Brace, World, 1958).
10. R. Blake and J. Mouton, *The Management Grid* (Houston: Gulf Publishing Co., 1964).
11. P. Drucker, *The Practice of Management* (New York: Harper and Row, 1954).
12. Fred Luthans and Robert Kreitner, *Organizational Behavior Modification* (Glenview: Scott, Foresman and Co., 1975).
13. E. J. Feeney, "At Emery Air Freight: Positive Reinforcement Boosts Performance," *Organizational Dynamics,* Vol. 1 No. 3 (Winter 1973), pp. 41–50.

DISCUSSION QUESTIONS

1. Do you think that, in most cases, resistance to an imposed change lasts indefinitely?
2. Is there any substance to the argument by many managers that their subordinates do not know as much as managers do about when and how a change should be effected?
3. Discuss the assertion that specialists brought into the organization to effect change merely act as an extension of the manager.
4. Explain why a T-group might develop high cohesiveness.
5. As a future manager, what might make you consider financing an OD effort with company funds?
6. Should supervisors and subordinates participate in the same T-group?

BIBLIOGRAPHY

Beckhard, Richard. "Strategies for Large System Change." *Sloan Management Review,* Vol. 16 No. 2 (Winter 1975), pp. 43–55.
Bobele, H. Kenneth and Peter Buchanan. "Behavior Modification: A Tool for Getting Things Done." *The Business Quarterly,* Vol. 40 No. 4 (Winter 1975), pp. 37–41.
Feeney, E. J. "At Emery Air Freight: Positive Reinforcement Boosts Performance." *Organizational Dynamics,* Vol. 1 No. 3 (Winter 1973), pp. 41–50.
Gibson, Charles H. "Volvo Increases Productivity Through Job Enrichment." *California Management Review,* Vol. 15 No. 4 (Summer 1973), pp. 64–66.

Hackman, J. Richard. "Is Job Enrichment Just a Fad?" *Harvard Business Review,* Vol. 53 No. 5 (September–October 1975), pp. 129–38.

Huse, Edgar F. *Organization Development and Change.* St. Paul: West Publishing Co., 1975.

Luthans, Fred and Robert Kreitner. *Organizational Behavior Modification.* Glenview: Scott, Foresman and Co., 1975.

Margulies, Newton and Anthony P. Raia. *Organization Development: Values, Process, and Technology.* New York: McGraw-Hill, 1972.

Zaleznik, Abraham. "Power and Politics in Organization Life." *Harvard Business Review,* Vol. 48 No. 3 (May–June 1970), pp. 47–60.

The Case of Deciding Which One Was Best

Joe Parsons was manager of the mechanical design section in the engineering department of Medco, Inc., a prominent manufacturer of hospital equipment. One evening toward the end of 1972 he was trying to compile a ranking of the engineers who reported to him in connection with the company's policy of awarding annual bonuses to the top 50 percent of the salaried employees in all departments, and found to his surprise that the newly instituted management by objectives program had not made the task any easier. He was completely convinced that the performance of at least eight of the twelve engineers in his section had improved since he had volunteered to try "managing by objectives," but now he was bogged down in trying to rank their contributions according to their value to the company. As a separate problem, he was going to have to decide what to do with the four engineers who had felt threatened by being put relatively on their own, and whose performance had actually declined.

Until 1971, Parsons' leadership style had been along the traditional lines of a boss giving specific and limited assignments to the people working under him. He set the goals that he expected to have accomplished, and the standards by which he would measure accomplishment. He kept a record for each of his engineers, on which he would note examples of good performance, and instances where the subordinate's performance exhibited shortcomings. At the end of each year he would meet privately with each of his people, and appraise them of how well they had done in his eyes. Then he would announce any raise or bonus that was forthcoming.

Parsons had been reading independently about management by objectives, and so was familiar with the concept when the president of Medco called a meeting of all management personnel in May 1970 for the purpose of hearing a talk on the subject by a professor from State University. At the end of the meeting, the president announced that he would like to try the new management approach on an experimental basis, and asked for some volunteer managers, who would first attend a six weeks' conference conducted by the professor. Joe Parsons was one of the volunteers.

Parsons introduced management by objectives to the people in his section in a way similar to that used previously by the president of the company. He had the professor give his talk, then explained that he had volunteered to try the program. He said that no one was forced to participate in the program, but for those who wanted to, the main objectives of the section that should be kept in mind were improvement in product quality and reduction in cost. A list of the assignments made to the section by the engineering department manager would be posted on the bulletin board. The participants were to choose the ones that they would like to work on, then prepare a plan as to how they would proceed, and develop a time-phase milepost schedule whereby their progress could be measured. They were invited to suggest any relaxation of restrictions in their job description that might be inhibiting. After these preparations each would be asked to discuss their plans with him, and with his approval could set about accomplishing the objectives that they had established for themselves. Review of their progress with him would be on the dates specified in their own plans.

Response to management by objectives was generally enthusiastic. Dave Young, whom Parsons rated as one of his top men, was the first to present his plan. "I think that we have all fallen into the habit of specifying unnecessary frills in our designs," Dave said. "For example, every knob on every one of our products is machine knurled. Knurling is an expensive process, and really adds nothing to the quality of our product. Another waste is our customary specification of seamless tubing. I think that with tests I can prove that welded tubing will do just as good a job, and it costs a lot less. We have machined parts that could just as well be die castings, with a substantial savings. I propose that my objective will be to effect an annual savings of $50,000 per year through design changes that will not deteriorate the quality of the product in any way. I will accomplish this in three months. I would like permission to contact vendors, because I would like to get price estimates on some of the ideas that I have."

"Your plan sounds fine, Dave," said Parsons. "Go ahead with it. However, I am afraid that we would start a war with purchasing if you began going to the vendors direct. You had better continue requisitioning estimates from them. What you might do, though, is get one of the buyers interested in working with you."

Mildred Wells was waiting to see Parsons as Young left the office.

"What I would like to do is take a crack at perfecting the German patents that we bought on the cine-radiography unit," Mildred said. "The unit is not quite right now, but I have been talking with a radiologist who has given me some ideas that I know can be developed. It will take a while to get the design ready for production, but I think that I can show you enough progress in three months to convince you that Medco will have the most accepted cine-radiography unit on the market."

"I was hoping that you would want to tackle this," said Parsons enthusiastically. "Let me suggest that you turn over everything that you develop to our patent attorney, Bob Allen, as soon as you finish it. That way he can get patent applications started immediately."

Over the next two weeks, all of Parsons' engineers discussed their objectives with him. Some plans sounded as promising as Young's and Wells', others had good possibilities, but a few were unimaginative. Parsons tried to stimulate the proposers of the latter plans, but it was apparent that what they really wanted was for him to tell them what to do. He decided to force these people to be on their own awhile; then if that didn't work he would try something else.

Dave Young asked Parsons for a review of his accomplishments ten days before his three months had expired. He was almost bursting with pride as he announced: "$50,000 savings in a year was just a drop in the bucket. I got Dick Hardesty in purchasing and Sam Buck in production to work with me as a team. We also got a salesman to evaluate what effect any changes that might be made would have on the product acceptability. Here is a report showing the details of every change that we propose. The conservative estimate of the annual savings is $117,000."

Before Mildred Wells reported on her progress, Joe Parsons received a call from Medco's sales manager, Allen Pruitt. Pruitt said: "I have taken the ideas that your engineer, Wells, has on the cine-radiography unit to the administrator of the Hillsboro Hospital, and he wants to buy the first one that we make." Parsons told Mildred about this the next day when Mildred came to see him.

"That's great," Mildred said. "And the patent attorney has filed four separate patent applications on my new designs which he says, with the German patents, will give us complete protection."

Parsons reviewed these incidents in his mind on the evening that he had allocated to ranking his subordinates. Under the company's reward system, which Parsons frankly didn't particularly like, first-place ranking was quite important. Who should receive this position, he pondered, Young or Wells?

DISCUSSION QUESTIONS

1. What would be the worst way for a company to try to get a management by objectives program started?
2. What are the dual—and not necessarily complementary—aspects of management by objectives?
3. In the Case of Deciding Which One Was Best, what performance appraisal method was Joe Parsons using prior to introducing management by objectives? What alternative conventional methods could he have considered? (See Chapter 18.)
4. In what way was Joe Parsons not completely candid with subordinates when he introduced management by objectives?
5. What problems do you see for Joe Parsons as a result of the performance reports of Dave Young and Mildred Wells?

Summary

In the final analysis, managers have successfully performed the leading function when organization members' behavior is resulting in organizational goal achievement. Rarely, however, is organizational reality so simple or so clearly defined. A more likely situation is one in which managers have been able to influence some people to behave in some desired ways and most of the balance of their behavior is a result of individual needs, motivations, personal and professional commitments, organizational communications and organizational climate. Most of these factors are only partially controlled by managers. It is more accurate to say that managers can influence these factors rather than control them. In performing the leading function, the chances that managers will be influential in bringing about desired organizational behavior will be improved to the extent they understand and can apply concepts and theories underlying these factors.

Leadership is a topic which has received a good deal of attention from, but has not led to a great deal of agreement among theorists and behavioral science researchers. The topic has been approached with attempts to develop a list of leadership traits or leadership styles which are optimum or necessary. A third approach to leadership introduces the elements of the situation as an important factor in determining successful leadership behavior. To improve the quality of their leadership behavior, managers are advised to consider the forces in themselves, in the follower, *and* in the situation. This implies that there is no best set of leadership traits or a leadership style which guarantees success. Rather, managers must rely on their judgment of the various forces to guide their decisions about appropriate leadership action.

People behave in ways that they hope will satisfy their needs. This assertion underlies much of the discussion of human needs and motivation. Needs have been said to exist in a hierarchy, ranging from physical, through safety, belonging and esteem up to the highest human need, that of needing to actualize one's fullest potential. Other needs that have been proposed to explain major segments of human behavior in organizations are needs for achievement, for affiliation, and for power. The need for power has been suggested to be a significant characteristic in differentiating between effective and ineffective managers.

The existence of two different kinds of influences on motivation in the workplace has been proposed. One set of influences are organizational responses designed to alleviate the unpleasant aspects of work. These have been labeled hygiene factors. The other set of influences are termed the "real" motivators and are elements in the workplace that respond to the higher levels of the human needs hierarchy.

A more complex view of human motivation proposes that it is the person's belief about the likelihood that a particular behavior will result in a particular outcome *and* the likelihood that the particular outcome will produce consequences that are satisfying that determines how a person behaves. Managers wishing to influence employee behavior must concern themselves with both relationships if they adopt this conceptual scheme.

Work groups exert a strong influence on motivation and behavior. Norms develop in groups as a consequence of their interpersonal interactions. These norms are powerful influences on group member behavior. Groups vary in the degree to which their members value group membership. Where membership is valued, managers can expect substantial conformity with group-imposed expectations of behavior.

Behavior modification proposes a method managers can use to influence behavior in organizations. Managers using behavior modification need not determine subordinate needs or satisfiers. Working from the observation that people tend to repeat behavior which they find satisfying and pleasant, the behavior modification approach suggests that managers determine what behavior they prefer in organizational members and then reward that behavior to encourage its repetition. Rewards and punishments can be linked to the particular behavior in a variety of ways.

Managers will find that the number and complexity of various motivation theories will not provide consistent advice in performing the leading function. Managers must select aspects from all the theories and models that seem to fit the manager's own views and the situation which the manager faces.

Managing an organization's professional employees presents special problems and issues. Professional employees represent a unique, valuable resource to the organization. At the same time, professionals have allegiances toward their profession which often are greater than their sense of obligation to the organization. Often, professional employees are asked to provide creative inputs and must be shielded from the numbing effects that standard procedures and practices can have on the expression of creative talent. In most cases, the pay and fringe benefits of professional employees are different from both the compensation levels within the employing organization *and* professionals in private practice outside the organization. Achieving practical levels of teamwork among practitioners from several professions is a monumental managerial task.

The success of managers' efforts to influence behavior are intimately tied to communications in an organization. Effective communication involves the successful transmission of an idea from one person to another person. Distortions can occur in both the media and the message. In organizations, communications can be one-way or two-way, upward, downward, and lateral. Communications can occur in different social configurations with different outcomes. Communication nets in the general form of circles, wheels, or stars will exhibit different transmission speeds, degrees of accuracy, and emotional consequences. Managers must carefully select communication modes, media, and messages to insure maximum effectiveness.

Interpersonal communications take up a lion's share of most managers' time. Skilled managers have learned good listening skills, and have learned how to reduce common barriers to effective interpersonal communications.

As organizations conduct their affairs and managers perform the leading function within them, it will become apparent that some changes in organizational behavior will require changes in the whole of the organization. Changes of this nature, which are designed to improve the effectiveness of the organization, are identified as organizational development (OD).

OD is based in values which support a spirit of inquiry, open communication, direct confrontation of organizational problems, and participative action strategies. OD endeavors will be time consuming and results cannot usually be expected immediately. OD techniques rely on management adopting a genuine collaborative style in effecting organizational changes.

Before an OD effort is launched

- certain minimum conditions must be present.
- the organizational target of the development effort must be clear.
- an organizational change model should be identified.
- power and conflict in the organization and in the change must be addressed.
- the role of the OD consultant must be clear.

A number of different techniques can be identified which have been used to effect improved organizational performance. Action research, the management grid, management by objectives (MBO), and organizational behavior modification are four common types. Most OD efforts will involve some combination of a variety of techniques and will be tailored to the specific needs of the organization, its membership, and its goals.

PART 6

Controlling

Part Six examines the managerial function of controlling. The control function is performed in various ways, but all are intended to measure the results of an organization's operations. Chapter 25 discusses the general nature of control, a corollary of planning. The construction of standards is explained, and a discussion follows on how controlling involves making corrections when actual events deviate from plans. Chapter 26 begins our discussion of the specialized aspects of control. This chapter concentrates on budgetary financial control, and control through the techniques of balance sheet analysis, breakeven analysis, and capital investment evaluation. Chapter 27 explores nonfinancial control devices including those used to control production, inventory, marketing, and research and development. Chapter 28 focuses on the systems approach to control, a topical issue in contemporary management literature. Chapter 29 is behavioral in nature. It examines human reactions to control methods designed to promote efficiency.

25 General Nature of Control

Control is the terminal function of management, in the sense that its purpose is to validate the functions of planning, organizing, staffing, and leading that precede it. In other words, control functions are performed to confirm that efforts are commensurate with results. Control is most intimately associated with planning, but is present in the performance of the other functions as well.

Control describes a specific task performed in all departments including the departments of finance, engineering, production, and marketing. Thus, in addition to assuring the effectiveness of the managerial functions, control also implies validation of the ways that operations are performed.

The feedback process is vital to the controlling function. After goals are formed and resources committed to achieving them, it is essential to have effective feedback of results. The most successful control systems employ feedback of probable *future* results, rather than of past outcomes. Modern forecasting techniques and computerization of data allow managers to achieve this ideal in an increasing number of control applications. The primary medium for feedback is the written report (in numerical or narrative terms); but common supplements are oral review and personal observation.

Of all the managerial functions, controlling has become the most mechanistic and indifferent to human concerns. Leading is concerned entirely with human behavior; the values involved in staffing are primarily humanistic rather than quantitative; the modern emphasis in organizing is on consideration of individuals and human needs; and planning (though moving toward quantitative approaches in most areas) still indicates a fresh awareness of human needs. However, controlling is almost completely objective, with quantitative methods assuming ever increasing dominance. In the process, human behavior, resistance, and attitudes seem to be overlooked, and the effectiveness of the function appears to be suffering as a result.

The prerequisite to the performance of the managerial function of controlling is the existence of comprehensive, dynamic plans covering all areas of a company's operations. Just as planning is the attempt to set the course of future events, controlling is the assurance that the course is followed, and that *actual* events are in phase with *planned* events. Thus, controlling is the corollary of planning; without plans, control would be impossible. And, conversely, without control mechanisms, planning would be a meaningless exercise. Controlling is needed to bring the plans to fruition.

Control is used in various contexts. It is sometimes offered as a synonym for *authority;* for example, managers are said to have certain subordinates under their control. On other occasions *controlling* is interchanged with *leading;* thus, statements are found to the effect that one managerial function includes controlling the actions of subordinates. There is a considerable amount of accuracy in both of these uses. However, it is suggested that to ascribe the term *controlling* to a specific and differentiated managerial function, a narrower description is required. We might say that the controlling function entails three distinct activities:

1. The establishment of standards by which the achievement of plans can be measured.
2. The comparison of performance results with these standards, and the seeking out of deviations.
3. The initiation of actions to correct continuance of the deviations or to modify the plans.

STANDARDS OF MEASUREMENT

Standards describe criterion that, when accomplished, signal the achievement of desired goals. Therefore, they must be specific to the individual plans. All standards have one common requirement: they should be expressed in numerical terms whenever possible. This requirement is critical because quantitative standards minimize the necessity for human judgment. If there is one number that expresses desired performance, and another that reflects what has actually been achieved, the two can be compared and an objective conclusion reached. Qualitative standards, on the other hand, are open to interpretation, which means that assessment of the achievement of plans may be distorted by personal biases.

The input-output concept can be used to set standards. Managers can set standards for both the input and output factors of an activity. Input factors, the resources committed to an activity, include labor, raw materials, and capital. A common unit of measurement for these factors is dollars, although labor hours and material weights may also be used. It should be plain that input factors are the costs of performing an activity. Output factors are the final products, services, or other results generated by an activity. These also may be expressed in dollars, but are often identified by such values as units of production or sales. Standards may also be set according to the criterion of time; that is, dates may be established for the completion of sequential mileposts, or subevents necessary for the accomplishment of a plan.

The input-output concept expresses outputs in relative terms. Thus, it is common to conceive of profitability as a ratio of sales to capital investment. Share of the market is also a commonly applied standard. In addition, proportional increases in such things as scale of operations constitute a popular measurement of achievement.

Bases for Constructing Standards

In setting standards, managers often tend to base them on past performance or on high hopes—neither of which can compare in effectiveness to objective analysis.

Past performance. Extrapolation from historical data is one usual method of constructing performance standards, the apparent theory being that even though past performance may not have been perfect, future performance certainly should not be worse. In using this method, standards expressed as ratios are often projected from past accomplishments and become minimum measurements of performance. For example, a firm that has never operated at less than 85 percent of capacity, has always earned at least 15 percent on invested capital, and has traditionally had more than 25 percent of the available market, will tend to project these ratios as cutoff points, so that problems will be indicated if they are not at least equaled. Some disadvantages of projecting past achievements as standards are the possibilities that inefficiencies will be perpetuated and changes (actual or predicted) will be overlooked.

High hopes. Aspiration is another basis for setting standards. Managers often subjectively establish standards higher than have been achieved through previous performance in the hope that the act of striving for them will result in some improvement, even though it is not likely. There is a danger in this approach, because people tend to be reluctant to even try to meet standards which they perceive to be unrealistic.

Objective analyses. A final method for setting standards, and the one that is by far the most effective, is to employ objective analyses to determine the ideal set of goals. It is often said that Frederick Taylor (Chapter 3) started the movement toward objective analysis with time and motion study for setting labor standards; and in recent years the quantitative methods for decision making (Chapter 9 and the appendixes) have been applied in many areas of a company's operation to determine possible standards.

Applying Standards

The reports which permit comparison of plans and actual events are necessarily of many varieties. Traditionally, a large proportion of these reports has been generated by a firm's accounting department, but a modern trend, caused by the increasing use of the computer, has companies moving toward centralizing reporting in a data-processing department. However, regardless of the source of reports, certain elements must be observed in measuring performance. These elements include pinpointing strategic factors, predicting deviations, using valid units of measurement, and distributing the report.

Pinpointing strategic factors. Because of the hosts of data that can be spewed from a reporting system, it is crucial that the strategic factors relevant to the achievement of each individual plan be identified. Factors are strategic if they make a significant difference between the success or failure of a plan, whereas nonstrategic factors may vary widely from plans, but have little effect on the final outcome. Reports should be designed to focus on the strategic factors. (See Chapters 6–10 on the planning function for discussions of the factors that are strategic to plans.)

Predicting deviations. The most meaningful reports are those that indicate deviations from plans before they occur. Such foresight is possible through sophisticated trend analysis, and enables managers to do something about potentially unfavorable conditions. If deviations cannot be predicted, the next best thing is to report them right after they have happened. In this way, corrective action may be taken to prevent a dangerous situation from getting out of control. It should be obvious that reports that tend to be ancient history are relatively useless. A manager can make little effective response to a report that reveals that plans are completely awry because of an event that went undetected three months before.

Using valid units of measurement. Events should be reported in valid units of measurement. For example, in reporting engineering accomplishments, it is far more meaningful to report mileposts achieved, as related to those that were scheduled, than to report the current status of expended engineering labor hours. Again, production status on a certain date is a more useful statistic than percent of plant capacity that was worked in the time period. Events that appear favorable when reported in one fashion, may, if reported in a way that more appropriately represents the condition, appear to be completely out of line.

Distributing the report. In each case, information should be transmitted to the manager who can do something about it, and to the higher-level manager who assesses whether appropriate action has been taken. In addition, reports should be sent to other managers whose own operations might be affected by the events. This probably is as far as the distribution of reports should go. Business firms are often blanketed with reports on deviations from plans. Frequently the manager who is most directly responsible for the cause of deviations is omitted.

Corrective Action

Depending on the severity of the deviations, corrective actions taken by a company will take the form of either short-term or long-term adjustments.

Short-term adjustments. Some deviations from planned events can be remedied by "fire-fighting" tactics, or short-term adjustments. Perhaps, for example, the responsible manager foresees that a deviation from plans is about to happen, and because this deviation was a contingency that was considered in the original planning effort, an alternative course was developed that can be adopted now that the contingency turns out to be a real fact. While all deviations may not be so easy to correct, some may be within the manager's ability to remedy, such as poor performance by individuals, underallocation of input resources, or inefficient use of resources. Some specific action can be used to handle each of these possible causes of deviation. Once the manager has isolated the cause and applied the action, the short-term crises should be resolved. The same tactics can be used, although with somewhat less effectiveness, to handle deviations of the immediate past that have been brought to the manager's attention.

Long-term adjustments. Deviations necessitating long-term adjustments are caused by factors that are built into the system itself. In such cases, the plans can be realized, theoretically, but short-term adjustments cannot improve deviations. As a result, responsible managers are frustrated by their ineffectiveness, their efforts are criticized by higher-level managers, and the chasm between plans and events becomes wider. The only solution lies in making significant, and probably long-term, adjustments in the total system.

The necessary adjustments may include a change of the method of organization, for instance, from functional to project, dropping or adding product lines, revamping the firms's capital structure, or vertical or horizontal merger. Often deviations that cannot be readily corrected are caused by the incompetence of the management team. For example, just after World War II a large wholesale grocery company in Los Angeles was forced to liquidate its assets because its management was comprised of elderly men who were no longer capable of operating the company in a highly competitive environment. At the time, the managers could not be satisfactorily replaced because of a national shortage of qualified managers.

DISCUSSION QUESTIONS

1. Why is controlling called the terminal function in management?
2. What is meant by "the feedback process"?
3. Discuss the close relationship between the planning and controlling functions.
4. How are standards established?
5. What are strategic factors?
6. Differentiate between short-term and long-term adjustments in correcting deviations.

BIBLIOGRAPHY

Dawson, Robert I. and Dorothy P. Carew. "Why Do Control Systems Fall Apart?" *Personnel,* Vol. 46 No. 3 (May–June 1969), pp. 8–16.

Fleming, John E. "The Spectrum of Management Control." *Advanced Management Journal,* Vol. 37 No. 2 (April 1972), pp. 54–61.

Koontz, Harold and Robert W. Bradspies. "Managing Through Feedback Control." *Business Horizons,* (June 1972), pp. 25–36.

Machin, John. "Measuring the Effectiveness of an Organization's Management Control Systems." *Management Decision,* (Winter 1973), pp. 260–79.

Sihler, William H. "Toward Better Management Control Systems." *California Management Review,* Vol. 14 No. 2 (Winter 1971), pp. 33–39.

Stroud, Bill. "Common Fallacies in Monitoring and Control." *Managerial Planning,* (July–August 1974), pp. 18–21.

The Case of the Slippery Siding Salesman

"I warned you six months ago that you were going to get into trouble because of Brooks and his high-pressure selling tactics," exclaimed Dominic Bianco, attorney for B and J Building Materials, Inc., and who was also on the firm's board of directors.

"What's the matter now?" nervously asked Joe Bradley, manager and part owner of the company.

"A group of the homeowners to whom Brooks and those crooks that he calls salespersons sold aluminum siding have hired an attorney, Tom Davis, to contest their contracts. Davis just called me about it," replied Bianco.

In an effort to bolster B and J's somewhat sagging earnings record with an allied product, Bradley had taken on a line of aluminum siding about a year previously. The product was made by a reputable manufacturer, and although expensive by the standards of the average homeowner, did improve the exterior of a house when installed over the original frame construction. Bradley hired an installation crew, and invested in an inventory of the siding. He advertised on television and in the newspaper, and when inquiries came in, two salespersons who had formerly worked in the hardware department of B and J for many years called on the homeowners and submitted price estimates. Sales were, however, extremely disappointing. In the first six months, only five installations had been sold.

While thinking about writing off the siding venture as a bad investment, Bradley received an impressive letter from a Mr. Mal Brooks. Brooks described himself as a highly successful developer of direct sales, cited the firms that he had worked for, his titles, and the dramatic increases in sales that he had effected. He said he now wanted the challenge of developing the aluminum siding market, and would like to meet with Mr. Bradley at 2:00 P.M. on the coming Friday.

The proposition that Brooks made was as follows: He would assume the management of a division to be created—the Aluminum Siding Division of B and J Building Materials, Inc., with the title of Vice-President. In the first month he would be on probation while he proved that he could sell ten installations. After that it would be considered a permanent arrangement, as long as sales increased 50 percent each month until they leveled off at thirty to thirty-five per month. His compensation would be a draw against a 10-percent commission on all installations. He would build a sales crew of about five salespersons, each of whom would have a draw against a 10-percent commission on every installation that they personally sold. A bank account would be set up for the division, and he would manage it. He would deposit the homeowners' down payments in it, and pay the salesforce advances out of it. Bradley was to open the account with $5000. Bradley was to leave all of the details of the aluminum siding business to him, and judge him by his sales performance. To protect Bradley, Brooks adamantly insisted that be become bonded.

Sales went as promised, and Bradley was delighted. The only sour notes were those sounded by Bianco at the monthly board meetings. Bianco called Bradley's attention to the scandalous "suede shoe gangs" who had exploited the aluminum siding market in other states. Through the local police department, he found that four of the five salespersons that Brooks had hired were ex-convicts, and that Brooks had been charged twice for extortion, although he had never been convicted. He said that he was sure that Brooks was not using the contract and warranty forms that he had prepared, but was employing forms of his own design. He prophesied that an indelible stain would be put on B and J's name, and now the action taken by the dissident homeowners confirmed his worst suspicions.

There was nothing for Bianco and Bradley to do but meet with Tom Davis, the homeowners' attorney. The following discussion took place in Davis' office:

"What are these people complaining about?" exploded Bradley. "They bought an aluminum siding installation, and they got it."

"Although this is far from the whole of it," Davis began, "even this statement isn't true. Don't you know that your own installation crew is so far behind that people who made down payments three months ago haven't had work started on their houses yet? And, don't you also know that your Mal Brooks lined up a fly-by-night construction outfit to make installations that were so badly done that the siding is falling off the houses?"

"No, I didn't," admitted Bradley.

"Their next step, after getting a homeowner to agree to buy an installation, was to clinch the financing arrangement," Davis went on. "Brooks had made a deal with a shady finance company to take the paper for 75 percent of the installation price. Although you have to look carefully to find it in the contract, interest is at 24 percent compounded on the original balance. Another interesting obscure clause in the contract is that the homeowner assigns a second mortgage on his property to the finance company. Then, to get the 25 percent cash down payment, the sales pressure must have been awesome to behold. People borrowed on their life insurance, took their children's education funds, and mortgaged their cars and furniture. You might say that they're adults and should know what they're doing, but if this goes to court I'm going to say that they are victims of unscrupulous and systematized chicanery."

"I had no idea that Brooks was using tactics like that," confessed Bradley.

"Mr. Bradley," Davis said sharply, "I know some judges who would say to you that you are either a liar or a fool."

When Bianco and Bradley got back to the company office, Bradley said, "I sure let it get out of control, didn't I?"

Bianco replied, "I'm not sure we know everything yet. Let's try to get Brooks in here."

About ten minutes after the request to locate Mal Brooks, Edna Wilson, Bradley's secretary and office manager, informed them that Brooks had checked out of his motel.

"We do have him bonded, don't we?" Bradley asked her.

"No, we don't," she replied. "On the first day that he was here he made a big show about getting an application form from the bonding company, but he never filled it out."

"Mrs. Wilson," said Bianco, "please find out what the balance is in the bank account of Aluminum Siding Division."

A few minutes later the phone rang. It was the bank manager. "I was going to call you anyway," he said. "The balance is now $15.83. Mr. Brooks made a withdrawal of close to $10,000 yesterday."

DISCUSSION QUESTIONS

1. Why are standards essential to the controlling function?

2. How does a student perform the controlling function while proceeding through a college course?

3. What long-term adjustments may students have to make when they assess the grade that they get in a course, as measured against the standard that they have set?

4. In the Case of the Slippery Siding Salesman, what standards did Joe Bradley have for control over Mal Brooks?

5. In what ways was Joe Bradley derelict in performing the controlling function?

The Case of the Newborn SPM

"One of the first things we have to do is establish regular calibration periods for all the shop gauges," said Stan Klopp, newly appointed quality control supervisor of Sum-ter Corporation, to his assistant Allen Tanaka. "The way it is now, company-owned gauges are checked whenever the tool-crib attendant happens to have the time, and it's been left to the mechanics to ask to have their personal gauges calibrated."

Sum-ter Corporation manufactures golf carts and snowmobiles. It has grown rapidly over its five-year life, and employs about three hundred people. A serious accident caused by defective brakes on one of its golf carts made John Woodward, president, realize the need for formal quality control. This decision led to the employment of Klopp, who was given pretty much of a free rein to set up appropriate quality-control procedures.

Klopp's conversation with Tanaka continued: "In addition to the lack of control over the shop gauges, I can't find any evidence that the master gauges have ever been checked."

"At the last place I worked," said Tanaka, "the procedure was to calibrate all shop gauges except screw plugs every two weeks. Screw plugs were checked after every use. Arrangements were made with the manufacturers of the master gauges for calibration every six months."

"That was my experience also," said Klopp. "I'll send a memorandum to the production manager asking that all gauges be assembled this weekend. We'll calibrate them, and make up a record card for each one. Then I'll get the production manager to tell his foreman to make sure that the calibration schedule is followed."

Stan and Allen patiently began to build quality-control procedures in this fashion. An early event that required their attention was a bearing that had been left out of each machine in a shipment of snowmobiles to Sum-ter's most important dealer. Upon investigation, Stan found out that the assembly shop had no procedure for assuring that all parts were included in a piece of equipment when it was put together. His action was to design a form with a space for the date and the equipment's serial number, and a listing of every part that was supposed to go in the machine. As the parts were assembled, they were to be checked off on a form, and a completed form for every machine that was assembled was to be sent to his office.

While Stan was working on the checklist procedure, he assigned Allen to the task of planning which parts were to be inspected at the machines as they were being processed, and which parts were to be sent to a central inspection station after they had been processed. It would be desirable to have all processes that were producing defective parts discovered before unnecessary costs were incurred, but the limiting factor was that some operations required inspection by apparatus that could not be moved about through the shop. Allen's approach was to prescribe decentralized inspection for all operations that could be examined by portable gauges, such as micrometers. Instructions were written calling for central inspection of operations requiring such apparatus as Starrett height gauges or electronic devices.

The next matter requiring attention was inspection of incoming materials at the receiving dock. Until the arrival of Klopp and Tanaka at Sum-ter, there had actually been no inspection of items made by vendors to the company's specifications. Foremost among these components were engines, transmissions, and castings. Stan and Allen worked out performance tests for engines and transmissions, and persuaded John Woodward to invest in an X-ray machine for inspecting castings for blow holes and cold shuts. They then had to decide between 100 percent inspection of critical items and statistical acceptance sampling. Because of the high cost of inspecting every item, they opted for sampling, and then had to develop a sampling plan for the purchasing department to incorporate in its purchase contracts.

The work with the purchasing department on sampling plans made Stan aware that the company had no objective basis for evaluating suppliers other than by price. Together with Bill Leslie, the purchasing agent, he developed a point evaluation system to rank vendors on the basis of the quality reports on incoming shipments.

A system for communicating Sumter's quality performance to the company's top management was an obvious need, and Allen designed a system called Quality Rejection Reports. The reports were issued monthly, and recapped the number of quality rejections, the cause for the rejections, and the recommended corrective actions.

When parts were rejected because of failure to meet quality standards, two actions were possible. They could either be reworked or scrapped. To make the rework decision a routine one, Stan developed a list of criteria for incurring the costs of rework, and another list which sent defective parts to the scrap heap.

After about three months of quality-control effort, Stan remarked to Allen as he surveyed the pile of memoranda on quality that had been written: "You know, we could use these instructions to write up a Quality Control Standard Procedures Manual. We could assign a copy to everybody in the company who needed one, and keep adding to it as we developed new procedures. We would also want to give notice of the revision of procedures. The SPM would be the source of reference on any question regarding Sum-ter's quality assurance program."

DISCUSSION QUESTIONS

Reference Case A. The Case of the Markets That Will Fade Away (Chapter 8)

1. Is it desirable that a firm commit all of its policies to writing?
2. How can an individual company (assume that it is a large one) exercise control over policies that are imposed by the government? By labor unions?
3. In Reference Case A, what is one of Petro's planning alternatives that should be formalized with the detail of a program?
4. In the Case of the Newborn SPM, how would you evaluate the development

of the Quality Control Standard Procedures Manual for Sum-ter Corporation? Are there any advantages to the way it was done? Could it have been done in another way?

5. Should quality-control procedures be developed by top management, instead of by middle managers such as Stan Klopp, with the help of his assistant?

26 Financial Control

As we emphasized in the preceding chapter, controlling is the managerial function concerned with assessing the extent to which plans are realized and correcting deviations. One aspect of controlling deals with standards and results expressed in financial terms. In other words, the units of measurement are dollars. Data for financial controls are usually derived from the organization's accounting statements. Although managers of an organization's various departmental units are ultimately responsible for the financial control of their own operations, in most organizations the executive heading the financial operation, and his or her staff, exercise considerable authority in establishing and implementing overall financial controls.

BUDGETARY FINANCIAL CONTROL

The interdependence of the controlling and planning functions is clearly evident in the technique known as *budgeting.* The first step in budgeting is to decide on the forms to be used in expressing the results of the company's operations. Ideally, the budget should be organized so that factors such as revenues can be aligned with expenses, cash fluctuations, and capital fund allocations. Next, company expectations regarding elements such as revenue, expenses, and cash flow should be recorded. These should be entered on the appropriate forms in numerical terms. Up to this point, budgeting is purely planning. When actual results are obtained, they are entered opposite the expected results, the differences are analyzed, and conclusions are reached regarding indicated actions. At this point the budget becomes a control device.

Figure 26-1. Operating Statement, Quarter Ending March 31, 1977.

	Actual ($000)	Actual Percent of Gross Sales	Budget ($000)	Budget Percent of Gross Sales	Variance* ($000)	Variance* Percent
Gross Sales	284.0	—	238.0	—	46.0	19
Less:						
Freight Out	14.2	5	4.8	2	(9.4)	(3.0)
Net Sales	269.8	95	233.2	98	36.6	(3.0)
Cost of Goods Sold:						
Direct Labor	83.2	29.3	64.3	27	(18.9)	(2.3)
Direct Materials	34.5	12.0	30.9	13	(3.6)	1.0
Overhead	58.5	21.0	52.4	22	(6.1)	1.0
Cost of Goods Sold	176.2	62.3	147.6	62	(28.6)	(0.3)
Gross Profit	93.6	32.7	85.6	36	8.0	(3.3)
Sales & Administrative:						
Sales Expense	68.2	24.0	38.1	16	(30.1)	(8.0)
Administrative Expense	24.0	8.5	23.8	10	(0.2)	1.5
Sales & Administrative	92.2	32.5	61.9	26	(30.3)	(6.5)
Net Profit	1.4	0.2	23.7	10	(22.3)	(9.8)

*Unfavorable variances in parentheses.

The typical firm will develop many types of budgets. Moreover, each type of budget will vary in the amount of detail it includes, depending on the organizational level for which it is prepared. In other words, budgets prepared for top-level management tend to be summaries; but the closer budgets get to the organizational level at which performance takes place, the more detailed they will be.

An Example of the Budgeting Process

The process of budgeting can be explained with reference to Figure 26-1, a simple operating statement (revenue and expense budget), plus a few supporting expense budgets—Figures 26-2 through 26-5. Refer to

Figure 26-2. Direct Labor Analysis, Quarter Ending March 31, 1977.

	Actual Hours	Budget Hours	Variance	Actual ($000)	Actual %GS	Budget ($000)	Budget %GS	Variance ($000)	Variance %
Foundry (Straight Time)	6400	6270	(130)	19.3		18.8	8		
" (Overtime)	1070	—	(1070)	4.8	8.5	—		(5.3)	(0.5)
Machine Shop (ST)	7300	7180	(120)	22.0		21.5	9		
" (OT)	1220	—	(1220)	5.5	9.7	—		(6.0)	(0.7)
Finishing Shop (ST)	3350	3200	(150)	10.0		9.6	4		
" (OT)	545	—	(545)	2.5	4.4	—		(2.9)	(0.4)
Assembly (ST)	5100	4800	(300)	15.4		14.4	6		
" (OT)	815	—	(815)	3.7	6.7	—		(4.7)	(0.7)
Total Direct Labor	25,800	21,450	(4350)	83.2	29.3	64.3	27	(18.9)	(2.3)

Figure 26-3. Direct Materials Analysis, Quarter Ending March 31, 1977.

	Actual		Budget		Variance	
	($000)	%GS	($000)	%GS	($000)	%
Raw Materials	17.5	6	16.5	7	(1.0)	1.0
Subcontracted Components	8.5	3	7.2	3	(1.3)	—
Purchased Parts	8.5	3	7.2	3	(1.3)	—
Total Direct Materials	34.5	12	30.9	13	(3.6)	1.0

these figures as we develop the following example that helps explain the budgeting process.

Sales performance. A general manager's first response to the operating statement presented in Figure 26-1 would be elation. To provide for a quarterly budget review, which the manager regards as an adequate means of control, the manager had the operating statement prepared immediately following March 31, and it confirms the sales manager's reports that gross sales for the quarter exceeded expectations by 19 percent. The major criterion of success or failure to managers of most small companies is sales performance, and an excess of this magnitude is usually regarded as a good omen. However, since this particular budget has been prepared with all elements represented as proportions of gross sales, as well as in absolute values, when the manager proceeds to the next two lines of the operating statement that initial elation may dampen. The expense of shipping the firm's product to its customers has gone sufficiently over the budget to lower the ratio of net sales to gross sales by 3 percent. Even at that, actual net sales exceeded the budgeted figure by $36,600, so things continue to look good.

Cost of goods sold. The firm expected to sell $238,000 worth of products. However, it sold $284,000 worth. Therefore, higher amounts for labor, materials, and overhead are not surprising. A disturbing item is the 2.3 percent higher ratio of direct labor to gross sales. This will have to be looked into later. Offsetting this higher ratio, however, are lower ratios of materials and overhead to gross sales; moreover, the ratio of

Figure 26-4. Overhead Analysis, Quarter Ending March 31, 1977.

	Actual		Budget		Variance	
	($000)	%GS	($000)	%GS	($000)	%
Indirect Labor	22.8	8	16.7	7	(6.1)	(1.0)
Salaries	11.9	4	11.9	5	—	1.0
Supplies	4.8	2	4.8	2	—	—
Depreciation	14.2	5	14.2	6	—	1.0
Power	2.4	1	2.4	1	—	—
Other	2.4	1	2.4	1	—	—
Total Overhead	58.5	21	52.4	22	(6.1)	1.0

Figure 26-5. Sales Analysis, Quarter Ending March 31, 1977.

	Total						Territory 1						Territory 2					
	Actual		Budget		Variance		Actual		Budget		Variance		Actual		Budget		Variance	
	$	%GS	$	%GS	$	%	$	%GS	$	%GS	$	%	$	%GS	$	%GS	$	%
Gross Sales	284.0	—	238.0	—	46.0	—	145.0	—	143.0	—	2	—	139.0	—	95.0	—	44.0	—
Less:																		
Freight Out	14.2	5	4.8	2	(9.4)	(3.0)	2.9	2	2.9	2	—	—	11.3	8.1	1.9	2	(9.4)	(6.1)
Net Sales	269.8	95	233.2	98	36.6	(3.0)	142.1	98	140.1	98	2	—	127.7	91.9	93.1	98	34.6	(6.1)
Sales Expense:																		
Salaries	22.7	8	19.1	8	(3.6)	—	11.6	8	11.5	8	(0.1)	—	11.1	8.0	7.6	8	(3.5)	—
Travel	25.6	9	9.5	4	(16.1)	(5.0)	5.8	4	5.7	4	(0.1)	—	19.8	14.2	3.8	4	(16.0)	(10.2)
Entertainment	19.9	7	9.5	4	(10.4)	(3.0)	5.8	4	5.7	4	(0.1)	—	14.1	10.2	3.8	4	(10.3)	(6.2)
Total Sales Expense	68.2	24	38.1	16	(30.1)	(8.0)	23.2	16	22.9	16	(0.3)	—	45.0	32.4	15.2	16	(29.8)	(16.4)

cost of goods sold to gross sales is only 0.3 percent above budget, which does not appear too alarming. Then, too, actual gross profit is $8000 higher than the budget figure, even though this amount represents a less favorable ratio to gross sales—32.7 percent, as compared with the 36 percent ratio that was budgeted.

Sales expenses. When the manager's analysis reaches the sales expense entries, all optimism will undoubtedly disappear. Take a look at the last line of Figure 26-5. It has cost $30,100 to generate the additional $46,000 in gross sales, and sales expense as a proportion of gross sales has gone 8 percent over budget. Even though administrative expense has held constant in absolute value, and is actually below the budget in relative amount, the ratio to gross sales of sales and administrative expense combined is over budget by 6.5 percent. The final blow is that profit only amounts to $1400, in comparison with a budgeted $23,700, and its ratio to gross sales is below the budget by 9.8 percent.

Investigating Deviations

The cost of freight out was an early clue that the additional sales were inordinately costly. High sales expense confirm this. In the face of these figures, the manager would turn first to the sales analysis schedule to get to the root of the problem. The total columns in Figure 26-5 indicate that travel and entertainment expenses, in addition to shipping cost, are sources of the trouble. Total travel relative to gross sales is 5 percent higher than budgeted, and entertainment, 3 percent. At this point the general manager may ask, "Have both sales territories generated excessive travel and entertainment increases?"

A look at the figures for Territory 1 discloses that nothing out of line has occurred. The actual sales produced in the territory were consistent with the volume that was planned; it cost no more to ship the product than the budgeted 2 percent; and the elements of salaries, travel, and entertainment were each satisfactorily within $100 of their budgets.

Territory 2 has a different story, however. It is in this territory that the sales increase has been bought at a high price. The 6.1 percent excess in freight and the 10.2 percent excess in travel, as ratios of gross sales, indicate that the sales force must be ranging far afield to find customers for their wares. In addition, the buyers must be receiving lavish entertainment in return for their purchasing favors, as is revealed by the 6.2 percent higher ratio for that element.

Taking Corrective Action

Reform must start with the manager responsible. In this case, it is obvious that the manager of Territory 2 is the guilty party. Salespersons in the territory were either encouraged to buy sales in order to make an impressive sales record, or lost control of their personal selling activities. The courses of action open to the general manager vary from discharging the sales manager to reprimanding the manager and giving the manager another chance. In real life, the specific action would be dictated by careful investigation of all of the circumstances.

Further Tracking

Once the increase in sales is diagnosed as a serious problem the general manager should try to pinpoint its effect on other phases of the company's operations. The operating statement showed that direct labor costs were in trouble, so Figure 26-2 warrants attention. Note that the manufacturing operation was budgeted for straight-time activity only, but that the increase in sales required overtime work. With the exception of the 50 percent higher labor cost for overtime hours, the manufacturing departments consistently stayed within their budgets. Figure 26-3 reveals that absolute cost of materials went over budget, as would be anticipated because more materials were needed for the increased goods produced. It is shown, however, that quantity discounts for raw materials apparently caused the ratio of this element to gross sales to go below budget by 1 percent.

Overhead elements, which tend to be fixed costs, are shown in Figure 26-4. These generally have remained constant with the budget in absolute terms, with salaries and depreciation under the budget in relative terms. One element, indirect labor, is above budget, both in dollars and percentage. An investigation would probably disclose that the unexpected increase in sales necessitated crash measures in scheduling, expediting, and shipping activities, which resulted in a need for additional people.

Budget Adjustments

Despite the fact that a serious problem was uncovered by budget analysis and can be corrected in the future, it should be apparent to the manager that quarterly reviews are insufficient. The budgeting system must be made more sophisticated so that potential variances can be detected before problems develop. In addition to remedying the budgeting defect, the unfortunate sales splurge probably developed other problems that can be isolated by nonbudgetary financial controls.

NONBUDGETARY FINANCIAL CONTROL

The control techniques in most business organizations employ dollars, or relationships between dollars, as the units of measurement, because dollars focus on the ultimate objective, which is profit. Controlling revenues and expenses by budgets, as described in the earlier parts of this chapter is one form of financial control; in addition, budgets will be developed for product lines, organizational departments, and many other aspects of a firm's operations. The convenience of using dollars as units of measurement leads to methods of financial control that are not strictly budgets, although the distinction may be somewhat shadowy. Three popular methods are balance sheet analysis, breakeven analysis, and capital investment evaluation.

Balance Sheet Analysis

Earlier, the budgeting process was explained using the example of the company whose operations got out of control. The same example will be used in the following explanation of balance sheet analysis.

The balance sheet. The conventional accounting device for expressing a firm's financial position at a given moment in time is the *balance sheet.* Assume that Figure 26-6 represents actual financial positions of the

Figure 26-6. Balance Sheet as of March 31, 1977.

	Quarter Ending 12/31/76 ($000)	Quarter Ending 3/31/77 ($000)	Plan Quarter Ending 6/30/77 ($000)
Current Assets:			
Cash	65	15	50
Accounts Receivable	110	156	115
Inventories	80	115	95
Total Current Assets	255	286	260
Fixed Assets			
Net Plant and Equipment	263	319	305
Total Assets	518	605	565
Current Liabilities			
Notes Payable	61	115	65
Accounts Payable	82	90	90
Total Current Liabilities	143	205	155
Long-Term Debt	150	200	200
Total Liabilities	293	405	355
Stockholders' Equity			
Common Stock	150	150	150
Net Retained Earnings	75	50	60
Total Stockholders' Equity	225	200	210
Total Liabilities and Equity	518	605	565

Figure 26-7. Ratio Analysis.

	Balance Sheets		
	12/31/76	3/31/77	6/30/77
Current Ratio	1.8:1	1.4:1	1.7:1
Quick Ratio	0.5:1	0.1:1	0.3:1
Equity/Debt Ratio	0.8:1	0.5:1	0.6:1

company discussed in our example for the past two time periods, and a projected position for the next time period. The firm is in trouble because of uncontrolled sales, but may not yet realize the full consequences.

Ratio Analysis.   Much can be learned about a firm's financial position by deriving the relationships between the various elements of the balance sheet. Ratios can be compared with accepted standards, to past records, or projected plans, to ascertain the state of the company's financial health. In Figure 26-7, the manager assesses the firm's position as of the end of March 1977 in comparison with the end of the preceding quarter, and finds that the runaway sales and the optimism they generated seriously hurt the company. With the planned corrective action in mind, the manager projects a balance sheet as of the end of the next quarter.

Current ratio.   One indication of a firm's ability to pay its short-term debts is its current ratio. This ratio is derived by dividing current assets by current liabilities. Since banks usually favor a current ratio of 2:1 when considering a loan application, you can see that the firm's current ratio of 1.4:1 is very unpromising. Its unusual sales activity drained cash and forced short-term borrowing to create working capital. The plan for the next quarter includes aggressive collection efforts to generate cash from receivables, and reducing the inventory. The short-term debt reduction will take a substantial part of the cash flow.

Quick ratio.   Derived by dividing cash by current liabilities, a quick ratio of 1:1 indicates a good cash position. Thus, with a ratio of 0.1:1, this firm is critically short of cash and will have difficulty surviving.

Equity/debt ratio.   The equity/debt ratio, derived by dividing equity (the value of the property less claims against it) by total liabilities, indicates where the real ownership of a firm lies. A 1:1 ratio is considered a safe one, yet in our example, where the ratio is 0.5:1, the creditors own more of the company than the stockholders. This happened because optimistic sales reports offered encouragement to borrow on long-term mortgages to buy new equipment, and, in addition, to pay dividends out of retained earnings. Now the company is stuck with the higher debt, and must slowly increase equity through profitable operations.

This example illustrates that the information contained in a reporting system may be adequate to permit control, but if it is out of date when it is received, effective control is impossible.

Breakeven Analysis

The term *breakeven* means that at some quantity of goods sold, a company's fixed costs will be recovered and from that point on, the difference between variable costs and sales revenue will be profit. Owners of small businesses are keenly sensitive to this breakeven point in their operations, perhaps because it can be calculated when conditions are simple. When a firm's operations become more complex, the breakeven point becomes more of a theoretical concept than a practical one.

Breakeven analysis can be explained by a simple graphic model (see Figure 26-8). Assume that a firm's fixed costs—that is, those costs such as rent, depreciation, and managers' salaries, which go on at a constant amount regardless of sales volume—are $100,000 per year. Assume that costs which vary with sales volume, such as labor and materials, are $1.50 per unit sold. The firm's total cost for any number of units sold would be $1.50 times the units sold (x) plus $100,000:

$$TC = 1.50x + \$100,000.$$

Assume that the selling price for each unit is $2.00. Sales revenue would then be $2.00 times the number of units sold:

$$S = \$2.00x.$$

The breakeven point is where sales revenue and total costs are equal, or where

$$\$2.00x = \$1.50x + \$100,000.$$

This point would be 200,000 units. Sales volume in excess of 200,000 units would produce a profit, as shown in the shaded portion of Figure 26-8.

Implicit in the concept of breakeven analysis is that fixed costs are really constant, and that variable costs are directly proportional to quantity. Unfortunately, some so-called fixed costs tend to change when quantity changes, and the so-called variable costs do not vary in direct proportion to sales volume. In the budgeting example developed earlier, more indirect workers had to be hired to cope with the disorder caused by unexpected sales, and it cost more to produce and to sell the additional units. The fact that these conditions are generally typical does not invalidate breakeven analysis; it simply means that it is difficult to apply with accuracy. Changes in fixed costs and variable costs must be calculated for each change in volume.

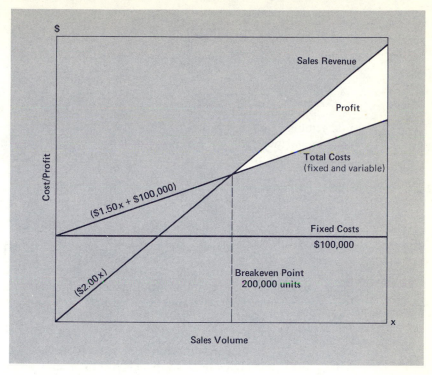

Figure 26-8. The Breakeven Point.

Capital Investment Evaluation

Most business firms are confronted each year with more demands for funds for equipment of various kinds than available investment capital. Therefore, firms must discriminate between the investment opportunities in such a way that the firm's available capital is rationed to the most promising investments. In addition, it must be assured that investment capital will earn enough over its economic life to pay for itself and generate a return consistent with some minimum standard. A conventional standard is the expected rate of return on the total of the firm's debt and equity capital, or in other words, how much interest is earned on the total investment.

Usually the investment opportunities will vary in several respects. They will require different amounts of capital, produce different amounts of absolute earnings, and have different economic lives. Therefore, it is essential that some common denominator be derived that would enable managers to compare investment opportunities.

Discounted rate of return. One popular method for evaluating investment opportunities is the discounted rate of return. The discounted rate of return is the interest rate at which the cost (negative value) of an investment, plus the *present* (positive) *value* of the estimated future flow of earnings from the investment, equal zero. This method takes into consideration the time value of money, or the fact that the sooner a promised sum of money is received, the greater its value.

Figure 26-9 illustrates the procedure for deriving this statistic. An investment opportunity has been carefully analyzed, and it has been determined that its cost will be $500,000. This is the negative value of the capital invested, or the money that flows out. The analysis shows that there will be a net flow of earnings of $125,000 from the investment for each year of its estimated five-year life. These are the positive values, before discounting, or the money that flows in. These data by themselves provide no clue to whether the investment should be undertaken, but the discounted rate of return does provide an index with which to evaluate the investment.

Look at Figure 26-9. At the present time or zero years from now, a dollar is worth a dollar at any interest rate, so the $500,000 that is paid out is at full value. A dollar that would be earned next year is worth $.94 now at an interest cost of 6 percent, and $.91 now at an interest cost of 10 percent. Therefore, the $125,000 that would be earned next year is only worth $118,000 now at 6 percent, and $114,000 now at 10 percent. The farther into the future money is received, the less value does that money have now, so the $125,000 annual earnings will have decreasing values as the times at which they will be received become more distant.

By adding the −$500,000 and the positive flow of earnings discounted at 6 percent, the net sum is $27,000. The net summation of −$500,000 and the positive flow of earnings discounted at 10 percent is −$25,000. Therefore, the effective rate of return is between 6 percent and 10 percent, and by interpolation is found to be 8 percent.

This technique can be used in many situations. Consider, for instance, a company that is examining 100 different investment opportunities. The discounted rates of return could be calculated for each of them. Then the

Figure 26-9. Discounted Rate of Return.

Year	Absolute Flow of Earnings ($000)	PVSP* 6%	Discounted Earnings @ 6% ($000)	PVSP* 10%	Discounted Earnings @ 10% ($000)
0	−500	1.00	−500	1.00	−500
1	125	0.94	118	0.91	114
2	125	0.89	111	0.83	104
3	125	0.84	105	0.75	94
4	125	0.79	99	0.68	85
5	125	0.75	94	0.62	78
Totals			27		−25

*Present value of a single payment.

investments could be arrayed, with the one yielding the highest discounted rate of return at the top of the list, then the next highest, and so on down to the lowest. Available capital could then be rationed to the opportunities high on the list until it was exhausted. The technique could also be used to preclude capital from ever being placed in low-return investments. If a firm has an objective of 15 percent return on its total capital, the investment we examined earlier that promised only 8 percent, or any other investment that promised less than 15 percent, would not be considered.

DISCUSSION QUESTIONS

1. What are the steps in the budgeting process?
2. How are variations between budgets and actual performance investigated?
3. What are some significant balance sheet ratios?
4. Explain the term "breakeven."
5. Why is capital investment evaluation so important to a business firm?

BIBLIOGRAPHY

Dunbar, Roger L. M. "Budgeting for Control." *Administrative Science Quarterly,* Vol. 16 No. 1 (March 1971), pp. 88–96.

Giglioni, Giovanni B. and Arthur G. Bedelan. "A Conspectus of Management Control Theory 1900–1972." *Academy of Management Journal,* (June 1974), pp. 292–305.

Mockler, Robert J. "The Corporate Control Job: Breaking the Mold." *Business Horizons,* (December 1970), pp. 73–77.

Seiler, Robert E. *Accounting Principles for Management: An Introduction.* Columbus: Charles E. Merrill, 1971.

Weston, J. Fred and Eugene F. Brigham. *Managerial Finance,* 4th ed. New York: Holt, Rinehart, and Winston, 1972.

The Case of the Salesman Who Did His Homework

The Bayou Land Company owned more than 400,000 acres of land in southern Louisiana. For a long time nothing much was done with the property except to collect royalties from the oil production on the extreme western sections, but starting in the 1950s the company began clearing and leveling the land for agricultural development. BLC, as the firm was known on the stock exchange, maintained a large fleet of earthmoving equipment for getting its land into productive condition, and repaired all of its equipment in its own extensive shop facilities.

Bill Paton was the shop superintendent, as well as acting purchasing agent for new equipment. "I don't act as purchasing agent as often as the equipment sales force would like me to," he often quipped, "because I believe in getting the last hour of life out of a tractor, or a blade, or a scraper. That's the way that I control the company's costs."

It was true that the equipment dealers and their salespersons in the area would like to see BLC replace its fleet at a faster rate. Paton had worked out a schedule whereby he annually submitted a capital expenditure request to BLC's directors for the replacement of one eighth of the equipment in terms of its original market value. Expressed differently, he expected to get eight years of life out of every piece of equipment. When equipment salespersons reminded him that construction companies using the same kind of equipment usually figured on a four- or five-year life, his response would be: "That's because they can't do their repairs as well, or as cheaply, as I can in this shop." The fact was that Paton's mechanics were good, and the equipment did last for eight years. As a result, the sales force tried to content themselves with their share of BLC's equipment that was bought each year. The dealers made money on the spare parts business, which did not reach BLC's top management attention but was a substantial yearly cost.

Kelley Grant was a young salesperson for Delta Tractor Company, which was owned and managed by his father. Kelley had been a business major at college, and seriously tried to apply some of the things that he had learned to improving his father's company. Getting BLC to change its equipment replacement policy, and assuring that Delta would gain a large share of the increased business, would certainly improve the firm's sales and profits. This Kelley set about to do.

While entertaining Bill Paton at lunch one day, Kelley made the comment: "Your company's annual report shows that most of the profits still come from oil royalties, and that the agricultural operation is only returning about 5 percent on its investment. Is this right?"

"Yes, it is," said Paton, who liked Kelley and respected his father. "Top management is trying every way possible to improve the return from agriculture, but nothing has worked so far."

"Your own department is part of the agriculture division, isn't it?" asked Kelley.

"Yes, I report to the division manager," replied Paton.

"Mr. Paton, I have an idea that might help you pick up some points with your company. I know that you keep excellent equipment records. Will you give me permission to work at night on these records, and see what I can come up with? Your security guard will be there, so that part of it will be all right, and I really think that I can help you bring your operation under better control."

Paton saw no reason for rejecting this request, and told Kelley to get started whenever he wanted to.

As crawler tractors represented two thirds of the number of pieces of equipment in BLC's fleet, Kelley began a detailed analysis of the records for every tractor that had ever been owned. He calculated the repair cost—parts and labor—for each year in each tractor's life, and the hours that the tractor was out of service because of repairs. As crawler tractors rented for $15.00 per hour, he used this figure to estimate the cost of down time. He then developed an average cost per year for repairs and down time. The rise in yearly costs as a tractor got older was impressive, especially the cost in the fifth year, which was the time when Paton always scheduled a complete major overhaul. However, there was an additional variable that Kelley wanted to include, which was the periodic operating improvements which the tractor manufacturers built into their products.

Kelley made an appointment with Bill Paton to make another proposition. "Mr. Paton," he said, "I am almost through with my analysis, but there is one more thing I want to do. Let Delta lend you two brand-new crawler tractors, with the increased horsepower and all of the other

improvements, for thirty days. Let's match how much dirt they move against the average dirt moved by all of your tractors over four years old."

Paton said, "I have a suspicion of what you are trying to prove, but go ahead, I haven't anything to lose."

At the end of the thirty-day period, Kelley worked up his comparative figures. Paton was obviously impressed. He said, "I guess I will have to concede that the old tractors have what you call an annual operating inferiority of $5000 in comparison with a new piece of equipment."

Kelley prepared his formal report, and took Paton to lunch to show it to him. "First," he said, "let's look at the average annual costs for a crawler tractor until it is four years old:

FIRST 4 YEARS OF A TRACTOR'S LIFE

Year	Repairs	Down Time	Total
1	$100	$45	$145
2	400	180	580
3	750	375	1125
4	1000	450	1450

"Next," Kelley said, "let's see how much a tractor costs, on the average, for its ages five through eight."

SECOND 4 YEARS OF A TRACTOR'S LIFE

Year	Repairs	Down Time	Operating Inferiority	Total
5	$15,000	$2400	$5000	$22,400
6	2,000	900	5000	7,900
7	4,000	1000	5000	10,000
8	6,000	1500	5000	12,500

"Now," Kelley went on, "let's say that the difference between the cost of a tractor one year old and a tractor five years old is the savings of a one-year-old-tractor, and the same with the difference between a two-year-old and a six-year-old, and so on. A new tractor costs $45,000, but you would get a $10,000 trade-in allowance for a four-year-old tractor, so the net cash outlay is $35,000. Suppose we find the discounted rate of return over four years for a new tractor that you buy instead of keeping an old one until it is eight years old."

Years	Net Flow of Savings	PVSP 4%	Discounted Savings @ 4%	PVSP 20%	Discounted Savings @ 20%
0	−$35,000	1.00	−$35,000	1.00	−$35,000
1	22,255	.96	21,400	.83	18,470
2	7,320	.93	6,800	.69	5,050
3	8,875	.89	7,900	.58	5,150
4	11,050	.86	9,500	.48	5,300
			10,600		−1,030

Discounted rate of return = 4% + (16% × 10,600/11,630) = 18.6%

"Mr. Paton," said Kelley quietly, "I suggest that your company's management will be pretty impressed when you show them how they can make over 18 percent on an investment."

"Young man, you have certainly taught an old dog some new tricks," said Paton, "and I promise that you won't regret the time that you have spent doing this study."

DISCUSSION QUESTIONS

1. In the balance sheet shown in the text (Figure 26-6), the company's assets increased from $518,000 to $605,000 in a three month period. Why could not this increase be interpreted to mean that things were going well?
2. In the breakeven point example, what would happen if the firm's sales volume were less than 200,000 units?
3. Why should the time value of money be incorporated in a model for evaluating investment opportunities?
4. In the Case of the Salesman Who Did His Homework, what theory is behind the assumption of an operating inferiority for productive equipment as it ages? What parallel might there be with an old automobile?
5. Also in the case presented, what implications do you see for personnel if BLC changes to a four-year life span for its earth-moving equipment? Are there other implications besides those affecting personnel?

27 Nonfinancial Control

Nonfinancial control differs from financial control mainly in the source of the data from which standards and results are derived. The previous chapter established that data for financial controls are usually derived from accounting statements. Data for nonfinancial control come from the operating plans and performance results of the organization's specialized processes. Nonfinancial control tends to be more directly exercised by the organization's departmental managers than by the financial managers of the organization. Although the unit of measurement for nonfinancial control may be dollars, it may also be units produced or sold, quantities ordered or in inventory, and ratios of various kinds. The techniques for nonfinancial control are numerous and can become very detailed. A few of the more general nonfinancial control methods are explained in this chapter.

PRODUCTION CONTROL

A production system is a complex of major and derivative plans, and control devices for implementing them. The effectiveness with which the system is controlled is measured by two standards, one having to do with the quantity and quality of the units produced (output), and the other with the employment of the resources committed to the operation (input). Control efforts to meet these standards must be balanced, because as much loss can be suffered by the inefficient use of a resource, such as labor, as can be incurred by failure to deliver the specified quality of goods in the required quantity at the proper time. Therefore, production control amounts to a descending order of parallel control procedures—there being at each level controls over output factors and input factors. In the descent, controls become increasingly detailed.

Aggregate Control

Few business firms produce only one product. The number of products that must be controlled in a typical company may range from a dozen to several hundred or more. However, looking at production control from the top, the first concern is with overall activity. And, because stable production effort is more efficient and less costly than fluctuating effort, aggregate control focuses on avoiding—to the extent possible—violent peaks and valleys in both inputs and outputs.

Figure 27-1 represents a company's forecast of the demand for the aggregate of its products and its production plan for meeting this demand. Both have been converted to direct labor hours. Of course, a host of plans must precede this graphic model. The timing of actual unit sales for each of the firm's products must be forecasted, then scheduled for production. The detailed plans for making the parts and assemblies for the various products must be integrated into the aggregate production plan, then smoothed to conform with the implied policy of a gradual buildup in production activity, a leveling-off period, and then a controlled decline. The implication is that for the first 190 days, excess production effort will be reflected in a moderate rise in inventories, followed by a period during which excess demand will be satisfied from inventory, and finally, another stage of slight inventory accumulation. The obvious objective of the plan is avoidance of cyclical swings in

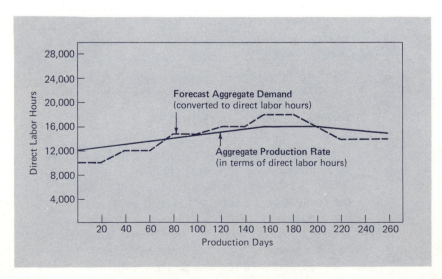

Figure 27-1.   Forecast Demand and Aggregate Production Plan.

employment, since total employment of all workers tends to be in proportion to direct labor hours.

Unfortunately, the future can never be predicted with precision. The incidence of such radical deviations of actual demand from forecasted demand in Figure 27-2, may be out of the ordinary. However, the model in the figure is designed to make the point that the central problem of production control is deciding what production changes, if any, will be made in response to differences between actual and forecasted demand. In the face of such differences, the choice of responses lies between two extremes. A firm may stay with its original plan and not adjust its production rate at all. The opposite extreme is to respond with 1 to 1 adjustments.

Costs of alternative actions. Regardless of the action a company takes in responding to differences in demand, the action will entail significant costs. Since production changes imply the hiring and laying off of workers, costs incurred include loss of investment in training, lower employee morale, poor community relations, and investment in re-training. Another costly result of production changes is either overtime pay or pay to direct workers for indirect work, such as maintenance, when they are retained despite a reduced production rate. Additional costs accrue simply from the disorder that accompanies a change in the rate of production.

The costs of holding to a stable production rate result from conditions associated with having high inventories when demand is appreciably lower than production, or a high volume of back orders (those for which customers have to wait for delivery) when demand is substantially higher

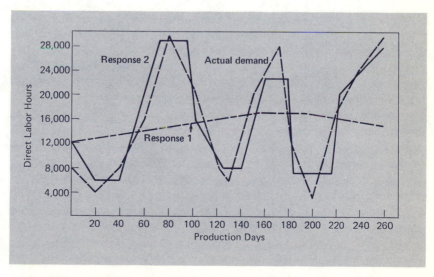

Figure 27-2. Actual Demand and Alternative Production Responses.

than production. Large inventories tie up capital, increase storage costs, entail higher taxes and insurance rates, and represent losses through obsolescence and deterioration. Back orders mean lost sales and forfeiting profit that would have come from them, because customers usually will buy from someone else when they cannot get what they want when they want it.

Optimal response rate. Figure 27-3 represents a manner of evaluating the two sets of costs discussed above. These costs run counter to each other: cost of production changes vs. costs of inventory or back orders. The objective of charting these so-called counter costs against *response rate* (the percentage of production change required for responding to the alternative demands) is to ascertain the optimal response rate—the point where the combination of the two sets of costs is minimal. A firm can develop a model like the one shown in Figure 27-3 from empirical data.

On the horizontal axis, degrees of production change in response to altered demand are in a scale ranging from zero to 100 percent. On the vertical axis calculated costs are arrayed for each degree of production change. Thus, it can be seen that at the optimal response rate, 0.3, the cost index is 6. At this point, the costs of inventory or back orders will vary in an inverse proportion to the cost of production changes (being less than 40 percent in this example). Therefore, as the response rate of

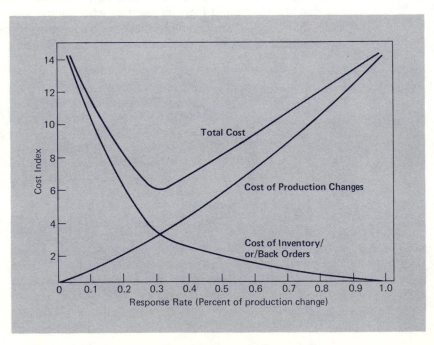

Figure 27-3. Counter Costs Affected by Response Rate.

production approaches 100 percent the costs of inventory or back orders approach zero. At some response rate, the combination of the two sets of costs will be at its lowest value. In Figure 27-3 the optimal response rate is a 30 percent adjustment of production to either a positive or negative difference between planned sales and actual sales. In other words, if planned sales were 100 units and actual sales turned out to be 150 units, then production would be increased to a rate of 115 units.

Intermediate Level of Control

At the intermediate control level, on the output factor side, schedules of finished goods production will have to be developed for each item in the firm's product line, and corrective measures instituted when schedules are not met or when demand changes require adjustments in the schedule.

A major problem with intermediate-level control of input factors is maintaining balanced employment in all of the specialized labor skill areas. Foundrymen cannot do assembly work, machinists are not competent to do electroplating, and, usually, spray painters are not qualified to operate a punch press. Yet the application of diverse labor skills in a production operation tends to be sequential; that is, in the making of a product, some are applied at the beginning, some in the middle, and some at the end. Control of schedules to prevent the layoff of some people when people with other skills are being hired is essential. Another input factor necessitating tight control is machinery. Schedules must be developed so that demand for specific machines is balanced; tools standing idle while others are swamped with work is a clue to poor machine control.

Control at the Basic Performance Level

A key feature of production control at the basic performance level is the breaking down of each work task into indivisible units, setting normal performance times for each unit, then totalling the unit times into a standard time for the task. The standard times provide the basis for controlling the efficiency of the labor resource.

Gantt charts. A traditional technique for controlling the output of a production operation is the Gantt chart. There are innumerable variations of this control device, Figure 27-4 illustrates one of them. In the figure, some quantity of an unmade part is scheduled for assembly in twenty working days. There is a sequence of operations that must be performed in making the part. Standard times are assumed to exist for each operation, so, working back from plating, the last operation, it can be determined when each preceding operation must begin and end in

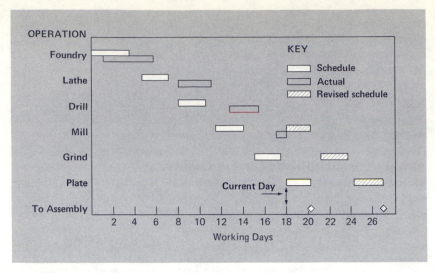

Figure 27-4.   Gantt Chart—Part Process Flow.

order to have the part completed by the scheduled date. An allowance of one day for inspection and transportation is scheduled between each operation.

As a study of the chart reveals, the operation is running late. Whatever kind of internal feedback system is in use at the plant—oral or written progress reports by the shop foremen, tracing and reporting on the movement of work by expediters, or transmission of shop information to the control center by computer—none of the three is really efficient. In any event, the part was a day late getting started in the foundry, and required a day longer than was planned for the casting operation. When it arrived in the machine shop, the scheduled lathe had been put on another job, and another delay resulted. Some other problems occurred, and finally it was realized that the part would have to be rescheduled. An incident of this kind can have an impact on a whole series of subsequent events, but the control system has given a somewhat belated, and, unfortunately, typical, warning that corrective action may have to be initiated.

Inventory control, which is a corollary of production control, is treated in the following section.

INVENTORY CONTROL

Few efforts are more crucial to the viability of a business organization than the effective control of inventories. Its accounting statements may show profitable operations, but if profits are inflexibly tied up in the inventory account, the managers may one day find themselves headed for bankruptcy court. Creditors are singularly uncooperative in accepting pieces of steel, semifinished parts, or gear boxes in lieu of cash when it is time to be paid. And an under-inventory position can be equally damaging. If operations are continually shut down or otherwise impaired by material shortages, costs can rise to the point where a company becomes unable to compete.

Inventory Responsibility

Because many aspects of inventory control can be routinized, it is often assumed that responsibility for the entire process can be relegated to personnel on a lower management level. It is true that procedures can be developed that will minimize the attention that top managers must direct to their firm's inventories. However, the policies for inventory control that the routine procedures are intended to implement must come from the managers with the most mature judgment. In fact, the few highly-critical inventory items may be directed by the personal decisions of top-level individuals in the organization structure.

A B C analysis. The prospect of exercising control over the thousands, or even tens of thousands, of individual items that comprise the total of a typical company's raw materials, in-process, finished goods, and supplies inventories would indeed be formidable were it not for A B C analysis. The essence of this method is that inventory items vary markedly in significant value, and that with any inventory—regardless of the firm or industry—a particular phenomenon will be at work. Figure 27-5 illustrates this phenomenon. Notice that approximately 10 percent of all the items in inventory (the A items) will be worth about 75 percent of the investment in inventory; 25 percent of all items (A + B) will be worth about 90 percent of the investment; and the bulk of the inventory items or about 75 percent (C), will be worth about 10 percent of the investment. It should be plain that the focus of inventory control should be on money, rather than numbers of items. Therefore, if extremely close control is exercised over the highly important A items, and as careful attention as is consistent with cost is directed to the B items, it can be said that the inventory is under control. Relatively speaking, what happens to the C items is not so important; thus, mechanical systems can be applied to them with a minimum of management decision making.

Inventory Control Systems

Inventory control systems generally are of two types, *fixed-reorder cycle* and *fixed-order quantity,* although combinations and variations of them are often designed for specific cases. Let's examine fixed-reorder cycles first.

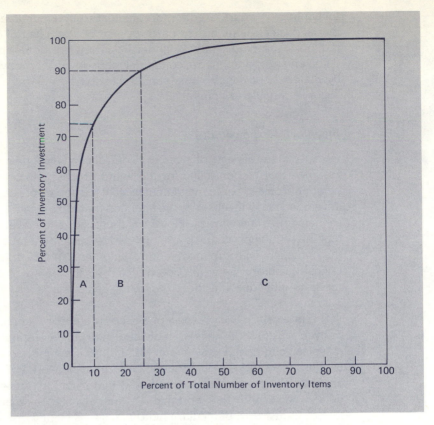

Figure 27-5. A B C Inventory Categories.

Fixed-reorder cycle. Under the fixed-reorder cycle system, the first step is to calculate usages for each inventory item for some minimum period of time, usually about one month. Periodically, such as every month, the balance of each item on hand is reviewed. Policies relative to some determined coverage in each classification of items for a future interval of time are guides in the replenishment of the various items. These policies normally originate with top management and reflect management's attitudes regarding consumer demand, availability of funds for inventory purposes, future prices and supply, and such forces as strike possibilities in vendor plants, war, or economic recession.

The stipulated coverage in the various inventory classifications will vary, depending on the factors mentioned. For example, the possibility of a strike in the steel industry might dictate a policy of a nine-month coverage for all raw steel items, while the prospect of a decline on copper prices might suggest a thirty-day inventory for copper-based items. Obviously, the fixed-reorder cycle system is most appropriate for the A and B inventory items, where the proportional size of dollar investment is large enough to warrant careful management attention to fluctuating coverage. Because the fixed-recorder cycle system is so much based on the subjective judgments of individual managers, details of its workings are difficult to describe. It is also not too amenable for use of mathematical models. For these reasons, it is not treated extensively in management literature.

Fixed-order quantity. Fixed-order quantity is a relatively mechanical inventory control system highly adaptable to operation through mathematical models, and now, by the computer. It is especially appropriate for C items.

Figure 27-6 graphically describes the theory of inventory control by fixed-order quantity. For each inventory item, the average rate of disbursement and the average time needed to replenish the stock—or the *lead time*—are determined. Then the maximum quantity that should ever be on hand at any time is calculated. These data make it possible to determine what size of inventory balance necessitates a replenishing order, and what size the order should be. No matter how much time has elapsed, an order is always placed when the balance reaches the order point. A safety stock is provided to compensate for inaccuracies in calculating disbursement rates and lead times.

The quantity ordered for any inventory item will obviously be a determinant of the amount of inventory carried for that item. When the order quantity is large, few orders will have to be placed annually to assure that sufficient stock is on hand to meet a year's requirements, but the costs of carrying the inventory will be high. As mentioned in the section on production control, these costs include the cost of capital tied up in inventory, warehouse rent and warehouse workers' salaries, taxes,

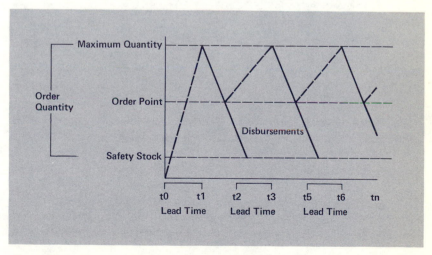

Figure 27-6.   Basic Concept of the Fixed-Order Quantity System. (Lead time designations of t0, t1, etc., are notations for time intervals.)

insurance, obsolescence, and deterioration. On the other hand, when the order quantity is small, inventory carrying costs will be commensurately reduced, but many orders must be placed each year to assure that stock on hand is adequate to avoid shortages. Ordering costs primarily include wages and salaries necessitated by placing and handling transactions, such as those involving purchasing, recording, follow-up, receiving, and inspection. In addition, the cost of supplies will be proportional to the number of orders placed. Thus, the most *economic order quantity* (EOQ) becomes a function of balancing the carrying costs (CC) against the ordering costs (OC).

Figure 27-7 illustrates a rise in carrying costs that occurs as the size of the order increases, and the decrease in ordering costs that occurs as the ordering quantity becomes larger. The economic order quantity for any inventory item is the point at which the curve for the combined costs is at its minimum point, or the point at which carrying costs and ordering costs have equal values.

It would be possible to calculate EOQ for all inventory items graphically, but it would be cumbersome and time-consuming. Instead, a mathematical model can be constructed that will greatly simplify the calculation and which, when programmed into a computer, makes the determination of EOQ virtually an instantaneous process.

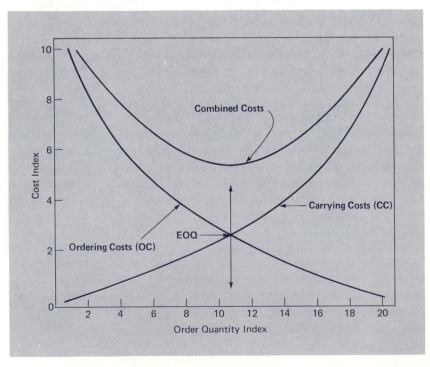

Figure 27-7. The Economic Order Quantity.

We have established that EOQ is at the order quantity point where CC = OC. Let us introduce some notation that will enable us to formulate a mathematical model. Let

Q = quantity,
U = annual usage of an inventory item,
A = total cost of placing an order,
 I = interest rate (time value of all carrying costs), and
C = total unit cost of an inventory item.

Then average carrying costs equal interest, times quantity, times unit cost, divided by 2:

$$CC = IQC/2.$$

And ordering costs equal annual usage, times the cost of placing an order, divided by the quantity ordered:

$$OC = UA/Q.$$

Now, if EOQ is at the point where CC = OC, then by substitution it is at the point where

$$IQC/2 = UA/Q$$

or, by cross multiplying the denominators, where

$$IQ^2C = 2UA,$$

and, by dividing both sides by IC, where

$$Q^2 = 2UA/IC.$$

Then, by deriving the square root of both sides, it is at the point where

$$Q = \sqrt{2UA/IC},$$

which is EOQ.
  The model

$$Q = \sqrt{2UA/IC}$$

is oversimplified, because it assumes linear disbursement rates, requires an exact knowledge of the interest rate of carrying costs, omits the possibility of quantity discounts, and assumes constant lead times. These defects are partially compensated for by the flatness of the combined cost curve in the area of the EOQ, which means that a mistake could be made in calculating Q, but that it would not be too important. In addition, it is mathematically possible to make the model more sophisticated by including some of the variables that have been omitted in this simple version.
  The appeal of the fixed-order quantity inventory control system employing the EOQ concept is that it reduces the incidence of subjective decision making. The facility with which the system can be adapted to the

computer is making it increasingly popular with all sizes and kinds of business firms as a method for controlling inventories on an objective basis.

MARKETING CONTROL

Profitability is the significant unit of measurement in the control of the marketing effort. Other common measurements, such as sales volume and market penetration, are useful supplements to profitability, but by themselves serve to conceal rather than reveal what is really happening as a result of committing resources to marketing operations.

Moreover, effective marketing control is achieved through detailed examinations of profitability, rather than aggregate measurements. It is necessary to fractionalize marketing into microsegments, and apply specific profitability standards to each of them. As a beginning, marketing might be divided into the following discrete areas for control: product line, selling effort per customer, marketing territories, and advertising.

Control of the Product Line

Decisions that bear on control of the product line have to do with assessing what stage in its life cycle a product has reached, detecting maldistributions of profits and effort, and eliminating unprofitable products.

Assessing a product's progression. Products generally can be subdivided into three categories:

- The approximately 80 percent of the new products introduced in the United States that never generate profitability.

- A large proportion of the remainder that have only temporary or spasmodic success.

- The small percentage of extremely profitable items that must cover the costs of the unsuccessful ones and, in addition, produce the profits that enable business firms to survive.

Few of even the most successful products enjoy unlimited life spans. Like the humans who conceive them, they have their struggling periods of infancy and adolescence, then they advance into productive maturity, and finally, they decline toward inevitable demise. Unsuccessful products often die after unbelievably long lives as infants.

Figure 27-8 depicts the typical life cycle of a successful product. The beginnings of all products are fundamentally the same. Resources of all kinds are committed to getting initial market acceptance, and there is an outpouring of funds without receiving anything in return. A critical

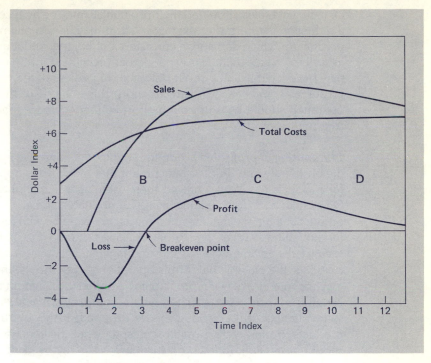

Figure 27-8. The Typical Life Cycle of a Successful Product.

control point for a new product is at A in the figure. Some products will never reach point A, and control is effective to the extent that this fact is realized before further losses are incurred. A second point of control is at B, where sales cover fixed costs, and the difference between variable costs and sales is profit.

Many products that pass point A never reach point B, and it is crucial that this prospect becomes known and the product "scrubbed" early in its life cycle. At point C, signs begin to suggest that the market's appetite for the product is becoming jaded and that returns are diminishing relative to the costs of generating sales. Finally, at point D the end is in sight. The control decision here is what to do with the venerable product that is coming to the close of its profitable life.

Detecting maldistributions of profits and effort.   An analysis of the product lines of most companies will disclose that relatively few items are sustaining the firm's profits, often with a disproportionate share of the total marketing effort. An essential marketing control is the determination of the relationship between effort and profitability for each item in the product line. For some items there may be a direct cause-and-effect relationship, and profitable items may be made more profitable by increasing the effort directed to them. Other items may not be affected by an increased sales effort and their profitability may be held constant with a reduction in effort. (For example, a firm may have a patent-protected product for which demand is consistent but limited, and it might be just as well to reduce the effort expended in promoting it.) Still other items may have a diminishing profit potential, regardless of the magnitude of resources committed to them. In short, this analysis of the marketing operation should be a thorough effort by managers to understand the true nature of their business.

Eliminating unprofitable products. Sentiment may have some place in the business world, but the attachment that many firms apparently feel for products that have outlived their usefulness is extremely wasteful. One explanation for retaining clearly unprofitable items in a company's product line may be that the company is preoccupied with total sales and market share—rather than profitability—as criteria for control. There seems to be an attitude with many managers that it is somehow immoral to reduce the scale of their firm's operations, even though the reduction may mean an increase in profitability. Another explanation may be that certain products are associated with a company's image, and it might suffer damage if the products were dropped. If this is true, then the products are indirectly profitable despite what the records show, and should be retained. However, in many cases myths grow up about a company's image which have no objective foundation.

Probably the main reason for the retention of unprofitable products, however, is that their unprofitability is not clearly recognized. In any event, a firm's marketing operation is out of control—aggregate profitability notwithstanding—if items are retained in the product line for reasons other than direct or indirect profitability.

Control of Selling Effort per Customer

An important analysis for marketing control is the differentiation between profitable and unprofitable customers. Basically, customers are classified according to the volume of their orders in relationship to the costs of generating those orders. Small-volume customers may be profitable if they require minimum sales effort. Conversely, large-volume customers may be unprofitable if the sales depend on unusual service, high transportation costs, special competitive allowances, or exorbitant entertainment expense. A manager hoping to increase the firm's profitable customers and decrease unprofitable customers is faced with a number of alternatives.

One obvious course of action in dealing with unprofitable customers is to reduce the sales effort to a level at which sales become profitable. At the same time, the released effort can be concentrated on existing or potential profitable accounts. Whenever a firm must buy its sales, its future is in jeopardy. Although a tapering off of the attractions that have induced sales from an unprofitable customer may lose the account, this loss would actually be a blessing.

Instead of reducing the sales effort, this factor could be held constant and gross billings to unprofitable customers could be increased. This can be accomplished by giving those customers a lower discount, which has the effect of increasing prices, or by adding a service charge to all invoices sufficient to cover the detailed items calling for extra cost.

A change in the distribution channel might be the answer. It often can be discerned from customer analysis that some accounts simply do not have the buying volume to justify a direct distribution channel. A manufacturer might profitably turn such accounts over to a wholesaler, or a wholesaler might direct small-volume customers to a retail outlet.

Canceling unprofitable accounts is another alternative. Probably all business firms have some customers who are simply not worth retaining. Feelings might be hurt and resentments aroused, but over the long run a company will be better off by following a control policy of periodically pruning its customer list of those accounts that have no potential of being anything but a drain on profitability.

Control of Marketing Territories

In most companies, an analysis of profit contribution by various sales territories will reveal that a relatively small proportion of the territories are providing the bulk of the profits. Moreover, analysts may discover that products that are sold profitably in some territories are markedly unsuccessful in other territories. Assuming that a comparison of the personal qualifications of the regional managers and salespersons has been made and has not been determined to be a variable, then several marketing control actions are possible.

First, the real market potential for a firm's products in the unprofitable territories should be evaluated. A company can easily extend itself into market areas where it really does not belong. If this appears to be the cause of low profits, managers should consider increasing sales effort to create demand for the products, turning the territories over to secondary distributors—such as wholesalers or jobbers—to handle, or pulling out of the barren lands altogether.

Another possible cause of low profits is uneven demand. Demand may exist in territories for part of the firm's product, but not for all of it. If this is the case sales effort is being wasted. Managers who recognize this situation should adjust marketing effort to the varying demand. Here the appropriate course of action would be to curtail efforts in selling the unwanted products and concentrate on the ones where profit can be realized.

Analysis might also suggest that part of the sales effort in the unprofitable territories be abandoned and the effort diverted to the territories where profits can be generated. In these successful territories, profits may respond to sales efforts and the increased effort will be rewarded, while in the unprofitable territories a reduction in the costs of sales efforts may make the operation profitable.

Control of Advertising Effort

Two important control devices monitor the effectiveness of the media employed to get a firm's advertising messages to consumers, and the extent of advertising expenses. Managers must analyze media effectiveness and determine the point of diminishing returns on media expenditures.

The effectiveness of the various forms of advertising media employed, such as television, radio, newspapers, magazines, and outdoor displays, varies with the product, the market, and consumer saturation. (It is assumed that the advertising concept is appropriate, and that the only object of inquiry is the media employed to convey it.) A firm's managers can analyze the media and bring the costs allocated to them under control by alternately emphasizing or reducing one form and holding the others constant. The effects of the change on sales should be compared to the relative costs associated with the change, and conclusions drawn. Another tactic is to use different media in different territories in an effort to isolate the most effective forms.

Typically, if the demand for a product is at all responsive to advertising, increased advertising will cause increased sales, up to a point. Beyond this point, the cost of further advertising to generate additional sales will be greater than the profit realized by the additional sales. This is a crucial control point, and one that is not easy to determine. Carefully designed market experiments offer the best solution to determining the point of diminishing returns. An example of such an experiment would be the soap company that selects a town in which to systematically increase its advertising, and carefully measures the effects of each increase on sales. Knowing when to stop expanding advertising, or when to reduce it, are among the most important decisions of marketing control.

CONTROL OF RESEARCH AND DEVELOPMENT

The environment of business operations of all kinds is now so dynamic that most companies of medium size and larger, and even very small firms whose products are of a technical nature, must prepare for the future. In most companies, the product or service presently offered must undergo substantial change within the next decade if the firm is to stay alive. The financial ability to get ready for the future is becoming one of the most powerful advantages that a large company has over a small one. But no matter how large it is, no company has the financial stamina

Are R and D Organizations Obsolete?

The key to success in R and D is excellence in technical work. Therefore, the effective organization must show that it places a high value on technical contribution. Many organizations say that technical work is important and that it will be rewarded, but they give all the important rewards to those in management roles. If an organization is going to keep talented people doing technical work, it must provide meaningful rewards to high-performing contributors. We see a need for improvements in the following areas.

Pay for performance, not position: The determination of who gets how much, with all the attendant questions of justice, is often so difficult and full of uncertainties that managers are willing to turn over the problem to an outside consulting company, which provides them with a plan or system. Unfortunately, such plans are usually built on the basis of a hierarchical system which considers factors, such as the number of people supervised, that do not reflect the needs of a professional organization.

The pay system needs to be flexible enough to allow managers to respond to movement through the career stages.

Some organizations may need to thoroughly redesign their pay systems. For a start, they should ask managers what they consider to be the important activities in the division, and then they should see if the people doing this work are receiving the highest pay. If they are not, the system is contributing to the problem of pulling the most talented people away from the important work of the organization.

Seek inputs in decision making: A critical incentive and reward for an experienced engineer or scientist is the confidence that he is influential in making important decisions. If a cadre of managers essentially makes all decisions based on the authority of their positions, it has a stifling effect on the entire organization. The organization loses out in that (a) poor decisions may be made because the managers did not seek valuable expertise, and (b) those who have the expertise but are not consulted may be less motivated to contribute to the organization.

We recognize that it is time consuming to get input from every person who thinks he has something to say about an important decision. However, managers who make use of the expertise of individual contributors have found that the practice pays handsome dividends.

Increase visibility for contributors: In many organizations, promotion into management is an important sign of success, and one reason is that is provides increased visibility. One engineer in a research lab complained that, every time something important happened at the lab, the managers got all the recognition. If the lab won a big contract, the local newspaper ran a story featuring a picture and an interview with the manager of the group—even if he was not primarily responsible for obtaining the contract.

The effective organization will avoid that type of publicity. Managers should work hard to see that high-performing individuals get recognition for their accomplishments. The people doing the work of the organization should have an opportunity to make presentations to the chief engineer and other top managers. They should be invited to important meetings with customers and suppliers.

to withstand for long the enormous drain of uncontrolled research and development projects. The first decision that must be made by a company looking to the future is what the scope of its R & D program will be.

The Nature and Extent of R & D

It is common to use the terms *research* and *development* together, as though they were a single activity. Sometimes they are, with *development* referring to the activity of getting a product which was discovered by the company's own research team ready for the commercial market. *Research* may, however, be an independent objective, without any intention by the firm of developing its own productive ideas. Where this is the case, a firm will sell the products of its research effort to other companies for development—companies that deliberately avoid the expense and frustration of research and look for likely ideas that can be acquired and commercially developed.

If a company is going to do research, it must consider whether its efforts will be directed toward pure research, research that *may* yield commercial applications, or toward research with determined commercial applications. With most companies, the decision will be for the latter, which then prompts the need for deciding in fairly specific terms what the objectives of its applied research are to be. Companies that buy their research ideas must have similar objectives when they evaluate promising research discoveries.

Budgeting the R & D Program

Having determined its R & D goals, the firm next must carefully assess the costs of achieving those goals over some future series of years. In most cases, these goals will not be attainable either cheaply or quickly. Often the firm will have to moderate its R & D ambitions in light of its ability to finance the effort, and achieve a balance between available money and the magnitude of its R & D program. When this is done, total annual budgets for R & D, projected over at least the next three to five years, should be prepared. The top managers should establish a strict policy that protects these budgets from invasion—even if business conditions should take a downturn. Managers are sometimes tempted to reallocate funds earmarked for R & D, but the practice has suicidal implications. When a firm's operations begin to turn sour, often the only rejuvenating factor will be some newly developed products.

The total budget for the R & D program, when established, should then have allocations made from it to specific projects that have been approved and are ready to get underway. This step entails some of the most careful decision making, because relatively few of these projects will ever pay off. The trick is to decide which are the most likely ones, and start them off with the most generous budgets. Some part of each year's total budget for R & D must be withheld, both to provide for the contingency of overruns of allocated budgets and for allocations to promising new projects that might come along in the interim. Control techniques applicable to an R & D budget are discussed later.

Staffing the R & D Effort

An effective director of an R & D program is an individual who can combine the attributes of a business manager and a scientist or research-oriented engineer. Simply having the general attributes of a good manager is not enough, because, as was mentioned in Chapter 22, professionally trained subordinates expect technical competence of the person they work under. Other reasons that the director must be professionally qualified, and possibly more compelling ones, are the abilities required to discriminate potentially productive research opportunities from those that are not, evaluate ongoing research and development projects, and select and train a professional staff. At the same time, the R & D director must demonstrate managerial ability in assuring that the program is under control and moving in a positive direction, in motivating scientists and engineers to put forth their maximum efforts, and in representing the program to senior managers in such a way as to sustain their confidence in it.

Criteria for selecting the professional staff should include diverse but complementary technical skills, a high tolerance for frustration, dedication to professional achievement, and a preference for the research environment over alternative working conditions. In addition to these personal characteristics, some recruits to the research staff should feel that they might like being managers, because potential managers of the individual projects must be identified and provided with the development opportunities that they need.

R & D Facilities

Some companies try to economize by mixing their R & D activities with their regular operations. This approach is only partially successful. Most often it causes confusion and disorder in the departmental areas concerned with engineering, testing, and manufacturing the firm's existing product line, and it also thwarts the creative processes so essential to the formulation of future product lines.

Ideally, an R & D budget should provide for working areas and experimental apparatus completely separate from the facilities devoted to regular operations. Many firms go so far as to establish their R & D programs in a different geographical area from where current products are engineered and manufactured. An R & D program should be looked upon as an independent operation, with everything provided to induce a climate where productivity will flourish.

Specific Control Techniques

The R & D program director is faced with the dilemma of having to be innovative in providing new products upon which the firm's future business will be based, but doing it while under both monetary and time limitations, and while exerting subtle and nonoppressive control.

The primary objectives of R & D control are to

- identify the projects that have no marketable potential while they are still in their early stages, so that they can be eliminated before further funds are wasted on them.

- assure that time, money, and manpower resources committed to promising projects are commensurate with their ultimate market worth.

One big problem with meeting these objectives is forecasting what flow of earnings might be realized from a product when the project is still in the embryonic stage. Another equally formidable problem is determining exactly where any project is at a given point in time, in terms of percent completed, and what additional resources will be required to have its end product ready for the market when the market is ready for it. The task of solving this latter problem is fraught with frustration, because a project may appear to be progressing beautifully up until its final testing, when it may utterly fail. Now the decision has to be made whether to scrub it or go back to the beginning and start again.

Essentially, R & D programs are controlled by means of periodic reports of progress relative to budgetary and scheduled milepost standards. The control process is upward flowing, with the individual project managers reporting their performance to the R & D director, who in turn summarizes the project reports in reviews to top management. Ascertaining the current status of funds actually committed to a project is, of course, easy, especially with computers available to collect and transmit cost data.

In Figure 27-9, a budgeted cumulative cost curve is shown, along with a curve depicting the actual cumulative expenditure of funds committed to the project's work order number. In the example, on the 50th day the project is approximately $8000 overrun. For the determination of the project's accomplishment, mileposts which presumably separate the project's mission into discrete stages are conventionally used. These reveal that the project is apparently 10 days behind schedule on the 50th day.

In reporting to the R & D director, the project manager in the case represented by the figure would explain the reasons for the negative budget and performance variances, and outline plans for corrective action. Often the variances will be due to the impossibility of estimating R & D effort with precision. But sometimes budgetary or schedule variances (or both as in the example), may be attributable to technical

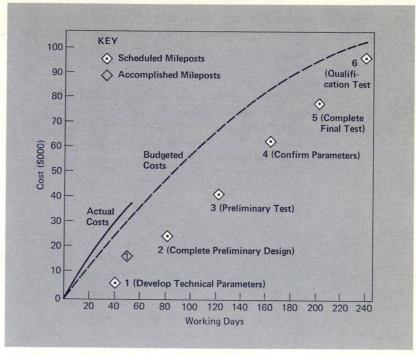

Figure 27-9. R & D Project Costs Vs. Accomplishment.

obstacles, which may or may not have ready solutions. In situations where obstacles are great and a project is very important, all of the technical wisdom and managerial acumen that the firm can muster must be directed to the decision of whether to continue or abandon the ailing project.

DISCUSSION QUESTIONS

1. Explain aggregate control.
2. What alternatives does a firm have when actual events differ from production plans?
3. Discuss the optimal response rate to a difference between actual events and production plans.
4. Explain the concept of a Gantt chart.
5. Discuss ABC analysis for inventory control.
6. Explain fixed reorder cycle and fixed order quantity inventory control systems.
7. Discuss the EOQ model.
8. Explain the theory of the product life cycle.
9. What alternatives exist for controlling selling effort per customer.
10. Explain how a firm's research and development effort may be controlled.

BIBLIOGRAPHY

Johnson, Richard A. William T. Newell and Roger C. Vergin. *Operations Management: A Systems Concept.* Boston: Houghton-Mifflin, 1972.

Lauffer, Arthur C. *Operations Management.* Cincinnati: South-Western, 1975.

Levin, McLaughlin, and Kottas Lamone. *Production/Operations Management.* New York: McGraw–Hill, 1972.

Shore, Barry. *Operations Management.* New York: McGraw–Hill, 1973.

Starr, Martin. *Production Management: Systems and Synthesis,* 2nd ed. Englewood Cliffs: Prentice Hall, 1972.

Vollman, Thomas E. *Operations Management: A Systems Building Approach.* Reading: Addison–Wesley, 1973.

The Case of the Greedy Tire Customer

When George Simmons, owner of Apex Tire & Recapping Company, hired young Bill Thompson as a tire salesman, he told him that the one thing he wanted him to do more than anything was to get back the California Construction Company's account.

Apex had enjoyed California's new tire and recapping business for many years, but approximately six months before the hiring of Thompson, California's new purchasing agent, Dan Delaney, had abruptly switched the bulk of his tire purchases to Apex's main competitor. As the volume of the account amounted to over $250,000 annually, its loss was a bitter blow to Simmons. Not only did Apex lose the fair profit that had always been earned on California's business, but the loss of the volume put the company in a lower discount bracket with the manufacturer that it represented, Goodwell Tire & Tire Rubber Company.

Bill Thompson began calling regularly on Dan Delaney, and quickly learned that he was quite amenable to being taken out to lunch at the most expensive places. These occasions worried Bill because he still was not getting any appreciable tire business from Delaney, although his expense account began to look excessive even to him.

One day he voiced these concerns to George Simmons, who listened attentively, then asked, "Do you think that you are making headway as far as getting back California's account?"

Bill answered, "Delaney told me yesterday that he was going to put a huge tire order out of bid, and that he hoped we would get it. He hinted that 40 per-cent off list was being talked about by our competitor."

"Wow! To go lower than that I would have to get help from the manufacturer," said Simmons. "However, let me see what I can do."

Goodwell wanted the business back as badly as Simmons did, and extended an additional discount. Apex bid 45 percent off list, and got California's order. George Simmons was happy about the order, but uneasy about the extremely slim profit margin. Bill Thompson was not nearly as jubilant as he thought he would be, because the cost of acceding to Delaney's thinly veiled demand for a dinner celebrating the order was close to $75.

Any thought that Apex had California's tire business back on a permanent basis was dispelled three months later when the competitor was given another order. Delaney's smug answer when Bill asked him why Apex lost the order was, "I guess your pencil needs sharpening. Another 5 percent makes a lot of difference."

Toward the end of that month, California Construction Company was awarded the contract to build a seven-mile stretch of freeway through the Sierras. It was to be a two-year job, and the order for heavy equipment tires that would have to be replaced during that period would probably run close to $300,000. Every tire dealer in the state hoped to be the exclusive supplier, and Delaney shrewdly played each one against the others.

Simmons, Thompson, and the Goodwell representative, Evan Peterson, discussed what strategy could be used to get the business for Apex. "It's a cinch to go for as low as 50 percent off list," said Simmons, "unless Delaney is lying to Bill, which I wouldn't put past him."

"In addition to price, Delaney is now hinting about having an inventory of tires consigned to the construction site, but not to be paid for until they are mounted on equipment." Bill said.

"The company might be willing to go for something like that if we were guaranteed to get the total business," Evan Peterson responded. "What we could do is handle the paper work through the main office and compensate Apex with a selling commission. I suggest that the three of us talk to Delaney."

Delaney sat quitely while George Simmons explained the proposition. "What we are doing is offering you a blanket deal, which is better than anything that you can get by asking for bids," was George's final remark.

"I'll have to admit that I am interested," Delaney responded. "Suppose I think about it, and I'll let Bill here know tomorrow at lunch."

"Do you know what he's asking for now?" Said Bill to Simmons and Peterson the next afternoon. "He wants us to furnish a tire-changing truck on the construction site at no cost, in addition to what we have already offered him."

"That's too much," said Simmons. "There is no way that we could supply a truck and break even."

"Now wait," Peterson said. "You figure the cost of a truck at $5.00 per hour. At 200 hours per month, that would be 2400 hours per year, or $12,000. Two years would be $24,000. Suppose Goodwell would pay half. Would you pay the other half to get the business?"

"Let's see how we would come out on the total account. We will never get all of California's local tire purchases, so assume that we will get half, or $125,000 per year. At the prices Delaney has driven us down to, we only net about 5 percent, not including Bill's expense account, so that is $6,250 per year, or $12,000 for two years. Our 2 percent commission on the freeway business would give us $6,000, or $18,500 total profit. Take out $12,000 for the truck, and the $1,000 a year that it looks like Bill is going to have to spend entertaining Delaney, and that leaves us $4,500 profit for two year's work. That's not much, but see if you can get it on this basis, Bill."

The next afternoon Bill phoned Simmons. "I just took Delaney to his office," Bill said. "What he wants now is for us to furnish a driver for the truck."

"Let's cross California Construction Company off our list," responded George Simmons wearily.

DISCUSSION QUESTIONS

1. If product profitability is such an important factor, how can you explain the tactic employed by supermarkets of deliberately selling some items at a loss?
2. What are some possible reasons for a product selling well in some territories yet being unsuccessful in others?
3. What would be some controls that a hardware store owner could use to determine whether people were reading his newspaper advertisements?

4. In the Case of the Greedy Tire Customer, why didn't George Simmons instruct Bill Thompson to recapture the large account on the basis of product and service quality, rather than price-cutting and entertainment?

5. What implications might Dan Delaney's tactics of playing competitors against each other in getting price and service concessions have for his own firm's long-term financial health, not to mention that of companies like Apex who vied for his orders?

The Case of Taking Too Big a Bite

Applied Computer Information, Inc. (ACI) had been formed in 1963 by Dave Whittlesey, Bill Coplen, and Renee Hawthorne, three former programmers of the largest computer hardware and software company in the industry. (Software is programming, of which the routines and subroutines for inventory control are an example.)

On the first day of their new venture, Dave said, "One thing that I think we have going for us is our similar backgrounds—all mathematicians, and with a combined experience of almost thirty years in developing software programs."

Their aggregate capital when they started, made up of their personal savings and what they could individually borrow, came to about $50,000. The initial project on which venture was based was a data bank program for storing real estate listings. Such information was in demand by real estate agencies all over the country, and by using time sharing on leased computers once the program was developed, ACI had the prospect of furnishing data to its customers for a profitable monthly fee.

At the end of six months, the program was still not developed, and ACI's owners realized that they had grossly underestimated the amount of money it would take to complete it. However, they were able to interest a private investment firm in ACI's exciting growth potential, and received new financing in the amount of $500,000 funded by convertible debentures. The new capital gave ACI the strength needed to develop and market its program, and by the beginning of 1965 the firm was operating well in the

black, and showed prospects of a sky-rocket growth.

In the following year, ACI developed two additional storage bank programs. One was for motor vehicle registrations, and the other, for consumer credit ratings. Both were within the capacity of ACI to handle the computer logic, and although there was growing competition in the software industry, ACI's good start gave it a marketing edge. The company continued to grow.

Upon the advice, and in fact, pressure, of the private investment firm that had come to ACI's rescue, ownership of the firm went public in 1966. Stock with a par value of $10 shot up to $80 as a result of the continued success of ACI's programs, plus speculation that computer software companies' brightest future still lay ahead. The investment firm sold out in 1967 and took its capital gain, and in that year ACI's sales were over $25 million.

Dave, Bill, and Renee had three new programs in the embryonic development stage in 1967. The objective of one was to provide daily information to entertainment ticket dealers regarding the availability of tickets to shows, concerts, athletic events, etc. The three founders of ACI, who by this time were sharing managerial responsibilities without any clear delineation of duties, envisaged this program as materializing into a steady "bread and butter" business, something like the ones to which the firm owed its present success. They estimated that the program could be developed for less than a million dollars. A more ambitious program was to provide on-line information concerning room reservations in hotels and major motels nationwide. A number of competitors were already trying to crack this nut, and the talk in the trade was that the potential annual revenues from a successful program would be upwards of $120 million. The third program on which ACI had started to incur development costs was of even broader dimensions. It involved computerizing supermarket check-out systems. Strong, rational arguments could be mustered for having a computer price the customer's grocery selection, receive payment and give change, including stamps, delete the purchases from the inventory balances, and prepare purchase orders to replenish the stock as it was reduced. Getting the first such system successfully on the market had such staggering growth possibilities according to the way that Dave, Bill, and Renee looked at things that they began envisaging their firm in the billion-dollar-a-year class.

The year of 1968 was one of tremendous outpourings of cash to get the new programs developed and get market acceptance for the promises that ACI's managers were making to potential customers. In addition, competition was beginning to dilute the firm's established revenues, and Dave, Bill, and Renee were so immersed in trying to broaden their product line that they lost sight of the need to diligently manage what they already had. The first major shock came when they realized that close to $5 million had been spent in starting the entertainment ticket program, and a market analyst whom they had tardily engaged

to study the actual potential revenue informed them that it would take at least ten years to recoup the investment. "You were simply shooting for too narrow a market," was the essence of his report.

The success of commercial airlines with computerized on-line systems for ticket reservations goaded ACI to continue dumping money into the hotel reservation program. The big hotel chains were all interested, but the technical problems of developing an integrated system appeared formidable. However, it was the competition of giant competitors that finally made it necessary for ACI to scrub this venture. When one big software company announced to a meeting of security analysts that it had budgeted $100 million for developing a program, and that it did not expect to break even for five years, Dave and his associates elected to take their loss of about $10 million.

The general business decline in 1969, plus the news of ACI's vicissitudes, resulted in a precipitous fall in the price of the company's stock. Moreover, its remaining development program, the supermarket system, ate up money as fast as it was poured in. Dave, Bill, and Renee frantically worked on the program while pioneering in the market, but the prospects that their efforts would result in any kind of an immediate payoff became increasingly dim. Finally, news that a competitor had installed a successful pilot system, but anticipated three or four more years of developing costs before it could be marketed successfully, made ACI decide to abandon this ship as well.

In June of 1971, with the company's

stock at $2 per share, Dave and his un-
happy associates met to discuss an impending creditor's action against ACI's
assets. "Well, I guess the big mistake that
we made was trying to take too big a
bite," was Dave's post-mortem remark.

DISCUSSION QUESTIONS

1. What major decision must precede a
   firm's determination of objectives for
   applied research and development?
   (See Chapter 6.)
2. What inferences can you draw concerning a given firm's R & D objectives and the allocation of funds to its
   R & D budget if its managers manifest
   a tendency to invade the R & D
   budget when business conditions take
   a downturn?
3. What would you think of having an experienced business manager and a scientist jointly head an R & D program?
   Under such an arrangement, which
   one should have final decision-making
   authority over disputed policies?
4. In the Case of Taking Too Big a Bite,
   what were the glaring weaknesses of
   ACI's R & D planning and control?
5. As of June 1971, what could Whittlesey and his associates do to save ACI?

28 A Systems Approach to Control

Systems theory has provided models for explaining relationships between interacting elements in the physical sciences for many years. More recently the theory has been applied to management processes and organizational entities. Fundamentally, systems theory is a way of thinking about and understanding real-world phenomena. It provides a conceptual framework for bringing natural combinations of dependent elements into sharper focus. Thinking about organizations from a systems point of view is particularly useful in examining the control functions in management. So, in this chapter we continue our discussion of the control function using a systems approach to control.

WHAT IS A SYSTEM?

Systems are usually described as a collection of interrelated parts often called subsystems, which exist within a given environment. An automobile is an example of a mechanical device that can be thought of in systems terms. Among its subsystems are an electrical subsystem, an exhaust subsystem, a guiding and control subsystem, and an energy conversion (motor and drive train) subsystem. The automobile takes fuel from outside its boundaries and converts it to energy which is used to move the machine according to the directions of the driver. Characteristically, a system is identified by the existence of a boundary which surrounds it, the inputs into the system which cross the boundary, and the processes occurring inside the system which convert inputs into system outputs. These outputs are then exported into the system's environment. The same elements can be employed to describe an organization. These elements and their relationship are pictured in Figure 28-1. Let's take a closer look at the parts of a system.

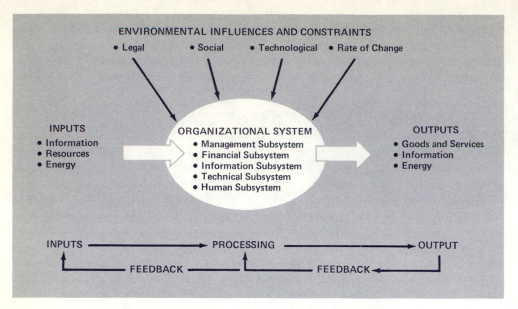

ENVIRONMENTAL INFLUENCES AND CONSTRAINTS
- Legal
- Social
- Technological
- Rate of Change

INPUTS
- Information
- Resources
- Energy

ORGANIZATIONAL SYSTEM
- Management Subsystem
- Financial Subsystem
- Information Subsystem
- Technical Subsystem
- Human Subsystem

OUTPUTS
- Goods and Services
- Information
- Energy

INPUTS ⟶ PROCESSING ⟶ OUTPUT
FEEDBACK — FEEDBACK

Figure 28-1.   An Organizational System Model.

Parts of a System

Inputs.   Inputs to an organizational system can take the form of information, resources, and energy. In our automobile example, fuel and air are imported to burn in the engine. A driver provides information and direction. When viewing a business as a system, the information input can be about the nature of the marketplace, the actions of competitors, or the levels of supply and demand. Resource inputs can take the form of financial resources, human skills, materials and equipment, and energy.

Organizational system.   A number of subsystems are usually found within the boundary of the larger organizational system. The interrelated actions of these subsystems will result in the conversion of the inputs into outputs which are exported back into the environment. The engine, fuel system, electrical circuits, and transmission of a car all contribute to the operation of the automobile. Subsystems which are usually identified in organizations include the management subsystem, and the financial, technical, information, and human subsystems. All these subsystems are interrelated so that a change which affects one will influence the other subsystems as well as the total system output. Systems thinking forces a recognition that organizational parts are interrelated. This attention on interaction is one of the conceptual benefits and strengths of systems analysis.

Outputs. All of the organizational subsystems operate to process the inputs and then export them to the environment. The automobile engine delivers energy to the wheels which moves the automobile. Gases that are produced by combustion are exhausted to the atmosphere. Organizational outputs can include the goods and services of the organization, information, and energy.

Environment. Surrounding a system is its environment. This environment can also be viewed as a collection of other related systems. It is critical to understand the nature of the environment and its relationship with the system in order to understand the system itself. Environmental influences on the system will be expressed through the legal, social, and cultural expectations and limits placed on the organization. Just as the interrelations of subsystems affect a system, any changes in the environment will be reflected in the systems process and outputs. Multinational firms which must operate simultaneously in several very different cultural environments are particularly aware of these environmental effects.

Boundaries. The boundary concept is crucial to an understanding of systems. It is the boundary which defines what is and what is not a part of the system. It is across the boundary that the system receives inputs and delivers its outputs to the environment. A boundary for an organizational system is arbitrarily defined. Usually a particular organizational boundary is defined to facilitate the understanding of the problem at hand. For example, the system boundaries defining a class in management could include the students and instructor or it might include only the students. Subsystem boundaries could differentiate students on the basis of sex, class standing, major, or any other criterion which would be useful in understanding class dynamics or behavior.

System Dynamics

The input-processing-output sequence that we have described is the generalized model for understanding a systems' operations. The *feedback loop* attached to that sequence (see Figure 28-1) is the feature that makes systems analysis so useful in understanding the management control function. Conceptually, the feedback loop indicates that the system is informed of the impact of its output on its environment. This information permits the system to adjust its processes in order to better achieve desired goals. It is this feedback that constitutes the first part of a control process. The second part of the control process involves issuing signals that permit or initiate corrective action to bring actual performance closer to desired performance. A thermostatic control on room temperature illustrates these ideas. Using feedback from its environment, the thermostat compares actual with desired room temperature. When a variance exists, the thermostat signals a heating or cooling system into operation. The output of those systems will alter room temperature until the desired level is reached. At that point the thermostat issues a signal which terminates the system's output.

IMPLICATIONS FOR ORGANIZATIONAL CONTROL

Many managers do not think about their organizations as systems. At the same time, though, they always have a continuing interest in the quality and quantities of their organizations' output. The systems approach to control emphasizes the interrelatedness of outputs and the inputs and processes leading to them. Recognizing these relationships will provide managers with powerful insights and opportunities for influencing organizational outputs.

Utilizing Feedback Loops

Feedback loops have been classified as open-loop and closed-loop. The thermostat is an example of what are often called closed-loop control systems. It is closed in that it requires no human intervention in its operation. Open-loop feedback is characterized by the existence of some kind of human intervention in the system. Most managerial controls are of this open-loop type. The feedback loop for information about students' class performance typically includes an input from the instructor. In that sense, the feedback loop is open. In some manufacturing situations, limits or tolerances are sensed automatically and corrective action is taken by the machine. In other types of manufacturing, tolerance must be checked and adjustments made by the machine operators, making it an open-loop feedback system.

Closed-loop control systems are limited in that the standards set must always be appropriate and not call for judgment. Either the output is or is not within tolerable limits. Open-loop control systems are more appropriate where there are less specific standards, or where the situation is so changeable that limits or tolerances in performance-ideal outcomes are subject to interpretations and judgment. For instance, the win-loss record of an athletic team is information about the output of that system. However, its usefulness as a criterion for judging that output will depend on the interpretation and judgment of those making the assessment. This human judgment intervention in the process makes it an example of an open-loop control system. In reality, few pure, closed-loop systems exist. More often, some degree of human intervention exists.

Fit Control Systems To Your Managerial Style

Organizations spend large amounts of money, time, and effort in designing and maintaining control systems. These systems are intended to enhance an organization's ability to coordinate the actions of its members and to identify problems as they arise. Often, however, instead of increasing organizational control these systems reduce the amount of effective control that the organization exercises.

Why does this happen? Our research and the research of others indicate that the problem often lies with the ways that managers use control systems. Most control systems, including budgetary, management information, and financial accounting systems, are essentially measurements. They regularly collect information about specific aspects of organizational performance.

The systems themselves are not capable of directly controlling organizational performance. Rather, they provide information to the managers who are in a position to exercise control. If managers use the information well, the control system works. If they use it poorly, the system may produce unintended effects.

Significantly, organizations seldom invest much effort in training managers to use control systems. Instead, most spend a lot of time designing, constructing, refining, and improving the technical aspects of their systems. The result is that while organizational control systems continually become more precise, accurate, and technologically sophisticated, two questions are often overlooked:

1

How effective is the system (and the way it is used) in doing what it is supposed to do?

2

How could the system be better used?

Recent research in a number of organizations has provided some answers to these questions. First, control systems influence the way organization members direct their energies on the job; the members are more likely to put time and effort into those areas covered by the systems. Second, how members respond to control systems depends largely on the way managers use the systems. Third, different managers develop different strategies for using control systems. Finally, each strategy has certain drawbacks and benefits.

Only when managers understand (a) how these systems influence the behavior of their subordinates and (b) what trade-offs occur in each control strategy can they learn to use organizational control systems effectively.

Problems Associated with the Feedback Process

In most managerial situations, the information carried along a feedback loop is subject to the same problems as accurate communications. The information can be distorted by its inherent ambiguity or by the perceptual idiosyncrasies of people in the feedback loop. The information may be qualitative and subjective which leaves room for differences in meaning between those generating the feedback and those receiving it for control purposes.

Delays between the generation of output and the measurement of data or behavior associated with the output result in what might be called "post-mortem examinations." These are of limited value because it is impossible to control past events. The idea is captured in the old adage about closing the barn door after the horse has run away. Under certain conditions—that is, when the purpose of the postmortem is to spot trends and apply remedies—the measurement of recent output provides a useful analytical case. However, the knowledge of a particular unfavorable event that happened some time previously is of minimal value in controlling present output.

The effectiveness of corrective adjustments is also obstructed by distortions and delays. For example, cyclical fluctuations can appear as negative trends which, if given time, will reverse and correct themselves. Delays in detecting this corrective tendency could result in adjustments being made to the system after it had run a complete cycle and had returned to a desired state. Such delays and distortions could enter the situation where the quarterly balance sheet showed accounts receivable to be unusually large—perhaps as much as double the amount of the average collection period. If a manager decides to correct the situation by initiating an aggressive collection policy, he or she might find that by the time it was carried out the delinquent customers had long since paid their bills. The aggressive collection policy would probably be offensive to the customers and could result in the loss of some of them.

Overreaction to variances can also cause another problem—it may unnecessarily amplify the adjustment process. This problem is complicated by long lead times in corrective actions. The effects of this sequence can be seen in situations where raw materials and supplies for an industry are anticipated to be in short supply in the future. Users will often try to stockpile such supplies. Such stockpiles give inaccurate feedback information to the suppliers about the level of demand for their product. If the product requires a relatively long lead time for its manufacture or processing, then the production schedules will need to be discounted to account for the excess demand created by the stockpiling.

Self-correcting, cyclical tendencies in a system and the hazards of overreacting suggest that the effective approach to control is achieved through frequent and timely reviews of output data, augmented by minor adjustments. Effective decisions in control are typically patient and plodding in nature, rather than heroic.

Cost of Control

A final consideration for control decisions involves the costs of control. Peter Drucker[1] has suggested that there are four categories of major "cost points" that occur in most organizations. These cost points account for the significant part of the total costs of the operation. Cost point categories are

- costs that contribute value added to the product.
- costs incurred in supporting production.
- costs incurred to make sure that nothing goes wrong.
- costs which are simply wasted and contribute nothing.

The manager should be most concerned with insuring that the costs he or she incurs in performing the control function are offset by commensurate benefits. The incremental cost of moving from 90 percent accuracy in the typing pool to 100 percent may be excessive when compared to the costs of resubmitting 10 percent of the work. Managers should keep in mind that the costs and benefits of control systems are not always measurable in financial terms. And, because control systems affect all other systems in the organization, absenteeism, labor turnover, reduced productivity, poor customer relations, loss of enthusiasm, and a dysfunctional organization climate can be the price of over zealous controls.

NOTES

1. Peter Drucker, *Managing for Results* (New York: Harper and Row, 1964).

DISCUSSION QUESTIONS

1. Describe a basketball team using systems concepts.
2. a. Systems' environments have been characterized as ranging from stable and predictable to turbulent and uncertain. How would you characterize a basketball team's environment?
   b. What implications do you think the nature of an organization's environment has on its control function?
3. "A good control system will accurately identify wrongdoers so that management can administer prompt and just punishment." Discuss.
4. "Open-loop feedback is generally better than closed-loop feedback." Discuss.

BIBLIOGRAPHY

Chase, Richard B. and Nicholas J. Aquilano. *Production and Operations Management: A Life Cycle Approach.* Homewood: Richard D. Irwin, Inc., 1973.

Camman, Cortlandt, and David A. Nadler. "Fit Control Systems to Your Managerial Style." *Harvard Business Review,* Vol. 54 No. 1 (January–February 1976), pp. 65–72.

Drucker, Peter F. *Managing for Results.* New York: Harper and Row, 1964.

Johnson, Richard A., Fremont E. Kast, and James E. Rosenzweig. *The Theory and Management of Systems,* 3rd edition. New York: McGraw-Hill Book Co., 1973.

Vaill, Peter B. "Industrial Engineering and Socio-Technical Systems." *Journal of Industrial Engineering,* Vol. 16 No. 9 (September 1967), pp. 530–38.

The Case of the Double Standards

"What we professors of management must do is communicate systems theory to operating managers in industry and convince them that they should begin applying it," said Dr. Ernest Talcott, chairman, to the other members of the management department of the College of Business Administration at Midwest State University. "The perfect opportunity will come at the forthcoming management seminar. I'm certainly going to stress it at the sessions I conduct."

The seminar that Dr. Talcott referred to was held annually at the college, and was directed to the upper-middle-level managers in the industrial firms of the area. The managers lived for a week in a dormitory, and attended morning, afternoon, and evening classes. The purpose of the seminar was to update the managers' formal business educations and stimulate them to apply the new management concepts.

True to his promise, Dr. Talcott focused entirely on systems theory in his part of the seminar. "And so," he went on in his third session, "you can see that the deliberate construction of a feedback loop in every operational process will permit a refinement of control not possible when output analysis is performed randomly. There isn't a single function that managers perform that can't be elevated to a higher standard through the application of systems theory."

"Are you open for questions, Dr. Talcott?" asked Lyle Peterson, the marketing manager for Elco Products, and a highly motivated student in the seminar.

"Of course, Mr. Peterson," said Dr. Talcott. "I want to know what you think about systems theory."

"How is systems theory being applied by educational institutions?" Lyle asked. "Or specifically, how are the schools of business administration using feedback loops to control the quality of their outputs—that is, the students who have graduated from them?"

"Perhaps you can explain a little more fully what you mean," said Dr. Talcott.

"Well, looking at the feedback model," said Lyle, "it would appear that the activating agent would be comprised of the professors. Input would be the various course contents, and the operation would be course requirements, schedules, instruction, examinations, and finally graduation. As I have suggested, output is young men and women entering business life. What standards do business schools have to measure the outputs of their system?"

"By standards, I suppose that my answer is that the grading system discriminates between various performance levels as students proceed through their educational programs," said Dr. Talcott.

"I think what Lyle is getting at is, what roles do you expect your outputs to perform during their business careers, and at what success levels, rather than what they do while, as students, they are still part of the operational process," volunteered Doug Lehman, credit manager of Litco Industries.

"We can point to many successful managers in this area who are graduates of Midwest's business school," answered Dr. Talcott.

"Yes, but do you have any systematic way of getting back information on all of your graduates?" Doug pressed. "Do you know what strengths may have been built into your outputs as a result of the inputs and the operation, and what weaknesses may exist in your outputs as a result of omissions or defects in the operation?"

"No, we don't have information of that kind," Dr. Talcott admitted.

"But if you did set up mechanisms to provide it," Lyle interjected, "wouldn't you benefit the educational program by permitting a comparison of the data relative to your graduate students with the standards expected of them? That is assuming, of course, that you have established standards."

"Yes, that would be quite useful," conceded Dr. Talcott.

"And if you found variances between what your students accomplish, or do, in business life, and what is expected of them, you could seek out means of correcting the differences, couldn't you?" Doug asked.

"Yes," answered Dr. Talcott, now obviously very cautious of his ground.

"This information could then be fed back to the professors, with recognition of the delays and distortions explicit in the model," said Lyle, as he resumed the questioning. "The professors could make the indicated revisions to the input, and to the standards, and the operation would presumably start producing improved outputs. Isn't this analogous to what you have been telling us that business managers should do with their processes?"

"Yes, the analogy is accurate," said Dr. Talcott.

"Then if there is an apparent potential application of the feedback loop model to educational systems, do you know of any business school that is seriously using it?" Lyle queried.

"No, I don't," Dr. Talcott answered.

"With due respect, sir," said Lyle, "aren't you advising business managers to do as professors preach, not as they practice?"

DISCUSSION QUESTIONS

1. While designing new control systems, or evaluating existing ones, what would a manager gain by keeping a systems model in mind?
2. Explain why a feedback loop is essential in any effective control system.
3. What are the advantages of frequent and timely processing of output data through the feedback loop?
4. In the Case of the Double Standards, what do you think of the feedback loop system proposed by Lyle Peterson for evaluating schools of business administration?
5. How many of Dr. Talcott's seminar students do you think may be impressed with the potential value of feedback loops built into control systems? How many do you think will diligently try to apply feedback control on their jobs?

29 Control Systems and Organizational Behavior

The broad objective of the control function is to effectively employ all the resources committed to an organization's operations. However, the fact that nonhuman resources depend on human effort for their utilization makes control, in the final analysis, the regulation of human performance.

This chapter will address a few of the issues which surface as humans anticipate and respond to organizational control systems. By recognizing the potential difficulties that control systems can generate with people, managers can design and implement their controls to minimize negative side-effects. People's natural resistance to controls is the first topic in the chapter addressing the behavior-control system intersection. Problems associated with performance standards that may inhibit good performance are covered next. The last sections of the chapter treat the impact of the managers' values and assumptions on controls and the problems associated with measuring human behavior.

A characteristic of conventional control processes as described in the preceding chapters is that they are relatively impersonal and are based on the assumption that human behavior will be rational. Potential problems surface when this impersonal rationality comes into contact with people who are often irrational and personally involved with organizational issues. This intersection may suggest why control in organizations is rarely as effective as it is meant to be.

In addition, organizational control systems often assume that there is solid agreement on the definition of the desired quality or quantity of output. As with rationality, people are noted for their capacity to be unpredictable in regard to their interpretation of organizational goals. People will behave in accordance with their own, perhaps unique, understanding of organizational expectations. Management may believe that organizational goals, objectives, and critical performance factors are perfectly clear. Yet subordinates will act and react on the basis of their own perceptions. These differences can cause headaches for managers trying to implement a control system.

NATURAL RESISTANCE TO CONTROL

Probably most people are ambivalent toward control. While most will concede that control is probably useful, and perhaps even necessary, they do not like having it applied to their own performance. The threatening aspect of having one's performance subjected to searching scrutiny is commonly felt by people on all occupational levels, no matter how high or low. The inventory clerk who is called on to account for the way seventeen years' supply of paper clips have accumulated is probably just as uncomfortable as the organization president who must account for a 300 percent overrun on a government contract. Some relief from being subject to controls comes to individuals who get to the upper levels in organizations in the sense that the number of people who can exercise control over them becomes smaller. However, at the lower levels of an organization, the control devices and control agents are multitudinous and the view upward can be oppressive.

Normally, the discomfort of being under the threat of personal controls is not alleviated by the manner in which employee performances are reviewed against standards. This is particularly so when performance shows a negative variance. A person can know few lonelier and more humbling experiences than trying to defend a budget or a schedule that has gotten out of control. While defending the poor performance may be a natural response, the effort does not really contribute much toward organizational goal achievement. Emphasis on the constructive aspects of the control system and minimal emphasis on punitive aspects will help to channel energy toward desirable organizational outputs.

Many individuals show a tendency to adapt to controls. They adapt even though their performance is not necessarily any better than those who do not adapt. They adapt even though they don't enjoy being controlled. Rather, they adapt in that they learn "how to play the game." There are ways to "beat" control systems, and perhaps the reason that some people are successful in organizations is that they have learned to use them. The distinction between coercing certain behavior by way of threats and the managerial control objective of bringing plans to reality is a real one. However, in the view of people in the organization, the distinction may become clouded. A management control system which requires first level supervisors to report to their managers whenever productivity falls to some predetermined level may be negatively interpreted by the supervisors. They may not see it as a positive policy, one that will lead to organizational goal achievement. Instead, they may see the reporting requirement as demeaning, a no-confidence vote, and a direct expression of management's lack of confidence in their ability to do their job. When these negative perceptions are prevalent, people will learn to adapt ways to circumvent the intent of control systems. Strategies that have been employed range from overloading the feedback communication system with masses of irrelevant information to the supplying of inaccurate information. Variances in the other direction can also cause responses unintended by management. For example, people have been known to pad budgets to give the impression of an efficiently run operation when actual costs have turned out to be less than the planned figure. In all of these instances, the "play the game" adaptations that people make not only defeat the control sytems but they consume resources which could be used for organizational goal achievement.

INHIBITIVE STANDARDS

Standards sometimes have the effect of making people who are expected to measure up to them feel resigned to failure rather than stimulated to extend their efforts. An undesired reaction to standards will often result when those standards are set in an arbitrary manner, when they are unrealistic, or when the standards are continually being shifted upward.

Standards set arbitrarily affect employee morale negatively—that is, such standards tend to lower morale. A typical example of an arbitrary standard is an order specifying that each department reduce its operating costs by 10 percent. Lower-level managers receiving such an order will accurately perceive it as evidence of laziness on the part of the senior managers. It certainly takes far less effort to issue a blanket edict of this kind than to diligently search out and correct the operations where serious cost excesses are occurring. Its most damaging impact on morale will be for those efficient managers whose costs are already pared to the bone. They can cut costs no further, yet they know that they will suffer in comparison with their peers who have deliberately maintained "fat" in their departments. They may become resentful as a result of the arbitrarily set standard.

Perception of standards as barriers, rather than stimuli to extended effort, also results from setting unrealistic standards. Frequently, individuals who are expected to accomplish the impossible will merely set their own standards at a level they can attain and resign themselves to suffer the consequences. Their attitude is something like that of a golfer who cannot shoot par on par-four holes longer than 400 yards. Since only a lucky fluke would enable the golfer to make par, he or she responds by establishing five as an acceptable score for the hole.

The impact of goals on motivation was discussed in Chapter 21. The implication for control systems management is that people will have

Fit Control Systems To Your Managerial Style

Influence on Subordinates

When an area is covered by a control system, organization members concentrate on improving their performance in the measured area. There are three reasons for this direction of energy:

1

Measurement of an area of activity indicates that top management feels the area is important and bears watching.

2

Managers generally use control system measures when they evaluate subordinate performance. Since the subordinate usually feels that the manager's evaluation influences his or her rewards, the subordinate tends to put energy into the measured areas.

3

It is easy for an organization member to see changes in performance measures that are part of the control system. If his performance is improving, this can be a source of personal satisfaction.

Effects of Control Systems

It appears that control systems direct how much energy subordinates put into an area, but how is this energy used? On one hand, subordinates may be motivated to increase their levels of performance, producing larger quantities or higher quality work.

On the other hand, measurement may cause subordinates to direct their efforts into "game playing" to "beat the system." Rather than performing well, employees often set low goals that can be easily met, manipulate measures to come out with the desired results, and actually sabotage the system's information base.

For example, a large government organization required each person to fill out a form accounting for the way he spent his time in 20-minute blocks. The intent was to motivate the employees to manage their time and to generate valid information about how much time they were allocating to different tasks. The result, however, was vastly different. The employees saw the system as an attempt to regiment their lives and activities.

Thus, instead of being a useful tool, the time sheets became a recreational activity. On Friday afternoons at the work break, employees got together to fill out their time sheets, each competing to see who could come up with the most preposterous record of activities. Needless to say, these records had no relation to actual work done. The system did not motivate people to increase performance; it motivated them to play games with the system.

different predispositions toward standards which measure their performance. Recall that people with a high need to achieve also have a corresponding need for feedback about how they are doing. In addition, they prefer to set their own goals at levels which are neither too easy nor impossible to achieve. Well-managed control systems should work particularly well with people who have a relatively high need for achievement.

In general, the reaction to standards set unrealistically high will be counterproductive to organizational goal achievement. People facing unattainable standards may simply ignore the standards. They may become passive and enervated, or they may try to resolve the dilemma by leaving the organization. None of these reactions is desirable or consistent with the intent of the control system of which the standards are a part.

Standards that are continually shifted upward represent another reason for people to react in ways that are counterproductive to the organization. Periodically raising the criteria for a normal day's work was a favorite tactic of the old-time efficiency experts in their attempts to set production records. This tactic is commonly used to goad a sales force to greater and greater efforts and has its analogy in the farm boy who, aspiring to greater strength, picked up the same calf each day as it grew to be a cow. People who are highly motivated within themselves will often achieve unbelievable goals as they shift their own standards upward. The essential difference centers on the decision to shift the standard. If an upward shift is imposed arbitrarily from an external source, the reaction is apt to be negative. Upward shifts which have been determined by the people expected to perform will not be similarly viewed.

Participation as a management concept has been discussed in the chapters on *leading*. One of the benefits of increased participation in decision making is an increased commitment to the decision. This is particularly true in the case of standards used to measure employee efforts. Surprisingly, people often set higher standards for themselves than would be set by an external control agent. For instance, when asked to judge the quality of their own work, students will often grade more severely than would the instructor. When a management by objectives procedure is in effect, the standards typically will be established through an interactive process involving the subordinate and the manager. In this instance, increases in standards have a good chance to enjoy the support, or at least agreement of the people directly involved.

MANAGEMENT VALUE AND ASSUMPTIONS

The issues of the managers' values and assumptions are critical in influencing the impact of a control system. What managers believe about the "proper" way to conduct organizational affairs and what they believe about the causes and forms of organizational behavior will be reflected in their own managerial behavior. The Theory X and Y assumptions proposed by McGregor and discussed in Chapter 21 are useful in illustrating this point. Recall that Theory X and Y are two different sets of assumptions that managers make about the basic nature of people. Theory X assumes that people basically dislike work, and will try to avoid it and responsibilities. As a consequence people need to be coerced or threatened with punishment to get them to perform adequately. Further, people prefer to be directed and want security above all. Theory Y assumes that work and play are both natural, that self-control is possible as well as external controls and threats, and that people can learn to accept and seek responsibilities. It should be kept in mind that it is the whole range of assumptions, beliefs, and values which are involved in influencing managerial behavior. The Theory X and Y example is a way of making the point by posing extremes. Actual situations will rarely be so polarized.

When Theory X assumptions are predominant in a manager's thinking, controls will be needed in order to get and keep lazy people at work. Furthermore, care must be taken to ensure that the workers continue to perform responsibly and in concert with organizational needs. When variances between actual and desired performance are discovered, then threats of sanctions, or the sanctions themselves are used to realign behavior in desired directions.

When assumptions similar to those of Theory Y are in operation, managerial control systems become a device aimed at assisting organizational members to perform better and achieve organizational goals and objectives as well as their own. Controls become ways to help members become more proficient, to grow, and to increase their competency.

PROBLEMS ASSOCIATED WITH MEASURING HUMAN PERFORMANCE

Previous chapters have stressed the efficiency of expressing measurements in numerical terms. With respect to human performance, however, not all variables can be expressed quantitatively nor measured objectively. This inability to quantify can often have discouraging effects on people at the time of their performance review. There are many tasks that people do in the service of organizational goal achievement which cannot be quantified. The patient development of subordinates' skills, the cultivation of customer good will, leadership quality, and the intensity of effort expended are examples. A control system that is focused solely on unit cost of production or net profitability completely overlooks the importance of these elements. Since rewards in most companies are bestowed on individuals who perform well when measured quantitatively, those who build for the future without numerically measurable short-term results may frequently be criticized in performance reviews and bypassed for raises and promotions. As a consequence, they might resort to a resigned conformity to the system or antipathy toward the company, or maybe even feel sufficiently indignant to quit outright.

Another problem related to measurement has to do with the frustrations employees can experience when important numerical data are omitted from the control system. An example of how such omissions can occur might be related to the preoccupation engineers can have with measurements of technical excellence in a product. Although these are unquestionably significant criteria in a control system, they must be weighed against other data such as time to develop a product, cost of production, and potential sale ability. When the latter factors are omitted, real frustration and discouragement for people in the other parts of the company will result.

Damaging Evaluations

The manager who must act on a negative evaluation of an employee's effort should consider the situation and options carefully. A nearsighted concern of managers with negative variances from desired objectives might obscure the fact that the variances could have been far worse than they actually were. Sometimes more credit is due an individual whose record shows negative variances, but whose outstanding performance kept them from being considerably worse, than is due more fortunate peers who were faced with easy challenges.

The impersonal objectivity with which control evaluations are frequently made can also be extremely damaging to the motivation of individuals. Standards are rarely inviolate, and variances often mean that the standards are wrong, rather than the performance. When no real effort has been extended by the monitor to identify the causes and reasons for the performance level, people who are punished or criticized for not performing up to expectations may sometimes defend themselves. However, in many instances they may simply adopt a contemptuous attitude toward the entire control system, and withdraw a little of their support and commitment to organizational goals.

Being evaluated for elements over which they have no control is another practice that can cause people to be bitter. Allocated costs to budgets afford one example. Managers whose budgets are continually overrun because of unexpected costs that are incurred outside their jurisdiction will soon become frustrated. Eventually they may even lose interest in trying to meet target costs that *are* within their control. Also, people will believe that they have been judged unfairly when an event or failure in another person's area of responsibility prevents them from meeting the standards set for their own performance. This is a common occurrence because of the interdependence often found between successive stages in an organization's total activity. For example, a student would be very discouraged if a term paper grade were reduced because of a missed due date which in turn was caused by a library reference that was not returned when due by another student. In business, a typical case would be a slipped production schedule, with blame laid on the production manager, when, actually, the cause was a combination of delay in receiving raw materials, a mandatory reduction in allowable manpower, and unanticipated engineering changes in the product.

Ineffective Adjustments

A number of factors can cause adjustments to be ineffective. Individuals often fail to respond to prescribed corrective action because they do not agree that the remedies are appropriate. In some instances, there may be disagreement with the conclusions drawn about the causes of the variances observed. In such situations, less than full commitment to a plan to reduce the variance can be expected. It is often the case that corrections do not represent one person's decision, but result from a pooling of judgments. Since there is frequently a difference of opinion in a group, there may be people who disagree with the outcome of the deliberations. Those who are in the minority may hope that events will prove them right rather than work to support the majority position. When the unwelcome corrective action is designated by an individual's supervisor, the latter might, rightly or wrongly, be perceived as lacking the authority to decide such matters and the subordinate may comply with a sufficient lack of enthusiasm to make the remedy ineffective.

Another common reason why adjustments intended to bring a system back into control are frequently ineffective is that the responsibility for implementing the correction is not clear-cut, and no single person is willing to assume the obligation risking failure and discredit. This situation is comparable to one in football where several defensive backs wait for one of the others to tackle an elusive open field runner. People instinctively seek to protect themselves and when a course of action has only a minimal chance of success, a common reaction is for people to try to avoid being directly associated with it.

Multiplicity of Controls

The typical middle manager in a modern organization, such as a machine-shop superintendent, is governed by a maze of controls. The objectives of these controls can often be in conflict with one another. To name but a few, there are production schedules, cost budgets, quality rejection reports, manpower ceilings, wage minimums and maximums, safety and health codes, overtime limitations, the union contract, and machine utilization standards. Individuals in all of the company's operations face similar controls.

The result is that people perceive that they cannot possibly win in terms of all of the standards by which they are measured. Typically they will choose the control which they think will result in the best impression if they comply with it and take the chance that success along this line will sustain them through failure along others. The frustration and demoralization attendant upon such a course are not difficult to imagine.

Perceived Inappropriateness of Control Agents

When employees feel control is being exercised by those who have no right to do so, problems may arise. Staff relationships can bring controls to bear on individuals by people other than the direct supervisor. For example, fair employment practices standards may be imposed by the personnel department. People may tolerate having their performances regulated by department supervisors, especially since the latter usually have the resources to reward and punish. But having controls established over internal activities by persons outside the subunit is often more than can be tolerated. Controls by outsiders is often termed *illegitimate* and is a central source of conflict between members of different departments.

A good subject for research is the formulation and testing of control designs which stimulate human effort as opposed to control systems which are primarily inhibitive.

DISCUSSION QUESTIONS

1. "What gets counted by the boss is what counts in organizations." Discuss.
2. Suppose a sixth grade class was performing substantially below the national and school norms on standardized tests of reading skill. How would a Theory X principal react? Theory Y?
3. In connection with labor disputes, air controllers have collectively and deliberately complied with all of the rules and regulations governing their job performance. This compliance has resulted in increased costs to the airlines, delays in operations and inconveniences to travelers. Discuss the control system implications of this phenomenon.
4. "No matter how carefully it is worded, a control system boils down to an evaluation of a person's performance and no one likes to be judged." Comment.

BIBLIOGRAPHY

Child, John. "Strategies of Control and Organizational Behavior." *Administrative Science Quarterly,* Vol. (March 1973), pp. 1–17.
Gibbons, C. C. "The Psychology of Budgeting." *Business Horizons,* (June 1972) pp. 47–58.

Huse, Edgar F., and James L. Bowditch. *Behavior in Organizations: A Systems Approach to Managing.* Reading: Addison-Wesley, 1973.

Ridgway, V. F. *"Dysfunctional Consequences of Performance Measurements." Administrative Science Quarterly,* (September 1956), pp. 240–47.

Tosi, Henry L. Jr. "The Human Effects of Budgeting Systems on Management." *MSU Business Topics,* (Autumn 1974), pp. 53–63.

The Case of the Controlled Controller

Jim Blakewell, a star lineman in college football, suffered a knee injury in his first year of pro ball. He then got a job in the production control department of Pilgrim Container Corporation, a large manufacturer of corrugated containers in the Midwest. Within a few years he rose to production control manager.

Under Jim's careful control of production schedules, Pilgrim gained a reputation among container buyers of always keeping its delivery promises. To accomplish this, Jim had developed standard lead times (intervals between receipt and delivery of orders) with built-in safety allowances for each item in the product line. For example, carload lots of one-color regular slotted containers (rsc's) had a lead time of six weeks. A week was added for two colors, for waxing, and for specialty boxes. Less-than-carload orders carried an extra week lead time because of the problem of economically fitting them into a production run. Pilgrim's sales force was generally happy with the support that they got from production control, but sometimes tried to persuade Jim to let them offer customers shorter lead times in order to capture desirable orders. This Jim adamantly refused to do, because, as he said, once he started making exceptions his whole control system would break down.

One such instance occurred when a salesman, Ollie Babcock, was convinced that he could get an initial order for containers from a major paint company. Jim had cooperated with Ollie in rushing the production of six sample boxes that had been used in the sales presentation, but turned deaf ears to Ollie's plea for four weeks' delivery of a carload trial order of one-color rcs's.

"Jim, you know you have an allowance built into your lead times," Ollie argued. "Most of my orders sit in the warehouse for a week before they are due to be delivered. And I am sure you could squeeze another week out for this order if you tried."

"That's right, I probably could," said Jim, "but if I did, within a day half of the sales force would be asking for four-week lead times. The plant can't work consistently to that kind of scheduling, and we would very soon start breaking our delivery commitments."

"I'm going to see Jones about it," said Ollie heatedly. "I don't think that you have the authority to control this tightly."

Art Jones was Pilgrim's sales manager, and was at the same organizational level in the company as Jim's boss, Bob Skinner, production manager. As Jim expected, he received a call from Skinner the morning following his dispute with Babcock.

"Jones is pretty upset at the possibility of losing that new order," Skinner said. "Is there anything that we should do to help him?"

Jim explained the position that he had taken regarding any relaxation of standard lead times.

"I am going to support you, of course," responded Skinner. "As far as I am concerned, you have complete control over production scheduling."

The first dampening of Jim's elation at having his decision upheld was the receipt of a memo from the personnel manager denying his request for a salary increase for his assistant. The explanation for the denial was that the individual was already at the top salary bracket for his job classification, and that if an exception was made in this case it could cause such a clamor for other exceptions that the entire salary structure would be threatened. Jim was honest enough to see the validity of the argument, and to also perceive the analogy to his own stand on not relaxing lead times, but it did irk him to realize how little control he had over conditions affecting his subordinates.

Pilgrim's paper mill was independent of the container manufacturing plant, but supplied the plant with its requirements for liner and corrugating medium materials. A source of conflict between mill personnel and plant personnel was the wide variation in the quality of the materials that the mill furnished. Some batches were so bad that the customers began to complain, and Lee Wing, the container plant quality control engineer, decided to take action. With Skinner's authorization, Wing set a control policy whereby he would stop further conversion of board that did not exceed the industry standard bursting strengths by at least 5 percent.

The impact of this policy hit Jim Blakewell on the same day that he received the memo from the personnel manager. The press foreman came to his office to tell him that Wing had condemned all of the 200-lb. bursting strength board then in the plant. Jim was horrified, because the action meant at least a two weeks' slippage of all of his production schedules. He immediately called Skinner and asked him to rescind Wing's order.

"I'm sorry, Jim, because I am as proud as you are of our scheduling performance," Skinner said. "However, the mill has to get the message that we won't accept shoddy materials, and getting the labor invested in the bad board charged back to them is one way of doing it."

"Yes, but the board almost comes up to the 200-lb. standard. Why don't we go ahead and use it, but warn the mill that we will reject the next bad batch?"

"No, now is the time to show them that we mean business," Skinner replied. "I am afraid that this is something that is outside your control."

Jim resignedly asked his secretary for some of the yellow pads that he used to block out schedule changes. In the place of the pads that he was accustomed to, she handed him some that were a dirty gray in color, and of a rough, abrasive texture.

"I knew you wouldn't like these, Mr. Blakewell," his secretary said, "so I called purchasing to see what caused the change from yellow ones. They are on a campaign to cut unnecessary costs, and they save 7¢ each on the gray pads."

DISCUSSION QUESTIONS

1. Suppose that you are a salesperson for a company that awards vacation trips and bonuses to individuals whose annual sales most greatly exceed quotas. The sales manager partially sets territory quotas, basing them on forecasts prepared by the sales force. What would be your objective in preparing your forecast? What would be the sales manager's objective in setting quotas? Knowing that objective, what strategy

would you use in preparing your forecast?

2. Should the same standards be applied to all individuals performing the same type of work?

3. What are the advantages and disadvantages of appointing a committee to correct a situation that has gotten out of control?

4. In the Case of the Controlled Controller, what do you think of Jim Blakewell's policy of making no exceptions to his six-week delivery policy?

5. How would you describe Jim Blakewell's general attitude toward control systems? Is it different from yours?

Summary

Controlling is the function that verifies the effective performance of the other managerial functions of planning, organizing, staffing, and leading. Although it is present in all functions, it is intimately associated with assuring that planning objectives are achieved. Controlling entails establishing standards, comparing actual events with the standards, and correcting deviations. Corrective actions may involve only short-term adjustments, or if the deviations are critical, may require major long-term adjustments to the operating system.

One aspect of controlling expresses standards and the actual events in financial terms. Budgeting is one form of financial control. Budgets vary in detail from top-level controls in which the data are expressed rather broadly and flexibly, down to operating level budgets that are precise and inflexible. Another financial control is balance sheet analysis in which a firm's financial position as of a point in time is evaluated by ratios. Breakeven analysis determines the volume of goods that must be sold to cover a firm's fixed costs. Beyond the breakeven point the difference between sales and variable costs is profit. Capital investment evaluation is a method for screening potentially profitable investments in plant, equipment, product line, and the like from those whose yield would not be sufficient to warrant investing company funds.

Nonfinancial control uses data for standards and actual events that are derived from the organization's processes. Production, inventory, and marketing control, and control of R&D are forms of nonfinancial control. Production control involves many detailed steps, but probably the most crucial is determining when and how to alter the production plan to conform to changing demands. An important feature of inventory control is the establishment of the most economical quantity of each inventory item to re-order when a stipulated balance has been reached. Another element of effective inventory control is the careful surveillance of the items in inventory that represent the largest dollar investment. A critical marketing control is monitoring a product through its life cycle. Other marketing controls include eliminating nonprofitable items in the product line, control of selling effort per customer, analysis of performance by sales territories, and assuring the most effective advertising effort. Control of research and development first requires looking at R&D expenditures as investments, and developing budgets for them. Then, budgeted costs and performance are compared with actual results, and variances are investigated and corrected.

In the systems approach to controlling, managers focus their attention on the relationships among the inputs, the internal processes, the outputs, and the environmental influences on the organization. The feedback loop is the element in a system that conveys information about the system's performance so that comparisons can be made between actual and desired output. Problems in the feedback loop can come about as a consequence of inaccuracies in communications, delays, and distortions. Action undertaken to correct deviations can sometimes be overzealous, and act to amplify the adjustment swings.

Applying control systems to the human element in organizations brings unique and sensitive problems to the manager. People do not consistently behave in a rational manner. Most conventional control systems are, by necessity and design, based on a rational approach to organizational affairs. Managers who are attempting to implement a control system must come to grips with these two facts. While most people can appreciate the need for organizational controls, they are often uncomfortable about having their own performance subjected to a control system review. People in organizations will create many innovative ways to avoid, disarm, or confuse a control system deemed to be inappropriate or unfair. Increased participation in the design and implementation of control systems by the people affected by it will often result in more commitment to work with the system rather than around or against it. A manager's assumptions about the basic nature of people will influence the design of control systems adopted and the manner in which they operate. Some problems that can develop for managers when controls are applied to an organization's human resources include

- inappropriate quantification of performance measures.
- negative reactions due to poorly handled performance evaluations.
- ineffective adjustments to variances between actual and desired performance.
- multiple, inconsistent expectations placed on organization members.

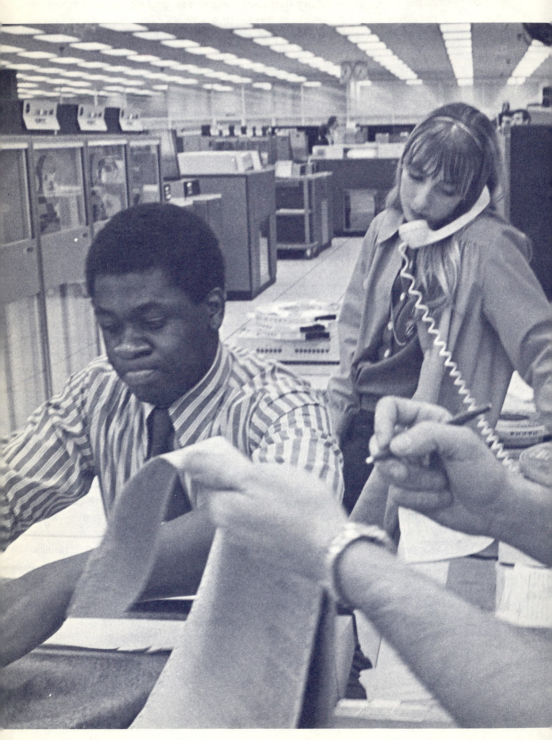

PART 7

Significant Factors in the Future of Management

In many respects, the future problems of managers bear a marked similarity to the problems of the past several decades. Threats of war, inflation, and high unemployment rates will continue to be apparently insoluble spectres. The state of the economy will alternately move ahead a few steps, and slide back a few steps, with, hopefully, a net gain every five or six years. The demands of trade unions may move toward more social gains and less toward direct economic increases, but they will still involve costs that managers must handle. Obsolescence of products and processes will continue, perhaps at an even faster rate, and preparation for change will become an even more necessary managerial behavior.

There will be a trend away from strictly localized operations as business firms widen the markets for their products and services. Multinational companies will be more common; the whole world will be the scene for the deployment of resources. Managers will be required to adapt to diverse cultures, in which values may be conflicting.

No book with the objectives of this one could do more than mention issues of the magnitude of those cited above. However, in coming to a close, some factors with which managers of the future will have to cope seem to merit special discussion. The computer has been with us for almost thirty years, but its significance to managers justifies its inclusion in Chapter 30. The importance of social issues has reached monumental proportions, and how managers respond to these pressures is discussed in Chapter 31. Chapter 32 is an innovative chapter for a book of this kind, because unlike practically all management texts, it deals with the real-life features of managing a small business, or entrepreneurship.

30 The Impact of the Computer

People following trends in management generally agree that the computer has become a highly significant factor in most organizations in the late 1970s. However, there have been varying predictions about how much additional influence the computer will exert in the coming decade. The extreme view is that computer technology will eventually take over managerial functions, and render managers, as they are now known, obsolete. An opposite view is that use of the computer will expand human managerial capability to proportions not now imagined.

In our attempt to project just what impact the computer may have on management of the future we will examine its characteristics and applications, assess what it may do to the job content and employment, consider some human consequences, and identify the implications for organizing and decision making.

THE CHARACTERISTICS OF THE COMPUTER

Two unique sets of characteristics have made the computer the powerful, though limited, tool that it is. One set consists of mechanical attributes—speed, accuracy, and memory—the other, its discriminatory attributes, contribute to its suitability for programming that enables it to choose from among alternatives.

- Mechanical attributes. The computer's incredible speed at making calculations—at least a million times faster than human skill—is its most distinctive characteristic. This capability permits data of unlimited variety to be collected, sorted, analyzed, and reported with a detail and immediacy completely impossible by any other means. In addition to improvements in data processing, the speed of the computer makes possible the ready solution of problems involving complex formulas, which otherwise, if achievable at all, might literally require thousands of worker-years.

The extreme accuracy of the computer is another singular characteristic. Unless people make mistakes in feeding data into the computer and telling it what to do with them, the output will be accurate. However, the computer will compound input errors, often with horrendous results.

A third mechanical attribute of the computer is its ability to store information in its memory cells. Thus, unlimited data can be put away for future use, then called upon and applied under appropriate conditions.

- Discriminatory attributes. Conditional transfer processes can be programmed into the computer, which permit it to discriminate between alternatives in a way somewhat like human thinking. The computer can learn a vast array of instructions, and then apply the proper instruction to a given situation. It can be taught to retrieve the right information from its memory cells. It can reach a decision point in its operation, and make the correct choice from among numerous possibilities. The computer learns to verify the results of its manipulation of data, and to know when one problem is finished and when to go to the next assignment.

  On the other hand, the computer cannot make intuitive discriminations in the way that humans get a "feel" for a situation. It has no values other than those put into it. There are no means for the computer to reach outside its programming to get additional information with which to refine its interpretations.

APPLICATIONS OF THE COMPUTER

The characteristics of the computer make it appropriate for use in many areas including data processing, real-time computation, automation, forecasting, simulation, and data storage and retrieval.

- Data processing. Manual handling of data has been almost entirely supplanted by computers in all but the smallest business firms in every type of industry. This has caused marked changes in the processing of accounting, inventory, production, and marketing data. The computer has completely altered the detail with which cost accounting records can be maintained and reported. A business organization's payroll calculations, record keeping, and check preparations are now almost entirely done by the computer; invoicing and payment transactions are also largely handled by computer.

Inventory control is another major usage. The computer assesses inventory balances, calculates requirements, writes requisitions, often selects suppliers and prepares purchase orders, calculates unit prices, and reports classified and aggregate totals as routine operations. In production, lot sizes are determined, schedules prepared, and daily, or even hourly, progress is reported. The marketing department can use computers to collect sales information of every conceivable classification, to determine prices and discounts, and to calculate commissions. The voluminous cost proposals required for bidding on government contracts are only possible with use of the computer.

- Real-time computation. Computers are increasingly being used to "post data up to real time," or to record and report events the instant they occur. Often the reporting is done via a television screen. The way election results are compiled and posted as vote subtotals are reported is a nonbusiness example of real-time computation. Sales information in a department store or supermarket can be similarly transmitted according to item, classification, dollar value, and many other breakdowns. Another fairly well-known example of real-time computation is the airlines' method for booking and reporting passenger reservations. And the nation's defense system is largely dependent on the computer's ability to interpret, analyze, report, and even initiate action on events as they take place.

- Automation: production process applications. Numerical-controlled machining of tools has been a technical advancement of immense proportions. Before the introduction of the computer, the process of cutting metal began with the development of engineering sketches. From these, detailed engineering drawings were prepared. Next came the making of the tooling, such as jigs, dies, and fixtures. Then the drawings and tooling were delivered to a machine tool, where a machinist would index the feed and speed mechanisms and guide the cutting tools to their work location. When the operation was completed, the machinist would inspect his or her work and then start the next piece.

  With numerical-controlled machining, this process is shortened drastically. A tape program is created from engineering design computations, bypassing all the intermediate stages described above. The tape contains detailed commands to the computer for running the machine tool. The tape is fed into the computer console of the machine tool, raw material is clamped on the bed of the machine, and the computer directs the machining of the part. The work is done faster and more accurately, and the costs of engineering drawings, tooling, and machinists' time are avoided. New costs, however, are imposed in the form of programming time and the investment in the computer.

In addition to numerical-controlled machining, the computer is being applied to an increasing number of process applications—indeed, in some instances, complete plants are run entirely by process applications. Plants that process constantly, such as those in the paper, steel, glass, and cement industries, have computers start the operations, check quality, make adjustments, change product mix, and report results.

- Forecasting. The characteristics of future conditions can be forecast by determining the functions of the related variables, establishing their coefficients, arranging the related sets in equation form, and solving the equations simultaneously. The complexity of this task would make it impossible by manual means. However, econometric models operated by the computer, such as the Wharton model at the University of Pennsylvania, are forecasting future economic conditions with improved precision each year. More and more companies are using the computer on an individual basis. The computers forecast sales, changes in consumer buying habits, manpower needs, prices, and other conditions.

- Simulation. The computer makes it possible to simulate inputs and outputs for unlimited alternatives and conclude from the reports that one decision is potentially the most effective. The costs of implementing the decision can then be undertaken with considerably improved confidence that the best possible course of action is under way. For more on simulations see Chapter 10. Without the computer, managers must try to determine which available alternative for any decision is likely to produce the most desirable results using the best judgment they can muster. Then they must proceed with that solution. They never know what might have happened if they had tried the others.

- Data banks. As indicated earlier in this section, the computer's memory capability makes it possible to continually feed it information that can be used for some future purpose. For example, computer data banks can be used to develop a manpower inventory, in which all pertinent data on each employee are stored. The magnitude of this information can be realized when it is related to a firm employing 50,000 people. In the future, whenever any data relating to personal characteristics or combinations of characteristics are required—such as, for example, the names of all unmarried cryogenics engineers in their thirties who speak Russian—the computer can instantly search its memory and print out the answer. Other uses for data banks include the storing of technical information, indexes of possible suppliers, court decisions, and applicable patents granted or applied for.

EFFECT OF AUTOMATION ON EMPLOYMENT
AND JOB CONTENT

Since the 1940s, when the widespread applications of the computer were first recognized, grave concern has been voiced in the United States over the possibility that the computer may eliminate millions of jobs. Some predict that the computer will lead to a national depression far more disastrous than the Great Depression of the 1930s. However, the record shows that in 1949, unemployment was running at a level of about 7 percent of the population available for work. By October 1976, with an expanded work force and computer applications in magnitudes not even imagined twenty years before, unemployment was still approximately 7 percent. We are not suggesting that the computer has reduced unemployment (the incidence of wars and inflation must be considered), only that the grim prognostications of widespread worker layoffs have not come to pass.

- Localized problems. Although there has been no widespread unemployment as a consequence of computerization, the computer has indisputably rendered many job skills obsolete. Significant numbers of people who have been displaced have acquired other skills, sometimes to their advantage. Conversely, some individuals, particularly older workers, have had their job careers terminated prematurely. To these people, national statistics do not mean much. Their lives have been directly affected, and for them the computer is the source of a serious social problem.

    The number of clerical workers—workers who would seem particularly vulnerable to being displaced—has actually increased in many firms after the introduction of the computer. In most instances the increase was not intended, because firms investing in computers thought the cost would be more than offset by a decrease in the clerical payroll. However, what seems to happen in such cases is that the computer generates so much more data than ever was produced before that additional people are required to handle, file, digest, and respond to the volume of paper work.

- Job content. Jobs that are subject to programming, and thus to elimination, are those that are routine—requiring limited skill and little initiative. Disappearing jobs include those at the supervisory and managerial level as well as the operating level. The new jobs that are necessitated by the computer—such as those of programmer or systems analyst—are in some way related to the computer, and they generally demand greater education and initiative than those that are displaced.

    Even jobs not directly related to the computer, in the way that those of programmer or systems analyst are, usually require a knowledge of it. In fact, some knowledge of the computer is becoming essential for practically all occupations, up to and including the professions. In many fields, such as accounting and engineering, high-level computer competence is becoming a required additional specialization. And, as implied in the discussion of the computer's applications, jobs in areas like inventory control, production control, market analysis, and credit and collection have become so oriented to the computer that the traditional ways of performing them have almost vanished.

HUMAN CONSEQUENCES

Changes as widespread as those attributable to the computer are sure to have profound human consequences. Members of business organizations who had to adapt to the computer era, have found that the changes often induce tension and fear. Some of that fear is legitimate, as it relates to the depersonalization of performance standards. However, fears arising from the need to learn computer-related skills are less well founded and can be conquered by individuals willing to face the challenges the computer represents.

- Tension. People in a range of occupations—in education, business, and the government—have experienced tension attributable to the computer. For the most part, they are persons who, having learned their job skills before the era of the computer, fear and resist it. Rather than adjusting to the computer, many appear to adopt on ostrich-like attitude, trying to ignore it and work around it as long as possible. This explains why the already impressive role of the computer is not even more dominant—many of its logical applications are still only being tried in a minimal way. In business, for example, trial and error is

DOONESBURY   by **Garry Trudeau**

Copyright, 1972, G. B. Trudeau/Distributed by Universal Press Syndicate.

The Impact of the Computer **459**

often being used where simulation (Chapter 10 and Appendix C) could yield better answers; in government, files of paper work are maintained to store information that could be stored in computer memories; and in education, professors often still require manually derived answers to problems appropriate to computer solution.

Alongside people in their twenties and thirties who have had exposure to the computer in school and can readily adapt to jobs of which it is an integral part, those in the older age group are apt to feel insecure and left out, perceiving themselves as old and obsolete before their chronological age indicates that they should. They are very conscious of the competition of youth, because young people with computer competence are being promoted into jobs at the middle-management level and above in increasing numbers.

- Dispelling the threat. Although many people have viewed the changes introduced by the computer as threatening, others have been more receptive toward them. There is no reason why we should not take a positive attitude toward the computer, for it is not so mysterious that people of normal intelligence cannot learn to live with it. Managers, in particular, can successfully learn to cope with the computer if they master the following essentials:

1. Develop the ability to communicate with computer specialists, and learn enough about their systems approach to analyzing problems to be able to digest their reports. Understanding a computer language, such as FORTRAN, is not important.
2. Learn what information can be obtained from the computer. If managers would simply put down all of the information that they would like to have in order to do their jobs better, they might be surprised to find out how much of it the computer can readily provide.
3. Determine the computer's practical limitations, and do not put insatiable demands on it. Reach a balance between what the computer can produce and the costs of obtaining it.
4. Capitalize on the added capability that the computer offers; that is, learn to view it as a highly competent assistant.

- Legitimate fear. For individuals in subordinate roles, the potential of the computer to depersonalize organizations is a basis for legitimate fear. In integrating job performance by computer and humans into a total system, the computer has reduced managers' reliance on subordinates' judgment and has caused jobs to be rigidly and impersonally defined. These aspects have been discussed in previous chapters, especially 5, 18, and 29.

Those contemplating the consequences of the computer in this light may fear that companies that are so systems-oriented might increase mechanization hoping to force apathetic and frustrated employees to work for company goals.

However, as indicated in earlier sections of this book, companies might well consider an alternative approach to motivating employees, namely, accommodating their organizations to human needs and using the computer to improve the probability of satisfying those needs. An encouraging sign of accommodation of organizations to human needs is the trend for business firms to experiment with "organization development," in which behavioral scientists help managers remove the causes for employee tensions, frustrations, and anxieties from the organizational environment. The computer can help in this effort by freeing managerial time from routine details so that more attention can be directed to "people" problems.

IMPLICATIONS FOR ORGANIZING AND DECISION MAKING

The computer's implications for organizing and decision making center chiefly upon the level in the organization at which decisions are to be made, the authority of computer specialists in contributing to decisions, and the type of decision factors for which the computer is best suited.

Decentralization or Centralization of Decision Making

A continuing debate over the influence of the computer centers on the issue of whether it will lead to decentralization or further centralization of decision making.

Arguments that the computer will foster centralization are based on the communication facility of the computer; the timely feedback to top management of complete and accurate information will enable relatively few individuals to make all the decisions necessary to maintain the system in a state of equilibrium. Consequently, some people believe that many middle-management levels will disappear, with charts of organization structure taking on a much flatter look. In other words, the key levels are envisioned to be those of top managers and operators, with some functional specialists in between.

Although there does seem to be a trend back toward centralization, in spite of the popularity the decentralization concept enjoyed in the 1950s and early 1960s, the computer is only one cause. When decision-making authority is withdrawn from middle management, it often is because decentralization has resulted in an organization's getting out of control, or because interactions with big government and big labor have required tighter interpretations of policies by business firms.

Despite the apparent trend back to more centralized decision making in business firms in the United States, it is possible that some decentralization may result from the computer. As we noted earlier, through real-time computation, senior managers have the capability of knowing precisely what is going on in their organizations at any time, and thus should be able to remedy situations that have gotten out of control. Therefore, it may be that the computer will permit the advantages of decentralization without the disadvantage of loss of control, which has been a problem in the past.

Reckoning with a New Kind of Specialist

As explained previously, the evolution of business organizations since 1900 has largely been characterized by the increase of specialists in so-called staff functions, such as personnel, purchasing, quality control, industrial engineering, and traffic. Obviously, computer technology has introduced another kind of specialist. Individuals who are trained in working with the computer are being placed either in centralized computer processing departments, or are being added to the staffs of central and supporting departments as technical advisers. Central computer processing departments have become major service organizations. Although in some cases they are part of the accounting operation, the trend seems for them to be independent of the accounting department, but with authority over many of the traditional accounting activities in modern guise, such as the development of specialized reports to managers. Computer technical advisers in operating departments quickly acquire prescriptive authority and become persons to reckon with in organizational power struggles.

Earlier, we discussed whether authority is delegated down from the top or rises by acceptance from the bottom. However, the computer is contributing to another view of the source of authority; current questions center on specialized functions. Some theorists question whether a great deal of authority is inherent in a specialized function. Computer expertise is a case in point. For example, senior managers in an organization may understand enough about the computer to use its capabilities and base a decision on its printout, but, unless they have unusual background, they must rely on specialists for the programming of the decision model, with its equations and weighting of variables. Such a reliance cannot fail to place the specialists in an authoritative role, because they can, in effect, limit the choice of the managers for whom they render service.

Differentiating Between Decision Factors

Inasmuch as the computer permits mechanization of decision making when factors can have numerical values assigned to them, it becomes necessary to differentiate between the kinds of factors involved in a decision. Some decisions will involve only quantitative factors, and others only nonquantitative ones, while a third kind will involve factors of both kinds.

Previous chapters, especially those dealing with planning, have stressed the value of quantitative analysis in facilitating decisions where all of the related factors have numerical values assigned to them. A problem such as whether optimal profit can be realized by making products A, B, and C in equal amounts or in varying proportions is an example. The typical organization will have hosts of operational decisions of this kind to make at all management levels. Where in the past they required a great deal of management time, the computer now permits them to be made routinely. And because they are completely objective, the location at which they are made can safely be delegated to secondary levels in the organization.

On the other hand, the difficulty of making sound managerial decisions in which none of the factors can be quantified has also been discussed in previous sections, especially those pertaining to the staffing and leading functions. Major decisions of this nature are the ones involving people. Such decisions are also made at all management levels. When a foreman tries to decide whether to promote Paul or Jim to task leader, the factors are the same as when the president deliberates over two candidates for a vice-president's spot. While the computer cannot assist directly in making these qualitative decisions, it can release managerial time for doing so through its capacity for handling the purely quantitative ones.

Certain decisions, which involve both quantitative and nonquantitative factors, must be based on computer evaluation and managerial judgment combined. For example, a computer can evaluate many alternate uses for funds available for capital investments, but it cannot objectively assess whether the funds should be put into a company cafeteria, whose only justification would be a possible improvement in employee morale because of convenience and low-cost nourishing meals. Thus, in deciding a capital budget, the firm's senior managers would have to balance the quantitative weights provided by the computer, and the subjective weight that they would have to assign to the cafeteria, and come to a partially objective, partially reasoned, rationing of funds.

If managers become so preoccupied with the computer's apparent efficiency that they attempt to mechanize all decision making, it will be in spite of the computer, which provides time for managers to humanize their organizations. Managers may lean toward completely mechanized decision making because of the difficulty of providing a motivational climate suited to each employee's requirements, and the present scarcity of information on how to carry out that objective.

From this overall discussion of the ways in which the computer is affecting management, a view emerges that managers will continue to plan, to organize, to staff, and to control, but their skill in performing these functions can be greatly enhanced through computerization of data. And, because the computer will release managerial time from the present routine of these functions and thus permit a greater focus on the leading function, it has the potential of contributing to the solution of human problems in organizations.

DISCUSSION QUESTIONS

1. Of the various applications of the computer that are listed in the chapter, which one seems to have potentially the most important use by the top managers of a business organization? For what reasons?
2. What are the implications of the computer for students who contemplate a business career?
3. Do you think the computer will reduce, or increase, the importance of middle managers in business organizations? Explain your views.
4. Do decisions made at the top management level in business organizations involve factors that can be quantified, or are they more concerned with human factors?
5. Select one application that you personally feel is appropriate for data banks, and explain your reasoning.

BIBLIOGRAPHY

"Business Takes a Second Look at Computers." *Business Week,* No. 2179 (June 5, 1971), p. 59.

Brady, Rodney H. "Computers and Top-Level Decision Making." *Harvard Business Review,* Vol. 45 No. 3 (July–August 1967), pp. 67–76.

Burck, Gilbert and the Fortune Editors. *The Computer Age and Its Potential for Management.* New York: Harper, 1965.

Dean, Neal J. "The Computer Comes of Age." *Harvard Business Review,* Vol. 46 No. 1 (January–February 1968), pp. 83–89.

Glaser, George. "Plain Talk About Computers." *Business Horizons,* Vol. 10 No. 3 (Fall 1967), pp. 33–38.

Malley, Francis J. "Report on the Computer Backlash." *S.A.M. Advanced Management Journal,* (April 1974).

Moan, Floyd E. "Does Management Practice Lag Behind Theory in the Computer Environment?" *Academy of Management Journal,* Vol. 16 No. 1 (March 1973), pp. 7–23.

The Case of the Elusive Cost Savings

"What I want to know is, when am I going to see the cost savings you promised when I let you talk me into that new-fangled computer system," demanded Janis Micovitch, semiretired but still domineering principal stockholder of Four Counties Machinery Company. "I want all of the facts brought out before this meeting adjourns today," was his ultimatum. The occasion was the monthly meeting of the Operating Management Committee.

Four Counties Machinery Company was the franchised dealer for a number of leading lines of industrial and construction machinery. It also operated a thriving used-machinery business. In addition, it depended on the sale of spare parts, which required the carrying of an inventory of close to 100,000 items, for a large part of its annual revenue. Besides its central operation in Los Angeles, it had 13 branch outlets in four Southern California counties. The number of employees in all job classifications ran around 750.

About three and one-half years earlier, a joint proposal was made to the Operating Management Committee by Bill Craig, inventory control manager, and John Simpson, accounting manager, that a feasibility study be made of computerizing the firm's perpetual inventory, payroll, and accounts payable systems. Craig thought that a computerized inventory control system might substantially reduce the firm's inventory investment, while at the same time increase the efficiency with which parts orders were filled from stock. Efficiency at that time was about 75 percent. Simpson thought a study would show that a com-

puterized accounting system would result in a marked improvement in accuracy and timeliness of paper-work processing. Both managers said that computer company sales force and articles in trade and business journals implied that the salaries of the clercial workers whose jobs would be done away with would pay for the cost of a computerized system. They felt that there was no moral issue involved in displacing workers, because new workers would simply not be hired to take the place of those lost by normal attrition.

When the proposal for a feasibility study was made, Micovitch, who still ran the company even though he had made his son-in-law, Tom Geiger, president, was against it. "We don't need anything like a computer in this business," he said. Finally, after about three months of patient selling by Craig and Simpson, he agreed to authorize an investigation. "However, it's going to be arranged by a sharp-pencil man like me," he stated, as he authorized the purchasing agent, Tom Downey, to have a study done. (Downey, who had been both his employee and close friend for forty years, was about the only one in the company whom Micovitch trusted.)

Downey talked with representatives of several of the computer manufacturers, and although each of them agreed to conduct a simple feasibility study at no cost to Four Counties Machinery Company, he was resentful of the similarity in their estimates of how much a "bundle" (hardware, software, and training) would cost. In order to get competition in price estimates, he called in a consulting firm, EDP Systems, Inc. EDP also agreed to do a no-cost study, but proposed that for a fee it would assist Downey in separately contracting for the computer equipment itself, the programming, and the training. Even with EDP's fee, the price estimate was considerably lower than those submitted by the computer manufacturers. As a result, Downey let EDP do the study.

EDP's study focused on the cost savings that would be effected by computerized systems. An abstract of the analysis is as follows:

Estimated Cost/Savings Comparison.

Computer System Costs:

Hardware lease cost ($4500 per month, 36 months)	$162,000	
Programming	29,000	
Training	18,000	
Salaries of personnel to run the system (36 months)	387,000	$596,000

Computer System Savings:

15 inventory clerks ($600 per month, 36 months)	$324,000	
18 accounting clerks ($500 per month, 36 months)	315,000	639,000
Saving over first 36 months		$ 43,000

After making the cost savings pitch, the EDP representative pointed out that the programming and training costs would be nonrecurring, so that the annual savings after the first three years would be even larger. Therefore, as the proposal went, Four Counties Machinery Company could have the efficiency of computerized systems, and save money besides.

On Tom Downey's assurance that the comparative costs were figured accurately, Micovitch let the computerized system be installed. Soon after that, Downey died.

After almost three years, each month's profit and loss statement showed increasing costs, prompting Micovitch's heated demand at the Operating Management Committee meeting.

"Let's first see how much this whole computer thing has cost," Micovitch stated. With obvious lack of enthusiasm for being the one who had to do it, Simpson showed him the following figures:

Computer System Actual Costs:

Hardware lease cost ($5700 per month, 34 months)	$193,800	
Programming	92,300	
Training	33,000	
Salaries of computer personnel (34 months)	469,000	
EDP consulting fee (27 months)	81,000	
Systems Control consulting fee (7 months)	28,000	$897,100

"What in blue blazes has happened." Micovitch exclaimed.

As calmly as he could, Simpson made his explanation: "EDP badly underestimated the lease cost of the peripheral equipment. Then the company that EDP subcontracted the programming to couldn't make it work on the computer that had been leased. In addition, our sales department wanted computerized market analysis, which required programming that hadn't been planned for. EDP also underestimated the various technicians that we would have to hire. EDP's estimate didn't include its own consulting fee which Mr. Downey had agreed to, and when we fired EDP seven months ago, we simply had to take on another consulting firm."

"Isn't that all just dandy?" Micovitch said. "Now where are those fabulous savings in clerical costs that I was told about?"

"We have eliminated all of the manual inventory posting," Craig reported, "but the additional work of analyzing the data that the computer puts out has meant that we have created a lot of new jobs. Actually, we have about the same number of people in inventory control as we had before. I do want to say this, however. We have had a lot of trouble getting the computerized system to function as it should, but it finally is and we are going to have some very positive results to show at the end of next year."

"The story is about the same in accounting as it is in Bill's operation," Simpson said. "It seems that, now the branch managers know that we have the computer, there is no end to the number and varieties of new reports that they want us to do for them. Like Bill, I have cut out most of the old manual posting jobs, but the new jobs that have been made are in higher salary brackets. I can show some net saving, but it would be less than $50,000 since we started the computer systems."

"Well, that just about does it," Micovitch exploded.

"I wish it did, sir," said Simpson. "Our office space is so crowded because of the amount of room that the computer equipment and the technicians occupy that we can't avoid adding on to the building. The architect estimates that it will cost about $250,000."

DISCUSSION QUESTIONS

1. Why did Micovitch resist attempts to persuade him to install a computer?
2. How has the computer affected the performance of Bill Craig and John Simpson?
3. How could other medium-sized companies benefit from the experience that Four Counties Machinery Company had in the Case of the Elusive Cost Savings?

31 Business Social Responsiveness

Clamors for various social reforms persistently reach public attention through the efforts of idealists whose personal value systems detect wrongs that should be rectified. Sometimes these reform movements crest in popularity, then ebb away like a tide, leaving only vague memories of once earthshaking philosophies. One such movement was to abolish all taxes except tax on land, which was proposed by the economist Henry George. In the 1930s there was "Technocracy," which swept the country through the oratory of a zealot named Townsend. Attempts to redistribute the personal wealth of the country through confiscatory inheritance taxes have periodic surges as potential panaceas for the inequities of the extremes of poor and rich population segments. In the 1960s however, a reform pressure that had been simmering for several decades reached the boiling point as the national issue of corporate social responsibility. Since then there has been a humiliating war, race riots and student rebellions, and the worst recession since the Great Depression of the early 1930s. Despite these distracting influences, by the late 1970s social responsibility, or as it is now more popularly called "social responsiveness" has demonstrated lasting qualities which suggest that business men and women can view it as one social issue with which they will have to deal permanently.

THE NATURE OF SOCIAL RESPONSIVENESS

Traditionally, profitability has been considered the prime responsibility of a business firm. In businesses where the owners and the managers are the same persons, this responsibility is fundamentally self-serving, because without profits their investment would be wiped out, and they could find their business careers forever blocked. In this era of professional managers performing their legal obligations to the corporate stockholders, these managers are dependent upon profitability to assure their personal rewards and continued employment. In addition to profits being the key responsibility of managers to the owners of businesses, a business without profits could not provide jobs, patronize suppliers, or pay taxes. Thus as a responsibility, a profitable operation must have the highest priority to business managers.

However, being sensitive to social issues, and responding to these issues supportively are concerns a manager must face in addition to shouldering legal and economic responsibilities. But, responsiveness to social issues and profit responsibility are not separate activities that managers perform independently. They should be perceived as being intimately related; together the two activities make up the total job of the responsible manager.

Since the 1960s, progress has been made in systematizing the definition of social issues. The harried but concerned business manager of that decade tried to respond to attacks of social irresponsibility by overreacting to topical waves of pressure, without a careful consideration of his or her most effective response to the totality of issues. For example, a firm like Ford Motor Company would define fulfillment of social responsibility by attempting to make several hundred young blacks employable. Several firms took the approach of Aerojet-General Corporation and set up subsidiary companies to be managed and staffed by blacks. Other firms, such as Union Carbide, upheld their social responsibility by installing filters on the smokestacks of their factories to reduce the emission of pollutants.

Fifteen years of attempts by business managers to cope with the demands of a new and unnatural role have resulted in a categorization of social issues. Some can only be handled indirectly, while others can be confronted with direct business actions. These categories are

1. Problems that are totally outside business and which in no way can honestly be attributed to business actions. Examples of such problems include the crime on the streets of most American cities, drug addiction (including alcohol), urban decay, the breakdown of institutions, like marriage and religion, and poverty.
2. Problems that result from the influence of business actions on the external environment. These problems include job displacement as a result of labor-saving machinery or plant relocation, quality of goods or services, hazardous products, and contaminating processes.
3. Problems that occur within the business firms, but which reflect social impacts. Examples are employment and promotion opportu-

nities for women and minorities, working conditions, and the ethics of business decision making.

In one sense the response of business managers to some problems in the latter two categories is being made easier because of government legislation. If there are laws prescribing how decisions must be made, then managers at least are relieved of the necessity of choosing. In the second category of problems, legislation at both the national and state levels specifies quality of foods and drugs. Each year consumer protection regulations are clamping down harder to prevent unsafe or unreliable products from being put on the market. Legislation emanating from state, county, and city levels is restraining manufacturers from polluting the atmosphere with emissions from both processes, such as disposal of wastes, and products, such as those from internal combustion engines. In the third category, the Civil Rights Act of 1964 and its amendments force business to abolish discriminatory employment practices. The Occupational Safety and Health Act of 1970 is intended to improve the quality of life in business organizations, and is having a significant impact on work rules, job content, and the overall work environment.

Legislation regulating the response of business to social issues notwithstanding, contemporary and future business executives will be increasingly faced with the necessity of considering the consequences of their actions on the external environment. There are few specific guidelines for business managers in their response to any of the unlegislated problems, so each firm will have to develop within itself the capacity to manage seemingly conflicting sets of demands, and at the same time keep the organization in equilibrium.

THE VARIABILITY OF SOCIAL ISSUES

Unfortunately for business managers, the relative priority of social issues is always changing. During the prosperous 1960s, smokestacks belching pollutants and waste products festering in rivers were popularly viewed as anathemas to society. However, the high unemployment rates of the 1970s have put a higher priority on jobs than on the protection of the environment. Energy scarcity fears seem to run in cycles. Following the oil price increases by the OPEC nations in 1973, there was a virtual energy panic, with this issue forging ahead of issues earlier considered far more pressing. By the middle 1970s, the crisis appeared to ease, and pressure on business managers to find new energy sources slackened noticeably. However, reliable predictions of energy demand/supply ratios for the 1980s strongly suggest the issue will become dominant again. Antidiscriminatory measures to provide equality in job opportunities for women, blacks, and other formerly underprivileged groups have run into counter-discrimination claims by white males.

The Pressure to Compromise Personal Ethics

Shaken by revelations of corporate bribery abroad and illegal campaign donations at home, executives have begun to wonder how widely spread is the pressure on managers to compromise personal ethics for company goals. Does such pressure exist in companies with no record of wrongdoing—even in companies that stress ethical conduct as management policy?

This week Pitney-Bowes Inc., the Stamford (Conn.) manufacturer of business equipment and a leader in the campaign for business ethics, provided a depressing answer. A majority of Pitney-Bowes managers, surveyed anonymously by the company, reported that indeed they do feel pressure to compromise personal ethics to achieve corporate goals.

Such pressures apparently exist widely in the business world. Results of the Pitney-Bowes study, made available to BUSINESS WEEK, resemble those of similar surveys conducted last year by Uniroyal Inc., the $2.2-billion rubber and plastics company, and by Associate Professor Archie B. Carroll III of the University of Georgia, who queried a random sample of corporate managers throughout the country. Seven out of 10 Uniroyal managers and 64% of Professor Carroll's respondents perceived company pressures on personal ethics. The Pitney-Bowes figure was 59%, rising to almost 70% among lower-level managers. All respondents—326 at P-B, 252 at Uniroyal, and 239 at the University of Georgia—replied anonymously.

At P-B, Fred T. Allen, chairman and chief executive officer, reacted to the study results by underscoring their importance during a management seminar on moral development last week at headquarters. He also prepared to send a letter on the survey's implications to all top company executives in the U.S. and abroad. In addition to plants in Canada, Mexico, Britain, Belgium, and West Germany, P-B has 13 overseas subsidiaries and 159 independent dealers outside the U.S. "I'd like to see what we can do about this," Allen says.

The other fellow. Among causes for Allen's concern were replies indicating that most managers believed that their peers would not refuse orders to market off-standard and possibly dangerous products (although an even larger majority insisted that they personally would reject such orders), and that they believed young managers automatically go along with their superiors to show loyalty, just like junior members of President Nixon's reelection committee.

Not that the survey news was all bad from a moralist's viewpoint. At both P-B and Uniroyal, 9 out of 10 respondents considered it unethical to turn in an incomplete report or to charge the expense account with a meal eaten in a relative's home. Other replies charted gray areas amid the black and white. Half or more of both groups would market off-standard items if they were not dangerous. Said one P-B respondent: "It would depend on the circumstances and what I had to lose. To a company, the individual is expendable."

Gifts. Corporate policy and industry practice clearly affected some responses, conspicuously those about giving and receiving gifts. Like many companies in the business equipment market, P-B has long emphasized a strict ban on such gifts. So it was hardly surprising that 80% of the P-B respondents said they would decline to give Christmas gifts to preferred customers and 92% said they would refuse to accept them (although one manager saw "nothing wrong with a bottle around the holidays").

Uniroyal, on the other hand, is a major contender in the hotly competitive commodities business, and the company bars only gifts worth more than $100. At Uniroyal, close to half of the respondents said they would give or accept gifts.

Other variations stemmed from differences in age, income, and work location of managers. At P-B, more pressure to compromise personal ethics was felt by managers under 35, earning under $30,000, and stationed at headquarters rather than in the field. But more older than younger managers favored an official code of ethics for businessmen.

Management's role. Overall, an overwhelming majority of respondents in both companies—9 out of 10—backed a code of ethics for business and the teaching of ethics in business schools. P-B's Allen found this heartening. "Managers want the leadership to show them what to do," he says. "They want to believe their particular job can be done with a high degree of ethics. It is up to corporate management to confirm this belief."

Allen also drew comfort from the widespread refusal to dismiss press reports on unethical business practices as evidence of antibusiness bias. Seventy percent of P-B respondents thought that press reports revealed a valid cause for concern and 20% thought that they would force corrective action by business. Another statistic appeared designed to cheer corporate officials everywhere: Almost all respondents felt that business ethics, however imperfect, were as good or better than the ethics of society at large.

Managerial ethics is a social issue for which a public clamor for correction will continue through the 1980s. This clamor will continue despite the fact that it is an "internal" issue. Public revulsion to such scandals as the Northrop Aircraft and Occidental Petroleum political contributions, the Lockheed and Gulf Oil briberies, and the Phillips Petroleum tax fraud will force a significant and convincing response by business. Like many of the issues to which business must respond, ethical behavior by managers must be instituted within the organization; there is no realistic way that ethics can be effectively mandated by legislature.

While the importance of other issues may fluctuate, there is undeniably an irreversible trend against the traditional business position that its sole consideration should be to carry out policies that lead to profits. In fact, over the short run social responsiveness will probably reduce profits. Even viewed in the long-term perspective, direct economic payoffs to business corporations resulting from being responsible social citizens will be elusive as far as quantitative measurements are concerned. For example, how can the costs of contributing to drug-education programs, making illiterate, culturally retarded young people employable, making factory processes pollution free, and losing sales to foreign countries who are indifferent to American ethical values ever be recovered? Yet American business must respond to these issues and many like them. The requirement for managers is to develop strategies that will result in both societal and economic efficiencies.

THE FUSION OF SOCIAL AND ECONOMIC STRATEGIES

It is both natural, and as has been stated, probably accurate, for managers to assume that responsiveness to social demands will reduce the resources available for profit generation over the short term. The implications of deliberate actions that negatively affect profits are apparently overlooked by the idealists who urge immediate strategies for coping with social issues, which must by necessity be incomplete. Strategies that will reduce profits without promise of long-term recovery will be unenthusiastically received by the debt and equity capital markets, and could lead to the inevitable demise of the corporations adopting them. Social responsiveness must be carefully thought out by business managers, and should probably start with the best forecasts that can be constructed as to the future patterns of social issues.

Social issues seem to start randomly and in a disorganized fashion, but at various pressure points simultaneously. As an issue gains momentum, it attracts powerful advocates who bring system and organization to it. Finally, concern about the issue peaks. It may then go in one of three directions. It may become totally accepted as an ingrained social institution. It may die for lack of realism. Or, it may subside temporarily, only to arise periodically with possible eventual acceptance.

One-time social issues that have become so accepted by business that to oppose them would be construed as abnormal behavior are so numerous as to defy counting. Some examples are the eight-hour day, payment for time not worked, such as vacations, holidays, and sick leave, health and accident insurance, abolition of child labor,—even the coffee break. An issue that appears to have died for lack of realism was the proposal by the Johnson-Humphrey administration that every individual in the United States below a certain income level be given a significant sum of money by the government. An issue that has not yet been accepted generally, but has the potential for becoming an eventual normal policy is the "portable pension," that would allow workers to carry their pension rights with them when they change jobs.

Business managers must become aware of incipient social issues, and acquire the ability to assess the probable urgency and durability of the issues. An initial strategy decision is whether to lead in responding to an issue, as for example, the Swift meat packing company did in retraining workers displaced by automation, or to wait for other business firms to do the pioneering work, then to step in when the problems and alternative solutions have been fully explored. Regardless of whether the business firm elects to lead or lag, in the future managers must learn to fuse social strategies with economic strategies.

Strategy decisions in the future will be incomplete if social demands and economic demands are considered separately. Every economic decision has social consequences, which must be weighted simultaneously with cost, sales and profit projections. Moving a plant may cause unemployment in the vacated location, the substitution of cheaper materials in a product may impair its safety, and temporary layoffs of the least senior employees may negate affirmative action efforts that led to the hiring of young blacks. Thus, the costs and benefits of every business decision must include both those that are measurable in economic terms, and those that are predictable in qualitative social terms.

MAKING SOCIAL RESPONSIVENESS A REALITY

Awareness of the need for social responsiveness must be part of the value system of the chief executive officer of the business organization and of his or her senior lieutenants. The top-level management of the company must be sensitive to the imperative nature of response to social demands. The implementation of social responsiveness will never be easy, and will be resisted not only by the corporate stockholders, who will perceive a potential dilution of their equity value, but also by middle-level managers who will be confused and threatened by a goal additional to that of profit generation. Thus, making social responsiveness a reality will be impossible if the policy-making level of management does not believe in it sincerely.

Within every business organization, there will be strong forces working against the addition of a new dimension to the firm's central objectives. The general trend toward adopting product organization by corporations complicates a centralized response to social demands, because, to a very large extent, the product divisions become autonomous. For example, where social responsiveness might have a high priority to the top management of a company like General Motors, it might have a very subordinate place in the value system of a central department manager, such as the head of the Chevrolet Division. Secondly, the financial reporting systems of business organizations are only constructed to provide information on the attainment of economic goals. Active efforts by managers to be socially responsive would probably result in the firm's reporting system showing negative variances in budgeted targets, but would be silent on the degree of achievement of social objectives. Thirdly, social demands conflict with a business manager's personal financial interests. To the extent that resources are diverted from economic goals to social goals, profitability in the manager's own productive lifetime is threatened, and with it, the consequential reduction in personal rewards that are a function of the profit system. Thus, the challenge to a socially responsive top-management team is to somehow inculcate the same motivation in all management levels.

Top management must implement social responsiveness slowly and painstakingly. An aggressive frontal attack might be suitable for launching a new product in a competitive market, but changing business attitudes toward acceptance of social demands requires patient and tolerant statesmanship. Senior management will almost always lack the expertise to design a socially responsive system, and to disseminate the details relative to its implementation, so specialists with extensive experience in such systems must be engaged. The pattern for responding to social demands must be convincingly established by top management, so that examples may be set for lower-level managers to follow. Finally, the performance appraisal system must incorporate criteria for measuring social achievements as well as economic accomplishments.

REPORTING SOCIAL RESPONSIVENESS

In the early 1970s, some imaginative schemes were created in which the performance of a business in response to social demands was cast in the same format as the firm's financial reports. The concept was highly programmed "social auditing," and results were displayed via the medium of "social balance sheets." An attempt was made to parallel accounting balance sheets in structure, with sections for social assets and social liabilities, with the difference between the two represented as the firm's net social accomplishments. Glowing promises were made for this technique, but by the late 1970s it appears to be generally abandoned in favor of less lofty reporting procedures.

The trend in corporate public accounting reporting for the past ten years has been toward increased "disclosure." A similar trend is evident in the so far informal requirement that business firms report responses to social demands. Whether regulations will be imposed making reporting on social responsiveness a legal requirement, like the Securities and Exchange Commission (SEC) regulations on financial reporting, is something that only time will tell, but the number of firms voluntarily making social reports is growing every year.

The business ethics issue is certainly going to require public disclosure by business firms, and reporting in this area will naturally lead to general reporting on all social issues. The social report must start with a clear-cut statement of objectives. Next there must be a description of the plan that the firm has devised for achieving its social goals. Finally, as in financial reporting, there must be a comparison of the plan with the accomplishments, an explanation of the variances between objectives and results, and a definition of the steps proposed to rectify the variances.

In summary, realistic business managers must accept that some form of disclosure about their firm's social responsiveness will be necessary, although not in the stylized format of a "social audit." The reporting should cover the company's "total" responsiveness package and not take the form of token publicity on some special programs, such as how many women were promoted to managerial positions last year, or what internal controls have been instituted to detect instances of bribery. The external reporting of response to social demands must derive from a complex system of internal objectives implemented by periodic reviews with provisions for corrective actions.

STAFF ASSISTANCE

Productive response to social demands requires specialized skills not usually present in the business firm embarking on a social responsiveness program. Therefore, companies above medium size who engage a specialist to assist in the transformation of a purely economic oriented business to one that has both economic and social goals will benefit considerably. There are problems in introducing a social responsiveness specialist into an organization, and in getting him or her accepted, but probably no more than with any other kind of a staff assistant.

The role of a social responsiveness specialist is to forecast trends in social issues; to assist in the formulation of the firm's objectives with regard to these objectives and in the development of implementing plans; and to serve as the catalyst in getting the objectives and implementing plans accepted throughout the organization. The person performing this role must have a high tolerance for ambiguity and frustration, because the job will, of necessity, be vaguely defined, and carry with it no formal authority. The specialist should be prepared for resistance ranging from passive acceptance all the way to active hostility, because he or she will be perceived as working against the traditional goals of a business organization.

The relationships that the specialist will have with managers at the product line or division level will require the greatest sensitivity and tact, because it is at this level that the selling of social responsiveness must be done. It is presumed that top management will already be sold on the need to respond to social issues, otherwise the specialist would not have been hired. In addition to stimulating a real commitment by the central department managers to social responsiveness, the specialist will also be required to design, implement, and monitor the internal systems that will make the achievement and reporting of social objectives possible.

DISCUSSION QUESTIONS

1. Explain the difference between social responsibility and social responsiveness.
2. What are some external factors that affect public demand for business social responsiveness?
3. Should social legislation be encouraged or opposed by business leaders?
4. Discuss some now commonly accepted employee benefits that started as controversial social issues.
5. How should a business firm implement a social responsiveness program?

BIBLIOGRAPHY

Ackerman, Robert W. "How Companies Respond to Social Demands." *Harvard Business Review,* Vol. 51 No. 4 (July–August 1973), pp. 88–98.

Bauer, Raymond A. and Dan H. Fenn, Jr. "What *is* a Corporate Social Audit?" *Harvard Business Review,* Vol. 51 No. 1 (January–February 1973), pp. 37–48.

Chamberlain, Neil. *The Limits of Corporate Responsibility.* New York: Basic Books, 1973.

Friedman, Milton. "The Social Responsibility of Business Is to Increase Profits." *New York Times Magazine,* (Sept. 13, 1970), p. 32.

Paluszek, John. "The Top Ten Social Responsibility Happenings of 1974." *Business and Society Review,* No. 12 (Winter 1974–75), pp. 26–29.

Votaw, Dow. "The Nature of Social Responsibility: You Can't Get There from Here." *Journal of Contemporary Business,* Vol. 2 No. 1 (Winter, 1973), pp. 1–20.

The Case of Who Gets the Slice of Pie

It had been the policy of Grayson Cast Steel Foundry, Inc., since the days when Henry Grayson, the founder, had put the company on a consistent profit-making basis, to annually donate 10 percent of the net profits to some socially worthwhile outside activity. The policy had lasted as something of a tradition, even after the Grayson heirs had sold most of their interest in the firm to a conglomerate, National Holdings, Inc., which operated Grayson as a semiautonomous subsidiary. At the board of directors' meeting held one month prior to the stockholders' meeting, when the distribution of the donation was always announced, John Pigot, chairman, asked for recommendations from the directors for recipients of the 1972 donation. It had been a good year for Grayson, and the fund available for donation, if the firm adhered to its past policy, amounted to $100,000. The matter of the donation was the last item on the agenda.

"Gentlemen," he began, "although some of you are new directors, I think you are all familiar with the company's policy of donating 10 percent of the annual net profits to some desirable community effort. As an officer and director of National Holdings, I can tell you that the parent company will not do anything to disturb the policy so long as the balance of the earnings is at a satisfactory level, and this board continues to endorse it. The subject at issue is the disposition of $100,000. Let us hear the recommendations, and when they have all been voiced we will vote, either for or against, each one on the slate. Mr. Carstairs, as the senior member of the board, what is your recommendation?"

"I know what Mr. Henry Grayson, Jr., would say if he were alive. This town is trying to raise funds to build a new hospital, and a $100,000 donation from us would give the campaign just the boost that it needs. If we donate this much, the other firms in town will also join the drive. I urge that Grayson contribute the entire amount to the new hospital."

"Very well, Mr. Carstairs," said Pigot, "your recommendation that the full donation go to the hospital is acknowledged. Gentlemen, let us withhold discussion of the recommendations until they have all been made, and just before we vote. Mr. Prentice, as another old-time director, what are your thoughts?"

"The colleges and universities in this country have never had a harder time meeting operating expenses, let alone getting any new building programs started, than they are having now. When the two Graysons were running this company the annual donation quite regularly went to either of their alma maters. I propose that we split the $100,000 this year between the two schools."

"Mr. Allen, you were here in the old days. What do you think we should do with the money?"

"The last conversation that I had with Mr. Henry Grayson, Jr., was on this subject, and I have repeatedly brought it up prior to the annual stockholders' meeting for the past four years. I think we should do something lasting for the arts—specifically, set up a Grayson Fellowship in Music. The $100,000 would provide a fellowship of about $5000 per year to a gifted student. We could have an annual competition in the local schools for the fellowship, and it would do more to help our community image than anything I know."

"All right. Mr. Allen has spoken for a Grayson Fellowship in Music. Now let's hear from the newer members of this board. Mr. Kelley, you are a labor relations attorney, and your background may give us a new slant on the most productive use for $100,000," invited Pigot.

"I can't criticize any of the recommendations that have been made," replied Kenneth T. Kelley, "but what I have in mind would be both socially beneficial and at the same time help the company. As everybody knows, this town has a hard core of unemployed people, particularly among the young blacks. Paradoxically, Grayson is having difficulty in getting good foundry workers. Now, what I am suggesting goes beyond a normal training program, because in that kind of a setup a company picks trainees who have all of the attributes to be successful. I propose that we select fifteen or twenty young men who appear untrainable, and who are therefore unemployable for any kind of a decent job. We would have to start with the very basics of work environment behavior. In many cases we would even have to teach the trainees to read. The content of jobs might have to be redesigned. Despite our care, some of the trainees would quit the program and we would lose our investment. It would take all of $100,000 to even get ten of the kind of young men I am talking about headed toward a useful life, but I hold that it would be worth it."

"That is an innovative thought, Mr. Kelley," answered Pigot. "Mr. Bergdorff, what is your recommendation?"

"I think that it is time to examine the policy itself. Let's remember that the Graysons were wealthy people, and making a donation of 10 percent of the net profits every year meant little to them personally. Now we have the stockholders of National Holdings to think about. Their interests should be our prime concern. They want growth or payout, or both, and if we continue to give away their money to the kinds of things that have been recommended here today we may find ourselves off the board. I propose that we use this $100,000 for an acquisition; for example, it would buy a controlling interest in the new die casting company in town that seems to have everything it needs for success except capital."

"I knew the policy was bound to be questioned sometime," John Pigot replied. "As a matter of fact, I am receiving letters and phone calls from stockholders complaining about it. I am confident that if this board agrees to continue it that I can sell it next month to most of the stockholders, but if Mr. Bergdorff is voicing a consensus, then we will have to make a change. Mr. McHenry, as our new president, perhaps your views should have been the first heard. However, I thought it would be better to hold you until last so that you can put all that has been said in perspective. What is your recommendation?"

"Because of the importance of our payroll to this town, the most valuable community contribution that Grayson can make is to stay viable. My assessment of our plant and equipment is that it is rapidly approaching obsolescence. In addition, our smokestacks for our oil furnaces are major causes of air pollution, and we should immediately start converting to all-electric furnaces. I can see substantial demands for capital improvements over the next five years, and it is to our own operations that our money should go, which indirectly fulfills our social responsibilities."

"Well, gentlemen, you have heard the recommendations," said Pigot. "Let us have a discussion of them before taking a vote."

DISCUSSION QUESTIONS

1. Would you support the idea that business leaders should assume a greater role in social reform? Why?
2. In the Case of Who Gets the Slice of Pie, the Grayson directors must make an important decision. How would you make it? What would be the consequences of your decision if it were the one adopted?

32 Entrepreneurship

The term "entrepreneur" was originally applied to the rational, anonymous responder to the forces of supply and demand in classical economic theory. Lately, however, it has been adopted internationally as the term for the creator and owner/manager of a small business. It has also come to mean a "risk taker," or men and women who deliberately sacrifice security and bureaucratic conformity for the potential rewards of economic independence. Small business is *not* a uniquely American characteristic; in fact, Napoleon alluded to England as a "nation of shopkeepers." However, the opportunity to create a business where none had existed before, and to nurture it to profitable maturity, harkens back to the days of Horatio Algier, and is known nostalgically as the "American Dream."

In this modern era of multi-billion dollar giant corporations, occasionally one hears prophecies of extinction for the successful entrepreneur. However, the fact is that, excluding farms, which are declining in numbers, there were more than double the amount of small businesses in the United States in 1975 than there were in 1945 (based on Survey of Current Business data). Moreover, there is an impressive number of huge corporations which started unbelievably small so recently that their creators are still active in the management of them. Included in this group are Hewlett-Packard, Polaroid, and TRW (formerly Ramo-Wooldridge). In this chapter we will assemble and present some key information pertinent to the aspiring entrepreneur.

DISTINCTIVE FEATURES OF SMALL BUSINESSES

Various methods are employed to define what criteria identify a "small" business. Popular measures of size include annual volume of sales and number of employees. Unfortunately, both criteria can be misleading, because a sales volume or employment statistic for a company in one industry might be enough to classify it as being small, whereas the same data for a firm in a different industry would establish it as relatively large. A manufacturing firm doing an annual sales volume of $2 million and employing 100 people would definitely be classified as small, but a restaurant or laundry generating the same statistics would probably not be considered small businesses in those industries.

Attempts to define small business more objectively have been made by the Small Business Administration (SBA) and the Committee for Economic Development (CED). The SBA defines a small business as "one which is independently owned and operated and not dominant in its field of operation." The SBA goes further, and states that for loan qualifying, a retailing or service company is small if it has less than $1 million in annual sales, a wholesaling firm is small if it has less than $5 million in annual sales, and a manufacturing firm is small if it has fewer than 250 employees.

The CED characterizes a small business as any firm where at least two of the following elements are present:

1. independent management (usually the managers are also owners).
2. owner-supplied capital.
3. mainly local area of operations.
4. relatively small size within the industry.

Let's examine these elements more closely. A small business is one where the manager owns a substantial part of the equity of the firm, or has personally arranged to borrow the main part of the debt capital with which the firm operates. Independent management means the owner/ manager is not under the control of a board of directors elected by outside stockholders. A large proportion of small businesses operate within a narrow geographical area often as confined as a neighborhood. The industry of which the small business is a part would probably not be affected by any action taken by the firm, such as exiting the industry altogether, raising or lowering price, changing marketing strategies, and so on. However, note that one of the characteristics may be present, and the firm would not necessarily be a small business. American Motors is a good example. Relative to General Motors, Ford, and Chrysler, AM is a midget, with only about 4 percent of the annual sales volume of the industry. However, AM's managers are professionals owning insignificant shares of the company's outstanding common stock, and are subject to control or complete removal by the board of directors. Also, American Motors' breadth of operations extends all over the world. So, American Motors is not a small business, even though one criterion qualifies it as such.

The term "small business" implies a variety of enterprises. It might imply the small plumber, painter, cabinetmaker kinds of operations, luncheonettes, barber and beauty shops, dry cleaning establishments, shoe repair shops, and all of the many other examples of businesses in direct contact with consumers. The primary contribution of such businesses is the performance of some specialized kind of labor. Probably for most of these companies there is no appreciation of capital, or, in other words, profits the businesses generate are really little more than salaries for the owner/managers. The payoffs from these kinds of small businesses are mostly hard work and constant pressure to survive, but they provide employment for the people owning and running them and they perform services that would be hard to imagine doing without.

Retail merchandise operations is another small business category. These companies supply goods from wholesalers or manufacturers to consumers, and include grocery stores, gasoline stations, drug stores, men's and women's shoe and clothing stores, and variety stores. Although many of these enterprises never grow much larger than the scale at which they start, others are able to expand under the direction of capable entrepreneurs, and over time develop an increase in value from retained earnings and potential earning power. These small businesses are cultivated and supported by the big corporations, because they serve as the end of the pipeline to the ultimate user of the producer's merchandise.

Small businesses may fall into a third category. Some supply goods manufactured or produced by companies at one level of business activity to companies at a subsequent level. Firms in the basic steel mill industry are one example. They produce steel sheets, plates, and structural forms from the raw materials of iron ore and scrap. Large manufacturers of products made from steel will purchase large volumes of steel direct from the mills, but the mills will reach the smaller users of steel through steel supply companies. Many steel supply companies are themselves large enough to not qualify as small businesses, but there are hundreds of steel supply companies in the small business category. Other examples of supply companies servicing other businesses include food wholesalers who sell to grocery stores ranging from the giant chains down to the "Mom and Pop" variety, and firms selling office supplies, welding supplies, or paper products. The list of the variety of specialized companies selling goods to other companies could be made almost infinite. The economic system of the United States is highly dependent on this kind of an operation. The role played by this type of small business is similar to retail operations in that the supply companies serve to store and sell the products of larger businesses. However, they differ from retail in the level of customers reached. Small businesses of the industrial supply company variety have the potential for being extremely profitable for the owner/manager.

Another group of small businesses perform production work for larger businesses on a subcontract basis. The work performed is usually to the specifications of the larger businesses, which are the customers, and is mainly on components of the customer's product line. Some examples of small businesses doing this type of work are machine shops, foundries, plating shops, and heat treating shops. Large companies are quite dependent on small businesses of this kind, because their specialization leads them to produce high quality work, they provide additional scheduling capacity for their customers, they often are more flexible in coping with change than their customers could be, and they can adapt to small production lot sizes, which is frequently difficult for large manufacturing operations. Small businesses doing subcontract work run the risk of having their customers pull back the work during times of recession, but there are risks in all businesses. Companies in this category frequently have the opportunity to develop their own proprietary products, and thereby become less dependent on the companies subcontracting to them.

The leisure or hospitality industry encompasses another small business form. This category includes boat marinas, restaurants, motels, ski lifts, bowling alleys, and the like. This is one of the fastest growing industries in the United States, although it had some setbacks in the recession of 1974–1975. In addition to being vulnerable to general business downturns, in many cases the industry is also vulnerable to weather. People want sun for water sports, and snow for cold weather sports, and a bad season or two can frequently break seemingly prosperous small businesses of this variety. Often resort living conditions are an advantage for the entrepreneur in this kind of business.

Although the variety of small businesses has not been exhausted in this discussion, we will examine only one other type of small business. This group is comprised of the companies that try to develop, manufacture, and sell products that the owner/manager has invented, or has otherwise acquired the patents or some distinguishing features. The mortality rate for ventures of this kind is extremely high, but the financial rewards for the successful entrepreneur in this kind of endeavor can be huge. This is where the classical success formula of starting a small business; generating extremely rapid growth; and selling out to the public through a stock offering, or to a large company for a handsome capital gain, has the best chances of working. In recent years, many success stories of this type have been related in some way to the electronics or computer industries. Of course, all successful entrepreneurs don't plan to sell their businesses; they pass them on to their heirs instead. There is a strong incentive to take the capital gain, however, because inheritance taxes may seriously erode the firm's working capital.

In an analysis of the role of small businesses, one fact stands out. Successful entrepreneurs with appropriately chosen products or services are an indispensable part of the economy of the nation, and share with the big corporations the responsibility of contributing significantly to economic advancement.

WHAT MAKES AN ENTREPRENEUR?

It must be made clear that the entrepreneurs who are the subjects of this chapter are the enterprising individuals who start and run businesses that provide jobs and make useful contributions to a subsystem of the economy. The unfortunate souls who are consistently on the marginal periphery of a business scene, either on the verge of going broke, or truly going broke, and who try going into business for themselves because they don't get a satisfactory job, are pitied—but do not qualify for attention in a textbook of this kind.

It seems to be fairly commonly agreed by writers on the topic of entrepreneurship that entrepreneurs are an unusual breed of people, and actually are not in too large a supply. An absolutely essential characteristic is a driving need to achieve. People with high n Ach are described in Chapter 21, "Human Needs and Motivation." We noted then that David McClelland has developed empirical evidence supporting the notion that need for achievement is a key ingredient for entrepreneurs. Keep in mind, however, that while n Ach is a requirement for success as an entrepreneur, it is not necessarily essential for those people who daydream about someday having a business of their own. This is an important distinction. The assumption is made here that most people in their 20s and 30s seriously think about starting a business. Entrepreneurs are the achievers who actually attain this objective; the majority of individuals find obstacles (real or imaginary), that keep them in the role of employees forever—regardless of what success they may reach in salary or wage positions.

In addition to being n Ach types, entrepreneurs possess other distinguishing characteristics. An uncommonly high level of courage is certainly a requirement for the men and women who volunteer for the initial and lasting traumas of small business enterprise. Except for the sources of assistance that are discussed later in the chapter, entrepreneurs knowingly step off the relatively secure and protective ledge of a paycheck type job into a dark and threatening unknown where survival is directly a function of individual capability. The entrepreneur makes a total commitment of his or her financial assets, because half-way ventures rarely pay off. If the small business doesn't make it, successful careers as employees are either retarded, or effectively rendered impossible. The ominous possibility of the stigma of bankruptcy is a dark cloud lurking subconsciously among the entrepreneur's unpleasant thoughts. A possible reduction in standard of living for years is a further sacrifice demanding the courage that it takes to be an entrepreneur. Starting and running a small business is not a game for weaklings.

A third personal quality absolutely essential for entrepreneurship is self-confidence. The entrepreneur must perceive ultimate success as only a matter of time. This, of course, does not mean that the entrepreneur is oblivious to the risks associated with small business because only a fool would be so "Pollyannish." However, the entrepreneur feels, and gives the impression in all of his or her actions, that provided a reasonable amount of luck, the risks will be overcome. This confidence will often be the deciding factor in the many tribulations faced by the entrepreneur between the time of starting a business and eventually knowing that it has become a success. Bankers may extend loans to entrepreneurs whose confidence in their ability to meet the payments inspires banker confidence in them. Trade creditors have been known to be unnaturally patient in waiting for their bills to be paid if entrepreneurs give the impression of complete confidence that banker faith in them has not been misplaced. When an entrepreneur's employees become anxious and worried about their jobs during the inevitable crises that befall all small businesses, it will be the perceived confidence of the boss that will motivate them to stay with the job and see the bad times through.

Need for achievement, courage, and self-confidence are the main personality factors that distinguish an entrepreneur. Other characteristics that are needed include judgment, ability to communicate, social skill in dealing with people, and integrity—but these elements are necessary in order for a person to be successful as an employee, and are therefore not exclusive to the entrepreneur. There is something else that is vital for the entrepreneur, however, and that is a technical knowledge of the business that he or she is going into. There are many causes for failures of small businesses and some of them are examined later in the chapter. Foremost among them is the ignorance of the aspiring entrepreneur of the specialized technical details that are associated with each separate kind of business. Probably the best way to get this knowledge is to serve a form of apprenticeship by working for someone else for a period of time. It may be acquired from the retiring owner of the business that the entrepreneur is buying out. Sellers of franchises often train franchisees in the technology of the franchised item. Regardless of how the knowledge is acquired, the entrepreneur is distinguished by an all encompassing knowledge of the business that is such a significant part of his or her life.

HOW TO START A SMALL BUSINESS

There are two relatively easy ways for an individual to become the owner/manager of a small business. One is through inheritance and the other is by marriage. There are thousands of instances where people who have acquired small businesses through either of these ways have built them into much sounder and more viable enterprises than they were when they got them. These means of acquisition are definitely not disparaged. However, the three ways of getting a business started that are discussed in this book are: forming a brand new company, buying an existing business, and becoming a franchisee.

Resolving to Start A Business

The decision to start a new small business should be justified in one or both of the following ways. A creative idea for producing a good or providing a service where nothing similar exists is one justification for starting a business from scratch. Edwin Land started Polaroid Corporation with an idea for a camera in which the film could be developed internally and from a small beginning revolutionized the amateur photography industry. Where competition exists, starting a new small business is justified when the aspiring entrepreneur has reason to believe that he or she can build a better product, or provide better service and thus grab a share of an existing market. Fisherman's Wharf in San Francisco, and La Cienega Boulevard in Los Angeles, have both seemed overcrowded with restaurants for the past ten years, but every year enterprising new restaurant managers find a niche in these restaurant locations.

Investigation. An imperative for those hoping to start a new business is a detailed study to determine the feasibility of the contemplated venture. Far too often this stage is overlooked as optimism dominates objectivity. The investigation of the feasibility of a new idea must start with a market analysis to determine the demand for the new product or service. Such an analysis must be conducted with a sample of the prospective customers of the new business. A venture one of your authors encountered concerned a product that would be incorporated in safety kits. Confidence that the product had merit was generated when a safety supply company contacted in the feasibility study placed an initial order for a half million units before production had even started.

The entrepreneur may carry out this important investigation alone, or hire a market research specialist to do it, or, as often happens, use surveys of consumer buying that have been conducted by universities or governmental agencies. Keep in mind that demand for a new idea must be firmly established. Room for a new business with an established product or service requires an equally diligent study. The person contemplating a new business must isolate the factors that warrant entering a competitive arena where adversaries are already in business. Factors that might support such a venture include an existing or potential population large enough to absorb a newcomer, sloppy service and inattention to customer demands by the established firms, or a promising exclusive product line offering advantages over the merchandise of the competition. The details of the surveys that should be made before a new business is started would themselves fill a book and become specialized according to the characteristics of the intended business, but conducting such an investigation is a *must* if the new business is to have a chance for survival.

Selecting a name.   From the time a new business is launched it will have to be called something. The choice of a company name is something like the choice of a spouse; once it is made, it is a pretty sticky thing to get rid of. Some guidelines that the aspiring entrepreneur should observe in deciding on a company name include the following:

1. The owner/manager's full name can be used for a business without any legal complications. However, if part of the name is used, or if the name is a fictitious one with some intended meaning to customers, it must be recorded with the clerk of the county in which the company intends to do business. If the company incorporates, the name becomes part of the articles of incorporation. If the name is partially the name of the owner/manager, or if it is a made-up one, the real names of the owners must be recorded. It is essential that a made-up name not have the appearance of being contrived to take business from a competitor with a similar name.
2. Make the name say something about the business to potential customers.
3. Often there is an advantage in coining a short, easily remembered name, and then educating the cusomers to recognize it through advertising. For example, Standard Oil Company of New Jersey changed its name to EXXON.
4. Some words in company names are worn out. For instance, "Fine Furnishings" and "Quality Jewelers" are names that seem overused.

Choosing a location.   For most businesses selling goods or services direct to the consumer, location is of paramount importance. A business catering to walk-in trade may find a low-rent building. However, if the rent is cheap because of an out-of-the-way location the total cost of using the building is high. An essential part of the investigation phase of starting a new business is a study of foot and auto traffic patterns. An additional element is availability of parking space. It is possible to attract customers to a location off the beaten path, but it will cost money in the form of advertising to do it. Choice of location for manufacturing or distributing companies must consider facilities for getting materials and finished goods in and out, such as railroad spurs and loading docks. Another location factor with companies of these kinds is proximity to a supply of suitable labor.

Buying An Existing Business

The steps that have been discussed that are crucial in starting a new business are also mandatory if a going business is to be purchased. That is, a thorough feasibility study should be conducted, the name examined for appropriateness—and a new name recorded if the old one is not suitable, and a careful assessment of the location carried out. If the feasibility and location studies do not reveal significant problems, buying an existing business can offer some distinct advantages over starting one from scratch. For one thing, there will be income right from the start from established customers. Secondly, the business will have ongoing relationships with suppliers and with banks. Third, the existing business will probably have some employees. This can be a blessing if the employees are trained and competent, or it can be a handicap if the employees don't know their jobs, or are carrying grievances that will be hard to overcome. However, buying an existing business calls for some additional steps that the prospective buyer must be sure not to avoid. The perspective buyer should

- *Engage a qualified attorney.* The buyer should have an attorney represent him or her in every matter that could be construed to be contractual, and engage an accountant to verify all financial facts submitted by the seller. Law and accounting are professions about which the aspiring entrepreneur probably knows very little. A fee paid for assistance of this kind will be repaid manyfold by the mistakes it prevents. This step is important regardless of how the small business is started, but it is essential if an existing business is purchased.

- *Determine the past and potential profitability of the business.* Do not accept the seller's word for the firm's profitability; require the seller to present audited business records of the past four or five years, plus tax returns. Carefully assess any conditions that could obstruct the continuance of the past profitability in the future. For example, in Lake Tahoe, a small town in California, there were three owner operated profitable grocery stores. However, Safeway put a store in the area, and within a year all three small stores were out of business.

- *Firmly establish what is being bought.* Have an appraisal made of the assets of the firm, and make sure that their price represents their true market value. Age the accounts receivable to assure that they don't include many uncollectible bills. Examine the inventory for current saleable merchandise; don't buy obsolete or damaged goods. Make certain that conventional depreciation has been charged against the fixed assets; remember that a business does not have to charge itself depreciation, and that profits can be misrepresented as a result. Ascertain what liabilities are being assumed, and assure that they are properly evaluated and deducted from the net assets.

- *Determine a basis for price negotiation.* Most business deals start with an offer to buy or sell, then there will be a counter offer, and so on, until both parties agree to a final figure. However, the buyer must have a sound basis upon which to begin negotiation. One method is to start with the net assets, plus any value placed on the intangible asset of the goodwill that is associated with a going business. Another method is to capitalize future earnings. This involves determining the rate of interest that the buyer wants, or is considered adequate for businesses with comparable risks, and dividing this decimal into the estimated net annual profits. For example, if a small business is estimated to net $15,000 a year in profits, and the buyer wants a 20 percent rate of interest, the negotiating base for the business would be $75,000. In this case, the buyer would expect to recover his or her investment in 5 years.

- *Pin down the seller's reasons for selling.* Many legitimate reasons exist for an owner/manager wanting to sell a business. Perhaps foremost is advancing age or illness of the seller, with a desire to sell the business and only be required to pay the capital gains tax. As we mentioned earlier, if an entrepreneur dies before selling the business, the inheritance tax can break the company. Also, the seller may want to enter a different business, leave the geographical area, or simply retire. Beware, however, of a seller who wants to take his or her capital gain, and then reenter the same business as a competitor of the buyer. An example was a plating company in a western city owned by a family whose last name was Faeth. The company was called the Faith Plating Company. The company was sold to a buyer who thought he was acquiring the goodwill built up by the company, but soon after the sale was consummated some members of the Faeth family started a new business in the same location called the Faeth Plating Company, and quickly got back most of their old customers.

- *Evaluate existing labor relations.* Intolerable labor relations can easily be inherited by the buyer of a business. They may have reached such a low point their resolution would drain entrepreneurial time and energy, and seriously obstruct the firm's profit and growth potentials. Also, existing union contracts may incorporate compensation, working conditions, or pension provisions so excessive that the costs may preclude the firm from being competitive. If possible the prospective buyer should meet with employees of the contemplated business acquisition, and exchange views and objectives with them. This would be in addition to a careful evaluation of any union contract.

Becoming a Franchisee

Franchising as a way of doing business has had a tremendous surge in the United States over the past twenty years, but actually the growth has been primarily in a specialized form of franchising. This growth has come through the advent of franchising companies. Several other franchising concepts go back to beyond the beginning of this century. Fundamentally, a *franchise* is a license entitling the holder to some exclusive right. One kind of a franchise is the right to include a manufacturer's product in a general line of similar products. For example, some hardware stores have a franchise to sell Black & Decker hand tools, or Fuller paint, some furniture stores have a franchise for Kroehler furniture, and some appliance stores have franchises for Frigidaire refrigerators or Panasonic television sets. A second distinct kind of a franchise entitles the franchisee to sell an entire line of products of a particular manufacturer. The franchisee is, in effect, a licensed dealer for the manufacturer. Examples include Chevrolet, Ford, and Chrysler-Plymouth dealers, Caterpillar and John Deere dealers, and Olivetti-Underwood and Burroughs dealers. Department store concessionaires constitute still another form of franchising. For example, the shoe department in a department store may be owned and operated by an entrepreneur who has a franchise from a manufacturer or distributor and a concession from the owners of the department store. However, what we've said about starting a new business and acquiring an existing business also applies to each of these three forms of franchising. The aspiring entrepreneur who acquires a franchise from a franchising company warrants special attention.

Franchising companies. Today display advertisements like the following are commonly found in the newspapers:

BE YOUR OWN BOSS

An unusual opportunity exists for an aggressive man or woman, or couple, to acquire an exclusive franchise to one of the most accepted new retail outlets in the country. No prior business experience is required—*we will train you.* All that you need is driving ambition, willingness for hard work, and $30,000 for inventory and fixtures. Reply Box xxx

There is no question that some franchises have been fantastic money makers. Names like McDonald's, Kentucky Fried Chicken, and Midas Muffler, are familiar in every town in the United States of any size, and in numerous foreign countries. The inimitable McDonald's store format is often a welcome sight to homesick American travelers in the Shinguku and Ginza districts of Tokyo or thousands of other places. However, there are numerous other franchises that have run into serious trouble in the 1970s, and hundreds of investors have sadly watched their time and money go down the drain. One famous franchise failure was Minnie Pearl's Chicken System.

Franchising companies are naturally in business to make money for themselves. They may do this in several ways. In one approach, the franchisee is carefully screened for business ability, and trained intensively in the company's style of operation. The franchising company generally receives an initial fee, and a percentage of the franchisee's gross volume. Other franchise companies make their profit primarily on the exclusive right to sell the franchisee all of the supplies and equipment used in the operation of the business. This includes signs, counters, menus, all foodstuffs, and even the paper napkins and plastic utensils.

A key factor to success in franchising lies in the consistently high quality service that customers can expect wherever they happen to be. This requires complete standardization of goods and services, which in turn requires considerable policing by the franchising company. For this reason franchise contracts tend to be extremely constraining on the franchisee, who may come to see "being his or her own boss" as a myth rather than a reality. Despite this discipline, franchisees are a fairly happy lot as long as they are making money. The really good franchising companies almost assure a qualified franchisee a successful small business through the training that they provide and the regimen that they require. However, there have been a number of "quick luck" franchising companies that have oversaturated markets, gouged franchisees with exorbitant prices for supplies and equipment, and provided only superficial management training, and failed to renew a franchise if the business didn't start making a profit. In this case, the franchising company would take over the operation for itself.

In summary, individuals who aspire to entrepreneurship through acquiring a franchise from a franchising company have several advantages that they would not have if they started a business from scratch. They have the advantages of training in successful, specialized business operation; they have a company name that is often nationally known; and they have company representatives from whom they can get advice. Franchises can be better opportunities than an existing business that is for sale because of up-to-date business practices and the advantage of the "guiding hand" of the franchising company. The individual considering a franchise should conduct a thorough additional investigation of the franchising company, its products or services, locations, exclusiveness of the franchise, and franchise terms, and then perform all of the other steps that have been recommended, regardless of how the small business is started.

FORMS OF BUSINESS ORGANIZATION

Decisions concerning organization form will have to be made in the early stages of a small business formation. Probably most men and women who have reached the point in life where a small business venture is being given serious consideration are aware that basically, there are three options open to them as to a business organization form—namely the single proprietorship, the general partnership, and the corporation. The discussion that follows describes these forms, and points out the characteristics of each in terms of liability, continuity, transferability, control, capital opportunities, and tax features.

The Single Proprietorship

Single proprietorship is the name given to a business where one individual is the owner and manager. From the earlier discussion of entrepreneurship, it might be inferred that the form of organization of entrepreneurships is always the single proprietorship. This is not true. For reasons that, hopefully, will be made clear, the entrepreneur will often choose the partnership or corporation forms. However, the single proprietorship is the easiest way of forming a business; the entrepreneur will at most only have to pay a small filing fee and be in business.

- *Liability.* The single proprietor is personally liable for all of the debts of the business. If he or she is unable to pay debts, creditors may legally claim all of the assets of the business, and also claim all of the proprietor's assets held outside the business, such as house, car, or savings.

- *Continuity.* Theoretically, a single proprietorship terminates upon the death of the owner, but a proper will may grant an executor testamentary powers to run the business until it can be sold or disposed of in some other way.

- *Transferability.* The single proprietor may sell or transfer all or any part of the business in any way that he or she chooses.

- *Control.* Except for any limitations imposed by creditors, the single proprietor is free to make all decisions and to exercise unilateral authority over all of the affairs of his or her business. There are no government regulations which affect the single proprietor specifically.

- *Capital Opportunities.* By definition the single proprietorship offers no opportunities to raise equity capital for the business. The only way to raise external capital is by short-term borrowing. This seriously limits the growth of the business.

- *Tax Features.* The single proprietor simply files a Form 1040, and the profits of the business are taxed as regular income.

In summary, the unlimited liability of the single proprietor, and the constriction on growth because of the inability to attract equity capital, generally relegates the single proprietorship as a form of organization to only the smallest of business operations.

The General Partnership

In the Uniform Partnership Act, a partnership is defined as a "voluntary association of two or more persons to carry on as co-owners a business for profit." A partnership may be formed as informally as a single proprietorship if the partners are simply using their own names as the name of the business, or it can involve a highly complicated "agreement of partnership" requiring expensive legal assistance.

- *Liability.* Partners are no more protected from personal responsibility for all debts incurred by the business than are single proprietors. Another liability feature of a partnership is that all partners risk a claim by creditors on their nonbusiness assets equally, regardless of any difference in the amount of capital contributed. There may be an agreement among the partners to share liabilities on a prorata basis, but such an agreement is not binding on the general public.

- *Continuity.* A partnership agreement can be formulated to assure continuance of the partnership in the event of the death of a partner. Without such an agreement, a partnership is dissolved upon the death of a partner.

- *Transferability.* An express agreement to the effect that a partner may sell or assign any portion of his or her interest in the partnership will permit transferability. If there is no such formal agreement, a transfer cannot be made if any of the partners are opposed to it.

- *Control.* There is little government regulation of partnerships, but internally, partners are subject to limitations on their authority by each other. Acts by one partner can legally bind other partners, and a majority of partners can effectively remove control from the minority. Partnerships can be arenas for bitter combats for control.

- *Capital Opportunities.* Partnerships can raise additional equity capital by accepting investments by additional partners, but the unlimited liability of partners for the debts of the partnership significantly discourages fund raising through equity sources. As with single proprietorships, this characteristic acts as a formidable barrier to growth.

- *Tax Features.* A partnership is not taxable itself, but there is a requirement to report partnership income to the Internal Revenue Service as a record of the income distributed to each partner. The partners report their share of partnership income as ordinary income on their individual tax returns.

Although partnerships permit greater growth possibilities than single proprietorships, and are a favored form of organization for some kinds of businesses, such as law firms, accounting firms, and brokerage offices, the unlimited liability feature works strongly against a wide adoption of the form.

The Corporation

A corporation is a legal entity, and is brought into being by statute. Statutory procedures for creating a corporation vary from state to state.

All states require the registration of the name of the corporation and the articles of incorporation. The corporation is a considerably more complicated and expensive form of organization for the entrepreneur to start with than the single proprietorship or the partnership.

- *Liability.* The distinctive characteristic of the corporation is that the owners are not personally liable for debts incurred by the corporation. In lieu of payment of corporate debts, creditors may only claim the assets of the corporation. The corporation is a legal "person," and can sue, or be sued, and own and sell property. Except in unusual circumstances, such as when owners of corporations personally guarantee repayment of loans to the corporation, the owners' assets are held by them separate and apart from the liabilities of the corporation.

- *Continuity.* The corporation is immortal until legally removed from existence. The comings and goings of its owners have no effect on its continued life.

- *Transferability.* The ownership of a corporation is represented by shares of stock. Shareholders may sell their interests allowing new owners of shares to enter the shareholder domain. One effect on the corporation of the ease of transferability is that new shareholders may elect new representatives to the corporation's board of directors, and thus threaten or usurp the control of the original shareholders.

- *Control.* The modern large corporation is legally controlled by the shareholders, but is practically controlled by the professional managers who are employed to run the firm. The small business that is incorporated is usually owned by the entrepreneur so that the distinction in control between a small corporation and a proprietorship or a corporation is minor.

- *Capital Opportunities.* A fundamental purpose of the corporation is to provide opportunites for the investment of equity capital through the medium of the various national and local stock markets. Therefore, corporations may grow through the sale of stock to the public. This vehicle for raising capital is not readily available to the small business, however, because investors want an inordinate amount of control and return on investment to induce them to take the risk of putting money in a small business, versus the lesser risk of the many large company alternatives.

- *Tax Features.* Corporations are taxed as legal entities, whereas proprietors and partners pay their business taxes on their individual returns. However, there is what seems to be an unfair tax feature of the corporation, which is called "double taxation." The corporation pays a tax on its profits. In addition, when some portion of the profits after taxation are paid to the shareholders of the corporation in the form of dividends, the profits are taxed again on the shareholders individual returns.

The choice between the single proprietorship, general partnership, and corporation forms of organization will be contingent upon the many variables that will be unique to each particular situation. In general, it can be said that the corporation is probably the most desirable form where even modest growth, freedom from personal liability, and continuity are considered to be significant factors.

DETERMINING REQUIRED INITIATING CAPITAL

One of the most common causes of failure of small business is starting with insufficient capital. Of course, what entrepreneurs usually do is start with all the capital that they can scrape together. Hewlett-Packard Company, one of the fantastic business successes of modern times, was started as a partnership in 1939 with $538. However, it is extremely important for the aspiring entrepreneur to make a serious attempt to determine how much beginning capital is really essential. A number of approaches to developing such an estimate can be employed, but one useful one is to work from industry ratios supplied in the Source Book of Statistics of Income, United States Treasury Department, and then to calculate nonrecurring initial costs.

Estimating Capital Requirements

Assume an individual wishes to start a retail building materials company, and an investigation of the market shows that he or she might reasonably expect a gross first year's sales of $120,000. A calculation of the initial cash requirement to get the business going for two months would be as shown in Figure 32-1. Thus, the aspiring entrepreneur is looking at a capital requirement of $45,000 to get the business illustrated in Figure 32-1 started. This, of course, is assuming that everything goes well. The next step is to determine how the beginning capital can be acquired, and after that, to make plans for working capital and capital for expansion.

OBTAINING CAPITAL

Insufficient capital nips a tremendous number of entrepreneurship dreams in the bud. There is definite justification for small business ambitions never getting beyond the dreaming stage because of lack of capital. An unestimable amount of personal savings are probably saved because the aspiring entrepreneur realizes that they represent insufficient capital, and is unaware of means to supplement them. Large, well-established businesses have a number of sources of capital, includ-

Figure 32-1.

Element	Average $/mo. on $120,000/yr. sales	Industry ratio	Initial cash required for 2 mos.
Sales	$10,000	100%	
Cost of goods sold	7,101	71.01%	$14,202[1]
Gross profit	2,899	28.99	
Fixed expenses			
Rent	94	0.94	188
Interest	51	0.51	102
Taxes	151	1.51	302
Depreciation	180	1.80	360
Utilities	125	1.25	250
Controllable expense			
Labor	1,032	10.32	2,064[2]
Supplies	196	1.96	392
Bad debts	53	.53	106
Repairs	47	.47	54
Total expenses	1,929	90.30	
Net Profit	970	9.70	$18,020

1. Inventory rate of turn 12 times per year.
2. Does not include owner's withdrawal

Initial cash requirement for 2 months operation	$18,020
Nonrecurring getting started costs:	
1. Furniture, fixtures, and equipment	10,800
2. Inventory reserve (50%)	3,400
3. Accounts receivable (30 days sales)	10,000
4. Advertising and promotion	500
5. Family living requirements for 2 months	800
Total Starting Capital Required	43,520
Add for Contingencies	1,480
Minimum Starting Capital	45,000

ing both equity, which includes forms of selling ownership, and debt, which includes various methods of borrowing, which are not available to small businesses. For all practical purposes, equity capital markets are closed to the small business owner. Friends and relatives may be persuaded to invest in the small company, or partners may be induced to put in money, or stock may be sold to risk "venture capitalists," but these alternatives virtually exhaust the sources of equity capital for small businesses, and they are often not satisfactory. So, the small business owner must explore the various methods of acquiring capital through borrowing. Debt financing, if used properly, can considerably expand the working capital base of the small business.

Debt Financing Alternatives

All businesses use debt financing to some extent. However, a company must not let debt get out of control. If it does, tragedy can strike even the largest of businesses. Loss of debt control ruined Lockheed Aircraft and Pennsylvania Central Railroad. The solution to avoiding an overdebt situation lies in managing the business so that key liquidity ratios—ratios of liabilities to assets—don't get out of line. For example, current assets (cash, accounts receivable, and inventory) should be at least twice as much as current liabilities (accounts payable, notes payable). Most banks use the following rule of thumb when reviewing loan applications: Total debt should at least be not more than equal to the owner's equity in the business. If the debt of the company is kept under control, the entrepreneur has three main sources of debt capital: trade credit, commercial banks, and the Small Business Administration.

Trade credit. Suppliers of materials, merchandise, and operating supplies to a new small business will extend trade credit if the small firm can demonstrate the ability to make payment when the invoice comes due. Most trade credit terms are for payment within thirty days after receipt of the goods, but the average interval between receipt and payment in the United States is forty-five days. This means that, in effect, a business can operate on its supplier's capital for over a month. There is a cost for the use of this capital, namely foregoing the usual 2 percent cash discount allowed if an invoice is paid within 10 days of receipt.

Small business owners may also buy furniture and equipment from suppliers on credit. The usual terms are a down payment, such as 25 percent, with the balance to be paid with interest over three to four years.

Commercial banks. The most important source of debt capital for the small business is commercial banks. Establishing a good working relationship with a bank should be one of the aspiring entrepreneur's priority items. Banks are veritable treasure houses of information about business conditions, markets, locations, consumer incomes (on a nonpersonal basis, of course), and other such valuable knowledge. In addition, people starting businesses should get to know their bankers before they are desperate for loans.

The small business owner should not look to banks to supply long-term debt capital. However, for short-term purposes, banks can be sources of financial strength to the entrepreneur who earns their confidence. Loans on a sixty to ninety day basis, secured only by the bank's belief in the borrower's ability to pay, can be continually renewed if the repayment prospects continue to be favorable. Loans of up to one year can be arranged with repayment on an installment basis. Equipment mortgages, with the equipment serving as collateral and payments arranged on an installment basis, can be negotiated for three to four years. When banks decide that collateral is necessary for even short-term loans, the small business operator may turn over accounts receivable, or pledge an inventory that is held in a bonded warehouse.

Banks can provide a variety of loans. In addition, banks differ in their specialization in loans. Some banks will have special departments to handle the needs of diverse businesses, such as construction, retailing, auto dealerships, and so on. Also, banks will differ in their inclinations to "ride out" bad times with their customers.

Small Businesses Administration (SBA). SBA is a Federal Agency set up for the explicit purpose of providing financial aid to small businesses. They generally look for the same measurements of a small businesses' strengths as banks, and usually require capital. They are authorized to assist small businesses by either guaranteeing a loan from a bank to the borrower of up to 90 percent of the loan or $350,000, whichever is smaller, or by making a direct loan of up to $100,000 to a qualifying small business. For an SBA checklist for going into business see page 500.

Small Business Investment Corporation or SBIC's were not mentioned as sources of equity capital in the introduction to this section, but they can be both equity and/or debt capital sources to the small business. They are licensed by the SBA, and are restricted to providing assistance to small businesses. SBIC's provide loans for longer terms than banks, and often use debentures for assisting small businesses needing financial help. A debenture is a loan which may be converted into stock at the borrower's option.

A Checklist For Going Into Business

As a conclusion to our discussion of entrepreneurship, the following checklist, prepared by the staff members of the Small Business Administration, asks questions that every aspiring entrepreneur should consider before venturing into such a challenging career.

Are You the Type?
1. Have you rated your personal traits such as leadership, organizing ability, perseverance, and physical energy?
2. Have you had some friends rate you on them?
3. Have you considered getting an associate whose strong points will compensate for your weak traits?

What Are Your Chances for Success?
4. Have you had any actual business experience?
5. Do you have special technical skills, such as those needed by a plumber, electrician, mechanic, or radio repairer?
6. Have you obtained some basic management experience working for someone else?
7. Have you analyzed the recent trend of business conditions (good or bad)?
8. Have you analyzed business conditions in the city and neighborhood where you want to locate?
9. Have you analyzed conditions in the line of business you are planning?
10. Have you determined what size business you plan to establish (dollar sales per year)?
11. Have you built up a detailed set of figures on how much capital you will need to launch the business?
12. Have you figured how much time you will need until the business income equals expenses?
13. Have you planned what net profit you believe you should make?
14. Will the net profit divided by the investment result in a rate you can return which compares favorably with the rate you can obtain from other investment opportunities?

How Much Capital Will You Need?
15. Have you worked out what income from sales or services you can reasonably expect in the first six months? the first year? the second year?
16. Do you know what net profit you can expect on these volumes?
17. Have you made a conservative forecast of expenses including a regular salary for yourself?
18. Have you compared this income with what you could make working for someone else?
19. Are you willing to risk uncertain or irregular income for the next year? two years?
20. Have you counted up how much actual money you have to invest in your business?
21. Do you have other assets which you could sell or on which you could borrow?
22. Have you some other source from which you could borrow money?

23. Have you talked to a banker?
24. Is the banker favorably impressed with your plan?
25. Do you have a financial reserve for unexpected needs?
26. Does your total capital, from all sources, cover your best estimates of the capital you will need?

Should You Share Ownership with Others?
27. Do you lack needed technical or management skills which can be most satisfactorily supplied by one or more partners?
28. Do you need the financial assistance of one or more partners?
29. Have you checked the features of each form or organization (individual proprietorship, partnership, corporation) to see which will best fit your situation?

Where Should You Locate?
30. Do you know how much space will be needed?
31. Do you know what type of building you will need?
32. Do you know of any special features you require in lighting, heating, ventilating, air conditioning, or parking facilities?
33. Have you listed the tools and equipment you need room for?
34. If the proposed location does not meet nearly all your requirements, is there a sound reason why you should not wait and continue seeking a more ideal location?
35. Have you checked the U.S. Census Bureau population figures?

Should You Buy a Going Business?
36. Have you considered the advantages and disadvantages of buying a going business?
37. Have you compared what it would take to equip and stock a new business with the price asked for the business you are considering?
38. Have you learned why the present owner wants to sell?
39. Have you checked the owner's claim about the business with reports from an independent accountant's analysis of the figures?
40. Have you checked with the company's suppliers to obtain their ideas of the value of the business?
41. Do the suppliers think well of the proposition?
42. Is the stock of merchandise a questionable buy? (Would a large proportion of it have to be disposed of at a loss? Is any of it out of date, unsalable, or not usable)?
43. Are the physical facilities old or in poor condition, and, hence overvalued?
44. Are you sure the accounts receivable are worth the asking price?
45. Is the present company's goodwill fairly valued?
46. Are you prepared to assume the liabilities, and are the creditors agreeable?
47. Has your lawyer checked to see if the title is good and if there is any lien against the assets?
48. Are there any back taxes to pay?
49. Have the sales been temporarily increased by conditions which are not likely to continue?

Are You Qualified to Supervise Buying and Selling?

50. Have you estimated your total stock requirements?
51. Do you know in what quantities users buy your product or service?
52. Do you know how often users buy your product or service?
53. Have you made a sales analysis to determine major lines to be carried?
54. Have you decided what characteristics you will require in your goods?
55. Have you set up a model stock assortment to follow in your buying?
56. Have you investigated whether it will be cheaper to buy large quantities infrequently or in small quantities frequently?
57. Have you weighted price differentials for large orders against capital and space tied up?
58. Have you decided what merchandise to buy direct from manufacturers?
59. Will you make your account more valuable to your suppliers by concentrating your buying with a few of them?
60. Have you worked out control plans to insure stocking the right quantities?

How Will You Price Your Products and Services?

61. Have you determined what prices you will have to charge to cover your costs and obtain profit?
62. Do these prices compare favorably with prices of competitors?

What Selling Methods Will You Use?

63. Have you studied the sales promotional methods used by competitors?
64. Have you outlined your own sales promotion policy?
65. Have you studied why customers will buy your product (service, price, quality, distinctive styling, others)?
66. Will you do outside selling?
67. Will you advertise in the newspaper?
68. Will you do direct mail advertising?
69. Will you use posters and handbills?
70. Will you use radio and television advertising?

How Will You Manage Personnel?

71. Will you be able to hire satisfactory employees, locally, to supply skills you lack?
72. Do you know what skills are necessary?
73. Have you checked the prevailing wage scales?
74. Have you a clear cut idea of what you plan to pay?
75. Have you considered hiring someone now employed by a competitor?
76. Have you checked on the pros and cons of doing so?
77. Have you planned your training procedures?

What Records Will You Keep?

78. Have you designed a suitable bookkeeping system that is ready to operate?
79. Have you planned a merchandise control system?
80. Have you obtained standard operating ratios for your type of business to use as guides?
81. Have you provided for additional records as necessary?
82. Have you designed a system to use to keep a check on costs?
83. Do you need any special forms?

84. Have you made adequate provision for having your record keeping done?

What Laws Will Affect You?
85. Have you investigated what, if any, licenses to do business are necessary?
86. Have you checked the health regulations?
87. Are your operations subject to interstate commerce regulations?
88. Have you seen your lawyer for advice on how to meet your legal responsibilities?

What Other Problems Will You Face?
89. Have you worked out a system for handling your tax requirements?
90. Have you arranged for adequate insurance coverage?
91. Have you worked out a way of building a management team?
92. Does your family (if any) agree that your proposed venture is sound?
93. Do you have enough capital to carry accounts receivable?
94. Will you sell for credit?
95. Have you worked out a definite returned goods policy?
96. Have you considered other management policies which must be established?
97. Have you planned how you will organize and assign the work?
98. Have you made a work plan for yourself?

Will You Keep Up to Date?
99. Have you a plan for keeping up with new developments in your line of business?
100. Have you a small group of qualified advisors from whom you can get help in solving new problems?

BIBLIOGRAPHY

Allen, Louis L. *Starting and Succeeding in Your Own Small Business*. New York: Grossett and Dunlap, 1968.

Baty, Gordon B. *Entrepreneurship: Playing to Win*. Reston: Reston, 1974.

Bollinger, Lynn L. and John S. Day. *Management of New Enterprises*. Homewood: Irwin, 1954.

Broom, H. N. and Justin G. Longenecker. *Small Business Management*, 3rd ed. Cincinnati: South-Western, 1971.

Fortune Editors. *Adventures in Small Business*. New York: McGraw-Hill, 1957.

Kelley, Pierce C. and Kenneth Lawyer. *How to Organize and Operate A Small Business*. Englewood-Cliffs: Prentice-Hall, 1961.

Marting, Elizabeth, ed. *Management for the Smaller Company*. New York: American Management Association, 1959.

Pickle, Hal B. and Royce L. Abrahamson. *Small Business Management*. New York: Wiley, 1976.

Summary

The eventual impact of the computer on the practice of management is still not clear. However, two sets of characteristics make the computer a powerful tool. One is its speed, accuracy, and memory, and the other is its problem solving capabilities. The computer has applications that render manual techniques obsolete. Automation of production processes is made possible by the computer, but fears that automation would lead to widespread unemployment have proven groundless. Because the computer involves new ways of doing things, it is threatening to the people in organizations who acquired job skills before its now common use. The computer may be a factor in recentralizing decision making, and it has generated a type of specialist who can use it to quantify decision making.

Business social reponsiveness is a national movement that business men and women will have to cope with permanently. The business manager has traditionally owed legal reponsibilities to corporate stockholders for profitable operations, but now, in addition, is being called upon to be responsive to social issues. Some categories of social issues are mandated by government legislation, but managers must be continually sensitive to incipient social issues that will be considered their responsibilities in the future. Managers must not treat economic responsibilities and social responsibilities separately, but must learn to fuse the strategies for dealing with each. The top managers of business organizations must be actively committed to social responsiveness, and assure that programs for realizing it are effectively implemented. It will be incumbent on managers of the future to devise means for publicly reporting their social issue actions and results.

Entrepreneur is the term popularly applied to the creator and owner/manager of a small business. Between the years 1945 and 1973 the number of small businesses in the United States doubled. However, identification of what constitutes a small business includes several different criteria. Small businesses cover a wide range of enterprises, including some specialized retail operations, suppliers to other businesses, subcontract firms, leisure industry firms, and small manufacturers. Entrepreneurs display personality characteristics that differ from those of employed workers or professionals. Three ways of getting a small business started are, 1) forming a brand new company, 2) buying an existing business, and 3) becoming a franchise. Forms of business organization include the single proprietorship, the general partnership, and the corporation. Estimating capital requirements and obtaining necessary capital are essential features in successfully starting a small business. Aspiring entrepreneurs should consult a checklist prepared by the Small Business Administration.

Appendixes

Critical-Path Scheduling

The planning technique known as critical-path scheduling can be explained simply by the example of a house-building project. Figure A-1 contains a list of events that must be done and the sequence for doing them. In addition, it gives the estimated time in days to complete each event, from the start of the event to the finish.

After the basic data are obtained for the required events, the sequence of their performance, and their estimated times—and this is probably the most difficult task the planner has to do—the next step is to develop a network analysis. Figure A-2 shows the network of events for the house-building project, with the circles representing the activities, and the connecting arrows representing the sequence in which they must be performed.

The next step in critical-path scheduling is to calculate the earliest start (ES) and the earliest finish (EF) for each event. The ES for any event is the latest EF of the immediately preceding events; and the EF for any event is its ES plus the estimated time for it to be completed. ES is conventionally entered to the left of the circle representing the event, and EF to the right of the circle. Figure A-3 shows the ES and EF for the events in the house-building project. Note that the process of calculating ES and EF is additive, beginning with the start event and ending with the finish event. [Refer to event (j) for an example of the calculation of ES

506

Figure A-1. The Sequence of Events and Estimated Times To Build a House.

Letter Designation for Event	Description of Event	Immediately Preceding Event	Estimated Time for Event (Days)
a	Start		0
b	Excavate and rough grade	a	2
c	Pour foundation	b	3
d	Erect frame and rough roof	c	5
e	Put on siding	d	5
f	Install sewer drains	c	1
g	Install rough plumbing	f	3
h	Install rough wiring	d	3
i	Install heating and ventilating	e	5
j	Erect interior walls and ceilings	g, h, i	8
k	Lay finish flooring	j	3
l	Install finish plumbing	k	3
m	Pour garage floor	c	2
n	Install fixtures	k, m	2
o	Install cabinet work	k	4
p	Finish roofing	e	3
q	Install gutters and downspouts	p	1
r	Paint	e, l, n, o	5
s	Finish electrical work	r	2
t	Lay carpet	r	3
u	Finish grading	q	2
v	Pour sidewalks and driveway	u	2
w	Finish	s, t, v	0

and EF. Since event (j) is preceded by event (g) with an EF of 9 days, event (h) with an EF of 13 days, and event (i) with an EF of 20 days, the latest EF of any event immediately preceding event (j) is 20 days, which becomes the ES of event (j). The estimated time to complete event (j) is 8 days. Thus the EF for event (j) is 20 days plus 8 days, or 28 days.]

Calculation of the latest start (LS) and latest finish (LF) for each event in the network is subtractive, or, in other words, the opposite of the calculation of the ES and EF. The LF for any event is the earliest LS of the immediately succeeding events; and the LS for any event is the LF for the event, minus the estimated time to complete it. LF is conventionally entered just to the right of the EF for the event, and LS just to the right of the ES. The LF for the total network is either some scheduled target time for completing the project, or, if there is no target time, the accumulated time at EF at the finish event.

Figure A-4 shows the LS and LF for the events in the project of building a house. It is emphasized again that the process of calculating LS and LF is subtractive, beginning with the finish event and ending with the start event. [Refer to event (k) for an example of the calculation of LS and LF. Since event (k) is succeeded by event (l) with an LS of 32 days, event (n) with an LS of 33 days, and event (o) with an LS of 31 days, the earliest LS of events immediately succeeding event (k) is 31 days, which

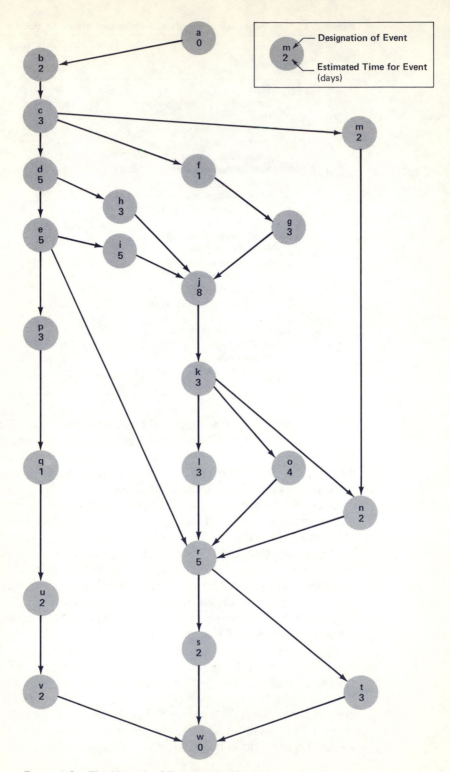

Figure A-2. The Network of Events to Build a House.

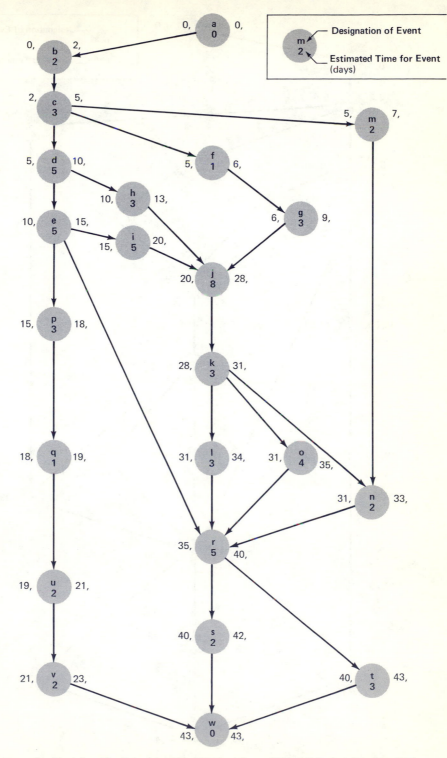

Figure A-3. The Development of Earliest Starts (ES) and Earliest Finishes (EF).

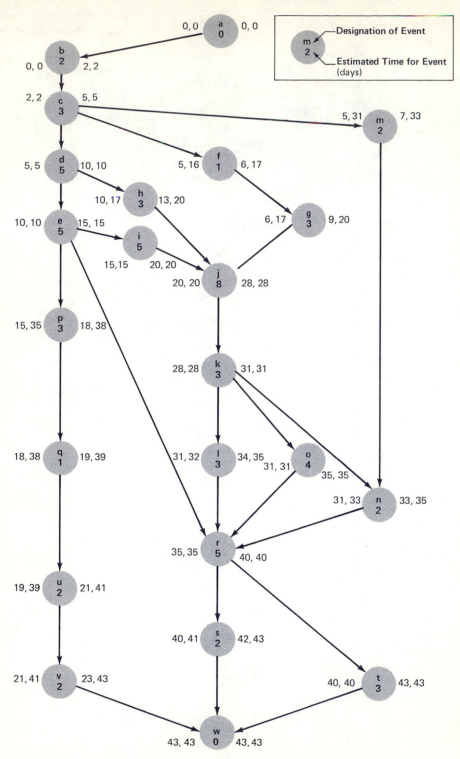

Figure A-4. The Development of Latest Starts (LS) and Latest Finishes (LF).

becomes the LF of event (k). The estimated time to complete event (k) is 3 days. Thus, the LS for event (k) is 31 days minus 3 days, or 28 days.]

After the ES, LS, EF, and LF for each event have been calculated, it is possible to calculate the total slack (TS) and free slack (FS) for each event. TS is the maximum amount of time that an event can be delayed beyond its ES without delaying the completion time of the project; it is calculated by subtracting the event's ES from its LS. Since each event that has the same TS as the difference between the EF and LF in the finish event cannot be delayed without delaying the completion time of the project by the same amount, all events of which this is true constitute the critical path of the network. FS is the maximum amount of time that an event can be delayed without delaying the ES of any other event in the network, and is calculated by subtracting an event's EF from the earliest ES of the event's immediate successors.

Figure A-5, which shows the TS and FS for each event in the house-building project, indicates that the TS in the finish event (w) is 0. Therefore 0 is the TS in the project—every event that has a TS of 0 is in the critical path. In Figure A-6, the heavy line connecting events with TS's of 0 traces the critical path through this particular network.

(A problem in critical-path scheduling is included at the end of Appendix A.)

Figure A-5. Total Slack and Free Slack in Each Event.

Event	Total Slack in Event	Free Slack in Event
a		
b	0	0
c	0	0
d	0	0
e	0	0
f	11	0
g	11	11
h	7	7
i	0	0
j	0	0
k	0	0
l	1	1
m	26	24
n	2	2
o	0	0
p	20	0
q	20	0
r	0	0
s	1	1
t	0	0
u	20	0
v	20	20
w	0	0

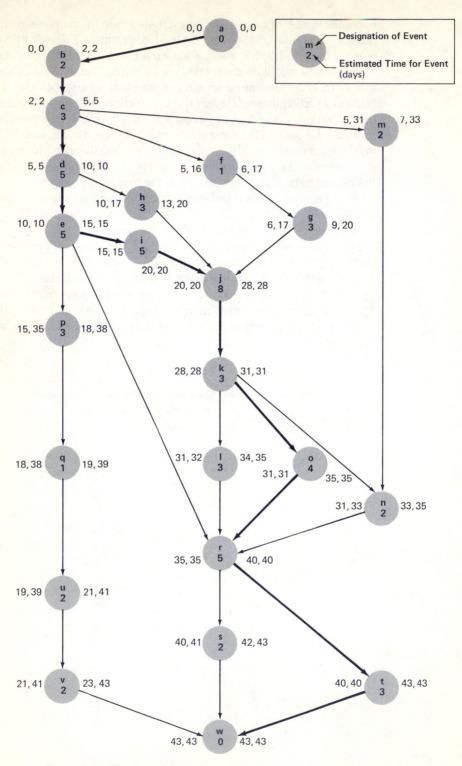

Figure A-6. The Critical Path Through the Network of Events to Build a House.

Problem

Listed below is a set of events, sequence requirements, and estimated event times for a construction project.

a. Prepare a network diagram.
b. Compute ES, EF, LS, and LF for each of the events.
c. Calculate TS and FS for each event.
d. Determine the critical path for the construction project.

Letter Designation for Event	Immediately Preceding Event	Estimated Time for Event (Days)
a	—	5
b	a	6
c	b	8
d	b	30
e	a	85
f	a	120
g	d	42
h	e,f,g	38
i	h	8
j	h	35
k	j,v	8
l	c	29
m	n,o	14
n	l	34
o	l	9
p	m	11
q	p,w	12
r	q	15
s	r	42
t	r	3
u	r	19
v	i,y	35
w	m	3
x	c	12
y	x	15
z	v	9
aa	a	15
bb	aa	8
cc	k	5
dd	s,t,u,z,bb	3
ee	cc,dd	5

Linear Programming

The planning technique of linear programming may be illustrated by a company that has a labor resource of 100 hours and an equipment resource of 80 hours. It has two products, A and B. Product A requires 1 hour of labor and 1 hour of equipment time to produce 100 units, and Product B requires 2 hours of labor and 1 hour of equipment time to produce 100 units. The profits made from Products A and B are $20.00 per 100 units, and $30,00 per 100 units, respectively.

The problem is how to allocate the limited resources of labor and equipment hours to the two products in a way to secure the highest possible combined profits.

Since the objective is to maximize profits, the objective function is said to be a maximizing one. It is expressed in mathematical form as:

$$f(max) = \$20(A) + \$30(B).$$

To find the amounts of A and B that can be substituted into the above equation to produce the highest profit, equations should be set up for labor and equipment and solved for the optimal values of A and B. However, there are constraints that must first be considered:

$$1(A) + 2(B) \leq 100 \text{ hours of labor.}$$
$$1(A) + (B) \leq 80 \text{ hours of equipment.}$$

That is, the combined total number of units of Product A (using 1 hour of labor per 100 units) and Product B (using 2 hours of labor per 100 units) cannot exceed 100 hours of labor. Nor can the total combined number of units of A and B (both using 1 hour of equipment time per 100 units) exceed 80 hours of equipment time.

Note that the above constraints are, so far, not equations but inequalities. They can be made into equations by adding another variable to each one of them. These variables are called "slack" variables. In symbolic form, slack variable C can be put in the first inequality, and slack variable D in the second. Because a rule of linear programming is that any variable that appears in one equation must appear in all equations in the same program, O(D) will be put into the first equation, and O(C) in the second. In the final solution of a linear program, slack variables may have positive values if some part of the resources are unused, or will equal zero if the resources can be allocated to the real variables with no remainder. After adding the slack variables, the constraining equations now appear as:

$$A + 2B + C + O(D) = 100.$$
$$A + B + O(C) + D = 80.$$

The slack variables must also appear in the objective function, and as no profit is realized from these variables, the profit coefficients are zero.

The objective function is now expressed as

$$f(max) = \$20(A) + \$30(B) + \$0(C) + \$0(D).$$

Now we are ready to solve for the optimal values of A and B. To do this, a form of algebra called Simplex has been developed. Simplex merely requires that some fundamental rules be followed, and if they are, any number of equations can be solved simultaneously. The process that Simplex follows is to start with a minimum feasible solution, and then to continue to improve the solution until an optimal solution is reached.

To begin, the constraining equations are put in a matrix form. Each row is an equation. A minimum feasible solution would be to allocate the constants to the slack variables. A conventional form for proceeding with the solution is shown in Figure B-1(a). (Note: the c_j values are obtained from the objective function.)

The next step is to calculate what is called the z_j row, which is derived by multiplying the profit for the variable in an equation times the values in each column for that equation, and adding the resulting product to the product obtained by multiplying the profit for the variable in the next equation times the values in each column for that equation.

Figure B-1(a). First Simplex Table.

Variable	Profit	Quantity	A (cj) $20	B (cj) $30	C (cj) $0	D (cj) $0
C	$0	100	1	2	1	0
D	$0	80	1	1	0	1

To demonstrate, C has a profit of $0. $0 times 100 = $0. D has a profit of $0. $0 times 80 = $0. And, $0 plus $0 = $0, which is the z_j value for the Profit column. Perform the same step for the A, B, C, D columns. When the slack variables are in the equation, zero is the sum in each case.

$$z_j \text{ row} \quad \$0 \quad 0 \quad 0 \quad 0 \quad 0$$

Now substract the z_j values for A, B, C, and D from the c_j values.

$$c_j\text{–}z_j \text{ row} \quad \$20 \quad \$30 \quad 0 \quad 0$$

The complete beginning solution is shown in Figure B-1(b).

What we want to do now is force a real variable, either A or B, into the solution, which in turn will drive a slack variable, either C or D, out of the solution. A Simplex rule is that if the objective function is a maximizing one, and in this case it is, then the variable to enter the solution is the one with the highest positive value in the c_j–z_j row. $30 is the highest positive value, so B will enter the solution. The variable leaving the solution will be the one with the lowest quotient obtained by dividing the

Figure B-1(b).   First Simplex Table Completed.

Variable	Profit	Quantity	A (cj) $20	B (cj) $30	C (cj) $0	D (cj) $0
C	$0	100	1	2	1	0
D	$0	80	1	1	0	1
zj	$0		0	0	0	0
cj–zj			$20	$30	0	0

number in the column of the variable entering the solution into the value in the Quantity column in the row. In the above case:

$$C = 100/2 = 50,$$
$$D = 80/1 = 80.$$

C has the lowest quotient, and will therefore leave the solution.

The next step is to find the values in the new row for which B is the variable. The way to do this is to divide the values in the old row for which C was the variable by what is called the "key number." The key number is the number at the intersection of the column headed by the variable entering the solution and the row headed by the variable leaving the solution. In this case, the key number is 2. An exception will be the value in the Profit column, which will be the cj value for B.

Old row: C $ 0   100   1   2   1   0
New row: B $30   50   ½   1   ½   0

As the entrance of B into the solution will affect the values in the row for which D is the variable, these values must be scaled down. Do this by subtracting from the old D row the values in the old C row, multiplied by a fraction composed of the number in the D row and B column as numerator and the key number as denominator.

Old D Row		New D Row
80	$- (100 \times \frac{1}{2}) =$	30
1	$- (\ \ 1 \times \frac{1}{2}) =$	$\frac{1}{2}$
1	$- (\ \ 2 \times \frac{1}{2}) =$	0
0	$- (\ \ 1 \times \frac{1}{2}) =$	$-\frac{1}{2}$
1	$- (\ \ 0 \times \frac{1}{2}) =$	1

It is now possible to take another step in the solution, refer to Figure B-2 for the demonstration of how the new rows for B and D are entered into the equation.

Find the zj row as in the first table, except now one of the multipliers is $30 instead of $0.

zj $1500 $15 $30 $15   0
cj–zj $ 5   0   −$15   0

This second trial solution in complete form is contained in Figure B-2.

Figure B-2. Second Simplex Table.

Variable	Profit	Quantity	A (cj) $20	B (cj) $30	C (cj) $0	D (cj) $0
B	$ 30	50	½	1	½	0
D	$ 0	30	½	0	−½	1
zj	$1500		$15	$30	$15	0
cj–zj			$ 5	0	−$15	0

With this second solution, the company would make a profit of $1500 by producing 5000 units of Product B. (Remember that in the original statement of the problem, the values were for 100 units. Thus, $50 \times 100 = 5000$ units.) However, a Simplex rule is that if the objective function is a maximizing one, an optimal solution has not been obtained until all positive values are driven out of the cj–zj row. One positive value, $5, remains, which means that A will enter the solution. Find the variable that will leave the solution as before:

$$B = 50/\tfrac{1}{2} = 100,$$
$$D = 30/\tfrac{1}{2} = 60.$$

D has the lowest quotient, and will therefore leave the solution.

Find the values in the new row for which A is the variable. Divide the values in the old D row by the new key number, which is ½—except for the interjection of A's cj value.

$$\text{Old row: D} \quad \$0 \quad 30 \quad \tfrac{1}{2} \quad 0 \quad -\tfrac{1}{2} \quad 1$$
$$\text{New row: A} \quad \$20 \quad 60 \quad 1 \quad 0 \quad -1 \quad 2$$

The introduction of A into the solution necessarily means that not as many units of B can be made. Therefore, the values in the row for which B is the variable must be scaled down. Do this by subtracting from the old B row the values in the old D row, multiplied by a fraction composed of the number in the B row and A column as numerator and the key number as denominator. This fraction is ½/½, which equals 1.

Old B Row		New B Row
50	− (30 × 1) =	20
½	− (½ × 1) =	0
1	− (0 × 1) =	1
½	− (−½ × 1) =	1
0	− (1 × 1) =	−1

Having obtained the values for the A and B rows, another step toward a solution may be made. Refer to Figure B-3, which contains the new values.

Find the zj row as in the first and second tables, except now one multiplier is $30 and the other multiplier is $20. To demonstrate, $30 times 20 plus $20 times 60 = $1800.

	zj	$1800	$20	$30	$10	$10
	cj–zj		0	0	–$10	–$10

As the objective function is a maximizing one, and as a Simplex rule is that an optimal solution in such a case is obtained when all positive values are driven out of the cj–zj row, the optimal solution has now been reached.

The company should produce 6000 units of Product A (60 × 100) and 2000 units of Product B (20 × 100) with the labor and equipment resources available, and as a result will generate a profit of $1800, which is the maximum possible under the resource constraints that exist.

Figure B-3. Third Simplex Table.

Variable	Profit	Quantity	A (cj) $20	B (cj) $30	C (cj) $0	D (cj) $0
B	$ 30	20	0	1	1	–1
A	$ 20	60	1	0	–1	2
zj	$1800		$20	$30	$10	$10
cj–zj			0	0	–$10	–$10

Problem

A widow has two recipes for making candy that have been passed down in her family. She wishes to supplement her small income by making and selling candy. She has obtained 150 pounds of sugar and 120 pounds of chocolate, which are the main ingredients for both recipes. Recipe A requires 1 pound of sugar and 1 pound of chocolate per gross pieces of candy. Recipe B requires 5 pounds of sugar and 3 pounds of chocolate per gross pieces. She estimates that she can make $7.00 profit per gross of the Recipe A candy, and $15.000 profit per gross of Recipe B.

How can she ration her sugar and chocolate to the two recipes and make the greatest profit?

Monte Carlo Simulation

Monte Carlo simulation can be illustrated by the case of a manufacturer's representative who sells a line of novelty items to department stores. A characteristic of the items is that they have a limited period of market popularity, ranging from six to twenty-four months. Wanting to maintain a line of ten active novelty items at all times, the representative has kept careful records of the market lives of his items over the past fifteen years. The records show that the specific life spans, and the percentage of items in the line corresponding to each one, have been as follows:

Market Life Spans	Percent of Items
6 months	5
9 months	15
12 months	20
15 months	25
18 months	20
21 months	10
24 months	5

At this point, the representative wants to determine how many new novelty items should be added to the line over the next three years in order to maintain an active line of ten items. The representative's starting line is composed of all brand new items.

The first step is to develop, from the past records, a cumulative frequency distribution curve of the novelty items. Figure C-1 shows the construction of the complete cumulative frequency distribution.

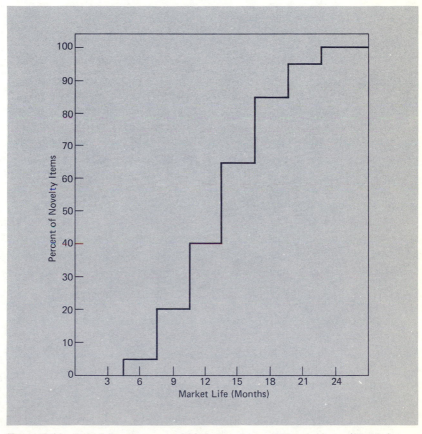

Figure C-1.   Cumulative Frequency Distribution, Lives of Novelty Items (Months).

The second step is to obtain, from the cumulative distributions, numbers that will designate specific lives of items for the simulation of thirty-six months of market experience. This is done by randomly selecting numbers between 0 and 100. There are many ways of generating random numbers, but the use of a city telephone directory can serve the purposes of this illustration. The directory can be opened to any page, and a number randomly pointed to. Its last two digits provide the first random number. Subsequent random numbers are obtained in the same manner.

Assume that the first number the manufacturer's representative has drawn is 31. As shown in Figure C-2, the representative would inscribe a horizontal line starting at 31 in the cumulative percentage column and extending to the point where it intersects the cumulative frequency distribution curve. He or she would then go back to the center of the interval bounded by the cumulative frequency distribution curve and inscribe a vertical line downward to the point where it intersects a

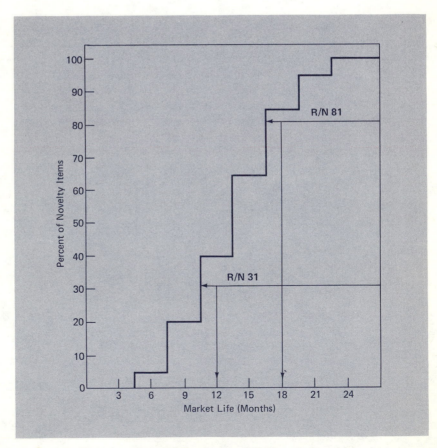

Figure C-2. Calculating Lives of Novelty Items. (R/N = random number.)

Figure C-3. Simulated Combined Lives of Ten Original Novelty Items and Their Replacements.

Item Number	Random Number	Probable Lives of Items in the Starting Line	Random Number	Combined Life of Items in Starting Line & First Replacements	Random Number	Combined Life of Items in Starting Line & First & Second Replacements
1	31	12	16	21x	41	36x
2	81	18	75	36	66	54
3	97	24	74	42	2	48
4	57	15	89	36	37	48
5	89	21	99	45	14	54
6	87	21	55	36	6	45
7	72	18	10	27x	98	51x
8	7	9	82	27x	35	39x
9	23	12	94	33	12	42
10	28	15	1	21x	43	36x

possible life of a novelty item. The possible life so intersected is twelve months, which is the probable life of the first item in the starting line. Assume that the next random number he obtains is 81. He or she would follow the same procedure to find that the probable life of the second item in the starting line is eighteen months.

As shown in Figure C-3, this process would be continued until the probable lives of all ten of the novelty items in the starting line were calculated; then the representative would calculate the probable lives of the items that would replace the items in the starting line. For example, the random number 16 indicates that the probable life of the replacement for the first item in the starting line is nine months. Nine months, plus the probable life of twelve months for the first item, equals twenty-one months, which is the probable combined life of the two items. The calculations are continued until all items in the starting line, plus their replacements, have a combined life of at least thirty-six months.

From Figure C-3, it can be seen that the manufacturer's representative can predict that over the next thirty-six months he or she will have to make one complete replacement of the ten novelty items carried in the line, and, in addition, will have to find second replacements for the four items marked x.

(A problem for the use of the simulation method is given at the end of Appendix C.)

Problem

Assume that a construction company has just purchased ten crawler tractors for a total cost of close to $1 million. The firm's top managers want to know approximately how many additional tractors will have to be bought over the next ten years to maintain a constant scale of operations. An analysis of equipment records shows that 10% of the crawler tractors bought by the firm in the past have worn out in three years; 20% have had to be replaced after four years; another 20%, after five years; 30%, six years; 15%, seven years; and 5%, eight years.

Approximately how many replacement tractors will have to be purchased over the next ten-year period?

Probability Decision Theory

A company that manufactures a line of mobile homes can be used to illustrate probability decision theory. To gain the advantages of mass production, it manufactures the homes in lots of varying sizes before receiving firm orders from dealers, and must hold the finished units in inventory until it sells them. The selling price to dealers is $7500 per unit, and if the homes can be moved out of inventory within 30 days of completion, the full expected profit of $750 per unit is realized. However, if the inventory period is extended, the combined cost of money tied up in inventory, storage, insurance, and taxes begins to erode the profit margin. A critical factor determining how long the finished mobile homes will remain in inventory is the prevailing interest rate on mortgages that ultimate buyers will secure to finance the purchase of the mobile homes from dealers.

The company's manager is trying to decide the best lot size for the next manufacturing order from alternative lot sizes of 100, 80, or 60 units. These alternatives will be called *strategies*. The manager is concerned with what the prevailing rate of interest will be when the mobile homes are completed, and although he or she cannot be sure what will happen, judgment tells the manager that the interest rate can go down .5 percent; it can remain the same as it is now; it can go up .5 percent; or it can even go up 1 percent. These possibilities will be called the *possible future states of nature*. Through reading and business contacts, the manager knows that there is not the same chance for each state of nature to occur. After careful consideration, the manager decides that there is only a 10 percent probability that the interest rate will go down, and only a 25 percent probability that it will stay the same. The manager decides that there is a 50 percent probability that it will go up .5 percent, and a 15 percent probability that it will go up 1 percent.

Analyzing the probable outcome of each of the alternative strategies relative to each of the possible future states of nature, the manager decides that if the interest rate goes down .5 percent, enough potential buyers will be attracted to the market to encourage dealers to stock up on mobile homes, and the firm's own production will move out of inventory rapidly enough to provide full profit with any of the three strategies. However, the manager detects buyer resistance to a long-term commitment at even the present interest rate, and knows that the larger the lot of mobile homes put into inventory, the slower will be the turnover, and hence the lower will be the average profit. When alternative strategies are projected into states of nature of interest rate increases, it becomes clear to the manager that if the firm manufactures 100 mobile homes, some of them will remain in inventory so long that the firm will actually lose money on them, and average profit will be substantially reduced.

Figure D-1 illustrates in matrix form how the manager can perform the analysis by considering a given state of nature momentarily to be certain, and then determining the outcome of each strategy under that condition. The outcome of each strategy/state of nature combination can be measured in terms of the probable profit payoff.

The final step that the manager must perform in order to make a decision consists of calculating the expected payoff for each alternative strategy (S1, S2, and S3 in the equations), weighted by the probabilities of each of the alternative states of nature. These calculations are as follows:

$$S1 = 75,000(.10) + 56,250(.25) + 37,500(.50) + 18,750(.15)$$
$$= \$43,125.$$
$$S2 = 60,000(.10) + 51,000(.25) + 39,000(.50) + 33,000(.15)$$
$$= \$43,200.$$
$$S3 = 45,000(.10) + 42,750(.25) + 33,750(.50) + 29,250(.15)$$
$$= \$36,450.$$

The manager's decision now becomes straightforward. There is no apparent reason to manufacture 100 or 60 mobile homes in preference to a lot of 80, after considering everything that can be predicted about the future. Although there is still the possibility that the interest rate will decrease by .5 percent, and a profit of $15,000 will be lost because of not having manufactured 100 mobile homes, the decision to manufacture 80 units appears to be the best one on the basis of present facts and estimates.

(A problem requiring the application of probability decision theory is included at the end of this appendix.)

Problem

Jim Lowe, a senior business student, won a $1000 first prize for a paper submitted in a contest sponsored by a national trade association. He wanted to maximize the value of the $1000 over the next year but recognized that there were certain risks involved with any investment he decided upon. Business conditions in the country could improve, and he thought that there was a 15 percent probability of that happening. If he invested in common stocks, improved conditions would result in an expected growth of his $1000 to $1300. Bond investment would yield a more modest growth to $1100. The $1000 invested in a combination of stocks and bonds should grow to $1200 under improved conditions.

Figure D-1. A Payoff Matrix of Various Strategy/State of Nature Combinations.

Alternative State of Nature / Alternative Strategies	N1: Interest rate decreases .5% (P) = 10%	N2: Interest rate remains constant (P) = 25%	N3: Interest rate increases .5% (P) = 50%	N4: Interest rate increases 1% (P) = 15%
S1: Manufacture 100 mobile homes	**Outcome:** Sell 100% of mobile homes at full profit. Payoff: $75,000	**Outcome:** Sell 50% at full profit, 50% at half profit. Payoff: $56,250	**Outcome:** Average one-half profit on all mobile homes sold. Payoff: $37,500	**Outcome:** Average one-quarter profit on all mobile homes sold. Payoff: $18,750
S2: Manufacture 80 mobile homes	**Outcome:** Sell 100% of mobile homes at full profit. Payoff: $60,000	**Outcome:** Sell 70% at full profit, 30% at half profit. Payoff: $51,000	**Outcome:** Sell 30% at full profit, 70% at half profit. Payoff: $39,000	**Outcome:** Sell 10% at full profit, 90% at half profit. Payoff: $33,000
S3: Manufacture 60 mobile homes	**Outcome:** Sell 100% of mobile homes at full profit. Payoff: $45,000	**Outcome:** Sell 90% at full profit, 10% at half profit. Payoff: $42,750	**Outcome:** Sell 50% at full profit, 50% at half profit. Payoff: $33,750	**Outcome:** Sell 30% at full profit, 70% at half profit. Payoff: $29,250

If business conditions remained unchanged, which Jim thought was 35 percent probable, a stock investment show grow to $1100, bonds to $1050, and a combination investment to $1075.

However, Jim was pessimistic, and thought that there was a 40 percent chance of a recession. In such a case, $1000 in stocks would drop in value to $800, and in bonds, to $950; and an investment half in stocks and half in bonds would be worth $875.

If a depression occurred, which Jim thought was only 10 percent probable, $1000 invested in stocks would be worth only $500 at the end of the year, a bond investment would fall to $900 in value, and a combination investment would depreciate to $700.

What was the end-of-year expected value for each of Jim's strategies? What should he have done with his $1000?

Glossary

A B C analysis In inventory control, differentiation between the 10 percent of the items that are worth about 75% of the investment (the A items); the 25% of the items that are worth about 90% of the investment (A and B items together) and the 75% of the items that are worth about 10% of the investment (the C items)

Acceptance sampling In statistical quality control, basing the acceptance or rejection of a lot on the characteristics of a sample

Acceptance theory of authority From Chester Barnard, the view that authority is accorded to superiors by their subordinates

Achievement need The chief motivator of persons who succeed, according to David C. McClelland, who classifies achievers as "n Ach" types

Action research A technique for organizational change that features an investigation-feedback-action cycle

Advisory relationships Interactions characterized by the extending of advice on work-related matters by a member of one department to a member of another department

Aggregate control Overall control of a firm's production operations, centered on determining the least costly way of accommodating production rate to consumer demand

Alternatives Various means by which objectives may be achieved

Amplification Distortion of communication through overreaction to stimuli

Authoritarian manager One who relies heavily on formal authority, who is an "order giver," and who mistrusts subordinates' ability to make decisions

Authority The right of a manager to make decisions within certain limitations, to assign duties to subordinates, and to require conformance by subordinates to what is expected of them

Back order An order for which the customer has to wait for delivery

Balance sheet Accounting statement of a firm's financial position at a given point in time

Ball of work concept A feeling ascribed to workers (by Frederick W.

Taylor) that available work is of a fixed amount and that it should be done slowly to make it last

Behavioral approach The use of the scientific method by psychologists, sociologists, and anthropologists in attempts to understand, explain, predict, and change human behavior in organizations

Behavior modification In motivation theory, an approach that uses the link between behavior and its consequences to develop desired behaviors

Bounded rationality In decision-making theory, the concept that asserts decision makers seek a "workable" rather than optimal solution because all factors affecting a problem cannot be determined

Brainstorming A group decision-making process designed to generate and evaluate alternative solutions

Breakeven point The point in the quantity of goods sold at which sales revenue and fixed costs are equal, and beyond which sales effort produces a profit

Budget A plan, expressed in numerical terms, which becomes a control device when actual results are analyzed and conclusions reached concerning indicated actions

Bureaucracy An impersonal, rational management system commonly associated with Max Weber and "red tape"

Central activities Broad elements of work associated with a firm's main income-producing operations

Centralization The reserving of decision-making authority for top managers

Charismatic leadership A natural, inspired form of leadership

Chief executive officer The top manager of an organization, in business often called the president or chairman of the board

Cohesiveness The close-knit character of a group that has attraction for its members

Collection period The length of time that it takes for a firm to be paid by its customers for the goods it has sold

Committee A formal group charged with either specific or general responsibilities associated with organizational goals

Communication The process whereby a message transmitted by a sender has some impact on the behavior of a receiver

Communication nets In communications theory, the various configurations of communication channels including wheel, star, and circle

Competition The striving, on an individual or organizational basis, for rewards that are in limited supply

Conflict, organizational Rivalry and hostility between members of different departments in an organization

Conformity Obedience to organizational procedures and norms of conduct

Contingency theory In management theory, the approach that notes there is no "one best way" to manage, that effective management depends on the environment, tasks, interpersonal relationships, and technology

Control by variables In statistical quality control, recording measured differences between inspected units, and drawing inferences from them

Controlling Assuring that actual results conform to plans

Coordinating Assuring that the contributions of individuals and departments in an organization are made as required, and that they are effectively linked together; or, the composite of the functions performed by all managers at all levels

Corporation A body formed and authorized by law to act as a single person in matters concerning the ownership and management of a business; this form of ownership is distinguished by its limited liability and stockholder ownership

Critical incident A technique for performance appraisal based on a record of significant impression—good and bad—made by subordinates

Critical-path scheduling A program type of plan that uses networks of events for planning and controlling the performance of activities

Current ratio An indicator of a firm's ability to pay its short-term debts, derived by dividing current assets by current liabilities

Data bank Computerized storage of information that can be used for some future purpose

Data processing The rapid and discriminatory handling of data and performing of processes by a computer in accord with instructions programmed into it

Decentralization Forcing decision-making authority down into lower levels of management

Decision making Choosing the means of achieving an objective from possible alternatives

Decode The act of converting a message from the language of the sender to a language the receiver understands

Departments Organizational units formed by grouping activities; also, activity groupings at a particular level

Development Provision of successive management experiences whereby candidates may grow to be managers

Discharge Termination of employment for violation of rules or incompetence

Discounted rate of return The interest rate at which the cost of an investment, and the present value of the estimated future flow of earnings from the investment, equal zero

Division of work The principle that large tasks should be divided into small ones, with people specializing in performing them

Down time Time that equipment is out of service for repairs or maintenance

Econometric model A series of complex simultaneous equations which simulate the operation of the total national economy or some segment of it—used in forecasting

Economic life The period throughout which the advantages of operating a piece of equipment outweigh the disadvantages

Economic order quantity The quantity ordered for an inventory item that is determined by balancing carrying costs against ordering costs

Empirical data Objective data from testing and observation, on which hypotheses or conclusions can be based

Employee-centered manager One who consistently represents the best interests of subordinates

Encode The act of preparing a message to be sent

Entrepreneur The creator, owner, and manager of a small business

Equity The value of a property less claims against it

Equity/debt ratio An indicator of the real ownership of a firm, derived by dividing equity by total liabilities

Esteem need The need that people have for self-respect and the respect of other people

Evaluative relationships Interactions between peers in different departments, characterized by informal performance evaluations

Examining for attributes In statistical quality control, discriminating between units that are good or bad according to some single quality standard

Expectancy theory of motivation The theory that says people act because they believe certain actions will bring about desired behaviors which will provide satisfaction

Extinction In behavior modification, the theory that behaviors are discontinued because no predictable consequence follows the behavior

Feedback In a control system, information concerning output that is communicated to the input source for the purpose of regulating performance

Feedback loop The circuit in an operational process which transmits feedback and permits control of output

Fire-fighting tactics Short-term adjustments for attacking problems as they arise, rather than systematic long-term plans

Fixed costs Costs, such as rent, depreciation, and managers' salaries, that go on at a constant amount regardless of sales volume

Forced-choice method A performance appraisal technique entailing the checking of statements on a review form that are most appropriate, and least appropriate, to the person being evaluated

Force field analysis In organization development, the practice of depicting organizational equilibrium as the result of driving and restraining forces

Forecasting Attempting to predict future events, such as demand for a firm's products or services

Franchise A license entitling holder to some special privilege

Frequency distribution Tabulated occurrence of certain events in some past time period—used in projecting the number of times such events may occur in the future

Fringe benefits Nonfinancial supplements to direct wages or salaries

Frustration Conscious recognition that certain needs are not being satisfied

Functional authority The right of members of one department to prescribe certain behavior for members of other departments

Functional boundary lines Sharp distinctions between activities and authority in different departments

Functional organization Grouping activities by the kind of work done

Functional-sequence relationships Interactions between members of different departments whose work is done in series to result in a product or service

Functions of managers The things that managers do when acting solely as managers

Gantt charts Traditional production control technique that compares work planned and completed to time elapsed

Geographical organization Grouping activities by the territorial location at which they are performed

Grade Technique for job evaluation based on development of classes or stages of skills, experience, and responsibility required to handle a job

Grapevine An unofficial, unauthorized channel of communication

Graphic rating scale In performance appraisal, a technique for measuring an individual's traits or performance characteristics

Grass roots inputs Feedback from lower levels in the organization

Hierarchy of authority The pyramid formed by management levels, in which authority increases and the number of positions decreases as ascent is made from bottom to top

Hierarchy of needs Abraham Maslow's arrangement of five basic needs into a sequence of ascending order, from physiological to self-actualization

Human relations A management approach preoccupied with assuring the contentment of workers with their jobs

Incentives Payoffs gained by taking some specific action (positive incentives), or punishments avoided by not taking some action (negative incentives)

Inducement-contribution balance In Chester Barnard's view, the equilibrium between the inducements that a member of an organization gets from the organization, and the contributions he or she makes in return

Illegitimate control Control brought to bear on employees by someone other than their direct supervisor

Informal organizations Instinctive groupings of people, without conscious purpose, within a formal organization

Input Resources committed to a production operation

Interview, nondirective The use of broad, general questions that permit interviewees to talk freely

Interview, patterned The technique of asking standard questions of all interviewees

Interview, stress An interview method designed to find out an interviewee's tolerance for stressful situations

Inventory A stock of goods in excess of immediate demand

Job The smallest subsystem or grouping of activities within an organization

Job description Statement identifying and describing the content and duties of a job

Job enlargement Broadening the scope of jobs, and making them richer in terms of variety, interest, and significance

Job enrichment Changes in jobs designed to provide increased opportunity for satisfaction of growth needs

Job evaluation Determination of the relative worth of jobs within an organization

Job grade The level occupied by different jobs having the same relative worth to the organization

Job rank In a simple form of job evaluation, the place of a job in the order of perceived importance

Job rotation Practice of encouraging holders of repetitive jobs to rotate periodically between a number of jobs

Job satisfaction A state of mind that varies in a favorable degree with the worker's positive impressions of the total job environment

Job specifications Statements of the personal qualifications required to properly perform jobs

Justice, corrective The system for remedying inequities in the administration of distributive justice

Justice, distributive The fair distribution to individuals of the good and bad things of life according to the way they are deserved

Lateral relationships Work-related interactions between members of different departments

Layoff Termination of employment because of lack of work, usually with the idea that the employee will be called back if business conditions improve

Lead time In inventory control, the scheduled interval between the placing and receipt of an order; in production control, the interval between receipt and delivery of an order

Leadership The ability of a manager to influence subordinates to accept the manager's interpretations of objectives, to follow the manager's ways of doing things, and to see that their personal goals can be achieved by consenting to the manager's authority over them

Leading Activating subordinates to perform their job tasks

Leading indicators Factors in the total economy, such as the gross national product or housing starts, that point to the direction that the economy may go

Life cycle The evolution of a successful product, from its development to market maturity and on into obsolescence

Line/staff concept The traditional distinction between line people (those who command) and staff people (those who advise them)

Linear programming A mathematical system for allocating resources to alternate uses to get best results

Long-term plan A set of alternative courses of action that, depending on external conditions, could lead a firm to achieve its basic objectives over an extended time period

Love or belongingness need The human need for affection and affiliation

Management The utilization of physical and human resources through coordinative efforts

Management by objectives A technique in which subordinates are encouraged to set their own objectives, plus the means whereby achievement of those objectives can be measured

Management grid A method of characterizing management styles according to two dimensions, concern for people and concern for tasks

Management principles General guides that have been abstracted from managerial experiences and deduction, such as those enunciated by Henri Fayol

Manpower inventory A detailed appraisal of the human resource of an organization

Manpower plan A systematic attempt to ensure the future availability of a firm's human resource in the proper quality and quantity

Market system The process in free enterprise in which price is considered the key factor in regulating supply and demand, with competition assuring equilibrium of power among firms in the market

Marketing control Techniques primarily concerned with applying specific profitability standards to discrete areas of control, such as product line, selling effort per customer, marketing territories, and advertising

Mathematics approach Approach to management that focuses on optimal decision making using mathematical models to describe current conditions and predict results

Maximizing function An optimal decision that generates the greatest possible profit, the highest output, and the highest return on investment

Minimizing function An optimal decision that produces the desired result at the lowest possible cost

Model A description or representation of a thing or a process, useful in decision making for predicting results obtainable from alternative solutions

Motivation The inducement of employees to extend their efforts for the good of the organization

Noise Extra energy in a communication channel

Norms Standards of behavior

Objectives Goals toward which plans are directed

One best way The most efficient way to do a job, used as the basis for setting minimum production rates

Open-door policy Provision for dissatisfied employees to bypass their immediate superior and present their case to a higher-level manager

Optimization Selection, from available alternatives, of the solution to a problem that is most effective in terms of the total system

Organization development The efforts of behavioralists, employing various educational strategies, to diagnose human problems that obstruct organization goals and to point to their correction

Organization development consultant A person professionally qualified to diagnose a need for change, prescribe the way to accomplish it, and assist in making it effective

Organizations Cooperative systems comprised of members consciously striving for a common purpose, the achievement of which is made possible by communication (from Chester Barnard)

Organizing Grouping activities into departments, assigning authority, and providing for coordination

Output Units produced in an operation

Participative management Involvement of people in decisions affecting them

Partnership A business owned by two or more persons, but not incorporated

Peer rating A performance appraisal method in which all members of a group with equal status evaluate each other

Performance appraisal The assessment of the way employees perform their assigned job duties

Physiological need The human requirement for elements, such as air, water, and food, that are essential to life

Planning Establishing an organization's objectives and determining the means for achieving them

Plural relationships Interactions between individuals in group meetings

Point method The use of a "point" value system to evaluate jobs

Policies Reflections of a firm's attitude on various issues, which set the course for actions on all organizational levels

Position One of the slots authorized for a job classification

Power politics The informal struggle for power within an organization

Primary level of management The level of managers in an organization who report directly to the chief executive officer

Probability decision theory A quantitative technique for making decisions under assumptions of what probably will happen

Procedures Step-by-step methods for performing specific actions

Product organization The grouping of activities required to turn out specific products or product lines

Production-centered manager One who focuses attention on output of work and is indifferent to subordinates' needs

Production control A complex of procedures for measuring input and output factors against standards, and for determining what adjustment to make if actual demand varies from forecasted demand

Productivity The ratio of output to the input of labor hours

Profit The surplus in excess of costs that a business firm realizes from its operations

Programmed instruction A classroom training method in which material to be learned is arranged into a sequence of steps, or frames, through which trainees proceed individually at a rate determined by their ability to correctly answer a question accompanying each frame

Programs (projects) Detailed long-term plans for accomplishing specific objectives.

Project organization The team or task-force approach to getting a particular job done, involving the temporary grouping of activities according to the requirements of the project or program

Punishment In behavior modification, the practice of following unwanted behavior with a displeasing consequence in an effort to stop the behavior

Quality control Assurance that goods produced or services rendered by a firm measure up to some specified quality standard

Quantitative techniques Methods for making decisions that employ mathematical forms—such methods including critical-path scheduling, linear programming, simulation, and probability decision theory

Quick ratio An indicator of a firm's cash position, derived by dividing cash by current liabilities

Rank order A method of performance appraisal in which relative values are applied to the performance characteristics of the people in the same job classification, thus placing them in the order of perceived merit

Rate of return The surplus that a firm receives from an investment after the investment is recovered

Real-time computation The recording and reporting of events by a computer the instant they occur

Recruitment The search for potential employees to fill job openings

Reinforcement schedule Pattern in which consequences follow behavior

Reliability of tests The capability of generating consistent test results over time

Research and development Two activities—often but not always combined in particular organizations—which include testing the product ideas and preparing likely products for the commercial market, respectively

Responsibility The obligation of a manager to properly execute authority

Retraining Teaching new skills to employees whose former jobs have become obsolete

Reward system A particular company's system of distributing raises, bonuses, and promotions for reasons of merit or seniority

Rules Stipulations concerning the personal conduct of employees in such matters as care of company property, times for starting and quitting, safety precautions, etc.

Safety need The compulsion that people have to feel secure from physical, social, and economic threats

Salary Compensation paid to a jobholder on a weekly, monthly, or yearly basis

Satisficing Selecting, from a limited number of alternative solutions, one that is satisfactory, though not necessarily optimal

Scalar chain The ladder-like chain of command linking superiors and subordinates from the top to the bottom of organizations

Scanlon Plan A group incentive system in which management and labor work together to improve productivity

Scatter diagram In job evaluation, a method used to equate compensation to job worth

Scientific management A philosophy, commonly associated with Frederick W. Taylor, dedicated to improving efficiency through the elimination of wasted effort

Screening Supplemental selection device used to assess skills and personality traits of job applicants

Self-actualization need The need people have to attain their full potential

Seniority An employee's length of service—with the company, in a department, or in a particular job classification

Sensitivity training A group process in which individuals learn of their impact on other people and of ways to correct negative behavior

Serendipity The occurrence of unforeseen positive events

Service relationships Interactions characterized by the rendering of specialized service by one department to other departments, such as recruiting and screening of job applicants by the personnel department

Shaping Reinforcement of behavior that is similar to desired behavior

Short-term plan Implementation of the long-term plan for the immediate period ahead—prepared in detail and intended to be carried out exactly as stated

Single proprietorship A business owned and managed by one person

Simulation Imitation of real conditions so that the outcome can be predicted

Single-purpose plan A plan applied to a single and probably nonrecurring series of future decisions, often called a program or project

Social responsibilities All responsibilities charged to a manager that are external to the obligations to the company's stockholders

Software Computer programming, rather than the equipment itself (hardware)

Span of control The number of subordinates that report directly to a manager

States of nature Conditions that determine the future domain of decision making including relative certainty, risk, and relative uncertainty

Staffing Developing and maintaining the human resource of an organization

Standing plans Policies, procedures, and rules intended as guides to decisions made regularly

Statistical analysis Sales forecast technique that attempts to isolate specific factors that tend to vary consistently with sales

Statistical quality control Use of sampling inspection for determining the probability that any sample is representative of the lot

Stockholders Owners of shares of stock in a corporation

Strategic factors Factors that most critically obstruct objectives and thus make a significant difference between the success or failure of a plan

Strategies Complex long-term plans focused on broad goals

Supporting activities Broad elements of work that back up, or assist, a firm's central activities

Systems theory A way of looking at every organization as part of a larger whole, in constant interaction with all other subsystems

Tactics Detailed short-term plans focused on specific goals

Task force A team comprised of people with different skills, assembled to work on a specific problem or project

Technical functions Things that people do on their jobs that are specific to a task and are nonmanagerial

Termination The action—either discharge or layoff—taken by a company to remove an employee from the payroll

Theory X/Theory Y Diametrically opposite views of worker motivation, pointed out by Douglas McGregor. In Theory X, workers are viewed as naturally lazy and resistant to work and must be strictly controlled by management; in Theory Y, workers are perceived as avidly seeking responsibility and capable of accomplishing great things on their own if given the opportunity

Training Teaching workers how to do some technical task

Trait theory of leadership The view that leadership could be predicted on the basis of the possession of certain traits

Unequal-status relationships (nonvertical) Interactions between members of different departments who are at different status levels

Unfreezing-change-refreezing In organization development, a process used to change an organization by discarding old routines, trying new ones, and if they are successful, making them routine

Unity of command The traditional principle that no subordinate should receive directions from more than one boss

Validity Accuracy of screening devices for selecting applicants—ascertainable by the subsequent performance on the job of those hired

Variable costs Costs, such as those for labor and material, that vary in proportion to a firm's sales volume

Vertical relationships Interactions between managers and the subordinates who report directly to them

Wage range The spread between the minimum and maximum compensation for a job grade

Wages Compensation paid to jobholders on an hourly or daily basis

Zone of indifference A term Chester Barnard used to designate the area occupied by the type of supervisory orders that workers regard as acceptable

Indexes

Name Index

Subject Index